Mediated Politics

Mediated Politics explores the changing media environments in contemporary democracy: the Internet, the decline of network news and
the daily newspaper; the growing tendency to treat election campaigns
as competing product advertisements; and the blurring line between
news and entertainment. By combining new developments in political
communication with core questions about politics and policy, a distinguished roster of international scholars offers new perspectives and
directions for further study.

Several broad questions emerge from the book: with ever-increasing
media outlets creating more specialized segments, are audiences treated
increasingly as consumers to be diverted rather than as citizens to be
informed? Are there implications for a sense of community? Should
media give people only what they want or also what they need to be
good citizens?

These and other tensions created by the changing nature of political
communication are covered in sections on the changing public sphere,
shifts in the nature of political communication, the new shape of public
opinion, transformations of political campaigns, and alterations in citizens' needs and involvement.

W. Lance Bennett is Professor of Political Science and Ruddick
C. Lawrence Professor of Communications at the University of
Washington.

Robert M. Entman is Professor of Communication and Head of the
Department of Communication at North Carolina State University.

COMMUNICATION, SOCIETY AND POLITICS

Editors

W. Lance Bennett, *University of Washington*

Robert M. Entman, *North Carolina State University*

Politics and relations among individuals in societies across the world are being transformed by new technologies for targeting individuals and by sophisticated methods for shaping personalized messages. The new technologies challenge boundaries of many kinds – between news, information, entertainment, and advertising; between media, with the arrival of the World Wide Web; and even between nations. *Communication, Society and Politics* probes the political and social impacts of these new communication systems in national, comparative, and global perspectives.

Mediated Politics

COMMUNICATION IN THE FUTURE OF DEMOCRACY

Edited by

W. Lance Bennett
University of Washington

Robert M. Entman
North Carolina State University

CAMBRIDGE
UNIVERSITY PRESS

CAMBRIDGE UNIVERSITY PRESS
Cambridge, New York, Melbourne, Madrid, Cape Town, Singapore, São Paulo

Cambridge University Press
40 West 20th Street, New York, NY 10011-4211, USA

www.cambridge.org
Information on this title: www.cambridge.org/9780521783569

First published 2001
Reprinted 2003, 2005

Printed in the United States of America

A catalog record for this publication is available from the British Library.

Library of Congress Cataloging in Publication Data

Mediated politics: communication in the future of democracy / edited by W. Lance
Bennett, Robert M. Entman.
p.   cm. – (Communication, society and politics)
Includes bibliographical references and index.
ISBN 0-521-78356-9
1. Communication in politics.   2. Communication – Political aspects.   3. Democracy.
I. Bennett, W. Lance.   II. Entman, Robert M.   III. Series.
JA85.M44   2000
320′01′4–dc21   00-023855

ISBN-13   978-0-521-78356-9 hardback
ISBN-10   0-521-78356-9 hardback

ISBN-13   978-0-521-78976-9 paperback
ISBN-10   0-521-78976-1 paperback

For our fathers:
Walt Bennett and Bernie Entman

Contents

List of Figures	*page* xii	
List of Tables	xiii	
Contributors	xv	
Preface	xxiii	
Acknowledgments	xxvii	

1 Mediated Politics: An Introduction   1
W. Lance Bennett and Robert M. Entman

Part 1   Democracy and the Public Sphere

2 The Public Sphere and the Net: Structure, Space, and
Communication   33
Peter Dahlgren

3 Promoting Political Engagement   56
William A. Gamson

4 The Internet and the Global Public Sphere   75
Colin Sparks

Part 2   Citizens, Consumers, and Media in Transition

5 Reporting and the Push for Market-Oriented Journalism:
Media Organizations as Businesses   99
Doug Underwood

6 Political Discourse and the Politics of Need: Discourses on
the Good Life in Cyberspace   117
Don Slater

7 Dividing Practices: Segmentation and Targeting in the
  Emerging Public Sphere   141
  Oscar H. Gandy, Jr.

8 Let Us Infotain You: Politics in the New Media
  Environment   160
  Michael X. Delli Carpini and Bruce A. Williams

9 The Future of the Institutional Media   182
  Timothy E. Cook

Part 3 Mediated Political Information and Public Opinion

10 Reframing Public Opinion as We Have Known It   203
   Robert M. Entman and Susan Herbst

11 Political Waves and Democratic Discourse: Terrorism Waves
   During the Oslo Peace Process   226
   Gadi Wolfsfeld

12 Monica Lewinsky and the Mainsprings of American Politics   252
   John Zaller

13 The Big Spin: Strategic Communication and the
   Transformation of Pluralist Democracy   279
   W. Lance Bennett and Jarol B. Manheim

14 The Impact of the New Media   299
   W. Russell Neuman

Part 4 Mediated Campaigns

15 Issue Advocacy in a Changing Discourse Environment   323
   Kathleen Hall Jamieson

16 Implications of Rival Visions of Electoral Campaigns   342
   C. Edwin Baker

17 Mediated Electoral Democracy: Campaigns, Incentives,
   and Reform   362
   Bruce I. Buchanan

18 "Americanization" Reconsidered: U.K.–U.S. Campaign
   Communication Comparisons Across Time   380
   Jay G. Blumler and Michael Gurevitch

Part 5 Citizens: Present and Future

19 Citizen Discourse and Political Participation: A Survey   407
    Roderick P. Hart

20 Adapting Political News to the Needs of Twenty-First
    Century Americans   433
    Doris A. Graber

21 National Identities and the Future of Democracy   453
    Wendy M. Rahn and Thomas J. Rudolph

22 Communication in the Future of Democracy: A Conclusion   468
    Robert M. Entman and W. Lance Bennett

    Index   481

Figures

Figure 4.1 Internet hosts in millions at January 1, 1998
and January 1, 1999   *page* 84
Figure 4.2 Growth of Internet hosts by domain name   88
Figure 10.1 Surveyed public support for defense spending
drops as spending increases   214
Figure 10.2 Surveyed opinion parallels media references to
Soviet threat   218
Figure 12.1 The effect of political information and partisanship
on attitudes toward the Lewinsky matter   257
Figure 12.2 Trends in partisan attachment and loyalty,
1952–1996   272
Figure 12.3 The impact of economic performance on
presidential elections   274
Figure 14.1 Characteristic normal distribution of public
opinion   306
Figure 14.2 Bimodal politics, France in the 1950s   307
Figure 14.3 Polarized views of racially based hiring preferences
(stratification)   308
Figure 14.4 Campaign interest by level of political knowledge   313
Figure 14.5 Sample issue item by level of political knowledge   314
Figure 14.6 Illustrative policy item: opinion distribution for
different knowledge levels   316
Figure 15.1 Television ad for the People for the American Way   332
Figure 16.1 Models of democracy and elections   350
Figure 17.1 The electoral triangle model   363
Figure 19.1 Range of writer appreciation   418
Figure 19.2 Significant correlations among political variables   423

Tables

Table 4.1 Percentages of U.S. households with a computer, modem, telephone, and e-mail 1994 and 1997 *page* 81

Table 4.2 Percentages of U.S. households with a computer ranked by income for 1997 82

Table 10.1 Surveyed opinion on defense spending increases and number of Soviet threat stories 217

Table 11.1 Number of articles about Beit Lid attack 237

Table 11.2 First day newspaper coverage of Beit Lid attack 239

Table 12.1 The effect of partisanship on responses to the Lewinsky scandal 256

Table 12.2 The "Lewinsky economy" in historical perspective 259

Table 12.3 Trends in Clinton job approval ratings in initial phase of Lewinsky matter 264

Table 14.1 Various issue items by level of political knowledge 315

Table 17.1 Media coverage categories 1988, 1992, and 1996, in percentages 370

Table 17.2 Voting and learning citizen incentives and disincentives 372

Table 19.1 Comparison of U.S. data to 10-city sample 411

Table 19.2 Survey of editors 414

Table 19.3 Respondents' attitudes toward writers 419

Table 19.4 Differences between writers and nonwriters 422

Table 19.5 Factor structure for main variables 424

Table 20.1 Age-related differences in following government and public affairs "most" plus "some of the time," 1966–1996 436

Table 20.2 Interest in technological innovations by generation: percent who are "definitely interested" 437

Table 20.3 News consumption attitudes and behaviors by age
groups   442
Table 20.4 "Regularly" and "sometimes" used news sources,
April 1996   443
Table 20.5 News interests by generation: percent of viewers
who are "very interested" in the topic   444
Table 21.1 Age and national identity in the United States   458
Table 21.2 Age and national identity in Europe   460
Table 21.3 Determinants of national identity and support for
the European Union   463

Contributors

C. Edwin Baker (Yale, J.D.; Stanford, B.A.), Nicholas F. Gallicchio Professor, University of Pennsylvania School of Law, has taught at Cornell, Texas, Oregon, and Toledo law schools and at Harvard's Kennedy School of Government and was a staff attorney for the ACLU. He presently teaches Constitutional Law, Mass Media Law, and related courses. He is the author of two books: *Advertising and a Democratic Press* (Princeton, 1994) and *Human Liberty and Freedom of Speech* (Oxford, 1989), and numerous articles about free speech, equality, property, law and economics, jurisprudence, and the mass media.

W. Lance Bennett is Ruddick C. Lawrence Professor of Communications and Professor of Political Science at the University of Washington. His work on the news media, public opinion, and political communication has appeared in the leading scholarly journals. He is the author of six books, including *News: The Politics of Illusion* and *The Governing Crisis: Media, Money, and Marketing in American Elections*, coeditor of *Taken by Storm: The Media, Public Opinion and U.S. Foreign Policy in the Gulf War*, and coauthor of *Democracy and the Marketplace of Ideas: Communication and Government in Sweden and the United States*. He has served as chair of the Political Communication Section of the American Political Science Association, and he received the Ithiel de Sola Pool Award and Lectureship of the American Political Science Association.

Jay G. Blumler is Emeritus Professor of the Social and Political Aspects of Broadcasting at the University of Leeds, England, and Emeritus Professor of Journalism at the University of Maryland. A Fellow and Past President of the International Communication Association and a founding coeditor of the *European Journal of Communication*, he has written extensively on the mass media and politics, including *The Crisis of Public Communication* (Routledge, 1995, with Michael Gurevitch) and "The Third Age of Political Communication: Influences and Features" (in Vol. 16, No. 3, 1999, of *Political Communication*, with Dennis Kavanagh).

Bruce I. Buchanan is Professor of Government at the University of Texas at Austin. He has written articles on presidential campaigns, White House organization, and public policy, and he is the author of *The Presidential Experience* (1978), *The Citizen's Presidency* (1987), *Electing a President* (1991), and *Renewing Presidential Politics* (1996). He served as research director for the Markle Foundation studies of the 1988, 1992, and 1996 presidential elections. He will synthesize these studies in a forthcoming book entitled *Presidential Campaigns and American Democracy*.

Timothy E. Cook is Fairleigh Dickinson, Jr., Professor of Political Science at Williams College, and Adjunct Professor of Public Policy at Harvard's Kennedy School of Government, where he has been long associated with the Shorenstein Center on Press, Politics, and Public Policy. He received his B.A. from Pomona College and his Ph.D. from the University of Wisconsin. Cook is the author of *Making Laws and Making News: Media Strategies in the U.S. House of Representatives* (Brookings, 1989) and *Governing with the News: The News Media as a Political Institution* (Chicago, 1998) and coauthor of *Crosstalk: Citizens, Candidates, and the Media in a Presidential Campaign* (Chicago, 1996).

Peter Dahlgren is Professor of Media and Communication, Lund University, Sweden. His research addresses the media, journalism, citizenship, and democracy, emphasizing various perspectives from social and cultural theory. In particular, he is interested in the notions of identity and civic culture and their relationship to democratic processes. He has published many articles and is the author of *Television and the Public Sphere* (Sage, 1995) and coeditor, with Colin Sparks, of *Journalism and Popular Culture* (Sage, 1992).

Michael X. Delli Carpini is Professor of Political Science at Barnard College and Columbia University. He holds the Ph.D. in political science from the University of Minnesota. He is author of *Stability and Change* *in American Politics: The Coming of Age of the Generation of the 1960's* (1986), editor of *Research in Micropolitics* (1995), and coauthor of *What Americans Know About Politics and Why It Matters* (1996).

Robert M. Entman is Professor and Head, Department of Communication, North Carolina State University. He served previously on the faculties at Northwestern and Duke and holds a Ph.D. in political science from Yale and an M.P.P. in policy analysis from the University of California (Berkeley). Dr. Entman has written *The Black Image in the White Mind: Media and Race in America* (University of Chicago Press, 2000, with Andrew Rojecki). He is also author of *Democracy Without Citizens: Media and the Decay of American Politics* (Oxford University Press, 1989), senior author of *Diversifying TV and Radio: Policies for Privatization and the Public Interest in Broadcasting* (Aspen Institute, 1998), and coauthor of *Media Power Politics* (Free Press, 1981, with D. L. Paletz). He serves as coeditor of the book series *Communication, Society and Politics* for Cambridge University Press with W. Lance Bennett.

William A. Gamson is a Professor of Sociology and codirects the Media Research and Action Project (MRAP) at Boston College. He is the author of *Talking Politics* (1992) and *The Strategy of Social Protest* (2nd Edition, 1990), among other books and articles on political discourse, the mass media, and social movements. He is a past president of the American Sociological Association.

Oscar H. Gandy, Jr., is the Herbert I. Schiller Information and Society Term Professor at the Annenberg School for Communication at the University of Pennsylvania. He is the author of *Communication and Race, The Panoptic Sort,* and *Beyond Agenda Setting,* in addition to numerous articles and chapters exploring privacy, race, power, and information technology. His current research interests include the strategic uses of social statistics. His Ph.D. in public affairs communication is from Stanford University.

Doris A. Graber is Professor of Political Science at the University of Illinois at Chicago. She has written numerous articles and books on political communication topics including *Verbal Behavior and Politics* (1976), *Processing the News: How People Tame the Information Tide* (1993), *Public Sector Communication: How Organizations Manage Information* (1992), *Media Power in Politics* (Fourth Edition, 2000), and

Mass Media and American Politics (Fifth Edition, 1996). Her forthcoming book, *Virtual Political Reality: Learning About Politics in the Audio-Visual Age* (2000), analyzes the political impact potential of audio-visuals in news broadcasts.

Michael Gurevitch is Professor at the College of Journalism, The University of Maryland. Prior to his current position he was on the faculty of The Open University in England. He is an author and coauthor of books, journal articles, and book chapters. His recent book is *The Crisis of Public Communication* (with Jay Blumler). He is also coeditor of *Mass Communication and Society* (1977), *Culture Society and the Media* (1982), and *Mass Media and Society* (1991 and 1995). He served as associate editor of the *Journal of Communication* and is currently a member of the editorial board of *Political Communication*.

Roderick P. Hart holds the Shivers Chair in Communication and Government at the University of Texas at Austin. He is the author of *Public Communication* (1975, 1983), *The Political Pulpit* (1977), *Verbal Style and the Presidency* (1984), *The Sound of Leadership* (1987), *Modern Rhetorical Criticism* (1990, 1997), *Seducing America* (1994), and *Campaign Talk: Why Elections Are Good for Us* (2000). He has received grant support from the Ford Foundation, Carnegie Foundation, Exxon Foundation, David Ross Foundation, University Research Institute, the Television and Politics Study Center, and the Kaltenborn Foundation. He has been named a Research Fellow of the International Communication Association and a Distinguished Scholar by the National Communication Association.

Susan Herbst is Professor of Political Science at Northwestern University. Her books include *Reading Public Opinion: How Political Actors View the Democratic Process* (University of Chicago Press, 1998), *Politics at the Margin* (Cambridge University Press, 1995), and *Numbered Voices: How Opinion Polls Have Shaped American Politics* (University of Chicago Press, 1994). She is editor, with Benjamin I. Page, of *Communication, Media and Public Opinion,* a book series at the University of Chicago Press.

Kathleen Hall Jamieson is Professor of Communication and Dean of The Annenberg School for Communication at the University of Pennsylvania. She is also director of the Annenberg Public Policy Center. She is the author or coauthor of nine books, including *Dirty Politics: Deception, Distraction and Democracy* (Oxford, 1992); *Beyond the Double Bind: Women and Leadership* (Oxford, 1995); *Packaging the Presidency*, which received the Speech Communication Association's Golden Anniversary Book Award; and *Eloquence in an Electronic Age*, which received the Winans-Wichelns Book Award. Her most recent book is *Spiral of Cynicism: Press and Public Good* (Oxford, 1997).

Jarol B. Manheim (Ph.D., Northwestern) is Professor of Media and Public Affairs and of Political Science at the George Washington University, where he was founding director of the School of Media and Public Affairs. Professor Manheim's research in strategic political communication has been published in the leading journals in political science, journalism, and mass communication. His most recent book, *Strategic Public Diplomacy and American Foreign Policy: The Evolution of Influence*, was published by Oxford University Press in 1994.

W. Russell Neuman is Professor of Communication at the Annenberg School, University of Pennsylvania, where he directs the Program on Information and Society at the Annenberg Public Policy Center. Professor Neuman's current research focuses on the impact of the advanced telecommunications and the economics and policy of new media technologies. His most recent book, coauthored with Lee McKnight and Richard Jay Solomon, *The Gordian Knot: Political Gridlock on the Information Highway*, was published by MIT Press.

Wendy M. Rahn is an Associate Professor of Political Science at the University of Minnesota. She coedits *Political Psychology*, the journal of the International Society of Political Psychology, and she is member of the National Election Studies Board of Overseers. Her current research interests include the relationship between affect and cognition, American national identity, and social capital.

Thomas J. Rudolph is a Ph.D. candidate in political science at the University of Minnesota. His research interests include political behavior, public opinion, and political psychology. He has published articles in the *Journal of Politics* and *Social Science Quarterly*.

Don Slater is Senior Lecturer in Sociology at Goldsmiths College, University of London. His research interests include consumer culture, economic sociology, and new information and communications technologies. Current work includes: *Consumer Culture and Modernity* (Polity Press, 1997); with Fran Tonkiss, *Market Societies and Modern Social Thought* (Polity Press, 2000); with Daniel Miller, *The Internet: An Ethnographic Approach* (Berg, 2000); and with Sean Nixon, *The Business of Advertising* (Arnold, 2000).

Colin Sparks is Professor of Media Studies in the Centre for Communication and Information Studies at the University of Westminster, in London, England. He has written widely on the media and the public sphere. His most recent book, *Communism, Capitalism and the Mass Media* (Sage, 1998), was on the democratization of the media after the fall of communism in Europe.

Doug Underwood is Associate Professor in the School of Communications at the University of Washington. He is the author of *When MBAs Rule the Newsroom*, which looks at the influence of the modern marketing movement on the journalism profession. A former political reporter with the *Seattle Times* and in the Washington, DC, bureau of the Gannett News Service, he is a regular contributor to the *Columbia Journalism Review*. He has recently completed a national survey of journalists' religious values and a book manuscript, *From Yahweh to Yahoo!*, which examines the connections between journalists' religious beliefs and their professional and ethical principles.

Bruce A. Williams is a Research Professor in the Institute of Communications Research at the University of Illinois at Urbana-Campaign. His most recent book, coauthored with Albert Matheny, is *Democracy, Dialogue and Environmental Disputes: The Contested Languages of Social Regulation* (Yale University Press). He is currently working with Michael Delli Carpini on a book-length elaboration of some of the arguments made in their contribution to this volume.

Gadi Wolfsfeld is Professor of Political Science at the Hebrew University of Jerusalem. Author of *Media and Political Conflict* (Cambridge, 1997), he holds a Ph.D. in political science from MIT. He is also co-editor of *Framing the Intifada* (Ablex, 1993) and author of *The Politics of Provocation* (SUNY, 1988).

John Zaller is Professor of Political Science at UCLA, where he specializes in public opinion, the mass media, and electoral politics. He has written *Nature and Origins of Mass Opinion* (Cambridge, 1992) and is currently working on *A Theory of Media Politics* (Chicago, forthcoming). His Ph.D. is from the University of California at Berkeley.

Preface

The study of political communication has reached a new level of maturity. Just as the field has attained recognition as a vital area of inquiry, however, the focus of its core concern, mass communication, faces radical transformation. New technologies for targeting individuals and sophisticated methods for shaping personalized messages have begun to reconstruct politics and relations among individuals in society. At the same time that the individual communication experience is changing rapidly, the public policy environment in many nations favors *laissez faire*, market solutions for issues ranging from distribution and use of bandwidth, to social responsibility in program content, to the cost and content of the messages in elections and public policy campaigns.

The coincidence of a new millennium with a new era of mediated communication offers a propitious moment to rethink the field of political communication. This book explores the changing media environments facing contemporary democracy and suggests new theoretical directions for the field. Since the communication environment raises profound questions about the role of citizens and the conduct of democracy, the book also considers important normative issues that emerge within this transformed communication landscape. By combining new developments in political communication with core questions about politics and policy, we hope in this volume to set new benchmarks and perspectives for development of the field.

We were fortunate in this enterprise to have two opportunities to gather as a group to debate and discuss the issues facing mediated democracies today. The generous funding of the Annenberg Public Policy Center at the University of Pennsylvania enabled workshops to be held in Washington, DC, and Philadelphia. Scholars from different nations and different intellectual perspectives cannot be counted on to agree on the same questions, much less the same answers. This lively group did not disappoint. However, we reached a surprising level of consensus on several broad tensions emerging in democratic societies as new communication technologies increasingly define, or at least "mediate," the human political experience.

First is the tension between diversity and commonality. The problem here concerns the levels of common identification required for living together. As media outlets proliferate and audiences are sliced and diced into more specialized segments, what will befall the common information space? The positive spin on the new trends is to stress the growing diversity in mediated information. More choice means more satisfaction for consumers and, perhaps, more chance for varied views to enter public discourse and contend for allegiance. However, the negative spin on these same trends would emphasize the fragmentation of the public. It seems likely that smaller, more homogeneous public spheres will arise alongside of, if not supplant, the larger, more heterogeneous public sphere that arguably dominated politics. In the old days when people could only choose between two to four TV channels and a newspaper or two, most citizens shared common mediated political experiences. What is the future of *imagined communities* as broad collective identifications give way to more focused, less geographically rooted communities that are more likely to be infused with consumer rather than political values?

A second and related political tension might be termed the problem of free information choice versus necessary citizen education. The problem here is one of information stratification and equality among publics: How much inequality of knowledge is sustainable in democracies? This concern arises from the age-old but newly compelling question of whether media should give people what they want, or rather should also give them what they need. In a predominantly commercial system such as the United States, profit pressures and audience calculations have never been far from the thoughts of media executives, but the economic trends of the late twentieth century have magnified them to a perhaps unprecedented degree. If, as it appears, market values will increasingly govern media behavior, both in the United States and elsewhere, we can predict some of the developments, as analyzed in this volume. These include a decrease in the quality of news as media compete desperately for audience attention; a corresponding distortion of news editorial choices by entertainment sensibilities; a blurring of once-clearer distinctions between advertising or promotional messages and news coverage; yet also an increase in the quality and number of specialized media targeting narrower audiences. All those trends together bespeak the conflict between the lurking potential of stratification in the efflorescence of media products and the relative equality that existed when some attempt to find a citizen-oriented information standard or common denominator ruled. The past was never halcyon, but it arguably featured higher-quality mass news media, clearer demarcations between news and entertainment or advertising – and also smaller numbers of specialized media outlets.

The third tension we see evolving in many democratic communication systems is between treating people as consumer audiences or as citizen publics. Whether this is even a conflict is a matter of some contention here. If we regard individuals merely as consumers of media products, some contributors suggest, we may be inviting diminution in the autonomy, political involvement, and representation of mass citizens in the policy sphere, along with a serious corruption of the electoral process. If we put the stress on citizenship, we will look for ways that communication media can and do enhance autonomy, encourage political involvement, and strengthen representation of ordinary people in the policy sphere. Other contributors to this volume feel this tension is overstated. They look at new communication trends and see no real change in political behavior or democratic functioning. Some even point to a democratizing potential inherent in the media's growing concern, enforced by the increasingly competitive market, with satisfying consumers.

The chapters that follow are informed by these epochal changes occurring in political communication and democratic politics. The comparative focus on the American case enables us to understand how changes that are affecting many nations are rolling through a particular political system. We hope that future analyses will introduce new comparative considerations based on other national and transnational cases and that these analyses will appear in this series.

Acknowledgments

This book was made possible through the generous funding of the Annenberg Policy Center at the University of Pennsylvania. The organization of the book and the content of the chapters evolved during the course of two workshops, one at the Annenberg Washington, D.C., Center and another at the Annenberg School for Communications at the University of Pennsylvania. The staff support at both meetings was superb. In particular, we would like to thank Debra Williams, Doug Rivlin, and Donna Burdamy. Dean Kathleen Hall Jamieson not only made these gatherings possible, but also minimized the usual red tape attached to conference grants. As a result, we were able to focus on the exchange of ideas and development of the book. Thanks, Kathleen. We also thank Alex Holzman for his interest in this project and his creative input to the Cambridge University Press series in which it appears. In addition, we thank Alissa Morris for her patient and effective handling of the many details involved with producing the book.

CHAPTER 1

Mediated Politics: An Introduction

W. Lance Bennett and Robert M. Entman

Mediated political communication has become central to politics and public life in contemporary democracies. Traditional features of politics persist, from old-fashioned door-to-door campaigning to party and social movement organizing. And people still engage in direct, unmediated political discussion with one another. However, many polities have reached a point where governance, along with a host of related processes such as opinion formation, could not occur in their present forms without various uses of media. Hence the title of this book.

Many of the political changes that ushered in the twenty-first century, from the declining importance of nationalism in most post-industrial democracies, to the shifting patterns of participation within them, are typically linked to media processes, either as causes or as adaptive mechanisms. While some aspects of civic life such as voting, party identification, and national sentiments have eroded in many nations, other activities such as joining causes, protesting unpopular policies, and forming new regional and global communities appear to be on the rise (Inglehart 1997; Archibugi, Held, and Kohler 1998). Political and academic debates question whether changing patterns of participation and identification pose alarming threats to the legitimacy of democratic governments, or whether they are simply routine, even liberating, adjustments to new global social and economic conditions (Bennett 1998; Pool 1990; Putnam 1993, 1995; Rahn and Transue 1998). Answering the core questions about citizen experience in the democratic process increasingly requires understanding the centrality of mediated political communication both in the governing process and in citizen perceptions of society and its problems.

DEMOCRACY AND THE PUBLIC SPHERE

The overarching purpose of this book is to explore how communication media affect the exchanges of information through which people decide how to think and act in politics. We accept a broad definition of politics as the "authoritative allocation of values" in society. Authority in this definition refers to the linkages between citizens and government through which power is conferred willingly by, or taken forcibly from, people to make decisions that regulate the flow of goods, services, health benefits, physical safety, and other values in society. It is clear in all democracies that personal power is not equal in matters of governance. Access to communication is one of the key measures of power and equality in modern democracies. People communicate both to make their values and interests (preferences) known, and to learn about the status of government activities affecting those preferences. Communication can shape power and participation in society in negative ways, by obscuring the motives and interests behind political decisions, or in positive ways, by promoting the involvement of citizens in those decisions.

People often understand when they are being deceived or excluded from aspects of government; the nature of communication in public life thus affects how people feel about politics and whether they feel that government legitimately represents them (Cappella and Jamieson 1997). As a result, the legitimacy of political authority has come under question as citizens in many nations view their elected authorities with increasing skepticism and suspicion. It is important to understand the degree to which the communication linkages among individuals, and between individuals and their governors, provide for information, interest formation, and representation that is agreeable and satisfying. To this end, we adopt two broad concepts through which to explore communication's impact on politics and government: the public sphere and the policy sphere.

PUBLIC SPHERE

Put simply, the public sphere refers to the areas of informal public life – from cafes, to Internet chat rooms, to the exchange of opinion in magazines and television talk programs – where citizens can go to explore social interests and conflicts. In this sphere, individuals have the freedom to judge the quality of their governmental decisions independently of censorship. The public sphere is comprised of *any and all loca-*

tions, physical or virtual, where ideas and feelings relevant to politics are transmitted or exchanged openly. We recognize that these definitions could encompass an e-mail exchange between two friends about whether, say, men are genetically sexist; a magazine article that discusses the high rate of fathering illegitimate children among professional athletes; and a television program that shows persistent, ostensibly comic misunderstandings between men and women who share a bathroom at a law firm. The definitional inclusiveness is intentional. One of the hallmarks of the emerging culture, boosted no doubt by the profusion of communication channels, is the permeability of boundaries separating the political from the nonpolitical and the private sphere from the public sphere. This book explores *transformations in politics and the public sphere that arise from the changing operations of new and old communication technologies.*

The idea of public sphere comes from the work of Jürgen Habermas (1989). In the ideal public sphere, all citizens have equal access to communication that is both independent of government constraint, and through its deliberative, consensus-building capacity, constrains the agendas and decisions of government in turn. Of course, this ideal has never been achieved, and it probably never will. As all students of politics understand, the liberation of governmental power from interest formations that exclude others (and, thereby, create permanent inequalities) is the fundamental, perhaps defining, challenge of democracy. Yet the public sphere serves theorists well as an ideal type – that is, as a construct against which different real-world approximations can be evaluated.

THE POLICY SPHERE

While it is important to recognize how people engage with and communicate their personal politics to others, often at some remove from government, it is equally important to assess the degree to which public deliberation – and whose deliberation – finds its way into the decisions of the state. In other words, we believe it important to recognize the distinction between politics as it occurs between citizens and governing institutions like legislatures or courts, and politics as it concerns power and values in informal social relationships. Discussions of matters seemingly remote from politics, such as food preferences or sports teams, may have political dimensions by our definition (e.g., Is it wrong to eat meat? Do professional athletes or owners make too much money, and should we boycott games when ticket prices get too high?). But even if the personal is (often) the political, it remains important to distinguish such exchanges from political discussions that directly address government policies. Therefore, we advance a second, finer distinction: between the public sphere and the policy sphere. The policy sphere is that subset of public sphere where ideas and feelings explicitly connect with – are communicated to, from, or about – government officials, parties, or candidates for office who may decide the outcomes of issues and conflicts facing society. None of the three earlier examples of public sphere discussions about gender and social behavior occur within the policy sphere. However, a radio documentary that investigated the effectiveness of "deadbeat parent" programs (i.e., government policies) designed to make absent parents maintain child support payments would embody a contribution to the policy sphere in the same general area.

If citizens are increasingly withdrawing into specialized communities or audience segments to pursue individual interests, as some of our contributors suggest, they may be practicing a species of politics and participating in a kind of public sphere. But we should not equate an Internet chat on which rifle does the best when hunting for deer with one about which candidate would do best as president or prime minister. There will always be citizens active in the policy sphere, and these political activists are the ones who will most affect how much everyone else in the society pays for taxes, gasoline, health care, and much else – including rifles and hunting licenses. Some of these activists may well applaud the withdrawal of masses from political engagement, as presumably a contracted policy sphere is easier to control. But at some point, if it shrivels enough, the policy sphere could become thoroughly unrepresentative, and the government undemocratic.

Many of the authors in this volume are concerned that important areas of the policy sphere lie beyond the grasp or interest of many citizens due to strategic communication that targets selected audiences and excludes others. A second, less direct but equally powerful force that discourages participation in the policy sphere is the commercialization of media in general and news organizations in particular. A broad survey of global media trends indicates that erosions of public media are accompanied by the crowding out of useful and compelling political content by commercial programming aimed at entertainment, lifestyle, and other consumer values (McChesney 1999). Without governments or other public regulatory entities to compel them, media corporations have little reason to embrace public service values.

4

The United States represents an advanced case of both these policy sphere trends: a relatively unregulated and highly commercialized media economy, and the application of enormously costly political communication technologies aimed at containing the scope and setting the terms of public involvement in many policy matters. In some areas, of course, there is lively and opinionated popular engagement. This pattern of engagement in the policy sphere exists largely on social policy matters that readily yield up emotional symbolism, such as welfare, abortion, and various civil rights issues. It is not coincidental that those issues often lead the nightly newscasts and find their way into the plots of movies and television entertainment programs, as noted in Gamson's chapter in this book. In other socially consequential areas such as the genetic engineering of food, or the rewriting of media and communications regulatory law, public engagement is dim, and news coverage is confined largely to science and business sections of elite newspapers. In the next section we suggest ways of understanding the unevenness of public involvement in the policy sphere that go beyond commonsense, individual-level accounts of publics as selectively apathetic, disinterested, or ignorant. Recognizing such explanations as post hoc or circular is a good start for building more systematic theories of political communication that illuminate democracy.

MEDIATED POLITICAL COMMUNICATION AND THE PUBLIC SPHERE

Mediated communication, from news programs to entertainment fare, serves important functions in the contemporary public sphere. It provides good or bad information, offers engaging or stupefying perspectives on social issues, stimulates conversations among friends or between strangers on trains, and offers a selection of political, scientific, and socially authoritative or dubious sources that audiences may accept or reject in thinking about social issues. Setting political communication within a broad definition of the public sphere encourages the broadest possible understanding of the ways in which communication affects politics and public life. Thinking about comparative differences in public spheres encourages scholars to take the production, content, distribution, and consumption of news, advertising, and other forms of publicity as important research topics in their own right. We believe that there is a tendency in some recent quantitative research to reduce political communication to an anemic relationship between abstracted message content and equally abstracted individual or aggregate responses.

Understanding the empirical relationships between mediated messages and political dispositions and behaviors is important, but it is also important to understand a number of other qualities of the larger political communication environment, including:

- The range or diversity of information and sources of information
- The frequency of various issues and themes
- The formats in which politically relevant information is presented, including the depth or detail of presentation, the employment of tabloid and entertainment styles, and the relative uses of narrative, analysis, and ideology
- The balance between broad social and narrow personal identity cues in message frames
- The ways in which members of the public engage with and communicate their reactions to political messages they have received from the media

In the case of news, for example, these political content patterns may vary according to the ownership of news organizations, the competition patterns among them, the professional norms that affect how journalists think about their reporting, and the ways in which audience's lifestyles and identifications affect patterns of information consumption. Understanding such constraints on news content can help explain the issue agendas that appear in the news, the ways in which issues are covered, and the kinds of signals to citizens about how they can use the information they are receiving. In the end, of course, we may return to the behavioral bottom line and ask how communication content shapes opinions and patterns of participation. However, given systemic factors surrounding the production, formatting, and distribution of political information, the interpretation of opinion or voting data makes problematic what some research takes as a given: how the political communication environment shapes both the information available and the ways ordinary people use it in thinking about politics.

In short, we seek to expand and bridge different ways of thinking about political communication in democratic societies. In the process, we hope to erase the arbitrary and unhelpful divide between theories of communication that are centered around how individuals process information and theories centered around the production and the qualities of the information that individuals are processing. Many scholars have focused on the degree to which individuals form independent and stable opinions in often noisy and politically manipulated information environments. From these perspectives, we gather that individuals often display remarkable degrees of stability in their judgments, and that this stability derives from information heuristics that simplify large, noisy volumes information (Sniderman, Brody, and Tetlock 1991; Page and Shapiro 1992; Lupia and McCubbins 1998). The important message from this research is that citizens often achieve impressive levels of rationality in their political thinking, despite being bombarded with strategic and often emotional political messages and despite the distractions of frequent media spectacles (see Zaller in Chap. 12).

This theoretical framing of the political communication process around individual (generally rational choice) models of information processing can also lead to an arbitrary distinction between political substance and media spectacle (Zaller 1998). This distinction may inflate individual rationality and independence in making substantive judgments, while discounting much political communication content as mere media spectacle and political hype. Scholars in this school tend to be critical of those who focus on how political information campaigns are assembled and implemented, and particularly critical of those who conclude that publics are often prisoners of poor information.

At the same time, those scholars who study the information processes that shape the news, create advertising messages, and target audiences often reply that on many important issues and policy questions, publics are prisoners of poor information. Many of the authors in this book, for example, note that large segments of the general population are strategically excluded in public information campaigns. Moreover, the messages aimed at targeted audiences are typically designed not to stimulate independent thinking by providing alternative understandings, but to draw out the audience's pretested, preexisting emotional concerns. Those who subscribe to this communication process orientation may concede that individuals are not necessarily duped by communication campaigns but admit that they are often excluded, seldom challenged, and unlikely to learn much in most policy processes.

Limiting our conception of political communication to either an individual-centered or an environment-centered perspective introduces serious biases into how we think about, and what we end up knowing about, democracy. For example, individual, opinion-centered approaches to political communication tend to study policy issues that are highly visible and frequently polled. It is our impression that even the bellwether surveys by the University of Michigan Center for Political Studies determine which issues will be asked about in a given election year based on the current, most widely publicized issues. This research practice makes sense given the limits on various environmental and communication variables that can be included in surveys, but it seriously constrains the usefulness of this *opinion-centered research* for building comparative democratic theory. For example, incorporating communication process perspectives makes it more likely that scholars – instead of (ironically) allowing themselves to be heavily influenced by media agendas – will explore the vast majority of public policy decisions that slip under the radar of media, polling, and public attention. Since the most publicized issues generate the most attention from pollsters, a common strategy of elites or interest groups is to dampen public awareness of many policy issues, restricting the sphere of conflict so they can better control outcomes (Schattschneider 1960).

In areas where efforts are made to actively discourage publicity, or where publicity efforts simply do not meet news values or commercial advertising prices, fewer polls are likely to be taken. Due to such selective variation in available data, researchers either end up with little information about opinion processes, or information that points to areas of ignorance and nonopinion. In addition, more salient and frequently polled issues are likely to have more psychologically independent and socially robust bases for judgment, making strategic communication efforts and various other news and media effects appear to be comparatively weak.

In short, abstracting individual characteristics, issues, and media content variables out of larger communication processes risks turning many communication effects into mere artifacts of available data. In addition, tracing communication patterns backward from the issues that are most highly polled also restricts our understanding of the dynamics of communication in the broader public sphere. For example, the public may find many opportunities for meaningful political engagement within the media spectacle of a government sex scandal, from issues of morality and sexual harassment to the exploration of class or gender based values (Lawrence, Bennett, and Hunt 1999). Yet these aspects of meaningful public engagement are easily overlooked if the issues in the scandal are reduced to partisan politics or leadership evaluations based on external economic conditions in society.

Finally, from a broader communication process model of the public sphere, the claim that citizens are not dupes may be narrowly true at the same time that it misses much of the political picture in which substantial publics are simply not involved (Entman 1989). Perhaps most importantly, the empirical discovery that all of the people are not swayed by all of the political messages, all of the time, hardly establishes a high standard for democratic achievement. In short, putting the main focus of mediated political communication on opinion responses to message content variables misses many other important and measurable characteristics of political communication on which the quality of democracy depends.

POLITICS IN MEDIATED SOCIETIES: THE UNITED STATES IN COMPARATIVE PERSPECTIVE

By the end of the twentieth century, virtually every country (democratic and otherwise) had seen a shift in the locus of influential political communication to the mass media. Even as the term *mass media* has become synonymous with collective communication experiences, we now witness the rise of competing channels and forms of information along with marketing technologies that shape specialized messages and target often narrow but strategically important audiences. This book explores the interactions between these communication systems and democratic politics with an eye toward citizen engagement, political values, and the quality of public life.

From cellular phones, to the Internet, to bigger screens and elaborate cable television systems to fill them up, citizens in many industrial nations spend increasing time and money on mediated communication services and products. Meanwhile, the nature of these communication products and services continues to undergo tectonic shifts. New communication and information technologies and increasing sophistication in the strategic use of traditional and new media have changed the ways people operate in both their public and private lives.

Although we focus primarily upon the United States, we bring explicitly comparative perspectives to this project, both to broaden its theoretical and empirical reach and to stimulate thinking about comparative frameworks for political communication. Comparative analysis is challenging for many reasons, not the least of which is that at some level of specificity, every nation, locality, institution, culture, and communication system is unique. At the other extreme, attempts to force generalizations for the sake of advancing contentious theories do not serve the cause of understanding political experience at the human level. We attempt in this volume to adopt a middle level theoretical approach to the democratic experience. This approach recognizes the United States as different from other democracies in important respects, including: the number and levels of governmental institutions, the unusual election and campaign financing procedures, and a media system unrivaled in its commercial basis and relative lack of government regulation. At the same time, the American case offers a rich basis for comparing the ways in which information is delivered to publics by various media and for evaluating the impact of such mediated communication on citizen values and consciousness, a sense of common purpose and identification, and engagement in political life. We also hope to stimulate comparative dialogue about the impact of market forces on media systems, the blurring of traditional boundaries between entertainment and news, and the political uses of new communication technologies. As noted in the next section, changes in markets, technologies, and political uses of media have swept the planet with breathtaking speed, transcending national and cultural boundaries, yet with effects in different nations that are as yet poorly understood. We offer a brief overview of commonly emerging aspects of democratic public spheres that merit greater empirical and theoretical attention.

MARKETS, TECHNOLOGIES, AND COMMUNICATION SYSTEMS

Fundamental changes in national and international communication systems began in the 1980s and accelerated for the rest of the century. Nations, such as Germany, Sweden, and England, with strong traditions of state regulation of communication systems have been affected by technological and policy developments that allow for *greater economic efficiency* in media markets of all kinds. Even the United States, already an extreme case of a free-market media system, has undergone an unprecedented period of mergers, deregulation, new channel creation, and equally important, something of a reformation in corporate and policy thinking about audiences, markets, and the social responsibility of the media. In the go-go business climate of the 1980s and 1990s, the government approved a dizzying array of mergers and combinations that created large media empires with diversified holdings in cable, broadcast, publishing, movies, and Internet services. A corresponding shift can be detected from an earlier time when smaller media companies – in compliance with stronger government regulations – proclaimed at least some public responsibility to the more recent corporate swagger that asserts primary obligation to stockholders' investments and the accompanying claim that consumer demand suffices as a measure of social accountability.

By the 1990s nations all over the world were bowing to the inexorable force of technological innovations that make it less expensive to engage in electronic communication. Governments opened up media markets just about everywhere, increasing competition among larger numbers of media outlets. This has produced in many cases a decrease in audience size for established mass media, chiefly daily newspapers and broadcast radio and television. Even as audiences for the traditional media shrank, they grew for such newer media as cable and satellite-delivered television and World Wide Web sites. The vastly increased number of outlets allowed for increased tailoring of media content to specific tastes of smaller groups. Programming resources that might once have gone to "least common denominator" productions acceptable but less than optimal for the majority of audience members shifted to production of shows more precisely suited for varying, smaller groups. Thus we see cable and satellite television networks for gourmet food lovers, golf lovers, old movie lovers, and so on. In state broadcast organizations such as the BBC in Britain, both news and entertainment programming decisions are increasingly subject to review based on audience research and an eye to ratings.

The decision calculus that determines "who gets to see, hear, or read what" is increasingly complex in both public and private media systems. Some observers suggest that open markets and competition enrich the flow of information to audiences, as in deals that bring international news services into China from sources such as Rupert Murdoch's News Corporation and Time Warner's CNN. Other ways of viewing these same developments suggest that competition occurs within constraints imposed by profits, product costs, and programming decisions based on market positions. For example, Murdoch himself canceled a book deal between one of his publishing companies and Chris Patton, the former British governor of Hong Kong, and a vocal critic of the transition to Chinese rule. Many observers alleged that Murdoch acted to avoid alienating the new Chinese rulers as they contemplated the terms of his entry into the Chinese cable television market.

Advocates of competition and government deregulation argue that enhancing economic efficiency is a good thing, since, by definition, it improves consumers' satisfaction levels at the lowest possible cost. However, the increasing penetration of market logic into the political aspects of communication also has disquieting implications. Above all, there is no reason to expect that competitive economic markets will automatically supply what economists call "public goods," such as (in this case) an informed citizenry or more democratic participation (Keane 1991; Tunstall and Palmer 1991). Even if consumers were willing to pay for such goods, there is no easy way for the market to capture revenues from providing them. Predictably, then, the supply of the goods may diminish even as economic efficiency flourishes in media markets. Under the old order of stronger government regulation (in the United States) and government-sponsored public service broadcasting (in most of the world's democracies), broadcasters and, in many cases, newspaper publishers were pushed to help fill these social needs – imperfectly, to be sure. But regulation virtually disappeared in the United States by 1990, and the public broadcasters in many nations now share the airwaves with commercial competitors. State broadcasting systems entering these competitive environments typically encounter loss of revenues, shrinking audiences and influence, and greater constraints in programming decisions (with important qualifications, as noted, for example, in Chap. 18, by Blumler and Gurevitch, on the United Kingdom).

The flip side of the market argument, then, is that under less competitive, less economically efficient systems, there are generally greater incentives and resources for the government and private media to promote educational, cultural, political, documentary, arts and literature, and public interest programming. These programming options based on considerations other than profits and audience demographics tend to be squeezed at the margin in market systems.

Even newspaper systems are affected by the new market trends. In England, for example, Mr. Murdoch owns both the leading tabloid, the *Sun*, and the leading prestige paper, the *Times of London*. Somehow the venerable *Times* neglected even to report Murdoch's decision to cancel publication of Governor Patton's book, despite the prominence of Mr. Patton and his awaited memoir, and despite the volume of controversy generated by the decision in other British media. In America, market forces long ago eliminated competing daily papers in most cities. More recently, the era of local ownership of the remaining papers has all but ended as well, with the acquisition of most newspapers by large publicly traded corporations whose managers are legally (and many would say, morally) obligated to maximize profits. Under private local ownership, newspapers could choose to use some of their revenues for features of little interest to most readers, or for standing up to advertiser pressure, or to honor the owner's sense of community involvement by covering the activities of government and civic groups. Today the local paper in most American towns is more likely to cover the latest killing spree than the city council debate about library funding, more likely to squeeze political features out in favor of food, fashion, sports, and weather, and more likely to run political coverage from its national syndicate rather than from local perspectives. These trends are signs of pressures to economize and to maximize profits, as Doug Underwood documents in Chap. 5.

All in all, then, the transition to a new century witnesses an unusual confluence of economic, technological, and policy changes that may have profound, though hardly clear implications for democracy. Consider just some of the specific changes underway.

THE DECLINE OF TRULY MASSIVE (E.G., NATIONAL) MASS MEDIA AUDIENCES. In the United States, for example, the national network television news and entertainment ratings measuring audience size shrank during the 1990s, in some cases by fully 50 percent. In some demographic groups at some times, cable has eclipsed broadcasting. For example, Nickelodeon often attracts more child viewers than the traditional big three broadcast networks, ABC, CBS, and NBC. Meanwhile, daily newspaper circulation continues its decades-long descent. One consequence of these trends is that increasing numbers of individuals enter mediated realities in which their traditional group memberships and sense of common social experience are less relevant. For political communication this may mean that both political inputs and citizen expectations have become more personalized, and thereby less likely to be satisfied by standard government action. For these and other reasons, social knowledge, interest in and support for government, and common political identifications have become less widely shared. Chap. 21, by Rahn and Rudolph, discusses these results in detail.

THE RISE OF THE INTERNET. In the Internet world, individual audience members split off into tens of thousands of different message environments at a given time, in contrast to the halcyon days of television's dominance, when tens of millions joined in simultaneously watching one of three or four shows. The transformation of the Internet into a new kind of highly segmented mass medium suggests a host of questions about the constitution of news, the common standards for creating and evaluating information, the formation of virtual political groups, and the potential decline of political organizations in society. Many of the contributors to this book touch upon various political or social implications of these developments in networked communication.

GROWTH OF ADVERTISING ON COMPUTER NETWORKS. As corporations have begun vigorously investing in the Internet, online advertising expenditures grew during the late 1990s at 20 to 30 percent per quarter, a rate that augurs profound change. Advertising was the engine that made American broadcast network television a dominant and fabulously profitable medium through the 1980s. Advertising goes to where the eyeballs are, and to the extent it alters its targets and channels, it both reflects and reinforces the changing locus of media power. One result of the rapid commercialization of the Internet is that its status as an independent, freely accessible, global forum may be quickly jeopardized. The Internet may develop just as American broadcasting did: after a somewhat anarchistic period of open access and high hopes for diversity, noncommercial sites will become marginalized, difficult to find, and not very influential. And as opposed to broadcasting where, as we have discussed, most nations operated until recently on different bases from that in the United States, the American commercial model could more or less completely and rapidly take over the Internet.

A visit to "virtual activist" sites such as Corporate Watch (British based) or Essential Information (American) illustrates both the sweep of global political networking made possible by the Internet and the level of concern among "Net activists" that commercialization of the Net will curtail a more democratic political future. Even the forms and selection of information that define what we think of as news are changing with the integration of advertising and editorial decisions, which has advanced more completely on the Net than in more traditional media. For example, commercial news sites typically link news and other information features to related products sold by advertisers on the site. Thus, a news story on terrorists in a CNN news site may be keyed to books on terrorism available through a sponsoring publisher or bookseller. Of course, this particular example could be viewed as a service to readers, indeed as a blow for literacy and informed citizenship – assuming the books highlighted are not exclusively those connected to Time Warner, which owns the Book-of-the-Month Club, Warner Books, and Little, Brown. Nonetheless, as consumer values, from health to entertainment interests, increasingly drive news decisions in general, the gatekeeping role of advertisers along with the intrusion of corporate public relations into news content decisions may all become more pronounced.

CONVERGENCE. Harbingers of the long-predicted convergence in media appeared by the late 1990s. Microsoft's Windows 98 desktop had icons for something it called "channels," meaning links to Web sites that look increasingly like interactive television channels that offer continually updated and integrated video, audio, and text. Various internet "gateways" such as America Online and Yahoo! also offered channels for direct links to shopping, travel, and entertainment industry sites. For the increasing numbers of households enjoying broadband connections to the Internet, RealPlayer offers desktop connections to a wide array of Web sites providing live video, including Bloomberg Financial Network, CNN Headline News, ABC News, the Comedy Channel, and ZDTV (computer information), as well as several dozen live radio feeds ranging from National Public Radio (United States) to Deutsche Welle (Germany) and CBC (Canada), to large choices of stations featuring rock, jazz, pop, classical, and country music, among others. Future services will provide arrays of computerized communication outlets comparable in variety to most cable and satellite television offerings, and, of course, far surpassing traditional over-the-air broadcasting. The time is near when fully integrated systems of computing, video, audio, phone, and mail will exist in the home for those who can afford it.

This future raises important questions about the technological "haves" and "have nots" in the future of democratic communication systems. It also generates concerns about the continuing shrinkage of the political universe as increasingly individualized expectations about political representation develop from such highly personalized communication links. With the advent of more personalized communication will come ever more sophisticated means of tracking consumer preferences for products, information services, entertainment on demand, and even political candidates and public policies. Interactivity is spawning a new era in which market research will be volunteered increasingly, if largely unknowingly, by consumers themselves, as an integrated feature of their daily media use.

SEGMENTATION. Beyond variety and convergence of communication media lie the even more important traits of interactivity and specialization. The new media give individual audience members the ability to tailor media choices to their particular interests. To some unpredictable

15

extent, the mass audience will increasingly peel off into ever-smaller niches. The traditional capacity of mass media to shape common experiences, promote shared discourse and agendas, and move public opinion will likely decline. Some observers celebrate the increasing individualization of political and social experience. However, the unanswered question that must be addressed in evaluating this new communication order is whether the representative processes on which all democracies depend – and which have developed from quite different social and communication circumstances in different societies – can aggregate increasingly segmented, individualized political demands, and channel them into coherent and legitimate public policies. One thing that we do know at this point is that reaching the fragmented public of this new communication order requires increasingly sophisticated communication strategies developed and implemented by professionals who typically operate beyond accountability to the ideals of democracy.

THE INCREASING PROFESSIONALIZATION OF POLITICAL COMMUNICATION. As Blumler and Kavanaugh (1999) view the last half-century of communication primarily in Western European, British, and North American settings, they note three markedly different political eras:

- Prior to the television age, political messages were constructed primarily through parties and interest associations and transmitted through those organizations and related civic groups to individuals. Such communication was characteristically ideological at its source, yet tempered by the pragmatic social exchanges required to forge alliances among organized groups in order to maximize power in the political arena.
- With the rise of mass media and national audiences, political communication gradually became professionalized, through the reliance on pollsters, image consultants, press strategists, performance coaches, and the routinization of relations between journalists and their political sources. The defining characteristic of political communication in this period (roughly bounded by the saturation of broadcast television and the rise of cable), was the mass marketing of symbols to forge broad identifications and mobilize large numbers of individuals, often outside of their local social affiliations.
- In the third era of political communication, professionalization of politics came of age. This period corresponds roughly to the rise

of direct-marketing methods, the proliferation of electronic channels, and the advent of new opinion-assessment technologies (e.g., focus groups, cognitive mapping, and political-performance evaluation through electronic audience feedback).

As noted in the "Segmentation" section, mass audiences have been broken down or segmented in the present era into strategically targeted groups for which highly personalized messages and delivery systems are constructed by the growing ranks of pollsters, strategists, and spin doctors who work behind the scenes of modern democracies. Politics is no longer a game for low budget amateurs. Journalists are increasingly outnumbered by public relations professionals who see placing stories in the news as the means of amplifying and authenticating their messages. With information selectively targeted to constructed publics, it is important to ask whether commonality of public engagement may diminish to the point of having democracies without citizens (Entman 1989).

OVERVIEW OF THE BOOK

The authors of this book have come together through two conferences and many e-mail exchanges to explore the effects of this new era of political communication on society and democratic politics. As noted above, we focus primarily on the United States, but use concepts and frameworks that encourage comparisons with other political systems. Throughout this exploration, we are reminded at various points that the trends we are exploring do not yield simplistic generalities about the prospects for democracy in our increasingly wired world. However, the trends that we identify do raise important issues that should be faced squarely by scholars, policy makers, and citizens alike. The alternative to careful study and policy formulation in every nation is to allow an otherwise unfathomable mix of forces such as new communication technologies, the political professionals who use those technologies, and the imperatives of global media and technology markets to determine the future of politics.

Democracy and the Public Sphere

Peter Dahlgren in Chap. 2 opens with a general discussion of conceptions of the public sphere, focusing on areas of controversy that are important for rethinking democratic theory in the media age. He then turns to the important question of whether the increasingly personalized medium of the Internet is likely to promote or undermine a more vibrant public life. At this embryonic stage, the Internet holds considerable democratic promise, but it also betrays individual proclivities to seek communities and information that do little to advance coherent citizen engagement on matters of public significance.

In Chap. 3, William Gamson examines the qualities of mediated public discourse that affect the prospects for citizen engagement on different issues in the United States and Germany. The importance of understanding how media systems interact with the public and the government is underscored by the differences in media discourse on a range of issues from abortion to nuclear power in the United States, and in the surprising contrast in abortion discourse in the American and German cases. It is clear that existing communication systems are capable of generating high quality discourse that motivates responsible citizen engagement. It is equally clear that such relatively sophisticated public discourse and public engagement is absent in many areas of politics. An important question emerging from Gamson's work is how – under what conditions – such engaging communication occurs, and whether it can be promoted across a broader range of issues facing society.

Perhaps the great irony of the growing person-to-person, or point-to-point communications capabilities on the planet is that their potential is not being harnessed systematically for coordinated, collective deliberation and decision making. Chap. 4, by Colin Sparks, explores the degree to which an increasingly wired globe permits individuals to engage in useful deliberative communication about the issues that arguably affect them in common. He introduces a variety of data suggesting that there is little likelihood either within nations or in the global context of attaining anything approaching an ideal (Habermasian) public sphere. While sheer volumes of information and communication may be rising, there is little evidence that the noisy exchange of human messages is finding political order through equality of citizen access or mechanisms for resolving political differences. Nor do many governments appear to be hard at work creating new communication channels beyond elections for linking various deliberative publics to momentous decisions affecting health, education, retirement security, moral codes, employment security, income, wealth and power distribution, business practices, genetic engineering, and the global environment.

It is ironic that the new technologies hold the potential for creating common communication across broad communities, yet there is little push either from civic-minded consumers or from social, economic, or political leaders in this direction. To the contrary, the opposing tendency toward ever more personalized, individually targeted communication may result in greater fragmentation of interests, social realities, and political impulses. Todd Gitlin has described this global tendency away from more coherent public spheres as resulting in increasingly isolated and fragmented "public sphericules" (Gitlin 1998). He argues that this technologically assisted centrifugal push away from common discourse also entails a widening gap between the wired and the unwired, the electronic haves and have nots: those who are included in political communication audiences, and those who are not. These concerns are expressed and explored throughout this book by Gandy, Entman and Herbst, Neuman, Bennett and Manheim, Jamieson, Buchanan, and Baker. The degree to which broad sections of the public are engaged in thinking, speaking, and acting on policy issues is the core measure of democracy. How mediated communication promotes or impedes such democratic engagement is the core of the earlier conceptual distinction between the *public sphere* (the patterns of public exchanges on all matters of social interest) and the *policy sphere* (those exchanges that are pertinent to formal political decisions).

Citizens, Consumers, and Media in Transition

Flowing from the above broad political definitions, we address a variety of questions about the role of citizens in electronic democracies, and about how communication systems may facilitate or frustrate citizen impact on the policy sphere. Many of the chapters address current communication fashions that treat members of the public as isolated consumers who pilot their own personal political destinies. A central question is whether the political fates of individuals addressed as consumers tend to involve realities, however personally stimulating, that are trapped within fragmenting public sphericules that offer few outlets for effective and satisfying participation in the policy sphere. At the core of this tension is the related question of whether citizens are shrinking from their citizen roles (measured in various trends of declining party loyalty, reduced voting, and greater antagonism toward government itself) because government is truly less relevant to personal lives, or because social realities based on such personal atomization make it hard to aggregate interests and achieve meaningful political representation.

As large national and global corporations increasingly absorb media outlets, the definition of both the products and their audiences inevitably shifts from social responsibility to profits. The United States represents a startling case of rapid commercialization and corporate merger of media. As Chap. 5, by Doug Underwood, indicates, the once clear divisions in news organizations between marketing the product and editorial decisions about what the product should be are disappearing rapidly. News organizations are increasingly driven by audience research that conflates cost and profit calculations with consumer demands. One result is that the amount of space devoted to detailed policy issues is shrinking (both because such material is relatively costly to produce, and because audiences that are treated as consumers prefer to consume information about movies, music, sports, food, fashion, and lifestyles).

In Chap. 6, Don Slater argues that as publics are more defined around consumer values, the discourses of public life become discourses of consumption far removed from the array of issues in the policy sphere. This holds for arenas ranging from shopping to the assertion of the supremacy of lifestyle freedoms, to the case that he examines here: the creation of communities dedicated to the use and exchange of pornography.

As personal pleasures of consumption become elevated over considerations of collective welfare, the political tendency is for relatively isolated communities to develop and to see government and policy intrusions as antagonistic. Thus, the public sphere becomes "consumed" with personal communication about consumption, while the policy sphere becomes negative and intrusive. And so we witness a global battle over the asserted right to trade freely in pornographic materials – a trade that is greatly facilitated by the new technologies of the Internet and the digital management of audio, visual, and text information. It is true that considerable policy sphere activity is dedicated to this question, but policy battles are often waged against those using the public communication space for purposes that others find objectionable. Indeed, the cyberpornographers see politics in the policy sphere as negative. They claim the right to be regarded as consumers alone, with a virtual society of their own, and many have effectively disowned any sense of a citizen's obligations to engage with other's concerns about the impact of pornographic communities on society as a whole. While the debate in the policy sphere buzzes around them, the pleasures of consumption displace consideration of important social questions raised in the policy sphere: Should children be eroticized? Does pornography degrade women and diminish the potential of human sexual intimacy?

If we step back again from Slater's specific case of electronic pornography trafficking, Gandy's analysis in Chap. 7 reveals that the growing tendency in most contemporary communication is to tap consumer values and to treat audiences as pockets of paying customers rather than as broad societies that should be addressed regardless of lifestyle or ability to consume. Gandy takes these concerns beyond the well-known arguments about the fragmentation of society and loss of collective experience that may be induced by contemporary technologies of audience segmentation and targeting (Turow 1997). He points to the growing numbers of citizens who, due to their poverty as consumers or their different lifestyles, are simply left out of society and politics because they are not linked by the commercial logic of communication.

If we look at the encroachment of consumer values in the public sphere and the resulting isolation that many people feel from the policy sphere, we can better appreciate the argument of Delli Carpini and Williams in Chap. 8 that information itself has been transformed in the bargain. Old categories such as news and entertainment make less and less sense, particularly in the highly commercialized American media context. We find expressions of public sphere politics in lifestyle dramas from soap operas to cop programs. Social conflicts and emerging norms are encoded, often in formulaic fashion, in movies, music, and entertainment television. And there is obvious blending of entertainment values into news.

In some ways, this blurring of genres may represent a welcome expansion of public sphere discourse. For example, to the extent that urban minorities are largely excluded from policy sphere deliberations about crime control, policing, economic development, or education, the convergence of communication forms may enable their political messages to be introduced into the public sphere through music, movies, and art (see Edelman 1995). However, the disconnect between such public sphere expression and policy sphere engagement may well damage the legitimacy of democratic government in the eyes of different groups. Alienation readily encompasses the rap artists who see policing and jail as means of excluding poor blacks from equal participation in society – and the shocked middle class parents who would cheerfully overlook the First Amendment to have government ban offensive lyrics about killing cops in rap songs.

Thus even as media consumers may enjoy growing choices in the marketplace, citizens in the United States and elsewhere may feel growing disaffection and disengagement from government. Ineffectual media responses to the problems of revivifying democratic governance, or, in some instances, media complicity in compounding the problems, animate this volume's concerns with the future of democracy. As Timothy Cook notes in Chap. 9 on the role of media in government, it is inconceivable to imagine governing in contemporary America without the strategic use of the news. At the same time, the growing public cynicism and distrust of the information contained in news reporting suggests that these essential political communication practices may be undermining the legitimacy of government itself.

Mediated Political Information and Public Opinion

Given the fragmentation of public spheres, and the sophistication of communication technologies to evaluate and attempt to shape audience behavior, we may need to rethink the very concept of public opinion. In Chap. 10, Entman and Herbst show how publics are in many ways created through the media framing process as information is packaged with audience reactions in mind, and audience reactions, in turn, inform future decisions about what stories the media tell and how they tell them. There are, to be sure, latent attitudes that give the public considerable independence and critical resistance to sheer fabrication of political images and public problems. However, the selection of images and problems from the available reserves of public considerations bears far greater scrutiny.

As Wolfsfeld argues in Chap. 11, there are other dynamics at work in the public opinion process, such as media portrayals of problems and crises that seem to trigger what he terms "waves" of public attention. This week we are overrun with terrorists. Next week it is a financial or sexual scandal at the highest levels of government. Then global warming looms in news accounts of droughts, floods, and other climatic catastrophes. These waves focus public attention on one problem, while withdrawing it from other possibilities. It is not that the problem *du jour* is not serious, or that people and politicians who keep the stories going via audience ratings and news management strategies are not genuinely interested in doing something about it. However, waves may fill the public sphere for a time with outpourings of popular concern that may not be well connected to policy processes or to sensible and enduring governmental responses. The rhythms of the media and government, and thus, public sphere and policy sphere, may be increasingly out of synch as the news cycle speeds up and the concentration of information fills individuals with alarm, while the policy process plods slowly and seemingly ineffectually on its own institutional clock.

To what extent is mediated political life characterized by such disjunctions between public attention and policy formation? Perhaps this view of instant media saturation of society with fleeting crises is unduly alarmist. Public waves may be no more hazardous to the health of contemporary democracy than were the spread of rumor and gossip to the quality of the Athenian polis. In Chap. 12, John Zaller argues that for all of the turbulence and disjunctures of mediated communication, members of the public continue to display remarkable stability and restraint in their judgments. Looking at one of the longest-lasting media waves to hit the American public, the sex scandal involving President Clinton that led to his impeachment, Zaller shows that despite the highly dramatic and persistent news and entertainment focus on presidential wrongdoing, public opinion remained consistently stable and supportive of Clinton. Thus, we are reminded that people are capable of remarkably independent public responses, even in the face of high levels of media spectacle and hype.

However, there may be ways to think about the effects of mediated communication beyond whether people continue to vote responsibly or resist the dramatized and scandalous implications of tabloid journalism. As noted earlier, for example, political spectacles may engage audiences at various levels that are worth paying attention to. For example, the Lewinsky scandal raised the interesting counterfactual question of how the public might have judged the president if his behavior constituted sexual harassment. There is evidence that public judgments about Clinton's relations with other women beyond Lewinsky, when considered with Lewinsky's strong assertion that their relationship was consensual, affected the common categorization of the affair in ways that protected Clinton's approval scores (Lawrence, Bennett, and Hunt 1999).

More generally, the uneasy distinction between media politics and substance inhibits more complex interpretations of political trends within the policy sphere. For example, although people may continue to vote on much the same basis as ever, note that decreasing numbers of people are voting. Moreover, many of those who continue to vote profess to be disgusted by the choices they are offered and by the ways in which candidates and parties communicate in the electoral process. Similarly, democratic theorists must consider that it was only a bare majority of members of the U.S. Congress (elected by the bare majority of those who bothered to vote) who attempted to remove a president from office – while the majority of citizens, who opposed impeachment, largely preferred to watch their usual entertainment programming instead of the televised drama of a governmental crisis. Saying that people are unaffected by the media spectacle while they employ self-interest considerations to judge events in the news misses what may be the most important workings of the policy sphere.

Chap. 13, by Bennett and Manheim, suggests that the uses of communication technologies to make strategic calculations about how to structure the perceptions and reactions of targeted audiences may have the more important effects of undermining the norms of informational transparency, reliability, and universality on which democratic legitimacy are based. Thus, democracy may continue to function at the most basic level of conducting elections, passing laws, and adjudicating disputes, but the sense of integrity and respect among the players and the popular trust in everyday communication about political affairs may be diminishing rapidly. In this light, Bennett and Manheim examine what may stand as the greatest governmental economic regulatory lawsuit of the century in the United States – the case against the computer software giant Microsoft. Their analysis suggests that the engagement of the judicial process may not represent so much an urgent or enlightened government response to a crisis in an important economic sector, as a key strategic component of a larger news and public relations campaign waged by business competitors against the targeted company.

Still, for all the strategic communicating and political dismantling of the public, when W. Russell Neuman (Chap. 14) looks for evidence that the bedrock of opinion has been eroded, he finds that the potential for broad publics persists in latent opinions that transcend narrow demographic differences. For all the onslaughts of media waves and strategic communication, the basis of a common political culture appears to be holding its own. Neuman's analysis may offer some optimism for restoring more satisfying linkages between publics and the policy sphere, as it reminds us that political culture is greater than the sum of its public, waves, and strategic messages.

There is a lesson here about media effects. Members of publics may behave responsibly and intelligently in the face of degraded communication, but they may devalue their political experience in the process. Many of the authors in this volume agree that a contemporary political dilemma is how to stop powerful groups and political actors from using communication in ways that undermine public interest and faith in government itself. Perhaps the current gap between the public and trust in the formal workings of government is greater in the United States than in other industrial democracies because markets and money so dominate the American political communication process. And nowhere is this domination more evident in what many regard as the cornerstone institution of the policy sphere, that is, election campaigns.

MEDIATED CAMPAIGNS

Many of the communication technologies and audience-targeting practices that define contemporary mediated politics were pioneered in election campaigns. For their part, the communication professionals who now run elections in most nations adapted many of these practices from marketing and advertising. Even as we understand the evolution of these communications trends, and even as we recognize their unpopular effects on the quality of political experience, it is difficult to figure out how to contain these practices as they spread from one nation to another. In the United States, for example, we find that nearly all policy issues routinely become wrapped in public relations campaigns. Moreover, these issue campaigns often invade elections in ways that give interest groups disproportionate influence over the terms and the tone of these democratically defining contests for power.

Nowhere are the excesses of political communication more protected by market ideology and cloaked in the rhetoric of freedom than in the United States, where court rulings on various attempts to limit spending on strategic communication have equated money with free speech itself. Several authors in this volume question whether money talks too loudly in politics. This theme enlivens Chaps. 15, 16, and 17, by Jamieson, Baker, and Buchanan, respectively, who introduce issues not often found in analyses of campaign communication.

Jamieson argues that the infusion of money in elections has transformed the nature of the process itself, from an evaluation of known candidates and parties to the saturation of the communication environment with often misleading and emotional issue campaigns funded by obscure cause groups. In this process, the important line between everyday issue politics and the larger agenda-setting function of elections has been blurred by communication technologies aimed at finding the issues that trigger votes. Moreover, traditional bases for judging persuasive communication, such as assessing the credibility of the source of information, may be short-circuited by constructing pseudonymous groups that only exist for the duration of a particular campaign.

In the American case, these issue campaigns (waged around taxes, abortion, gun control, and other volatile "hot button" issues) often affect how voters think about parties and candidates, but they are not officially produced and run by parties. This elaborate deception in the election process is due in large part to the successful efforts of parties and their financial backers to circumvent laws that restrict the amount of private money that can enter publicly financed election campaigns. Thus, the comparatively modest American attempts to keep wealthy interests from buying elections has yielded a deceptive system of surrogate political groups who can buy enough advertising space and air time to set the tone of an entire election or public policy debate.

Chap. 16, by Baker, and Chap. 17, by Buchanan, address the difficulties in regulating these communication practices, even though both voters and politicians tend to agree that they are undermining the quality of elections, citizen involvement, and government itself. Baker suggests that we rethink the very meaning, and even downplay the importance, of elections in an effort to regain control over what goes on in them. He argues that the courts and media scholars alike tend to place elections on the highest pedestal of democratic free speech. This not only belies the often limited discourse that goes on in campaigns, but it creates a rhetorical barrier to redesigning campaign communications so that they may better serve the basic function of finding the best people to fill government jobs. Buchanan argues that elections remain the sole arena of broad collective political engagement, and as such, deserve their special status. He proposes that campaign communication practices can be reformed through incentives for voters and candidates to communicate as creatively as possible about society and its future.

Chap. 18, by Blumler and Gurevitch, puts the American electoral dilemma in comparative perspective. While campaign communications in Britain have become more "Americanized" over the course of recent elections, fundamental differences in media systems produce important differences in election coverage. Despite notable changes over time, both the BBC and the British press have maintained higher profile issue coverage and fuller presentations of party and candidate positions than do the American media. The British election that reaches voters in the papers and on TV is, in their view, less disruptively "mediated" than its

American counterpart. How long British distinctiveness will persist in the face of the pressures documented throughout the book remains to be seen.

CITIZENS: PRESENT AND FUTURE

The book closes by looking squarely at the qualities of citizenship that are shaped by, and expressed through, mediated politics. Chap. 19, by Roderick Hart, reconstructs something of the citizen ideal, by looking at profiles of people who wrote letters to their local newspapers. Hart argues that these public communiqués offer important insights about political culture and shows how they can be analyzed as expressions of public opinion and civic values. The new technologies may augment opportunities for this form of participation.

Doris Graber in Chap. 20 turns to the citizens of the future, challenging the alarmist belief that younger generations are inherently turned off to politics and have little interest in news and public affairs. Graber presents data suggesting that a large part the problem involves the impatience of these "cybercitizens" with traditional linear forms of information presentation. She argues that the means for reconnecting younger generations to politics involve placing the media focus on politics where they live and producing news with more creative visual and interactive presentations of information. If Graber is right, citizens of the future will demand interactive information rather than the edited and passively transmitted media formats of the present day. This optimistic look at the future offers a vision of political communication based on technologies that already exist in entertainment and consumer realms.

The exploration of citizens in the new democratic context concludes in Chap. 21 with Rahn and Rudolph's look at the impact of globalization and materialism on patterns of political identification. They note that whatever forms democracy may take in the future, it must accommodate citizens that are more individualistic and less committed to collective identifications such as nationalism than past generations. This returns us to earlier questions about how to aggregate the increasingly fragmented interests of publics in the policy sphere, while raising an important question about a materialist age: How much self-interested behavior can democracy withstand?

In Chap. 22, we return to draw out key themes from different chapters and present an agenda of questions that might guide future efforts to understand the problems and prospects that the new political communication presents for democracy. This discussion translates the American case into useful terms for comparative analysis by adapting Robert Dahl's continuum of the development of polyarchy as a tool for evaluating the ways in which information is communicated within different democratic systems. This discussion suggests how we can better understand both the effects and the democratic potential of mediated political communication through comparative research.

References

Archibugi, Daniele, David Held, and Martin Kohler (Eds.) (1998). *Re-imagining Political Community: Studies in Cosmopolitan Democracy.* Stanford: Stanford University Press.

Bennett, W. Lance (1998). "The UnCivic Culture: Communication, Identity, and the Rise of Lifestyle Politics." *PS: Political Science and Politics,* 31 (December):741–761.

Blumler, Jay G., and Dennis Kavanaugh (1998). "The Third Age of Political Communication: Influences and Features." *Political Communication,* 16 (July–September):209–230.

Cappella, Joseph N., and Kathleen Hall Jamieson (1997). *Spiral of Cynicism: The Press and the Public Good.* New York: Oxford University Press.

Edelman, Murray (1995). *From Art to Politics: How Artistic Creations Shape Political Conceptions.* Chicago: University of Chicago Press.

Entman, Robert M. (1989). *Democracy without Citizens: Media and the Decay of American Politics.* New York: Oxford University Press.

Gitlin, Todd (1998). "Public Spheres or Public Sphericules?" in James Curran and Tamar Liebes (Eds.), *Media, Ritual, and Identity.* London: Routledge, pp. 168–174.

Habermas, Jürgen (1989). *Structural Transformation of the Public Sphere: An Inquiry into a Category of Bourgeois Society.* Trans., Thomas Burger and Frederick Lawrence. Cambridge, MA: MIT Press.

Inglehart, Ronald (1997). *Modernization and Postmodernization: Cultural, Economic, and Political Change in 43 Societies.* Princeton, NJ: Princeton University Press.

Keane, John (1991). *The Media and Democracy.* Cambridge: Polity Press.

Lawrence, Regina G., W. Lance Bennett, and Valerie Hunt (1999). "Making Sense of Monica: Media Politics and the Lewinsky Scandal." Paper presented at the Annual Meeting of the American Political Science Association, Atlanta.

Lupia, Arthur, and Matthew D. McCubbins (1998). *The Democratic Dilemma: Can Citizens Learn What They Need to Know?* New York: Cambridge University Press.

McChesney, Robert M. (1999). *Rich Media, Poor Democracies.* Urbana, IL: University of Illinois Press.

Page, Benjamin I., and Robert Y. Shapiro (1992). *The Rational Public.* Chicago: University of Chicago Press.

Pool, Ithiel de Sola (1990). *Technologies Without Boundaries: On Telecommunication in a Global Age.* Cambridge, MA: Harvard University Press.

Putnam, Robert D. (1993). *Making Democracy Work.* Princeton: Princeton University Press.

(1995). "Tuning In, Tuning Out: The Strange Disappearance of Social Capital in America." *PS: Political Science and Politics,* 28 (December): 664–683.

Rahn, Wendy M., and John Transue (1998). "Social Trust and Value Change: The Decline of Social Capital in American Youth." *Political Psychology*, 19(3):545–566.

Schattshneider, E. E. (1960). *The Semi-Sovereign People: A Realist's View of Democracy in America.* New York: Holt, Rinehart and Winston.

Sniderman, Paul A., Richard A. Brody, and Philip E. Tetlock (1991). *Reasoning and Choice: Explorations in Political Psychology.* New York: Cambridge University Press.

Tunstall, Jeremy, and Michael Palmer (1991). *Media Moguls.* London: Routledge.

Turow, Joseph (1997). *Breaking Up America: Advertisers and the New Media World.* Chicago: University of Chicago Press.

Zaller, John R. (1998). "Monica Lewinsky's Contribution to Political Science," *PS: Political Science and Politics*, 31(June):182–189.

PART 1

Democracy and the
Public Sphere

The Public Sphere and the Net:
Structure, Space, and Communication

Peter Dahlgren

While the public sphere as a general notion appears in a variety of ways in the writings of many authors in the twentith century, such as Walter Lippman, Hannah Arendt, and John Dewey, most people today associate the concept with Jürgen Habermas's particular version. Written in the early 1960s, his original text was translated into English only a decade ago (Habermas 1989). Since this translation, use of the concept has grown considerably in the Anglo-American world. Over the years there have been many critical interventions around the concept (see Calhoun 1992, for the best collection), and while Habermas has not attempted a full-scale reformulation of the public sphere, it is clear that his view of the concept is evolving as his work in other areas develops (Habermas 1996). While I cannot here trace all the contributions and debates around the public sphere (I probe the concept more extensively in Dahlgren 1995), my aim in this presentation is to briefly sketch the main features of the original argument, but looking at it from the standpoint of three interrelated dimensions: structural, spatial, and communicative. After summarizing the major dilemmas facing the late modern public sphere, I turn to the Internet and look at how its dominant features relate to the democratic ideals embodied in the idea of the public sphere.

In its original formulation, the public sphere as described by Habermas consists of the institutional space where political will formation takes place, via the unfettered flow of relevant information and ideas. Mediated and face-to-face interactions constitute this space. After an extensive historical overview, Habermas arrives at the view that what he calls a public sphere began to emerge within the bourgeois classes of Western Europe in the late eighteenth and early nineteenth centuries. The institutional basis for this public sphere consisted of an array of milieu and media, such as clubs, salons, coffee houses, newspapers, books, and pamphlets, all of which in various (though incomplete) ways manifested Enlightenment ideals of the human pursuit of knowledge and freedom. For Habermas, the key here was not only the institutional basis, but also the manner in which communication took place in this burgeoning public sphere. However imperfectly, he saw that interaction in this social space embodied the ideals of reason, that is, the Enlightenment goals of rational thinking, argument, and discussion. In his notion of the public as a rational, dialogic process, Habermas's account of communication and democracy bears similarities with that of John Dewey.

As he continues with his historical narrative, Habermas sees the public sphere growing and deepening in the first few decades of the nineteenth century with the spread of mass literacy and the press. Then gradually the decay sets in. Journalism increasingly loses its claim to reason; public discourse degenerates into public relations. As the logic of commercialism increasingly shapes the operations of the media, the domain of rationality diminishes. Moving into the twentieth century, Habermas observes with pessimism the trivialization of politics, not least in the electronic media, the industrialization of public opinion, the transformation of publics from discursive to consuming collectivities, and an array of other ills that many other critics have also often noted.

Perhaps the first thing to be said about Habermas's historical account is that it bears many of the markings of the original Frankfurt School of critical theory, including a critique of "mass society" and a neo-Marxian perspective of advanced capitalism and the cultural industries. There is also a decidedly nostalgic quality to the analysis, the sense that there once was an historical opening, which then became closed off. There is also some ambiguity: It is not fully clear whether what Habermas describes is an ideological self-appraisal of a particular class, an empirical reality of an historical situation, or a normative vision. Habermas certainly sees the limits of this bourgeois public sphere, not least in class terms – and feminists have been quick to point out the gender limitations – but there remains something powerfully compelling for him (and many of his readers) about this budding public sphere and its significance for Western democracy. More recently, Habermas (in Calhoun 1992) seems to take a less militantly pessimistic view of the public sphere than in his original exposition.

Analytic differences can be seen between those who accept that what we have today qualifies as a public sphere and those (e.g., Colin Sparks in Chap. 4) who do not. These critics argue that the public sphere has yet to be achieved, but the concept is useful as a normative vision. I take the view that it *is* meaningful to speak about a public sphere that does exist today, but by any standard of evaluation it is in a dismal state. In practical terms, however, the normative horizons from the liberal or progressive traditions that promote "good journalism" or "information in the public interest" are not so different from ideals about the media inspired by the framework of the public sphere. Chap. 3, by William Gamson, is an excellent example of engaged research on the media that meshes very well with the public sphere ideal. As has often been said in the past, the genuine realization of liberal ideals would have truly radical implications for society.

Gradually, the public sphere has entered into more common usage: Its Frankfurt School origins are not always emphasized. The term often connotes the realm of media, politics, and opinion processes in a more general, descriptive way. In some usages, the concept veers toward the larger sociocultural realm, as I discuss next. In Chap. 1, Lance Bennett and Robert Entman concern themselves with what they call the policy sphere, which is the specific domain of the public sphere that has to do with media representations relating to concrete governmental decision making. This pluralization of the concept, and its insertion into other kinds of intellectual discourses, can no doubt generate some conceptual issues. Yet, fundamentally, the notion of the public sphere invites us to reflect upon the relationships among media, communication, and democracy. Rather than artificially trying to force a full consensus, at this point, it seems more productive to acknowledge different inflections of the concept and understand how each relates to the protean ideal of democracy. In the following discussion, I highlight three inseparable dimensions of the public sphere, each of which raises sets of issues having to do with the character of democracy.

NECESSARY STRUCTURES

The structural dimension has to do with the larger institutional features that set important parameters for the public sphere. At bottom, the public sphere rests upon the idea of universality, the norm that it must be accessible to all citizens of society. This puts key institutional aspects of the media into the limelight. If the media are a dominant feature of the public sphere, they must be technically, economically, culturally, and linguistically within reach of society's members; any a priori exclusions of any segment of the population collides with democracy's claim to universalism. Seen from this angle, the vision of a public sphere raises questions about media policy and economics, ownership and control, the role of market forces and regulation, issues of the privatization of information, corporate power, and so forth. In this volume, Chaps. 5 and 7 by Doug Underwood and Oscar Gandy, respectively, address themes of this kind. The practical tasks of shaping media policy are often conceptually complicated and politically difficult, given the array of competing interests at stake. However, promoting the idea of the public sphere, which builds on the ideal of something common and shared to which all citizens are entitled, becomes all the more challenging in an era when market forces have such a strong influence in forming policy.

Institutionally, the modern media are in the midst of a pervasive global restructuring, yielding fewer but larger global conglomerates, which in turn further accentuates the processes of commodification (cf. Herman and McChesney 1997). In terms of communicative practices, most serious analyses of journalistic practices in the press and on television – as manifested in routine political and social coverage as well as in election campaigns – come to dismal conclusions (cf. Blumler and Gurevitch 1995). While popularization can and has been in many cases a positive development, bringing more people into the public sphere, by most accounts today popularization is degenerating into trivialization and sensationalism. The ideals of journalism are increasingly subordinated to the imperatives of market. For example, the boundaries between journalism and popular culture are becoming ever more porous, as Michael Delli Carpini and Bruce Williams point out in their contribution to this volume (see also Dahlgren and Sparks 1992). Those journalists, editors, and producers still committed to quality journalism (whose definitions of course vary) struggle to find new formats that will satisfy the economic conditions, take into account shifts in audiences' expectations and horizons, and yet fulfill journalistic ideals. Chap. 20, by Doris Graber, explicitly addresses this theme.

Beyond the institutions of the media lie the socioeconomic structures of society as a whole. The public sphere is predicated on interaction between citizens and not just on the institutions of the media, and this interaction is of course shaped by social hierarchies, economics, work circumstances, welfare, and education. Such factors tend often to be disregarded in, for example, discussions about declining participation in the formal political system (see Bennett 1998), and "apathy" and other ills are often treated as expressions of citizens' seemingly enigmatic subjectivity, decontextualized from material circumstances. The importance of these factors leads us directly into the classic arguments like those of T. H. Marshall (1950) for the necessity of securing the *social* conditions of citizenship if democracy is to function. Needless to say, the weight that should be accorded such arguments is politically contested, especially now that welfare state traditions are eroding in the face of neoliberal initiatives.

Finally, the relationship of political structures and the decision-making processes to the public sphere is of central concern. Colin Sparks in Chap. 3 makes the important point that while we tend to link together the public sphere and democracy, there is no a priori theoretical reason why democratic structures and processes necessarily arise in conjunction with a public sphere. Indeed, the historical situation that Habermas originally analyzed had at best only a very rudimentary democratic character. Democracy today, though different in character, is arguably still in a highly problematic state. A blooming public sphere per se does not guarantee a democracy; it is a necessary but not sufficient ingredient.

SPATIAL BOUNDARIES: EXPANSIVE AND RESTRICTIVE

In the past decade, the humanities and social sciences have become increasingly sensitive to spatial dimensions of social and cultural processes; the where is catching up in importance with the what, the who, the why, and the how. The spatial involves more than simple geography; it readily becomes an analytic dimension in a world where space can be constituted by communication processes that may be quite indifferent to place. The constitution of social space via modern communication technologies, and their separation from place, can be said to have begun with the invention of the telegraph, with its protodigital code and its capacity to trasmit signals over large distances in almost no time. Both the mass media and interactive media like the Net play a very important role in constituting space in the modern world.

In looking at the public sphere as a space, we should first of all take note of its relationship to another major space, namely the market. The mass media have contributed to spaces of public visibility, where the world and its current affairs are, via various modes of representation, available to most citizens. Given the institutional factors of political economy that shape the media, however, it becomes increasingly difficult for them to maintain a space for the public sphere that is separate and distinct from the imperatives of the market. The market, conceived of as a communicative space, operates on and through the media with its own logic, to which the public sphere must accommodate. This is nothing new, of course; much of the media's origins can be traced to the need for the distribution of economic news, and the problematic character of the commercial media has long been analyzed by critics.

Rather, the point here is that from the standpoint of communicative space in the media, the market and the public sphere in the media present very different profiles: the one robust, expansive, and ideologically ascendant; the other frail, diminutive, and on the defensive. In the press and on television, the spaces available to the public sphere are comparatively restricted; we speak about the "news media," but only a small portion of the media's output concerns journalism and the public sphere. Our everyday lives are saturated by media culture, but the public sphere remains a minor feature of the total output.

If the public sphere on the one hand is implicated with the market, on the other hand this space has also become increasingly interwoven with private space, to the point that the distinctions between public and private space are not always so self-evident as they seem to have been in the past (cf. Thompson 1995). For example, the public space of the media is to a great extent intertwined with the private space of the home: Media reception is still mostly a domestic activity. Further, the public sphere often deals with private matters, such as the personal lives of politicians and celebrities or general topics having to do with "lifestyle" questions or moral issues about how we live (e.g., abortion). This blurring of public and private spheres is a key feature of late modern culture (cf. Fornäs 1995; see also Weintraub and Kumar 1997), and whether we should applaud or bemoan this development is still an open question.

While communicative space becomes more independent of place, issues of the relationship between place and space remain very current. One normative requisite for the public sphere in this regard, over which there is not much controversy, is the congruence between geographical political entities and the public sphere as a communicative space. Geographical political entities define territorial place, yet the boundaries of public spheres are not always congruent with political boundaries. Among the mass media, for example, broadcast television in

Europe has, since its origins, spilled across boundaries, while much satellite television today is predicated precisely on transnational accessibility. Yet, there is no real public sphere, based on television or any other medium, that is congruent with the political boundaries of the transnational European Union. Most citizens of the European Union have to use national public spheres to participate discursively in this supranational political body.

A second, related spatial theme is the question of whether the public sphere within a nation-state is or should be singular or plural. Some observers (e.g., Colin Sparks in Chap. 4; Garnham 1992) make the case that for politics to function at a national level, there must not only be congruence between political boundaries and the boundaries of the public sphere, but the public sphere itself must be an overarching, unifying one. This public sphere would largely be defined by the dominant mass media of the society. However fragmented the public sphere may seem, the normative argument is that we must strive for a unified space that follows shared discursive procedures and creates a communicative forum that is (at least in principle) all-inclusive. While it is easy to agree on this goal, I am compelled to point to the sociological implausibility of such a goal, given the heterogeneous character of late modern societies.

In fact, it can be argued that the goal of a unitary public sphere actually risks marginalizing and suppressing the diversity of complex societies, acting as a restrictive and disciplinarian force. Differences in experience, identity, modes of expression, and so on can easily become subordinated in a unitary public sphere. Democracy needs multiple and alternative public spheres (see Negt and Kluge 1993; Fraser 1992; Verstraeten 1996). The ideal of a unified citizenry all engaged in talking in the same discursive mode in a singular space seems a bit stilted given today's societal landscape. Indeed, Habermas's own views seem to have shifted rather dramatically in this direction, as Rousiley C. M. Maia (forthcoming) points out. Habermas (1996) now understands the public sphere as consisting of a seemingly ungraspable myriad of distinct but also overlapping, interweaving, communicative spaces.

What we have is the tension between a restrictive and an expansive view of the public sphere, with corresponding assumptions about democracy. Both positions have their merit; both have their pitfalls. Carried too far, the restricted concept of the public sphere risks cementing the formal political arena at the expense of extrasystemic political expression and activity, and cutting off opinion formation from its roots

in everyday experience. On the other hand, the expansive view, in col-
lapsing the public sphere into civil society, loses analytic and empirical
clarity; the public sphere as such ceases to be a specific referent; and
the contact with practical politics fades. The policy sphere of governmental decision making that Bennett and Entman discuss in Chap. 1
becomes blurred. This conceptual tension of the public sphere does not
seem to lend itself to easy resolution.

If we try to retain the best of both positions, much pivots on the
notion of "the political." We must certainly keep in focus the practical
business of politics, yet also acknowledge the origins of people's political views in the intricate spaces of their everyday lives. This does not
mean that every facet of the sociocultural domain is always of immediate relevance from the standpoint of the public sphere or for analyzing politics. Rather than predefining a seemingly endless terrain and
labeling it the public sphere, it would be more productive to be alert
to the fact that the boundaries of the public sphere are always to some
extent fluid, in flux. This is precisely because the concept of the political embodies a constant force field between the potential and the actual:
It is always to some degree in the process of becoming. Our understanding of what is political at any point in time is a social construction, shaped in part by power itself. Thus, the boundaries of the public
sphere, as a communicative space, are always to some extent both ana-
lytically negotiable and politically contestable. I will return to this theme
in the next section.

COMMUNICATIVE ACTION

Habermas repositions his understanding of the public sphere in the
light of his work from recent decades on systems theory and in particular communication pragmatics (Habermas 1996). The public sphere
is now incorporated into a perspective that emphasizes his theory of
communicative action, understood as the discursive negotiation of
norms and values, based on intersubjectivity and linguistic–cultural
competence. Communicative action and the mode of rationality it
builds on are distinct from, and irreducible to, strategic action and
instrumental rationality. Strategic action is goal-oriented and manipulative; communicative action aims for mutual understanding, trust, and
shared knowledge (a helpful presentation and modification of Habermas's complex scheme is found in Fornäs 1995). Thus, it is not surprising that what evolves from this in political terms is a view of

democracy that emphasizes communication among people; democracy at bottom concerns people freely communicating with each other. In this regard, Habermas's position is often logically associated with "deliberative democracy." (See Benhabib 1996 for a collection of essays exploring this theme.)

While the distinction between communicative and strategic action may seem abstract or (even worse) academic, it is important to grasp the basic principle that Habermas posits and defends here (these perspectives derive from Habermas 1984, 1987). He argues that we must at least assume the theoretic possibility that people can have the normative intentions of arriving at shared understandings in a nonmanipulative manner, and they can have the communicative capacity to interact in ways congruent with these intentions. (Here his views certainly overlap with many other social and linguistic theorists.) Obviously, people are not always communicating like this. In fact, it is one of Habermas's major theses that normatively based communication between people – which is the fundamental logic of the "life-world" of our daily reality – is increasingly being eroded by the strategic logic and instrumental rationality of the "system," that is, by the underlying imperatives of power and markets.

From the standpoint of the media, the perspective of communicative action is the entry point to many of the familiar questions about media representations. While criteria of truth, accuracy, fairness, and other qualities having to do with the empirical validity of media portrayals are all relevant here, the perspective of communicative action also requires that we look at systematic communication patterns in the media. This involves the modes of communication itself. Many common research themes ranging from questions about comprehension levels to popularization, infotainment, and modes of audience address exemplify these concerns. For example, how are media audiences positioned in relation to the world (and to the media), what role are they offered, to what extent do the representations make possible critical reflection, and what identities are fostered?

Despite the media being the key resource for much of the talk among citizens, it is discussion as such that makes the public sphere "come alive." Where such interaction takes place, among whom, under what circumstances, through what kinds of communicative processes, and with what competencies are all issues that open up a whole field of microsociology and political communication. What kinds of factors promote or obstruct intersubjective understanding in everyday encounters? However we may choose to draw the actual boundaries of the public sphere, it is clear that these themes readily intersect with important areas of the sociocultural domain. I am thinking here of those everyday values, norms, practices, and procedures that may promote or hinder democratic virtues (however understood), including forms of interaction among citizens (cf. Dahlgren 1997; Mouffe 1993) and even "civility" itself (cf. Hefner 1998). Further, people's identities as citizens (however defined), with their sense of belonging to – and their perceived possibilities for participating in – societal development (cf. Clarke 1996) are also highly relevant.

People's sense of what topics are of political relevance is always an ongoing process. One can say that communicative action not only contributes to intersubjective understanding in discussions, but also to the ongoing definitions of politics – and therefore of the public sphere itself. Thus, our concern for the public sphere must include how its boundaries are discursively constructed, maintained, and altered. What kinds of issues are legitimate as political questions? Which are not, and why not? What is at stake in the maintenance of the present borders? How and at what point do things become political (or not) in the convoluted, criss-crossing streams of communicative flows? We need to be alert to the processes whereby "the political" communicatively emerges (the women's movement, for example, provides many good examples). In other words, we must see the construction – and the constriction – of the spaces of the public sphere in the media and via citizen interaction as themselves potentially contested and political. At bottom, the public sphere is not a given fact, but rather an accomplishment, to be defended and in need of extension.

DEMOCRATIC DEFICITS

The condition of democracy in Western democracies varies between countries, but some general trends are apparent. The arena of official politics does not command the degree of support and participation it has in the past. Voter turnouts are declining, even in countries such as Sweden, which has had considerable stability in its electoral patterns over the earlier postwar decades. Party loyalty is declining, especially among the young. The formal political system of most Western nations appears stagnant, reactive rather than proactive, eclipsed by developments in the realms of large-scale capitalism and technological innovations. A corrosive climate of cynicism is emerging in many places. This cannot be understood as merely a response to the media, though this is no doubt part of it. Rather, this atmosphere of "antipolitics" must also be seen as the consequence of the inability of the political system to meet social expectations. Economic insecurity, unemployment, low wages, declining social services, and growing class cleavages are all part of the picture. If the causes are complex, it is nonetheless clear that what we are faced with is a serious erosion of the civic engagement.

Carl Boggs (1997) calls this withdrawal from the arena of the common concerns and politics "the great retreat" into "enclave consciousness," away from larger collective identities and community sensibilities. He refers to a 1995 survey of 240,000 college freshman, which finds that fewer than one third say they keep up with current events, and only 16 percent say they ever discuss politics. He adds, however, in an acerbic afterthought, that given the banality of contemporary formal politics, it is hard to imagine the students responding differently. The extensive demoralization with formal politics that the survey suggests is a theme addressed by many today (cf. Sandel 1996). We have a crisis of civic culture and citizenship (cf. Mosco 1997), which can be linked to a more pervasive cultural malaise (e.g. Bellah et al. 1985). Many people in Western societies seem to have at best very rudimentary identities as citizens, as members and potential participants of political society. They do not feel that they are a part of a larger democratic project, even if they may enter into a variety of media-based communities based on consumption, as Chap. 6, by Don Slater, suggests.

At the same time, there is counter evidence that evokes a different train of thought. From her fieldwork, Nina Eliasoph (1997), for example, finds that in the microcosms of everyday life people reveal that what may appear on the surface as apathy toward politics and contemporary issues disguises something else. In discursive situations she finds that they are actually working very hard to *avoid* the political, to refrain from contextualizing their life circumstances in terms of public issues. Thus, political disengagement may not necessarily be the "easy way out," but rather something that, whatever the motivations, requires a concerted effort. Seemingly, the potential for political engagement stubbornly remains.

It is precisely this kind of ambivalence that holds the door open for constructive thinking about a democratic future. The growing withdrawal from the official politics must be interpreted as responses to the present arrangements of power and the current ways in which the political system operates. The ostensible political apathy, disenchantment, and disaffiliation from the established political system may not necessarily signal a disinterest in politics per se. That is, if we look beyond formal electoral politics, we can see various signs that suggest that many people have not abandoned engagement with politics, but rather have refocused their political attention outside the parliamentarian systems. Or they are in the process of redefining just what constitutes the political (Mulgan 1994; Mouffe 1993). Observers see a strong shift to what is called lifestyle politics (cf. Bennett 1998), which is characterized by personalized rather than collective engagement, and a stronger emphasis on single issues rather than overarching platforms or ideologies. The various manifestations of so-called new social movements can also be seen in this light.

In coming to terms with the state of democracy today or in reflecting on how it has been in the past, obviously many factors have to be weighed. It would certainly be misguided to simply look at the media as some sort of barometer of democratic well-being, ignoring all the other important social, economic, and cultural forces at play. Yet, it could be argued that the relative importance of the media in the functioning of democracy has continued to increase in the modern period. Indeed, this is precisely one of the key arguments that Habermas makes in his original contribution on the public sphere, and which other contemporary scholars hold as well (cf. Thompson 1995). To grasp the character of modern democracy, it is imperative to incorporate perspectives on the media and their interplay with other social forces. Certainly this has been done in a sustained way over the past three decades. Even if there are divergent interpretations about the media's roles in the political process, it is fair to say that our knowledge today is quite extensive about the contributions of the traditional media (chiefly newspapers, television, and radio) to a democratic public sphere. The Internet as a new media phenomenon, however, is far-reaching; its emergence has been dramatic; and its impact on politics needs to be investigated.

The significance of the Internet for democracy lies not just in the fact that it is a new medium, but also in that it arises in an historical context characterized by such profound uncertainties. Much of the received wisdom about what democracy is or how it should function seems not to correspond in an encouraging manner with the realities at the end of the century. Applying the normative vision of the public sphere does not lead to uplifting conclusions. What these developments promise for the future of democracy is hard to tell at this point, but they are a central feature of the present situation into which the Internet makes its intervention. Against this backdrop, let us now look at the Internet from the standpoint of the public sphere. I first look at the Net as a growing phenomenon, and then turn to consider aspects about its structures, spaces, and communicative modes as an element of the public sphere. This will help us to get a sense of its democratic potential.

THE SPREADING NET

We can first note a simple pattern: a new medium is introduced, swathed in utopian rhetoric about how it will benefit society and enhance democracy. This cheery prognosis comes not only from those engaged in marketing it, but also from some voices within academia and other intellectual corners. Then, with little delay, come the dystopian pronouncements, often from more marginalized voices who forecast that the medium in question will, on the contrary, signal a downturn in the quality of social life or democracy. Later, the direction of the developments often suggests that there were elements of truth to both sets of predictions, yet the truth itself is no mere splitting of the difference between them. Rather, the outcome – if one can artificially take some point in time to investigate what "finally" happened – is complex and multivalent. The Net is no exception here; it is a sort of vast moving target, undergoing a rapid development. Our knowledge about it quickly becomes outdated, and my reflections here can only be suggestive.

With the growth of the Net there has followed a surge of literature about it. Along with the popular techno self-help books and cybercultural manifestations, there are already a number of useful academic/ intellectual texts available. (e.g., Kitchen 1998; Holmes 1997; Jones 1997; Loader 1997, 1998; Porter 1997; Sardar and Ravetz 1996; Tsagarousianou et al. 1998). Journals are arranging special issues or sections dealing with the Net (e.g., *Constellations* 1997). A good deal of this literature takes up the Net's role in democracy, with various points of departure (Barnett 1997). Popular books and magazines readily polarize on the theme of the Net's contribution to democracy, with guru-like optimists like Rheingold (1993) and consumer-oriented enthusiasts like Katz (1997) stacking up against reflex pessimists such as Slouka (1995). Yet even the academic interventions display a spectrum of views, ranging from the bleak prospects sketched by Thu Nguyen and Alexander (1996) to the more hopeful tone displayed in literature that emphasizes practical utility in specific settings (e.g., many of the texts in the collection by Kiesler 1997).

Other academic efforts are more concerned with situating the Net within larger theoretic frameworks analyzing the development of late modern society; Castell's (1996) contribution is notable here. We find interventions from the perspective of critical political economy of information technology (IT) (Sussman 1997), the media (Herman and McChesney 1997), the Net, and the computer industry more specifically (Newman 1998). A good number of these contributions address the Internet from the perspective of democracy, and some specifically in relation to the public sphere (cf. Poster 1997; Thornton 1996). The initial point to be made about Internet in regard to the public sphere is that the consequences today appear quite mixed. This ambivalent view will no doubt remain even as the Net continues to expand in its reach and develop in its technical possibilities. We cannot reduce the complexity of the Net or its impact to a singular, unequivocally positive or negative evaluation.

This becomes self-evident if we take even a cursory glance at the several kinds of communication possibilities that the Net offers today. First, though not part of its original profile, the Net in its current phase can be seen as an extension of mass media. On-line versions of television, radio stations, news services, and daily newspapers constitute a considerable degree of net activity, with many major mass media now having an on-line presence. These versions offer extensions of the original "one-to-many" logic of the mass media, with the addition of their hypertext, archival, and interactive capacities. Traditional media audiences are becoming more selective about – and interactive with – the media organizations they use. At the same time, the move to on-line journalism is altering the ideals of journalism and the way that it gets done (cf. Bardoel 1996), though it is still too early to draw conclusions. Certainly the archival possibilities many of these services offer can be of great significance for those citizens who are motivated to use them. And the Internet can even be used to generate public "media events" in ways that remind us of the older mass media (e.g., the on-line release of the Clinton-Lewinsky transcripts).

Second, the Internet also offers one-to-many communication via the Web sites that in principle (though not in practice) anybody can set up, including governments, businesses, financial advisers, interest groups, political and civic activists, hobbyists, and fan clubs. Interactivity takes off from this bulletin-board function as interested parties connect with and explore Web sites, with a snowballing effect of contacts and responses. The rapid growth of the market on the Net is manifested in part by the intense growth of commercial Web sites.

Third, this leads directly to the interactive, many-to-many mode of communication typified by Usenet news groups and chat rooms. Globally, there are tens of thousands of such discussion groups, with many fading out and new ones taking off all the time. Also, all the various forms of networking, enacted by an endless variety of institutions and collectivities, must be included in this many-to-many communication. People link up not just to talk, but also to get things done, including achieving political goals.

Finally, e-mail is the one-to-one kind of communication for which the post office is the paradigmatic model. As with the post office, mass mailings are often done via e-mail, but the core of this part of the Internet remains dyadic in its communicative form.

Net use is massive, but far from universal. Counting net users is notoriously difficult, and there are of course interests at stake in the numbers derived. According to Neilsen Media Research, 79 million North Americans were using the Net in September 1998, which is an increase of 36 percent from the previous year. Even if we give or take many million or question the details of how Net use is defined in such research, it is still undeniable that the Net's development and spread over the past few years is having an enormous impact on media structures and patterns of use. In Sweden, it is estimated that half the population now has access to the Net. The sociological profile of those who use the Net is by now well understood: There is a strong bias toward affluent males with a high degree of cultural capital. The economics and cultural competencies required to become an on-line citizen will prevent the Net from becoming genuinely universal far beyond the foreseeable future. While we can expect significant inroads down the socioeconomic ladder and a certain degree of leveling of the differences between users and nonusers, there will be strong limits to these trends.

Turning to interactivity on the Net, in the most ambitious empirical study to date of the Net and political activity, Hill and Hughes (1998) looked at, among other things, Web pages and Usenet groups. They find that 6.6 percent of the approximately 3000 Usenet groups they could locate were referenced by the word "politics." By comparison, "computers" appeared in 38.2 percent of the newsgroups, "sex" in 23.3 percent, "movies" in 10.7 percent, "TV" in 9 percent, "religion" in 6.3 percent, and "recipes" in 3.4 percent. To put it mildly, politics is not the overwhelming focus of most Net use.

However, Hill and Hughes note that the Net does add something significant for those who use it: Of the sites that had to do with politics, they find that about 20 percent fall outside the political mainstream reflected by the traditional media. In other words, for its users, the Net can expand the political margins of the public sphere. In the United States, Hill and Hughes note the paradox that most Internet users lean toward the liberal end of the political spectrum; conservatives are a minority in terms of numbers. However, in looking at the political activity among Usenet groups and other manifestations of political engagement on the Internet, there is a clear conservative dominance. The conclusion they draw is that thus far the right wing has been more ambitious, organized, and well-financed and has taken more initiative in terms of using the Net.

In the use of the Net as an extension of the older media, Hill and Hughes observe that people favor a few specialized news providers, much as they do with the mass media. Also, they are often probing deeper into something that they have seen in the traditional mass media; they are getting more, but largely not very different information. In contrast to some postmodern theorizing, this suggests that the Internet does not change people so much; rather, it tends to allow them to do what they usually do, but do it better. We should add, however, that this may change with increasing experience of the Net and its capacity for interactivity. It seems that few people become political information junkies via the Net; in all likelihood, they already were before they became Net users.

The picture that comes into focus counsels sobriety in regard to easy optimism or pessimism. A massive sea change in political life is not yet apparent. As indicated, access to the Net is far from universal, and only a small portion of those who use the Net do so in ways that seemingly pertain to the public sphere. However, looking to the decades ahead, the "cyberspace divide," based as it ultimately is on material conditions (Loader 1998), may well prove to be a key issue regarding the social grounds of citizenship. The growing gap between information haves and have-nots in the digital age threatens to become a serious destabilizing factor for democratic life.

NET STRUCTURES

The nonuniversal character of the Net is derived from the basic facts of its institutional structures. As Herman and McChesney (1997) point out, the U.S. Telecommunications Act of 1996 was a major step that basically cemented the role of market mechanisms in the development of the Internet. This holds true even outside the United States, given that many of the commercial actors in cyberspace are transnational corporations. Within the European Union there is a similar thrust, with the Net's infrastructure in telecommunications industries at least partially privatized in all member countries of European Union.

In essence, the Internet is a question for consumers, not for citizens (cf. Schiller 1999); there is effectively no general policy or concrete regulation that intervenes on behalf of the public interest to enhance access. Situated at the forefront of the growing convergence between broadcasting, telephony, and the computer industries, the Internet looms today as a Klondike. The economics of the Internet are at present still rather turbulent; the Net is not yet firmly integrated into the existing global media empires. But in all the flurry generated by the various actors seeking private profit, there is no compelling force or presence that espouses collective, social needs. Herman and McChesney (1997) comment that it is not just business-to-customer sales that are growing on the Net, but also business-to-business. They quote IBM's head of networking (p. 131), who says that by the year 2000 the Internet may well be "the world's largest, deepest, fastest, and most secure marketplace."

Today, the Internet and IT more generally are not only areas of investment but also technologies on which power is increasingly dependent: financial actors and conglomerates, as well as governments. The Net has become a major focus of interest for the corporate world, even for its own internal operations. As the Swedish researchers Ilshammar and Larsmo (1999) observe, this creates a policy dilemma. On the one hand, power interests prefer an unregulated Net, which can be steered by capital, but on the other hand, they want this space to be relatively secure; an anarchic Net is seen as a possible threat. The potential conflict with industry-led regulation and the ideals of free speech are obvious. It is questionable if the public at present has any rights on the Net outside of their roles as capitalists or consumers; the emerging structure is aimed to address the needs of business and affluent consumers. Attempts have been made by governments to formalize cyberspace regulation, with the goal of protecting citizens from harmful Internet content and uses, but thus far the results are inconclusive. The regulation of the Internet is still in the process of being formed, and there are many important issues with few easy solutions. Such questions as access, censorship, copyright, privacy, freedom of speech, and libel are still being grappled with. As Kitchen (1998) notes, the legal conflicts around regulation reflect the larger power struggle to define the Net's future.

ON-LINE SPACES AND COMMUNICATION

As with the traditional mass media just noted, the public sphere generally on the Internet is small in scale compared to the growing space occupied by the market. Despite these structural constraints, the Net does make a positive contribution to the public sphere and has the potential to do even more. The Internet not only offers its users vast communicative spaces in which to travel, visit, and participate, but also allows them to collectively generate new spaces, by launching Web sites, news groups, chat rooms, networks, action groups, and so on. Further, the hypertext structure of much Internet material, and the links often provided, allow for very extensive "interspatiality," the capacity to move freely between different communicative spaces. On-line services often can provide accessible data banks for a good deal of previously published materials. Also, individuals are increasingly able to select from an enormous array of on-line output, customizing their own mix of news, opinion, and other information. From the standpoint of the public sphere, these are of course attractive attributes.

The Net contributes to the multiplicity of the public sphere, embodying the virtues of the expansive perspective. At the same time, this raises precisely the issues that supporters of the restrictive view have taken up: Many of the separate public spheres in the form of news groups and chat rooms remain very separate. They become spaces for bonding among like-minded individuals, with limited openings for (and civility toward) ideas that challenge basic premises (cf. Fisher et al. 1996). How opinion generation and flows in these spheres will link up with the more mainstream sphere remains to be investigated. However, we should not ignore that the communicative space created by even a few activists can translate into real life activity; extraparliamentarian politics becomes more feasible with the Net. For example, environmental groups can use the Net not only for collective identity and opinion generation, but also to coordinate public actions. We also have examples of Net-based transnational opinion mobilization, which bypasses national boundaries, albeit carried out by a very small number of engaged citizens.

Interactivity with the formal political system, in the form of contact with parties and elected officials, does appear to be extensive. Swedish data suggest that this space was not very well populated in the national elections in the autumn of 1998, contrary to expectations. In Sweden, it seems that the Net is being used for simple, practical contact with the authorities (information about social services). Governments can selectively and strategically release information on the Net, but for citizens to dig deeper and get access to other kinds of information on-line, there are often economic hindrances. Even governments seem to treat the Net as a money-making venture; for example, both the U.S. and Swedish governments charge high costs for certain kinds of on-line information. The Net by itself does not lead to more open government or accountability of power.

While the Net may offer opportunities to enter into public space to many people who otherwise would not have done so, it is questionable to assume that the availability of the technology itself will have significant impact on the overall patterns of political engagement. According to Hill and Hughes (1998), the evidence thus far suggests that the Net is a tool, a resource for those with political involvement, but that it generally does not recruit large numbers of new citizens to the public sphere. The Net is not by itself likely to counter the "great withdrawal" from mainstream politics, nor give rise to mass-based, extraparliamentarian alternatives. It probably will not alter present constellations of power, but can at best serve to generate more counter-public spheres, as well as deepen – and widen – the dominant, mainstream public sphere. Certainly many of the concerns of traditional media analysis (e.g., accuracy in representing reality) apply to the Net in its role as a new mass medium. The problem of tracing and identifying sources, for example, becomes all the more difficult in cyberspace.

Habermas's notion of intersubjective communicative action manifests itself on the Net, even if it is marginalized and threatened by the spread of strategic action, that is, instrumental and manipulative communication shaped by the logic of economics and power. While all discursive interaction has its structural and contextual limitations, the fact that open-ended, noncontrolled communication does exist in some spaces on the Net is a cornerstone for its role in the public sphere. This discursive quality permits ongoing discussion not only of existing political issues, but holds open the possibility of introducing new issues, that is, of defining the field of the political. This quality is in a sense constitutive of the public sphere itself. That it is modest in scope and on the defensive is of course indicative of the democracy's contemporary condition.

Communication on-line and "virtual relationships" have specific features; they are text-centered, make use largely of terse writing styles, and are also usually characterized by the absence of auditory, visual, and tactile cues. We must ask – and further investigate – how these attributes enable and limit people's sense of shared purpose and collective self-understanding. Anonymity and deception on the Internet are easy; at the same time, the lack of traditional social markings in Net interaction may also be seen as enabling, allowing voices to come forward that might otherwise not be heard.

The disembodied character of on-line communication and its lack of moorings to geographic place suggest, however, that there are limits to the kinds of intersubjectivity that the Net can help us achieve in the context of the public sphere. What place can we find for political commitment within the playful environment of the Net, when we can so easily switch off or move on to something more fun if we feel bored? The Net tends to undermine the significance or geographic space, yet territorial parameters simply do not vanish: Governments still protect their borders, people still maintain geogaphically based identities, and there is still local social life to be lived. And much of social life, not least its political concerns, is premised on place and its demarcations.

TWO CHEERS FOR THE NET

The Internet promises and delivers a lot. It can empower us, it can widen our worlds, it can offer us seemingly endless information, it can help us get in touch with people who share our interests. It can entertain, it can tantalize, it can tempt. It can also absorb and engulf us, drenching us in more information than we can ever use. It can promote our identities as consumers, but also, with some effort on our part, allow us to cultivate our identities as citizens. Will the Net help deliver a better democracy? The Net does have a capacity to enhance the public sphere, though it seems not to dramatically transform political life. It allows new communicative spaces to develop – alternative public spheres – even if the paths to the centers of political decision making are often far removed. Its structural features make any thought of universalism highly unrealistic, yet at the same time, only a small part of all Net activity at present has to do with politics and the public sphere. Mostly the Net is used for other things. The Internet clearly offers opportunities for the motivated. The questions today are not so much how the Internet will change political life, but rather, what might motivate more people to see themselves as citizens of a democracy, to engage in the political and – for those with access – make use of the possibilities that the Net still offers. Some of the answers may be found on the Net itself, but most reside in our real social circumstances.

REFERENCES

Bardoel, Jo (1996). "Beyond Journalism: A Profession Between Information Society and Civil Society." *European Journal of Communication*, 11(3):283–302.

Barnett, Steven (1997). "New Media, Old Problems: New Technology and the Political Process," *European Journal of Communication*, 12(2):193–218.

Bellah, Robert et al. (1985). *Habits of the Heart*. New York: Perennial Library.

Benhabib, Seyla (Ed.) (1996). *Democracy and Difference: Contesting the Boundaries of the Political*. Princeton, NJ: Princeton University Press.

Bennett, Lance (1998). "The Uncivic Culture: Communication, Identity, and the Rise of Lifestyle Politics." The Ithiel de Sola Pool Lecture. Annual meeting of the American Political Science Association, Boston.

Blumler, Jay, and Michael Gurevitch (1995). *The Crisis of Public Communication*. London: Routledge.

Boggs, Carl (1997). "The Great Retreat: Decline of the Public Sphere in Late Twentieth-century America." *Theory and Society*, 26:741–780.

Calhoun, Craig (Ed.) (1992). *Habermas and the Public Sphere*. Cambridge, Mass: MIT Press.

Castells, Manuel (1996). *The Rise of the Network Society*. Oxford: Basil Blackwell.

Clarke, Paul Barry (1996). *Deep Citizenship*. London: Pluto Press.

Constellations 4(2), (1997). Special section, "Democratizing Technology/Technologizing Democracy."

Dahlgren, Peter (1995). *Television and the Public Sphere*. London: Sage.

    (1997). "Enhancing the Civic Ideal in TV Journalism," in K. Brants et al. (Eds.), *The Media in Question*. London: Sage.

    and Colin Sparks, (Eds.) (1992). *Journalism and Popular Culture*. London: Sage.

Eliasoph, Nina (1997) " 'Close to Home': The Work of Avoiding Politics." *Theory and Society*, 26:5 605–647.

Fisher, Bonnie, Michael Margolis, and David Resnick (1996). "Breaking Ground on the Virtual Frontier: Surveying Civic Life on the Internet." *American Sociologist*, 27:11–25.

Fornäs, Johan (1995). *Culture Theory and Late Modernity*. London: Sage.

Fraser, Nancy (1992). "Rethinking the Public Sphere: A Contribution to the Critique of Actually Existing Democracy." in Craig Calhoun (ed.), *Habermas and the Public Sphere*. Cambridge, MA: MIT Press, pp. 109–142.

Garnham, Nicholas (1992). "The Media and the Public Sphere," in C. Calhoun (Ed.), *Habermas and the Public Sphere*. Cambridge, MA: MIT Press, PP. 359–374.

Habermas, Jürgen (1984/1987). *The Theory of Communicative Action*. (2 Vols.) Cambridge: Polity Press.

(1989). *The Structural Transformation of the Public Sphere*. Cambridge: Polity Press.

(1996). *Between Facts and Norms*. Cambridge, MA: MIT Press.

Hefner, Robert H. (1998). "Civil Society: Cultural Possibility of a Modern Ideal." *Society*, 35(3) March/April 16–27.

Herman, Edward, and Robert McChesney (1997). *The Global Media*. London: Cassell.

Hill, Kevin A., and John E. Hughes (1998) *Cyberpolitics: Citizen Activism in the Age of the Internet*. Lanham, MD: Rowman & Littlefield.

Holmes, David (Ed.) (1997). *Virtual Politics: Identity and Community in Cyberspace*. London: Sage.

Ilshammar, Lars, and Ola Larsmo (1999). *Net.wars*. Stockholm: Atlas.

Jones, Steven G. (Ed.) (1997). *Virtual Culture*. London: Sage.

Katz, Jon (1997). "The digital citizen." *Wired*, December. www.w\red.com.

Keisler, Sara (Ed.) (1997). *Culture of the Internet*. Mahwah, NJ: Lawrence Erlbaum Associates.

Kitchen, Rob (1998). *Cyberspace: The World in Two Wires*. New York: John Wiley and Sons.

Loader, Brian D. (Ed.) (1997). *The Governance of Cyberspace*. London: Routledge.

(Ed.) (1998). *Cyberspace Divide*. London: Routledge.

Maia, Rousiley C. M. (forthcoming). "The Role of the Media in Pre-structuring the Public Sphere." *Media, Culture and Society*.

Marshall, T. H. (1950). *Citizenship and Social Class*. Cambridge: Cambridge University Press.

Mouffe, Chantal (1993). *The Return of the Political*. London: Verso.

Mosco, Vincent (1997). "Citizenship and the Technopoles." *Javnost/The Public*, 4(4):35–45.

Mulgan, Geoff (1994). *Politics in an Antipolitical Age*. Cambridge: Polity Press.

Negt, Oskar, and Alexander Kluge (1993). *The Public Sphere and Experience*. Minneapolis: University of Minnesota Press.

Newman, Nathan (1998). "From Microsoft Word to Microsoft World: How Microsoft is Building a Global Monopoly" (A Netaction White Paper). http://netaction.org/msoft/worldMSWord2World.tx.

Porter, David (Ed.) (1997). *Internet Culture*. London: Routledge.

Poster, Mark (1997). "Cyberdemocracy: The Internet and the Public Sphere," in Holmes, *Virtual Politics*, and Porter *Internet Culture*.

Rheingold, Howard (1993). *The Virtual Community: Homesteading on the Electronic Frontier*. New York: Harper Perennial.

Sandel, Michael (1996). *Democracy's Discontent*. Cambridge, MA: The Belknap Press of Harvard University Press.

Sardar, Ziauddin, and Jerome Ravetz (Eds.) (1996). *Cyberfutures*. London: Pluto.

Schiller, Dan (1999). *Digital Capitalism*. Cambridge, MA: MIT Press.

Slouka, Mark (1995). *War of the Worlds: Cyberspace and the High-Tech Assault on Reality*. New York: Basic Books.

Sussman, Gerald (1997). *Communication, Technology and Politics in the Information Age.* London: Sage.

Thompson, John B. (1995). *The Media and Modernity.* Cambridge: Polity Press.

Thornton, Alinta (1996). "Will the Internet Revitalize Democracy in the Public Sphere? http://www.au/democracy/intro.htl."

Thu Nguyen, Dan, and Alexander, Jon (1996). "The Coming of Cyberspace and the End of the Polity," in B. Shields (Ed.), *Cultures of Internet.* London: Sage.

Tsagarousianou, Roza, Damian Tambini, and Cathy Bryan (Eds.) (1998). *Cyberdemocracy: Technologies, Cities and Civic Networks.* London: Routledge.

Weintraub, Jeff, and Krishan Kumar (Eds.) (1997). *Public and Private in Thought and Practice.* Chicago: University of Chicago Press.

Verstraeten, Hans (1996). "The Media and the Transformation of the Public Sphere. A Contribution for a Critical Political Economy of the Public Sphere." *European Journal of Communication,* 11(3):347–370.

CHAPTER 3

Promoting Political Engagement

William A. Gamson

In the voluminous literature on the quality of public discourse, there is a recurrent theme that, in a democracy, public discourse can and should empower citizens, give them voice and agency, build community, and help citizens to act on behalf of their interests and values. The normative standard here is one of engaging citizens in the democratic process through their active participation in the public sphere.

One important strand of democratic theory rejects this normative standard. Its proponents argue that it is natural and even desirable for citizens to be passive, quiescent, and limited in their political participation in a well-functioning, party-led, representative democracy. In such a *limited citizenship* model, the citizen's role is to choose periodically who among competing teams of would-be office holders will exercise public authority.[1] Open competition for citizen votes ensures responsiveness and accountability. If people don't like what they are getting, they can vote the rascals out. In the interim between elections, officials need to respond to problems that are technically complex, and most people have neither the inclination nor the ability to master the issues involved.

To expect citizens to be actively engaged in public life is seen by advocates of this view as at best wishful thinking, what Baker (1998) in summarizing this theory characterizes as a "romantic but idle fantasy." At worst, encouraging such engagement obstructs and complicates the problems of democratic governance by politicizing and oversimplifying complex problems that require skilled leadership and technical expertise. The media retain an important role in this theory – for example, exposure of corruption and incompetence and providing decision makers with reliable information, including information about public concerns. But the media do not need to promote civic engagement or even reflection and discussion.

Going beyond limited citizenship models, other strands of democratic theory call for a more participatory citizen role. In one form or another, this theme runs through the theories of Habermas and his followers, that is, in participatory democratic theory, civic republican theory, feminist theory, communitarian democratic theory, and social movement theory. A common normative thread is the desirability of maximizing the participation of citizens in the public decisions that affect their lives. To do this, they should, to the extent feasible, be active participants in the public sphere as part of an ongoing process.

Barber (1984, p. 151) calls his version *strong democracy*:

> Strong democracy is defined by politics in the participatory mode: literally it is self-government by citizens rather than representative government in the name of citizens. Active citizens govern themselves directly here, not necessarily at every level and in every instance, but frequently enough and in particular when basic policies are being decided and when significant power is deployed. Self-government is carried on through institutions designed to facilitate ongoing civic participation in agenda-setting, deliberation, legislation, and policy implementation (in the form of "common work").

In this tradition, preferences and abilities for judging public issues emerge in the process of public deliberation, and that participation transforms individuals into public citizens. To quote Barber (1984, p. 151) again:

> In place of a search for a pre-political independent ground or for an immutable rational plan, strong democracy relies on participation in an evolving problem-solving community that creates public ends where there were none before by means of its own activity . . . In such communities, public ends are neither extrapolated from absolutes nor "discovered" in a preexisting "hidden consensus." They are literally forged through the act of public participation, created through common deliberation and common action and the effect that deliberation and action have on interests, which change shape and direction when subjected to these participatory processes.

Public participation, then, is meaningful for the outcome of the political process, for the individual's self-development as a citizen, and for increasing the collective capacity of citizens to act on their own behalf. As Dahlgren (1991, pp. 2, 11) puts it, the public sphere should provide

> the institutional sites where popular political will should take form and citizens should be able to constitute themselves as active agents in the political process . . . The goal is to establish structures of broadcasting in the public interest . . . which optimize diversity in terms of information, viewpoints and forms of expression, and which foster full and active citizenship.

COLLECTIVE ACTION FRAMES

Let's accept this normative standard and ask *how* the media can help to engage people as citizens and how we would know how well they were succeeding. Given the many-faceted nature of the task, we need a more specified model of the nature of citizen action that the media is expected to facilitate. The model I have in mind draws on theories of contentious politics and, more specifically, the concept of *collective action frames.*

These frames, to quote Snow and Benford (1992, p. 137), are "action oriented sets of beliefs and meanings that inspire and legitimate social movement activities and campaigns." They offer ways of understanding that imply the need for and desirability of some form of action. Ryan (1991) and Gamson (1992) unpack the concept into three components: injustice, identity, and agency.

The *injustice* component refers to the moral indignation expressed in this form of political consciousness. This is not merely a cognitive or intellectual judgment about what is equitable but also what cognitive psychologists call a *hot cognition* – one that is laden with emotion (see Zajonc 1980). An injustice frame requires an awareness of motivated human actors who carry some of the onus for bringing about harm and suffering.

The *identity* component refers to the process of defining a *we*, typically but not necessarily in opposition to some *they* who have different interests or values. Without an adversarial component, the potential target of collective action is likely to remain an abstraction – hunger, disease, poverty, or war, for example. Collective action requires a consciousness of human agents whose policies or practices must be changed and a *we* who will help to bring the change about. The central question here is whether the mass media support and encourage grassroots constituencies in their attempts to articulate and develop a sense of themselves as a community of action.[2]

The *agency* component refers to the consciousness that it is possible to alter conditions or policies through collective action. Collective action frames imply some sense of collective efficacy and deny the immutability of some undesirable situation. They empower people by defining them as potential agents of their own history. They suggest not merely that something can be done but that *we* can do something.

This paper focuses on the agency component and, in particular, on ways in which the media can encourage or discourage the development of collective agency among citizens. Do the mass media provide this cultural tool for encouraging political engagement, that is, to support and encourage a sense that by acting together, grassroots constituencies can take actions that influence the policies and conditions that affect their daily lives?

COLLECTIVE AGENCY

It would be surprising, indeed, to find such support and encouragement, given the powerful arguments of most analysts and close observers of American media. The forces discouraging a sense of agency among the vast majority of the citizenry are overwhelming. Culture and social structure combine to induce collective helplessness. Only individual escape seems possible, typically through some kind of liberating educational experience that strips the scales from one's eyes and opens opportunities. Most citizens remain subject to sociocultural forces that systematically remove from their consciousness any sense that collectively they can alter the conditions and terms of their daily lives.

Everyday life and public policy are experienced as separate realms because we have a national political economy that is dominated by centralized, hierarchical, national corporations and a national state. This structural impediment to collective agency is reinforced by a political culture that operates to produce quiescence and passivity. Merelman (1984, p. 1) tells us that a

> loosely bounded culture prevents Americans from controlling their political and social destinies, for the world which loose boundedness portrays is not the world of political and social

structures that actually exists. It is, instead, a shadowland, which gives Americans little real purchase on the massive, hierarchical political and economic structures that dominate their lives.

Merelman analyzes the role of television in particular in promoting a loosely bounded culture that backs people away from politics and directs them toward a private vision of the self in the world.

Edelman (1988) points to the powerful social control that is exercised, largely unconsciously, through the manipulation of symbolism used in "constructing the political spectacle." Problems, enemies, crises, and leaders are constantly being constructed and reconstructed to create a series of threats and reassurances. To take it in is to be taken in by it. "For most of the human race," Edelman writes in his conclusion, "political history has been a record of the triumph of mystification over strategies to maximize well-being." Rebellious collective action can even buttress the dominant world view by helping political elites in their construction of a stable enemy or threat that justifies their policies and provides a legitimation for political repression.

Bennett (1988, p. xii) observes how the structure and culture of news production combine to limit popular participation. "As long as the distribution of power is narrow and decision processes are closed," he argues, "journalists will never be free of their dependence on the small group of public relations experts, official spokespersons, and powerful leaders whose self-serving pronouncements have become firmly established as the bulk of the daily news."

Furthermore, these "advertisements for authority" are surrounded by other reports "that convey fearful images of violent crime, economic insecurity, and nuclear war. Such images reinforce public support for political authorities who promise order, security, and responsive political solutions." Granting that people take it all with a grain of salt, Bennett argues that even minimal acceptance of basic assumptions about political reality is enough to discourage most people from participating actively in the political process.

It is no wonder, Bennett concludes, that few Americans become involved politically and "most cannot imagine how they could make a political difference." One can break out by reading specialized publications with a broader range of discourse, but "those who take the time to do so may find themselves unable to communicate with the majority who remain trapped on the other side of the wall of mass media imagery" (1988, p. xv).

The result of these sociocultural forces, then, is not a blind acceptance of official portraits of reality but a pervasive cynicism about politics among most of the citizenry. Their practical political wisdom tells them, as Flacks (1988, p. 88) puts it, that "the authority set-up is more or less stupid and predatory. The best way to deal with it is to try to make your own way, taking what you can, giving back what you must – while always being on the lookout for space and opportunity to enhance your freedom." Gans (1988, p. 70), reviewing the many reasons for people to avoid political activities, is led to conclude that "it is surprising to find any citizen activity taking place at all."

Looking for Cracks

And yet it does. There are clearly moments when people do take it upon themselves to do more than evade or transcend the terms and conditions of their daily lives and behave as collective agents who can change them. At some level, they harbor a sense of potential agency. Are social scientists, in emphasizing how this culture of quiescence is produced and maintained, themselves promulgating yet another set of reasons for inaction, another discouragement of agency? Where are the cracks where some idea of collective action stays alive, ready to grow and prosper under the proper conditions, as it did so dramatically and to everyone's surprise in Eastern Europe, for example?

Our examination of media discourse is a search for these cracks. More specifically, we look for one or more of the following ways in which the mass media, albeit unintentionally, can encourage a sense of collective agency:

- By giving social movements and the collective actions that they engage in a prominent place in the discourse on public policy issues. By doing so, even when the coverage is largely unfavorable, it provides images of citizens engaging in politics and thereby making a difference. It suggests that other power holders are, at a minimum, taking them seriously as players.
- When it depicts the population being affected by public policies, it can present them as potential agents who are or might become involved in some form of collective action to influence those policies – not merely as a social category who are individually affected by these policies and need protection or consideration.
- It can help to bridge experiential knowledge and public discourse, helping people to integrate the language of the lifeworld with

policy discourse. This encourages agency by opening discursive opportunities for constituencies whose claim to standing in the public discourse rests heavily on their experiential knowledge.

The presence of these cracks in the general mass media tendency to discourage collective agency varies substantially from issue to issue. On some issues, the cracks seem few and far between, while on others they are a virtual chasm – indeed, one would have to conclude that the media appear to encourage collective agency. I will confine my attention here to five issues on which I already have, from previous research, copious and systematic samples of media discourse: troubled industry, the Arab-Israeli conflict, abortion, affirmative action, and nuclear power.[3]

EXAMINING MEDIA DISCOURSE

TROUBLED INDUSTRY

In the late 1970s, the American steel industry was in trouble. Among the efforts to do something about the situation, one involved a significant citizen action – a community effort by workers and other citizens in the Mahoning Valley area in Ohio to buy and run the Youngstown Sheet and Tube Company. Sheet and Tube had been acquired in 1969 by a New Orleans-based conglomerate, the Lykes Corporation, which had used it as a cash cow. Rather than modernizing the plant, Lykes used its cash flow to service the debt it had assumed in buying Sheet and Tube and to finance other new acquisitions.

In 1977, it tried to sell the depleted company but found no buyers among other foreign and domestic steel companies; in September, it announced that it would permanently close its largest mill in the area, laying off 4,100 employees. An estimated 3,600 additional jobs would be lost through effects on local suppliers and retail businesses. In response, a broad group of religious leaders formed the Ecumenical Coalition of the Mahoning Valley to search for a solution to the crisis. At the suggestions of local steelworkers, they began exploring the possibility of a combined worker-community buyout. Alperowitz and Faux (1982, p. 355) describe it as embodying "concerns for jobs rather than welfare, for self-help and widespread participation rather than dependence on absentee decision-makers."

The new company was to be known as Community Steel, directed by a fifteen-member board with six members elected by the company's workers, six by stockholders, and three by a broadly based community corporation. Thousands of residents pledged savings to a fund that would purchase the factory, and the coalition received a grant from the Department of Housing and Urban Development (HUD) to conduct a feasibility study. Eventually, the plan faltered when the Carter administration failed to support the needed loan guarantees, but the two-year Youngstown effort was clearly the largest and most significant attempt to convert a plant to worker-community ownership.

Was it visible in national media discourse? When covering a continuing issue such as the decline of the troubled steel industry, journalists look for a topical peg on which to hang their stories. The Carter Administration provided one when it offered a six-point plan to deal with the problems of the steel industry late in the fall of 1977. If there was a story in the Youngstown effort begun a couple of months earlier, this was an excellent opportunity to include it. It was receiving extensive coverage in local media. Grassroots efforts of this sort are novel enough to be newsworthy, and it was too soon at the moment to know what the outcome would be. HUD Secretary Patricia Harris was calling for "new models of community involvement to solve these problems" (Alperovitz and Faux 1982, p. 355).

We sampled a two-week period after the announcement of the administration's plan for aiding the steel industry. The sample included the editorial and op ed pages of a regionally stratified sample of the fifty largest circulation metropolitan daily newspapers, the evening news coverage of the three major networks, and two editions each of the three major newsmagazines.[4] Our sample yielded six opinion columns, five cartoons, and three newsmagazine stories on the steel industry, but no network television coverage. We searched this sample in vain for *any* reference to citizen action in the Mahoning Valley in the heart of the steel industry.

Steelworkers appeared in all six opinion columns but never as agents. There were numerous references to workers as victims, losing their jobs. But James Reston (column, December 2, 1977) thought they partly brought it on themselves, chiding American workers who "increasingly condemn the integrity of work and reject the authority of their managers" and quoting approvingly from a former Nixon administration Labor Department official who claimed that workers "no longer think that hard work pays off" and "increasingly resist authority in their companies, communities, churches, or governments."

Worker action did appear allegorically in an Art Buchwald column (December 11, 1977) in the form of a "delegation of elves" confronting

Santa Claus about the lack of work in Santa's toy factory. Santa explains that "it's out of my hands," since he has sold out to a conglomerate that only cares about the bottom line. One elf "demands" to know why he sold out in the first place, and Santa explains how he needed capital and couldn't compete. "You know how I feel about you little fellows," Santa tells the elves. "I've worked with you all my life. But what can I do when the Japanese start dumping Farrah Fawcett dolls down every chimney at a quarter of the price that we can make them for up here?" The elves sadly accept a Christmas of unemployment as Santa tells them, "I'm sorry, but that's the way the beach ball bounces." So much for cracks in the mass media on troubled industry.

ARAB-ISRAELI CONFLICT

Domestic citizen action by Americans with ties to the old country is a routine part of the reporting of foreign conflicts. Rallies and demonstrations by ethnic groups are expected, are duly reported, and typically scrutinized for their electoral relevance – that is, for clues to the behavior of a voting bloc. It becomes especially newsworthy when any large ethnic group is upset with elected officials belonging to a party that the group has supported in the past. The general message here implicitly encourages citizen action: If domestic ethnic groups are substantial in size and cohesive – and hence have significant electoral leverage – collective action is important.

Coverage of citizen action on the Arab-Israeli conflict fits this general picture, but with some complications. Collective action by people in other countries has frequently been a central part of the story, but domestic citizen action has been strictly a routine ethnic sidebar. From 1948 to the mid-1970s, rallies by American Jewish groups in support of Israel during its various wars were a standard part of the coverage. During the October 1973 war, for example, *Time* Magazine wrote, "Rallies, marches and meetings are being held everywhere." The article described events in Los Angeles and Chicago while showing a picture of a large group of demonstrators with signs and Israeli flags, with the caption, "New Yorkers gathered at City Hall to demonstrate their support of Israel in Middle East War." Smaller demonstrations by Arab-Americans in support of the Arab protagonists in the war were also noted in passing.

By 1982, domestic citizen action was still an ethnic story, but with a new twist. We sampled media discourse during the Israeli invasion of Lebanon and shortly after the massacres at the Sabra and Shatilla refugee camps by Lebanese Christian forces under Israeli control. *Newsweek* contrasted the flurry of "muted" protests by American Jews compared with the more vocal critics in Israel itself. The caption accompanying two pictures of demonstrations used a quote, "There is a need to speak out," and labeled them "Anti-Begin protests in Boston and San Francisco."

It is difficult to find in this coverage any overall tendency to render citizen action invisible. When action occurs, it is given its due as part of the story. But it is invariably framed as part of the ethnic politics of the Jewish and, to a less extent, the Arab-American community. The subtext is that citizen action on the Arab-Israeli issue is relevant only insofar as it expresses the concerns and identities of these two particular ethnic groups. For the more than 95 percent of Americans who have no strong ties with either group, citizen action on the Arab-Israeli conflict is implicitly defined as irrelevant in media discourse.

AFFIRMATIVE ACTION

The story of agency in media discourse on affirmative action is complicated; citizen action once had a prominent place but faded rapidly in the 1980s. We sampled media discourse for a two-week period following three Supreme Court decisions in 1978 – (Bakke), 1979 (Weber), and 1984 (Memphis Firefighters) – and found a dramatic shift in the centrality of the civil rights movement.

One can see this change most dramatically in the way the story was treated on television. Visually, affirmative action was originally linked to the civil rights movement and to contemporary expressions that implied its continuing relevance. In 1978, all three networks showed footage of a demonstration by women and minorities in San Francisco protesting the Bakke decision. There were shots of pickets and marchers, of signs and banners saying "Fight racism, Overturn Bakke" and "Abajo con Bakke" (Down with Bakke). Heroes and heroines of the civil rights movement such as Julian Bond, Jesse Jackson, and Coretta Scott King were interviewed, along with spokespersons for the NAACP, the Urban League, the Southern Christian Leadership Conference (SCLC), and the Congressional Black Caucus. They were, of course, identified in print as well as orally. ABC showed shots of Martin Luther King at a White House ceremony with President Lyndon Johnson for the signing of the Civil Rights Act.

By the next year, at the time of the Weber decision, this same visual message was still there but had become more muted. Two of the networks showed the NAACP convention in Louisville, and ABC included audience shots of black men and women singing, clapping hands, and swaying to music. CBS did not cover the convention but used numerous spokespersons for civil rights groups.

This positive imagery of the civil rights movement in the late 1970s certainly did not put media coverage at odds with official discourse. Eleanor Holmes Norton, a black woman, headed the Equal Opportunity Employment Commission (EEOC) and was the Carter administration's principal spokesperson on the issue. She had a long history of participation in both the civil rights and women's movements. The inclination of journalists to adopt official frames worked in this instance to support a sympathetic view of the civil rights movement and citizen action associated with it.

By 1984, official discourse on affirmative action had undergone a shift. At the beginning of the Reagan administration, internal differences apparently prevented full backing of the efforts led by Assistant Attorney General William Bradford Reynolds to ban all "color-conscious programs." By 1984, when the Supreme Court confronted the conflict between affirmative action and seniority in deciding who should be fired first in the Memphis firefighters case, the Reynolds group had won the internal battle. The Justice Department filed briefs in this and other cases, arguing that all race-conscious programs were illegal, even when adopted in response to undeniable past discrimination against blacks. When the Supreme Court upheld the primacy of seniority even though it might mean that most of those laid off were minorities who were recently hired under an affirmative action agreement, Reynolds called the decision "exhilarating" and Solicitor General Rex Lee said, "It's a slam dunk."

In contrast to the coverage of earlier decisions, the civil rights movement had virtually disappeared from the visual coverage of the issue and appeared in ways that obscured or denied its relevance. No pickets, marchers, or any other symbol of social movement activity appeared on any of the television news programs, nor did any icons of the civil rights movement. The NAACP was the only civil rights organization represented by spokespersons. Furthermore, on two of the three networks, Reagan administration officials hailed the decision against the Memphis affirmative action program as pro-civil rights. Clarence Pendleton, chairman of the Civil Rights Commission (and black), applauded the decision as "a mighty blow for civil rights, not a mighty blow against civil rights."

In sum, national media discourse on affirmative action did portray citizen action as part of the story, even when the news peg rested on Supreme Court decisions that are supposedly insulated from popular pressure. The civil rights movement is a story about ordinary people making history; it legitimizes, albeit retrospectively, collective action as a positive force for change. On this issue, then, media discourse does not uniformly discourage a sense of collective agency among the citizenry; in some contexts, it can even be seen to support it.

But every silver lining has a cloud. This piece of the story was present only during the period in which official discourse supported the goals of civil rights activists. When official discourse shifted from sympathetic to unsympathetic, the affirmative action media story shifted as well; the civil rights movement lost its visibility, and citizen action lost its relevance in media discourse on the issue.

Abortion

If there were cracks in the media discouragement of collective action on affirmative action, they have become chasms on the abortion issue. Indeed, it is hard to imagine how there could be more encouragement of collective agency than we find here. First of all, there is extensive coverage of two social movements, both of which involve grassroots citizen action – an antiabortion movement with a direct action component spearheaded by Operation Rescue, and an abortion rights movement spearheaded by a variety of grassroots organizations. Citizen action is a very central part of the media story on abortion.

Beyond this, there are two more subtle ways in which U.S. abortion coverage encourages agency. Ferree and Gamson (1999) distinguish two different ways in which abortion discourse can be gendered: (a) Women can be presented as active *agents* who are capable of making meaningful moral decisions and of influencing public policies that limit their choice, and (b) women can be presented as *objects* or victims of policies, and as a part of a class needing protection in their vulnerability. We saw the distinction operating earlier in the discussion of the role of steelworkers in the problems besetting their industry.

German and American abortion discourses have both become increasingly gendered in the past 30 years, in part as a consequence of the rise of supranational feminism and the overall visibility of women as political beings.[5] The specific gendering of American discourse places women as agents whose privacy rights allow them to "choose." In Germany, in contrast, media discourse defines women as the objects of state policy, as those who should be "helped, not punished" in their weakness and vulnerability. This formulation leaves virtually no rhetorical place for advocates of the view that women are free and autonomous decision makers who can morally choose to terminate a pregnancy. As a result, such spokespersons as Christina Schenk, a feminist PDS parliamentarian from the East, are isolated and attacked as radical and immoral by even her proliberalization "allies" (Lennox 1995).

Finally, and most subtly, U.S. abortion discourse enables a sense of agency by broadening the norms of legitimate expression in public discourse in ways that favor grassroots constituencies. Young (1996) argues that the norms and practices governing policy discourse privilege certain forms of presentation over others. In particular, they favor speech that is dispassionate and disembodied. They presuppose an opposition between mind and body, reason and emotion. They favor argument over narrative, decontexualized arguments from general principles over contextualized arguments rooted in concrete circumstances, and statistical data over experiential knowledge. They separate the language of the life-world from discourse on public policy.[6]

These practices are relevant for the issue of civic engagement because they encourage passivity and nonparticipation, and they do it selectively. The more boisterous style and practice of the plebeian public sphere is disparaged and subject to charges of incivility. The more embodied-speech culture of women is disparaged as emotional rather than rational.

The exclusionary character of these practices is especially evident on an issue such as abortion. Consider the implications of discounting experiential knowledge and storytelling – the primary currency of the life-world. The existential experience of the dilemmas of an unwanted pregnancy is gender specific. If one rules out such contributions in the policy discourse, the silencing falls unequally on men and women.

Caution is in order, however, on how much and in what ways the removal of the silencing promotes the kind of civic engagement that leads to citizen action. At best, it opens discursive opportunities, but whether and how much this actually increases a sense of agency depends on other factors. Narrative and experiential knowledge in a discourse does not translate into agency unless collective actors exist to tie the lessons of such stories to public policy.

Journalists often appropriate the experience of the life-world for "human interest" stories that individualize social problems, taking the story without the lesson. To translate this into a sense of agency, movements, parties, and other collective actors must draw out policy lessons that identify targets for efforts at change. When a woman publicly speaks out about her own experience of an unwanted pregnancy, she is adding her story to a set of such stories, bearing collective witness. And the implications for abortion policies are very much part of the collective story.

In practice, it is possible for a given discourse to meet an expanded definition of a reasoned and deliberative public sphere without excluding the voices of those with less cultural power. To do this, it must provide a way of integrating the language of the life-world into the policy discourse. A discourse that fails to do this discourages civic engagement.

In fact, there is strong evidence that U.S. media discourse on abortion does an excellent job of doing this. In our comparative study of abortion discourse in Germany and the United States (Ferree et al. 2000), we examined two U.S. and two German newspapers over a thirty-year span. Personal narratives often appeared in our American newspaper sample (in contrast to very rarely in the German sample), thereby legitimating the appropriateness of experiential knowledge.

In sum, U.S. media discourse on abortion appears to meet the criteria for promoting political engagement quite well. It presents repeated examples of grassroots organizations and social movements as players who must be taken seriously. It presents women as active *agents* who have the right to make decisions and be strongly involved in setting public policy on the issue rather than as *objects* of state policy needing protection in their vulnerability. In legitimating experiential knowledge and personal narratives, it opens discursive opportunities for women, presenting them as agents. Taken as a whole, including primetime television dramatizations, media discourse on abortion concretizes public discourse and helps to counteract excessive abstraction. It helps to bridge private and public spheres by translating between political policy discourse and the language of the life-world. In doing so, it helps to integrate experiential knowledge with media discourse.

NUCLEAR POWER

Citizen action became part of the nuclear power story with the rise of the anti-nuclear-power movement in the 1970s. One of its major accomplishments was to trigger particular media practices that opened the discourse – but in restricted ways. Before the 1970s, journalists did not apply the balance norm to nuclear power; its application is triggered by controversy. Operationally, this requires either extensive or dramatic citizen action by challengers or public opposition to nuclear power policies by powerful elites – neither of which occurred until the early 1970s.

The anti-nuclear-power movement, like many movements, consisted of a broad coalition of movement organizations with different frames on nuclear power and different strategies for changing nuclear policy. The anti-nuclear-power movement was most likely to be represented in the media by spokespersons for the Union of Concerned Scientists (UCS), with Ralph Nader in second place. Spokespersons for direct action groups such as the Clamshell Alliance were rare, although their actions – especially the 1977 site occupation of the Seabrook, New Hampshire, nuclear reactor – sometimes drew extensive coverage.

We sampled media discourse in a two-week period in the spring of 1977, covering both the Seabrook action and an effort by President Jimmy Carter to gain international support for controlling the spread of nuclear technology. Our sample yielded fifteen television segments, two newsmagazine accounts, six cartoons, and five opinion columns. Television coverage focused exclusively on the visually rich collective action at Seabrook and its aftermath, driving the Carter initiative out of the picture.

The demonstrators were presented relatively sympathetically in newsmagazine coverage. Both *Time* and *Newsweek* mentioned their commitment to nonviolence, and *Newsweek* added their exclusion of drugs, weapons, and fighting. The accompanying photographs reinforced the television images of backpackers; *Newsweek* called them "scruffy" and mentioned playing frisbee, playing guitars, and reading Thoreau. *Time* also quoted the publisher of the Manchester Union Leader, William Loeb, who likened the Clamshell Alliance to "Nazi storm troopers under Hitler," but characterized him in a discrediting way as an "abrasive conservative."

The cartoons and columns, with one exception, ignored the antinuclear movement in their commentary on the issue. Only Jeremiah Murphy (column, May 2, 1977) brought in antinuclear protestors, linking them with 1960s images of antiway protestors – scruffy beards, longish hair, and braless women. Some of them, he wrote, "really don't know what they are protesting and – far worse – don't care."

After 1977, whether it was treated sympathetically or not, the anti-nuclear-power movement had become a visible, established part of media discourse on the issue. When we sampled media coverage after the Chernobyl accident, we found all three television networks showing American or European antinuclear protestors, with a total of eight separate instances. The protestors' signs reminded viewers that "Chernobyl can happen here" or "Chernobyl is everywhere."

Unlike affirmative action, no national administration has ever promoted or supported citizen action on nuclear power. Media attentiveness, in this case, occurred in spite of official discouragement. And even though no collective action since 1977 has come close to the national visibility of the Seabrook occupation, the antinuclear movement has succeeded in keeping citizen action visible in the issue discourse. Again, the generalization that media discourse uniformly suppresses any sense of collective agency seems seriously misleading for nuclear power.

CONCLUSION

I make no claim that this close analysis of media discourse on these five issues forces us to abandon the generalization that American media discourse discourages the idea that ordinary citizens can alter the conditions and terms of their daily lives through their own actions. But while this message comes through clearly on some issues, on others, the opposite seems to be the case. On some issues, a sense of collective agency is nurtured.

The case for discouragement is strongest on troubled industry. Significant citizen action in the steel industry, undertaken with a degree of official encouragement, nevertheless remained invisible in national media discourse. It is only slightly less true for the Arab-Israeli conflict, where citizen action by Americans is present and treated sympathetically. However, it is presented in the context of ethnic politics and, by implication, is only relevant and encouraged for Jewish Americans and Arab-Americans as a legitimate expression. By implication, citizen action by others or foreign policy actions in anything except an ethnic context is rendered irrelevant.

On affirmative action, citizen action was visible when an administration sympathetic to the civil rights movement was in power and became largely invisible when official discourse turned unsympathetic. Official sympathy for citizen action, then, may alter its normal disparagement or invisibility and encourage journalists to treat such collective actors as relevant players in the policy arena.

On both abortion and nuclear power, however, one finds consistent encouragement of a sense of agency in media discourse. On abortion, U.S. media discourse (in contrast to such discourse in Germany) emphasizes the role of social movements as important players whose collective actions can and do influence policy. It tends to portray women in particular as agents who decide on courses of action rather than as passive objects in need of protection. And it encourages a mode of discourse that helps groups who are often excluded through taken-for-granted discursive practices to bring their experiential knowledge and personal stories to bear in discussions of abortion policy. On nuclear power, media encouragement of collective agency has occurred even though it serves no official agenda to have antinuke protestors taken so seriously that they might provide potential models for the next community where one might wish to construct a nuclear reactor.

The media role in portraying collective agency seems, to a substantial degree, issue specific and variable rather than constant. If I were to offer a tentative generalization, it would focus on the type of issue. Discouragement seems most impregnable on those issues involving class-based action by workers to challenge economic inequality. Elite unity on such discouragement seems to include the mass media in its orbit. On some issues, such as affirmative action and abortion, elite interests seem less fundamentally engaged or more divided. Official encouragement or discouragement can make journalists more or less sensitive to official cues about the legitimacy and efficacy of citizen action. But on nuclear power, media encouragement for collective agency has taken place even in the face of no official encouragement and the substantial economic stakes of a major industry in promoting quiescence.

If there are some surprises here, perhaps it indicates an overemphasis by social scientists on how media discourse contributes to social control. It clearly does in many respects on many issues, but there is enormous variability and numerous cracks in the media monolith. Media coverage frequently and inadvertently keeps alive and helps transmit images of group protest, treats citizens as potential agents, and challenges exclusion by opening the rules governing policy discourse.

Media-amplified images of successful citizen action on one issue can generalize and transfer to other issues. The repertoire of collective action presented on a broad range of political issues in media discourse – of boycotts, strikes, and demonstrations, for example – can be divorced from the particular issue context in which they occur and applied to other issues. Hence, one must be cautious about the argument that the media does nothing to encourage a sense of collective agency.

NOTES

1. One classic articulation of this theory is Schumpeter's *Capitalism, Socialism, and Democracy* (1942). This version of democratic theory is often called "elitist democracy," but this is not a term that its advocates would embrace.
2. This question is explored in detail in "Collective Identity and the Mass Media" (Gamson 1998).
3. The research on all of the issues except abortion is reported in greater detail in Gamson (1992). The abortion data are reported in Gamson (1999), and in Ferree et al. (2000).
4. The details of this sampling design are reported in Gamson (1992).
5. The data summarized here are reported more fully in Ferree et al. (2000).
6. This argument is developed more fully in Gamson (1999).

REFERENCES

Alperovitz, Gar, and Jeff Faux (1982). "The Youngstown Project," in Frank Lindenfeld and Joyce Rothschild-Whitt (Eds.), *Workplace Democracy and Social Change.* Boston: Porter Sergent, pp. 353–369.

Baker, C. Edwin (1998). "The Media that Citizens Need." *University of Pennsylvania Law Review,* 147:317–407.

Barber, Benjamin (1984). *Strong Democracy: Participatory Politics for a New Age.* Berkeley: University of California Press.

Bennett, W. Lance (1988). *News: The Politics of Illusion.* Second Edition. White Plains, NY: Longman.

Dahlgren, Peter (1991). "Introduction," in Peter Dahlgren and Colin Sparks (Eds.), *Communication and Citizenship: Journalism and the Public Sphere.* London: Routledge, pp. 1–24.

Edelman, Murray J. (1988). *Constructing the Political Spectacle.* Chicago: University of Chicago Press.

Ferree, Myra Marx, and William A. Gamson (1999). "The Gendering of Abortion Discourse," in Donatella della Porta, Hanspeter Kriesi, and Dieter Rucht (Eds.), *Social Movements in a Globalizing World.* New York: St. Martin's Press, pp. 40–56.

Ferree, Myra Marx, William A. Gamson, Jürgen Gerhards, and Dieter Rucht (2000). *Shaping Abortion Discourse: Democracy and the Public Sphere in Germany and the United States.* New York: Cambridge University Press.

Flacks, Richard (1988). *Making History.* New York: Columbia University Press.

Gamson, William A. (1992). *Talking Politics.* New York: Cambridge University Press.

(1998). "Collective Identity and the Mass Media." Chapter prepared for Minnesota Symposium on Political Psychology volume, Gene Borgida and John L. Sullivan (Eds.). New York: Cambridge University Press.

(1999). "Policy Discourse and the Language of the Life-World," in Jürgen Gerhards and Ronald Hitzler (Eds.), *Eigenwilligkeit und Rationalität sozialer Prozesse.* Opladen/Wiesbaden: Westdeutscher Verlag, pp. 127–144.

Gans, Herbert (1988). *Middle American Individualism*. New York: The Free Press.

Lennox, Sara (1995). "Debating Abortion after 1989." Unpublished manuscript, Dept. of Comparative Literature, University of Massachusetts.

Merelman, Richard M. (1984). *Making Something of Ourselves: On Culture and Politics in the United States*. Berkeley: University of California Press.

Ryan, Charlotte (1991). *Prime Time Activism*. Boston: South End Press.

Schumpeter, Joseph A. (1942). *Capitalism, Socialism, and Democracy*. New York: Harper.

Snow, David A., and Robert D. Benford (1992). "Master Frames and Cycles of Protest," in Aldon Morris and Carol Mueller (Eds.), *Frontiers of Social Movement Theory*. New Haven, CT: Yale University Press.

Young, Iris Marian (1996). "Communication and the Other: Beyond Deliberative Democracy," in Seyla Benhabib (Ed.), *Democracy and Difference*. Princeton: Princeton University Press, pp. 120–135.

Zajonc, Robert B. (1980). "Feeling and Thinking: Preferences Need No Inferences." *American Psychologist*, 35:151–175.

CHAPTER 4

The Internet and the Global Public Sphere

Colin Sparks

INTRODUCTION

The issue discussed in this chapter has been vividly illustrated by the recent world financial crisis. Major decisions, affecting the lives of millions of people, have been made by organizations like the World Bank and the International Monetary Fund (IMF). Many of these decisions have been made in secret by appointees over whom there is no democratic control. Such proceedings have been criticized, not only by those whose lives have been transformed by the changes, but also by people wholly committed to the operations of international capitalism. Jeffrey Sachs, panegyrist for the freest of free markets and the most enthusiastic advocate of shock therapy for ailing economies from Poland to Peru, is one such critic. Writing about the IMF in the *Financial Times*, the main newspaper of European business, he argued that the "situation was out of hand" and that there had to be a new openness and debate about its policies (Sachs 1997). The same general point has been made more formally and academically by other writers (Garnham 1992; Hjarvard 1993). The development of a global economy, and of political institutions that operate at the supranational level, call for the creation of a global public sphere. In this forum their policies can be subjected to the same kind of rational scrutiny as that which, in principle, those of the United States, or any other country with democratic pretensions, experience.

This chapter will explore some of the issues involved in that challenge. I will first make some brief remarks clarifying the ways in which I am here using the term "public sphere." I will then go on to review the ways in which the traditional media of press and broadcasting have been able to adapt to this new situation. I will consider the extent to which the new interactive media, and in particular the Internet, have modified our understanding of the issues involved. I will then conclude with a discussion of how far the democratic potential of these new technologies is likely to be realized.

THE GLOBAL AND THE PUBLIC SPHERE

The dominant contemporary view of globalisation sees its fully developed form as a recent phase of human history, distinct from earlier epochs (Robertson 1992). Among the unique features of this new age is the increasing importance of symbolic exchanges, and the emergence of genuinely global media (Waters 1996). These media, and their content, must be understood as radically distinct from the media characteristic of earlier periods, which they systematically marginalize (Herman and McChesney 1997). In the strongest versions of this theory, they are not the international projections of particular states or cultures but the bearers of a new global culture. The epoch of globalization is radically different from the preceding age of imperialism, in the media as well as in politics and economics (Tomlinson 1997). Global media, if indeed they do exist, form the necessary material framework for any global public sphere that might exist or emerge.

The concept of the *public sphere* is a more contentious one. Both Bennett and Entman in their introduction to this book and Dahlgren in Chap. 2 review some of the problems involved. Here, I want to make four brief points about the way in which the term is being used in this chapter:

1. The empirical status of the concept has been subject to numerous critiques (for example, from a massive literature: Fraser 1992; Curran 1991; Schudson 1992; LeMahieu 1988; Scannell 1989). Taken together, these suggest that the public sphere as an embodied reality does not exist today and has never existed in the past. The only justification for retaining the concept in circulation must therefore be its normative status.

2. Although the emergence of approximations to the public sphere has been historically bound up with the struggle for political democracy, there is not a direct link between the two. The classical bourgeois public sphere that Habermas identified in eighteenth-century England was only tenuously connected even to the most minimal forms of democratic politics. If we then investigate

whether a global public sphere is coming into being, we are not disqualified a priori because of the absence of global democracy.

3. One of the major criticisms of the original formulations of the public sphere has been upon its singularity. It has been argued that, "In the present conjuncture, the scope and location of conflicts are many and varied . . . The autonomous movements institute a plurality of public spheres" (Keane 1984, p. 29; original emphasis). This chapter is predicated upon the contrary insistence that, if the term is to retain any validity and utility, *public sphere* must be taken as singular. To the extent that any social movement or philosophy subscribes to a notion of the collective self-determination of social life, it must in principle be prepared to present its arguments in such a way as to be intelligible to the remainder of society (Garnham 1992, pp. 368–72).

4. To the extent that it is linked with a theory of democracy, the concept of the public sphere has a bias toward direct and participatory theories. A classic formulation was that the concept of the public sphere is "a realm of our social life in which something approaching public opinion can be formed" (Habermas 1974, p. 49). The stress in the concept of the public sphere is upon the active and participatory role of the public in the formation of their common opinion.

The discussion of the global public sphere in this chapter is therefore marked by two concerns: first, whether any media that might be thought to be vehicles of such a global process actually exist, and, second, whether they are structured in such a way as to allow an inclusive discussion between equal parties, directed at reaching a common agreement. Naturally, we would not expect to find any such utopian arrangement existing in the contemporary world. Rather, we will be concerned to discover whether it is possible to discern developments that tend toward achieving those goals.

THE TRADITIONAL MEDIA

The traditional media, that is, the press and broadcasting, are the main embodiments of the actually existing approximations to the public sphere within the current state system. The extent to which they are satisfactory embodiments varies from country to country but it is generally recognized that, even in the best cases, they fall short of the ideal in at least three main ways:

1. There are limitations on what may be said. The various forms of state censorship are well known, but the limitations imposed by the market, concentrations of ownership, and dependence upon advertising revenue are also important.
2. The existing media superserve social elites. The serious press tends to be the preserve of the upper social groups, excluding largely for economic reasons the poor. In broadcasting, the move toward niche channels and the rise of subscription services of various types undermine the universalism of the free-to-air broadcasters.
3. The dominant media in most countries are large-scale undertakings, and profitable operation at this level entails professional production. These media professionals effectively ration public discourse in our societies. The room for genuinely public access is very small, being restricted to specialized channels on cable or the letters page in the printed press, or similar marginal sites.

All of these factors taken together tend to make the existing media rather poor representatives of the public sphere, even within the most democratic of nations.

These problems are intensified when we consider how far these same media embody a global public sphere. Numerous studies of the national media have shown how international news flows tend to be dominated by the elite states, and by elite groups within those states (Alleyne 1997; Galtung and Vincent 1992, pp. 31–70; Gerbner et al. 1993). There are very limited grounds for claiming that they constitute the makings of a global public sphere.

There are, however, some media that might properly be considered international, even global. There are some news channels, of which the most famous is CNN, that aspire to be global in their reporting and in their transmission. There are newspapers and magazines that attempt to be global in their reporting and circulation. At present, at least, these media fail to constitute the basis of a public sphere for at least three reasons:

1. The extent to which they are genuinely global, or even international, is limited. The *Wall Street Journal,* in all its editions, is essentially a U.S. newspaper; the *Financial Times,* in all its editions, is essentially a British newspaper. The same is true for all "global" products. While there is a circulation of television images around

the world, these are generally mediated by national broadcasters before reaching their audiences (Gurevitch et al. 1991, pp.214–15).

2. The audience for these products is very small indeed. In the United States, CNN has, in normal years, around a 1 percent market share. Even in the great crisis of the Gulf War, it only commanded around 3 percent of the audience (Greenberg and Levy 1997, p. 139). In the United Kingdom in 1998, CNN had a 0.1 percent audience share, up from the unmeasurably small audience of the previous year. The same is true of the international newspapers.

3. The audience they have is an elite one. Its members tend to be extremely rich and disproportionately powerful. The average income of readers of the *Wall Street Journal Europe*, for example, is more than $100,000 a year. Second, this audience is very much at home in English, or sometimes Spanish. The number of native speakers of either of these languages is tiny compared to the world population, and the number of people who have a good working knowledge is still small.

Overall, then, we can say that the existing mass media are even more inadequate as vehicles for a genuinely global public sphere than they are at the level of the state. They serve a very small and very rich audience, and they devote disproportionate (at least in crude population terms) attention to the news of elite states (Sparks 1998).

THE NEW MEDIA

The new media, and in particular computer mediated communication (CMC) as embodied in the Internet, hold out the promise of overcoming many of the limitations of the existing mass media (Rheingold 1995, p. 14). There are those for whom the development of CMC marks the destruction of the state as historically constituted and its replacement with other forms of social organization (Negroponte 1995; Dyson 1997).[1] Others see CMC as enabling a new constituency that can act to revive existing democratic structures and perhaps build new ones (Watson 1997). It is worth spelling out some of the ways in which the Internet is claimed to provide a solution to some of the problems identified above:

1. The basic communication protocols are designed to be transparent and are, therefore, in principle global (IITF 1998, p. 5).

2. The basic model of communication is interactive. The domination of social communication by those with the resources necessary to operate a newspaper or television station is negated in favor of drastically reduced entry barriers (Foreman 1995, p. 2).

3. The electronic nature of communication ensures that the accidents of place, that have been so convincing an argument against the more participatory forms of democracy, are no longer at all important (Fernback 1997).

4. The anonymity of the IP address serves to disguise many of those social markers (age, gender, ethnic origin, accent, and so on) that in practice serve to either validate or disqualify the opinions of speakers in direct social interaction (Mitra 1997, p. 73).[2]

5. The basic design of the system was generated with the exchange of scientific information in mind, and therefore it is particularly suited to the kind of textualized discursive practices that are characteristic of the Enlightenment definition of rational political debate.

6. The searchable architecture of the system makes it easy to distribute and organize the information necessary to reach informed decisions on any matter.

These advantages, and there are no doubt others, are so real and so important as to give some credibility even to the most messianic of the prophets of electronic democracy. There are numerous accounts of experiments, in the United States and elsewhere, in which the potential of this technology has been embodied in real democratic structures, with variable results (Tsagarousianou et al. 1998). Most of the projects studied have been local, but there is no reason why they cannot be applied to the broader question of a global public sphere.

WHO'S WIRED?

If it is in principle possible to conceive of the Internet constituting the vehicle for a global public sphere, then the key question is the empirical one of discovering how far the ideal of every citizen having the power to communicate with every other citizen is being realized. The fact that something is an empirical question does not mean that it is a simple question. In this case, it is very hard indeed to give a definitive answer. The main problem is the relative novelty of the technology. By far the maturest Internet environment is that of the United States. To

Table 4.1. *Percentages of U.S. households with a computer, modem telephone, and e-mail 1994 and 1997*

	Computer	Modem	Phone	E-mail
1994	24.1	11	93.8	3.4
1997	36.6	26.3	93.8	16.9

Source: NTIA, 1998: Chart One.

the extent that the diffusion of this technology throughout society can be studied empirically, it is here. But even here, reliable data are limited in scope, and the time series are short. Any snapshot of provision or usage thus tends to be misleading. There is simply not enough evidence to allow us to distinguish with certainty between the projections of exponential growth and the forecasts of limited availability.

Studies of Internet use in the United States give widely diverging figures for penetration rates, partly depending upon the date and the methodology of the survey employed. For the purposes of this paper, I have chosen to look at the most "official" rather than the most recent surveys: those produced by the U.S. Census Bureau from 48,000 door-to-door interviews in October 1994 and October 1997. The size and provenance of these surveys makes them particularly likely to be reliable. The data were collected and analyzed to investigate whether there are any systematic patterns of social exclusion operating in access to telecommunications and computing facilities in the United States.[3] The fact that there have been two surveys using the same methodology means that we can make at least hesitant projections. It is important to note that what the survey measures is not whether people actually use the Internet, or even whether they have a connection to the Internet, but the extent to which they have, in their households, a cluster of enabling technologies.[4] Not surprisingly, as Table 4.1 shows, the report found that there was rapid overall growth in the diffusion of these technologies. But there were also marked social differences in the penetration levels of telephones, computers, and on-line access. Table 4.2 illustrates one of the many divisions found by the survey. Differences of this kind were found along a number of axes, most notably race–origin, rural–urban, and educational level. We should not be surprised by these sorts of results. It is a well-established characteristic of diffusion patterns that the early adopters will tend to come dispropor-

Table 4.2. *Percentages of U.S. households with a computer ranked by income for 1997*

Household income	U.S. as a whole
Under $5,000	16.5
$5,000–9,999	9.9
$10,000–14,999	12.9
$15,000–19,999	17.4
$20,000–24,999	23.0
$25,000–34,999	31.7
$35,000–49,999	45.6
$50,000–74,999	60.6
$75,000+	75.9

Source: NTIA, 1998: Chart 11.

tionately from groups that have high incomes and other forms of social privilege (Rogers 1995, p. 269). We might therefore expect that over the time it takes for the classic s-curve to be completed the inequalities in access to the Internet will diminish and these technologies will become, like television, more or less universal. As Table 4.1 shows, the telephone was found in 93.8 percent of U.S. households in 1997, a percentage that had not changed since the first survey in 1994. We might therefore expect that the other electronic devices studied here would continue to grow until diffusion was almost complete. In fact, there is strong evidence against such a positive conclusion, at least in the short term. In the first place, we need to recall that the telephone has taken around 100 years to reach its current high level of diffusion in the United States. It is sustained at this level even today by the provision of (federally mandated) state subsidies for the poorest families (NTIA 1997, pp. 2–3). Secondly, although the telephone has achieved a very high level of diffusion, there remain important differences between different social groups. Thus, the lowest diffusion rate, of 74.4 percent, is found among rural Americans with an income of under $5,000. The highest, on the other hand, is a rate of 99.1 percent among rural Americans with an income of more than $75,000 (NTIA 1998, Chart 3).

More importantly, perhaps, the evidence suggests that, at least over a short period, the gap between rich and poor, and between whites and others, has expanded significantly. As the report notes with regard to income:

Although all income groups are now [i.e., 1997 as compared with 1994] more likely to own a computer, the penetration levels for those at higher incomes have grown more significantly. As a result, the gap in computer ownership levels between higher-income households and lower-income households has expanded in the last three years. (NTIA 1998, p. 3)

Not only do the rich and the white have more access to computers and associated technologies, but also these technologies are diffusing more rapidly among such people than among the relatively disadvantaged of U.S. society. This pattern of a broadening gap is repeated across most of the combinations of income and race/origin, with the notable exception of the category "other, not hispanic" (NTIA 1998, Charts 15–15d).

Once we move outside the borders of the United States, the pattern of diffusion is generally far less complete. The factors that facilitate Internet adoption in the United States – very rich population, cheap equipment, low telecommunications charges with free local calls, a widespread innovation-oriented social psychology with regard to technology, etc. – are not widely duplicated elsewhere in the developed world. Once one moves beyond the magic circle of rich countries, of course, the gap widens dramatically.

It is very difficult to say precisely how wide the gaps are, since the problems of data reliability in the rest of the world are at least as great as in the United States. One possible approach is through host and domain names, but a location in cyberspace does not necessarily correspond to a location in physical space: an Internet address can be *http://www.xxxx.co.uk*, and the physical company can actually be located in Vermont. We can, however get some idea of the orders of magnitude involved if we compare the size of the top twelve groupings of hosts with the number of hosts registered with domain names in the world's two most populous countries for 1998 and 1999. The results are represented in Figure 4.1.[5] As this evidence makes strikingly clear, the less-developed countries are much less provided for than are the developed countries, and this gap appears to be growing. Obviously, on this evidence, even in the United States, the Internet is today very far from having the inclusiveness that is distinctive of a public sphere, and which Rheingold and other writers have identified as its key enabling characteristic. Even in the most advanced and developed of online environments, it is still only a minority of people who have the technology that enables them to communicate in the ways predicted by the enthusiasts

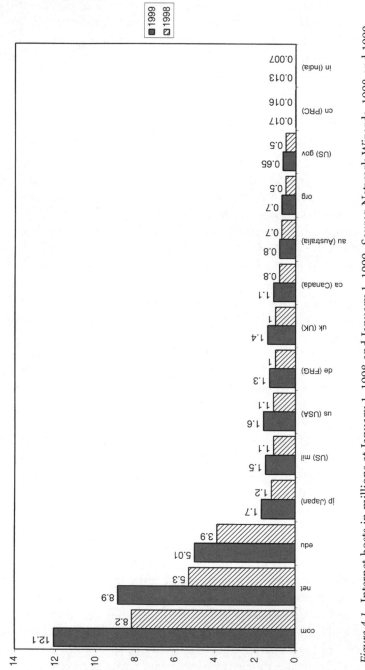

Figure 4.1. Internet hosts in millions at January 1, 1998 and January 1, 1999. *Source:* Network Wizards, 1998 and 1999.

for cyberdemocracy. When we broaden our interests to the global dimension, it becomes impossible to consider the Internet as anything remotely resembling a public sphere. The exclusions are too great and too obvious to be ignored by serious social theorists.

There are two possible responses to this sort of evidence. One is to abandon serious social theory, perhaps note in passing that such inequalities exist, and then to pass swiftly on to a discussion of the supposed implications of "communicative abundance" (Keane 1998). Dismissing the experience of the vast majority of the world's population has little to recommend it from the point of view of democratic theory. A more valuable response is to say that it is early yet, which it certainly is, and that as time passes, these differences, if not eradicated, will at least be smoothed out. In due course, "everyone" will have the technology to access the public sphere of the Internet, in the same way that "everyone" has the technology (functioning eyeballs and functional literacy) needed to access the public sphere of the press and television. It is a characteristic of diffusion processes that there are early adopters, late majority, laggards, and so on. The fact that there are differences in diffusion between different social groups at this point, and that they appear to be growing, is a normal function of the diffusion process, and in due course they will be eliminated. It is commonly observed that the effect of the early phases of the diffusion of a particular innovation are marked by a widening of the gap in acceptance, followed later by a narrowing as diffusion approaches 100 percent (Rogers 1986, pp. 170–72). This argument, bolstered by the experience of the diffusion of television sets in the United States, is the one used by enthusiasts like Louis Rossetto, CEO of *Wired*. He argues that today's "have nots" are really "have laters," and that in time the market will sort it all out (Bollier 1997, pp. 7–8). Those worried about the time taken for diffusion to be completed can propose policy initiatives to attempt to minimize the lag and reduce the lingering effects of exclusion. For example, these problems can be addressed by using the educational system as a change agent, providing subsidies and incentives for targeted groups of non-adopters to modify their behavior, and by the provision of public access in libraries and community centers. On a global scale, the richer countries can adopt programs to spread the benefits of connectivity to the developing world.

There are several grounds for thinking that this optimistic scenario might be flawed. In the first place, projection in the social sciences, particularly on the basis of such a limited time series, is notoriously unreliable. It might possibly be true that one can envisage the complete diffusion of these technologies within the United States within the next decade. The time scale for most of the world's population, however, must realistically be set as rather longer than "in the first half of the twenty-first century" envisaged by enthusiasts (Foreman 1995, p. 7). The scale of existing international aid projects makes it unlikely that this slow development will be short-circuited: The United States Agency for International Development, for example, has a project called the "Leland Initiative" designed to assist African countries improve Internet connections. It has a five-year total budget of $15 million (USAID 1998).

Second, in order for a genuinely global public sphere to evolve, it would be necessary not only for the cluster of technologies to be in place, but also for there to be a common language of communication. At present, English is the effective mandatory language of the Internet. Estimates suggest that around 80 percent of Internet traffic is in English (Babel 1997). In one recent calculation, there are 91 million native English speakers accessing the Internet, as against 4.6 million native speakers of Mandarin and Cantonese (Headcount 1999). Machine translation is primitive and development slow, so it is unlikely that this obstacle to open communication will be easily overcome. For both of these reasons, it will probably be quite some time before we will be able to think of the Internet as even an approximation to a global public sphere.

The most substantial problem, however, is the unresolved issue of whether the technology will in fact ever diffuse throughout the population of the United States, let alone the world. Diffusion studies apply with respect to a particular population defined with reference to a particular innovation, not to a general population. In the classic case, hybrid seed corn diffused to all Iowa cereal farmers, not to all residents of the state of Iowa. Clearly, some technologies, for example, television and (eventually) the telephone, have diffused more or less completely throughout the general population of all residents of the state of Iowa. The unanswered question is whether the Internet is like seed-corn or like television. If the answer is "television," then sooner or later there will be universal service, and sooner or later there will be a global public sphere. If the answer is "seed-corn," then the technology will diffuse within that specific group to which it is appropriate, and never directly affect the lives of the rest of the population. If the latter is the case, then the Internet cannot be the technological basis for a global public sphere.

Since the evidence is very limited, views can legitimately differ on this issue. My own preference is for the view that the Internet is not like either television or seed-corn: it is at present a composite technology. Many innovations are characterized by the fact that they are "reinvented" in the process of adoption; the telephone, computer, and Internet are all innovations with a very high degree of reinventability. This set of technologies has already been reinvented in a variety of ways: scientific data transfer, personal messaging, public discussion, research, entertainment, electronic commerce, education, and no doubt many others. Some of these reinventions are corn-like (for example, e-commerce), others are television-like (for example, Web TV), but so far they have all been contained in more or less the same technological envelope. This is not necessarily optimal for all of the various functions. There is no reason for this to continue, and already there is some evidence that the entertainment functions – the television-like reinventions – are migrating back toward enhanced televisions, which offer much greater functionality in important areas. If that were to be generalized, then there would be a technological divergence between those users primarily oriented to the kinds of communication central to the debate about the public sphere and those who prefer an improved version of televisual communication.

The issue can be seen as whether the Internet will evolve as a productive technology (seed-corn) or a leisure technology (television), or whether it can continue as both (telephone). Current evidence seems to suggest a "productive" orientation. As Figure 4.2 shows, the Internet itself is evolving more and more toward domination by commercial sites. These are not predominantly engaged in communication with consumers like you and me, but with other businesses. One recent estimate by the OECD found that business-to-business e-commerce activity accounted for at least 80 percent of the current total, and that this domination was likely to continue into the future (OECD 1998, p. 3). The signs are that it will not be "the Internet," with the wonderful egalitarian interactivity that we all know and admire, that diffuses. On the contrary, there could well be a technological divergence that will result in the diffusion of "the Internet" among businesses and one group of citizens, and the diffusion of quite different and much less interactive technologies to the rest.[6]

We already know, from evidence regarding existing media preferences, that the propensity to seek information related to public enlightenment and the propensity to engage in political action are socially

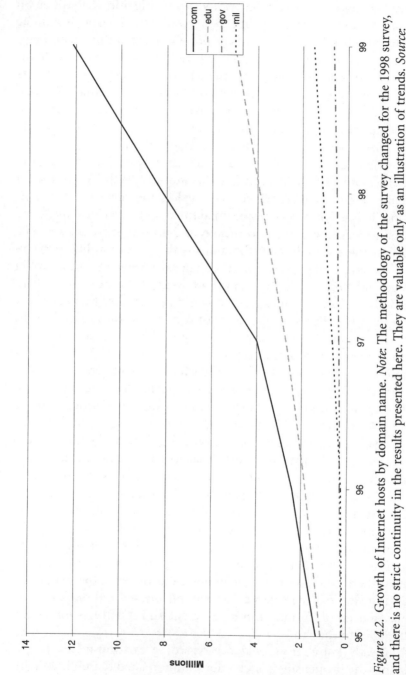

Figure 4.2. Growth of Internet hosts by domain name. *Note:* The methodology of the survey changed for the 1998 survey, and there is no strict continuity in the results presented here. They are valuable only as an illustration of trends. *Source:* Network Wizards, 1995–1999.

patterned in normal times toward elite social groups. We can therefore reasonably suggest that the differential patterns of diffusion noted here are in fact the early evidence of this kind of technological divergence. If that were the case, then the fully interactive mode of communication would remain the preserve of a minority rather than becoming a genuinely public property.

As an enabling technology that permits citizens to know more about the world, to put forward their views, to listen to discussions, and to reach an informed decision, the Internet is unrivalled since the *agora* of classical antiquity (Jones 1960, pp. 46–47). But, despite their international nature, despite their riches of information, and despite the glorious abundance of debate, the global media, both old and new, fall a very long way short of the ideal notion of a public sphere. They have clear limits that exclude the voices and the interests of a majority of the world's population. These exclusions operate every bit as completely and permanently as did the laws of Athenian citizenship. Unless and until these limits are overcome, there will be no sign of a global public sphere.

CONCLUSIONS: THE TOPOGRAPHY OF
THE PUBLIC SPHERE

Such bald statements, however true they may be, run the risk of being accused of missing the point. After all, there is certainly something going on. The global media do exist and they do have audiences. The newspapers and magazines with global ambitions are avidly read around the world. CNN, and, for that matter, the BBC Radio World Service, have loyal, if rather small, audiences in almost every country. On the Internet, there are masses of data sources, discussion groups, and other forms of communication linking people around the world. It is only reasonable to enquire: If this seething public life is not a public sphere, then what is it?

The answer to that question brings us back to what I call the topography of the public sphere. In the opening passage of their classic analysis of the limits of the bourgeois public sphere, Negt and Kluge wrote that

Federal elections, Olympic ceremonies, the actions of a commando unit, a theater premiere – all are considered as public events. Other events of overwhelming public significance, such as

89

childrearing, factory work, and watching television within one's own four walls, are considered private. The real social experiences of human beings, produced in everyday life and work, cut across such divisions. (Negt and Kluge 1993, p. xliii)

Public and private are not self-evident and naturally distinct categories. On the contrary, aspects of social reality can pass from one to another and back again over time, be located differently in different cultures, or be public for one group but not for another. What is more, the fact that an event is public, in that it is generally known, does not necessarily bring it into the public sphere. Negt and Kluge point to the fact that since its inception bourgeois democracy has engaged in a struggle to define the limits of public power and public debate so as to try to exclude, among other things, issues of property ownership. In this, it has recently been very successful, at least in the United States and the United Kingdom. The majority of what constitutes the global media falls within the limits of the bourgeois topography of the public sphere. Those media that challenge such limits, either in traditional or electronic form, eke out a marginal existence on the fringes of economic viability. But the bourgeois topography of the public sphere is never secure. There is always the danger that external opposition, or internal contradiction, will bring issues of property into the forefront of public debate.

This instability is particularly apparent at the global level. We can find in the global media, and in particular on the Internet, all sorts of things – some clearly public, some clearly private. Business news has a prominent place in the old global media like the *Financial Times*. As we have seen, various kinds of commercial information and commercial transactions find a prominent place on the Internet. To the extent that the global media, old and new, are fora in which the owners of property debate and supervise their property, they constitute what I have elsewhere called a private sphere (Sparks 1998). Some of this is open to the public, but its status, as a matter of public concern, is problematic. As an abstract principle, what I do with my private property is not a public matter, but in contemporary reality things are more complicated. The size and importance of the productive units of the modern economy mean that there is no hard and fast line, even in the bourgeois public sphere, between the "private" world of the business transaction and the "public" world of matters of general interest. A sovereign default is recognized as a matter of public interest, but the bankruptcy of a small business is not. A collapse of the stock market is recognized as a matter of public interest, but the price of the shares in a small company is not. In principle, however, all this material pertains to private information that guides individuals and corporations in the disposal of their property, and it only becomes a public issue to the extent that it encroaches on the general interest. Whether this material falls into the private or public sphere is thus a hotly contested issue, even within wholly bourgeois circles. This instability has always been present in the public sphere, and it is what constitutes its irreducible radical core. There has always been the possibility that the rational scrutiny of public life will lead to the conclusion that some, or all, private property is an obstacle to the general good and should be socialized, or at the very least regulated.

It is precisely the power of private property to produce public catastrophe that provokes calls for the creation of a global public sphere. It is private capital that destabilizes currencies and whole economies, that reverses decades of prosperity in one frantic burst of speculation, that drives millions back below even the World Bank's definition of the poverty line (an income of $1 per day). Completely unfettered capital operating on a global stage, apparently outside the control of any existing state, reveals the limits of the existing public spheres very starkly. Even Sachs, whose commitment to the capitalist system is beyond question, is appalled by the power of unaccountable global organizations, and seeks to open their doings to public debate. But to seek to open this debate is to return to the radical implications of the original concept of a public sphere. The rulers of the global economy have their arcania of power every bit as much as did the monarchs of the eighteenth century. Their business, they believe, is none of our business.

Over time, the public spheres of the developed states have become naturalized and the radical nature of their origins obscured. A battery of resources – coercion, political concessions, habit, nationalism, and xenophobia; the logic of the media industries; and, above all, the outstanding success of the capitalist system in raising the overall standard of living – have worked to make the limits of the bourgeois public sphere accepted by most people, most of the time. It is only in moments of crisis and social upheaval that the mass of the population starts to question the existing topography of the public sphere. The global public sphere, if it comes in to being at all, will be born with none of this restrictive paraphernalia. Its nature and limits will be a matter for debate and contestation from the start. The circumstances of its birth will be ones in which the immediate existential consequences of the untrammelled exercise of the rights to private property in the means of production will be evident to millions. They will also be ones in which the effective global public power is demonstrably quite beyond the control of the vast majority of the people over whom it is exercised. To the extent that it is a public sphere, it will be open to the voices of precisely those people who today are largely excluded from debates over global politics and economics.

The core of truth in the prophesies of the enthusiasts for computer-mediated communication is located here. They are right to say that this technology does provide the potential basis for such a global debate. One can certainly find on the Internet information and opinions that transgress the limits of the bourgeois public sphere. One can certainly see in the electronic activities of political and social groups the dim outlines of a new *agora*. But these are the minority usages at present. In its origins, the Internet was a child of the needs of the U.S. military. Today, that has changed: The majority of effort going in to the development of the Internet is designed to render it a more perfect instrument for business. It is the discourse of business that dominates cyberspace. The bulk of the frenetic activity on the Internet lies outside of the public sphere, so long as we accept the definitions of its limits as those of the bourgeois public sphere. The *agora*, of course, was the marketplace of Athens, as well as the physical site of the classical public sphere. But before the meetings of the assembly of citizens, it was the duty of the Council to close all of the market stalls in order to make room for the business of the city.

NOTES

1. Many of these enthusiasts for the Internet are, consciously or unconsciously, anarchists (usually right-wing anarchists), and it would be reasonable to say that the extreme position is that the Internet will do away with democracy by rendering it obsolete along with all other forms of government.
2. We should note an important counterargument put forward by Mark Poster, who claims that physical presence, as the embodiment of a stable identity, was the necessary guarantor of authenticity in the traditional public sphere. Since this is absent from the Internet, there can be no stable identities and thus no progress towards consensus (*http://www.wired.com/wired/3.11/departments/poster.if.html*). Poster confuses the attributes of corporeal beings with the attributes of communication.
3. I have used the report's own classifications here, most notably the category of "race": "Race is defined as a concept used by individuals as a self-identification of 'biological stock'" (NTIA 1998, p. 5).

4. That is, telephone connection, computer, and modem, plus those who have access to on-line services. It is, of course, reasonable to assume that this latter means, in the vast majority of cases, Internet access.

5. We cannot assume that all .com, .edu, .net, and .org addresses are in the United States, although many are. While .mil addresses are those of the U.S. military, this organization is notoriously not confined to the United States. So, while it is certain that the number of hosts in the physical United States is greater than that of any other country, and probably greater by an order of magnitude, we can't find a reliable figure from these data.

6. It might be that there is a marketing-driven pressure that will override these social distinctions and result in most, if not all, U.S. homes having the requisite technology within the next few years. We may admit that this is a possibility, but we would then note that one of the known characteristics of home computers is that usage patterns are highly skewed toward a minority of heavy users: "A common finding in research on new communication systems is that only 10 percent of the users represent 50 percent of all uses, with the other 90 percent of users making up the other 50 percent of uses" (Rogers 1986, p. 125). Even if everyone had the capability to access the Internet, it seems likely that relatively few would use it intensively and that television, in one form or another, would remain the dominant domestic leisure technology.

REFERENCES

Alleyen, M. D. (1997). *News Revolution: Political and Economic Decisions about Global Information*. Basingstoke: Macmillan.

Babel (1997). "Web Languages Hit Parade." The Babel Project. http://www.isoc.org.8080/palmares.html.

Bollier, D. (1997). "Social Venture Capital for Universal Electronic Communications: A Conference Report." The Markle Foundation and the Aspen Institute. http://www.iaginteractive.com/emfa/venture.htm.

Curran, J. (1991). "Rethinking the media as a public sphere," in P. Dahlgren, and C. Sparks (Eds.), *Communication and Citizenship*. London: Routledge, pp. 38–42.

Dyson, E. (1997). *Release 2.0: A design for living in the Digital Age*. New York: Viking.

Fernback, J. (1997). "The Individual within the Collective: Virtual Ideology and the Realization of Collective Principles," in S. G. Jones (Ed.), *Virtual Culture: Identity and Community in Cybersociety*. London: Sage, pp. 36–54.

Foreman, W. (1995). *Creative Democracy and the Internet*. Martinez, CA: Centre for the Evolution of Democracy. http://www.cedemocracy.org/4chap1.html.

Fraser, N. (1992). "Rethinking the Public Sphere. A Contribution to the Critique of Actually Existing Democracy," in C. Calhoun (Ed.), *Habermas and the Public Sphere* Cambridge, MS: MIT Press, pp. 109–142.

Galtung, J., and R. C. Vincent (1992). *Global Glasnost: Toward a New World Information and Communication Order?* Cresskill, NJ: Hampton Press.

Garnham, N. (1992). "The Media and the Public Sphere," in C. Calhoun (Ed.), *Habermas and the Public Sphere* Cambridge, MS: MIT Press, pp. 359–76.

Gerbner, G., H. Mowlana, and K. Nordenstreng (Eds.), (1993). *The Global Media Debate: Its Rise, Fall and Renewal*. Norwood, NJ: Ablex.

Greenberg, B. S., and M. Levy (1997). "Television in the Changing Communication Environment: Audience and Content Trends in US Television." *Studies of Broadcasting*, 33:131–74.

Gurevitch, M., M. R. Levy, and I. Roeh (1991). "The global newsroom: convergences and diversities in the globalization of television news," in P. Dahlgren and C. Sparks (Eds.), *Communication and Citizenship*. London: Routledge, pp. 195–216.

Habermas, J. (1974). "The Public Sphere: An Encyclopedia Article (1964)." *New German Critique*, 1(3):49–55.

Headcount (1998). "Who.s Online by Language." Headcount. http://www.headcount.com/.

Herman, E. S., and R. W. McChesney (1997). *The Global Media: the New Missionaries of Global Capitalism*. London: Cassell.

Hjarvard, S. (1993). "Pan-European Television News: Toward a European Political Public Sphere?," in P. Drummond, R. Patterson, and J. Willis (Eds.), *National Identity and Europe* London: BFI, pp. 71–94.

IITF (1998). "The Global Information Infrastructure: Agenda for Cooperation." Information Infrastructure Task Force. http://www.iitf.nist.gov/documents/docs/gii/giiagend.html.

Jones, A. H. M. (1960). *Athenian Democracy*. Oxford: Basil Blackwell.

Keane, J. (1984). *Public Life and Late Capitalism: Toward a Socialist Theory of Democracy*. Cambridge: Cambridge University Press.

(1998). *Public Life In the Era of Communicative Abundance*. London: Centre for the Study of Democracy.

Le Mahieu, D. (1988). *A Culture for Democracy*. Oxford: Clarendon Press.

Mitra, A. (1997). "Virtual Commonality: Looking for India on the Internet," in S. G. Jones (Ed.), *Virtual Culture: Identity and Community in Cybersociety*. London: Sage, pp. 55–79.

Negroponte, N. (1995). *Being Digital*. London: Coronet.

Negt, O., and A. Kluge (1993). *Public Sphere and Experience: Toward an Analysis of the Bourgeois and Proletarian Public Sphere*. Minneapolis: University of Minnesota Press.

Network Wizards (1995). "Internet Domain Survey, January 1995." Network Wizards. http://www.nw.com/zone.

(1996). "Internet Domain Survey, January 1996." Network Wizards. http://www.nw.com/zone.

(1997). "Internet Domain Survey, January 1997." Network Wizards. http://www.nw.com/zone.

(1998). "Internet Domain Survey, January 1998." Network Wizards. http://www.nw.com/zone.

(1999). "Internet Domain Survey, January 1999." Network Wizards. http://www.nw.com/zone.

NTIA (1997). "The New Universal Service: NTIA.s Guide for Users." National Telecommunications and Information Administration. http://www.ntia.doc.gov/opadhome/uniserve/univweb.htm.

(1998). "Falling Through the Net II: New Data on the Digital Divide." National Telecommunications and Information Administration. http://www.ntia.doc.gov/ntiahome/net2/falling.html.

OECD (1998). "The Economic and Social Impacts of Electronic Commerce: Preliminary Findings and Research Agenda. Report Summary." Organization for Economic Co-operation and Development. http://www.oecd.org/subject/e_commerce/ summary.htm.

Rheingold, H. (1995). *The Virtual Community: Surfing the Internet.* London: Minerva.

Robertson, R. (1992). *Globalization: Social Theory and Global Culture.* London: Sage.

Rogers, E. M. (1986). *Communication Technology: The New Media in Society.* New York: The Free Press.

——— (1995). *Diffusion of Innovations,* Fourth Edition. New York: The Free Press.

Sachs, Jeffrey (1997). "Personal View: 'Power Unto Itself,'" *Financial Times,* 11 December, pp. 1–18.

Scannell, P. (1989). "Public service broadcasting and modern public life." *Media, Culture and Society,* 11(2):135–66.

Schudson, M. (1992). "Was There Ever a Public Sphere?" in C. Calhoun (Ed.), *Habermas and the Public Sphere.* Cambridge, Mass: The MIT Press, pp. 143–163.

Sparks, C. (1998). "A Global Public Sphere?," in D. Thussu (Ed.), *Electronic Empires.* London: Edward Arnold, pp. 108–124.

Tomlinson, J. (1997). "Cultural Globalization and Cultural Imperialism," in A. Mohammadi (Ed.), *International Communication and Globalization.* London: Sage, pp. 170–190.

Tsagarousianou, R., D. Tambin, and C. Bryan (Eds.), (1998). *Cyberdemocracy: Technology, Cities and Civic Networks.* London: Routledge.

USAID (1998). "*USAID Leland Initiative: Africa Global Information Infrastructure Project.*" United States Agency for International Development. http://www.Info.usaid.gov/regions/afr/leland.

Waters, M. (1995). *Globalization.* London: Routledge.

Watson, N. (1997). "Why We Argue About Virtual Community: A Case Study of the Phish.Net Fan Community," in S. G. Jones (Ed.), *Virtual Culture: Identity and Community in Cybersociety.* London: Sage, pp. 103–122.

PART 2

Citizens, Consumers, and Media
in Transition

Reporting and the Push for Market-Oriented Journalism: Media Organizations as Businesses

Doug Underwood

The tension within American news organizations between treating readers as "customers" or as "citizens" is well illustrated at the *Minneapolis Star Tribune*, where publisher Joel Kramer explained to a 1995 meeting of the American Society of Newspaper Editors: "In Minneapolis, we're saying that marketing is part of journalism. Editors are making decisions along these lines. Their newspaper has been structured around customer units. The editor is also responsible for looking out for readers and profits." (Manzella 1998, p. 60)

The *Star Tribune* has adopted many of the faddish new management techniques to deal with the realities of market-driven journalism: The traditional newsroom beat system of cops, courts, and city hall has been restructured into topic teams designed to make coverage meet perceived reader interests; editors have broken down the traditional walls between the news and business departments and work with their business-side colleagues to fashion the newspaper's marketing strategy; and the newspaper has been redesigned with more graphics, pull-out boxes, and easy-to-read bulleted items to make it more "reader-friendly."[1]

But much of this has upset journalists in the *Star Tribune* newsroom who feel the newspaper is now more dedicated to the task of making money, meeting marketing goals, and serving advertiser needs than it is to the traditional public service role of informing the public and serving as a watchdog of government and business.

"These guys are wringing their hands when they are making 20 percent return on equity," Mike Meyers, a veteran *Star Tribune* business reporter, says of the newspaper's executives. ". . . The First Amendment wasn't written for return on equity. When I got into the business I never encountered this. What has changed in the 1990's is that editors now have a dual responsibility . . . a counting house responsibility."

"I dislike the superficiality that comes with dressing up the news to make it easier to read," adds a longtime *Star Tribune* copy editor, who calls the newspaper's constant emphasis upon brief copy and at-a-glance summaries "anti-intellectual" and something that underestimates the intelligence of readers.[2]

This chapter will explore this tension – whether to treat the audience as consumers or as citizens – within the context of the marketing-oriented strategies that have made their way into media organizations as they try to maintain high levels of profits and respond to the lifestyle and perceived interests of their audience. Key elements of the analysis will include the impact of these strategies upon coverage of public life and the public sector; the success of marketing strategies in stemming audience erosion; the moves to integrate popular and consumer culture into the definition of the news; and the efforts to retain a meaningful "public sphere" where intelligent dialogue about public life can be sustained.

THE AUDIENCE: CONSUMERS OR CITIZENS?

The marketing and bottom-line influence upon today's media organizations has become ever more evident since the days when *USA Today*, the preeminent example of a newspaper created whole cloth out of marketing surveys, was founded in the early 1980s. Today it seems that the intertwining of news with marketing goals is everywhere:

- In the tabloid techniques adopted by ratings-fixated local television stations and the network television newsmagazines
- In the embrace of splashy visual techniques and news-you-can-use items by newspapers desperate to stem a four decade long readership slide
- In the explosion of salacious copy and scandal coverage in traditional media outlets and on the Internet
- In the mixing of entertainment, crime, and gossip with the news by television organizations trying to hold onto their audience
- And in the "synergy" of relentlessly expanding media conglomerates eager to treat the news as a "product" to be recast for the publicity, promotional, and marketing purposes of their integrated media holdings.

Equally intense has become the debate about what all this means to the public service mission of journalism – and particularly the attention paid to the traditional oversight role of government. Traditionalists, like the *Star Tribune* staffers, say serious-minded journalism that treats readers as citizens and focuses upon what they need to know to perform their democratic duties is being overwhelmed by the media marketer's vision of the public as busy, distracted, fulfillment-seeking consumers who must be pleased at all costs even if it means abandoning the higher traditions of the profession (For works that discuss this trend, see Underwood 1993; Kurtz 1993; Squires 1993; McManus 1994; Demers 1996).

In this new marketer's paradigm, audience research and marketing programs reign supreme. The definition of news has been recast so that it is defined as what is "relevant" to the audience. As a result, at many newspapers, the traditional beat structure, where since the early 1800s reporters have focused on coverage of politics, government, the courts, and police, has been replaced with thematic coverage that is built around self-help, family, and financial issues viewed as personally meaningful to readers. This coverage – which usually is adopted in concert with graphic redesigns; an intense focus upon localized and lifestyle topics; and lots of lists, tips, and information that is viewed as useful to readers – is also driven by the perception of news managers that the public is not interested in the complex issues that make up routine coverage of public bodies and the bureaucracy (Underwood 1998a; Stepp 1992). In place of the traditional, cover-the-meetings-and-grind-out-the-copy-about-the-activities of government, daily newspapers are giving their audience special projects and thematic packages written by reporters and reporting teams with little sustained contact with public agencies and investigative projects that often are aimed at winning prizes as much as rooting out abuses. Newspapers are presenting stories about medicine, health, diet, and personal finances that are geared to what market researchers believe touch readers personally. And, everything is packaged in lay-outs with computer-generated graphics that often put as much emphasis upon design and eye-catching appeal as substance (Stepp 1991).

This view is even more prevalent in ratings-driven television news. Here, the thinking among news managers and news consultants goes, if an issue isn't highly controversial or can't be sensationalized, it doesn't make the newscast. On local, over-the-airwaves television, viewers get a steady diet of ratings-driven crime news, celebrity coverage, and cutesy stories about animals (with the excessive coverage of crime and violence having a particularly deleterious impact upon the public psyche, the critics say). Meanwhile, the three major television news networks (CBS, NBC, and ABC) have cut back news staffs, virtually dropped out of the business of doing serious documentaries, diverted more resources to their hyped and often sensationalized news magazines, and taken to doing their own audience-friendly feature stories and news-you-can-use items (Tucher 1997; Kimball 1994).

In this environment, mayors and local council members complain that the press never shows up to cover their activities anymore – or, if it does, it invariably highlights controversy or tries to make everything out to be a scandal in ways that give the public a distorted view of public life. State legislatures are virtually never covered by local television (unless, of course, the issues are sexy or involve controversy or dispute), and many newspapers are cutting back on their coverage of the state capital (Layton and Walton 1998). Congress and the president still are the targets of intense press coverage. But, as the Monica Lewinsky scandal has shown, the national press has become obsessed with scandal, partisan disputes, and whatever else it believes will build audience and ratings (as witnessed by the growth of a beltway punditocracy with "attitude" who specialize in taking partisan jibes at each other on the new television political "shout" shows). The mundane activities of government (and the federal bureaucracy or the internal committee doings of Congress, in particular) are left largely unexamined. International affairs – never a strong point with the insular American media – are getting short shrift, as both newspapers and the television networks have cut back their overseas bureaus and ceded much of the coverage of foreign news to CNN. Coverage of business – again never a strong suit of the American press (particularly if those business interests involve advertisers or companies with powerful financial influence in the community) – has grown even more servile, with almost breathless attention paid to the stock market, the growth of the high technology industry, issues surrounding global trade, and anything else perceived as of interest to a public now deeply invested in mutual funds and the financial markets.

STAGNANT CIRCULATION; SLIPPING RATINGS

Despite these changes, there is little evidence that the move toward market-oriented journalism – including the abandonment of traditional government coverage – has done anything to improve the prospects of the media business. Although most media organizations are enormously profitable, with earnings margins much higher than the typical industry average, daily commercial newspapers and free, over-the-airwaves, broadcast television have seen their audience stagnating or eroding – and little has stemmed the decline. Daily newspapers have been on a four-decade-long slide as measured by daily newspaper readership household penetration, and the trend has grown slightly worse in recent years. Both national and local over-the-airwaves television have seen an enormous erosion in their audience since the 1970s as cable and satellite stations have chewed into their audience and turned the television dial into a cornucopia of choices. And now the arrival of the Internet has left executives of both newspapers and television worrying that their very medium of communication may be on the way out.

Since the late 1970s, when news executives started worrying seriously about these trends, both newspaper and television executives have jumped into marketing in a big way. While marketing solutions and the move toward "journalism lite" are still treated as orthodoxy in many media circles, few companies can show any improvement in their circulation rates as a result of adopting marketing-oriented solutions. The most dramatic example of this has been *USA Today*, which despite its splashy graphics, its brief text, and its self-conscious efforts to be "television in print," has failed to attract advertisers and, before recently turning a small profit, lost over $1 billion for its parent company, Gannett. during its first years of existence. Likewise, the Knight Ridder Co. abandoned its experiment with the Boca Raton, Florida, *News*, where the company's much-touted efforts to build circulation by redesigning the newspaper around light features, trendy graphics, and reader-relevant news showed little circulation success. Most recently, Mark Willes, a former cereal company executive and new publisher of the *Los Angeles Times*, has created controversy within the industry with his ambitious goals to build circulation by installing business-side executives in the newsroom and requiring editors to work with marketing, circulation, and advertising people to help develop new editorial products and to search for new ways to meet revenue and readership targets. Again, although recent reports show Willes's changes haven't eased circulation problems, newspapers all around the country are following suit by integrating news and business functions and putting editors and reporters through business literacy training (Underwood 1998b).

A handful of news organizations – particularly some of the larger prestige newspapers like the *New York Times,* the *Boston Globe,* the *Philadelphia Enquirer,* and the *Washington Post* – have rejected the *USA Today* approach and instead have decided to build readership by producing in-depth, informative journalism designed to appeal to an educated audience interested in public affairs (Gladney 1992). But other newspapers, such as the *Atlanta Journal and Constitution,* once the South's most respected newspaper, have decided to go in the other direction. In the early 1990s, the *Journal and Constitution*'s parent company, Cox Co., hired Bill Kovach, a respected *New York Times* editor, then abruptly replaced him with Ron Martin, the former *USA Today* editor, who redesigned the newspaper around color and graphics, more lifestyle stories, and more attention to marketing and reader interests. The differing philosophies of Kovach, who believes dailies must build readership through the solid, contextual coverage of public affairs that television doesn't do, and Martin, who believes that newspapers must compete with television on television's terms, are seen as a watershed debate in the industry. But, based on stagnant readership rates under the tenure of both editors, the question of what can be done to turn around the prospects of daily newspapers hasn't yet been answered (Shumate 1992).

The complexity of the problem facing today's newspaper editors is expressed by Leo Bogart, the widely respected media research specialist, who believes that news executives overemphasize marketing solutions and underestimate the public's interest in serious public affairs coverage. Bogart's research has found consistently high levels of audience interest for state, national, government and political, and international news. And Bogart believes that news editors regularly discount the public's interest in serious news as opposed to sports, entertainment, cultural, and fashion coverage (although, to confuse matters, he also notes that the public puts a much higher priority than editors upon such items as action line columns, news summaries, comic strips, astrology columns, and homemaking features) (Bogart 1989).

Researchers Klaus Schoenbach and Lori Bergen also question whether the "truisms" that have come to guide market-oriented editors – for example, the more local coverage and the more color graphics, the better; newspaper readers like bits of information rather than long stories; writing should be simple and entertaining – are supported by audience research. Schoenbach and Bergen throw cold water upon a whole host of "copying" strategies of newspapers – the mimicking of television by the presentation of graphs and brief sound-bite type stories, the use of magazine-style layouts, the focus on design strategies based largely on the tastes of designers – as effective methods for taking advantage of the special connection that newspapers have with their readers. Instead, they suggest that newspapers focus their strategies, and their audience research, on the questions that capitalize upon newspapers' unique appeal (Schoenbach and Bergen 1998): What are the limits of a more hedonistic, less serious, approach to news? How long should articles be to hold readers' attention but provide enough context and background? How do inserts and special sections detract from the newspaper's portability? What can newspapers do to balance the needs of sophisticated with less educated readers? These questions point to the essence of the problem that faces newspapers that seek to attract news readers by adopting strategies that offend their traditional reading base. In fact, a number of newspaper executives have come to question the wisdom of chasing after marginal, television-oriented readers (who probably won't stick with newspapers anyway) by "dumbing down" the newspaper in ways that undermine its credibility with its better educated, more informed readership.

Television news, in its own way, also has struggled with the problems created by a too mindless embrace of market-driven strategies. More and more, traditional, free, over-the-airwaves broadcast news has withdrawn from the world of serious news coverage into entertainment and left the field of public affairs coverage to CNN, C-Span, public television, local all-news cable channels, and Internet programming like MSNBC. In this way, network and local television have begun to follow in the path of radio. Most commercial radio stations dropped their news programming after the federal government deregulated them in the early 1980s and left news programming to the handful of all-news radio stations that still practice journalism (Grossman 1998). While the three traditional networks (ABC, CBS, and NBC) still put out strong newscasts, their audience has been shrinking (along with the general network television audience).[3] The rise of the ratings-oriented network news magazines, combined with the near-total emphasis local broadcast news puts upon crime and entertainment stories, has driven many of those who seek to be seriously informed away from free, over-the-airwaves television news.

And yet, it may be that television news organizations arc forsaking one of their strongest attributes. Audience surveys show that the public still puts its greatest trust in the credibility of television broadcast news of all kinds, despite what the critics have called the "trashing" of television news by market-oriented consultants and news executives (Newport and Saad 1998). Local, over-the-airwaves television, in particular, has struggled in an environment of declining ratings by trying to maintain what it can of a mass audience by holding those attracted to the lowest common denominator – crime and violence, accidents, catastrophes, sex, celebrity coverage, and gossip. The fact that the more discriminating audience has gravitated away doesn't much seem to bother local TV news executives – even if, as they are reluctant to admit, they are paying an increasingly high price in the scorn that is heaped upon them by media critics and citizens upset with the distorted lens through which they present the picture of community.

MEDIATED COVERAGE

Ironically, as traditional mainstream news organizations have cut back their serious coverage of public affairs, other institutions have taken to more aggressively trying to manage the news. Public relations has been one of the greatest growth industries both within government and business during the 1980s and 1990s, and few large organizations are without bevies of sophisticated professionals bent upon managing press strategy. In many areas of both state and national government, particularly bureaucratic agencies, coverage by the press is so minimal that what news is generated comes almost completely via press releases from self-interested sources. Think tanks – particularly with partisan political connections – have sprung up in Washington, D.C., and state capitals with the avowed intent to shape media, and thus public, opinion through a steady flow of reports, research studies, and the availability of experts. Political "spinning" and the use of political consultants and media campaign specialists is so endemic that reporters regularly are accused of relying on "spin doctors" almost exclusively to frame political debate. Direct political advertising by candidates and interest groups fills the television screens not only at election time, but whenever major issues come up in Congress or appear as state or local initiative measures. Interest groups routinely plan strategies that coordinate lobbying, public relations blitzes, direct television advertising, and initiative campaigns as a way to win over public support.

These campaigns to essentially circumvent the traditional "gatekeeper" role of the media are based, at least in part, upon the recognition of the media's withdrawal from serious, analytical coverage of complex issues, and the growing ease with which market-oriented journalists can be manipulated. Mark Hertsgaard, in his analysis of the strategies of the public-relations-savvy Reagan Administration, came to the conclusion that Reagan's aides were able to control the media agenda so effectively, and thus successfully stage media events, because media corporations have come to treat news largely as "a commodity to be bought and sold." By tailoring Reagan's program toward what met the visual and information needs of the media (television in particular), the images that Reagan's people wanted communicated passed almost directly to the public, despite the resentment of some television reporters that the demands of their medium handcuffed their ability to frame the debate with sufficient skepticism and in-depth analysis (Hertsgaard 1988).

Candidates, too, have adjusted to the void in serious political discourse left by media that have become increasingly wedded to superficial, poll-driven coverage, the use of public relations wizards, sound-bite analysis of issues, and glib political punditry. The 1992 presidential race, in particular, stands out for the way Ross Perot and Bill Clinton used alternative forms of media, town meetings, and in-depth political advertising as a method to directly connect with voters and to discuss issues in more depth. Still, attack ads, fueled by ever-larger contributions from special interest groups, continue to drive much political debate. The spectacle of television journalists lamenting the corruption of money in the political process, all the while watching their bosses line the company coffers with paid political advertising, has made the public only more cynical about big media's complicity in the debasement of political discussion. The perception, too, that the media's hunger for ratings increasingly shapes political discourse has also left members of the public shaking their collective heads, as has been the case with the Monica Lewinsky scandal, where saturation reporting and a near obsession of the Washington, D.C., press corps with the subject persisted despite polls showing that Americans were disgusted with the coverage and wanted to move the national discussion to other things. (Of course, those ratings wouldn't be so high if the public – of two minds, as is often the case – weren't watching in large numbers.)

The advent of the Internet, and its growing importance in conveying news and political information, has only added to the chaotic environment of public affairs coverage. On the positive side, boosters of new media note the direct and interactive capabilities of electronic computer information systems to allow the public access to large volumes of government information and government proceedings without the filter of traditional media. Many hail this as a revolutionary development, and some, such as Leonard Grossman, the former president of NBC News, predict that new media will lead to electronic plebiscites and dramatic, new ways of involving the public more directly in the decision-making processes of public life (Grossman 1995). This is the theme of Peter Dahlgren and Colin Sparks in Chaps. 2 and 4, respectively, who probe the question of whether the Internet and the growth of cyberspace have the potential to lead to the emergence of a global public sphere where public issues can be dealt with in a new and exciting fashion (Sparks 1998; Dahlgren 1998).

But those who worry about the darker side of new media fear that the volumes of data available in the information age may actually overwhelm intelligent public decision making and undermine the traditional standards that have guided ethical and intelligent professional journalistic judgment. Again, as the Monica Lewinsky scandal has shown, the Internet is increasingly the vehicle where public debate is fostered, as witnessed by the drama drummed up when the House Judiciary committee released first the Kenneth Starr report and then the video clip of President Clinton's grand jury testimony via the Internet. In fact, the Internet drove the Monica Lewinsky story in ways that deeply troubled journalists. For example, it was Matt Drudge, an Internet reporter who traffics in political gossip, who "broke" the story in January 1998 after *Newsweek* magazine, exercising traditional professional caution, decided to hold off on the story until it was more confident of its sources. In the same way, it was *Salon*, an Internet magazine, that revealed the story of House Judiciary committee chair Henry Hyde's long-ago affair after other mainstream media organizations had passed on it. And, of course, it has been on the Internet that a myriad of stories – ranging from the basest allegations against President Clinton to the wildest conspiracy theories – are kept alive alongside the Web pages of traditional media outlets. As excited as people may be about this access to a wide-open cyberspace environment, it is clear that we are paying a price for the loss of trusted editors operating in the old gatekeeper role who kept the public agenda focused on the high road.

A NEW PARADIGM?

In this brave new world of undifferentiated media diffusion and unfiltered and entertainment-driven news coverage, there are those who say that journalism, as it has been known, must be redefined to fit the circumstances of today. The best-known claim has been made by television critic Jon Katz, who argues that there is a "New News," blending Hollywood films and television culture, pop music and pop art, celebrity magazines, tabloid telecasts, and home video, which has become the new informational discourse, particularly among the young. He contrasts this with the "Old News" of the traditional media – formal, balanced, stilted – which he sees as ossified and dying (Katz 1992). Other commentators have picked up on this theme, including Michael X. Delli Carpini and Bruce A. Williams, who argue in Chap. 8 that the walls that separate public affairs from popular culture are breaking down, and that journalists and political scientists would be wise to expand their definition and interpretation of news to include more entertainment-oriented programming (Delli Carpini and Williams 1998).

Many journalists, as we have seen, have already incorporated this thinking into their modern marketing practices. Consumer-oriented newspaper editors, with an eye always on their market research, comfortably have embraced the notion that news must be redefined to fit the changing orientation of a modern population, increasingly wedded to entertainment, lifestyle issues, and parochial concerns. In television, in particular, a preponderance of news executives accept that entertainment values dictate the parameters of their business, and few resist as television news becomes more blended with entertainment programming and television journalism more reflective of tabloid values. Highbrows who don't accept mass taste, say television news executives, should feel free to gravitate toward public television, specialty public affairs publications, or other "intelligent" media sources.

Still, the handful of media executives who resist market thinking argue that it is more important for news organizations to treat the audience as citizens, and it is by connecting to readers' desire for community, their belief in democracy, and their willingness to tackle social problems that audience respect is maintained and long-term loyalty built. This is the philosophy that underlies the "public" or "civic" journalism movement where journalists are encouraged to get involved with citizens and public officials in solving community problems rather than commenting from the sidelines. This campaign, spearheaded by New York University professor Jay Rosen and former *Wichita Eagle* editor Davis "Buzz" Merritt, Jr., has caught on at many news organizations, despite the objections of journalists who believe it runs counter to traditional journalistic notions of detachment and objectivity (Rosen

1996; Merritt 1995). In fact, this movement has been embraced with almost religious fervor – particularly in journalism academic circles – by those who see it as one of the few bright hopes for a media world otherwise sinking beneath commercial imperatives. (Some critics, though, also have noted that the civic journalism movement, with its credo of involving citizens to help set the news agenda, has certain similarities to the marketing movement, with its emphasis upon focus groups and reader-relevant news and in fact has been subsumed by the marketing forces at certain news organizations).

THE DEBATE OVER THE SHIFTING PUBLIC SPHERE

Interestingly, the changing nature of modern media and its influence upon public life has shifted the discussion within academic circles from debates about the traditional journalistic role as "gate-keepers" and "agenda-setters" within powerful media organizations with the capacity to control public debate to a broader examination of a global media system that is growing more diffused and more centralized at the same time. Academic critics often view the growth of global media conglomerates and the increasing commercialization of media programming with deep concern. And they have kept alive their nostalgia for the political life of the ancient Greek city-states by looking for mechanisms – particularly in their enthusiasm for the interactivity of new media or the practice of civic journalism – that will allow for direct, individual-to-individual, voter-to-voter forums for high-minded discussion of public issues. Postmodern and leftist academic scholars of communications and political science have been particularly attracted to the theories of media sociologist Jürgen Habermas, who argues that feudal and courtly life in Europe was increasingly undermined by an emerging "public sphere" that has come to shape the economic and personal relations in modern civil society.[4] In his writings, Habermas holds out the seventeenth- and eighteenth-century salons and coffee houses in England and France as the model of a milieu where educated elites gathered to discuss public affairs and where the early periodical press exercised widescale influence. This expression of a public sphere quickly died out, Habermas says, as the periodical press became larger and more commercialized and absorbed rational-critical debate in a manufactured world of image creation and opinion management (Habermas 1989). The fascination of academics for Habermas's notion of the public sphere can seem a bit baffling until one recognizes how much what

Habermas is talking about resembles the gathering of intellectuals within academia who still long for a time when civil discourse was high-minded, elitist, privileged, and bourgeois in nature.

Leftists and postmodernists take from Habermas their justification for trying to withdraw from the "hegemonous" influence of news framed by capitalist media institutions and look to alternative sources – whether it is Web sites, zines, leftist opinion magazines, the few remaining alternative publications, or academic journals – for the communication of their interpretation of events free from the influence of the economic status quo. The right's solution to a media structure that it, in turn, believes is culturally liberal in orientation is to organize boycotts (such as the boycott of the Disney Company because of its policy of benefits for gays), threaten stockholder takeovers (as Senator Jesse Helms did with CBS), establish pressure group organizations (such as Reed Irvine's media criticism organizations), and establish its own alternative news sources (such as conservative talk radio and Rupert Murdoch's creation of the FOX network's avowedly conservative news). Both the critics of the left and the right decry, for very different reasons, the marketing and entertainment orientation of the mainstream commercial mass media. But as global media conglomerates grow and the news from an increasingly diffused media seems ever more commercialized and anarchic, few on the political spectrum look to reform of the internal workings of the media – or the reassertion of traditional moral and ethical professional standards – to help the news media out of its malaise, or to rescue a public whose political discourse has been transformed by the commercial imperatives of the media marketplace.

CONCLUSION

Many mainstream journalism professionals dedicated to the cause of serious public service journalism feel a sense of despair at the prospects they face. Everywhere they look they see their professional standards eroded: by the sense that they are working in a dying industry; by the fear that the public may not be interested in complex public issues or in-depth coverage of public affairs; by the emergence of the Internet and talk radio as places where gossip, opinion, and dubious information have replaced news gathered the traditional way; by the notion that young people take movies, video, and entertainment programming more seriously than they do real news; by the media's turning to tabloid techniques to appeal to a cynical and uninvolved public; by the synergistic expansion of the global media conglomerates; and by the relentless dedication to marketing and the bottom line that they see from their employers. For too many news professionals, the cause of treating their audience as citizens rather than consumers seems to be a lost cause.

But this kind of defeatist thinking lacks historical perspective. Ever since Marshall McLuhan argued that the medium is the message, modern individuals have come to believe that the changing nature of the media inexorably changes society and the way we are as individuals. There can be no doubt that the mediated environment of modern life has a transformative effect on the psyches of all of us who are bombarded with media messages. But the cause of journalism and the values that professional journalists hold as sacred – the search for truth, the commitment to the public good, the importance of community and the sanctity of the individual lives within it – still work as an island of principle, and a powerful one at that, amid the currents of chaos and change in the commercial media marketplace. Those who would give up on the attempts to reform the commercial mass media – or at least to hold the line to preserve journalistic autonomy and integrity within the modern newsroom – risk abandoning the territory to the marketers, the synergizers, the bean counters, and the forces of the global media conglomerates. Mainstream commercial media organizations still provide much of the information – or, at least, the credible information – upon which society's communications pyramid is erected. We might wish that the trends that seem to be engulfing the cause of good journalism in the morass of entertainment, marketing, and excess profit-making would go away – but they aren't likely to do so. And no amount of talk-show chatter, civic journalism forums, or new media access to government data will be able to compensate for the public service work of serious journalistic organizations or to substitute for intelligent analysis of public affairs by dedicated media professionals.

Since the days of Horace Greeley, Joseph Pulitzer, and E.W. Scripps, American journalists have been able to carry on the tradition of enterprising, truth-seeking, reform-oriented, watchdog journalism despite the commercial demands of their mainstream media employers. That doesn't mean the tension hasn't often been high and the good fight difficult to sustain. As Neal Shine, the former publisher of the *Detroit Free Press*, puts it, journalists' fear of the "cataclysmic trend" of bottom-line journalism ignores the fact that "there has never been a newspaper publisher who, from the moment he or she first decided to put ink to paper, did not understand that a prudent business course should probably involve making a profit." (Manzella 1998, p. 52) But most journalists also recognize the dangers, as Douglas Birkhead does, of forgetting to distinguish their professional ethic from the business needs of their employers (Birkhead 1986). Journalists need support in their efforts to resist the trendy solutions of market-oriented news managers who are pressing them to quantify production, package the news as a product, and incorporate the business interests of their bosses into all that they do. In the same way, we should look for encouragement from those media organizations that seem to be having doubts about the effectiveness of pursuing purely marketplace strategies and that see their future in the production of meaningful, contextual, in-depth journalism for an informed public.

In defending these traditions, the public, too, will benefit from the fundamental principles of enterprise journalism that have animated the profession since James Gordon Bennett made the police, the courthouse, and the Congress the core of his coverage and put the public service mission at the heart of the journalistic enterprise. After all, some members of the public may believe that they can do it all themselves – by using their computers to sort through masses of often incomplete and self-serving data on the Internet, by trying to interpret government proceedings directly on cable television, by hoping to make sense of attack ads and direct mail campaigns, and by attending civic journalism public forums. But these methods – as much as they may be romanticized as the Information Age's way to return to the ideal of Greek democracy – have their limitations. Even with so much direct citizen access to electronic data, the judgment of professional journalists dedicated to coverage of public life and unencumbered by the restraints of marketplace journalism still offer a profound counterweight to the forces that threaten to undermine the bedrock traditions of a profession that has for so long played a vital role in the sustenance of American democracy.

I have argued here that, for the most part, modern media organizations have tipped the balance toward treating their audience as consumers rather than citizens. But is it possible that the divide between citizens and consumers is an artificial one? Quality journalism produced by good journalists – serious and informative, but also compelling and interesting – can always serve as a bridge. We also must accept the fact that the effort to gauge public opinion is as much a matter of art as of science. In a time when many elements of the population seem turned off to politics and public life, it may not be remarkable to find market-minded news executives believing that less focus upon public affairs is what the public wants. But the interplay between what the public wants and what news executives believe the public wants is complex and often open to miscalculation. Journalism grew out of the soil of public affairs and always has been intertwined with public life. Those news executives who happily take the news down some new path may wake up to find that, in the long run, their franchise isn't worth much.

NOTES

1. These observations are based upon conversations with employees and interviews I have done with reporters covering aspects of the *Star Tribune*'s adoption of various market-oriented strategies for an article in the *Columbia Journalism Review* (Underwood 1998b).
2. Telephone interviews with the author, November 1997.
3. While the network audience has been dropping steadily since the advent of cable television, in recent years there is some indication that the audience numbers for the networks have been stabilizing (particularly if one considers the growth provided by the new networks like Fox and Warner).
4. See a particularly good discussion of Habermas in John B. Thompson (1995). Also note references to Habermas in the papers of Sparks (1998), Dahlgren (1998), Gandy, Jr. (1998), and Gamson (1998), and in their chapters in this book.

REFERENCES

Birkhead, Douglas (1986). "News Media Ethics and the Management of Professionals." *Journal of Mass Media Ethics*, 1(Spring/Summer):37–46.

Bogart, Leo (1989). *Press and Public: Who Reads What, When, Where, and Why in American Newspapers*. Hillsdale, NJ: Erlbaum.

Delli Carpini, Michael X., and Bruce A. Williams (1998). "Let Us Entertain You: The Politics of Popular Media." Paper presented to Mediated Politics conference, Annenberg Public Policy Center, Washington, DC.

Demers, David Pearce (1996). *The Menace of the Corporate Newspaper: Fact or Fiction?* Ames: Iowa State University Press.

Dahlgren, Peter (1998). "The Net and the Public Sphere: Media Logic, Civic Culture and Democracy." Paper presented to Mediated Politics conference, Annenberg Public Policy Center, Washington, DC.

Gamson, William A. (1998). "Promoting Political Engagement." Paper presented to Mediated Politics conference, Annenberg Public Policy Center, Washington, DC.

Gandy, Jr., Oscar H. (1998). "Dividing Practices: Segmentation, Targeting, and the Shaping of Political Identity." Paper presented to Mediated Politics conference, Annenberg Public Policy Center, Washington, DC.

Gladney, George Albert (1992). "The McPaper Revolution?: *USA Today*-style Innovation at Large U.S. Dailies." *Newspaper Research Journal,* 13(Winter/Spring):54–71.

Grossman, Lawrence K. (1998). "The Death of Radio Reporting: Will TV Be Next?" *Columbia Journalism Review,* 37(September/October):61–62.

———— (1995). *The Electronic Republic: Reshaping American Democracy in the Information Age.* New York: Viking.

Habermas, Jurgen (1989). *The Structural Transformation of the Public Sphere: An Inquiry into a Category of Bourgeois Society.* Cambridge: Polity Press.

Hertsgaard, Mark (1988). *On Bended Knee: The Press and the Reagan Presidency.* New York: Farrar Straus Giroux.

Katz, Jon (1992). "Rock, Rap and Movies Bring You the News." *Rolling Stone* (March 5):33, 36–37, 40, 78.

Kimball, Penn (1994). *Downsizing the News: Network Cutbacks in the Nation's Capital.* Washington, DC: The Woodrow Wilson Center Press.

Kurtz, Howard (1993). *Media Circus: The Trouble with America's Newspapers.* New York: Times Books.

Layton, Charles, and Mary Walton (1998). "Missing the Story at the Statehouse". *American Journalism Review,* 20(July/August):42–57.

McManus, John H (1994). *Market-Driven Journalism: Let the Citizen Beware?* Thousand Oaks, CA: Sage.

Manzella, Joseph (1998). *Elite Newspeople: Ideology and Revitalization in Print Journalism.* Unpublished manuscript.

Merritt, Davis "Buzz" (1995). *Public Journalism and Public Life: Why Telling the News Is Not Enough.* Hillsdale, NJ: Erlbaum.

Newport, Frank, and Lydia Saad (1998). "A Matter of Trust." *American Journalism Review,* 20(July/August):30–33.

Rosen, Jay (1996). *Getting the Connections Right: Public Journalism and the Troubles in the Press.* New York: Twentieth Century Fund Press.

Schoenbach, Klaus, and Lori Bergen (1998). "Readership Research: Challenges and Chances." *Newspaper Research Journal,* 19(Spring):88–102.

Shumate, Richard. (1992). "Life after Kovach." *Washington Journalism Review,* 14(September):28–32.

Sparks, Colin (1998). "Beyond National Politics: The Emergence of a Global Public Sphere?" Paper presented to Mediated Politics conference, Annenberg Public Policy Center, Washington, DC.

Squires, James D. (1993). *Read All About It: The Corporate Takeover of America's Newspapers.* New York: Times Books.

Stepp, Carl Sessions (1992). "Of the People, By the People, Bore the People." *Washington Journalism Review,* 14(March):24–26.

———— (1991). "When Readers Design the News." *Washington Journalism Review,* 13(April):20–24.

Thompson, John B. (1995). *The Media and Modernity: A Social Theory of the Media.* Stanford, CA: Stanford University Press.

Tucher, Andie (1997). "You News." *Columbia Journalism Review,* 36(May/June):26–31.

Underwood, Doug (1998a). "Market Research and the Audience for Political News," in Doris Graber, Denis McQuail, Pippa Norris (Eds.), *The Politics of News: The News of Politics.* Washington, DC: Congressional Quarterly Press, pp. 171–192.

(1998b). "It's Not Just in L.A." *Columbia Journalism Review,* 36(January/February):24–26.

(1993). *When MBAs Rule the Newsroom: How the Marketers and Managers Are Reshaping Today's Media.* New York: Columbia University Press.

CHAPTER 6

Political Discourse and the Politics of Need: Discourses on the Good Life in Cyberspace

Don Slater

INTRODUCTION

Where in the modern world do we locate politics and political communication? What counts as political discourse? It is obviously too restrictive to identify "the political" with an explicitly political sphere and with people acting as explicitly political agents. Indeed, this would paradoxically mean evading some of the central political issues of modernity: A concern that politics, or "real politics," is disappearing from public life, migrating to and invading other social spaces, colonizing and interfering in them. As several papers in this project show, the study of political communications seems haunted by the suspicion that the explicitly political has been emptied of meaning and reduced to mere appearances: *Real* politics happens – is sought or inflicted – elsewhere.

We must therefore start from a broader sense of the political and look at the manner in which public discourses on social ends and social means are distributed across different social spheres, and indeed at ways in which an explicitly political realm is displaced by or relates to other realms. In particular, this chapter starts from an extraordinarily long-term theme within modernity, the idea that consumerist discourses continually displace or replace real politics, or that consumerism represents for many a valued freedom *from* politics, a retreat from the political as a compromised sphere. This argument is presented from many different positions but always rounds on the same point: that modern subjects experience "discourses through and about objects" (Leiss et al. 1986) as a more satisfying or convincing mode of articulating the good life than they do the public sphere of action and speech. The political sphere, it is frequently argued, has given ground to the private sphere as the place in which questions of purpose and meaning are pursued, and this private sphere is in turn dominated by an essentially consumerist self-understanding: We come to relate self to society through notions of private choice among needs-satisfying commodities. It is as consumers rather than citizens that we understand ourselves politically and are politically addressed and constituted in any meaningful sense.

This concern with the migration of the (real) political comes powerfully to the fore in relation to the new electronic arenas of communications. This is so because although participants and commentators from very diverse positions see in the Internet new forms and forums of political engagement, a new public sphere, there is nonetheless a strong suspicion that its "politics" are dominated more by consumerist and free market models of choice than by democratic procedures of discussion and deliberation. This concern is intensified by the context of its emergence: The seeming triumph of a neoliberalism that regards free market behavior and institutions as models for all social domains and of a postmodernism that argues that "the social" is already dead, replaced by the desires of fragmented but choosing subjects.

POLITICS OF NEEDS

Part of the problem of understanding the relation between consumerism and democratic politics is that most modern thought assumes that needs and consumption should properly be defined *outside* the political domain; politics, like the marketplace, is supposedly limited to competing attempts to gain satisfaction of needs or interests that were in fact defined elsewhere (in nature, in culture, and in unexplained "subjective preferences"). Needs are a kind of independent variable. In contrast to this approach, let us begin by defining the political in such a way that the connection between needs and public discourse will appear intrinsic and normative rather than as an aberration or problem: Discussions of needs and consumption are intrinsically political, and intrinsic to politics, because they advance claims to live a particular form of life (they involve claims about how life ought to be lived) and they advance claims on social resources. As argued previously in a Habermasian vein (Slater 1997a; Slater 1997b) drawing on the work of Soper (1981, 1990; also Doyal and Gough 1991), to say, "I need something" is not to make a private or individual statement: First, it is to say that I need *x in order to* accomplish some end that I deem worthy and desirable. Need statements are therefore bound up with questions of social purpose and interest, and specifically make sense in terms of forms of life that one wants to achieve or reproduce. By the same token, they are not merely individual statements of preference but statements about social and cultural priorities, about the nature of the good life. They are ultimately legitimated by reference to socially shared values (such as health, autonomy, "civilization," etc). Second, by extension, statements of needs are also claims to social resources, implicitly arguing that a good society *should* provide symbolic or material resources to meet these needs and thus to accomplish desired end states. To debate needs publicly therefore means to engage in public debate on both the nature of the good life and the way in which social resources are allocated between competing visions, or between members seeking access to that good life. It is through claims about needs that we can publicly debate the ends rather than merely the means of social life.

"Needs," in this argument, do not refer to something that is fixed in human nature or biology, which therefore lies beyond political dispute. On the contrary, it is in attempting to define or dispute needs that we are most thoroughly political because we are drawn into the game of articulating and offering good grounds for our vision of the good life. Neither can needs be reduced to subjective, inexplicable, arbitrary desires or wants of individuals, thus placing them outside the domain of politics on the grounds that they are not subject to rational public discussion. The crucial step in this argument, and the crucial tension, is to recognize that although people are never simply hungry but are always hungry for foods that make sense within a culturally defined form of life, this cultural hunger is not a mere individual whim and not a private matter: it is through such senses of need that we experience and attempt to reproduce valued collective lives.

As Soper (1981, p. 2) put it, the question of human needs is really the question of value in human affairs, "a question concerned with the worth of human productions and their consequences and with the grounds upon which value is accorded to them." Theoretical and practical attempts to *solve* the question of needs once and for all, rather than to formulate it as an ever-open issue, are profoundly antipolitical. We need

> to confront the fact that questions of politics are not to be solved by appeal to "human needs," but are, on the contrary, only posed as political questions properly speaking when they are posed in the form of a question about human needs. (1981, p. 2)

Conversely, anything that places needs outside politics, or removes needs from political debate, would appear deeply problematic to both politics but also to discourses on needs: It would make politics empty or technocratic (concerned merely with meeting needs that are never themselves opened up to processes of collective will formation and are treated as beyond rational discussion), or it would make consumption purely individual and private, that is, "consumerist." The argument is that this is exactly what happens. One can identify three very broad positions on the politics of need: First, a range of critical theories start from the idea that modern political economy is dominated by a formal rationality that increases the productive ability to meet needs but at the cost of subjecting those needs to a capitalist or industrial order. That order can only be critiqued by asserting a substantive rationality – "real needs" or else a nonalienated logic of human development – by which we might judge the ends sought – and not merely the means employed – by modern social orders. Real politics is identified with substantive needs, but at the cost of treating needs as something defined outside of and in opposition to actual politics. Critical theories of all sorts were largely defined in distinction to forms of liberal and utilitarian constructions of need, which constitute the second position: here, needs are rendered indistinguishable from wants, preferences, or desires. From the liberal perspective, they are – and normatively *should* be – outside politics in the sense that they are private to the individual and cannot be rationally debated: literally, *de gustibus non est disputandem.* The public sphere, in this view, is properly a domain of purely formal rationality, allowing the rational pursuit of already privately defined ends. To treat issues of needs as public political matters would be an assault on both political freedom and market efficiency. Thirdly, and finally, poststructuralist (and loosely allied postmodernist) positions produce a compelling critique of critical theory on the grounds that it essentializes needs, thereby depoliticizing them; and a compelling critique of liberalism on the grounds that it assumes a coherent and rational ego – a choosing subject – that is capable of knowing its own needs, calculating them rationally and pursuing them without contradiction or ambivalence. This critique contains two further planks: a critique of identity and of political identities as the representation of preexistent interests (e.g., Butler 1990; 1993); and the critique of freedom as a strategy of governmentality (Burchell et al. 1991; Rose 1999). And yet it is at least arguable that this critique, while politicizing the views of those it opposes, and while powerfully connecting politics to desire, nonetheless formulates politics in ways that make it very difficult to distinguish from simple consumerism: It moves away from any connection between needs and rational political debate. Needs may no longer be matters of mere individual preference, but they are no more than matters of local and incommensurable language games that cannot be subjected to communicatively rational discourse.

Let us now explore these positions in a bit more detail in order to see how this opposition between needs and politics informs thinking about both consumerism and political communication.

CLASSICAL AND CRITICAL THEORY

The separation of a private domain of needs from a public domain of politics was constitutive of classical thought, entered into modern thought in the eighteenth century by way of neo-classicism and the revival of Stoicism that so influenced even the most stalwart of liberals such as Hume and Smith, and persists into the classical tradition of social theory through such various thinkers as Tocqueville and Marx. The argument, most powerfully articulated by Hannah Arendt (1958), is that in the classical world needs and the labor by which they are met were confined to a private realm of the *oikos*, the household economy, which is also the domain of the unfree (slaves, women, and children) and the insignificant. One rises into the glory of the political to the extent that one is able to insulate a sphere of action from the ephemeral grind, from the eternal cycle of bodily reproduction, and from its extended form – trade – which promotes enslavement to the pursuit of material gain. The move from labor to action is not only a move from the private to the public, but also from the ephemeral to the eternal, from the confines of an individual life to generalizable interests as motives for great deeds, for actions that endure. Arendt crucially connects the political to forms of communication that have no place in the private domain, are inconceivable there, most notably the arts of narration, the immortalizing of the deed in story. Narration commemorates or honors the citizen's transcendence of the constraining temporalities and obligations of need, a transcendence that constitutes the political as such.

The fact that this use of the concept of need to separate the private from the public rested on the subjugation of most of the population to unfree private labor and on removing them from speech and narration – from history – has not made it any less powerful as a motif in critical theory. To the contrary, the classical perspective provides abiding utopian images that link the political to a postscarcity world in which collective human development is decoupled from the mere meeting of basic needs of survival and daily reproduction, in which (some) humans move from nature to culture by moving beyond the exigencies of bodily reproduction. Marx's narration of a move beyond the realm of necessity into a realm of freedom conjures up a technical production of hyperabundance that would allow the development of individuals who are "rich in needs," but needs of a grand rather than mundane sort, the needs of one who can conceive of being a philosopher in the morning and a fisherman in the afternoon. Marx is only one example of a crucial theme in political counterdiscourse that imagines that the efficient – and indeed depoliticized – management or administration of productive forces should allow the political as such to whither away into a deeper collectivity of materially unconstrained human development. Much of the bitter irony of critical theory (in Arendt most powerfully) stems from a sense that politics has indeed been reduced to the efficient administration of things (including reified persons) but in the interests of the productive system as an end in itself, as an apotheosis of need, rather than as a means to that deeper human development. Arendt's final dictum on modernity is that we have all become consumers by virtue of being entirely circumscribed by labor and need.

Hence the separation of the private from the public along the fault line of necessity comes to appear as a utopian moment by which to critique the actual invasion of the public by private interests: Capitalism imposes necessity on the population and requires the rule of labor as part of the law of surplus value. It is within this kind of argument – and we have simply followed one, Marxist variant of it; the conservative, Leavisite version has a similar structure – that the consumerist communications media of advertising, marketing, and design come to appear as politically central, as somehow representing the *real* false politics of modernity. We can pursue this in terms of three major themes from critical theory:

First, there is the civic republican argument that the public sphere and civic virtue are being undermined and ultimately replaced by an exclusive concern with private interests: social place is identified not with citizenship but consumerism. Advertising is profoundly political in its fundamental message that value, meaning, personal empowerment, and social place are to be identified with private satisfactions within a steadily rising consumption norm. It is not the public but the private sphere that is defined as the domain of freedom; there is a freedom from politics, rather than a freedom from need, which is at the consumerist source of modern social membership.

Second, critical theory characterizes capitalist modernity in terms of a split between production and consumption whereby the relation between needs and resources is mediated and mystified by the market. Neither the qualitative content nor the distribution of production is transparently connected to processes of collective will formation, to determination by a politics of need. To the contrary, critical theory tends to see a reversed process in which individual needs are determined by the functional requirements of capitalist profit. Advertising exemplifies a technology of needs, a commercial power to organize needs, as well as an ideological structure that displaces politics by obscuring social structure, rendering invisible real social needs, interests, and contradictions. In particular, it obscures real interests as defined by critical theory (those determined by relations of production) as much as it mystifies real need. In commodity fetishism arguments, advertising places us in a postpolitical or postideological world in which there are no classes and no inequalities that cannot be overcome through fantasy aspirations or immanent social mobility and there is no scarcity or crisis.

Third, critical theory, drawing on Weber and Simmel as well as Marx, argues for the increasingly technocratic character of modern governance. Questions of value, the good, and the substantive ends of governance are increasingly removed from the public sphere, from rationality and collective decision making, and are made increasingly a matter of private, irrational, individual, or household choice. Politics in twentieth-century liberal democracy has been largely about the formal efficiency and increasing the quantitative scale by which it "delivers the goods" (the nature of those goods being determined by private and individual agendas). Indeed, even the needs of the public are not ends in themselves but are necessary means to achieving stable economic growth. Advertising, critical theory argues, is essential in establishing the overall framework and in instituting a system of unending and ever-renewed desires that ensure future sales of capitalism's ever-increasing output.

RECONSTITUTING POLITICS

The themes foregrounded by traditional critical theory have come under at least two kinds of devastating and (probably) decisive attack. First, a withering critical assault has been made on their reliance on knowledge of "real needs" and their claim to be able to distinguish these from the false or artificial needs that emerge from consumer capitalism. This assault is as much based on populist politics as on philosophical antifoundationalism: The idea of identity as active self-constitution has completely replaced models of determination; the critic's claim to know the real needs of others and to use this knowledge to judge both social provision and the social member's experienced wants and desires is treated as a move of oppression rather than critique (Poster 1995). Second, a focus on structural transformations – post–Fordism, post-modernity, neoliberalism – that render critical theory empirically out of touch: The spectacles of contemporary commodity culture do not so much hide political interests as reconstitute them according to new logics. As a result of the cultural revolutions of the 1980s (neoliberalism, enterprise culture, marketization), advertising and consumer culture have become the paradigms for politics, the preeminent place for discourses on needs, choice, and both individual and social purposes. In contrast to earlier critical theory, the current concern is less with the displacement of politics by consumer culture and rather more with the way in which consumer culture seems to provide a model for all social action, including the political.

In the post-1980s political environment, critical theory seems to face a hyperconsumerism that is more readily grasped by liberal or post-structuralist thought. Neoliberalism sought to reconstruct all politics on the basis of consumer choice, reducing both collective interests and a politics of need to the level of subjective and individual wants. This cannot be understood by referring to notions of "real needs" as a means of critiquing "misrepresented" ones. Both liberalism and poststructuralism, on the other hand, seem able to attend to the sense in which modern social subjects relate to themselves and the world through their relation to their own needs, through a relationship of reflexivity and choice (Giddens 1991; Bauman 1993; Beck 1992). In the following paragraphs, I contrast critical theory's concerns about advertising with the kinds of issues that contemporary theory raises.

First, if critical theory attacked a world in which life retreated into the private domain, we now see the extrapolation of the model of the private choosing individual to the entire social domain through marketization, either by privatizing public institutions or reconstituting them on a commercial, consumer-oriented basis. In terms of communications, what is striking is both the mode and the channels of address. Corporate communications and overarching modes of addressing all publics as consumer constituencies (PR, customer relations, personnel management) have overtaken and subsumed advertising.

Second, whereas critical theory bemoaned the mystification and invisibility of social structure, contemporary theory declares the death of the social, including the death of representable political constituencies based in structurally organized identities. This is a process of both disaggregation and culturalization of the very notion of identity, sometimes summarized in the notion of neotribalism (Bauman 1988; Maffesoli 1989). Identity is produced out of cultural materials of representation, appearance, and self-definition. These symbolic materials are seen as almost exclusively bound up with (or supplied by) commercial capitalism and consumer culture, which again becomes the basis of what would otherwise be political discourse; conversely, politics is reconstituted as a sphere that does not so much represent constituencies as endorse and reflect ever-shifting cultural identities.

Third, whereas critical theory was concerned with a split between a formally rational, technocratic public sphere and a private sphere of substantive but false needs, contemporary theory emphasizes an increasingly technocratic relation to the self within the private sphere, summarized in notions like enterprise culture and self-management (Keat and Abercrombie 1991; Keat et al. 1994; Rose 1992). Self-identity is a production for which one is responsible and that requires values of self-reflexivity, constant monitoring, knowledge, and expertise (Giddens 1991), the end result being not so much achievement of substantive goals as the fulfilment of formal ends of social place, identity, and membership on any acceptable basis. The need for identity seems to displace all other needs.

We therefore seem to be facing the complete subsumption of all relevant political questions under consumerist notions of choice and desire. It is in this new intellectual, social, and communicative context that we need to think through the position of new communications media as political spaces.

A CASE STUDY: INTERNET AND PORNOGRAPHY

I want to pursue some of these themes by way of a case study concerning the Internet. The reason that "cyberspace" is so interesting for these kinds of debates is that it seems to operate from a position beyond the split between needs and politics. That at least apparently underlies the claims emerging from a range of poststructuralist, postmodern, cyberfeminist, and cyberutopian discourses, which argue that virtuality allows for the deconstruction of fixed identities, including fixed political identities, alliances, and formations. Cyberspace has become the prime locus of both hopes and fears concerning transformations in the nature of identity, sociality, and public communications. More specifically it has become a kind of test case for poststructuralist claims to challenge both critical theory and liberal versions of the relation between needs and politics, about the proper location and shape of the political. Actual or potential relations in cyberspace would appear to cut against both the fixed needs of traditional critical theory and the fixed and coherent choosing subject of liberal theory: in a condition of virtuality, the argument goes, all forms of identity are self-evidently discursive performances; politics cannot take the form of "representing" preexisting interests or needs and identities (for discussions see, for example, Bassett 1997; de Landa 1991; Dery 1994; Featherstone and Burrows 1995; Haraway 1991; Kroker and Weinstein 1994; Plant 1997; Porter 1997; Poster 1995; Springer 1996; Stone 1996; Turkle 1995).

Cyberspace appears as the natural site of a "third way": participants act neither as coherent egos making rational choices nor as objects of manipulation or subjects of false needs but rather as hybrids or cyborgs, as discursive subjects who are self-evidently and self-consciously treating their needs and identities as constructs and performances. The claim that both interpersonal relations and a more general public sphere may take this form on-line usually rests on a notion of virtuality and disembodiment: Bodies no longer act as anchors for identities; rather the body is left behind as identities are enacted in dematerialized spaces that the new technology makes available.

In particular, these claims raise two questions: whether this is indeed how cyberspace is experienced and used by participants; and, to the extent that these claims are true, how are discourses on needs related to the political? To what extent are on-line political assumptions bound up with consumerist understandings of needs and identities; in what respects are needs and "questions of value in human affairs" opened up to political discourse? Can we (or participants) distinguish the performative view of cyberspace from garden-variety consumerism? The material on which this exploration centers arises from about eighteen months of ethnographic engagement with amateur (noncommercial and nonprofessional) collectors and traders of pornography (or "sexpics" in the local vocabulary), mainly in the setting of Internet relay chat (IRC), but also in the context of the WWW and usenet (Slater 1998;

Rival, Slater, and Miller 1998; Slater forthcoming). Participants in the sexpics scene on IRC traded and collected sexually explicit digitized material (photographs, drawings, texts, video clips, sounds), as well as engaged in eroticized relationships ranging from flirtation to cybersex, as well as friendships and long-term relationships. Both the trading and the enacted sexuality took place within a stream of real-time chatting and within complex social orders that made otherwise private consumption activities public both to other participants and to ethnographic study.

Although this is probably odd material with which to look at either consumerism or political discourse, on-line pornography and sexuality are in fact highly consequential topics for assessing cyberspace as a political domain. First, this is a quantitatively enormous arena, involving tens of thousands of people and accounting for a disproportionate amount of Net activity. Second, it addresses the conceptual core of claims about the uniqueness of cyberspace because of the way the relation between bodies and sexual identities are implicated and challenged; we might therefore use it to test expectations about on-line sexual politics. Third, in terms of conventional politics, pornography and "netsex" have played a disproportionate role in defining the politics of cyberspace and the politics within it. This came to a head in the battle over the American Communications Decency Act (CDA), discussed in this chapter. The three-way battle among America's familial morality, its first amendment, and its business culture have dominated both the virtual and the real globe. It is more than likely that different relations to needs, identities, and politics are evidenced in other Internet sites, including others oriented to sexuality, but that does not detract from the quantitative, conceptual, or political consequentiality of this one.

Above all, on-line pornography is not so odd a case as a vehicle for exploring the issues presented in the first part of this chapter, precisely because what one can observe is the way in which needs – the needs of sexuality, sociality, and free interaction that are all profoundly close to identities and ways of life – are articulated in a public space. Are forms of sexual identity formulated as private consumerist choices or as claims to publicly and rationally debatable notions of the "good life"? It is a particularly strong case insofar as sexuality is something that has more generally been placed ambiguously in relation to the personal and the political, being alternatively relegated to a matter of private individual desire and reclaimed as a matter of public political concern and intervention.

The argument explored in my other articles based on this research tends toward the conclusion that participants in these settings and activities took a consumerist stance toward sexuality, pornography, the Internet, and, in some respects, each other. That is to say, in contrast to poststructuralist hopes and expectations, they tended to see themselves as coherent subjects, with knowledge of their own needs, on the basis of which they made choices between available exchangeable goods. Moreover, their explicitly political positions – most notably around the CDA – tended to be formulated in terms of consumerist freedoms to make unfettered choices between possible goods. The aim here is not to dismiss cyberspace in general, or even these particular participants in it, as merely consumerist and therefore as uninteresting or as merely another example of the debasement of political potentials into vapid consumerist indulgence. Rather, I am interested in the ways in which participants formulated and acted on their patch of cyberspace: The picture includes an inconsistent mixture of themes from critical theory, liberalism, and poststructuralism. However, I demonstrate that consumerism is still very much part of that admixture, defining political positions and subjects on-line.

While space precludes a detailed ethnographic presentation, I'll present findings under three themes: first, the relation between needs and identities; second, utopian images of needs and consumption; third, the relationships among concepts of need, consumption, and freedom as exemplified in political opposition to the CDA. The overall argument is that participants embrace a relationship to their own needs that is at once consumerist (treating needs as private and opposed to the political domain) and yet anticommercial as well as opposed to government and public interference. They embrace a utopian notion of consumption as their core politics, a notion in which needs can be indulged in total freedom, a freedom defined not only in opposition to political regulation but also in opposition to *payment*. In the consumer utopia of net libertarianism, everything is "free" in every sense.

FIXING NEEDS AND IDENTITIES

In some respects, the orientation of sexpics traders on IRC and amateur Web sites is almost too self-evidently consumerist. The images (and other representations) they traded were either scanned in directly from commercial pornography or – in the case of so-called amateur or personal pics – from photos putatively taken by and of nonprofessionals and slavishly followed the conventions of mainstream commercial pornography. Participants never altered or creatively engaged with image files (despite readily accessible techniques to do so) but treated them as reified and objectified commodities to be chosen, stored, and exchanged just like any other consumer good. In one extensive subculture within the subculture – people who collected master "scans" of Playboy-style images with the highest production values – the orientation to the digital files as objects was conventionally fetishistic: These image files were treated as auratic objects by their collectors, who aimed at complete and authoritative collections of scanned series.

These conventional consumerist themes extended to the kinds of sexualities enacted by participants. Despite using a language of experimentation in which participants claimed that they were free to enact or represent any sexuality they could dream up, they in fact stayed extremely close to the standard conventions of mainstream pornography. Above all, male heterosexist norms were absolute: male participants and the men depicted in the representations traded had to be heterosexual; female identities, performed or depicted, were assumed to be bisexual, as consuming and consumed by anyone. There are obviously other scenes that are oriented to a self-declared gay identity and others with less rigorous boundaries. However, the huge – and in many respects normative – scene studied here was significantly constituted around these absolute exclusions and inclusions. Moreover, in contrast to poststructuralist expectations regarding hybridity of identity and the heroic figure of the cyborg, pariah sexualities were dealt with by absolute exclusion: There was no sense that sexual identities were in any way constructed through these exclusions; rather a variety of identities – from the simply gay to the pedophilic or bestial – were constructed as absolute *other* and as taboo in ways not open to discursive understanding or discussion, and on the basis of normative dictates unproblematically imported off-line.

Within the standard conventions and sexual orientations, participants generally maintained a sense of distance between the identity of the choosing subject and its acts of choosing. Although participants took it as self-evident that when on-line people *performed* identities, their *real* identities were not generally felt to be challenged or changed by those performances. The model of the relation among self, needs, and society that participants usually articulate is one concerned with repression: There is a real self whose desires cannot be acted out IRL (in real life) but that can be safely enjoyed on-line. At most, there is a desire to transform mundane off-line life by injecting stimulation or entertainment from on-line sexual activities (either porn or fantasies), but in general they act on the basis that people enter the on-line sexpics scene – as they would any marketplace – with already given needs and identities that they would like to satisfy by selecting from a range of goods. The position accords best with critical theory or liberalism rather than poststructuralist versions: Identities are externally related to needs (people "have" needs, and know which needs they have) rather than being seen in terms of an internal relationship in which desires and identities are mutually constitutive. This grounds a politics closely bound up with consumer choice: It is always a question of sovereignty, of bending the object world to the satisfaction of given needs.

Finally, as reported more extensively in Slater (1998), notions of authenticity are more significant in on-line life than is acknowledged by most commentators. Participants consistently acted on the basis that the identities of those with whom they interacted were simply performances. However, this led them to make a distinction between real identities and merely realistic performances, and thus to retain authenticity as a criterion for judging what was going on. On the one hand, they generally treated all on-line identity claims with complete cynicism, on the basis that *nothing* said on-line should be accepted as true, however realistic the performance, and therefore should not be treated seriously. This did not conflict with satisfying a vast range of desires and wants so long as they were treated lightly and at a distance from the (real) self. On the other hand, participants would only allow on-line relationships to touch what they regarded as their real needs and identities insofar as they felt that they could authenticate the other and their identity claims, could regard the other not as a mere performance but as a real person with a fixed – hence ethically accountable and trustworthy – identity.

PORNOTOPIA AND CONSUMERIST UTOPIAS

In these respects, then, we can describe the sexual politics of the sexpics scene as modeled on the figure of the consumer, both in its conventionality and in the exclusions operated in order to separate the chooser from both the things chosen and those not chosen. Yet despite these exclusions and distinctions, the deeper politics of the sexpics scene – the politics that arose from the way in which their discourses on needs and satisfactions actually articulated visions of the good life and "questions of value in human affairs" – was characterized by the denial of all exclusions, boundaries, and limits and by an unceasing drive to dedif-ferentiation, to use the language of postmodernism. I want to charac-terize participants' utopian vision of the good life by the term *pornotopia*.

Pornotopia is a utopian fantasy constructed through the conjunction of (1) unrestricted sexual stimulation and expression with (2) unlim-ited consumption of inexhaustible and free gratifications that renders notions of scarcity and economic value redundant, in (3) a space that is itself beyond the limitations of time, space, and bodily boundaries. That is to say, pornotopia is more than a promise of sexual pleasures; it projects a vision of the good life as a consumer utopia in a virtual paradise. In this vision of the pleasure principle achieved, *the political* can only appear as a reality principle that threatens paradise with restrictions and imposes the notion of scarcity on its hyperabundance; at the same time, participants' sense of *real politics* therefore takes the form of defending paradise through a Net libertarianism that attacks not only all political authority but also all commercial power as, in prin-ciple, destructive of pornotopia.

First, in analyzing the sexpics trading scene, we are dealing with a pornotopia in a few clearcut respects: The supply of sexually explicit material is both inexhaustible and free. One could never come to the end of these images whose supply is constantly fed and renewed by the streams of industry, amateurs, usenet, and so on. The stream of sexual representation may also be renewed at any moment by another, less literal, process: Given the textual nature of IRC interactions, all events, conversations, and interactive others can be eroticized at any moment; as in the close connection between sexpics trading and cybersex, participants' performed identities constantly merge with the porno-graphy they trade; they themselves constantly enter the stream of representation.

The supply of material is not only postscarcity in the sense of being limitless but also in being free: there are no prices to remind one of scarcity or of barriers to access and gratification. In fact, we will qualify this point next: The IRC sexpics are rife with quasi-prices, while modes of regulating exchange are positive obsessions among participants. Nonetheless, this subsists alongside with the fantasy of pornotopia as in principle inexhaustible and free, postscarcity (Slater forthcoming).

Second, in this respect, pornography, sexpics trading, and IRC as such are experienced as similar and convergent fantasy spaces. Just as pornography provides a fantasy of inexhaustible desire and complete gratification, IRC is itself treated as a place of limitless desire and gratification because one experiences a loss of a sense of time, space, and embodiment. Time is felt to be inexhaustible (people will stay in IRC dream-time for hour after hour, decoupling it from real-life time scales to do with eating, going to the toilet, doing domestic or paid work; real-life time scales from around the world can be merged within the dream-time zone of IRC); space is dedifferentiated into the virtual IRC space in which presences that cannot meet in real life can easily interact; identity performances are detached from the limits of identifiable bodily attributes such as sex, race, age, and beauty. All of these provide a sense that absolutely anything may happen; that time, space, and (virtual) embodiment are governed directly by desire and individual or collective/interactive fantasy.

Third, both porn and IRC, and their conjuncture, are experienced by participants as places of pure consumption in which production, labor, and effort are either rendered invisible or else are themselves eroticized and collapsed into consumption. For example, when questioned about how the pictures were taken (particularly in relation to issues such as safe sex or exploitation within the porn industry), the typical responses treat production as moments of consumer choice. The models, it is argued, know what they are doing and choose to do it; they are talked about in a fantasy register in which the moment of taking the picture is treated as an erotic experience for both model and photographer; there is a huge valuation placed on "amateur" and "personal" pics, in which the picture is understood to be embedded in an erotic and *real* relationship that is untouched by commercial, contractual, or professional relationships. Similarly, IRC is understood as a space that is not to be commercialized or regulated by labor. It is constituted out of voluntary leisure, entertainment, and hobbyist connections, or connections of pure leisure-time sociability. (It is neither coincidental nor insignificant that many informants were actually in their workplaces.)

Finally, there is an ambivalent orientation toward this limitlessness, which I might characterize as perverse calculation or perverse quantification. By this I mean that participants can be ambivalent toward the limitlessness of cyberspace, sexuality, and consumption, feeling a need to map or organize it, but in ways that do not overtly limit it. For example, *perverse quantification* is evidenced in Web site or IRC listings and categorizations of pictures, or (particular female-denominated) participants' claims about the range of their sexual desires or experience: These will always be excessive and impossible, seeking through the process of listing to evoke the inexhaustibility of their world; by trying to enumerate you can demonstrate that pornotopia cannot be contained. This constant enumeration and mapping of geometries of sexual combination harks back very directly to the pornography of de Sade as characterized by Adorno and Horkheimer (1979), Carter (1979), and Lasch (1979) (see also Hunt 1993): a mixed metaphor that evokes both the boundless productivity of modern capitalist forces of production and at the same time the instrumental rationality – the game of mastery and limitation – that occasions it.

This brings us back to the notion of postscarcity and of freedom in the sense of the absence of payment and prices, and can alert us to certain conundrums in which the denizens of pornotopia feel trapped: The limitlessness of on-line sexuality, while utopian, is also problematic in various ways. Despite the utopian discourse of limitlessness, in practice participants demonstrate not only a concern but a positive obsession with regulating this immensity. The clearest and omnipresent example of this is the ubiquity of the quasi-prices and exchange ratios governing the trade of their virtual objects. As discussed in Slater (forthcoming), IRC sexpics participants are constantly concerned with *quid pro quos*, with reciprocity, with not getting ripped off, with ensuring that no one gets anything for nothing, even though everything they want is actually or ideally hyperabundant. They behave as if they are accumulating capital and engaging in contractual obligations. The (somewhat Durkheimian) argument that could account for this is that it is not in fact the case that sexpics participants regulate their exchanges of pictures because they want to ensure that they get equity in exchange; quite the contrary, they need to reify their virtual objects in the form of consumable and exchangeable commodities *so that* they may enforce regulations and hence constitute themselves as an ethical community. That is to say, in the local world view, people's articulated politics is one of total freedom (both lack of prices and lack of restraints), yet the politics they practice is absolutely the opposite: They constantly attempt to turn the digital files they exchange into consumer objects within price structures or other systems of valuation in order to generate a sense of ethical community between accountable individuals.

CENSORSHIP, COMMERCE, AND POLITICS

In many respects, then, the sexpics trading scene reflects the mainstream classical tradition. Needs are constituted as part of the private domain of the choosing individual; freedom means a freedom *from* politics – and true politics involves defending the individual from a debased or oppressive political realm. These people should be heroes to neoliberals, falsely conscious victims to critical theory, and the despair of poststructuralist hopes. We will now confirm these judgments in terms of the politically explicit issue of censorship: I want to argue that the main position from which "netizens" – particularly those involved in sexual material – opposed the CDA involved a libertarianism that was in crucial respects formed in relation to these images of a consumerist pornotopia.

In a famous formulation, netizens defined censorship as "noise," around which information reroutes itself to maintain its essential freedom. The essence of cyberspace inheres in this freedom, in its frontier-like quality of being both a place apart from the mainstream world – not legitimately subject to its interference – and at the same time internally undifferentiated, a matter of pure, untrammelled, and entirely voluntaristic flow from one social conjuncture to another. In point of fact, cybersexual morality is closely bound up with that of the mainstream world – it is in many respects conventional, as we have seen, and mainstream morality is often imposed through intensive self-censorship in order to preempt external interference. Nonetheless, the idea of censorship is anathema on-line. In cyberland, the normative way of dealing with undifferentiated flows is to ensure that they can be unproblematically construed as the results of knowledgeable individual choices. Hence the key defense against censorship was first to argue that no one could accidentally happen upon pornography and then to ensure this through various technical mechanisms (e.g., entry pages carrying explicit warnings as to what would be encountered if you clicked a button, "netnanny" services, paid password systems, etc), and second to argue that the appropriate model for cyberspace was the distributed voluntarism of the telephone system rather than the centralized gatekeeping characteristic of broadcast media. The CDA's explicit embrace of the latter model arose from a neoconservative paternalism, which raised the hackles of every brand of libertarian from way left to way right, from NRA and militia types for whom the right to bear porn was threatened by the same oppressive governmentality that threatened their guns (and in both cases, no doubt, their masculinity) to the most enlightened wings of "queer politics" activists who felt equally threatened by religious and feminist fundamentalists. It was distinctly a case of the strangest bedfellows all around, one whose deepest irony is probably only now emerging in the form of the Lewinsky debacle: The Internet distribution of the Starr Report would have been prevented by the porn-screening software that would have been legislatively imposed on the public by precisely the same Republicans who so strongly believed the public needed to know the very detailed truth of the President's sexual activities.

What is interesting is the relationship between the breadth of libertarian resistance to censorship and the CDA, on the one hand, and the utopia of boundless consumption that I have characterized as pornotopia, on the other. This is best understood through a theme I raised earlier: the connection between two notions of freedom that made up pornotopia as a utopian vision of the limitless. Netizens believed that cyberspace in general and sexpics on IRC in particular represented a free place apart from the mainstream world not only in that there was complete freedom of choice and gratification but also that all goods were "free" in an economic-commercial sense of being beyond both scarcity and price. Moreover, they saw these two forms of freedom as inseparable and mutual conditions: Lose one and you lose the other. This partly arises from a general Net libertarianism that sees itself as a free community based on equal and cooperative reciprocity, on communality rather than private self-interest (a self-image that does go against the grain of the constant stress on individual choice). Price is seen as an impurity that enters by way of commercial forces that offend against the caring, sharing, shareware spirit of the Net and its more anarchist or at least trusting economic principle of "what goes around comes around."

More specifically, political freedom and free goods were somehow inseparable premises in the sense that moves toward censorship seemed to Net libertarians inevitably to result in the imposition of prices, markets, and commercialization, while commercialization would result in the incursion of big business forces carrying out regulatory functions in conjunction, or at least cahoots, with big government. All of these forces represented a diremption, that is, a splitting up, of the fantastic dreamscape of pornotopia, the cutting of it up through barriers to the free flow of desire and gratification.

To be specific, on the one hand, moves towards both censorship and self-censorship seemed to coincide with a massive commercialization of on-line pornography. IRC managed to maintain itself as a relatively autonomous sphere, although subject to major incursions of blanket advertising by businesses (in the form of timed channel messages and of messages that appear to be from other participants but actually lure one to commercial Web sites). On the Web, the problem is that the gateways erected to ensure that all encounters with pornography were individually chosen ones were also capable of acting as commercial gateways or tollbooths. Business arose to sell passwords to protected sites; entry pages with lurid warnings could operate equally as the basis of extensive and increasingly elaborate teaser campaigns, complete with free samples. In order to be free from politics, one might well lose one's freedom from commerce. Moreover, in the legally unclear period under the shadow of the CDA, from 1996 to 1997, commercial operations were able and willing to take on the financial and legal risks that private citizens or consumers would and could not: In February 1996, all subscribers to the Blue Ribbon campaign against Net censorship blacked out their Web sites in protest and also in worry; most of them never came back.

In essence, then, the dominant tenor of on-line libertarianism, evidenced among sexpics traders as much as elsewhere, is a consumerism whose utopianism leads it to be nonetheless anticommercial, to combat the restrictions enacted by big business as much as by big government, and, particularly, to fear their conjunction in the process of censorship. The root of this is their conceptualization of a politics of need rooted in a fantasy of abundance that opposes both politics and economics as such. The good life is characterized by a consumption that absorbs all other social moments.

This characterization might help us make sense of Andrew Ross's (1998) vivid summing up of the state of play at the explicitly political level:

> But for those weaned on old media definitions of public communication, the geography of the Web is a strange landscape to host a new public sphere. After all, it was the Web that brought us the shopping malls and cyberstores, the advertisers, the financial real estate, indeed the entire world of commercial agents in hot pursuit of good addresses from which to promote and shop their wares. Once the barbarians were on the Web, there was no looking back. While distasteful to Net purists, the new commercial presence had little difficulty, initially at least, in fitting in with the open architectural milieu of Net culture. Nothing in the house religion of Net libertarianism seemed at odds with the laissez-faire ideals of the corporations. Except, of course, when it came to paying for the

stuff ("information wants to be free" is a Net mantra). A free market and freedom of speech are one thing; free products and shareware ethics are another. They are inevitably at odds. (Ross 1998)

Net libertarianism is perfectly compatible with a general *laissez-faire* perspective; but corporations are not *laissez faire* any more than liberal democratic governments believe in radical participatory democracy. Netizens share with business the language of choice and free exchange, but it has a different meaning for them and they live it out in a different – utopic – space. This space does indeed have deeper resonances and echoes within the political imaginary of the West, specifically in American political imaginary. Specifically, insofar as the dream of cyberspace as a place of limitless consumption is part and parcel of a political conception of a place of unlimited freedom, then "frontier" metaphors – images of the American frontier – have always been apt. Cyberspace always yearned to be established as a place apart, a place to be filled by the unbounded imagination and the political experiment, a stage set for the year zero of modern history. It is a utopia – contra Plato – dependent on a space in which authority structures and external regulation are considered to be neither legitimate nor practicable. Hence, Ross aptly compares Net libertarianism with the ethos of militias and survivalists: Certainly, it is a survivalism that moves beyond the liberal defense of a free market to map out entire worlds apart from both government and business, new frontiers where (cyber)pioneers may roam free and where the private individual as ultimate value is safely preserved. This meeting of all sides of the spectrum at the shrine of radical individualism, in which market models move into a utopian vision of complete liberty, is not new but actually a regular beat in the pulse of – particularly American – political vision, as argued by Brown (1997). For sexpics traders, the Net was meant to be a haven from all forms of modernizing bigness and a return to self-making and self-choosing, the small, the cooperative, and the homespun. The ethos is therefore anti-commercial in significant respects: Again, this is a long-running theme in the sense that big business can be seen as an equal or greater threat to *the consumer* (the little individual attempting to maintain freedom to maneuver in the sense of free choice) as the government. The ranchers and railwaymen, the robber barons and motor companies that American populism and progressivism confronted reappear on the electronic frontier in the form of Microsoft and Intel as well as the big porn businesses. They are understood to be far more effective regulators than government is and therefore a far more potent threat to Net freedoms.

CONCLUSION

Where do we locate politics, then? In cyberspace – or at least in the restricted basis for this case study – we seem to confront a classic face-off between private needs and public discourse, between consumerism and politics, between democracy as a utopia of private choice and a public sphere of communicative rationality. The new communicative space rather neatly, if extremely, replicates a classic structure of Western thought in which needs oppose the political space rather than constituting the grounds on which the fundamental political issues of value and the good life might not only be framed but made open to democratic discourse. This is most disappointing in relation to poststructuralist hopes that cyberspace might destabilize those notions of needs, bodies, and identities that so powerfully fix and essentialize people, reducing politics to the mere representation of interests that are assumed to unproblematically preexist it: Netizens still seem to require or at least seem unwilling to give up ways of framing needs, identities, and choice that are conventional in profound respects. We seem to be witnessing in this case another retreat from politics into a private and consumerist (in this case utopian) version of need.

REFERENCES

Adorno, T., and M. Horkheimer (1979). *Dialectic of Enlightenment.* London: Verso.
Arendt, H. (1958). *The Human Condition.* Chicago: University of Chicago Press.
Bassett, C. (1997). "Virtually Gendered: Life in an On-line World," in K. Gelder and S. Thornton (Eds.), *The Subcultures Reader.* London: Routledge, pp. 537–550.
Bauman, Z. (1988). *Freedom.* Milton Keynes: Open University Press.
 (1993). *Postmodern Ethics.* Oxford: Blackwell.
Beck, U. (1992). *Risk Society: Towards a New Modernity.* London: Sage.
Brown, S. L. (1997). "The Free Market as Salvation from Government: the Anarcho-capitalist View," in J. G. Carrier (Ed.), *Meanings of the Market: The Free Market in Western Culture.* Oxford: Berg, pp. 99–128.
Burchell, C., C. Gordon, and P. Miller (1991). *The Foucault Effect: Studies in Governmentality.* London: Harvester/Wheatsheaf.
Butler, J. (1990). *Gender Trouble: Feminism and the Subversion of Identity.* London: Routledge.
 (1993). *Bodies That Matter.* London: Routledge.

Carter, A. (1979). *The Sadeian Woman: An Exercise in Cultural History*. London: Virago.

de Landa, M. (1991). *War in the Age of Intelligent Machines*. New York: Zone Books.

Dery, M. (Ed.) (1994). *Flame Wars: The Discourse of Cyberculture*. London: Duke University Press.

Doyal, L., and I. Gough (1991). *A Theory of Human Needs*. London: Macmillan.

Featherstone, M., and R. Burrows (Eds.) (1995). *Cyberspace, Cyberbodies, Cyberpunk: Cultures of Technological Embodiment*. London: Routledge.

Giddens, A. (1991). *Modernity and Self-Identity: Self and Society in the Late Modern Age*. Cambridge: Polity.

Haraway, D. (1991). *Simians, Cyborgs and Women: The Reinvention of Nature*. London: Free Association Books.

Hunt, L. (Ed.) (1993). *The Invention of Pornography: Obscenity and the Origins of Modernity. 1500–1800*, New York: Zone Books.

Keat, R., and N. Abercrombie (Eds.) (1991). *Enterprise Culture*. London: Routledge.

Keat, R., N. Whiteley, and N. Abercrombie (1994). *The Authority of the Consumer*. London: Routledge.

Kroker, A., and M. Weinstein (1994). *Data Trash: The Theory of the Virtual Class*. Montreal: New World Perspectives.

Lasch, C. (1979). *The Culture of Narcissism*. London: Abacus.

Leiss, W., S. Kline, and S. Jhally (1986). *Social Communication in Advertising: Persons, Products & Images of Well-Being*. London: Methuen.

Maffesoli, M. (1996). *The Time of the Tribes*. London: Sage.

Plant, S. (1997). *Zeros and Ones: Digital Women and the New Technoculture*. London: Fourth Estate.

Porter, D. (Ed.) (1997). *Internet Culture*. London: Routledge.

Poster, M. (1995). *The Second Media Age*. Cambridge: Polity Press.

Rival, L., D. Slater, and D. Miller (1998). "Sex and Sociality: Comparative Ethnography of Sexual Objectification." *Theory, Culture and Society*, 15(3–4):295–322.

Rose, N. (1992). "Governing the Enterprising Self," in P. Heelas and P. Morris (Eds.), *The Values of the Enterprise Culture: The Moral Debate*. London: Routledge, pp. 141–164.

(1999). *Powers of Freedom: Reframing Political Thought*. Cambridge: Cambridge University Press.

Ross, A. (1998). *Real Love: In Pursuit of Cultural Justice*. New York: New York University Press.

Slater, D. R. (1997a). *Consumer Culture and Modernity*. Cambridge: Polity Press.

(1997b). "Consumer Culture and the Politics of Need," in M. Nava, et al. (Eds.) *Buy This Book: Contemporary Issues in Advertising and Consumption*. London: Routledge, pp. 51–63.

(1998). "Trading Sexpics on IRC: Embodiment and Authenticity on the Internet," *Body and Society* 4(4):91–117.

(Forthcoming). "Consumption without scarcity: exchange and normativity in an Internet setting," in D. Miller, et al. (Eds.) *Commercial Cultures*. London: Berg.

Soper, K. (1981). *On Human Needs: Open and Closed Theories in a Marxist Perspective*. Sussex: Harvester Press.

(1990). *Troubled Pleasures: Writings on Politics, Gender and Hedonism.* London: Verso.

Springer, C. (1996). *Electronic Eros: Bodies and Desire in the Postindustrial Age.* Austin, TX: University of Texas Press.

Stone, A. R. (1996). *The War of Desire and Technology at the Close of the Mechanical Age.* Cambridge, MA: MIT Press.

Turkle, S. (1995). *Life on the Screen: Identity in the Age of the Internet.* New York: Simon and Schuster.

CHAPTER 7

Dividing Practices: Segmentation and Targeting in the Emerging Public Sphere

Oscar H. Gandy, Jr.

INTRODUCTION

I argue in this chapter that the public sphere, including that which is emerging in cyberspace, is increasingly subject to the distorting influence of technologies developed to enhance commercial marketing: specifically segmentation and targeting.

While some will argue that politics has always been subject to a variety of techniques governed by the admonition to "divide and conquer," I will suggest that the computer and the telecommunications networks that enable them to share vast quantities of information represent a difference in breadth and depth that requires our attention, if not our concern.

While we are well served by the reminder that "garbage in" usually results in a substantial increment of "garbage out," it should also be recognized that the impact of flawed strategy is often just as harmful as one that is well-informed but intentionally misdirected. The analyses, constructions, and predictions that are derived from campaign management software, or consultants' reports, while almost certain to be in error, will still nevertheless have an impact on the quality of deliberation and the public policies that eventually emerge. They will also have an impact upon the relations between people who depend upon and help to nourish the public sphere.

THE DEMOCRATIC PUBLIC SPHERE

From Habermas we have the view that democratically constituted opinion- and will-formation depends on the supply of informal public opinions that, ideally, develop in structures of an unsubverted political public sphere (Habermas 1998, p. 308). Habermas underscores the importance of deliberation to the democratic process. As a means of arriving at the public will as a reflection of public opinion, deliberation can be understood to have an identifiable functional utility. However, there are assumptions about several requirements that are necessary if deliberation is to serve its democratic function well. Among the most important requirements is that deliberation be inclusive – no one should be excluded, and all should have an equal chance to enter into and take part in discussion and debate (Habermas 1998, p. 305). Segmentation and targeting is in direct conflict with these requirements in that the effect, if not the primary purpose, of segmentation and targeting is the *exclusion* of participants who are deemed unlikely to support the preferred view.

There are also distinctions to be explored that take account of the fact that people may have the same "rights," but the circumstances they face in attempting to exercise those rights means that the rights they enjoy are far from equivalent. Habermas recognizes that "the structures of the public sphere reflect unavoidable asymmetries in the availability of information, that is, unequal chances to have access to the generation, validation, shaping, and presentation of messages" (Habermas 1998, p. 325). He also notes that there are "accidental inequalities," such as those produced by individual differences in abilities related to communication and sense making. But neither the structural nor the accidental constraints are what should concern us at this point. Instead, we should be concerned about the purposeful, strategic interventions that produce the inequalities that generate distortions within the public sphere. (Similar concerns with strategic intervention are explored in Chap. 15, by Jamieson, and Chap. 13, by Bennett and Manheim.)

Habermas warns that responses to the increasing complexity within social systems invite particular forms of distortion in the public sphere and accelerate the degradation of the public opinion that they generate. Specifically, he suggests that the "actor roles that increasingly professionalize and multiply with organizational complexity and range of media are, of course, furnished with unequal opportunities for exerting influence" (Habermas 1998, pp. 363–364).

There are other aspects of democratic theory that are relevant to this class of concerns. They have to do with the ways in which pluralist theory has had to be modified to account for the different sorts of inequality that emerge and are reified by the political structure. With regard to interest group politics, Habermas suggests that because "the composition of interest groups is in fact highly selective, because members are largely inactive and have little influence on organizational policy, it was now assumed that power struggles are essentially conducted by elites" (Habermas 1998, p. 332). This is only partially correct. These days, power struggles are being conducted on *behalf* of elites by a growing cadre of professionals – the political consultants.

Consultants

It is important to recognize that the *technology* to which Ellul referred (Ellul 1964) was not limited to what we understand as hardware and software, but included the individuals who have developed special skills and tokens of qualification, and who offer their services to the highest bidders in the market. Political consultants or operatives have emerged as a highly specialized auxiliary service function. They have their own professional organization, The American Association of Political Consultants, which has something of a code of professional ethics.[1] A masters degree is offered by George Washington University through its Graduate School of Political Management, and they keep up to date with advances in the field by reading articles in their major trade journal *Campaigns & Elections* (Tobe 1995). While it is difficult to estimate the demand for their services, there are estimates that at the top as many as two dozen professionals earn more than $500,000 a year in fees (Rust 1994).

Concerned about the social impact of what they estimate to be a $3-billion-dollar industry, the Pew Charitable Trusts recently awarded American University's Campaign Management Institute $1.4 million to assist the industry in "doing well, while doing good."[2] In addition to helping the industry to revise its code of conduct, the Pew grant is supposed to support an analysis of the ways in which political campaigns affect the performance of government. There are few signs that Pew, or the industry their grant is designed to support, is likely to question the challenges to democracy that this professionalization represents.

Among the functions served by these political operatives is the design of communications strategies. Consultants advise candidates on what to say, how to say it, and who to or not to say it. In the words of one of the innovators in the field, Matthew Reese, the purpose of segmentation and targeting, which has been informed by sophisticated research, is to be able to deliver "different – and compelling – truths" to precisely the right segments (Ganz 1994). The result of this strategy means that depending upon the skills and resources available to the political organization, increasingly greater numbers of unique but related "campaigns" will be designed and presented to narrower and narrower constituencies. Ganz reports that the number of geodemographic groups targeted for electoral campaigns varies from 60 to 1,200. He estimates that the typical congressional campaign will have around 300 different groups targeted. Because referenda are not linked so clearly to political parties, the number and variety of targeted groups may be larger, depending upon the amount of money available to the organization.

Many consultants are identified with particular parties, or with particular ideological perspectives. However, the fact that they are commercial entities means that their first consideration is whether their activities produce a profit. The public interest is, if anything, a secondary concern. Financial success is linked to a record of substantially more "wins" than losses, and this concern for success will be reflected in the choice of issues, candidates, and strategies. Choices in each of these areas will reflect a profit or utility-maximizing logic, and social consequences are either ignored or subordinated (Edmondson 1986).

This is not to suggest that one cannot identify political consultants who have pursued contracts with what we might identify as good, progressive organizations, fighting on the right side of issues that matter to us. Wired Strategies, a Washington-based, Internet-savvy, full-service agency, has a really impressive list of clients. They went to the defense of chief petty officer Timothy McVeigh, who was threatened with expulsion from the Navy because his superiors suspected he was gay. They have a long history of supporting the efforts of the Children's Defense Fund, and they claim responsibility for designing and maintaining the Web presence of the ACLU. At the same time, it is clear from their publicity that Wired Strategies is engaged in issue management and political marketing. They rely on a toolkit of public relations that includes oppositional research (Shalit 1994). In their promotional materials, Wired Strategies notes that "the Internet is an easy place for corporations, organizations, politicians, and private individuals to lose complete control over their message or reputation. If you need to create, monitor, or repair a message or reputation, let Wired Strategies help you factor an Internet-marketing component into your legislative and corporate strategies."[3]

When consultants enter contracts in support of lobbying or grassroots mobilization, it is not unusual to see performance contracts specified such that payments are made in terms of the number of documented contacts with members of Congress. Different rates will be set for letters, telephone calls, and personal contact, reflecting both the cost of producing them and the effect each has on the representative's response to constituents (Clark 1993).

Depending upon the budgets available for a given campaign, political marketing consultants can provide tests of campaign spots that they have inserted within actual broadcasts. Under the guise of evaluating television programming, the influence of ads viewed under more natural conditions can be assessed. Consultants are also critical in designing and implementing a series of strategic polls that help to sharpen the focus of segmentation and targeting efforts. In demonstrating the importance of very large samples asking a limited number of questions, consultants are able to include current opinions and issues, as well as precise lifestyle and demographic information into the targeting algorithm. In one case, a consultant suggests that:

> For example, it is important to know that a Republican candidate should target white men in his/her communication, but it is even more important to know whether these should be young men or older men – well off, not so well off, or across the board in income. These smaller subgroups of white men respond to different messages, live in different parts of town, and watch different news programs and TV shows. Using this increased precision in targeting research greatly improves direct mail strategy, broadcast buys, cable buys and radio segmentation." (Hamilton 1995)

Segmentation and targeting, even in the defense of what we might identify as important social goals, is in my view damaging to the public sphere.

SEGMENTATION AND TARGETING

As a political technology derived from its origins in commercial marketing, segmentation and targeting is quite simple to understand and implement as a competitive strategy. Populations are divided into smaller segments, presumably reflecting tastes, preferences, interests, needs, and propensities that bear some identifiable relationship to political issues. The rationale behind segmentation is that different backgrounds and interests, and perhaps even cognitive styles, require different sorts of persuasive appeals. It is rational, in that it makes good economic sense, to focus one's limited resources upon the most favorable prospects, and ignoring those who, if they can be moved at all, will only be moved at great cost. Segmentation is akin to the military strategy of *triage*. Divide the wounded into three groups: (1) those who will survive on their own and (2) those who are likely to die, no matter what you do, and then concentrate your limited resources on (3) those who remain. The discourse of political marketing is often filled with metaphors more appropriate to war than to consensus, so I guess we ought not be surprised that military strategies have found a welcomed home.

The delivery of specially tailored messages to particular segments is what we refer to as targeting. This too is a rational strategy. It takes account of the fact that not all appeals work equally well with all audiences. Not all examples resonate with the experiences of men and women, whites and African Americans, or Yuppies and people who live on the street. Informed with knowledge about attitudes, opinions, lifestyles, and expectations, targeting seeks to increase the probability that a persuasive message achieves its intended result.

Theoretically, there are no limits to the narrowness of the segment, and the uniqueness of the targeted appeal. Of course, in practice, there are limits aplenty. They have to do with the availability of information that enables reliable classification of individuals, or communities, or regions into segments. This is a problem involving the quality of both data and theory. Segments are not naturally occurring. Segments are the products of theoretical models and analytical techniques that vary from simple classification by political party, or registration status, to sophisticated psychographic assessments developed with the aid of neural networks or other form of artificial intelligence. The more sophisticated the model, the more narrow the segments, and the greater the demand for information.

There is also the problem of delivering the targeted message. Strategic decisions about targeting involve an assessment of the cost and availability of channels of communication or message delivery that can be used to reach the target. Underlying cost considerations is a concern about accuracy and timing. In the realm of politics, accuracy means not only avoiding the waste of scarce resources, but it also means not delivering strategic resources "to the other side." I have referred to the ability to target narrowly and to assure reception as "addressability and verifiability," and political strategists have to continually evaluate different technical systems in terms of their efficiency in this regard (Gandy 1995).

Segmentation and targeting are tightly linked. Increases in sophistication in segmentation cannot provide benefits if the messages cannot be delivered on time and to the right targets. Narrowness in segments is closely matched by movements in media from mass toward narrow and, ultimately, toward individualized forms of distribution.

THE TECHNOLOGY OF SEGMENTATION AND TARGETING

It should be clear that the number and variety of channels of communication have increased dramatically. While there is an appropriate concern about increased concentration in media ownership, there is no denying the fact that the number of uniquely defined media channels has expanded almost exponentially. What remains unclear is whether this expansion in channel availability actually results in improved opportunities for segmentation and targeting as some adherents claim (Sohinki 1996).

The degree that different media channels reflect identifiable differences in consumer tastes and preferences is the degree to which those channels might support segmentation and targeting. The assumption is that on at least *one* criterion used for segmentation, the differences between "audiences" will be greater *between* than *within* channels. Upon reflection, we can readily imagine the kinds of differences in audience characteristics that might be seen as relevant for political segmentation. That is, we can easily identify magazines, radio stations, and even television networks and specific programs that attract audiences that can be differentiated on the basis of age, race, and social class (McCarty and Shrum 1993). A well-established industry, with a host of technical resources, exists to serve commercial and now political strategists in finding the right medium to reach the right audience at the right price (Donnelly 1996).

In some cases the choice of medium reflects the primary characteristics of the segmentation strategy. Although networked computers seem likely to reduce the importance of locale or "place" in the array of segmentation options, geographic information systems (GIS) and thematic mapping represent another powerful resource, which is increasingly being put to use for political marketing through newspapers, direct mail, telephone, and when necessary, door-to-door contact. Organized under the general heading of "geodemographic clustering systems," segmentation strategies based on census and other information linked to specific locales have made much of the adage "birds of a feather flock together."

The leading products and services that are provided by political strategists utilize statistical clustering routines to classify neighborhoods defined by zip codes or census tracts into as many as sixty different types of neighborhoods. The fact that there are only sixty, rather than 260 million cluster types, reflects the need to reduce the complexity within a population according to some informed theory about what matters most to those interested in segmentation. These factors are likely to vary across time, and existing cluster models are likely to be more useful to some interests than to others.

One model produces forty clusters from sixty-one variables, or measured characteristics. The racial and ethnic composition of neighborhoods has emerged as a more important feature of the clusters in the 1990s than those produced in earlier years (Mitchell 1995). By adding data from other sources, such as automotive registrations, neighborhoods can be defined in terms of the predominance of imports or four-wheel-drive sport utility vehicles. By adding data from sources within the "voter file industry," political profiles of communities can be generated that include levels of political involvement (Beiler 1990). Increasingly, cluster models include information about media use that is of central importance to decisions about targeting.

Most firms offering geodemographic clustering can produce much finer gradations below the level of census block groups that might involve 340 households. Because of the increased availability of individualized data, including data gathered from credit records, clustering models are increasingly able to target households and the individuals within them. This level of detail allows political operatives to identify and isolate the highly educated, politically active "urban pioneers" that might otherwise be missed by schemes based on census blocks or neighborhood demographics.

More sophisticated, though perhaps less reliable, ways of characterizing individuals are continually being introduced into the toolkits of marketing researchers. As lifestyle and psychographic segmentation trickles down to the desktop of the middle-level specialist in political marketing, practitioners in the upper reaches of the profession are attempting to iron out the wrinkles in still more imaginative but untested approaches to understanding the citizen or consumer. Many are developing reliable ways to segment individuals on the basis of their values (McCarty and Shrum 1993) and the ways they "feel" about attitude objects. Evaluative assessment can obviously be extended to include political candidates (Pirito 1990) as well as consumer products

(Grigsby 1996). Even more specific information about individuals is derived from the numerous transactions that they make in their daily lives as consumers (Corbin 1994). In this way the growth in segmentation and targeting, even if used only for the purpose of marketing commercial goods, represents a dangerous wedge being thrust into the social fabric.

Recently, Joseph Turow has charged American advertisers with "breaking up America" in ways that he believes are ultimately threatening to the nation (Turow 1997). He suggests that we might distinguish between media that help to build and improve the social collective and those that sharpen the distinctions among segments within society. Among the many insights that Turow provides, one of the most useful is the evidence that suggests that media planners not only assess the character of segments, but are increasingly providing signals akin to the signs posted on gated communities that are designed to keep "undesirables" out. Thus, from Turow's perspective, it seems likely that the audience segments of mainstream media will become increasingly homogeneous with respect to the lifestyles that are relevant to marketers of consumer goods.

In Turow's words, "the trajectory is clear. A desire to label people so that they may be separated into primary media communities is transforming the way that television is programmed, the way newspapers are 'zoned,' the way that magazines are printed, and the way cultural events are produced and promoted" (Turow 1997, p. 6). He has little doubt that this orientation will be reflected in the emerging media environment of 500 television channels and an unlimited number of infostops along the Information Superhighway.

Richard Sclove argues that technology ought to be understood as a social structure that helps to define and regulate social life. In his view, technology "produces its most profound social effects indirectly – and generally in concert with other, seemingly unrelated technologies" (Sclove 1995, p. 90). There is little doubt that the Internet can facilitate democratic participation. But it also seems clear that the Internet is following the path of other media toward the demands of entertainment and marketing, and away from the ideals of information for the public good (Barber et al. 1998). Structurally, one can also see the Internet as representing a threat to what we have traditionally understood as community. The virtual community, to the extent that it exists at all, is quite different from the face-to-face communities that are the basis for local political action. To the extent that virtual communities are both reflections of and reinforcements for strategic efforts at segmentation and targeting, I would suggest that the Internet will not realize its potential.

The incredibly rapid growth of the Internet, fueled in large part by the frenzied dash to identify and realize the commercial potential of the World Wide Web, represents a significant transformation of the terrain upon which political communication takes place. The Internet environment differs in vitally important ways from the largely one-way, source-driven character of traditional media. Numerous false starts and dead ends have marked attempts to apply broadcast models to a client-server environment in which users engage in more active search for information. It seems unlikely that such an approach will ultimately succeed.

The challenge to be faced by those who would use the Internet to continue the segmentation and targeting of the citizen/consumer is to develop the equivalent of "peoplemeters" that would quietly but efficiently gather information about what kinds of people go where, for what kinds of information. While the competition has been fierce, and the volume of hype almost deafening, it seems likely that both industry standards and industry leaders will emerge to provide the guidance that strategic communicators will require in order to segment and target the citizens/consumers navigating the information clouds in cyberspace.

Among the resources that will be important in this process is the ability to assign individuals to analytical categories, using theories about interest and responsiveness. Because the costs of capturing, storing, and then searching for information in machine-readable form continue to decline, an increasing number of "information entrepreneurs" have emerged to engage in the process of "data mining" in search of marketable value (Gandy 1993, 1996). A great many database services are available that provide on-line access to information about the citizen/consumer. While much of the information used for political segmentation and targeting is from public records, an army of compilers has emerged to arrange this information into formats that ease its integration into computer profiles and prospect lists. There are other sources as well.

At the same time that the thousands of usenet newsgroups provide an important opportunity for citizens to engage in political discussion, participation in those groups indirectly provides information that can be used by strategists to characterize the participants as targets. Several search engines can be used to explore the massive archives of political talk that these newsgroups invite (Conhaim 1996), and some, like DejaNews,[4] provide a variety of ways to "profile" those who participate in newsgroup discussions. Such profiles become the basis for political segmentation.

POLLS AND SURVEYS

In developing segments and targeted messages, political strategists rely heavily on traditional forms of survey research to shape their understanding of similarities and differences within the population (Hamilton 1995). In recognition that information gathered by telephone interviewers generally provided sterile, quantitative data, political operatives also included focus groups as sources of information. Political strategists understand, at least as well as the social scientists who have been critical of opinion polling, that much of the reported change in what passes as public opinion actually reflects subtle changes in the questions that are being asked (Zaller 1992), rather than meaningful changes in opinion.

Some suggest that the differences in response also reflect the substantial differences among people with regard to specific aspects of larger issues. One observer argues that "every issue is really a basket of issues. Choice vs. abortion vs. gender selection vs. legality vs. morality vs. privacy vs. parental consent vs. father's rights vs. rape/incest exceptions, ad infinitum" (Johnson 1992). There seem to be at least as many subissues connected in some meaningful way to the debates about affirmative action.

There are also important differences among polls designed to characterize the population as a whole, and those polls that are used to characterize individuals. Polling is increasingly used to characterize individuals and to enhance voter files. This information is then used to determine how these individuals might be approached and nurtured, or avoided in the future (Belier 1990). One organization, Political Marketing Service, emphasizes the efficiency with which it can "match voters to issues. Since we call every voter in your district, we can measure the response to a candidate's view on any issue and identify the voters who support that issue and the ones who oppose it" (Political Marketing Service, 1998).

Unlike mainstream public opinion pollsters, there is no expectation or requirement that confidentiality be assured to individuals who respond to inquiries from political operatives. Indeed, the Code of

Professional Ethics signed by the members of the American Association of Political Consultants seems more concerned with the treatment of colleagues and clients than citizens or the democratic process (AAPC 1997).

While there has been much said and written about the differences among media that affect their usefulness for the delivery of targeted messages, there is also the expectation that digital convergence will reduce those differences in the future (Baldwin et al. 1995). Indeed, there is also speculation that the nature of delivery systems in the future will mean that each commercial or political ad that is displayed in the home or office will have been targeted to an identifiable individual (Johnson 1992). There is already evidence of such individualized marketing in the real-time dynamic adjustments made to Web pages, which reflects some level of assumed knowledge about visitors to that site. While the widespread use of such microtargeting is somewhat off in the future, there is much work being done by political strategists in assessing the similarities, differences, and trade-offs in cost and effectiveness among snail mail, e-mail, and voice mail, as well as among satellite, broadcast, cable, tape, disc, and remote servers as means of delivering audiovisual appeals and representations to different segments.

Grassroots Lobbying and Issues Management

Historically, political consultants and their strategic resources had been applied primarily to the goal of electing candidates to public office, but in recent years we have observed a shift in their attention toward the management of public issues, or what one observer refers to as "campaigns without candidates" (Clark 1993). The fact that the clients for these consultants' services are primarily corporations and interest groups is yet another basis for our concern about the status of the public sphere (Mitchell 1998). The creation of a fictional citizen, the corporate person, is among the most important events in the transformation of modern politics. Corporate resources applied to the orchestration of political engagement by real citizens has not only been legitimized, but has become a way of life for many political consultants.

Ron Faucheux has written extensively on grassroots lobbying as an essential component of corporate special interest campaigns (Faucheux 1994). The logic behind these campaigns is that politicians respond favorably to demonstrations of public concern about policy issues. While social movements have engaged in grassroots mobilization in support of civil rights and other social concerns, the use of such strategies by the corporate sector is a relatively recent phenomenon. Nevertheless, the demand for professional services in support of these campaigns now exceeds $800 million a year (Faucheux 1994).

Because they are frequently the targets of consumerist regulation, some industries such as tobacco, waste disposal, restaurants, and, of course, the health insurance industry have taken an early lead in developing sophisticated techniques for issue management. A large part of that effort is public relations (Tucker and Trumpfheller 1993). Public relations practitioners like to think of their role as akin to that of a radar, or advance warning system, in that their expertise is most useful when they are able to anticipate "conditions, pressures, events or trends that may seriously undermine the mission of an organization." (Tucker and Trumpfheller 1993:36). Strategies that go beyond identification often involve efforts to mobilize opposition or support for specific legislation or regulations. Early involvement is vital to the extent that it allows organizations to help shape the ways in which issues and options are understood. Issue management campaigns are frequently organized through their industry trade associations.

Problems in designing segmentation and targeting strategies that arise in grassroots campaigns are no less problematic than those that are directed toward the general population. The need to gather and process information about members of an association or industry group remains substantial. Constituent research helps strategic planners identify the differential sensitivities that exist within and among associations that are often brought together in emergency coalitions in response to a perceived threat or a strategic opportunity. For critical communications researchers, there are interesting questions to be explored in understanding just which factors lead an industrial, service, or member association to develop its own grassroots lobbying specialists, rather than to rely on commercial services in the market. While an emphasis on resource mobilization seems to have gone into retreat within the community of social movement theorists (Morris and Mueller 1992), I would suggest that problems of identity are not as critical within the corporate sector. As a result, it is important to understand how perceived risk and other environmental assessments function within the strategic models of these organizations.

Because the focus of grassroots lobbying is on individual issues and legislative initiatives rather than periodic elections, the need to communicate with "grassroots activists" can emerge suddenly and require an almost instant response. The use of mail, telephone, and more recently, electronic mail and computer conferences to mobilize constituents to action requires continually updated voter lists. Lists may include assessments of both the likelihood that the individual will produce the "contact" with the legislator, or other policy target, as well as an assessment of how meaningful contact from that particular individual might be. These assessments are the basis upon which segmentation within an already specialized group will proceed.

While we might think of the telephone as a relatively well-established and stable technology, we should note that when combined with functions enabled by computerization, the telephone becomes a cost-effective means for delivering targeted communications and gathering relevant data. Current advances in telephone management are described under the rubric of "predictive dialing." This time-management system for telephone banks integrates automatic dialing with live operators. Its use in segmentation is based upon the ease with which calls can be limited to callers who match preferred demographics, or who have responded appropriately to earlier contacts (Conrad 1994). Some systems enable an agreeable contact to be immediately "patched-in" or connected to the office of the public official being targeted in a grass-roots campaign.

One company, Political Marketing Services, based in Las Vegas, claims it can personally contact 500,000 voters a day,[5] and it promises that its targeted messages will go only to voters who agree with the candidates' positions on key issues. It refers to its targeting strategy as "voter isolation." They are unusual within the field in that they resist the logic of sampling. Instead, they attempt to call every voter in the district in order to gather information on candidate and issue support. It is on the basis of individual profiles that targeted messages are sent.

Not all issues require, or rely entirely on, the more expensive, narrowly targeted communications that the telephone and e-mail provide. The mobilization effort organized by the Health Insurance Association of America included an expenditure of $15 million for the broadcast of the now infamous "Harry and Louise" spots. The spots were released in specific markets, and relied heavily on CNN and cable television. By including an 800 number with most of the spots, the campaign was able to recruit some 40,000 "activists" who generated more than 200,000 contacts with members of Congress (Faucheux 1994). Other campaigns have involved buys of space in magazines and newspapers that still enable a reasonable degree of targeting at a competitive cost per thousand.

Corporate campaigns also rely heavily on communications targeted to employees, shareholders, suppliers, and clients. Here as well, specialized knowledge is required in order to ensure that appeals don't annoy friends or arouse the opposition. Corporations have to walk a narrow line between coercion and the activation of self-interest in their efforts to mobilize internal or associated grassroots support. Public relations consultants often assist corporate executives in identifying potential constituents among employees and associates (Heath et al. 1995).

THREATS TO THE PUBLIC SPHERE

If full and equal participation in the public sphere is a fundamental requirement for the realization of the goals of the idealized democracy, then the use of segmentation and targeting by political consultants is a serious threat. First, as Ganz (1994) suggests, because campaign management relies on public opinion polling, which allows political actors to "know" the public without having any direct relationship to it, it is unlikely that the distance between individuals and political machines will be bridged through meaningful, face-to-face interaction. Where a campaign requires direct contact, as in the mobilization of grassroots support, contact is likely to be made by part-time employees, rather than the community volunteers who once went door-to-door (Faucheux 1994). Indeed, the creation of "instant organizations" has become a hallmark of issue politics in an age of professionally managed campaigns. The use of instant organization usually entails "paid door-to-door or telephone canvassers using prepared scripts to solicit voter support and who are paid on a per head or bounty basis" (Ganz 1994). As with the public opinion poll, there is no direct or continuing relationship between the citizens, those who provide the political equivalent of grunt work, and those who manage the campaigns – to say nothing of the candidates for office. Political pollsters note that "increasing cynicism, alienation, and information overload have created a disconnect between voters and their government." Rather than recognizing that they bear some responsibility for this state of affairs, these consultants suggest instead that *even more* polling will be required to discover what and how people think about political issues (Hamilton 1995).

Second, because the purpose of targeting is to focus on individuals within segments that are by definition smaller fractions of the electorate, sizeable portions of the population are excluded from the flow of communication (Hughes 1994). Ganz argues that over the last few decades, it has been the goal of campaign consultants to "reduce the universe" of voters (Ganz 1994). The decline in voter participation is undoubtedly the result of a strategy of focusing campaign resources on that segment of "likely voters," that is, those who are likely to vote the right way.

Because outreach and mobilization strategies are informed by models that rely on past voting behavior, we should expect to validate a self-fulfilling prophesy. People who are deemed unlikely to vote because they did not vote in the last election are less likely to be contacted in a "get out the vote" drive. As an example, Ganz notes that despite the great range of problems that confronted the citizens of Los Angeles, both campaigns in the last mayoralty election followed a strategy of universe reduction. As a result only 25 percent of the electorate turned out to vote. These consultants seemed more concerned about the fact that their strategies might eliminate the wrong voter than they were about the impact they were having on the political process (Hughes 1994).

Excluding persons from the flow of information because they have been deemed unlikely to vote means that the people who are most in need of information are least likely to receive it. This is akin to the consequences that flow from advertiser support for newspapers, magazines, and other fee-based media. Advertisers are interested in reaching those segments of the population with more resources and a higher probability of purchasing expensive consumer goods and services. They are willing to provide "information subsidies" that reduce the expenses that this population would ordinarily have to face in acquiring the information (Gandy 1982). They will not support media that have the wrong audience profile. Thus, the wealthy pay less than they might, and the poor find that the information they need is not available at any price (Baker 1994). The logic that informs commercial advertising thus works to degrade the quality of political content in the press. When that logic makes its way into the management of electoral and issue campaigns, it has the same effect – the widening of the knowledge and information gap between the haves and the have-nots.

The formulation of public issues and political concerns into targeted appeals reflects the influence of strategic resources. It is therefore also likely that perspectives that are reflective of and potentially more relevant to those who are most marginalized by "politics as usual" are perspectives that are likely to be ignored in most campaigns. This ultimately means that those who are most in need of exposure to and experience in formulating political discourse are least likely to have such experience (Gandy 1988). As a result, their ability to articulate their concerns remains underdeveloped (Ganz 1994).

There are a number of other consequences that flow from increased reliance on political consultants who use the twin technologies of segmentation and targeting. Reliance on political consultants and the use of marketing techniques may also be contributing to the level of political disengagement that Putnam describes as a loss in social capital (Putnam 1995). The kind of interpersonal trust that is traditionally generated and reinforced through face-to-face contact has been allowed to decay in the wake of an approach to politics that devalues volunteerism and reduces participation to the act of writing a check.

While there are any number of explanations for the emergence of single issue and identity politics as a defining characteristic of the modern public sphere (Eder 1993; Obershall 1995), the logic of segmentation emphasizes the value of difference over the value of commonality. Because strategic communication is designed to mobilize individuals as members of groups with common interests at risk, rather than as members of a larger complex whose interests are served through compromise, political discourse is bound to be combative, rather than cooperative. As Cappella and Jamieson argue, the result is an escalating spiral of cynicism and a withdrawal from the public sphere (Cappella and Jamieson 1997).

NOTES

1. Viewed on June 3, 1998 at http://www.theaapc.org/ethics.htm.
2. Press release issued June 30, 1997, viewed on June 8, 1998 at http://www.pewtrusts.com/docs/consult.html.
3. Viewed on June 2, 1998 at http://www.wiredstrategies.com/whatisws.html.
4. Located at http://www.dejanews.com.
5. Viewed on April 18, 1998 at http://www.hostmasters.net/molmkt/pms1.htm.

REFERENCES

AAPC (American Association of Political Consultants) (1997). "Code of Professional Ethics." http://www.theaapc.org/ethics.htm.
Baker, C. E. (1994). *Advertising and a Democratic Press.* Princeton, NJ: Princeton University Press.
Baldwin, T., D. S. McVoy, and C. Steinfeld (1995). *Convergence: Integrating Media, Information, & Communication.* Thousand Oaks, CA: Sage.
Barber, B., K. Mattson, and J. Peterson (1998). "The State of 'Electronically Enhanced Democracy': A Survey of the Internet." New Brunswick, NJ: The Walt Whitman Center for the Culture and Politics of Democracy.

Beiler, D. (1990). "Precision Politics: Technology and Circumstance Are Pushing Voter Files into the Driver's Seat of the Campaign Bandwagon, but Who's Got the Keys?" *Campaigns & Elections*, Nexis/Lexis, February–March.

Cappella, J., and K. Jamieson (1997). *The Spiral of Cynicism: The Press and the Public Good.* New York: Oxford University Press.

Clark, M. (1993). "Selling Issues." *Campaigns & Elections*, 14:26.

Conhaim, W. (1996). "The Internet: Linking Up to a Global Network." *Link-Up*, 13:5.

Conrad, R. (1994). "Winning Votes on the Information Super-highway." *Campaigns & Elections*. Nexis/Lexis.

Corbin, H. (1994). "Tracking the New Thinkers." *Public Relations Quarterly*, 39(4):38.

Donnelly, W. J. (1996). *Planning Media: Strategy and Imagination.* Upper Saddle River, NJ: Prentice Hall.

Eder, K. (1993). *New Politics of Class: Social Movements and Cultural Dynamics in Advanced Societies.* London: Sage.

Edmondson, B. (1986). "The Political Sell." *American Demographics*, 8:27.

Ellul, J. (1964). *The Technological Society.* New York: Vintage Books.

Faucheux, R. (1994). The Grassroots Explosion. *Campaigns & Elections*, 16:20.

Gandy, O. H. (1982). *Beyond Agenda Setting. Information Subsidies and Public Policy.* Norwood, NJ: Ablex.

 (1988). "The Political Economy of Communications Competence." in V. Mosco and J. Wasko (Eds.), *The Political Economy of Information.* Madison, Wisconsin: University of Wisconsin Press, pp. 108–124.

 (1993). *The Panoptic Sort. A Political Economy of Personal Information.* Boulder, Colorado: Westview Press.

 (1995). "Tracking the Audience. Personal Information and Privacy." In A. M. John Downing, Annabelle Sreberny-Mohammadi, *Questioning the Media. A Critical Introduction.* Thousand Oaks, CA: Sage, pp. 221–237.

 (1996). "Legitimate Business Interests: No End in Sight? An Inquiry into the Status of Privacy in Cyberspace." *The University of Chicago Legal Forum*, 1996:77–137.

Ganz, M. (1994). "Voters in the Crosshairs: Elections and Voter Turnout." *Current*, 362:4.

Grigsby, J. (1996). "Vote-by-mail: A Catalyst for Change in Political Marketing." *Public Relations Quarterly*, 41(3):31.

Habermas, J. (1998). *Between Facts and Norms: Contributions to a Discourse Theory of Law and Democracy.* Boston: MIT Press.

Hamilton, W. (1995). *Political Polling: From the Beginning to the Center of American Election Campaigns.* Boulder, CO: Westview Press.

Heath, R., W. Douglas, and M. Russell (1995). "Constituency Building: Determining Employee's Willingness to Participate in Corporate Political Activities." *Public Relations Research*, 7(4):273.

Hughes, R. H. (1994). "Hitting the Mark: Targeting by Turnout." *Campaigns & Elections*, 15:24.

Johnson, W. (1992). "First, do no harm: Targeting Voters without Boosting Your Own Negatives." *Campaigns & Elections*, Nexis/Lexis Search.

McCarty, J., and L. J. Shrum (1993). "The Role of Personal Values and Demographics in Predicting Television Viewing Behavior: Implications for Theory and Application." *Journal of Advertising*, 22(4):77.

Mitchell, S. (1995). "Birds of a Feather." *American Demographics*, 17:40.

Mitchell, A. (1998). "A New Form of Lobbying Puts Public Face on Private Interest." *New York Times*: A1.

Morris, A., and C. Mueller (Eds.) (1992). *Frontiers in Social Movement Theory.* New Haven: Yale University Press.

Obershall, A. (1995). *Social Movements. Ideologies, Interest & Identities.* New Brunswick, NJ: Transaction Publishers.

Pirito, R. (1990). "Measuring Minds in the 1990s," *American Demographics*, 12(12):30.

Political Marketing Service (1998). "Get personal." http://www.hostmasters.net/polmkt/pms1.htm.

Putnam, R. (1995). "Bowling alone." *Journal of Democracy*, 6:77.

Rust, M. (1994). "The Growing Rolls of Political Consultants." *Insight on the News*, 10:18.

Sclove, R. (1995). "Making Technology Democratic." in J. Brook and I. Boal (Eds.), *Resisting the Virtual Life: The Culture and Politics of Information.* San Francisco: City Light Books, pp. 85–101.

Shalit, R. (1994). "The Oppo Boom: Smearing for Profit Takes Off." *The New Republic*, 210:16.

Sohinki, J. (1996). "Cable Power." *Campaigns & Elections*, February: 26.

Tobe, F. (1995). "Effective Slate Mailers: How Personalized Top-to-Bottom Voter Cards Can Produce Votes." *Campaigns & Elections*, 16(6):40.

Tucker, K., and B. Trumpfheller (1993). "Building an Issues Management System." *Public Relations Journal*, 49(11):36.

Turow, J. (1997). *Breaking Up America: Advertisers and the New Media World.* Chicago: University of Chicago Press.

Zaller, J. (1992). *The Nature and Origins of Mass Opinion.* New York: Cambridge University Press.

CHAPTER 8

Let Us Infotain You: Politics in the New Media Environment

Michael X. Delli Carpini and Bruce A. Williams

Political beliefs and actions spring from assumptions, biases, and news reports. In this critical sense politics is a drama taking place in an assumed and reported world that evokes threats and hopes, a world people do not directly observe or touch. . . . The models, scenarios, narratives, and images into which audiences for political news translate that news are social capital, not individual inventions. They come from works of art in all genres: novels, paintings, stories, films, dramas, television sitcoms, striking rumors, even memorable jokes. For each type of news report there is likely to be a small set of striking images that are influential with large numbers of people, both spectators of the political scene and policymakers themselves.

Murray Edelman, *From Art to Politics* (p. 1)

We are living in an era where the wall between news and entertainment has been eaten away like the cartilage of David Crosby's septum.

Al Franken, Chief Political Correspondent,
Comedy Central

Political communications scholars, members of the press, and political elites have traditionally distinguished between entertainment and nonentertainment media. It is in public affairs media in general and news media in particular that politics is assumed to reside, and it is to this part of the media that the public is assumed to turn when engaging the political world. *Politics*, in this view, is a distinct and self-contained part of public life, and *citizen* is one role among many played by individuals. As a former network television executive put it, in the civic education of the American public, entertainment programming is recess.

But people, politics, and the media are far more complex than this. Individuals are *simultaneously* citizens, consumers, audiences, family members, workers, and so forth.[1] Politics is built on deep-seated cultural values and beliefs that are imbedded in the seemingly nonpolitical aspects of public and private life. Entertainment media often provide factual information, stimulate social and political debate, and critique government, while public affairs media are all too often diversionary, contextless, and politically irrelevant.

In this chapter we build upon the premises contained in the opening quote from Edelman: that politics is largely a mediated experience; that political attitudes and actions result from the interpretation of new information through the lenses of previously held assumptions and beliefs; and that these lenses are socially constructed from a range of shared cultural sources. We also agree with Edelman that this has always been the case, and so to the extent that researchers have ignored or downplayed entertainment media, popular culture, art, and so forth, in the construction of both news and public opinion, we have missed a critical component of this process.[2]

But we further argue that this omission is not a coincidence. Rather it has been supported by a set of understandable but ultimately artificial structures and practices of the media, academic researchers, and political elites that distinguish fact from opinion, public affairs from popular culture, news from nonnews, and citizens/consumers from experts/producers. These walls – in place throughout most of this century – are rapidly eroding, the result of changing communications technologies, the new economics of mass media, and broader cultural trends. This erosion not only makes more obvious the political significance of popular culture in the social construction and interpretation of the news, but also makes the very distinction between news and nonnews increasingly untenable. The resulting media environment is rearranging traditional power relationships as the authority of journalists, public officials, and other political gatekeepers is increasingly challenged by other producers of political and social meaning – including the public itself.

To explore these issues, we first critically analyze the distinction between public affairs and entertainment media, the way this distinction has become reified, and the reasons for its recent erosion. Media coverage of the Lewinsky-Clinton scandal (and its precursors) provide us with a rich example of this erosion, and of the new power struggle over defining and framing the public agenda that it has unleashed. We conclude by discussing the role of the public in this new media environment, suggesting that while traditional gatekeepers have lost much of their agenda-setting authority, it is unclear who, if anyone, has taken their place.

THE INHERENT ARBITRARINESS OF THE NEWS – ENTERTAINMENT DISTINCTION

Despite the seeming naturalness of the distinction between news and entertainment media, it is remarkably difficult to identify the characteristics upon which this distinction is based. In fact, it is difficult – we would argue impossible – to articulate a theoretically useful definition of this distinction. The opposite of *news* is not *entertainment*, as the news is often diversionary or amusing (the definition of entertainment) and what is called "entertainment" is often neither. One might instead use the terms *public affairs* media and *popular* media, but these distinctions also collapse under the slightest scrutiny. Does the definition of public affairs media require that it be *un*popular? Does the broadcasting of a presidential address shift from public affairs to popular media because it is watched by too many people? And how does one classify the many magazine stories, novels, movies, television shows – in all their rapidly changing formats such as melodramas, docudramas, docusoaps, and talk shows – that address issues of public concern? Clearly the concept of popular media does not provide a counterpoint to public affairs. To the contrary, the "public" in public affairs indicates that the issues discussed are of importance to a substantial segment of the citizenry, and most of what is studied under this heading *is* popular by any reasonable definition of the term.

The difficulty in even *naming* the categories upon which we base so fundamental a distinction is more than semantics. Rather it highlights the artificiality of this distinction. A more fruitful approach might be to identify the key characteristics that are assumed to distinguish politically relevant from politically irrelevant media. But this does more to blur than clarify the traditional news/nonnews categories. Public affairs media address real-world issues of relevance to a significant percentage of the citizenry, but so, too, does much of what traditionally falls outside of this genre: one would be hard pressed to find *any* substantive topic covered in the news that has not also been the subject of ostensibly nonnews media. And public affairs media generally, and the news more specifically, regularly address issues of culture, celebrity, and personality.

Attempting to define public affairs media in broader strokes also does little to resolve this conceptual dilemma. Walter Lippmann defined news as "the signalizing of an event" (Lippmann 1922). And yet entertainment media often play this role, drawing the public's attention to issues and events of social and political import (Delli Carpini and Williams 1994a; Fiske 1996). In short, all of the usual characteristics we associate with news or public affairs media can be found in other media, and those we associate with popular or entertainment media can be found in the news. We do not conclude from this that *all* media are equally relevant to politics or useful to democratic discourse. Rather we suggest that our traditional categories fail as a way of making such distinctions; that they are social constructions that tell us more about the distribution of political power than about the political relevance of different genres. Further, we argue that these categories are rapidly losing what power they once had to privilege certain gatekeepers and genres in the process of constructing political reality. Before exploring the implications of this changing media environment, however, it is instructive to examine how the current categories emerged and were supported, and why they have been eroding in recent years.

THE "WALLING OFF" OF NEWS AND THE CREATION OF AN INFORMATION ELITE

The now familiar distinction between news and entertainment can be traced in large part to the first several decades of the twentieth century, when economic, technological, political, and sociocultural changes redefined the roles of the mass media, citizens, and elites.[3] Growing centralization of ownership and decreasing competition in the printed press, coupled with the rise of an inherently centralized and expensive electronic media, threatened one of the presumed requisites of liberal democracy: a diverse marketplace of ideas. At the same time, the economics and politics of American life were becoming increasingly nationalized (Lears 1983; Hanson 1985). In this centralized and nation-alized environment, inherent tensions between the economic, enter-tainment, and civic goals of the media became increasingly difficult to ignore (Peterson 1956).

Adding to this sense of unease, social science research and real-world events in Europe and the United States throughout the first half of the twentieth century raised concerns regarding the stability of democratic systems and the civic capacity of democratic citizens (Berelson 1952; Schumpeter 1942). The public was increasingly seen as an inchoate, dis-engaged mass that was susceptible to manipulation by the media and that required protection from the media's propagandizing power (Lippmann 1925).

Concerns about the proper role of both the media and citizens led to greater emphasis on the role of experts, an emphasis that was part of broader attempts to distinguish elites from the masses in the first decades of the twentieth century. Progressive Era efforts to define government as the province of specially trained experts rather than easily corrupted elected officials or ignorant citizens have been well-chronicled. In a similar vein, Levine (1988) describes the ways in which dramatic changes in American society during the Progressive Era – industrialization, immigration, urbanization, and so forth – challenged existing cultural, social, and political definitions of what it meant to be American. In response, elites in a wide range of cultural arenas – theater, literature, museums, musical performance – sought to impose and protect their own definitions of American identity by developing aes-thetic standards, rules of audience behavior, canons of "meritorious" art and literature, and other practices that constructed a new distinction between elite and mass audiences. The result was the elevation and cel-ebration of that which was enjoyed by elites and a parallel devaluation of "the popular."

Driven in large part by the technological, economic, and cultural changes just discussed, three conceptual distinctions of importance to current theorizing about the media had emerged by the second half of this century. First, the news media were separated from entertainment media, with the former viewed as most directly responsible for fulfill-ing the media's civic function. Second, within the news media, fact became distinguished from opinion, and news reporting increasingly strove to be accurate, objective, and balanced (ostensibly obviating the need for a decentralized, competitive press). And third, the public was distinguished from media professionals and policy experts, with the former viewed as passive, easily manipulated consumers of information, and the latter as information gatekeepers who took primary responsibility for determining and representing the public interest.

These distinctions were maintained through a set of institutional structures and processes:[4]

- The division of media organizations into separate news and entertainment divisions
- The assumption that public affairs programing would be free from (or less tied to) expectations of profitability
- Trade distinctions between news and entertainment media
- The physical layout and labeling of segments of publications and programs so as to distinguish news from analysis or opinion, and "hard" news from "soft" news or features
- The routinization of program schedules (e.g., local news in the early evening followed immediately by national news; local news again at 10 or 11 PM; political talk shows on Sunday mornings)
- The professionalization of journalists
- The development of formal and informal standard operating procedures to assist in determining newsworthiness

The limited number of television stations available to citizens (from one to five from the 1950s through at least the early 1980s), most or all of which broadcast news at the same time, also reinforced the news–entertainment distinction.

Distinctions between public affairs and popular media were also maintained by the nature of their respective audiences. Readers of prestige news magazines and newspapers and viewers of public affairs broadcasting were a self-selected segment of the population – a more elite social, economic, and political strata of citizens. This elite audience signaled the serious nature of what was being read or watched, distinguishing it from popular media. As with the distinction between high brow and low brow culture (Levine 1988), the politically significant and insignificant were defined as much by the organization of producing institutions and the makeup of the audience as by actual content.

In sum, the structural walling off of news from nonnews reified what was essentially a socially constructed distinction. As Schudson notes, the ideal of objective, professional journalists emerged "precisely when the impossibility of overcoming subjectivity in presenting the news was widely accepted and . . . precisely *because* subjectivity had come to be regarded as inevitable" (1978, p. 157; emphasis added). Readers and viewers were signaled that something was news *because* it was on the evening news or the front page of the newspaper and that something was opinion *because* it appeared on the opinion page or was labeled as such on the evening news. Likewise, the *nonpolitical* was defined in part by where and when it appeared, how it was labeled, who presented it, and who attended to it.

THE BREAKDOWN OF THE NEWS–ENTERTAINMENT DISTINCTION

The media environment in the United States has changed dramatically in the last fifteen years, spurred in part by the proliferation of VCRs and remote television controls, the availability of cable and satellite television, the growth of the Internet and World Wide Web, the horizontal and vertical integration of the media through conglomerates, and so forth. These changes have dramatically increased the amount and range of information that is readily available, the speed with which it becomes available, and the opportunities for interactive mass communications (Abramson et al. 1988). They are also leading to a convergence (or at least blurring) of types of media, ownership of media, and media genres.

This new media environment is a hostile one for maintaining the always fragile distinction between public affairs and entertainment. The division of media organizations into separate news, entertainment, and sports divisions, while still in place, has become more porous, and thus journalists, management executives, public officials, and entertainers can develop celebrity identities that transcend any specific job description and allow them to move freely between both types of media and decreasingly distinct genres. In turn, the distinction between fact and opinion or analysis is much less clearly identified by simple rules such as where it appears, who is saying it, or how it is labeled. Public affairs time slots have become overwhelmed by the range of options open to citizens: Traditional news can be gotten any time of the day through cable or the Web, or equally ignored at any time of the day. Even the standard operating procedures, routines, and beats that determined newsworthiness have become subject to reconsideration both from within and outside the journalistic profession

(Rosen 1999). As audiences themselves absorb these changes and the resulting erosion of formerly commonsense distinctions, they too begin to move freely among media and genres (Delli Carpini and Williams 1994b).

Economic changes, many of which are the direct result of this new media environment, have further eroded the news–entertainment distinction. News divisions, once accepted as the industry's concession to the public good, are increasingly seen as potential sources of revenue. The downsizing of news organizations makes it increasingly difficult to perform their journalistic function with the same degree of care as in the past. Many of the federal regulations designed to assure at least a minimal amount of public affairs broadcasting and some degree of fairness and access have been dismantled or allowed to go unenforced. The growing centralization of the media into a handful of international communications conglomerates with interests in film, music, cable, and broadcast television increases the pressure for profit and further blur the line between news and entertainment (Bagdikian 1992).

In short, the new media are creating an environment that is increasingly incompatible with the structures and practices that maintained the news–entertainment distinction for most of this century. As these walls crumble, the form and content of news and entertainment come to resemble each other more closely, laying bare what has always been a socially constructed distinction.[5] What is clear is that this new media environment presents a direct challenge to the authority of elites – journalists, policy experts, public officials, academics, and the like – who served as gatekeepers under the old system. Less clear is to whom, if anyone, this authority has shifted. To some extent it is returning to the public, as they play a more active role in constructing social and political meaning out of the mix of mediated narratives with which they are presented. At the same time, there is evidence that new or marginalized groups, along with new or formerly nonpolitical media, are playing a more central role in setting and framing the public agenda. And, keeping in mind the first several decades of this century, it is quite possible that traditional media and political elites will emerge from the current period of flux having reasserted their gatekeeping role in some new form. In the next section we illustrate the blurring line between entertainment and news, and its complex impact on the agenda-setting process, by closely examining media coverage of the Lewinsky-Clinton spectacle.[6]

SEX, LIES, AND VIDEOTAPES: A CASE STUDY OF THE
NEW MEDIA POLITICS

In mid-January 1992 *The Star*, a national tabloid specializing in stories about the personal lives of celebrities, published a story in which Gennifer Flowers claimed to have had a twelve-year affair with Bill Clinton, then the frontrunner for the Democratic nomination for president of the United States. The story was initially downplayed in the mainstream press, in part because the allegations were two years old. It was also initially ignored because the *Star*, described in one mainstream newspaper article as better than most of the national tabloids, but still a step below the *National Enquirer*, was deemed an unreliable news source.[7]

The decision by Bill and Hillary Clinton to directly address the issue by appearing on *60 Minutes* (a choice based in part because the show would air immediately following the Super Bowl) brought the issue more centrally into the mainstream press. The Clintons, who helped perfect the art of using the nontraditional press, also appeared on shows like *Prime Time Live*, *Donahue*, *The Arsenio Hall Show*, and *MTV* either to directly refute or to deflect the issue. While the Clintons' efforts were successful in rallying public support and partially diffusing the issue, the alleged affair had gained some legitimacy within the mainstream press as a campaign issue – members of the press could point to the existence of legitimate sources (for example, the Clintons themselves) and to the fact that other traditional news outlets were covering the story, to justify their expanded coverage. The press could also justify covering what was initially defined as a private matter by focusing on the issue of "lying to the public."

Nearly seven years later the Clinton presidency stood at the brink of dissolution, rocked by another sex scandal and another controversial Star(r) report – this time that of Independent Counsel Kenneth Starr – focusing on an alleged affair between President Clinton and a White House intern named Monica Lewinsky. By the fall of 1998 all notions that one could make clear-cut distinctions between serious and less serious news outlets, even between news and nonnews genres, had been effectively destroyed. Whether one started the day by listening to National Public Radio or Howard Stern, watching *Good Morning America* or *CNN*, reading the *New York Times* or the *Star*, the topic was the same.[8] Viewers of daytime talk shows such as NBC's *Leeza* could watch a panel – consisting of a Washington newspaper correspondent, a public relations expert who works with celebrities, a gossip columnist, and a television star who had gone through a very public divorce – discuss the way Hillary Clinton was handling the media spotlight. An Internet search under the heading "Monica Lewinsky" would produce over 12,000 options, ranging from breaking news reports to "the Monica Lewinsky Fan Club." E-mails sharing the latest Clinton-Lewinsky jokes were commonplace in offices around the country. The early evening local and national news competed not only with each other, but with the on-line *Drudge Report* (50,000 hits per day at the height of the scandal, a large proportion of which were mainstream journalists themselves) and television tabloid shows like *Entertainment Tonight*, *Hard Copy*, and *A Current Affair* (the latter two whose names had taken on interesting double meanings) for the latest details and interpretations of the scandal. Prime time dramas and comedies either made direct references to the scandal, or their usual fare of sex, infidelity, power, and conspiracy took on new meanings. Cable talk shows like *Hardball* and *Rivera Live*, and all-news cable networks like MSNBC, became virtually "all-Monica, all the time." Late evening news was no different, to be followed into the wee hours by more "discussion" of the scandal by news anchor Ted Koppel; comedians Jay Leno, David Letterman, Bill Maher, and Conan O'Brien; and crossover personalities like sportscaster-turned-newscaster Keith Oberman. One could literally spend 24 hours a day watching, listening to, and reading about the Clinton scandal. More tellingly, one could do so without ever tuning in or picking up a traditional news source.

Reflecting the ability of the new media to obliterate both time and space, the story flowed across national borders, where it also crossed genres and audiences. For example, while serious commentary in Israeli newspapers focused on the impact of the scandal on prospects for a Middle East peace settlement, commercials for spot removers on Israeli television spoofed the scandal (private detectives searching Lewinsky's closet are distressed to find a can of the advertiser's spot remover lying next to "the" dress). Similarly, the scandal dominated the mainstream British press and was also used in commercials to sell a newspaper's weekly job listings (a Clinton impersonator asks his aide why he should be interested in the new job listings, since he already has a job. After a pause, he says, "Oh yeah, maybe I should take a look.").

It is obvious that any approach to political communication based upon clear-cut distinctions between fact and opinion or public affairs and entertainment is of little help in understanding the dynamics of media coverage of the Clinton sex scandals as they developed between 1992 and 1998. While there are a number of frameworks one might use to attempt to make sense of this new world of mediated politics, two concepts – *hyperreality* and *multiaxiality* – are particularly applicable.

HYPERREALITY. For Fiske (1996), the central unit of analysis in studying the media (and the driving force in public discourse) is not objective reality, but "media events."[9] According to Fiske,

> The term *media event* is an indication that in a postmodern world we can no longer rely on a stable relationship or clear distinction between a "real" event and its mediated representation. Consequently, we can no longer work with the idea that the "real" is more important, significant, or even "true" than the representation. A media event, then, is not a mere representation of what happened, but it has its own reality, which gathers up into itself the reality of the event that may or may not have preceded it. (Fiske 1996, p. 2)

The intertwining of an event and its mediated representation produces what Baudrillard has called "hyperreality," and which Fiske defines as "a postmodern sense of the real that accounts for our loss of certainty in being able to distinguish clearly and hierarchically between reality and its representation, and being able to distinguish clearly and hierarchically between the modes of its representation" (p. 62).

The Lewinsky-Clinton scandal is nothing if not hyperreal. The questions of fact in the case – did Clinton engage in sex with Lewinsky? Did he lie about it? Did he commit perjury? – are *inextricably* tied to and ultimately overshadowed by the representations of these issues – Clinton's televised denial of sexual relations to the American public; the barrage of interpretations by partisan pundits, lawyers, and comedians; the nonstop release of rumors, leaks, and reports; the sounds and images of private phone conversations and grand jury testimony. The representation of these issues on the news, talk shows, and entertainment programs all build on the same set of mediated facts but deploy them in distinct ways. On other occasions these interpretations intersect, as on shows like *Politically Incorrect*, where guests drawn from entertainment, academia, politics, and the news media discuss contemporary issues like the Clinton-Lewinsky scandal.

These sometimes distinct, sometimes changing, and sometimes intersecting genres blur any notions of a hierarchy between fact and fiction, or news and nonnews. For all the information available, and the speed with which it is available (President Clinton received the Starr report from Congress only an hour before the rest of the American Public did), there is no consensus on the facts or their significance because there is no longer a clear distinction between facts and their representation. In a world in which we have the ability to use the science of DNA testing to "prove" the occurrence of an event, but in which such evidence has no guarantee of carrying any more authority than a comedian's satirical comment or a lawyer's definition of sex, what does it mean to talk about the objective facts?[10]

The hyperreality of the Clinton-Lewinsky scandal is perhaps best exemplified by recalling that it began as a result of an investigation of a decades-old land deal. The intersection of Whitewater with Gennifer Flowers, Paula Jones, Katherine Willey, Linda Tripp, and Monica Lewinsky, as well as with the alleged misuse of FBI files and the firings at the White House travel office was not illogical – one can certainly reconstruct the connections between potential misuse of power, the intimidation of witnesses, and so forth. But it was the dynamics of the media environment that transformed these incidents into a media event with its own complex and shifting meaning. In this hyperreal world, the specific facts become mere vehicles for discussion of more deep-seated, foundational issues about the human condition – political corruption, public and private trust, sexual mores, workplace harassment, personal relationships, and the like.

From this perspective, the Clinton-Lewinsky scandal was as much rooted in events as diverse as Watergate, the political and cultural movements of the 1960s, and the O. J. Simpson, Louise Woodward, and JonBenet Ramsey trials, as in the Whitewater or Paula Jones cases. It was also rooted in popular culture genres (films, television dramas and comedies, novels, and music), which address many of the same foundational issues. Sometimes these connections were obvious – terms like "Whitewatergate," "Filegate," "Travelgate," and "Fornigate" tied the Clinton scandals to those of the Nixon administration and in doing so tied the former to the long-standing public cynicism about government the latter engenders. Films like *Wag The Dog*, *Primary Colors*, and *An American President*, or television shows like *Spin City* – direct commentaries on the contemporary state of politics – occasionally became part of the discourse about the Clinton-Lewinsky scandal. For example, when the United States bombed a Sudanese pharmaceutical plant that was allegedly manufacturing chemical weapons, Kenneth Starr was asked by a reporter whether he had seen *Wag The Dog* (in which a fictional president creates a fake war as a diversion from a sex scandal), and if he saw any parallels. If he didn't, Saddam Hussein did: Earlier in the year, Iraqi television broadcast a pirated copy of the movie at the height of tensions over U.N. weapons inspections and U.S. threats to launch air strikes. And an MSNBC story noted that a statement by President Clinton explaining his initial concerns over ordering the strike sounded remarkably like one made by the fictional president in *An American President* under similar circumstances.

Often, however, the connections between popular culture and the Clinton scandal were more subtle, based on the similarity of the underlying issues, values, or beliefs that were tapped rather than on direct references to contemporary politics. But this larger media environment, even when it never made specific reference to the Clinton sex scandal, was critically important in setting the context in which the scandal was interpreted.

MULTIAXIALITY. To argue that the new media environment creates a hyperreality in which reality and its representation begin to blur is not to say that this process occurs outside the realm of politics. As Fiske notes,

> [public discourse] is language in social use; language accented with its history of domination, subordination, and resistance; language marked by the social conditions of its use and its users; it is politicized, power-bearing language employed to extend or defend the interests of its discursive community. (Fiske 1996, p. 3)

The hyperreality of postmodern media events does not change this, but instead creates what Fiske calls *multiaxiality*: "As hyperreality dissolves stable categories of modes of representation, so multiaxiality transforms any stability of categories into the fluidities of power" (p. 65).

While Fiske focuses on the core axes of class, race, and gender in his discussion of public discourse, the concept of multiaxiality can be used to better understand the changing nature of mediated political discourse more broadly. Traditionally, the political agenda has been shaped by a symbiotic relationship between mainstream political actors and major news outlets (Bennett 1988; Hallin 1986, pp. 115–119). In this relationship, the media act as a monolithic gatekeeper, while a limited set of political elites vie with each other to shape the agenda and how it is framed. The public is reduced to the role of passive consumer, whose own attention to and interpretation of events is constrained by this limited information environment.

This single axis system has been transformed in two ways. First, the expansion of politically relevant media and the blurring of genres leads to a struggle within the media itself for the role of authoritative gatekeeper. And second, the expansion of media outlets and the obliterating of the normal news cycle create new opportunities for non-mainstream political actors to influence the setting and framing of the political agenda.

The new media environment presents a challenge to mainstream journalists in their roles of agenda setter and issue framer. It is telling that throughout the Clinton sex scandals the mainstream press frequently paused to reflect on is own role, and to try to clarify (for itself and the public) what constitutes newsworthiness.[11] But the existence of multiple news outlets (cable news or talk shows, radio call-in shows, conservative publications like the *American Spectator*), quasi-news outlets (*Hard Copy, A Current Affair*), entertainment media (*The Tonight Show, Late Night with David Letterman*), and the Internet (e.g., *The Drudge Report*), all of which were in some sense covering the scandals, made it difficult for either the mainstream press or political elites to ignore or downplay them.

The impact of this multiaxial media environment can be seen in the pattern of coverage that characterized the Paula Jones incident.[12] While mainstream coverage ebbed and flowed throughout most of 1994 (driven largely by events in the civil suit), and all but disappeared throughout all of 1995 (as a result of legal appeals that put much of the case on hold), a number of alternative media outlets stuck consistently to the story, keeping the issue firmly on this subterranean agenda.

It was not until 1997 that the Paula Jones issue became an ongoing news story in the mainstream press, driven largely by events surrounding the civil suit and the increasingly inflammatory rhetoric coming from both the Clinton and the Jones camps. While in some ways this increased attention suggests that the mainstream news media had recaptured control of the political agenda, most of the stories written or aired during this period were initially generated through leaks, reports, and rumors that first emerged over the Internet, from conservative publications and the cable talk shows. Thus, while the mainstream press had more firmly embraced the issue as newsworthy, it was still reacting to an agenda that was being framed largely by others. Mainstream news sources like the evening news and the prestige newspapers were also disadvantaged by the collapse of the normal twice-a-day news cycle and its rapid replacement with 24-hours-a-day breaking news (Kurtz 1998).

For all the attention generated by the Paula Jones case, it paled in comparison to the explosion of coverage that began with the allegation in January 1998 of President Clinton's affair with a White House intern. The last ten days of that month generated more newspaper stories around the country than all the articles and commentaries written on Gennifer Flowers and Paula Jones combined. While journalists continued to periodically stop and reflect on whether this was a topic worthy of so much attention, or to lament the decline in journalistic standards in reporting, by 1998 the mainstream news media had essentially succumbed to the new system. Alternative media figures (most notably, Matt Drudge) continued to indirectly shape mainstream media coverage, but also emerged as commentators or guests on serious news shows like *Meet the Press*. At the same time, mainstream print journalists and news reporters appeared with greater frequency on network and cable talk shows, both a reflection of their increased celebrity and a concession to the shifting balance of power in the media. Major publications like *Newsweek*, the *New York Times*, and the *Washington Post* prepublished and updated their stories on the Internet, allowing the public to see the normally hidden process of constructing the news. Competing news outlets began to use each other – and in at least one case indirectly used *itself* – as sources for their stories.[13] The commentary of comedians like Jay Leno, David Letterman, Bill Maher, and Al Franken occasionally became the topic of the next day's news stories, while the day's news was increasingly the subject of that evening's monologue.

In short, in the six-year period from the publication of the *Star* expose to the publication of the *Starr* report, traditional journalism lost its position as the central gatekeeper of the nation's political agenda. For most of that period (arguably through 1997) the news media attempted to play its traditional role and found that the political agenda was being set without them. As a result it adapted to the new rules by increasingly mimicking the form and substance of its new media competitors.

Just as the new information environment created multiple axes of power within the media, it also created new axes among the political actors who shape the media's agenda. Authoritative sources have been traditionally limited to a largely mainstream political, economic, and social elite: elected officials, spokespersons for major interest groups, and so forth. These sources, while attempting to shape the media environment in ways that would benefit their particular political agenda, understood and largely operated within the rules of traditional journalism. But the new media environment, with its multiple points of access and more continuous news cycle, has increased the opportunities for less mainstream individuals and groups to influence public discourse. This was certainly the case with the Clinton scandals.

While falling short of Hillary Clinton's claim of "a vast right-wing conspiracy," the attacks on Bill Clinton's financial and sexual behavior were orchestrated in large part by the religious and partisan far right. Of particular interest to us is the way this traditionally marginalized group effectively exploited the new media environment to create new axes of power.[14] For example, when Gennifer Flowers first went public with her affair, her contract with the *Star* was negotiated by John Hudgens, an Arkansas businessman who had been press secretary to two of Clinton's Republican challengers for governor. And it was Floyd Brown (head of the independent *Presidential Victory Committee* that produced the infamous "Willie Horton" political spot in 1988) who set up the 900 number where callers could listen to excerpts from the taped conversations between Clinton and Flowers. The Flowers affair was also kept in the news when ultraconservative congressman Robert Dornan read the entire *Star* expose into the Congressional Record while being broadcast on *C-Span*.

In December 1993, the *American Spectator*, a conservative monthly magazine, published the first reports that then Governor Clinton had used state troopers to facilitate his rendevous with Flowers and other women. The troopers' lawyer was Cliff Jackson, a former Oxford classmate of Bill Clinton and more recent critic who had been the source of the story about Clinton's draft dodging during the Vietnam war. It was Jackson who approached the *American Spectator* about doing the "troopergate" story, which was then picked up first by CNN and then by other major news outlets. Jackson also organized the 1994 news conference (sponsored by the *Conservative Political Action Conference*) in which Paula Jones announced her intent to file a sexual harassment suit against Clinton.

The Jones story was also initially kept in the news through conservative publications like the *Washington Times* and the *National Review*. When the mainstream press failed to cover the story with enough vigor, the conservative media watchdog group, *Accuracy in Media*, ran ads in the *Washington Post* and the *New York Times* criticizing them for ignoring the issue. By this time Floyd Brown, now heading an organization called *Citizens United*, was acting as a clearinghouse for incriminating information about Clinton and providing leads to conservative G.O.P. congressional aides and reporters from both mainstream and nonmainstream media. The religious right also played an important role in maintaining the anti-Clinton media campaign. Jerry Falwell produced and distributed a video entitled *Circles of Power*, which "documented" a host of alleged ethical and moral violations of the President. And television evangelist and one-time Republican presidential candidate Pat Robertson interviewed Paula Jones on his nationally televised program.

Conservative groups found other creative ways to draw media attention to the Clinton scandals. In 1996 former F.B.I. agent Gary Aldrich published *Unlimited Access*, which alleged numerous (largely unsubstantiated) improprieties within the Clinton White House. In addition to becoming a bestseller, which was released in paperback as the Lewinsky scandal was at its peak, it was also given away free as an incentive to join the *Conservative Book Club*. In 1997 the *Free Congress Foundation* ran radio spots in Washington, D.C., offering to pay any "victims of Bill Clinton" who would step forward and tell their story. And in that same year *Judicial Watch*, headed by Larry Klayman, initiated a suit on behalf of *State Farm Insurance* policyholders, alleging that the company wrongly paid for some of President Clinton's legal bills as a result of a personal liability policy he held. The suit allowed Klayman to depose a number of Clinton administration people and ask about a wide range of topics. Klayman then became a regular guest on a number of talk shows such as *Rivera Live*, where he aired selected portions of the videotaped depositions.

While garnering some support from mainstream conservatives and Republicans, by and large this loosely knit network of conservative foundations, public officials, private citizens, and media organizations operated outside the normal chain of command. This was essentially an insurgency movement that was able to influence the public agenda through newly emerging axes of mediated political power. And though generally failing in more traditional institutional settings (e.g., the courts), they succeeded in influencing the political agenda by exploiting the new media environment through first using the right wing press, then the new media (the Internet, cable talk shows, etc.), and ultimately the mainstream press.[15]

THE "PUBLIC" IN THE NEW MEDIA ENVIRONMENT

The Clinton sex scandals provide a useful example of the blurring line between media outlets and genres, and the challenge this presents for traditional gatekeepers. But this case study raises a number of issues as well. While we think the evidence is strong that the new media environment allowed nonmainstream conservative groups to set the *media's* agenda, its impact on the *public's* agenda is much less obvious. Public opinion polls throughout this period showed remarkably little movement, and much of the movement that did occur was in the direction of *increased* support for the president – exactly the opposite of what traditional agenda-setting, framing, and priming theory would predict (Zaller 1998).[16]

This stability could be interpreted as evidence that in the new media environment, the "public" (collectively and as separate economic, political, and cultural communities) is free to construct its own interpretation of political reality. Opinion surveys and media-market analyses suggest that the public followed the ongoing story (through a variety of media) and knew the central issues and facts. Yet despite the efforts of the President's supporters and detractors to frame the issue, a large majority of the public created their own narrative that was consistent with neither group's interpretation: The president had an affair and lied about it to the public in his deposition and testimony (despite his denials). This affair (and other allegations of sexual misconduct) lowered their estimation of Clinton's already questionable moral character (despite his attempts to salvage his image). At the same time, and in the face of concerted efforts by Clinton's detractors, the public consistently separated this issue from his ability to govern, said that it was ultimately a private matter, and opposed resignation or impeachment, instead favoring either dropping the issue or imposing some form of mild censure. Arguably, the ultimate resolution of the scandal (with the significant exception of the President's impeachment) was closer to the public's preferred outcome than that of either the President or his opponents.

But there is another, less optimistic interpretation of these events and public reaction to them. While Clinton ultimately remained in office, his sexual infidelity (and his opponents' exploitation of this personal failing) shaped a substantial part of the media's agenda for six years and dominated it for another year; led to the impeachment of a popularly elected president for the first time in U.S. history; and turned both the public's and the government's attention away from other, more substantive issues. And all this was done with maximum media attention and minimal public response. From this perspective, the public's attention to this unfolding drama was no different than it might have been to a particularly engrossing episode of *ER*, *The X-Files*, or *The Jerry Springer Show*. In short, national politics had been reduced to a sometimes amusing, sometimes melodramatic, but seldom relevant spectator sport.[17]

Both of these interpretations of public reaction to the Clinton sex scandals suggest that media events may play a greater role in setting the public agenda than in framing it.[18] But determining whether reaction to such mediated events reflects an autonomous, reasoning public or massive public indifference is crucial to understanding the current and future state of democracy in the United States. We can offer no evidence or argument for reaching such a determination. But we are convinced that the answer lies in developing theories of mediated politics that are more compatible with the fluidities of power emerging from the hyperreal, multiaxial media environment in which we now live. We are also convinced that developing such theories will require abandoning our always artificial, but now almost certainly untenable, assumptions about the distinction between news and entertainment media.

Notes

1. The tendency to distinguish these roles reflects the general failure of liberal–democratic political theory to adequately address the complex relationship between citizenship and consumption (what Miller [1998] calls the consumer-citizen couplet). On this general issue, see Chaps. 5, 6, and 7, by Underwood, Slater, and Gandy, respectively.

2. In this regard we believe that the study of political communication has much to learn from the theoretically rich approaches to these issues found in the cultural studies literature.

3. Debates over the appropriate role of the media, citizens, and elites; attempts to distinguish between fact and opinion; efforts to define high and low culture; and the other issues discussed in this section predate this period, of course. Our point is that the first several decades of the twentieth century were particularly significant in this regard, and shaped much of what we have come to treat as natural in the current mediated political environment.

4. Many of these distinctions were formerly codified in the 1920s through the early 1950s by, among others, the Federal Radio (1927) and Federal Communications (1934) Commissions; professional associations such as the American Society of Newspaper Editors (1922), the National Association of Broadcasters (1923), and

the Newspapers Guild (1933); the privately funded Commission on Freedom of the Press (1947); and codes of conduct created by the movie (1930), radio (1937) and television (1952) industries (Emery and Emery 1988; Peterson 1956).

5. Whether this "merging" of news and entertainment results in an actual change in the form and content of both genres, or simply means that producers and consumers of mediated messages treat this information differently is an empirical question we do not address. Our strong suspicion (based on some initial research) is that the content of the news has increasingly addressed issues of celebrity, culture, and so forth, and presents information in a way that is more self-conciously entertaining. Entertainment media has always directly and indirectly addressed issues of political and social import, so here the difference may be more in how this information is interpreted and used (Delli Carpini and Williams 1994b). We suspect, however, that even ostensibly entertainment genres are more likely (and able, given new technology) to situate their story lines, etc., in real world events and issues.

6. The following discussion of media coverage of the Clinton sex scandals is based on a systematic review of that coverage using *Nexus* and Internet searches, as well as on an in-depth, though somewhat less exhaustive, review of broadcast and cable coverage.

7. The blurring between news and entertainment is exemplified by the fact that the *National Enquirer's* own reputation had been enhanced and begrudgingly acknowledged by members of the mainstream press as a result of its reporting during the O. J. Simpson trial.

8. In this regard, media coverage of the Clinton-Lewinsky scandal takes on characteristics of "waves" as developed in Chap. 11, by Wolfsfeld.

9. The concept of a media event has also been used by Dayan and Katz (1994). While the two uses are similar in some ways (and share much in common with Wolfsfeld's notion of "waves" in Chap. 11), there are several important differences. For Fiske, media events provide opportunities for marginalized publics to enter mainstream discourse by using such events to draw attention to their concerns (much as the O. J. Simpson trial or Clarence Thomas–Anita Hill hearings raised broader issues of race and gender). For Dayan and Katz, however, media events have the potential to tap into shared foundational beliefs that can unify seemingly disparate segments of society: while various media may cover the event in different ways, underlying assumptions about the public agenda are *shared* across both outlets and audiences (as with the death of Princess Diana or the explosion of the space shuttle). In our view the Clinton scandals come closer to Fiske's than Dayan's and Katz's type of media event.

10. Of course, the DNA evidence did lead Clinton to finally acknowledge his sexual relationship with Lewinsky, but had little discernible or lasting effect on public opinion. Indeed, in the O. J. Simpson case, the science of DNA testing itself could be challenged by further appeals to science, to beliefs in the corruption or ineptness of the police, and to inherent assumptions of racism, reducing this evidence to the status of opinion at best, and even to "proof" that Mr. Simpson was being set up, and thus was not guilty.

11. Recent attempts by the news media to "police" itself also point to this crisis in defining journalism: for example, the firing of several reporters and columnists at the *Boston Globe* and *Washington Post* for inaccurate reporting, the resignation of a

local newscaster in protest over the hiring of talk show host Jerry Springer, the decision by ABC to not air a docudrama by Oliver Stone about the downing of TWA Flight 800 out of fear that it would confuse viewers, the ongoing criticism of "public journalism" by mainstream members of the press, and so forth.

12. A similar pattern existed for coverage of the Gennifer Flowers scandal, though shorter in duration.

13. One major news organization published what later turned out to be an erroneous story on its Web site. The story was then picked up from the Web site by a competitor, leading the first news organization to reaffirm the story using the second organization's story as confirmation!

14. While in the case of the Clinton sex scandals it was conservative groups outside the mainstream that were best able to exploit the new media environment, we make no claims that this was the only possibility: In other circumstances and certainly for other issues, very different groups could be equally successful.

15. The Republican losses in the 1998 congressional elections, resulting in part from their failed strategy regarding the Clinton-Lewinsky scandal and the subsequent meltdown within the G.O.P. leadership, suggest the extent to which established elites within the party had lost control of their own agenda.

16. But see Keeter (1999) for an argument suggesting that political-science theories of presidential approval may account for this pattern of stability and change.

17. The fact that the public's reaction to charges of sexual *harassment* in the Paula Jones or Katherine Willey cases (or to alleged campaign finance violations by the Clinton-Gore campaign) were similar to those expressed in the Monica Lewinsky case supports this rather pessimistic view. Perhaps more tellingly, the involvement of U.S. military forces in Kosovo could not hold the public's attention at all.

18. Unexplored in this chapter is the impact of the new media environment in the absence of an overriding media event. We suspect that under these quite common circumstances the typical pattern may be a fracturing of the ability of the media or political elites (mainstream or not) to even set an agenda that holds the attention of anything like a majority of the public.

References

Abramson, Jeffrey, Christopher Arterton, and Gary Orren (1988). *The Electronic Commonwealth.* New York: Basic Books.

Bagdikian, Ben (1992). *The Media Monopoly.* Boston: Beacon Press.

Bennett, Lance (1988). *News: The Politics of Illusion* (2nd ed.). New York: Longman.

Berelson, Bernard (1952). "Democratic Theory and Public Opinion." *Public Opinion Quarterly,* 16:313–330.

Dayan, Daniel, and Elihu Katz (1994). *Media Events.* Cambridge, MA: Harvard University Press.

Delli Carpini, Michael X., and Bruce Williams (1994a). " 'Fictional' and 'Non-Fictional' Television Celebrates Earthday." *Cultural Studies,* 8:74–98.

(1994b). "Methods, Metaphors, and Media Research: The Use of Television in Political Conversations." *Communication Research,* 21:782–812.

Edelman, Murray (1995). *From Art to Politics.* Chicago: University of Chicago Press.

Emery, Michael, and Edwin Emery (1988). *The Press and America*. Englewood Cliffs, NJ: Prentice Hall.

Fiske, John (1996). *Media Matters*. Minneapolis: University of Minnesota Press.

Hallin, Daniel (1986). *The Uncensored War*. Berkeley, CA: University of California Press.

Hanson, Russell (1985). *The Democratic Imagination*. Princeton: Princeton University Press.

Keeter, Scott (1999). "The Perplexing Case of Public Opinion About the Clinton Scandal." Paper presented at the annual conference of the American Association for Public Opinion Research. St. Petersburg, FL.

Kurtz, Howard (1998). *Spin Cycle*. New York: Touchstone Books.

Lears, T. J. Jackson (1983). "From Salvation to Self-Realization: Advertising and the Therapeutic Roots of Consumer Culture, 1880–1930." In Richard Wightman Fox and T. J. Jackson Lears (Eds.), *The Culture of Consumption*. New York: Pantheon Books.

Levine, Lawrence (1988). *Highbrow/Lowbrow*. Cambridge, Mass.: Harvard University Press.

Lippmann, Walter (1922). *Public Opinion*. New York: The Free Press.

(1925). *The Phantom Public*. New York: Harcourt, Brace.

Miller, Toby (1998). *Technologies of Truth: Cultural Citizenship and the Popular Media*. Minneapolis: University of Minnesota Press.

Peterson, Theodore (1956). "The Social Responsibility Theory." In Fred Siebert, Theodore Peterson, and Wilbur Schramm, *Four Theories of the Press*. Urbana, IL: University of Illinois Press, pp. 73–104.

Rosen, Jay (1999). *What Journalists Are For*. New Haven: Yale University Press.

Schudson, Michael (1978). *Discovering the News*. New York: Basic Books.

Schumpeter, Joseph (1942). *Capitalism, Socialism, and Democracy*. New York: Harper and Row.

Zaller, John R. (1998). "Monica Lewinsky's Contribution to Political Science. *PS: Political Science and Politics* 31(2):182–189.

CHAPTER 9

The Future of the Institutional Media

Timothy E. Cook

Nowadays, almost everyone assumes the news media are powerful in one way or another. How, when, where, and why this occurs, and for good or for ill, brings considerably less consensus. Different conceptions of journalism and theories of what shapes the news and thus of the news media's power abound (see Gans 1979, pp. 78–79). Journalists protest that they hold a mirror up to reality, a notion that has been debunked by the constant preference over time for only certain newsmakers, subject matters, and storylines. Critics on various points on the left–right continuum contend instead that biased news stems from journalists' particular ideological stances – whether their own or that of the news organization for which they work (Lichter et al. 1986, p. 1996) – yet this begs the question of how this can occur given journalists' explicit and conscientious exclusion of personal values and dogged pursuit of neutrality, if not objectivity (Tuchman 1972; Gans 1979; Weaver and Wilhoit 1996).

Perhaps the dominant explanation among scholars is the role of the news media as organizations having to crank out a predictable amount of news weekly, daily, even hourly nowadays, even though what is news is all but undefinable. In the process of "routinizing the unexpected" (Tuchman 1973), the organizational approach contends that the news gravitates only toward those news sources and subject matters that can easily and efficiently provide opportunities for news on a regular, recurring basis. Although the organizational approach helps us understand the role of powerful authoritative sources, the centrality of news beats and the repetition of news formulas (e.g., Epstein 1973; Sigal 1973; Tuchman 1978), there is much that cannot be explained by it. In particular, the need to routinely produce the news has little impact in and of itself on the political content of the news. As Eliasoph (1988) convincingly showed in her study of an alternative news outlet, the radio station KPFA, both mainstream and radical news can easily be produced by the same routines. Moreover, as Gans (1979) noted, organizations may create new values, but, at least as often, they reflect the values that are built into the very structure of the organization (see also Selznick 1957). Most of all, the organizational approach to the news cannot explain why there is such apparent similarity in news content from one outlet to the next. Organizations, after all, might well be expected to craft distinctive approaches as their goals and clienteles vary. Yet although we know that different news outlets have considerably different audiences, which actors and which stories are newsworthy, and for what reasons, are remarkably alike.

One way to answer this puzzle of media power, as I have argued elsewhere (Cook 1998), is to envision the media as a collective institution. Similar to other such collective institutions (see Powell and DiMaggio 1991), news organizations are structured similarly to achieve similar goals, in part because of transorganizational norms of professionalism, in part because of operating in similar political environments, and above all because of the abiding uncertainty of what is important and interesting enough to be considered news. I proposed the following definition: "Institutions are social patterns of behavior identifiable across the organizations that are generally seen within a society to preside over a particular social sphere" (Cook 1998, p. 70). Three questions then had to be answered for me to be able to conclude that the news media did, in fact, constitute a political institution: "First, can we conclude that the news media create the news based on distinctive roles, routines, rules, and procedures? Second, have these practices evolved and endured over time and do they extend across news organizations? And finally, are the news media viewed by newspersons themselves, as well as those who are not, as together presiding over a given part of social and political life?" (Cook 1998, p. 71)

Indeed, research has suggested that these questions can and should be answered affirmatively. As a consequence, the news media have become an institution wielding, advertently or not, collective power. Not simply because the public relies upon the media for their information about politics but because officials use the news to communicate with each other and influence the all-important context for decision making, the news media are now a crucial intermediary implicated in day-to-day governance at least as much as a means to connect officials and the public. The dilemma emerges in the tenuous links to citizenship, given the ascendancy of communication that relies upon private financing, that sees its audiences less as participants to be mobilized than consumers to be reached by advertisers and that consequently focuses on certain news values that have little or less to do with the quality of public policy. The growing importance of the news media to officialdom then suggests an increasing incursion of news values into the very processes of decision making in government.

Yet there is nothing inevitable about this set of developments. Indeed, as I have shown (Cook 1998, Chaps. 2–3), both politics and journalism shift because of governmental decisions about public policies toward the news media and/or of technological possibilities that create new openings for new kinds of journalism. And the developments of 1998 imply new challenges to the future of the media as a collective political institution.

Take the Lewinsky scandal, which was characterized both by the role of narrowcast cable channels that have profited from the presence of a continuing saga in the form of a scandal to build and hold audiences at low cost, and by indications of the role of the Internet, as the story was broken by a gossip Web site run by Matt Drudge (who eschewed traditional norms of journalism) and then was propelled by on-line releases, such as the report of independent counsel Kenneth Starr. In short, 1998 encapsulated the lessening dominance of any single news outlet (or single set of news outlets, such as network news). The first two characteristics of an institution seem, on the face of it, to be undermined by the expanding range of news outlets and the deteriorating market share of each individual news outlet. In particular, we may wonder whether the onetime homogeneity of the news media – and the boundaries around the profession of journalism – are breaking down. In other words, both the "distinctive roles, routines, rules, and procedures" of American journalism, as well as the extension of those practices across a wide range of news outlets, may be eroding.

A second aspect of the Lewinsky scandal – the dramatic rise in disaffection from the news media reflected in public opinion polls across 1998 through its aftermath – also raises intriguing questions about the durability of the institutional media. President Clinton's job performance ratings actually went up in the first days of the scandal, particularly after his 1998 State of the Union Message. A poll that the Pew Research Center for the People and the Press conducted from January 30 to February 2, 1998, suggested that Clinton's approval ratings improved in part because of antipathy to the news media: "Sympathy for a president beleaguered by a press perceived as biased and inaccurate is an important element in Clinton's support." (Pew 1998c, p. 1) After the conclusion of the impeachment trial in early 1999, the public was still unhappy, as another Pew poll conducted February 18–21, 1999, revealed: "The . . . clear and consistent trend is discontent with the news media. Public criticism of press practices and coverage of the Clinton-Lewinsky scandal continues. And the negative view of the news media now extends to its values, with growing numbers of Americans describing the press as immoral, unprofessional and uncaring about the country" (Pew 1999a, p. 1). These results bring home to us what is possibly a new fact of life for journalists and journalism: that the news media and journalists have moved from being highly respected in the wake of Watergate in the 1970s to disliked and disdained in the 1990s. The third characteristic of the institution that I described here, namely whether it is widely accepted as presiding over a certain part of social and political life, is endangered when public opinion begins to question its legitimacy. As Dennis (1975, p. 189) asked about another intermediary institution, the political party system, "Are we able to say with any assurance that public goodwill has reached a dangerously depleted level – a point low enough to make the institution unable to withstand major new stresses during the coming years?" Thus I wish to explore the state and implications of the growing disaffection, recorded in recent public opinion surveys, of citizens toward the news media and toward journalists.

DOES THE RISE OF NARROWCASTING SPELL THE END OF PACK JOURNALISM?

In the 1970s, it was commonplace to refer to the way in which the two-party system was displaced by the three-network system. The accelerating collapse of the audience for the three broadcast networks of CBS, ABC, and NBC makes this a quaintly historical bon mot. As surveys of the Pew Research Center (1998a, p. 2) have revealed, the number of respondents who say they regularly view cable news (CNN, CNBC, MSNBC, or Fox News) is just about the same as for network news broadcasts – adding up the nightly news and the newsmagazine shows and the morning shows – once one folds in other cable channels with formats and subjects borrowed from the news, for example, ESPN (sports) and the Weather Channel. Indeed, this same report suggested that there was no dominant mass audience any more; instead, the report used cluster analysis to show six different news audiences with different habits, levels of attention, and preferences for news. These audiences are largely distinguished by their attention to particular broadcast and print news outlets, not to mention the burgeoning opportunities afforded by the Internet and the Web.

On the surface, the greater diversification of the news audience would seem to suggest that we can no longer think of the news media as a single institution. Indeed, it does appear that the news habits of Americans are becoming even more varied if not more haphazard than they were in the past (cf. Graber 1984; Robinson and Levy 1986). The percentage of survey respondents who report watching only television news fell in Pew reports from 30% in 1993 to 15% in 1998 (Pew 1998a, p. 1). When asked which news outlets they attended to the day before, over half the respondents reported not reading a newspaper, listening to radio news, or reading a magazine, and around 40% did not watch any television news at all (Pew 1998a, Q8–Q13). Yet the lack of overlap of the news audiences means that only 14% of the survey respondents reported spending no time attending to the news the previous day (Pew 1998a, Section 3, p. 1). Add to this the growing number of survey respondents who reported checking the Web or the Internet for news,[1] and one could imagine a qualitatively different political system from the 1970s with its focus on a neatly delineated set of national news media.

Likewise, all news outlets are more sensitive than was the case in the 1970s to the bottom line of economic pressures – in part because a guaranteed audience is no longer there, in part because of the rise in publicly traded media companies that are now being judged for profit margins much like any other corporations. We might not then be surprised if journalists' onetime autonomy, particularly their apparent ability to neglect if not ignore their mass audiences, might be severely cut back, and in favor of greater attention to their more distinct niche audiences. In addition, the growing competition offered by the Internet for the news could produce a new set of sources of the news.

But has this clear rise in "narrowcasting" produced a wide array of differing understandings and interpretations of the news? To judge from the latest round of indispensable surveys of full-time journalists working for mass outlets, conducted by Weaver and Wilhoit (1996), and a recent survey of a representative sample of working journalists by the Pew Research Center (1999b) between November 1998 and February 1999, the answer must be no. The roles endorsed for the news media are startlingly constant over time and across different news organizations by medium and by focus (national or local). Weaver and Wilhoit, for instance, report strong emphasis on interpreting government claims and disseminating objective information (1996, Figure 4.2), and a strong rejection of the role of journalists setting the political agenda. Similarly, the Pew Research Center survey (1999b, Q4) revealed that journalists regard others joining the profession overwhelmingly for "providing people with information they need in their lives" and "having the chance to uncover wrongdoing," far more than "working to reform society" or "helping to create a sense of community." Journalists exhibited much lower job satisfaction in 1992 than in either 1971 or 1982 (1999b, Figure 3.13), in no small part because their perceived autonomy had also shrunk substantially, in turn attributed to "inadequate staff, time and space" (1999b, Figures 3.2 to 3.5). At least in the early 1990s, then, journalists' complaints (which are many) about the decline of standards in the news says less about being pushed to reflect audience wishes and more about lacking the resources to do the good job they once perceive they did.

Reporters engage in increased self-criticism and disgruntlement about the job they do. In survey responses from 1995 and 1999, journalists now fret about the decline of the news media's credibility and criticize the news for failing to distinguish between reporting and commentary, for factual errors and for being out of touch with their audiences. Yet these answers presuppose the same criteria for quality journalism that have existed for decades. Indeed, there is continuing strong endorsement for the value of objectivity as a systematic method for attaining "a true and accurate account of an event" (Pew 1999b, Q6–Q7). Most strikingly, remarkable consensus on the "core principles" of journalism, with large majorities (usually well over 70%) of both national and local journalists (print and television) emphasizing "getting the facts right," "getting both sides of the story," "not publishing rumors," "providing at least two sources to confirm a story based on anonymous sources," "making your reader/viewer/listener your first obligation," "keeping some distance from the people you cover," "always remaining neutral," and "keeping the business people out of the newsroom" (Pew 1999b, Q24).

In sum, the multiplication of different news outlets has not been matched by a diversification of approaches to journalism. More fully, the homogeneity of the news across different news outlets, if anything, has probably been strengthened rather than weakened by recent developments. To grasp this point, we only need to recall the truism that profits can be achieved either by boosting revenue or cutting cost. Judging from the evidence provided by Doug Underwood in Chap. 5, at least for *political* coverage, cost-cutting seems to have had the most impressive impact. For one thing, news broadcasts, as well as newspapers, have sought to emphasize more service-oriented "news that you can use," traditionally more popular than the Washington fare that was the heart of reporting up until the 1980s and that was drastically reduced by the early 1990s (see Kimball 1994). In addition, newspapers have redesigned their format to increase typeface size and white space, all of which ends up shrinking the news hole further at a time when political news is under greater competition from service-oriented news. In other words, the service orientation of the news media has changed the content of political news less than it has reduced the amount of space and time available for it.

Networks and newspapers alike have tended to close down bureaus as one way to present a favorable bottom line. The creation of news now relies ever more on outside reports – whether pools of reporters or news services of one sort or another – to provide them with the content that reporters could remake into stories for their news outlets without ever having to leave the newsroom. McManus's (1994) pioneering work on "market-driven journalism" at three California local television news operations showed how the diminishing resources provided to reporters inevitably meant a greater reactivity to the news and an expanding dependence on the story suggestions of other news outlets, such as local daily newspapers. Yet matters have changed differently than we might have expected. We don't see simply old wine in new bottles, as has occurred with Internet Web sites linked to existing news organizations that provide Web surfers with a brand-name assurance of quality and credibility (Davis 1999, Chap. 2). Instead, we also see greater *explicit and formal collaboration* between journalists in the creation of news.

The classic studies from the 1970s (e.g. Crouse 1973; Sigal 1973; Tuchman 1978; Gans 1979; Fishman 1980) not only identified pack journalism but stressed informal reasons for its presence. They stressed how reporters sought to minimize the inevitable uncertainty of what was nonfictional news on a daily basis. In order to give their superiors a product that could routinely be accepted as authoritative enough to be in the news, they tended either to turn to each other on the news beat or to rely upon certain news outlets, such as the wire services or the *New York Times*, to give an agreed-upon indication of what was news.

These *informal* mechanisms have not been displaced but have been succeeded by ever more *formal* modes of cooperation between organizations in the production of news. Perhaps the best example here is NBC, which, faced with the dispersion of their audience, has been most aggressive in spinning off two additional cable channels – MSNBC, as part of a collaboration with Microsoft to integrate an all-news cable channel with an interactive Web site, and CNBC, focused in particular on business news (from the perspective of business) and drawing nowadays on a deal with the *Wall Street Journal* to provide its writers for commentary and insight – which then feed back into the home network's programming, as when MSNBC's commentator Laura Ingraham is enlisted to serve as a talking head on NBC's morning show, *Today*, or when CNBC's Ron Insana provides a film story for *NBC Nightly News*. The collaboration between *Time* magazine and CNN may have become at least momentarily infamous in 1998 for a story on the U.S. Army's use of nerve gas in Vietnam that both organizations ultimately felt obliged to retract, yet indicates how the common ownership of the two outlets now pushes a common content. Add the greater tendency nowadays for journalists from one news outlet to serve as sources for others, sometimes with the encouragement of bonuses from their home organization for appearing on someone else's show. It soon becomes clear that the more widespread dispersion of the news audience and the possible multiplication of news outlets says very little per se about the diversity of news content itself. Homogeneity of the news, it appears, seems to be alive and well – for better or worse.

DOES THE GROWING PUBLIC CRITICISM OF THE MEDIA AND OF JOURNALISM SUGGEST A "LEGITIMACY CRISIS" FOR THE FOURTH BRANCH?

If the news media still act as a transorganizational institution, recent public opinion polls show just how much the legitimacy of that institution has dipped. The General Social Survey (GSS) annually asks respondents to report the confidence they had in various "leaders" of national institutions (FitzSimon and McGill 1995; W. L. Bennett 1998, Figure 1). In the early 1970s, the press was ranked highly,[2] about equal to the military and usually far more favorably than Congress or the executive branch. Around 1982, the press slipped in public evaluation to the lower levels of Congress and the executive branch, and all three slumped further in the public's estimation in the early 1990s.

Moreover, there has been a more qualitative shift in the public's views toward the news media from the 1970s, where we can first gauge public opinion, through the 1990s. The portrait from the 1970s, continuing on into the 1980s, is of a generally favorable set of public attitudes toward the news media. Lipset and Schneider (1987), reanalyzing Harris and NORC surveys from 1966 through 1986, concluded that confidence in the press was only weakly associated with confidence in other institutions. They suggested that "the press" and organized religion are "'guiding' institutions, outside the normal political and economic order, and to some extent 'critics' of that order" (Lipset and Schneider 1987, p. 65).

The apparent public support for restrictions on press access during the U.S. invasion of Grenada in 1983 clearly worried reporters. Yet reviews of contemporaneous poll results (Gergen 1984; Schneider and Lewis 1985; Whitney 1985; Robinson and Kohut 1988) implied that public criticism may have been relatively limited. Critical of what they saw as a general tendency for the news media to be unfair, biased, and preoccupied with bad news, the public was satisfied with the overall performance of the news outlets with which they were most familiar, rarely provided a majority in favor of government restrictions on the media (ones that reporters strongly opposed), and even viewed the news media as a whole more positively than other institutions.

By the 1990s, however, the news media were no longer immune from the overall decline in institutions that had begun in the early 1970s. Now, as S. Bennett (1998) has found in the 1996 GSS, the correlation of measures of confidence in the news media and in other leaders is significantly positive, in part because public ratings of the news media's performance, independence, fairness, ethics, and completeness all fell more rapidly from the 1980s to the 1990s than they had from the 1970s to the 1980s (see also FitzSimon and McGill 1995).

Data from a Harris survey taken directly after the 1996 general election (Smith and Lichter 1997) and Pew Research Center polls over the last three years fill out this portrait of disapproval of the news media as a whole. Let's examine first the level of confidence that citizens have in the news media. When given a choice between saying "the news media helps society to solve its problems" or "the news media gets in the way of society solving its problems," the public chose, by a 2-to-1 margin, the latter in February 1998 (Pew 1998c, Q6). Although a minority opted for agreeing that "criticism by the press keeps political leaders from doing their job," the percentage grew from 23% in August 1989 to 39% in February 1998 and 31% in February 1999 (Pew 1999b, Q20). Strong majorities – considerably more so than in 1985 – of the public opted for saying "news organizations generally" "don't care about the people they report on" and "try to cover up their mistakes" with significant increases over time in the public's propensity to accuse them of being "immoral," of "hurting democracy," of "not [being] professional" and of being "too critical of America" (Pew 1999b, Q23). The distrust of the news media extends to journalists, particularly regarding their honesty and ethics, on which a Gallup poll in 1994 ranked them below most other professionals, higher only than "advertising practitioners," "congressmen," "insurance salesmen," and "car salesmen" (FitzSimon and McGill 1995, Table 7).

It does appear then that the public's trust in the news media has eroded considerably, raising questions about the public *legitimacy* of news media power. When asked directly, citizens largely say "the news media have too much influence over what happens in the world today"; in the Harris poll from late 1996, 58% said "too much," 7% "too little," and 33% "just about the right amount" (Smith and Lichter 1997, Exhibit 3–4). Consequently, the past reticence about governmental intervention to improve the news has diminished (Smith and Lichter 1997, Exhibit 6–1).

Does this decline in the trust given to the news media and to journalists then suggest a crisis for the institutional media? After all, these findings would seem to undermine the conclusion I reached (in Cook 1998, p. 70), which suggested that the news media, as a political and social institution, "are expected to preside over a societal and/or political sector" by both elites and the mass public. Yet the public's apparent lack of confidence in the news media as a whole may or may not undermine the institutional place of the news media very much, given two other factors.

First, we need to distinguish between confidence in the news media as a whole and support for particular news outlets. It may be that while the public is skittish about trusting the news media, they still find their overall day-to-day performance to be adequate. Just as the public usually dislikes Congress far more than its own representative in Congress or often disapproves of the health care system in the United States at the same time they approve of their own physician or sees discrimination against women occurring frequently in the world at large but rarely in their immediate surroundings, citizens may disapprove of the news media as a whole or of journalists taken as a group yet still be satisfied with the news outlets to which they attend.

Indeed, this bifurcation of support was already recognizable in poll results in the 1980s that showed consistently stronger criticism of the "news media" compared to their hometown newspaper and to either local or network television news (Schneider and Lewis 1985: Table 2).

> When it comes to the press, people are very familiar with the newspaper that lands on their front porch every day. Television, particularly network television, is more remote. 'The media' represents a distant and abstract force, and people are reluctant to offer unqualified praise for powerful institutions that are removed from their daily experience . . . When people think of the media, they probably think of a powerful institution, the role it plays in society, and the kind of people who work for it, as opposed to specific newspapers or television programs or news stories. (Schneider and Lewis 1985, p. 10)

The most important recent study of approval of national political institutions, Hibbing and Theiss-Morse's *Congress as Public Enemy* (1995), also elucidates citizens' understandings and evaluations of a collective political institution such as the news media. Even in 1992, a year of unusual political anger and disaffection, the American public was highly favorable to the institutional structure itself of Congress, the least popular of the three branches of government. By contrast, the gap between approval of the institution and approval of its members, substantial for all three branches, was especially large with Congress, leading the authors to conclude that the famous phenomenon of the public approving one's representative while disliking Congress was not so much the contrast of individual and institution, but the difference between what citizens knew about their particular member and about all members of Congress as a whole: "People think about Congress in terms of its members primarily because their exposure to Congress usually comes through the actions of the membership" (Hibbing and Theiss-Morse 1995, p. 107).

Like Congress, the work of journalists is increasingly visible to the public. And similarly, there is often negative news about the sloppy processes, ethical missteps, and mistakes of both members of Congress and journalists[3] – not to mention often unrelenting criticism against both of them from the spin control of the White House – that can serve as data about Congress and its members as a whole and about the news media and journalists as a whole. And as with Congress, the public appears disinclined to give the news media any slack. For instance, a *Newsweek* poll conducted in July 1998, after a series of well-publicized journalistic mishaps and scandals, asked its respondents, "Do you see these recent cases of media inaccuracy as isolated incidents involving a few specific reporters and news organizations, or do they make you less likely to trust the news media's reporting in general?" Thirty percent chose the former, 62% the latter.[4]

Yet though the public's more day-to-day support often tends toward the negative, it has been fairly volatile. And the public continues to be satisfied and positive about the individual news outlets they use, much more so than they are about the institutional news media or institutional actors of journalists. The Pew Research Center's (1998c, Q4) early 1998 survey shows continued strong approval for local television news (81% saying that their "overall opinion" is very or mostly favorable), network television news (76%), "the daily newspaper you are most familiar with" (74%), "cable news networks such as CNN or MSNBC" (71%), though less so for "large nationally influential newspapers such as the *New York Times* and the *Washington Post* (47%). Most strikingly, these figures have been remarkably stable, bouncing around within a limited range since they were first asked for all but cable in the summer of 1985.

To be sure, as the Pew Research Center (1998a) documented in the spring of 1998, news is less important as a pleasurable daily activity (especially among younger cohorts). Large audiences follow national and international news only when big stories have already drawn their attention.[5] However, the general lack of confidence that the people accord to the news media or to journalists does not prevent them from approving the day-to-day practice of the news outlets they attend to.

Second, the public has never been, for better or worse, pivotal to the ability of the news media to act as an intermediary political institution. After all, the utility of the news media in achieving political and policy goals of government officials and activists can be accomplished without the public directly weighing in. Much of what the media do – particularly in Washington but elsewhere in American politics as well – is to facilitate communication within and among policy elites at least as much as from those elites to the public at large. Moreover, the effect of coverage is not necessarily to mobilize the public so much as expand the perceived salience of an issue, and thereby enhance the extent to which political actors may have to account for their actions (or even more problematic, their inactions) down the road, whether or not that accounting ever takes place (Price 1978; Arnold 1990). To recall what I once heard as the first rule of lobbying, "People act differently when they know they're being watched."

Since my book appeared, two new indications have emerged to reinforce how much the public is out of the loop – even when political actors are called upon to gauge "public opinion." One is Herbst's (1998) exploration in the Illinois state capital of political actors' concepts of public opinion. She found from conversations with activists, statehouse beat journalists, and legislative staffers that only the activists tended to rely on polls as key measures of what the public thought. Her results underscore longstanding conclusions of sociological research on journalists: They tend to disdain if not fear their mass audiences; the main way in which they overtly attend to their readers and viewers is by softening the news; and the greater profit-mindedness of the news media is handled less by attending closely to the audience and more by cutting costs. Of particular importance is Herbst's finding that, even nowadays with the omnipresence of polls, the legislative staffers tended to see media coverage as being a better (not simply more immediately available) indicator of public opinion than surveys themselves.

Herbst's qualitative work has found quantitative confirmation from a survey conducted by the Pew Research Center (1998d) of 81 members of Congress, 98 presidential appointees, and 151 civil servants in the Senior Executive Service. All three sets of respondents show relatively high disagreement with the statement that "Americans know enough about issues to form wise opinions about what should be done".[6] In addition, they were likely not to rely on polls, even among members of Congress, for instance, who viewed the public more favorably than their executive branch colleagues. When asked about their principal sources of information on how the public feels about issues – and, importantly, allowed multiple responses – legislators pointed to personal contacts (59%), letters and phone calls (36%), and even the media (31%) before public opinion polls (24%). Moreover, 76% of presidential appointees and 84% of civil servants listed the media as a main source of information about public opinion. This poll also provides impressive additional quantitative evidence of the extent to which Washington leaders are far heavier consumers of news than the public as a whole (cf. Weiss 1974). In addition to near-unanimous regular reading of the *Washing-*

ton Post, strong majorities of all three groups reported regularly or sometimes watching network news and CNN, listening to NPR, and reading the *New York Times* and the *Wall Street Journal* (Pew 1998d, Q31). Familiarity in this case does not breed contempt. All three sets of elite respondents replied that their overall opinion of the news media was very or mostly favorable – 61% of members of Congress, 60% of presidential appointees, and 62% of senior civil servants – substantially higher than the 50% of the general public who gave that ranking to the same question in a contemporary survey (Pew 1998d, Q6).

In short, the declining legitimacy of the news media as a whole among the public has obscured citizens' continuingly strong endorsement of the job that their preferred news outlets are doing, not to mention the esteem of Washington elites, who not only see communication as a key purpose of their work and tend not merely to be heavier news consumers but also evaluate the news media more favorably than the public as a whole. And such attitudes do not even address the extent to which the news media, whether one likes them or not, are helpful for elites doing their jobs and for the mass public seeking to reassure themselves that nothing happened in the previous week/day/hour that they needed to know and act upon. The news media, in short, could well be performing as an intermediary political institution, especially though not exclusively among political elites, regardless of their public popularity or perceived legitimacy.

CONCLUSION

Neither technology nor economics nor the shifting attitudes of the public will, in and of themselves, provoke a decline of the news media's new, largely inadvertent, role as an intermediary political institution. Instead, the continued power that the news media hold owes much to the calculations of political actors who, seeking to get something done in an ever more complex and balky political system, turn to the news media to help them accomplish their goals. The news media's power is then not because the people are in thrall to them. On the contrary, if political elites acted differently, the power of the news media might well be drastically diminished. But in an increasingly complicated, quite possibly ungovernable, political system, the news media provide a key resource for political elites and activists to get something done; that is unlikely to change in the absence of stark shifts in the makeup and structure of the political system as a whole.

Just because the news hole for politics is diminishing and therefore less accessible to any given political actor, and just because it is more difficult to target a particular news outlet or set of news outlets that will reach the majority of the American people, in the way that, say, Ronald Reagan's White House aimed for (if not at) the network news, we cannot say that political actors will become any less media-minded. Certainly a lesson of the early months of the Clinton presidency was that an end-run around the Washington press corps, via the circuit extended interviews that candidate Clinton had used so well, was unlikely to be enough publicity in and of itself. And whatever else the Starr Report might symbolize, its release by the House Judiciary Committee over the Internet has also been taken by some to signal a new era of political communication where members of the Washington elite can directly link up to the public instantaneously; yet in fact, if the Pew Research Center's (1998b) figures are correct, just under half of their survey respondents in mid-September 1998 had read "any part of the actual report," and of those, around 22% had read it on-line – an impressive amount, perhaps, but inflated by the Pew Center's acceptance of multiple responses, and fewer than those who said they had read it in a newspaper (56% of the report readers) or had heard excerpts on television (30% of the report readers). Whatever direct information citizens or other members of the elite receive seems still to be put into the context of the communication provided by the news media.

Ironically, the multiplication of news sources only makes it more imperative for political actors to target the media. In a way, I am reminded of words I wrote almost a decade ago about members of the U.S. House of Representatives that, now, probably extends to any political actors wanting to exert influence through the news:

Press secretaries [to House members] rarely rely on any one medium because none satisfies all four of their crucial criteria: access, a large audience, high credibility, and control of the final product . . . Outlets with large audiences and high credibility, such as television, offer less access and control over the final message. Those that provide easy access and substantial control, such as local weeklies and newsletters, offer small audiences and only moderate credibility. The one medium that performs least poorly in all these criteria is the local daily newspaper. But press secretaries cannot concentrate exclusively on them: getting publicity is simply too uncertain a process. As far as House press operations are concerned, the more lines of communication, the better (Cook 1989, p. 100).

In short, we should not expect the news media to move away from being a political institution, nor should we anticipate that political actors will become frustrated and try to find other ways of governing. True, there are still empirical questions that remain to be answered. The argument I set forth here was inspired by Cater's (1959) initial formulation that saw the press as becoming a "fourth branch of government" because of the unique American system of, in Neustadt's (1960) words, "separated institutions sharing power." It may be, however, that the rise of the news media as a political institution has less to do with the arrangement of the U.S. Constitution, and more to do with the news media themselves. And if it is true that the news media beyond the United States are becoming "Americanized" themselves, as globalization and privatization take hold, the news media may have emerged as an intermediary and at least partially independent political institution in other countries as well. Clearly, comparative work needs to be carried out if we are to understand whether it is the legally established political system, the public policies thereby pursued, or the nature of the press itself within a country that ends up politically empowering the news media.

And such research seems eminently worth pursuing, given the ways in which the news media do not contribute well to the current state and future prospects of a democratic political system. Throughout the twentieth century, the American news media have tended to see their audiences less as citizens requiring information to intercede in politics and more as consumers seeking ways to spend their disposable income (Baldasty 1992). And as political elites find getting into the news increasingly beneficial for their policies and programmatic goals, they have had to adapt their activities to the news values that do not contribute much to good, let alone democratic decision making. The irony then is that a "free press," conceived as a "bulwark of liberty," does less to enhance the people's performance as citizens, and much more to bolster the economic power of news organizations and the political power of elites.

NOTES

1. Polls asking respondents if they went on-line for news at least once a week show an increase from 4% in 1995 to 20% in 1998 (Pew Research Center 1998a).

2. I put "the press" in quotes to note that we may have strong question effects if we ask, variously, "the press," "the news media," "reporters," "journalists," etc.

3. Ironically, the attention that one news outlets gives to journalistic mistakes are part of what Bennett et al. (1985) call "repair work," designed to boost the authority of the news and safeguard the agreed-upon methods from criticism. Like Tuchman's (1972) "strategic ritual of objectivity," we may wonder if it works on the mass public as effectively as we once thought – though whether it works on the journalists themselves may be another matter.

4. *Newsweek* poll conducted by Princeton Survey Research Associates, July 9–10, 1998, question R09, accessed from the POLL archive of the Roper Center for Public Opinion Research, University of Connecticut. See also the Media Studies Center poll discussed by McClain (1998) that noted that relatively few people had heard of the June scandals (the highest was 42% reporting hearing of the CNN/*Time* retraction of the nerve gas report) but large majorities concluded that journalists often or sometimes: invent stories, plagiarize, use unethical or illegal tactics, and have factual errors.

5. "A substantial minority of Americans (46%) *only* follow national news when something major is happening and an even greater number (63%) react the same way to international news. Only local news attracts a large regular audience that is not event driven – 61% of Americans follow it most of the time" (Pew Center 1998a, p. 2).

6. Not surprisingly, legislators were more positive toward the public, with 31% agreeing, compared to 13% of presidential appointees and 14% of civil servants (Pew 1998d, p. 1).

REFERENCES

Arnold, R. Douglas (1990). *The Logic of Congressional Action*. New Haven: Yale University Press.

Baldasty, Gerald J. (1992). *The Commercialization of News in the Nineteenth Century*. Madison: University of Wisconsin Press.

Bennett, Stephen (1998). "Trust in Government, Trust in the Media: Is There a connection?" Paper presented at the research roundtable series, Shorenstein Center, Kennedy School of Government, Harvard, September 28.

Bennett, W. Lance (1998). "The UnCivic Culture: Communication, Identity, and the Rise of Lifestyle Politics." Ithiel de Sola Pool lecture delivered at American Political Science Association annual meeting, Boston.

Bennett, W. Lance, Lynne A. Gressett, and William Haltom (1985). "Repairing the News: A Case Study of the News Paradigm." *Journal of Communication*, 35(2):50–68.

Cater, Douglass (1959). *The Fourth Branch of Government*. Boston: Houghton Mifflin.

Cook, Timothy E. (1989). *Making Laws and Making News*. Washington, DC: Brookings Institution.

(1998). *Governing with the News*. Chicago: University of Chicago Press.

Crouse Timothy (1973). *The Boys on the Bus*. New York: Ballantine.

Davis, Richard (1999). *The Web of Politics*. New York: Oxford University Press.

Dennis, Jack (1975). Trends in public support for the American party system. *British Journal of Political Science*, 5:187–230.

Eliasoph, Nina (1988). "Routines and the Making of Oppositional News." *Critical Studies in Mass Communication,* 5:313–334.

Epstein, Edward Jay (1973). *News from Nowhere: Television and the News.* New York: Vintage.

Fishman, Mark (1980). *Manufacturing the News.* Austin: University of Texas Press.

FitzSimon, Martha, and Lawrence T. McGill (1995). "The Citizen as Media Critic." *Media Studies Journal,* 9(2):91–101.

Gans, Herbert J. (1979). *Deciding What's News.* New York: Vintage.

Gergen, David R. (1984). The message to the media. *Public Opinion,* 7(2):5–8.

Graber, Doris A. (1984). *Processing the News.* New York: Longman.

Herbst, Susan (1998). *Reading Public Opinion.* Chicago: University of Chicago Press.

Hibbing, John, and Elizabeth Theiss-Morse (1995). *Congress as Public Enemy.* New York: Cambridge University Press.

Kimball, Penn (1994). *Downsizing the News.* Washington, DC: Woodrow Wilson Center Press.

Lichter, S. Robert, Stanley Rothman, and Linda S. Lichter (1986). *The Media Elite.* Bethesda, MD: Adler and Adler.

Lipset, Seymour Martin, and William Schneider (1987). *The Confidence Gap* (rev. ed.). Baltimore: Johns Hopkins University Press.

McClain, Dylan Loeb (1998). "Scandals Don't Much Harm an Already Bad Reputation." *New York Times* (October 19, 1998): C4 (New England edition).

McManus, John (1994). *Market-Driven Journalism.* Newbury Park, CA: Sage.

Neustadt, Richard E. (1960). *Presidential Power.* New York: Wiley.

Page, Benjamin I. (1996). *Who Deliberates?* Chicago: University of Chicago Press.

Pew Research Center for the People and the Press (1998a). "Internet News Takes Off: Event-driven News Audiences." Press release, June 8. Available on-line at http://www.people-press.org/med98rpt.htm, with questionnaire results at http://www.people-press.org/med98que.htm.

(1998b). "Pew's Poll Numbers: Clinton Moral Authority Slips: Phone Calls, Not Polls, May Sway Congress: 20 Million Go Online for Starr Report." Press release, September 17. Available on-line at http://www.people-press.org/starrrpt.htm with questionnaire results at http://www.people-press.org/starrque.htm.

(1998c). Popular Policies and Unpopular Press Lift Clinton Ratings: Scandal Reporting Faulted for Bias and Inaccuracy." Press release, February 6. Available on-line at http://www.people-press.org/feb98rpt.htm with questionnaire results at http://www.people-press.org/feb98que.htm.

(1998d). "Washington Leaders Wary of Public Opinion: Public Appetite for Government Misjudged." Press release, April 17. Available on-line at http://www.people-press.org/leadrpt.htm with questionnaire results at http://www.people-press.org/leadque.htm.

(1999a). "Public Votes for Continuity and Change in 2000: Big Doubts About News Media's Values." Press release, February 25. Available on-line at http://www.people-press.org/feb99rpt.htm with questionnaire results at http://www.people-press.org/feb99que.htm.

(1999b). "Striking the Balance: Audience Interests, Business Pressures and Journalists' Values." Press release, March 30. Available on-line at http://www.people-press.org/press99rpt.htm with questionnaire results at http://www.people-press.org/press99que.htm.

Powell, Walter W., and Paul J. DiMaggio (Eds.) (1991). *The New Institutionalism in Organizational Analysis.* Chicago: University of Chicago Press.

Price, David E. (1978). "Policy Making in Congressional Committees." *American Political Science Review,* 72:548–574.

Robinson, John, and Mark Levy (1986). *The Main Source.* Beverly Hills, CA: Sage.

Robinson, Michael J., and Andrew Kohut (1988). "Believability and the Press." *Public Opinion Quarterly,* 52:174–189.

Schneider, William, and I. A. Lewis (1985). "Views on the News." *Public Opinion,* 8(4):6–11, 58–59.

Selznick, Philip (1957). *Leadership in Administration.* Evanston, IL: Row, Peterson and Company.

Sigal, Leon V. (1973). *Reporters and Officials.* Lexington, MA: D.C. Heath.

Smith, Ted J. III, and S. Robert Lichter (1997). *What the People Want from the Press.* Washington, DC: Center for Media and Public Affairs.

Tuchman, Gaye (1972). "Objectivity as Strategic Ritual: An Examination of Newsmen's Notions of Objectivity." *American Journal of Sociology,* 77:660–679.

(1973). Making News by Doing Work: Routinizing the Unexpected. *American Journal of Sociology,* 78:110–131.

(1978). *Making News.* New York: Free Press.

Weaver, David H., and G. Cleveland Wilhoit (1996). *The American Journalist in the 1990s.* Mahwah, NJ: Lawrence Erlbaum Associates.

Weiss, Carol H. (1974). "What America's Leaders Read." *Public Opinion Quarterly* 38:1–22.

Whitney, D. Charles (1985). "The Media and the People – Americans' Experience with the News Media: a Fifty-Year Review." Gannett Center Working Paper.

PART 3

Mediated Political Information and Public Opinion

CHAPTER 10

Reframing Public Opinion as We Have Known It

Robert M. Entman and Susan Herbst

The continuing controversies over media effects on public opinion and democracy can be traced in part to uncertainties about what public opinion is. "Public opinion" is a useful fiction that actually refers to several distinct phenomena, many of them crucially shaped by the current media system. The process of framing – selecting, highlighting, and sorting into a coherent narrative some facts or observations and deleting many others – is critical to the formation of this convenient fiction. Yet the framing process could be altered dramatically by new channels and processes of mediated communication. If that happens, public opinion as we have known it will likely be transformed, altering the way democracy has (imperfectly) worked since mass media became central to its operation. We shall differentiate *public opinion*, by which we mean the loose, usually undefined, and thoroughly protean term used by just about everyone from academics to journalists to citizens and politicans, from four referents that we define more precisely. Once we understand these distinctions we can understand better how *current* mass media influence politics, and how well the public gets represented in a democratic political process shaped by the traditional mass media. Profound changes in the media system now underway demand both far greater conceptual clarity and creative new means of getting at the theoretical concerns that underlie social scientists' longstanding attention to the role of public opinion in democracy.

Those invoking public opinion seem usually to mean the *comprehensive preferences of the majority of individuals on an issue.* (Sometimes they also refer to the other side, to a single minority preference on the issue.) That is, observers imply or say that the majority would gain subjective utility if a particular policy were enacted or candidate elected. By "comprehensive preferences" we mean that most assertions about public opinion imply that a majority of Americans actually would prefer, say, a balanced budget amendment to the U.S. Constitution taking into account all other possible policy outcomes. There are many well-known problems with the assumptions built into such readings of the public's sentiments. Among the sources of these uncertainties are measurement problems, contradictions in beliefs, sentiments based in debatable perceptions that with alteration might change radically, aggregation dilemmas (i.e., the indeterminacy of majority opinion as soon as we consider trade-offs among more than two issues at the same time),[1] and nonattitudes (i.e., the absence of real opinions about many issues).

This is not to say that individuals don't have real (if perhaps evanescent) preferences, but discovering what they are and what they'd be with altered information, distinguishing real ones from nonattitudes and erroneously measured ones, determining trade-offs and then aggregating them into a useful summary characterization require selecting aspects of reality and ignoring many others – or framing (Entman 1993). When people invoke public opinion, then, they selectively highlight some elements of the difficult-to-know reality of individuals' thinking and omit lots of others. The current media system, because it gathers elites and mass publics into a common information space that largely highlights and repeats the same themes, facilitates this framing process and thus a sense that public opinion is a meaningful concept.

Yet a fair reading of all the survey evidence on any issue most often yields a shrug of the shoulders. Consider the balanced budget. In a March 1995 ABC/Washington Post survey, respondents' support for a budget-balancing amendment to the U.S. Constitution was premised on one condition: that it not lead to cuts in Social Security. Nearly 80 percent favored the amendment, but eight in ten respondents also rejected the idea that balancing the budget would require Social Security cuts; a smaller majority, 58 percent, said tax increases wouldn't be necessary either. If it came to a choice, 72 percent said protecting Social Security was more important than balancing the budget. Did public opinion favor the balanced budget amendment or not? Events between 1995 and 1998 reveal that it *was* necessary to raise taxes to balance the budget (at least if we wanted to by 1998 or any foreseeable future). Does that mean public opinion in March 1995 actually opposed a balanced budget? Or that if asked in 1998, a majority of Americans would have preferred at that time to repeal the Bush and Clinton tax increases (mostly on the rich) rather than putting up with the budget being balanced that year – and with attendant benefits such as low mortgage and unemployment rates?

Another example comes from the prewar debate on Iraq in 1990. As Mueller (1994, p. 82) writes:

> While it is possible to argue from some data that there was something of a movement toward greater hawkishness during this period, other data indicate something of a movement toward dovishness, and there are considerable data to suggest that there was no change at all.

Mueller's book-length study documents that the looming and then ongoing war was subjected to perhaps the most intense, even fulsome, public opinion surveying of any short-term policy issue ever. Yet Mueller shows that the total does not yield a clear picture of real public desires or even a clear survey majority prior to the war.

We cannot know public opinion definitively, via either surveys or other forms of evidence, which are at least as problematic and subject to framing. But this doesn't mean the opinions of ordinary members of the public are irrelevant to the democratic process, or that media have no real influence on them. We identify four referents of the term public opinion. They are more consistently knowable, they are influenced by mass media, and they affect government.

As preface: We are not arguing that mediated politics caused certain referents or types of public opinion to appear on the American political scene, but simply that mediated politics valorizes some meanings of public opinion over others. Many of the referents we discuss in the next section have long been found in political discourse – before the age of broadcast media, for example. Yet they appear, disappear, and reappear when they are deemed useful by powerful institutions and actors (on the historical contingency of public opinion referents, see Habermas 1989 or Herbst 1993).

REFERENTS OF PUBLIC OPINION

The four referents of public opinion are not, by any means, the only possible forms public opinion might take within the context of public discourse and policy making. And this simple four-fold classification does not reflect the long intellectual history of combat over the meaning of public opinion (see Herbst 1993). Yet for the purposes of understanding the ways public opinion is evoked at the end of the twentieth century, in national policy debates and legislative action, delineating these four forms of public opinion proves illuminating.

Mass Opinion

The first form of public opinion is *mass opinion*. This is the aggregation or summation of individual preferences as tabulated through opinion polls, referenda, or elections. It is simply the "will of all" that Rousseau wrote about in *The Social Contract* (1762): the result of adding citizen opinions together, regardless of how informed or tightly held these beliefs happen to be. Mass opinion is vital to a democracy, as Rousseau knew and as we today know. There are times when policy issues are fairly straightforward and a simple query to the public about its preferences yields a useful aggregate. One instance is capital punishment. This is a topic about which most people appear to have strong and consistent opinions: Most citizens have wrestled with the topic and really do know how they feel. Yet, most issues are unlike this: They are fluid social, economic, and political problems far from most persons' confident grasp. They may opine so forcefully and confidently on capital punishment because crime and punishment are something they feel they understand, that they are or could be close to. But to voice preferences on the Israeli-Palestinian question or Social Security demands a fairly intricate and historically informed sort of political knowledge. So mass opinion is useful in some instances, when details are within the comprehension of most, but on many other issues, lack of understanding about all aspects of the issue prevents typical citizens from producing a considered opinion.

Some have argued for *low information rationality* (Popkin 1991; Lupia and McCubbins 1998), noting that mass opinion – the opinions we get from polling, for example – is useful because people need very few cues to produce a rational opinion or an opinion that reflects their own interests. This paradigm has many appeals, but its deficiencies outweigh them, including its lack of much empirical support. Few who care about democracy, who believe that citizens should be engaged in discourse and in the policy-making process, should be happy with low information rationality. Yes, people get cues from elites about which way to lean when casting a vote or deciding between two crude alternatives. But one cannot become an educated and subtle-minded citizen in any democracy by remaining mostly ignorant and taking cues from political parties or elites whom they seem to agree with.

Mass opinion, then, is problematic because it is not informed opinion. There are, undoubtedly, many respondents in a typical opinion poll who are the kinds of citizens we applaud in democratic theorizing – well-informed, motivated to learn about policy, and engaged in argumentation with friends, neighbors, and colleagues. But most respondents are not "ideal" citizens, and indeed the uneven information levels among citizens skew results of opinion polls – chief indicators of mass opinion – in significant and troubling ways (Althaus 1998). Most worrisome is that mass opinion, because it is not typically reflective of thoughtful, informed citizen preferences (polls, for example, are often brief or conducted before extended public debate has occurred) are quite malleable. The media, in particular, have great ability to shape mass opinion through framing issues in particular ways, limiting certain types of information in their reporting on public affairs, and the like. We now have decades of research that demonstrate how media influence mass opinion, but it is important to keep in mind that mass opinion can be swayed because it is – at base and in the main – unstable and superficial.

ACTIVATED PUBLIC OPINION

The second type of public opinion of import here is what we call *activated public opinion*. These are the opinions of engaged, informed, and organized citizens – those who are mobilizable during campaign periods and between elections as well. Political science tells us who these citizens are: party loyalists, local community activists, interest group spokespersons, opinion leaders, and others who pay close attention to the political realm. Policy makers have long heeded activated public opinion because it is the public opinion that matters most often in day-to-day policy making, as empirical research has begun to demonstrate (Herbst 1998a; Jacobs and Shapiro 2000). Indeed, Herbert Blumer (1948) argued that mass opinion is not particularly useful because it ignores the sociological truth about politics: People with power and resources, closely engaged in politics, compose the public opinion that matters. Blumer argued fiercely against the interchangeability of mass opinion (polling data) and public opinion, because he believed that they were far from synonymous if we are to describe political reality.

Interestingly, the media are not as influential on the politically engaged because they have strong opinions, formed with consideration and tied to coherent and deeply felt ideology. Unlike mass opinion, which is more likely swayed by the mass media, highly educated and engaged citizens are most often resistant to messages that run counter to their belief systems very much in the ways that Klapper (1960) first wrote about selective exposure and retention of media content. On one level, and from the perspective of democratic theory, the fact that citizens in this group resist (and indeed argue with) media content coming into their living rooms is comforting: These are people who know how they feel and hold tight to their preferences. Yet, the citizens who fit under the category of activated public opinion are small in number, as we have known for some time now (e.g., Converse 1964). The ideal public sphere would be teeming with active citizens, but at the close of the twentieth century, the United States and other industrialized democracies were far from Jürgen Habermas's (1989) ideal state of public communication.

LATENT PUBLIC OPINION

The third category is what V. O. Key called *latent public opinion* (Key 1961; Zaller 1998) – the fundamental public preferences that underlie more fleeting and superficial opinions we find when conducting polls of the mass public. Latent opinion, in short, is where public opinion will "end up" after a policy debate has progressed or what people truly feel beneath all the chaos and shifting opinion we see in the heat of democratic practice. The most successful leaders are those who can sense latent opinion – who understand the dynamics of public opinion beneath the discursive chaos. In the nineteenth century, for example, party bosses were excellent at sensing latent opinion (see Herbst 1993). They had such a thorough understanding of public preferences, gained through sustained political experience and close contact with constituents, that they could predict with some accuracy where – at the end of the day – public opinion would be. Key knew that latent opinion was difficult to measure, but he also understood, in ways that have been lost in the political science literature (see Zaller 1998), that this form of opinion was different from mass opinion and mattered quite a lot in the policy-making process. From our perspective, it is likely that the effective politician measures latent opinion – perhaps the most important form of public opinion – through multiple venues: mass opinion measures (polls), activated opinion, communication with colleagues, experience in politics, and – most nebulously – an instinct for what his or her constituencies truly value. One might argue, in fact, that if a leader understands the latter – the fundamental, core values of majorities – he or she can ignore opinion polls and other superficial measures of public opinion altogether. A dangerous game, no doubt, but tempting in an age when polls conflict, survey response rates drop, and people remain as uninformed about politics as ever.

PERCEIVED MAJORITIES

The final referent that observers who invoke public opinion may wittingly or unwittingly be describing is *perceived majorities*. Perceived majorities are the perceptions held by most observers, including journalists, politicians, and members of the public themselves, of where the majority of the public stands on an issue. This is the convenient fiction observers use to characterize the comprehensive preferences of a majority of citizens despite all the problems we've seen in accepting any such summary labels as valid. Media may not affect the *actual* sentiments of individual citizens. And those sentiments may typically be more complicated or superficial or volatile than suggested by confident descriptions of what "the American people believe" or "the public demands." Still, news reports do shape the majority opinions that are widely *perceived* to exist. By helping to form these perceived majorities, a kind of reification of public opinion (Herbst 1993, p. 46; cf. Lippmann 1925 and Bordieu 1979) media reports may affect the actions of governing elites and perhaps the other aspects of public opinion (i.e., mass opinion, activated opinion, and latent opinion). If the media keep asserting that the public holds a particular view, the resulting perceptions of public desires – perceived majorities – can shape actual behavior by government and citizens. Many of the strategic campaigns described by Bennett and Manheim in Chap. 13 are designed to influence, or actually influence, perceived majorities rather than mass opinion itself.

Congruence between the majority sentiments widely perceived to exist and those that actually obtain (insofar as we can know them) is best conceived as a variable. For example, during most of the Reagan administration, media were replete with assertions of his great popularity with Americans. Yet presidential approval polls during his first term actually made him the least popular president, on average, since systematic polling began (King and Schudson 1991). Nonetheless, the widely shared perception of Reagan as massively popular bolstered his political clout. Politicians and journalists frequently ignore survey results in characterizing public opinion, in part because the data are often so contradictory and in part because neglecting polls is strategically useful. Since they can usually find some poll somewhere that backs their preferred reading of majority sentiment, elites typically just sound off about what the people allegedly believe. Significant political capital goes into the contest among politicians and groups to induce the media to depict majority opinion in desired ways. A 1998 survey of Congress members ($n = 81$), presidential appointees ($n = 98$), and Senior Executive Service workers ($n = 151$) (Pew 1998) suggests that such investments of political energy in shaping media depictions of public opinion are indeed worthwhile. The survey found that news media reports rather than polls provide the most important source for executive branch elites' perceptions of "public opinion."

Why are typologies of public opinion referents useful to scholars? For one thing, these typologies underscore the dynamic nature of discourse about public opinion. As Habermas has so clearly demonstrated, public opinion is a moving, historically situated target, and our language for discussing it must therefore be complex, subtle, and exacting. Typologies enable scholars to discern which referent is being used by a particular actor or institution, and also force us to ask why others are inappropriate or are ignored. Second, political actors themselves hold varied meanings of public opinion in their heads, simultaneously, so even in the unlikely event that scholars could come to consensus on a meaning of public opinion, real political actors could not and would not (see Herbst 1998). Finally, if we are ever to trace the impact or impotence of public opinion in politics, we can only do so by looking for its multiple forms. If we stay focused on only one referent or way of defining public opinion, we miss others and therefore miss their effects on the political process.

REPRESENTATION OF PUBLIC OPINION

Exactly how can the aforementioned conceptual distinctions enhance understanding of public opinion and democracy? In this section we illustrate the usefulness by focusing on the representation of public opinion, specifically with respect to defense spending. Recently the dominant trend in scholarly discussions has been to offer optimistic readings of how well public opinion is represented in U.S. democracy. We suggest that such complaisant interpretations of public opinion's putatively powerful impacts require further specification and qualification in light of our distinctions.

To come up with a reading of public opinion requires *framing*, that is, selecting and highlighting some elements of alleged public sentiments while neglecting other elements. As we wrote in the first section, on most public policy issues there is no determinate public opinion; what scholars are really talking about when they probe the representation of public opinion is *mass opinion*. The framing process that produces mass opinion is a product of both strategic and haphazard interactions among media, government, events, and pollsters. Executive branch and congressional party leaders seek to dominate mass opinion (and its perception by others with political power) by trying to impose their framing of public opinion on media coverage. In a somewhat analogous way, scholars claiming to represent public opinion through their research data and analyses also engage in framing. Since they have no way of truly capturing public thinking in all its dimensions, they actually employ selected aspects of public sentiment captured by polls – they use mass opinion as a surrogate for public opinion, and this creates difficulties for empirical theory and normative judgment.

There are numerous studies in political science that choose a particular referent for public opinion – often the aggregation of individual opinions – and then draw conclusions about broad opinion dynamics from there, building theory about democratic practice. For example, in their important work on the relationship between public opinion and public policy directions, Page and Shapiro (1992) rely solely on survey data as referent of public opinion. This is justifiable given the focus of their argument, but does mean that other forms or referents of public opinion that fail to influence policy or influence it in entirely different ways than aggregate opinion are omitted. For this essay, we'd like to examine another study – the influential article on representation of public opinion in defense policy by Thomas Hartley and Bruce Russett (1992). They link normative democratic theory with empirical data to ask "Who governs military spending in the United States?" They answer that "public opinion" helps "govern." Hartley and Russett's study (cf. Bartels 1991) demonstrates the difficulty of reaching such a conclusion; for, despite their creativity, the authors neglect problems of measurement, causality, and variation. We cannot conclude, as these authors do, that the public consistently exerts significant independent impact over foreign and defense policy makers. If much of the public opinion to which these authors say officials respond is actually mass opinion, then we may not have much of an empirical basis for inferring anything definitive about which way the power flows. A close examination of this research is worthwhile because it typifies the dominant, sanguine thrust in empirical studies of public opinion and democracy toward the end of the century. It exemplifies the problems that arise when the conceptual complexities of measuring and understanding public opinion are too readily passed over.

The study finds that between 1965 and 1990, "changes in public opinion consistently exert an effect on changes in military spending." (Hartley and Russett 1992, p. 905). It measures public opinion by responses to a single, repeatedly used survey question: whether government is spending too little, too much, or about the right amount on defense. Changes in the levels of too little (or too much) responses significantly predict alteration in the total defense obligations Congress approves (p. 907). On this basis Hartley and Russett argue that, judging by the case of defense spending, Congress is responsive to public opinion, fulfilling its representative duties according to at least one reasonable version of democracy. In essence, Russett and Hartley claim that the large increases in defense spending of those years were *responses to independent changes in the defense policy preferences that led to a majority of Americans favoring higher spending*. To assess the findings and inferences here, we focus on the period encompassing the Carter and Reagan administrations (1977–89), which saw the widest swings in public sentiment and thus the best opportunity for congressional responsiveness, although similar arguments could be made for the Johnson and Nixon years.

The Hartley–Russett piece, like most in this realm, neglects the many imperfections of survey research in practice and even in theory as a means of discerning individuals' genuine beliefs and preferences (Schuman and Presser 1981; Zaller 1992). It also passes over the difficulties of aggregating individual responses to identify a singular public opinion. We know that surveys through the 1970s and 1980s registered consistent support for higher levels of government services *and* lower taxes *and* lower deficits. What is the real public opinion to which Congress should or could have responded? Indeed, in this case as in most, we cannot even determine a clear mass opinion, let alone true preference rankings and preferred trade-offs. As Bartels (1991, p. 466) notes, there were simultaneous public demands for "social programs, tax reduction, and fiscal responsibility," which "manifestly limited the ability of Congress to respond to each of them separately." In this sense, it would appear nearly arbitrary to pick one dimension where mass opinion and Congressional action coincide, while neglecting others where they did not and draw any general conclusions on government responsiveness.

On some issues, the aggregate of the public's responses to polls – mass opinion – can be quite stable over many years. But mass opinion on any *specific* proposal is usually measured when it is politically relevant, such as during an election or a congressional vote. This point highlights the limitation of the Yankelovich theory (cf. Page and Shapiro 1992), that public opinion may be ignorant and volatile when an issue first emerges but then matures and settles down as the public in aggregate has a chance to learn and deliberate. For political purposes, in the typical case the public may not have enough time to deliberate, because the government has moved on to new issues before sufficient time has passed. What we usually get in polls is opinion at the early stage, when the public's answers are most unstable and susceptible to framing effects. In any case, though mass opinion might consistently back, say, a balanced budget and lower taxes, the relevance and congruence of these apple pie generalities to specific policy proposals before legislatures, executive agencies, and courts is usually problematic. Making them line up, for example, by claiming a particular law fulfills majority preferences, requires framing: selecting some manifestations of public sentiment and some elements of the law, and ignoring many others.

It seems difficult to justify selecting one strain of opinion tapped by the single defense spending question, while ignoring the indubitable failure of Congress to respond to other strains. Congress failed to insist that Reagan approach nuclear negotiations seriously in his first term (see Talbott 1984 on Reagan's negotiating approach), let alone to approve a nuclear freeze. Yet surveys showed the majorities favoring such action, often by upward of 75 percent (Entman and Rojecki 1993). If, reversing the Hartley–Russett approach, one used the survey data only on the nuclear freeze while ignoring the data on defense spending, one might well conclude Congress was entirely unresponsive to the public in the defense policy area.

Most noticeable in this period is the lack of representation from 1982 to 1985, when Congress raised defense spending despite the sharp dovish turn in mass opinion. Surveyed sentiment shifted even more sharply away from defense spending during this time than it had turned toward support between 1977 and 1981, so if Congress was responsive to altered public sentiment, we would expect a cut in defense by 1982 or 1983. Yet defense spending began declining in real terms only in *fiscal 1990*. Consider Figure 10.1, showing spending and survey results for 1980–90. Defense allocations kept growing as public support declined.

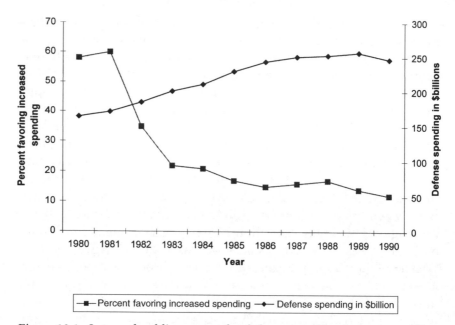

Figure 10.1. Surveyed public support for defense spending drops as spending increases. *Source:* Historical tables, *Budget of the United States Government, Fiscal 1992*, pp. 69–70; constant 1982 dollars. Survey data from Hartley and Russett.

The *rate* of growth in spending began slowing notably in fiscal 1987 (Entman and Rojecki 1993), which might have been a response to perceived majorities. But counting decisions that persist for eight years (1982–89) against both the overall dovish *movement* in opinion and the dovish *plurality* as "democratic responsiveness" would stretch most theories of democracy, including Hartley and Russett's, beyond recognition. To be sure, one major reason for continued budget growth during this period is that long-term commitments to weapons systems had been made in previous years (rarely does Congress stop after paying for half a submarine or bomber). More important, spending momentum is reinforced by electoral incentives in specific Congressional districts where military spending is more than a pork barrel and more like a lifeline; their representatives often exert disproportionate influence over defense budgets. But these points only underscore the complexity of generalizing about government responsiveness to public opinion.

Further, although surveys did not ask, surely few Americans preferred defense money to be spent with poor congressional analysis and oversight, by a Pentagon bureaucracy ill-prepared to handle rapid growth and tending to place first priority on turf and prestige rather than on securing the most effective national defense. Yet Congress did allow bureaucratic mismanagement to flourish, as the Pentagon procurement scandal and many studies of noncriminal behavior confirm – not to mention Congressional deliberation on specific projects suffused with pork barrel and logrolling considerations (see Stubbing 1986). Unless we classify only positive acts, not failures to act (or act responsibly), as part of the legislative response, Congress's neglect of careful analysis and oversight suggests a lack of responsiveness to public desires.

Beyond this, available data cannot tell us whether the public wanted the magnitude of increase approved by Congress during the 1980s. A much smaller increase might have been enough to satisfy most Americans. This seems especially likely in view of many other poll findings, some from the very surveys on "more" or "less" government spending that Hartley and Russett use, of large majorities desiring higher budgets for crime fighting, education, health care, or other domestic priorities (Page and Shapiro 1992, Chaps. 2, 4). For example, in 1982 the net polling position (percentage saying "cut back" spending subtracted from that saying "expand") was +52 percent for education, +43 percent for Social Security, and −10 percent for defense (Rielly 1991, p. 11). If respondents had been asked questions directly posing trade-offs (e.g., Would you like to have a 3-percent increase on defense and 3-percent on education and environment, or a 6-percent increase on defense and nothing on education and environment?), majorities even during the most hawkish years might well have favored a much lower defense increase than occurred.

In relying on some poll evidence to conclude that the public really preferred to raise defense spending as much as Congress did, instead of alternative uses of the money, then, scholars must ignore much other polling data. Include all the information at once and the notion of an identifiable public opinion (or "popular will," using Riker's term) dissolves – except as a convenient fiction for political strategists. The cyclical majority problem means that a majority might prefer a to b and c (say, defense spending increases to education increases and tax cuts), but a majority composed of different people might prefer b to a and c (i.e., education over the other two), and a still differently composed majority might most prefer *c* (tax cuts). The cycle goes around with no "correct" resolution. The decision among the three is determined by the structure of political rules and strategic interaction of decision makers, most importantly the framing of the choices so that a particular dimension of the trade-off is highlighted and others repressed (Riker 1986). Acknowledging this requires a far more circumscribed understanding of democratic responsiveness than invoked by Hartley and Russett and many others, including Zaller in Chap. 12, who write on public opinion and democracy. The larger point is that public opinion includes a variety of individual preferences and intensities, contradictions and harmonies, which are varyingly susceptible to measurement and aggregation (cf. Herbst 1993, 1998b; see Page and Shapiro 1992, pp. 263–74 on the twists and turns in public and elite opinion). As for measuring government response, aside from whatever Congress as a whole decided, the degree to which individual legislators were responding to mass opinion also varied from member to member. Many voting for increased spending had long propagated alarmist readings of Soviet intentions and thus "responded" to mass opinion or activated public opinion they helped engender, while others more genuinely responded, voting for more spending than they seemed to prefer personally (Bartels 1991).

In this jumbled spiral, this double helix, of reciprocal influences, movements, and resistances among elites and mass public, empirical research should at the minimum recognize that neither the public's actual individual preferences nor mass opinion registered in surveys change entirely independently. To their credit, Hartley and Russett do raise the possibility that public opinion is a dependent variable, but they conclude that changes in defense spending do not cause parallel changes in opinion. Hence, they argue, public opinion is an independent causal force shaping defense policy. However, their failure to detect a statistical relationship between actual level of defense spending and the public's preferred defense budgetary direction raises an important puzzle. It would be difficult to understand, let alone represent, a citizenry that remained indifferent to current levels of defense spending when deciding whether budgets should increase or decrease. The poll response itself could not be interpreted – a "too little" or a "too much" response would appear meaningless – if we assume respondents do not know or assess current spending levels. Yet just such a disengaged public and empty survey responses are implied if we accept Hartley and Russett's finding that spending levels have no influence on mass opinion. Thus, in discussing the representation by government of public

Table 10.1. *Surveyed opinion on defense spending increases and number of Soviet threat stories*

Year	Percent favor more spending	Number of USSR threat stories
1977	33	149
1978	37	176
1979	40	232
1980	58	527
1981	60	385
1982	35	305
1983	22	432
1984	21	212
1985	17	186
1986	15	170
1987	16	211
1988	17	154
1989	14	103
1990	12	139

Source: Hartley and Russett (Percent favor more spending); Analysis by authors of *Washington Post* coverage (Number of USSR threat stories).

opinion, the dilemma of causality cannot be neglected: Where did the opinions aggregated into the public opinion come from? In fact, the degree of Soviet threat represented in the mass media corresponds closely to the movement of mass opinion. The data displayed in Table 10.1 result from searching all *Washington Post* stories, beginning in 1977 when computer archives were first available, where the words "Russia" or "Soviet" were juxtaposed within twenty-five words of the words aggression, buildup, or threat. Each story was checked to ensure the assertions containing the terms did refer to the USSR's actions or intentions (spending opinion data from Hartley and Russett 1990, p. 909). The relationship also graphs nicely, as shown in Figure 10.2.

The correlation is quite high for this kind of research (Pearson's $r = 0.69$, $p < 0.01$), and the measure is not even very refined. With enough searching and fine tuning one could probably come up with a media statistic that matched the movement of public opinion even more precisely.[2] Indeed, if the media measure were entered into the Hartley–Russett calculations and the survey data omitted, one might conclude

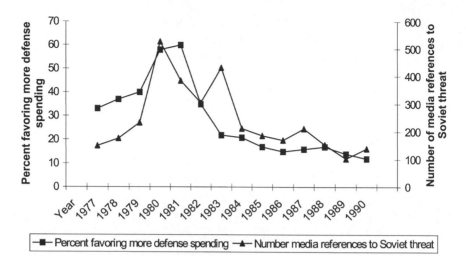

Figure 10.2. Surveyed opinion parallels media references to Soviet threat. *Source*: Hartley and Russett (Percent favoring more defense spending); analysis by the authors of *Washington Post* coverage (Media references to Soviet threats).

that Congress is highly responsive to *media images* rather than to public opinion. Our purpose is not to argue that position, but rather to emphasize the usefulness of distinguishing among different referents of public opinion for grasping the intermingling, simultaneous forces shaping both public sentiments and government decisions.

On balance, it appears unwarranted for Hartley and Russett to assert that their results offer "strong evidence" that public opinion exerts independent influence over policy (pp. 911–12), and thus that "institutions that maintain public control over government" are not "losing their efficacy." To have "strong" evidence for public *control*, research would have to show that mass opinion not only influences but is independent of elite pronouncements, government policy, and media messages. To supplement the terminology of independence and control, and the statistical methods implied by the terms, research should begin exploring the possibility of a public and government locked in interdependent embrace (cf. Jacobs and Shapiro 1992 for further consideration of this issue for the Johnson administration). Untangling the relationships here is enormously difficult: Perceived public sentiments are influenced by elites and policy; all three influence and are influenced by media; and obtainable measures of elite and mass opinion, of policy, and of media content are deeply problematic. Short of acknowledging and probing this complexity, evidence for the independent influence of public opinion on policy, or for democratic control of government by the public, is likely to fall short.

The dramatic divergence between surveyed opinion and public policy during most of the 1980s suggests the need to develop more inclusive models that can explain the many spells of clear unresponsiveness as well as those that seem to indicate responsiveness, the episodes where mass opinion changes independent of elite information blitzes and the instances where Americans seem either to voice eager support of the White House or remain quiescent despite government policy that violates their expressed policy desires. Public opinion – actually, mass opinion – appears to be a sporadic constraint, not a controlling force to which government develops any kind of one-to-one correspondence. Meanwhile, greater attention should be paid to the impacts of activated opinion and perceived majorities in reinforcing policy choices that, like the defense spending hikes of the 1980s, clash with indicators of mass opinion.

ENHANCED STUDY OF PUBLIC OPINION

With the example of defense spending, and in light of our earlier critique of public opinion research, it might seem that we are arguing against the usefulness of surveying. We are not, and to disregard survey methodology as a way of sensing *some aspect* of public opinion would be wrongheaded. The challenge to opinion researchers is to discern the conditions in which different forms of public opinion matter and conditions in which they do not. Let us work through examples where the forms of public opinion noted in this chapter seem most important from an analytical standpoint.

Mass opinion, as a form of public opinion, has its limitations, as noted. It is in many ways the least robust, most malleable, most tentative of all opinion forms. Mass opinion data need to be treated with great care as a result, and should not be bandied about without significant caution and qualification. On the other hand, there are cases where the issues are straightforward, where information is easily accessed by the public, and where citizens talk about the issue and therefore have considered opinions. An example with a clear majority in mass opinion was the 1998 public debate over whether Congress should pursue the impeachment of President Clinton for allegedly perjuring himself and covering up his malfeasance. Through 1998, mass opinion in surveys and in the election results spoke clearly against pursuing impeachment. And this should have been meaningful to representatives in Congress, regardless of their own personal views or views of activated publics. In the case of potential impeachment, the public's survey responses embodied an underlying force and intelligence because the alleged misdeeds were straightforward and the public had been inundated with information about them. In addition, most Americans had engaged in discussion of the issue with family, colleagues, or neighbors, so their opinions were arrived at after some argument and consideration. This is not to say that mass opinion was immutable, but it does seem a moment where mass opinion had a legitimate call to be heeded at least to some extent by politicians. In the event, and prior to their surprisingly weak showing in the 1998 elections, the Republican majority was unmoved by mass opinion, choosing to pursue impeachment vigorously. Many different motivations no doubt propelled Republicans' choice to act against mass opinion, some of them noble, others base, and it may well have been the right decision. Regardless, here (unlike in the case of defense spending), we have both the real world conditions and the data to draw more confident inferences about the degree to which the GOP manifested democratic responsiveness to mass opinion in the United States.[3] Other cases like this would require careful scrutiny.

Activated opinion is vital in any democracy. It is our fantasy, as scholars working to improve democratic practice, that most citizens become part of active publics – writing letters, protesting, forming local political discussion groups, and so forth. But in reality, activated publics are quite small. They are unrepresentative as well, if one is interested in representing a large sector of the American public. Yet if we are to understand the policy-making process, active publics are the ones to watch, and activated public opinion is the entity to measure – active citizens are the ones most often getting represented. In our research about legislative policy staff and who represents public opinion to them (Herbst 1998a) we found that on complex matters that involve trade-offs (tax hikes for education, for example) interest groups – one form of activated public opinion – were more important to staffers than mass opinion could ever be. Most residents of Illinois governed by its legislature are either unaware of particular, complex policy issues or find it difficult to think about trade-offs, while interest groups are skilled at these sorts of analyses. Important also is that interest groups are engaged in the political process, realizing the potential impacts of legislative action. So, for the analyst attempting to understand how public opinion plays a role in policymaking in a legislative setting, it is best to put aside mass opinion in favor of probing activated public opinion.

Latent opinion is an interesting concept in theory, but has remained since Key described it elusive for purposes of policy analysis. One possibility is to look to culture, that is, underlying values and norms, that might help us to predict with more accuracy where public opinion may end up, after the dust of a heated policy debate settles. The study of culture is complex, and while we have an overwhelmingly large array of artifacts that might "tip us off" about underlying societal norms and values (e.g., media content), political scientists have not developed sophisticated tools for the study of culture. Fortunately, we have models in other fields – particularly sociology and cultural history – that we can borrow to discern the infrastructure of American values that help form the somewhat nebulous latent opinion V. O. Key wrote about, with popular entertainment, as Delli Carpini and Williams argue in Chap. 8, a particularly promising vehicle (see Herbst 1998b for examples of analytical tools).

Perceived majorities are perhaps less elusive, at least in theory. One might survey elites (as the Pew Foundation 1998 has about other matters) or mass publics and ask them to describe what they believe to be majority sentiments on a range of issues. Responses in turn could be correlated to media use and behavioral variables. At the same time, media references to the "public mood," the way "most people feel," and the like might be toted up as another form of evidence for wide circulation of claims about "public opinion" that may or may not match other referents. If we are correct in suspecting that perceived majorities often motivate elite behavior on the one hand or legitimize it on the other, careful scholarly attention to the phenomenon would enhance understanding of the play of power in modern mediated democracies.

TOWARD THE FUTURE OF PUBLIC OPINION
AND DEMOCRACY

One implicit argument we have been making in this chapter is that public opinion and mass media are so often conflated and so intricately intertwined that we must consolidate the study of media and public opinion. This was the project of the Columbia School decades ago, and it is a project that must be resuscitated if we are to understand the dynamics of politics and social life in America or any other democracy. Due to the increasing specialization of academic subfields and the great advances in survey methodology, we have allowed opinion research to become disconnected to the study of communication – an odd occurrence that might surprise Paul Lazarsfeld if he were alive today. In this essay, and in this book, we encourage vigilant and simultaneous attention to the interaction of media and public opinion. Political actors themselves understand this conflation (see Herbst 1998a), and it is time we recognize this as well.

In this chapter we described the current public opinion system, based on the framing of political information and data on public opinion by a mass media infrastructure that is crumbling around us. The traditional sources, nightly television news programs and daily newspapers, face growing competition from information genres like talk radio, on-line chat rooms, 24-hour satellite news channels, and customized news reports delivered by e-mail and Web site. Most of these new sources are international if not global, potentially creating a much more complex flow of information and disrupting the media's (and elites') ability to establish dominant frames. Just as important is the competition from increasingly attractive, highly targeted, and differentiated entertainment media whose growing political content may (as Delli Carpini and Williams suggest in Chap. 8) alter media effects on the public opinion system.

In studying the emerging system, predictions are hazardous. But we know the existing public opinion system has relied upon common discourse experiences that might be altered with the rise of so many differentiated channels of mediated communication (cf. Gandy in Chap. 7). Tendencies in the new system are contradictory. The centrifugal push of decentralization and differentiation of communication channels combines with the centripetal pull of allowing more individuals to communicate with each other directly, creating the *potential* for flatter power hierarchies and emergence of what Gamson in Chap. 3 calls "collective action frames" among certain groups. On the other hand, economic and cultural forces may continue to yield largely common political communication experiences for most people. Globalizing communication infrastructures and economic markets could create a steep international hierarchy in which the perspectives of a few countries will dominate the world's mediated communication experiences. Domestically, stratification could also increase: Educated elites might have extraordinarily greater opportunities to gather and share political information among themselves, while the bottom 85 percent fiddle with their remote controls and joysticks (cf. Chap. 14, by Neuman).

Given the several referents of public opinion, and the likely influence of traditional media in shaping them, it may not be an exaggeration to suggest the very nature of public opinion as previously deployed in the political process could change significantly. Will rhetorical invocations of public opinion, based upon selective readings of polls or deliberate conflation of activated with mass opinion succeed if common public space deteriorates? How will democracy and government legitimacy be affected if assertions about public opinion become less credible?

Beyond this, will individuals' actual preferences (not aggregated into public opinion) become more informed or less? Will any decline of common public communication experiences provide individuals more control over their responses to pollsters' preframed questions – as hinted by the apparent majority who denied the relevance of President Clinton's sex life to his job performance during 1998 (Zaller's finding in Chap. 12)? Will this fragmentation of the information commons also make crystallization of latent public opinion and its conversion into an influential political force more difficult? The task facing scholars will be to make sense of the emerging public opinion system, using a more differentiated conception of public opinion and a far broader range of sources and approaches than hitherto employed.

Notes

1. Aggregating even well-reasoned and priority-ordered mass preferences in some sensible way often presents insurmountable difficulties. In Riker's (1986) words: "The popular will is defined only as long as the issue dimensions are restricted. Once issue dimensions multiply, the popular will is irresolute. Slight changes in dimensions induce disequilibrium." This is another way of saying that typical invocations of public opinion ignore trade-offs.

2. The year 1983 is an outlier, because of the March "evil empire" speech and the Autumn crisis over the Soviets' destruction of Korean Airlines Flight 007. With these four months removed, threat references average 28 per month, so the "normalized" annual total would be 336. Entering 336 negative references for 1983 brings the correlation to $r = 0.77$ ($p < 0.001$). Negative references dropped to a near-average twenty-five in December 1983, were twenty-seven in January 1984 and so forth, so the use of a normal average of twenty-eight seems right. A second measure was employed that counted *net* references to Soviet aggression, buildup, and threat. The measure reported in the text is the total assertions that Soviets were aggressive, building up, and threatening. The net measure subtracts from this the total assertions saying the Soviets were not aggressive, building up, or threatening. These counter-frame assertions remained fairly low, averaging twenty-five per year from 1977

through 1988. In 1989 they jumped to 137 and in 1990 to 254. The correlation of the net measure with the defense spending opinion is $r = 0.68$ ($p < 0.01$), compared with 0.69 for negative images only as reported in the text. The correlation using the correction for 1983 is 0.74 ($p < 0.001$), compared with the 0.77 in the text. Hence the relationship seems quite robust.

3. It is possible that GOP members did not ignore public opinion but rather that they responded to some combination of mass, activated, latent, and perceived majority opinion *within specific Congressional districts, states, and personal electoral coalitions.* If this is indeed what motivated the legislative majority, then whether such responsiveness equates to democratic representation is beyond the scope of this essay.

REFERENCES

Althaus, Scott (1998). "Information Effects in Collective Preferences." *American Political Science Review*, 92:545–558.

Bartels, Larry M. (1991). "Constituency Opinion and Congressional Policy Making: The Reagan Defense Buildup." *American Political Science Review* 85:457–75.

Blumer, Herbert (1948). "Public Opinion and Public Opinion Polling." *American Sociological Review* 13:242–9.

Bordieu, Pierre (1979). "Public Opinion Does Not Exist." In Armand Mattelart and Seth Siegelaub (Eds.), *Communication and Class Struggle*. New York: International General.

Converse, Philip E. (1964). "The Nature of Belief Systems in Mass Publics." In David Apter (Ed.), *Ideology and Its Discontents*. Glencoe, IL: Free Press.

Entman, Robert M. (1993). "Framing: Toward Clarification of a Fractured Paradigm." *Journal of Communication* 43(4):51–58.

Entman, Robert M., and Andrew Rojecki (1993). "Freezing out the Public: Elite and Media Framing of the U.S. Anti-Nuclear Movement." *Political Communication* 10:151–167.

Habermas, Jürgen (1989). *The Structural Transformation of the Public Sphere: An Inquiry into a Category of Bourgeois Society*. Cambridge, MA: MIT Press.

Hartley, Thomas, and Bruce Russett (1992). "Public Opinion and the Common Defense." *American Political Science Review* 86:905–15.

Herbst, Susan (1998a). *Reading Public Opinion: How Political Actors View the Democratic Process*. Chicago: University of Chicago Press.

(1998b). "Rousseau Meets Opinion Research: Re-Introducing the General Will." Paper presented at the Kennedy School, Harvard University, October 26.

(1993). *Numbered Voices: How Opinion Polling Has Shaped American Politics*. Chicago: University of Chicago Press.

Jacobs, Lawrence R., and Robert Y. Shapiro (2000). *Politicians Don't Pander: Political Manipulation and the Loss of Democratic Responsiveness*. Chicago: University of Chicago Press.

(1992). "Leadership and Responsiveness: Some New Evidence on the Johnson Presidency." Paper presented at the Annual Meeting of the American Political Science Association, Chicago, September 3–6.

Key, V. O. (1961). *Public Opinion and American Democracy*. New York: Knopf.

King, Elliot, and Michael Schudson (1991). "The Myth of the Great Communicator." *Columbia Journalism Review* 26(November/December):37–39.

Klapper, Joseph (1960). *The Effects of Mass Communication.* Glencoe, IL: The Free Press.

Lippmann, Walter (1925). *The Phantom Public.* New York: Harcourt Brace.

Lupia, Arthur, and Mathew McCubbins (1998). *The Democratic Dilemma: Can Citizens Learn What They Need to Know?* New York: Cambridge University Press.

Mueller, John E. (1994). *Policy and Opinion in the Gulf War.* Chicago: University of Chicago Press.

Page, Benjamin I., and Robert Y. Shapiro (1992). *The Rational Public.* Chicago: University of Chicago Press.

Pew Center on the People and the Press (1998). *Public Appetite for Government Misjudged.* (April 17). (http://www.people-press.org/leadrpt.htm)

Popkin, Samuel (1991). *The Reasoning Voter: Communication and Persuasion in Presidential Campaigns.* Chicago: University of Chicago Press.

Rielly, John E. (1991). *American Public Opinion and U.S. Foreign Policy 1991.* Chicago: Chicago Council on Foreign Relations.

Riker, William (1986). *The Art of Political Manipulation.* New Haven: Yale University Press.

Schuman, Howard, and Stanley Presser (1981). *Questions and Answers in Attitude Surveys: Experiments on Question Form, Wording, and Context.* New York: Academic Press.

Stubbing, Richard (1986). *The Defense Game.* New York: Harper and Row.

Talbott, Strobe (1984). *Deadly Gambits.* New York: Knopf.

Zaller, John (1998). "Coming to Grips with V. O. Key's Concept of Latent Opinion." Paper presented at the Symposium in Honor of Philip Converse, Boston, MA.

   (1992). *The Nature and Origins of Mass Opinion.* New York: Cambridge University Press.

CHAPTER 11

Political Waves and Democratic Discourse: Terrorism Waves During the Oslo Peace Process

Gadi Wolfsfeld

The modern political process can be thought of as a series of cycles in which leaders, publics, and the press focus attention on a narrow number of public issues and events for a limited period of time. The initiation of these cycles, or political waves, is marked by a dramatic increase in media coverage about an issue, an increase in public reactions by political leaders and activists concerning the topic, and an increase in discussions about the issue among the general public (Downs 1972; Hilgartner and Bosk 1988; Linsky 1991; Mathes and Fetch 1991; McCombs and Hua 1995). After reaching a certain peak in public attention, such waves either die of their own accord or are replaced by new waves. The study of these waves can provide important insights into a wide range of issues that confront researchers in the fields of political science, communication, and sociology.

Political waves can be defined as *sudden and significant changes in the political environment that are characterized by a substantial increase in the amount of public attention centered on a political issue or event.* Whereas this is the first time that the term *political wave* is being used in the literature, it is important to carefully specify its meaning.

The first thing to note is that the unit of analysis is the political environment. The political environment refers to the aggregate of private and public beliefs, discourse, and behaviors concerning political matters within a particular setting and time (Wolfsfeld 1997a). It is a "macro" concept referring to the political "situation" at a given time and place. What issues are people talking about? What are various leaders doing and how are people reacting to these activities? How are the news media covering political issues at that particular time and place? What is the distribution of opinion on a particular issue? What are the most common interpretive frames being employed to explain and evaluate what is happening in the political realm?

The political environment is constantly changing. Political issues come and go, some actors become more prominent, while others fade into the background. The study of political waves looks at rapid changes in the ways in which a given society relates to events and issues. The goal of research in this area is to better understand how leaders, the press, and citizens initiate, amplify, understand, and react to these waves and what the implications of this dynamic are for democratic discourse.

The focus on the political environment distinguishes this approach from related issues concerning "news cycles" or "feeding frenzies" (Sabato 1991). While the news media play an important role in defining and amplifying such waves, they rarely initiate them.[1] It is critical to understand how political actors initiate such waves and how they and the public react to them. While a broader perspective makes research more complex, it provides a richer and more authentic understanding of the phenomenon.

Finally, something should be said about what is meant by a "sudden and significant change in the political environment." I am referring to cases in which certain events and/or issues dominate the public agenda for at least several days. There are many periods when *no* single issue dominates the public agenda, and therefore not all waves are replaced by other waves.

The amount of coverage granted by the various news media is clearly the most convenient indicator of such a change. It is important, however, to keep in mind the difference between the indicator and the phenomenon itself. Political waves also include changes in attention by leaders, activists, and the public. Many of these people also depend on the news media as their major indicator for evaluating the state of the political environment. Researchers have little choice but to do the same. Despite the dangers associated with this approach, it does provide a convenient measure for the size and duration of political waves. The greater the number of news articles and broadcast items about a particular issue or event appearing in a prominent position in all of the mainstream media, the larger the wave.

There can be separate waves about the same issue. A topic – such as the Monica Lewinsky scandal – can rise and fall, only to rise again. Nevertheless, because there are so many short-lived waves, it makes more sense to define each individual episode as a separate wave. This is also important because of the very different political context in which each wave takes place.

In this chapter we shall limit our theoretical and empirical focus to two sets of actors who are especially sensitive to the rise and fall of political waves: political antagonists and those working in the news media. The goal of the piece is to explain something about the initiation of political waves, the role the news play in amplifying and structuring waves, and the impact this dynamic has on the political process.

Political antagonists invest a good deal of time and resources in an ongoing struggle for control over the political environment (Wolfsfeld 1997a). Some have used the term "permanent campaign" to describe this phenomenon (Blumler and Kavanaugh 1999; Pfetsch 1998). The increasing sense of urgency makes the political environment much more volatile. Political actors must be prepared for sudden shifts in climate that can alter the strategic position of the various antagonists.

Those with political power are often in the best position to *initiate* political waves. This is an important advantage because those who initiate such cycles can often influence how the political climate will change because of the wave. President Reagan's "Star Wars" strategy, Prime Minister Thatcher's decision to go to war over the Falklands, President Bush's actions to contest the Iraqi invasion of Kuwait, and Prime Minister Rabin's decision to sign an interim agreement with the PLO are all good examples of such initiatives. Weaker antagonists, on the other hand, are usually forced to react to waves initiated by others.

THE ROLE OF THE NEWS MEDIA

The news media are the primary agents for amplifying political waves and providing them with structure. The press has a vested interest in promoting waves because such stories serve to dramatically expand audience size. The growing emphasis on "infotainment" and the "tabloidization" of news suggests that such waves will become an increasingly important part of political discourse around the world (see Chap. 8, by Delli Carpini and Williams, and Chap. 13, by Bennett and Manheim).

Fallows (1994) and Patterson (1998) make similar arguments about the ways in which the modern news media cover politics. Fallows argues that news has become an "endless stream of emergencies" presented within "artificial short-lived intensity." He found thirty such emergencies during the first two months of the Clinton Presidency, many of which proved to be much less significant than they were portrayed. Patterson found a massive rise in the number of news stories that were considered urgent in the 1990s as compared to stories in the 1960s.

The media provide structure to political waves in two major ways. First, they provide *temporal structure* in that they are the primary agents deciding when a wave begins and when it ends. The decision of editors that a story is either hot or dead has significant consequences for leaders, activists, and publics. While such evaluations are clearly related to the flow of external events, the news media maintain their own internal clocks (Trumbo 1996). The ongoing search for novelty means that political waves will rarely go on for more than a few days.

One finds a significant amount of agreement among the news media about the time span of a wave. This is a fascinating phenomenon that provides important evidence about the power of journalistic norms and routines. While a certain amount of this correspondence can be attributed to the news media monitoring each other, there appears to be an unspoken agreement among editors about how long a news story should last. This is one of a number of routines that lowers the amount of diversity in media coverage. It is rooted in a rigid professional culture whose rules come to be taken for granted by journalists in the Western world.

The news media also provide *narrative structure* to political waves (Gamson et al. 1992; McComas and Shanahan 1999). They do so by providing citizens with a fairly common view of the major actors, events, and themes. The construction and impact of media frames has become a major area of research in political communication (for reviews, see Entman 1993; Scheufele 1999). Here we are interested in understanding how the adoption of a particular media frame influences the construction of news stories and interactions with various antagonists. The fact that the same basic story line is repeated in so many different media is likely to lead many people to accept it as a common point of reference.

Once a wave has been identified, the news media become massive search engines looking for any information and events that can be linked to the story. The best evidence on this point is provided by German scholars studying what they call "key events" (Brosius and Eps 1995; Kepplinger and Habermeir 1995). They found convincing evidence that such events change the criteria for the news selection, giving the false impression that there had subsequently been a rise in similar events such as traffic fatalities, cases of AIDS, and attacks on aliens and asylum seekers in Germany. The change in political context that is associated with political waves leads to a change in how the news media process information.

These same processes also take place within the context of routine reporting. The major difference is that when the media deal with waves everything becomes intensified. The issue dominates news coverage to such an extent that few can avoid knowing about it. Journalists go into crisis mode and frantically search for any stories that can be thematically linked to the issue. The changes in the political environment associated with major waves have an impact on antagonists, journalists, and the public.

INFLUENCES ON THE POLITICAL PROCESS

When a particular issue becomes "the story" being covered by all of the news media, political actors are forced to react. The news media thus become important agents not only in establishing leaders' political agenda but also in accelerating the pace of decision making. Patterson (1998, p. 65), in his important essay on time and news, also talks about this problem: "In Western democracies, the politics of time is increasingly the politics of news time, often with adverse consequences for policy and opinion."

On the international level this phenomenon is known as the "CNN effect" (Livingston 1997), but a similar process can also occur on the domestic scene. One example is provided in a study by Ungar (1992). The summer of 1988 proved to be particularly hot, and the news media decided that the culprit was global warming. Leaders in the United States, Canada, and Britain were all forced to propose solutions for the problem. In hindsight, it seems that el niño – which became the hot topic in 1997–98 – provided a much better explanation for the sudden change in weather.

When story lines run in a particular direction it can influence antagonists' tactics and strategies and their political fortunes. The shooting at Columbine High School in April 1999 provides an excellent example. The massive amount of publicity associated with that event provided an important opportunity for gun control advocates to rally support for new legislation. The NRA stood as the accused in that incident and was forced to devote a considerable amount of time and resources to damage control. The entertainment industry also came under serious attack, leading to a number of policy changes.

The publicity associated with political waves has an especially powerful impact on weaker antagonists. If they become one of the principal actors in the story line their level of political standing can dramatically increase. Media status can often be converted to political status. If the publicity is also in the right direction, it can also have a major impact on mobilization efforts. Social movements are often forced to wait for such critical moments to make progress (Joppke 1991; Staggenborg 1993; Ungar 1992). Clinton's threat to attack Iraq in February 1998, for example, provided an important opportunity for the mobilization of antiwar movements in the United States.

One of the only ways for weaker antagonists to *initiate* a political wave is through political violence. The largest waves are generated through acts of terrorism, and this will be the focus of the present analysis. Most of the literature in this field deals with the symbiotic relationship between journalists and terrorists (see, for example, Nacos 1996; Paletz and Shmid 1992; Picard 1993; Schaffert 1992; Weimann 1994). The emphasis in this study will be to look at terrorists as simply one more type of antagonist attempting to influence the political environment. Many "back-door challengers" (Wolfsfeld 1997a) turn to political violence in order to get their message through, and the media's addiction to excitement assures such groups a prominent place on the public agenda.

RESEARCH STRATEGY

This chapter seeks to provide evidence in support of three major arguments: (1) Political antagonists often initiate political waves as a means of furthering political goals and the news media play a central role in this strategy. (2) The news media play an important role in constructing the political environment by amplifying political waves and by providing them with temporal and narrative structures. (3) Changes in the political environment associated with political waves have important influences on the interactions between journalists and antagonists and on the political process.

The research will focus on a major bout of terrorism that Israel endured between October 1994 and January 1995. The Rabin government was attempting to convince the Israeli public about the benefits of the Oslo peace process. The right-wing opposition in Israel was firmly against the accords, arguing that concessions to the Palestinians would endanger Israeli security. There were also two major Palestinian groups opposed to the agreement: Hamas and the Islamic Jihad. They carried out a number of attacks during this period in an attempt to derail the accords, each of which led to political waves of grief and anger in Israel.

The research I carried out was part of a larger study looking at the role of the Israeli news media in the Oslo peace process (Wolfsfeld 1997b, c). The topic of political waves was one part of this project that employed two major methodologies. The first consisted of turning to expert informants who knew about the norms and routines that characterized their behavior during the waves. These transcripts will be used to demonstrate the reasoning behind the initiation of political waves (argument 1) and how journalists and antagonists deal with the onset of waves (argument 3). The second set of data comes from a content analysis of newspaper coverage concerning one particular wave: the terrorist attack at the Beit Lid junction that took place on January 23, 1995. This part of the analysis will allow us to look at the questions concerning the media's role in amplifying and structuring political waves (argument 2).

Semistructured interviews were carried out with a wide selection of political leaders, advisors, and journalists who were all involved in creating the news about the Oslo peace process. A total of forty-one individuals were questioned over a period that lasted from July 1994 to December 1995. This period runs from about a year after the breakthrough at Oslo to a month after the Rabin assassination. Interviews were carried out with representatives from the Rabin/Peres governments (seven interviews), the Israeli opposition parties (eight interviews), the Palestinian authority (six interviews), and the Palestinian opposition (seven interviews). The major criterion for being interviewed was that the individual had an ongoing relationship with the Israeli press concerning the Oslo peace process. Thirteen journalists were interviewed who had covered the peace process for newspapers, television, and radio. The journalists were selected based on the importance of their news organ and their area of responsibility. Most interviews lasted for about an hour. All were taped and then transcribed.

The fact that we were able to carry out interviews with members of the Islamic Hamas movement provided a unique opportunity to better understand their motivations and strategies in initiating terrorism waves. The leaders who were interviewed were members of the "political" wing of the movement, which is separate from the "military" branch that carries out the actual attacks. The operating assumption was that these leaders were in a position to tell us something about the role of the media played in the movement's overall strategy.

Semistructured interviews use a standard set of questions but also provide the flexibility of following up interesting leads that emerge during the sessions. While this particular analysis deals specifically with terrorism waves, the larger study also looks at other types of waves that occurred during this period. Leaders and advisers were asked about issues such as

- The amount of organization and resources devoted to dealing with the news media
- Media strategies
- The structure and nature of the ongoing relationships with reporters
- Periods of conflict and cooperation with reporters
- Perceptions about the degree of success in getting their frames about the peace process into the news media
- Perceptions about the degree of success other antagonists were having
- The influence of political bias on their ability to promote their messages
- The influence of political context on their ability to promote their messages
- Perceptions about any changes that have occurred in media images of the Palestinians since the breakthrough at Oslo
- The influence of the media on the process itself.

Journalists were asked many of these same questions and also about issues such as

- The varying abilities of antagonists to use the news media
- Journalistic norms and practices for covering the peace process
- Dilemmas about the coverage of peace ceremonies on the one hand and terrorist attacks on the other
- The influence of waves on journalistic routines
- The relative status of different assignments associated with the peace process

- Perceptions about the changes in the way Palestinians have been covered in recent years
- Perceptions about differences among the news media in their coverage of the peace process.

The Beit Lid case study looked at all of the newspaper articles that appeared in the three major newspapers in Israel during the four days following the attack (January 24–26, 1995). *Yediot Achronot* is by far the most popular newspaper in Israel and is characterized by a mostly tabloid format, but also employs some of the more serious journalists in Israel. *Ma'ariv* has an almost identical format to *Yediot,* and is the second most popular newspaper. *Ha'aretz* is considered a "quality" newspaper and is read by a much smaller, more elite section of the population.

The discussion will be divided into three parts, which coincide to the three arguments already formulated. The section titled "the Initiation of Terrorism Waves" will deal with the logic behind the initiation of terrorism waves. Starting with this perspective serves as an important reminder that the news media are one element in a much larger world of politics. The section on "The Media Construction of Political Waves" deals with the specific example of Beit Lid in an attempt to illustrate the role the news media play in amplifying and structuring such waves. The final section, "The Impact of Changes in the Political Environment," looks at the influence these changes had on interactions between journalists and the various political actors and on the political process.

THE INITIATION OF TERRORISM WAVES

The first two years of the Oslo peace process were marked by an unusually high number of emotional highs and lows. The Israeli public was led from the thrill of the initial breakthrough to the despair over buses being blown up in terrorist attacks, from the signing of the peace treaty with Jordan to the assassination of Prime Minister Rabin. All of these waves were based on genuinely important events.

The period between October of 1994 and January of 1995 was particularly unsettling. There had been a terrorist attack in Jerusalem on October 9 and the kidnapping of an Israeli soldier, Nachshon Wachsman, a few days later. The kidnapping drama lasted several days with video tapes from his captors being shown on Israeli television.

Wachsman was then killed in the attempt to rescue him. On October 17, Rabin and Peres initialed a peace agreement with Jordan. This was a tremendous breakthrough in the Arab-Israeli conflict. On October 19, the Islamic Hamas movement struck again by blowing up a bus in the middle of Tel Aviv, killing twenty-two people. Four days later, after days of media hype, the formal signing of the Israeli-Jordanian peace treaty took place on October 26, attended by President Clinton. In December, Rabin, Peres, and Yassar Arafat were awarded the Oslo peace prize for their historic agreement.

The final terrorist attack of this period took place at the Beit Lid junction on January 22. The well-known interchange is not far from Tel Aviv and serves as a major transfer point for hundreds of Israeli soldiers traveling to and from their bases. Two suicide bombers blew themselves up on that morning, killing twenty people and wounding sixty-five. The resulting tide of sorrow and anger once again swept through the country.

The decision to use violence is an ideological decision. The media are seen as convenient tools that increase the impact of those acts. The major movement behind the bout of terrorism that struck Israel during this period was the Islamic Hamas movement. This movement is opposed to the Oslo accords signed by Israel and the PLO and represents the largest opposition to the Arafat regime. Hamas opposes any recognition of the state of Israel, and the movement's goal is to establish an Islamic state in all of Palestine.

As with many opposition movements, Hamas employs political violence as a means of establishing standing (Gamson and Wolfsfeld 1993). There is little doubt that Hamas was very successful using this strategy. They became major players, and their movement and their attacks had a powerful and detrimental impact on the Oslo peace process. One of the Hamas leaders talked directly about the use of "military actions" as a means of achieving standing:

> The military actions are just a means of getting the message across to the Israeli society to get the minimal conditions of Hamas. Our message is clear. The military actions come in order to pressure the Israeli decision-makers to pay attention to what we say and to hear our opinions and our demands. We want Israeli citizens to come to a conclusion that there will be no peace without negotiating with the Hamas movement. (author's interview 25, June 8, 1995)

The Israeli news media play a critical role is this strategy. This does not mean, as some might argue, that a lack of news coverage would eliminate terrorism. The news media are, however, considered powerful tools for amplifying the impact of the attacks. Ironically, many of the Hamas people who were interviewed found the "Zionist" press a more efficient tool than their own, not only for sending messages to the Israelis, but also to their own people. One of the leaders put it this way:

> The enemy can sometimes serve us indirectly. We don't have any large news institutions that will publicize and cover the things that we're interested in . . . So in the end, the Hamas actions force the media to report and relate to the activities and positions of the movement. I want to use the military actions to prove my abilities on both the local and regional level. The Israeli press helps with this. Therefore, through my military action I am trying to pass a message that Hamas is a central force among the Palestinians and it is impossible to ignore it. (author's interview 35, June 8, 1995)

In order to ensure the maximum impact, movement leaders must ensure that dealing with the news media is an integral part of the operational plan:

> The military actions of the Hamas are carried out by the Az Aldin Elkasam unit. After every action of those units always comes a press release on the action carried out, explaining their claims or their demands. Before carrying out every action they prepare a press release including films and pictures about what needs to be shown or explained. Thus, the media dimension is very important in this context. (author's interview 25, June 8, 1995)

It is a mistake, however, to see terrorism as a publicity stunt. It is rooted in desperation and a deep-seated anger against a more powerful force. The media increase the effectiveness of such actions by amplifying the message to the point where none of the parties can ignore it. It is hardly surprising, therefore, that those who carry out such acts will do everything in their power to ensure that they get the maximum amount of coverage for their actions. In this sense, at least, those who carry out terrorism are no different from any other political antagonist. They want to initiate political waves that will allow them the maximum amount of public attention.

Table 11.1. *Number of articles about Beit Lid attack*

Newspaper	Jan. 23	Jan. 24	Jan. 25	Jan. 26
Yediot	30	17	13	0
Ma'ariv	29	29	14	0
Ha'aretz	21	19	17	2
Total	80	65	44	2

THE MEDIA CONSTRUCTION OF POLITICAL WAVES

The purpose of this section is to examine the role of the news media in amplifying and providing structure to political waves. The newspaper coverage of the terrorist attack at Beit Lid provides graphic evidence on this point.

As noted, the attack on Beit Lid took place in the early morning of January 22, 1995.[2] The number of articles published in the three major newspapers is detailed in Table 11.1. This table is important, for it provides evidence of how the news media both amplified and provided temporal structure to such waves. As can been seen, it is a massive amount of attention: 191 articles in three newspapers over an extremely short period of time. These numbers do not even include the large number of pictures, which, in the two popular papers (*Yediot Achronot* and *Ma'ariv*) often took up an entire tabloid page.

What is fascinating is that the wave ends as abruptly as it begins, and it does so at exactly the same moment in all three newspapers. While *Ha'aretz* published two articles on January 26, the story is basically over on January 25. The event that had been so enormously important to Israel just three days before was no longer worth mentioning. The sudden drop is not related to the start of any new wave: There was only routine coverage on January 26. All of the editors came to the same conclusion at the same time: The story was dead. The problem of terrorism was apparently no longer worth discussing until it happened again.

This decision about the temporal structure of the story has important implications for both the government and the opposition. The government is no longer under pressure to find an immediate solution to the problem, and the opposition finds it more difficult to exploit this issue as a means of gaining access to the media.

Amplification not only comes from the amount of space devoted to the attack, it also comes from the exaggerated, emotional tone of the coverage. The ways in which the Israeli media deal with such incidents is remarkable. The national radio stations put on special "emergency tapes" consisting of slow, mostly sad music in Hebrew. Television and radio halt all normal programming and dedicate their programming to an "open line": continual news and discussions by leaders, analysts, and citizens. There is no other news; there are no other topics. The attacks are considered a national trauma that the entire community must endure together.

The newspapers – which will be the focus here – played a critical role in this emotional catharsis. A summary of the first day's coverage in the three newspapers is presented in Table 11.2. The front pages of the two most popular papers were covered with portrait photographs of the dead staring out at the readers. The massive red headline in *Yediot Achronot* read: "The Children that Won't Return." The *Ma'ariv* headline was "With Tears of Rage." A short biographical piece was written about every victim and his or her grieving family.

An incredible amount of space was devoted to the pictures and reports of the horror and grief. On the first day *Ma'ariv* devoted ten full pages, and *Yediot*, nine full pages. On the second day (not shown) *Ma'ariv* devoted another ten full pages, and *Yediot* gave another nine pages. The stories included appalling stories by eyewitnesses and the victims' families.

The coverage in the more quality newspaper *Ha'aretz* provides an important contrast, for it illustrates that the same event can be covered in a much less emotional style. Here the emphasis is on detached analysis rather than emotional catharsis. Thus, the first day's headline read: "19 Killed from the Two Bombs at Beit Lid Junction; Closure Imposed on the Territories." The portraits of the victims were placed on page 3. Perhaps even more important is the fact that there were also other news stories on the front page and throughout the newspaper, including other stories relating to the Arab-Israeli conflict. These differences in tone also continued into the second day. As noted, the popular newspapers devoted a massive amount of attention to the funerals and national mourning. *Ha'aretz*, on the other hand, printed almost nothing along this line.

Perhaps there is no objective means of deciding which type of coverage is more appropriate. Eyewitnesses to the horror of a terrorist attack would probably react like the two popular newspapers. What is clear is the fact that the vast majority of Israelis are exposed to the more sensationalist, emotional coverage – which is then reinforced by

Table 11.2. *First day newspaper coverage of Beit Lid attack*

Newspaper	Page	Headline	Visuals*
Yediot Achronot	1	The Children Who Won't Return	Individual pictures of victims
	2, 3	Red Berets Soaked in Blood	Weeping soldier holding bloody shirt[a]
	4, 5	The Children Who left for the Army and Won't Return	Portrait pictures of two victims
	6, 7	In One Moment the Intersection Turned into a Deadly Field	Sister kissing wounded brother[a]
	8, 9	Death on the Way to the Base: Stories from the Booby Trap	Shocked medic[b]; overhead picture of site[b]
	10	I Saw by the Coffee House People Whose Entire Head Was Burned, All Those Hands . . .	Crying soldier being held/led by second soldier
Ma'ariv	1	With Tears of Rage Complete Closure of Territories	Individual pictures of victims
	2, 3	Death on the Way to the Base	Sapper going through debris[b]; female soldier crying
	4, 5	19 Black Frames [obituary notices]	Medic treating wounded
	6, 7	The Curse of Renne Cassain: 2 Dead Yesterday, 6 Within Last Half Year	Shocked soldier being held by second soldier[a]
	8	Booby Trap at Parachute Junction: The Dead	Picture of one victim
	9	The Terrorist Ran Towards the Wounded and the Dead and Blew Himself Up	Scenes of bodies wounded and dead at site
	10	"It Was a Terrible Massacre"	Medics comforting weeping civilians
Ha'aretz	1	19 Killed in Two Bombs at Parachute Junction; Closure Placed on the Territories; The Islamic Jihad Accepts Responsibility; Beilin to Al-Baz: We Will Consider Signing the Nuclear Non-Proliferation Treaty	Sappers going through debris
	2	The Terrorist Blew Himself Up Next to the Soldiers That Were Treating Their Friends	Diagram of site; religious workers standing next to bodies

Table 11.2. *(cont.)*

Newspaper	Page	Headline	Visuals*
	3	Those Killed in the Attack: 18 Soldiers, Including One Woman Soldier, and a Civilian	Individual pictures of victims
	4	Rabin: In the Intermediate Time-Span, the Entrance of Palestinians to the Sovereign Territory of Israel Must Be Prevented; In the Security Offices There Are Discussion about Possible Actions Against Terrorism: "The Intelligence Operations Will Be Increased"; Parachute Junction: Among the Most Crowed, and an Old Site for Terrorist Attacks	None
	5	"I Am Looking for My Friend," said the Pale Girl; Senior Members of Likud Party Reject [President] Weisman's Call of Unity Government	Wounded being unloaded from helicopter at hospital
	6	Islamic Jihad Leaflet: "Our Heroes Blew Up the Transportation Station of the Zionist Soldiers"; Yaasar Arafat Called Rabin to Condemn the Attack, and to Send Condolences to the Families; Hamas Supporters Suggest Stopping the Violent Actions in Exchange for Israeli Withdrawal from West Bank	Picture of one of the attackers; picture of "The Engineer"

a Visuals taking up full tabloid page.
b Visuals taking up half of a tabloid page.

the horrific images being shown on television. Leaders operating in a political environment that was defined by the *Ha'aretz* tone might be in a better position to think about more long-range policies concerning terrorism. As discussed, this apparently was the situation before the rise in sensationalist news coverage in Israel.

NARRATIVE STRUCTURE

The news media also provide a narrative structure to political waves by providing an authoritative account of the major actors and events associated with a wave, and by thematically organizing information in ways that serve both their own professional interests and the cultural sensitivities of their audience. The construction of a narrative structure should be seen as a joint effort among journalists, antagonists, and the public.

News coverage of disaster waves, which include terrorism, run along fairly predictable lines. The news media construct stories that correspond with public reactions to the event: sorrow over the loss of human life, anger at any who can be held responsible, and an intensive search for some type of solution. There are also more "technical" stories that provide details about how the disaster took place.

The Beit Lid story ran along just these lines. In addition to the technical details of the incident, the news stories centered on three major themes: grief over the dead and wounded, anger at the Palestinians, and an almost desperate search for some way to prevent future acts of terror. The Israeli media conducted a massive search for any information that could be related to these three themes. Given time constraints and the enormous amount of space allocated to the story, journalists had little choice but to lower their normal standards of evaluation. Stories that would not normally be considered worthy of publication were included because they could be easily integrated into existing slots.

The stories about the horror and mourning in the two popular newspapers were structured by using *organizing captions* to thematically connect a number of different stories under the same headings. This is a standard routine for covering waves in Israel and even includes a (literal) frame to indicate which stories fall under the same heading. The first day's organizing captions centered on the initial shock: "Death on the Way to the Base" (*Yediot Achronot*, January 23, 1995, pp. 3–11) and "Hell [Tofet] at Paratroopers Junction" (*Ma'ariv*, pp. 2–10). The second day focused on the theme that the whole country was suffering: "The Country Is Crying" (*Ma'ariv*, pp. 2–11), "A Country in Mourning" (*Yediot Achronot*, January 24, 1995, pp. 1,3,5,7,9). These captions not only provided a structural link to the stories, but also allowed the editor to integrate the many photo images into the overall narrative.

Decisions about narrative structure influence the collection of information. A good example of this process is the decision by *Ha'aretz* not to put a major emphasis on the grief and mourning theme. Because of this decision, no reporters were sent to cover the many funerals taking place on the second day of the coverage. These journalists were then assigned to cover the other aspects of the story deemed to be more important by *Ha'aretz* editors.

The stories about grief and mourning were already described in detail. The discussion turns then to the stories having to do with the other two themes: anger at the Palestinians and the search for solutions. The rage against the Palestinians and the accompanying doubts about the peace process was an important theme in all three days of coverage. The anger was directed at all the Palestinians and specifically at Arafat. Examining these news stories one gets a better understanding of how sources, journalists, and publics cooperate in constructing such items (see also Just et al. 1996).

There were a large number of stories denigrating Arafat and the Palestinian leadership. The President of Israel was one of the first to open the attack by suggesting that "maybe" Arafat is not "the right partner" and that "the peace talks should be suspended." The front page of *Yediot Achronot* (January 23, 1995) concluded that Arafat had been reluctant to condemn the attack. A story in *Ha'aretz*, based on information supplied by a former advisor to the previous government, talked about an audio tape in which Arafat was purported to have stated that "we are all suicide bombers" (*Ha'aretz*, January 23, 1995, p. 5). There was no information about how long he had had the tape, but this was clearly an appropriate time to release it and publish a story about it. The next day *Ha'aretz* published an article that contained a leaked report from the meeting of the Rabin government: "Security forces at the government meeting: Arafat is not keeping his commitment to operate against extremists" (January 24, 1995, p. 5b). *Yediot* had a similar story suggesting that a secret report prepared by the military's legal department suggested that the PLO was constantly breaking the agreement (January 24, 1995, p. 3). Here too, no information was given about when the report had been written. Other stories focussed on calls by various leaders to end all cultural contacts with the Palestinians and on those Palestinian groups who were "celebrating" the attack on Beit Lid.

All of these items illustrate how a story line is constructed during a wave. Once the initial theme has been established, journalists look for any information that can provide empirical support for that theme, and their sources are eager to supply it. The theme in this case centers on the anger against the Palestinians.

The third important theme in the coverage centered on the frantic search for solutions. None of the remedies presented withstood the test of time and terrorism continued unabated. But people wanted answers, and given the extremely high level of anxiety, leaders had to come up with something.

Prime Minister Rabin's speech to the nation on the night of the attack became the center point of these discussions. As noted by his adviser, the goal of this speech was to "calm" the people. Part of the strategy was to promise revenge: "We will destroy the murderers: no border will stop us," and a dramatic message to the terrorists: "We will come after you and we will win." The other part was a grand plan for "separation" from the territories using some type of fence or electronic border that would provide a means for controlling the inflow of Palestinians. Rabin's separation proposal provided the news media with an important new angle for the terrorism story, a means of filling the enormous news hole that had been created by the attack. Politicians, experts, and citizens could all express their views on the desirability and feasibility of the plan.

There were also many other solutions that were suggested for dealing with terrorism, all of which proved ephemeral. The government announced that they would close the territories, not release the Palestinian prisoners as had been promised, and would expand their attacks on the terrorist infrastructure. The police announced that they would use an additional helicopter to increase control on the border. One reporter suggested that the families of suicide bombers should be expelled to another country. A government minister proposed that Israel forbid Palestinian Muslims to come to the mosques in Jerusalem during the holy month of Ramadan "so they will know there is a price for mayhem." One of the religious parties claimed that the real cause of terrorism was that Rabin did not observe the Jewish Sabbath.

The search for a solution provides a fitting end to the narrative. The story begins with the shock and grief over the loss of life, continues with the rage towards the perpetuators, and concludes with a number of proposals for revenge. The sad truth is that there are never any short-term solutions to terrorism, especially when suicide bombers are involved. Nevertheless, given the enormous amount of grief and fear associated with such waves, such a message would be culturally unacceptable. The end of the wave brings a certain relief. Terrorism is no longer an issue worth discussing and the political process moves on to other topics. The story – at least for a time – is over.

THE IMPACT OF CHANGES IN THE
POLITICAL ENVIRONMENT

Acts of terrorism are a major jolt to any political system. Political leaders, activists, and journalists all abandon their normal routines and move into a crisis mode of operation. Nevertheless, all of these actors have been through previous waves, and thus they have established routines for dealing with them.

Every terrorist attack during this period was considered a major failure for the Rabin government. Israelis had been promised an end to violence; terrorism was seen as a clear indication that the Oslo accords were not working. There was no doubt that this wave was considered a government failure; the direction of the wave was very clear. The euphoria in the early days of Oslo was being replaced by the need for damage control. The cultural resonance of competing frames varies along with changes in political context (Wolfsfeld 1997a). One of Rabin's advisors talked about these changes in fortune:

> In certain areas my message is the main message. In other instances it is the message of the opposition or other forces that influence the final journalistic product. For example, when it comes to terrorism, you have to remember that I don't have a strong explanation for the terrorism issue. I am hurt by terrorism as much as the opposition. I just say that if I stop the process it would be a mistake, because they would only increase terrorism . . . The problem is that when there is a wave of terror my explanation is not strong, and the explanation or the inputs of the opposition to stop the process are just as powerful or even more powerful than mine. (author's interview 3, May 17, 1995)

Almost every one of the journalists we spoke to supported the Oslo peace process. Yet the relationship with the Rabin government became strained and even hostile in the midst of these waves. Reporters were caught up within the surge of pessimism and doubt. Liebes (1998, p. 79) made a similar point in her study of "disaster marathons," in which Israeli television stops its normal broadcasting and focuses exclusively on a major calamity. These become, she says, "degradation ceremonies" in which the Prime Minister and the Chief-of-Staff are grilled about their culpability. A political reporter who was interviewed in May 1995 described the relationship between the political mood and support for the peace process:

I think it depends on when you are talking about. If you are talking about September of '93 [start of the Oslo process], then yes [we supported it], if you are talking about the day when the peace agreement was signed with Jordan, then yes. But those are not representative days. You have to ask about a day like today. The journalists, including those in the middle politically, are influenced by the atmosphere and I think many support it less, much less than they supported it before. When it comes down to it, they reflect the general political mood, they can't detach themselves from it. (author's interview 6, May 11, 1995)

It is impossible to isolate the extent to which the news media are creating the mood or mostly amplifying it. As noted, however, the sensationalist coverage of terrorism in Israel is a relatively recent development. In the 1970s and early 1980s, terrorism coverage was much less extensive and emotional. Unfortunately, making decisions without public hysteria is no longer possible. Another Rabin advisor was asked about the public mood during these waves:

Anxiety, fear, extreme attitudes on all sides. One side says give it all up, and the other side says we should kill all the Arabs. And the emotional excitement [Hitragshut] that never existed before. (author's interview 4, March 19, 1995)

In the wake of the first two incidents – the Wachsman kidnapping and the bomb on Dizengoff street – Rabin held extremely trying press conferences in which he attempted to defend himself. The journalists – so enthusiastic only a few months before – battered him with questions and accusations. They wanted answers and they wanted them immediately. Rabin was no longer confident or in control; his performance was weak and unconvincing. After the third attack in Beit Lid, Rabin asked for television time in order to speak directly to the people and avoid the hostile reporters. His chief advisor talked about that decision:

Those three incidents, Beit Lid, Wachsman, and Dizengoff were three unsuccessful things. All three were unsuccessful. Because carrying out a press conference in the midst of hysteria is worst than if you shut up. The reporters are hysterical, and the Prime Minister gets angry with them and answers them hysterically and the results are terrible . . . We thought that the broadcast from his room here, with the flag, would be more calming. We thought that would work. Maybe we didn't succeed. (author's interview 4, March 19, 1995)

The terrorist attacks provided an important opportunity for the parliamentary opposition to promote its frames against the Oslo process. They had argued all along that the giving in to Palestinian demands would encourage violence. The terrorist attacks provided graphic "proof" that Oslo had failed. As the death toll grew, so did their case against Oslo. The major goal of the opposition political parties was to have the debate over Oslo framed as a conflict over security instead of an internal debate over the chances for peace. When terrorism was everyone's major concern, the need for greater security became self-evident.

Terrorist waves also offered important opportunities for the right-wing movements that were opposed to Oslo. In many ways they were much more effective than the political parties in getting the message across. As with any movement, they were forced to wait for the proper event in order to mobilize their members and sympathizers. Within hours of every terrorist attack, people were in the streets all over the country. People were angry, and it was up to the movements to channel that anger. One of the opposition spokespeople put it this way:

Everything I plan is planned in advance, but even the advanced planning takes into account that things happen from now to now. So if you're going to plan a demonstration in Kings of Israel Square [major site for massive demonstrations], you need a trigger in order to do it. So people say, "O.K., when something happens, when they sign an agreement, when they don't sign an agreement, when the security situation gets bad, then we'll put that plan into action. (author's interview 18, August 18, 1995)

The changes in the political environment also had an impact on the relationship between the Israeli journalists and the Palestinian leadership under Arafat.[3] They too were placed on the defensive during every terrorist wave. At the very least it appeared that Arafat was incapable of controlling Hamas; at the worst, that he was cooperating with them. The emphasis on dramatic events made it difficult for the Palestinian leadership to compete with Hamas. A PLO leader argued that the emphasis of the Israeli media on terrorism was destroying the peace process.

> I think the Israeli media in general, and Israeli television in particular is not passing on our message, or to be more exact it is passing on the unusual situation like the bombing at Beit Lid. They are using the articles and the pictures to inflame the situation rather than to calm it. The Israeli press and especially the Israeli television should be reporting in a way that helps the peace process. They attack the Palestinians for the Hamas actions as if all of the Palestinians are carrying out these kinds of acts, and they're trying to destroy the peace process. But if they really want peace then the Israeli television should be telling the Israeli viewer about the other side of the Palestinian people. (author's interview 26, January 16, 1995)

The message of antagonists is always constructed within a particular political context. Just as the Israeli leaders had to change their message in light of the wave of terrorism, so did the Palestinian leadership.

In many ways the terrorism waves accomplished exactly what they were supposed to. They served as powerful counterweights to the euphoric waves that accompanied the peace ceremonies. By January 1995, after the three incidents discussed in this chapter, public support for the Oslo peace process dropped to an all-time low (Tami Steinmentz Institute 1996). The terrorism waves increased the political standing of Hamas and lowered the legitimacy of the Arafat government. All of the leaders, activists, and journalists were forced to adjust themselves to the new reality. The news media cannot be held responsible for either the initiation of the terrorism wave or for how the various actors chose to react to it. They did, however, play an important role in the social construction of that reality.

CONCLUSION

A healthy democracy demands that citizens have a reasonable opportunity to deliberate on the major topics of the day (Fishkin 1991). The predominance of political waves, along with many other developments in modern politics and journalism, inhibit any such consideration. Instead, citizens are taken for a ride on an emotional roller coaster where external events often rush by in a blur of drama and action. It is a thrilling ride, which explains why so many people are willing to line up for it every day. However, one leaves dizzy and slightly off balance, in no condition to make any serious decisions about public issues.

The news media's need to portray politics as a series of exciting episodes is clearly related to the increasingly thin line between entertainment and news. Political leaders are forced to adapt to this constructed reality, and this in turn has a significant impact on the political process itself. The need for a quick, well-packaged response becomes a central priority. Other, often equally important issues are ignored.

It is true that the political and media environment in Israel may be especially prone to such waves. It is a country that has many ongoing security threats and an extremely centralized news media. All of the important news media are organized at the national level, and this increases the tendency to monitor one another and to move as a pack. But political waves increase the size of the audience in every country, and this provides an important incentive for journalists. While there may be an unusually high number of political waves in Israel, the need for big, exciting stories is universal.

There is one positive aspect of political waves. The onset of waves encourages a wide range of citizens to become engaged in the political process. The fact that a large number of citizens talk and think about political issues – however briefly and simplistically – is a more democratic solution than leaving politics to the elite few. While the political indifference has never been a problem in Israel, it is a concern in many Western countries.

The difficulty is that the mass public is being exposed to a narrow and unrealistic understanding of the issues at stake. The debate over the Oslo peace process is a perfect example of this problem. The euphoria in the early stages of the process was as unrealistic as the despair that gripped the society in the wake of terrorism. The early stages of the peace process were also a joint production between leaders and the press. The grand "peace ceremonies" staged by the Rabin government certainly made it seem as if the Arab-Israeli conflict was coming to an end. The news media are always looking for closure. They are not equipped to deal with a long, historical process such as the Middle East conflict.

This then is the inherent trade-off associated with the way the news media deal with political waves. The onset of waves provides important opportunities for a large segment of the population to become involved in the political process. Citizens have a chance to be exposed to a massive amount of information in a relatively short time, and many are motivated to discuss and debate the issues of the day. The problem is that the norms and routines for covering such waves have a profound influence on how issues are presented. Individual incidents become more important than processes, and drama is often valued over substance. Political leaders find themselves under increasing pressure to provide short-term solutions to long-term problems. The challenge for leaders, journalists, and citizens is to look beyond the turbulence associated with waves in an attempt to focus on the larger picture.

NOTES

1. The media initiate political waves when they uncover scandals and the like. One might also point to those cases in which the news media turn a small event into a big story. In general, however, the media are more likely to *react* to major events than to create them.
2. The Beit Lid Attack was carried out by the Islamic Jihad movement rather than Hamas. There is no indication, however, that this fact had any impact whatsoever on either the coverage or the reaction of the political leadership in Israel.
3. The analysis is only concerned with the political environment in Israel and not that which existed in the Palestinian Authority. Such an analysis could only be carried out by an expert on that society.

REFERENCES

Blumler, J. G., and D. Kavanaugh (1999). "The Third Age of Political Communication: Influences and Features." *Political Communication*, 14(3):209–230.

Brosius, H., and P. Epp (1995). "Prototyping through Key Events: News Selection in the Case of Violence Against Aliens and Asylum Seekers in Germany." *European Journal of Communication*, 10:391–412.

Downs, A. (1972). "Up and Down with Ecology – The "issue-attention cycle." *Public Interest*, 28:38–50.

Entman, R. (1993). "Framing: Towards Clarification of a Fractured Paradigm." *Journal of Communication*, 43:51–58.

Fallows, J. (1994). "Did you have a good week?" *The Atlantic Monthly*, 274:32–33.

Fishkin, J. S. (1991). *Democracy and Deliberation: New Directions for Democratic Reform.* New Haven, CT: Yale University Press.

Gamson, W. A., D. Croteau, W. Hoynes, and T. Sasson (1992). "Media Images and the Social Construction of Reality." *Annual Review of Sociology*, 18:373–393.

Gamson, W. A., and G. Wolfsfeld (1993). "Movements and the Media as Interacting Systems." *Annals of the American Academy of Political and Social Science*, 528:114–125.

Hilgartner, S., and C. Bosk (1988). "The Rise and Fall of Social Problems: A Public Arenas Model." *American Journal of Sociology*, 94:53–78.

Joppke, C. (1991). "Social Movements During Cycles of Issue Attention: The Decline of Anti-Nuclear Energy Movements in West Germany and the U.S.A." *British Journal of Sociology*, 42:43–60.

Just, M., A. Crigler, D. E. Alger, T. E. Cook, M. Kern, and D. M. West (1996). *Crosstalk: Citizens, Candidates, and the Media in a Presidential Election.* Chicago: University of Chicago Press.

Kepplinger, H. M., and J. Habermeir (1995). "The Impact of Key Events on the Presentation of Reality." *European Journal of Communication*, 10:371–390.

Liebes, T. (1998). "Television and Disaster Marathons: A Danger for Democratic Processes." In T. Liebes and J. Curran (Eds.), *Media, Culture, and Identity*, London: Routledge.

Linsky, M. (1991). *Impact: How the Press Affects Federal Policy Making.* New York: W.W. Norton.

Livingston, S. (1997). "Clarifying the CNN Effect: An Examination of Media Effects According to the Type of Military Intervention." Research Paper R-18, Cambridge, MA: The Joan Shorenstein Center on the Press, Politics, and Public Policy, Kennedy School of Government, Harvard University.

Mathes R., and B. Pfetsch (1991). "The Role of the Alternative Press in the Agenda-Building Process: Spill Over Effects and Media Opinion-Leadership." *European Journal of Communication*, 6:33–62.

McComas, K., and J. Shanahan (1999). Telling Stories about Global Climate Change: Measuring the Impact of Narratives on Issue Cycles." *Communication Research*, 26:30–57.

McCombs, M., and Z. Jian-Hua (1995). "Capacity, Diversity, and Volatility of the Public Agenda – Trends from 1954 to 1994." *Public Opinion Quarterly*, 59:495–525.

Nacos, B. L. (1996). *Terrorism and the Media: From the Iran Hostage Crisis to the World Trade Center Bombing.* New York: Columbia University Press.

Paletz, D., and A. P. Schmid (Eds.) (1992). *Terrorism and the Media.* Newbury Park, CA: Sage.

Patterson, T. (1998). "Time and News: The Media's Limitations as an Instrument of Democracy." *International Political Science Review*, 19:55–68.

Pfetsch, B. (1998). "Government News Management." In D. Graber, D. McQuail, and P. Norris (Eds.), *The Politics of News: The News of Politics.* Washington, DC: CQ Press.

Picard, R. (1993). *Media Portrayals of Terrorism: Functions and Meanings of News Coverage.* Ames, IA: Iowa State University Press.

Sabato, L. J. (1991). *Feeding Frenzy: How Attack Journalism Has Transformed American Politics.* New York: The Free Press.

Schaffert, R. W. (1992). *Mass Media and International Terrorism: A Quantitative Analysis.* New York: Praeger.

Scheufele, D. A. (1999). "Framing as a Theory of Media Effects." *Journal of Communication*, 49:103–122.

Staggenborg, S. (1993). "Critical Events and the Mobilization of the Pro-Choice Movement." *Political Sociology*, 6:319–345.

Tami Steinmetz Institute (1996). "The 'peace indicator' project: First findings." Ramat Aviv: Tel Aviv University [Hebrew].

Trumbo, C. (1996). "Constructing Climate Change: Claims and Frames in U.S. News Coverage of an Environmental Issue." *Public Understanding of Science,* 5:269–283.

Ungar, S. (1992). "The Rise and (Relative) Decline of Global Warming as a Social Problem." *The Sociological Quarterly,* 33:483–501.

Weimann, G. (1994). *The Theater of Terror: Mass Media and International Terrorism.* New York: Longman.

Wolfsfeld, Gadi (1997a). *Media and Political Conflict: News from the Middle East.* Cambridge: Cambridge University Press.

(1997b). "Fair Weather Friends: The Varying Role of the News Media in the Arab-Israeli peace process." *Political Communication,* 1997, 14:29–48.

(1997c). Promoting Peace through the News Media: Some Initial Lessons from the Peace Process." *Harvard International Journal of Press/Politics,* 2:52–70.

CHAPTER 12

Monica Lewinsky and the Mainsprings of American Politics

John Zaller

Just before news of a sexual relationship between Bill Clinton and Monica Lewinsky became the talk of the nation, the president's job approval rating stood at 60 percent. Ten days later, following intense media coverage of the affair, Clinton's approval ratings, as measured by the same polling organizations, had risen to about 70 percent.[1] Thus, the president not only survived the first round of Monicagate; he seemed to prosper.

Several months later, Clinton pulled off another miracle. One of the most enduring regularities of American politics is that the president's party loses seats in the House of Representatives in midterm elections. In the 1998 midterms, with the Congress threatening to impeach the president for lying to cover up his sexual misbehavior, a big loss for Clinton's party seemed especially likely. But when the votes were counted, the Democrats had actually gained seats in Congress, thereby surprising political scientists and maddening Clinton's enemies.

If anyone had previously doubted it, these two occurrences should be taken as final evidence that media frenzies over personal shortcomings are not the driving force of American politics. Stories of personal scandal can sell newspapers and provide opposition politicians with ammunition for rhetorical attack, but they do not in the end seem to make much difference for public opinion or national politics.

What, then, does move public opinion? What forces do drive American politics?

The argument of this chapter – hardly novel but sufficiently under-

I thank Fred Greenstein for pressing me to write this chapter. He, Larry Bartels, Lance Bennett, Richard Brody, Barbara Geddes, and Nelson Polsby also made helpful comments on earlier drafts.

appreciated that it bears making – is that presidents and their parties rise and fall in the public's esteem mainly according to how effectively they govern.[2] Political accountability for war and peace, prosperity and recession, policies that work and policies that don't – these are the mainsprings of American politics. Other things can matter, but accountability for the condition of the country and for the enactment of effective policies matter most of all. The significant contribution of the Lewinsky scandal to the understanding of American politics has been to drive home this lesson as never before.

It is often claimed that traditional American politics has been shattered by two transforming developments, the decline of political parties and the rise of new communication technologies, such as the Internet and political talk radio. The effect, it is argued, has been to unhinge American politics from its traditional moorings and to make public opinion prey to media-driven fads and contagion. I argue in this essay that this view is wrong, and I shall use the Lewinsky affair as exhibit A. More specifically, I shall argue that, in the Lewinsky matter as in presidential politics more generally:

- Political parties, though given up for dead by many political analysts, are still the most important vehicle by which Americans relate to politics and hold leaders accountable.
- Despite the rise of new forms of communication that might have been expected to destabilize it, American public opinion, at least as regards presidential politics, is no more volatile now than in the past.
- Political fundamentals tend to trump media hype in national politics. By this I mean that politicians who can claim the high ground of peace, prosperity, and moderation have dominated presidential politics through most of this century and will continue to do so.

HOW DID CLINTON SURVIVE?

The main issue in the Lewinsky scandal was not Clinton's relationship with Lewinsky; it was whether he tried illegally to cover up that relationship. In testimony before an Arkansas court over a separate matter,[3] Clinton was asked whether he had ever had a sexual relationship with Lewinsky. The legal rationale for asking that question of the President of the United States was to establish whether Clinton had a pattern of sexual relations with underlings. Having sworn an oath to tell the truth, Clinton denied having sexual relations with Lewinsky.

The scandal became public when an Internet journalist, Matt Drudge, reported that Independent Prosecutor Ken Starr was looking into the Lewinsky matter. Starr was charged with investigating Clinton's role in a series of business transactions in Arkansas in the early 1980s that were known as the Whitewater case. Sex in the White House had nothing to do with Whitewater, but Starr suspected that Bill and Hillary Clinton had encouraged witnesses to deny their involvement in Whitewater, and he suspected that Bill Clinton had similarly urged Lewinsky to lie in the Arkansas court case. An alleged pattern of encouraging witnesses to lie was the legal rationale for Starr's investigation into Clinton's personal life. Starr never did bring charges against the Clintons over Whitewater, but his investigation of the President for perjury and witness tampering in the Lewinsky case made the president's sexual behavior a major news story.

When the Lewinsky story broke, the nation's mass media gave it the kind of saturation coverage that political stories rarely get. There were special programs on TV, cover stories in the news magazines, and cable and talk radio programs whose fare was "All Monica, all the time." Not since the O. J. Simpson murder trial did America have such a titillating news story.

It is hard to blame the media for its saturation coverage. For one thing, it was clear from the first day that the scandal might lead to impeachment in the House of Representatives – as, in fact, it eventually did. For another, there is much natural interest in a story about a president who cheats on the First Lady, lies to cover it up, but gets caught anyway, and has hell to pay. Thus, news outlets that gave heavy coverage to the Lewinsky matter saw their ratings rise. To mention three examples: When *Time* magazine put Monica Lewinsky on the cover early in the scandal, it sold 350,000 newstand copies, compared with 250,000 normally. When Lewinsky appeared on ABC's 20/20 to tell her side of the story to journalist Barbara Walters, 50 million viewers tuned in, making it one of the most heavily watched news programs in TV history. Hillary Clinton's appearance on NBC's *Today* show to deny her husband's affair with Lewinsky enabled *Today* to achieve the highest weekly audience ratings in its history.

Not only were news organizations lavish in their coverage of the Lewinsky matter; they were also lavish in their sponsorship of public opinion polls about it. Every major media poll took numerous soundings of national opinion, even though such polls are expensive to do and have no direct effect on audience ratings. The expectation was that the president's public support would drain away as the scandal continued, and each major news organization wanted to be able to document the president's fall with its own poll numbers.

As it turned out, the president' support never fell. After the first ten days, there was almost no change in support for Clinton. Insofar as opinion did shift, it tended to drift very slowly downward in quiet times and to bounce back when "the big guy" came under threat. Events that might have been expected to hurt the President – Kathleen Willey's charge on CBS's 60 Minutes that Clinton groped her breasts when she sought help in getting a job; release of Clinton's televised grand jury testimony in which he denied a sexual relationship with Lewinsky; the Starr report, with its graphic descriptions of sexual encounters in a hallway just off the Oval Office; the House of Representatives vote to impeach him – all either helped him or had no effect on his poll standings.

Altogether, there was so little movement in the polls that it is hard to get any sense of the dynamics of public opinion. The key question thus becomes: Why so much stability in public opinion amidst the Lewinsky scandal?

Party loyalty is a large part of the answer. A large political science literature has shown that most Americans, especially most who bother to vote, develop party attachments sometime in their youth or early adulthood and maintain those attachments through the rest of their lives. Partisan conversion does occur, but the main story is one of partisan loyalty. (In the 1960s and 1970s, there was evidence of erosion in party loyalty. But more recent data show that early reports of the demise of party were greatly exaggerated, as we shall see here.)

Table 12.1 gives examples of the importance of party loyalty in the public's reaction to the Lewinsky scandal. By margins of about four-to-one, self-described Republicans were more likely than self-described Democrats to believe that Clinton's transgressions were public rather than private matters, to believe that Ken Starr's investigation was impartial rather than partisan, and to believe that Clinton should be impeached if he wouldn't resign. Differences were even bigger among more zealous partisans. For example, 74 percent of self-described strong Republicans, compared to 6 percent of strong Democrats, thought Clinton should be impeached (these data not in Table 12.1).

One might suspect that strong partisanship of the kind in Table 12.1

Table 12.1. *The effect of partisanship on responses to the Lewinsky scandal*

If [Clinton] does not resign, should he be impeached?

	Republicans	Independents	Democrats
Yes	54.2%	27.8	10.6
No	41.8	69.5	88.0
Don't know	4.1	2.6	1.4
	100%	100	100
N = 1270			

Do you think of this whole situation (the Clinton-Lewinsky matter) more as a PRIVATE MATTER having to do with Bill Clinton's personal life, or more a PUBLIC MATTER having to do with Bill Clinton's job as President?

	Republicans	Independents	Democrats
Public matter	57.4	24.2	15.0
Private matter	36.6	66.7	80.4
Don't know	6.0	9.2	4.6
	100%	100	100
N = 1273			

Do you think Kenneth Starr, the Independent Counsel investigating Whitewater and other issues, is mostly conducting an IMPARTIAL INVESTIGATION to find out if anything illegal occurred or is mostly conducting a PARTISAN INVESTIGATION to damage Bill Clinton?

	Republicans	Independents	Democrats
Impartial Investigation	52.1	17.1	11.1
Partisan Investigation	41.6	65.1	84.1
Don't know/Can't choose	6.2	17.8	4.7
	100%	100	100
N = 1273			

Note: Cell entries are percent giving the indicated response. Partisanship is measured by the standard party question, as described in connection with Figure 12.2.
Source: *1998 National Election Study.*

occurs mainly among the politically ignorant and uninformed. The opposite, however, is the case: As can be seen in Figure 12.1, highly informed persons had the strongest partisan reaction to the Lewinsky scandal. Poorly informed citizens, for their part, showed only a hint of partisanship. (In Figure 12.1, "political information" is measured by

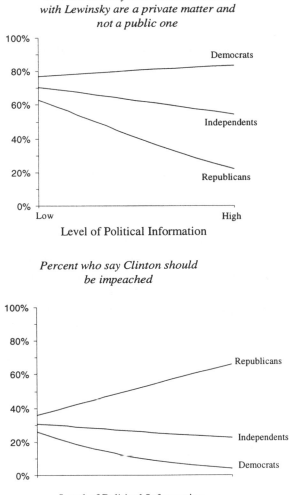

Figure 12.1. The effect of political information and partisanship on attitudes toward the Lewinsky matter. *Source: National Election Study*, 1998.

questions about basic political facts, such as which party controls Congress.)

The pattern of party-based polarization of opinion shown in Figure 12.1 is entirely normal in American politics. It arises whenever, as occurred in the Lewinsky case, party elites take opposing positions on an issue (Zaller 1992). This basic fact of American politics is highly relevant to understanding the public's response to the Lewinsky scandal. For with the opinions of most Americans, especially those most heavily exposed to news of the scandal, stubbornly anchored in partisan attachments, it was hard for the media to have much effect on public opinion.

Yet partisans are not always so loyal. Every president, including Clinton, has experienced ups and downs in public support. Hence, if Clinton's support remained high during the scandal, something more is needed to explain why. I therefore offer the following explanation: The performance criteria by which Americans normally judge presidents remained favorable to Clinton throughout the year in which Lewinsky was in the headlines.

One of the most important of these performance criteria is the condition of the national economy. As many know from the movie *War Room*, Clinton's media consultants ran his 1992 presidential campaign on the theme that "It's the economy, stupid." This was their way of reminding themselves and voters that the 1991–92 recession, which began under incumbent President George Bush, should be the most important issue in the 1992 election. Much evidence supports the claim that such recessions do, in fact, have a powerful effect on presidential elections. It appears, for example, that about half of the variance in the outcomes of presidential elections is explained by economic conditions in the country at the time of the vote, as we shall see in this chapter.

The Lewinsky scandal did not, of course, take place at the time of a presidential election. But economic conditions affect a president's poll ratings even when there is no election going on (MacKuen, Erikson, and Stimson 1992). To understand the effect of economic prosperity on Clinton's popularity amid the Lewinsky scandal, one must view the "Lewinsky economy" – that is, economic conditions in the year of the scandal – in historical perspective. Table 12.2 provides the information to do this. From data in this table, we see that, from the end of World War II to 1998, average personal income in the United States rose about 1.89 percent per year. From the end of the Vietnam War to 1998, it rose an average of 1.51 percent per year. But in the year of the Lewinsky scandal, personal income rose 2.25 percent, which is roughly 50 percent above the norm in the post–Vietnam era.

If these growth rates seem small, keep in mind two things. First, a strong economy means that more people have jobs, feel secure about their jobs, and hence feel secure about their future more generally.

Table 12.2. *The "Lewinsky economy" in historical perspective*

Average annual gain in personal income:	
Since World War II (1946 to 1998)	+1.89%
Since Vietnam War (1974 to 1998)	+1.51%
During Jimmy Carter presidency (1977 to 1980)	+1.80%
During Ronald Reagan presidency (1981 to 1988)	+2.14%
During George Bush presidency (1989 to 1992)	+0.58%
During Clinton presidency (1993 to 1998)	+1.52%
During year of Lewinsky scandal (1998)	*+2.25%*
Year of Nixon's resignation over Watergate (1974)	*−1.67%*

Note: The data are average annual percent change in Real Disposable Income, adjusted to per capita rates to reflect change in U.S. population.
Sources: *Survey of Current Business*, August 1998, and September 1999, p. D6, and U.S. Department of Census Web page: http://www.census.gov/.

Second, even small annual growth rates add up over the years in the manner of compound interest. Thus, an annual increase of 1.89 percent per year for the 52-year period 1946 to 1998 compounds to an increase of 265 percent in per person income over the whole period. (This figure is based on the standard formula for compound interest – that is, $(1.0189)^{52} = 2.65$, which is 265 percent.) For the 24-year period from the end of the Vietnam War to 1998, an annual increase of 1.51 percent compounds to an overall increase of 43 percent.

A comparison of growth rates under Presidents Bush and Clinton is illuminating. If the average growth rate during Clinton's presidency – 1.52 percent from 1993 through the end of 1998 – were sustained over a 25-year period, it would produce a 46 percent increase in national income. If, in contrast, the average income gain during Bush's term (0.58 percent per year) were compounded over a 25-year period, it would produce a mere 16 percent increase in national income. If one wonders why Bill Clinton won election for a second term as president and then survived the Lewinsky scandal, and why George Bush lost the presidency after one term, one need look no further than this comparison for a big part of the answer.

But there is another comparison in Table 12.2 that is even more telling. It concerns the Watergate scandal, which came to a climax in August 1974 and resulted in Richard Nixon being forced from office. Unhappily for President Nixon, 1974 was a year in which change in personal income was actually negative, namely, −1.67 percent. This was the single worst annual income figure since the Great Depression.

Nor was a weak economy Nixon's only economic headache during Watergate. The Organization of Petroleum Exporting Countries (OPEC) also imposed an oil boycott on the United States and other importers. One effect was gasoline shortages so severe that Americans were forced to wait hours in line to buy gasoline – when they could get gasoline at all. Another was to set off a bout of high inflation. The combination of high inflation and a faltering economy was without precedent and gave rise to a new term, "stagflation," meaning economic stagnation plus inflation.

If, then, one wonders why Bill Clinton escaped Monicagate and Richard Nixon was driven from office over Watergate, one would be wise to take account of the differences in economic conditions in the two periods. Americans tend to keep presidents who, by luck or skill, preside over prosperous times, and to get rid of presidents who preside over economic disasters.

I shall provide a more systematic account of the effect of economic conditions on presidential politics in the section on "The Mainsprings of American Politics." I wish now to move on to other factors affecting the public's assessment of presidential performance. For, as Brody (1991) has shown, essentially everything that happens in the way of "good news" for the president's political program boosts the president's job approval ratings. My account will focus on two factors in particular.

One big but easy-to-overlook determinant of presidential popularity is, as I suggested earlier, peace – or at least the absence of costly war. It is almost impossible for a president to maintain popular support when Americans are fighting and dying in combat (Mueller 1973). Popular support for Presidents Harry Truman and Lyndon Johnson was so damaged by bloody wars that, despite fairly good economies, they both chose to retire from office rather than run for reelection.[4] Earlier on, Abraham Lincoln won reelection in 1864 by a slim margin amid the carnage of the Civil War (and despite the fact that southern states were not voting); the party of World War I leader Woodrow Wilson was massively repudiated in the first election after that war ended; and even Franklin Roosevelt faced declining popularity as a result of the casualties suffered in World War II.[5]

Perhaps the clearest evidence that war and peace affect poll ratings has been provided by Clinton himself. After maintaining job approval ratings in the range of 60 to 70 percent throughout the Lewinsky scandal, his ratings fell into the range of 50 to 55 percent approval when the War in Kosovo seemed to be bogging down. And this was a war in which the United States did not suffer a single battlefield casualty! Thus, what intense media coverage of a sex scandal could not accomplish in a year, the hint of an unsuccessful war – coming after the Lewinsky scandal was over – accomplished within a few weeks.

Besides peace and a strong economy, a third big performance factor in presidential popularity is the ability to pick policies that voters like. The temptation for many politicians is to follow an ideological agenda, serving up policies that are either too liberal or too conservative for the bulk of voters, who tend to cluster in "the middle of the (ideological) road." Thus, ideological moderation, in contrast to ideological extremism, tends to make for successful presidencies.

This was a lesson that Clinton learned the hard way, through voter rejection of his overly liberal policies in the 1994 congressional elections. But once Clinton learned the lesson of moderation, he learned it very well. Friend and foe alike say that, after major missteps in his first two years in office, he developed unusual skill in figuring out what middle-of-the-road voters wanted and giving it to them.

The story of Clinton's trek to the ideological center is as follows. Clinton came into office in 1992 committed to equal rights for homosexuals and some form of national health insurance. Both ideas were popular with ideological activists in the Democratic party – that is, people who volunteer their time and money to work for party candidates – and Clinton began his presidency by trying to enact policies that these groups favored. Polls suggested these policies might be popular with the public as well, but that turned out to be wrong. Clinton's proposals for gays in the military and government-controlled health insurance quickly became controversial with the general public, making him seem extreme. The result was "The Revolution of 1994," in which voters turned against Clinton and the Democrats in the congressional elections of that year by giving Republicans control of Congress for the first time since 1954. The centerpiece of the successful Republican campaign was emphasis on Clinton's unpopular liberal policies (Jacobson 1997).

Stung by voter rejection of his party in 1994, Clinton trimmed his ideological sails and began paying attention to what centrist voters wanted (Morris 1999). As the 1996 election neared, the Democratic president faced a particularly tough choice on welfare reform. The Republican Congress was pushing a proposal to end federal responsibility for welfare (Aid to Families with Dependent Children, or AFDC) by turning it over to state government, but the idea was adamantly opposed by Democratic party activists and probably by Clinton himself. But the Republican proposal was popular with centrist voters, so after considerable hesitation, Clinton went along. Clinton also managed to seize the center ground in his battle with the Republican-controlled Congress on how to balance the budget. Clinton stood firmly against cuts to Medicare and Social Security, while Republicans wanted to restrain spending on both. This made Clinton seem moderate and the Republican budget-cutters like extremists.

Although systematic evidence is thin, Clinton's move to the ideological center after the 1994 midterm election seems to have helped his job approval ratings. His ratings were lower at the midpoint of his first term, when the economy was strong but he was identified with policies like gays in the military, than at the end of this term, when the economy was weaker but he had remade himself as a centrist. Clinton's average job approval rating in Gallup polls taken in the sixth, seventh, and eighth quarters of his term averaged 44.3 percent, and the average percent change in personal income in these same quarters was 4.7 percent. But in quarters fourteen through sixteen of his first term, these figures were 55.5 and 1.5. This evidence, though scarcely definitive, suggests that ideological moderation may be as important to high poll ratings as economic prosperity. I shall have more to say about ideological moderation in a later section.

The question under examination in this section has been why Clinton's public support remained high during a year in which charges of adultery and perjury by the President were the country's top news story. I have offered two answers. The first is that much of the public is highly partisan in its reaction to politics and that Clinton derived solid support from people who are predisposed to support almost any Democrat. (Of course, Republican presidents enjoy the same benefit from their partisan base when they occupy the White House.) Second, the public normally holds presidents accountable for the general condition of the country and for the policies they advance, and on both counts, Clinton was on solid ground at the time of the Lewinsky scandal.

EFFECTS OF MEDIA COVERAGE

Although public support for Clinton was generally steady throughout the year of the scandal, there was one point at which opinion did fluctuate: Just after the media broke news of the scandal, Clinton's job approval ratings fell about 5 to 6 percentage points in three days. But then, amid continuing heavy media coverage, support for Clinton bounced back 15 points over the next week or so, for a net gain of about 10 points. In this section, I shall look closely at this episode to see what it reveals about the nature of media influence on public opinion.

Let us begin by examining levels of public support for Clinton in polls taken just before, during, and after the Lewinsky story broke. These polls – everything I can find on the Internet – are summarized in Table 12.3. Although question wordings differ somewhat, all polls refer to Clinton's job performance as president. Also reported in Table 12.3 are the results of a content analysis of TV news coverage of the Lewinsky scandal during this period.

The media content analysis, as shown in the top three rows of Table 12.3, gives average minutes per network news program that were favorable or unfavorable to Clinton. Favorable references include Clinton's denials of an affair with Lewinsky, attacks on Independent Prosecutor Ken Starr by Clinton allies, statements of support for Clinton from allies, and any other information (including nonscandal information) that might tend to enhance public support for the President. Unfavorable references include all statements indicating that the President did have an affair with Lewinsky or tried to cover it up, attacks on Clinton or defense of Starr, and any other information that might tend to undermine public support for Clinton. It is worth emphasizing that politicians rather than journalists initiated part of the news being summarized in Table 12.3. Thus, some of what I have classified as positive or negative "media coverage" might also be called "partisan attacks" or "partisan defenses" by politicians.

What the content analysis shows is that the media frenzy began with two days of heavily negative coverage, but that coverage was relatively balanced after that (given that the sex scandal continued to be in the news at all). Positive coverage consisted mainly of denials that Clinton had a relationship with Lewinsky and attacks on Starr for pursuing the matter. If the first two days of coverage are set aside, the remaining period has about as many positive minutes as negative ones, including two days on which Clinton's coverage was actually positive.

I have divided the poll data into four partly overlapping periods to reflect trends in the content and opinion data. As Table 12.3 shows, the first two days of heavily negative scandal reportage seemed to have a big

Table 12.3. *Trends in Clinton job approval ratings in initial phase of Lewinsky matter*

	Story Pre-event Baseline	Breaks Jan. 21	22	23	24	25	26	Before speech 27	After speech 27	28	29	30	31	Feb. 1	Change
Network TV News Content															
Positive news minutes		0.7	2.0	4.2	2.5	2.4	2.9	4.9		4.6	1.9	4.0			
Negative news minutes		7.9	8.3	5.3	5.2	1.6	5.3	3.4		1.5	2.4	2.4			
Net news (positive minus negative)		−7.2	−6.3	−1.1	−2.8	+0.8	−2.5	+1.5		+3.1	−0.4	+1.6			
Phase I: Initial frenzy (first two days)															
NBC News	62 (1/18)		61												−1
CBS News–*NYT*	58 (1/18)		55												−3
ABC News	62 (1/13)				57										−6
Time/CNN	59 (1/15)			52											−7
Newsweek	61 (1/18)			54											−7
Gallup	60 (1/18)				58										−2
ABC News–*Wash. Post*	59 (1/19)				51										−8

Phase II: Run up to State of Union address

Source														Diff
NBC					61	63								+2
CBS News/NYT		55		56	61	57								+2
ABC News				57	59	60								+3
Gallup		58		60	59		67							+9

Phase III: State of Union address

Source														Diff
ABC News						60	60							0
NBC						63	63		68					+5
CBS (respondents asked ahead to watch speech)							73							16?

Phase IV: State of Union address plus post speech events

Source														Diff
Gallup							67	67	69					+2
CBS News						57		73					72	+15
ABC News						60				68	69			+9
Los Angeles Times				59								68		+9
Times/CNN		52									68	68		

| **Simple Averages** | 60 | 58 | 53 | 56 | 59 | 60 | 67 | 67 | 70 | 68 | 69 | 68 | 70 | |

Note: Cell entries are percent who approve Clinton's job performance in a given poll.
Sources: For sources of polls, see a PC Excel file called "Lewpols" on my Web page, www.sscnet.ucla.edu/polisci/faculty/zaller/. Sizes and designs of polls vary.

impact on opinion. On the basis of a half-dozen polls, Clinton's support seems to have dropped about six or seven points.

The scandal broke on a Wednesday, with the most heavily negative coverage on that day and Thursday. From Friday on, coverage was more balanced and public support for the President rose. By Monday, Clinton had regained everything lost in the first two days, and in Tuesday's Gallup poll, support for the President rose above pre–Lewinsky levels. There were two notable events in this period, both of which got heavy news coverage. The first was Clinton's appearance at a televised press conference on Monday to make an emotional denial of a sexual relationship with Lewinsky. "I did not have sex with that woman, Ms. Lewinsky," the president said. The other notable event was Hillary Clinton's appearance on NBC's *Today* show on Tuesday morning, where she charged that the Lewinsky matter was the product of a right-wing conspiracy against her husband. One basis of her claim was that Starr was a Republican with long-standing ties to conservative organizations. Perhaps more importantly to an enthralled nation, the *Today* show appearance seemed an example of Hillary "standing by her man."

If there is any particular break or spike in the opinion data, it is the Tuesday Gallup poll, which was taken early that evening. It was therefore able to reflect news of Hillary Clinton's appearance on the *Today* show in the morning. Indeed, the poll was taken just as many Americans were getting news of Mrs. Clinton's appearance on the evening news programs. With this news so vivid in many Americans' minds, this Gallup poll may have overstated the lasting importance of Mrs. Clinton's defense of the president on public opinion. But however this may be, the poll taken following her *Today* show appearance showed a gain of 8 percentage points from the day before, a difference that achieves conventional levels of statistical significance.

Clinton's State of the Union address occurred later on Tuesday evening, the end of the seventh day since the Lewinsky story broke and the same day as his wife's appearance on *Today*. The speech attracted an unusually large audience, presumably because people wanted to see how the crisis-stricken President would perform. According to pundits and commentators, he performed extremely well. "Good speech, too bad," as one commentator put it, thus suggesting that any good effects from the speech would be wasted.[6]

Two national surveys were taken immediately after the speech. From baselines on the day before the State of the Union address — and therefore also before Hillary Clinton's defense of the president – one survey showed no change and the other showed a gain of 5 points, for an average gain of 2.5 percent. [7] There was also a CBS poll involving re-interviews with a panel of respondents who had been asked by telephone to watch the speech so that they could be polled afterward. This survey found that Clinton' postspeech job approval rating was 73 percent. No immediate prespeech baseline is available for this poll, but if we use the best baseline we have – Clinton's 57-percent job approval in the CBS-NYT poll from the day before the speech – then the combination of the speech and Mrs. Clinton's defense netted the president some 16 percentage points in support.

A little back-of-the-envelope arithmetic shows that these two sets of post-speech results – an average 2.5-percent gain in two polls and a 16-point gain among those asked to watch the speech – are not as far apart as they might seem. According to the Nielsen research firm, 53.1 million Americans saw the speech.[8] This is a lot of people, but only about 25 percent of the adult population. If 16 percent of the 25 percent who watched the speech became more supportive of the president, the overall increase in public support would be only 4.0 percentage points $(0.16 \times 0.25 = 0.04)$. If we assume that viewership of the speech was higher than 25 percent among those asked to watch it in preparation for a survey but still well under 100 percent – say, about 50 percent – then there is no disagreement among the three polls on the size of the "speech plus Hillary" effect.

In the days after the speech, Clinton's job approval rate may have risen a bit more. From the bottom panel of Table 12.3, this gain appears to have been about 3 percentage points. But this gain, if real, is small in relation to gains that had already occurred.

From this analysis of poll trends and media coverage, an important conclusion follows: Although media coverage may explain the drop in Clinton's support in the first few days of the scandal, it cannot explain the rebound, and it especially cannot explain how Clinton ended up with more support than he started with. Thus, a theory that public support for Clinton responded mechanically to media coverage – dropping with bad coverage, rising with good coverage – cannot adequately explain the public's response to the Lewinsky scandal.

From this conclusion, a second follows: That to understand what moved public opinion in this case, analysts (such as me) must move beyond simple counts of the amounts of "favorable coverage" and "unfavorable coverage" in the media, as examined so far. But how to do this? What can be done to study the dynamics of opinion change besides tallying amounts of positive and negative media coverage?

I propose that the best way to make sense of the dynamics of public opinion in this case is to analyze the particular events that occurred rather than media coverage of these events. Hence I posit that there were essentially three events in the first days of the Lewinsky scandal. The first was the release of information that the independent prosecutor was investigating charges that the President had lied to an Arkansas Grand Jury about his sexual relationship with Lewinsky. Information about Lewinsky's interrogation by law enforcement officials and her attempts at a plea bargain would all be counted as part of this compound event. As would be expected, the effect of this event was to undermine Clinton's public support, as shown in Table 12.3. The second event was Clinton's protestation of innocence at a press conference, with Hillary Clinton's appearance on *Today* counted as part of this same claim of innocence. Poll data suggest that this event – Clinton's public defense of himself – helped the President. The third event was Clinton's State of the Union address, which also probably helped the president.

Such an argument goes against the grain of much media analysis, which tends to view the media, rather than the events the media reports, as being influential. Often the focus on media content, apart from the underlying events, does seem appropriate. But in this case, the pattern of evidence points to the importance of events rather than media coverage of those events.[9]

This argument also goes against the grain of analysis that emphasizes the capacity of "powerful mass media" to shape the views of "ignorant and gullible" masses. For if there is one lesson that the Lewinsky scandal has demonstrated, it is that, however poorly informed, psychologically driven, and "mass-mediated" public opinion may be, it is capable of recognizing and focusing on its own conception of what matters.

If, then, the public was more persuaded by Clinton's protestation of innocence than by Starr's accusations of sex and perjury, the next question is why. Why did the public seem to believe Clinton rather than Starr?

One possibility is that Clinton's denials were simply very credible. But I find this hard to accept. Clinton was a man with a well-known reputation for womanizing, and while he was denying an affair with Lewinsky, Lewinsky was semipublicly negotiating a plea bargain with Starr. If, under these circumstances, the public believed Clinton, it was because it wanted to. It turned out, moreover, that even after Starr did lay out evidence that left little doubt as to Clinton's guilt on the perjury charge, most of the public continued to back Clinton.

I suggest, therefore, that we consider the political context that made the public want to believe Clinton's self-defense, namely, his record of achievement in office. Clinton made an excellent statement of this record in his State of the Union address. Although, as we have seen, the address reached too few people and came too late to explain the bulk of Clinton's recovery in the polls, it is reasonable to suppose that the presidential record that the speech touted was apprehended to some degree by the majority of the public.

Clinton speech was, first of all, a celebration of a list of "accomplishments" that would be any President's dream: The economy during Clinton's second term was the strongest in twenty-five years, the federal budget was on the verge of balance for the first time in twenty years, the crime rate was falling rapidly for the first time in living memory, and the country was at peace. In the main section of the speech, the President proposed a series of programs designed to appeal to the ideological center, as exemplified by a plan to use surplus funds to put Social Security on a sound footing, improve public education, and build more highways. Thus, what the president trumpeted in the State of the Union address – and what he would presumably continue by remaining in office – was a record of peace, prosperity, and moderation. Or, more succinctly, it was a record of "political substance." This record was so unassailable that, to much of what the President said in the State of the Union address, the Republican leadership could only offer polite applause.

To argue, as I am, that the public stays focused on a bottom line consisting of peace, prosperity, and moderation is not to say that the public is either wise or virtuous. For one thing, its sense of substance seems, in the aggregate, quite amoral – much more like "what have you done for me lately?" than such traditional ideals as freedom, equality, or justice. Nor is it clear that the public's decision criteria are very sophisticated. Suppose, for example, that the Watergate investigation of Richard Nixon had taken place in the context of Bill Clinton's booming economy rather than, as was the case, in the context of gasoline shortages, high inflation, and high unemployment. Would Nixon have been forced from office in a good economy? Or, if Clinton had been saddled with the economic conditions that existed during Watergate, would he have been driven from office as Nixon was? These are, I believe, real questions, and the fact that they are does not speak well for the public's wisdom or virtue.

THE MAINSPRINGS OF AMERICAN POLITICS

A few years after he left the presidency, Lyndon Johnson was asked by a TV news producer what had changed in American politics since the 1930s when he came to Washington as a young Texas congressman.

> "You guys, [Johnson replied], without even reflecting. "All you guys in the media. All of politics has changed because of you. You've broken all the [party] machines and the ties between us in the Congress and the city machines. You've given us a new kind of people." A certain disdain passed over his face. "Teddy, Tunney.[10] They're your creations, your puppets. No machine could ever create a Teddy Kennedy. Only you guys. They're all yours. Your product." (Halberstam 1979, pp. 15–16)

The view that the rise of the mass media has destroyed political parties is widely spread among observers of American politics. So is another: That the new style of media-driven politics is more given to fad, excess, and instability than the regime of political parties that it replaced.

"Every election, at every level of political activity, became a new throw of the dice, and the electorate behaved differently each time, with the ordering of choice among many voters between the parties increasingly unpredictable from contest to contest," writes historian Joel Silbey (1994, pp. 16–17). Martin Wattenberg (1991) has likewise argued that parties' ability to polarize opinion into rival camps [has] weakened, creating a vacuum in the structure of electoral attitudes. Voters were thus set politically adrift and subject to volatile electoral swings" (p. 2). This development has in turn led to "the rise of candidate-centered politics" and to what Walter Dean Burnham calls a "volcanic instability" in American politics.

Such language is much too strong for the current reality of American politics, at least in regard to presidential politics. All of politics has *not* changed, and, in particular, it has *not* become unusually volatile. It continues, as in the past, to be dominated by political parties and by voters whose demands on parties can be summarized as peace, prosperity, and moderation. Politicians who can fulfill these demands thrive and those who can't are returned to private life, more or less regardless of what the media say about it. American politics in the late twentieth century was, in short, a politics of tough-minded substance. Thus, the public's steady support for Clinton in the midst of a sex scandal is not exceptional in American politics; it is the rule.

Evidence bearing on these issues is quite easy to marshal. I begin with the notion that presidential elections have become less stable. In the period from 1900 to 1964, the average swing in the presidential vote from one election to the next was 7.7 points, including any effects of third-party candidates on the vote. In the period from 1968 to 1996, the comparable swing was essentially the same, 8.12 points.[11]

It is also possible to measure instability within each election campaign. Starting in 1948, the Gallup organization has regularly measured public support for the major party candidates in January of the election year, just after the party conventions in August, and in the first week of October. In the period from 1948 to 1964, the average swing from January to the[12] election was 14.8 percent; in the period from 1968 to 1996, this figure was 14.9. The comparable figures for the swing from the post-convention period to election day are 4.7 percent for the early period and 5.1 percent for the recent period. And finally, figures for average swing from early October to election day are 4.0 percent and 4.3 percent.[13]

The claim of "volcanic instability" thus fails to get much support from data on presidential elections. Let us now evaluate the claim that there has been a dramatic decline in American parties. One way to measure the importance of parties is to measure allegiance to parties among members of the voting public. If voters continue to profess allegiance to parties in large numbers, and if they continue to vote loyally for the party to which they declare allegiance, it would be hard to argue that parties are weak.

With this in mind, we shall examine responses to the following question, which was put to a representative sample of citizens in each election year from 1952 to 1996: "Generally speaking, do you usually think of yourself as a Republican, a Democrat, an independent or what?"

Respondents who claimed to identify with a party were asked in a follow-up question whether they were strong or not so strong partisans. Respondents who initially said they were independents were asked if they were closer to one of the parties. Based on these questions, each respondent has been given a score on a scale that runs from 3 (strong partisan) to 0 (pure independent). The average of these responses, calculated separately for voters and nonvoters, is shown in the top part of

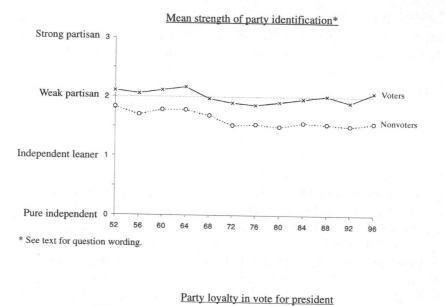

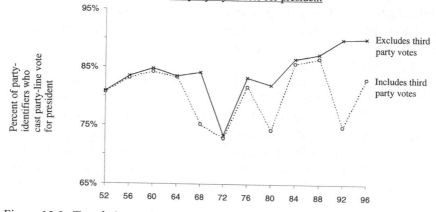

Figure 12.2. Trends in partisan attachment and loyalty, 1952–1996. *Source: National Election Studies* cumulative file.

Figure 12.2. As can be seen, there was a modest dip in support for parties in the late 1960s and 1970s. But for persons who cast ballots in presidential elections, party allegiance is as strong as it has been since surveys began to measure it. Among nonvoters, party allegiance has recovered less well from the dip in the 1970s and is now 15 percent below what it was in 1952. But since, by definition, nonvoters do not vote, this decline has no direct effect on the electoral system.

The lower half of Figure 12.2 displays party loyalty for voters who express any degree of attachment to a party – that is, voters are strongly or weakly attached to a party or say they are closer to a party. The party loyalty rates for these voters, as shown in the lower panel in Figure 12.2, disclose little if any tendency toward a long-term decline. Except for the McGovern–Nixon election in 1972 and the appearance of well-publicized third-party candidates, party loyalty rates have been about 80 percent since the NES first began measuring party identification in 1952. The main story here is "no important change."

Thus, my conclusion from Figure 12.2 is that the attachment of voters to parties is about as strong as it has been at any time in 50 years, and that voters are about as loyal to their parties as they have ever been in this period.

This conclusion requires one qualification: Voting participation in presidential elections has fallen from about 60 percent in the 1950s to about 50 percent in the 1990s. The decline in voting participation is quite real and quite important. But, for citizens who still vote, party attachment certainly appears to be alive and well.

If, as these data show, presidential elections are neither more volatile nor less partisan than in the past, perhaps they are, as President Bush said of the 1992 election, more "wacky" than they were in the past. Perhaps, that is, Americans are about as changeable as they used to be, but are changing in ways that are strange, difficult to predict, or somehow irrational.

This does not seem to be happening either. In fact, the trend is in the other direction: The outcomes of presidential elections are, if anything, more intelligible and easier to explain in recent decades. They also appear to involve more party accountability than in the past.

To show this, I have gathered data on the effect of economic conditions on presidential elections for two time periods – one period before the rise of modern media politics, and one after its rise. The purpose is to see whether accountability for the economic condition of the country has changed from the earlier period to the later one.

These data are shown in Figure 12.3. The left-hand graph is for presidential elections from 1940 to 1964; the right-hand graph is for the elections from 1968 to 1996. In each graph, the horizontal axis shows the performance of the national economy, namely, the percentage change in per capita real disposable income for the average American in the calendar year of the election.[14] For example, the left-hand figure shows that in the year of the 1960 election, there was essentially no

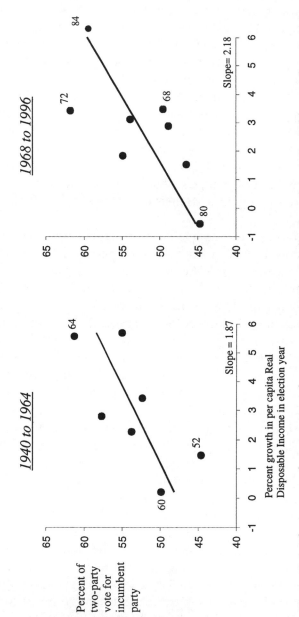

Figure 12.3. The impact of economic performance on presidential elections. *Source:* See Table 12.2 for source of economic data.

growth in personal income. In 1964, by contrast, average income rose by about 5 percent.

The vertical axis shows the percent of the vote won by the incumbent presidential party. Thus, in 1960, it can be seen that the candidate of the incumbent party got just under 50 percent of the vote and lost the election. (This was the election in which John Kennedy beat Richard Nixon to become the first Catholic to win the presidency.) But in 1964, when the economy was much stronger, the incumbent party won with 61 percent of the vote.

In the same way, each of the points in Figure 12.3 refers to a particular election between 1940 and 1996. Several of the more famous elections are labeled, such as the 1980 and 1984 elections. As the figure shows, Ronald Reagan, running as the challenger to incumbent Jimmy Carter, won the 1980 election when the incumbent was burdened with a bad economy; Reagan then won a landslide reelection in 1984 when the economy was very strong. Looking at the overall pattern, one can see that the points tend to form a line running from the lower left to the upper right, as summarized by the solid lines. What this trend shows is that the incumbent party does well in presidential elections when the economy is good and poorly when it is bad.

Note, moreover, that this trend is nothing new. The relationship between economic performance and vote for the incumbent party is about as strong in the era of Media Politics (1968 to 1996) as in the preceding period (1940 to 1964). Thus, politics in the current era does *not* seem to be either wacky or strange. It seems, as in the recent past, to reflect a healthy concern for the performance of the incumbent party.

Although this analysis has focused heavily on the effect of economic conditions, it does not follow that the economy is the only thing voters care about. They are not so foolish. For example, as noted earlier, voters dislike bloody wars and tend to punish presidents who allow the country to become entangled in them. However, voters also appear to dislike "peaceniks" – candidates who call for peace at any price. What voters do like are presidents who can keep the country's enemies at bay without having to fight them in wars. Through much of the "Cold War" with the former Soviet Union, the Republican party was favored by voters who believed that it could, in the common phrase of that day, "contain communism" without the need to fight wars.

Ideological moderation, as noted earlier, is another important factor in presidential politics. It is, however, somewhat difficult to find unambiguous evidence of its importance. The reason is that presidential candidates are increasingly aware of the importance of moderation and so rarely stray for long from the middle of the ideological road. (We saw earlier that Clinton did stray from the middle-of-the-road early in his first term, but returned to the center when he got into trouble for it.) When both parties run centrist candidates for president, as they do nowadays, it is hard to find evidence that ideological moderation matters.

Nonetheless, some systematic evidence is available. In a study of presidential elections from 1948 to 1980, Rosenstone (1983) found that a candidate's ideological distance from the center of state opinion was a strong determinant of vote share at the state level. Working with national-level data, I have found that this relationship holds for elections from 1948 to 1996 (Zaller 1998). (There are, however, significant methodological issues in measuring the effects of ideological moderation, which are beyond the scope of this chapter.)

SUMMARY

The argument of this chapter has been that Clinton and the Democratic party escaped the Lewinsky scandal with little political damage because most Americans cared more about peace, prosperity, and moderation under Clinton than about Clinton's personal shortcomings and the lies he told to keep them secret. More generally, political accountability for the condition of the country and for the policies the President advocates matter a great deal in American politics, and personal aspects of presidential character and performance matter relatively little.

Concerning my last point, it might be argued that the public's lack of concern about private sexual misbehavior is different from lack of concern about character in general. Perhaps. But it is not obvious that voter concern about character has ever been very great. For example, Richard Nixon's peculiar shortcomings were deeply felt by a large number of voters from the moment he stepped onto the national stage in the 1940s. Further, the concerns about Nixon's character were at least as serious as any that have been raised about Clinton's. Yet Nixon was elected to the presidency twice, once over Hubert Humphrey, a man whose sterling character has been almost universally acknowledged. Nixon's campaign against Humphrey was, of course, framed by urban riots and a stalemated war in Asia, and in these circumstances, Nixon chose to emphasize substance rather than character. "When you're in trouble," he told voters in the 1968 presidential campaign, "you don't turn to the men who got you in trouble to get you out of it. I say we can't be led in the 70s by the men who stumbled in the 60s."[15] Voters agreed with this emphasis, as they almost always do.

NOTES

1. Documentation of the sources of polls cited in this paper may be found in a PC Excel 5.0 file, Lewpols, on my Web page, http:/www.sscnet.ucla.edu/polisci/faculty/zaller/.
2. See Key (1966) and Fiorina (1981).
3. The case was the Paula Jones civil lawsuit over charges that Clinton had sexually harassed her in 1991, when he was Governor of Arkansas.
4. The Gulf War showed that wars costing few American lives do not harm popularity, but neither do they much help over the long run.
5. See Baum and Kernell (1999) for the effect of war casualties on Franklin Roosevelt's job approval ratings.
6. Peter Jennings, quoting an anonymous politician.
7. These estimates are imprecise. The baseline for the ABC poll was actually January 25–26, with a sample of 1,023. The size of the ABC postspeech survey was 528. The NBC pre- and postspeech surveys both have reported sizes of 405. Assuming simple random sampling (which is too generous), the standard error of a difference of means on the ABC polls is 2.6 percent. Thus, it is very possible that the true effect of the speech might be 2.5 points and yet the two ABC polls might find no effect. The standard error for the difference of the two NBC polls is 3.4 points. With corrections for cluster sampling, these standard errors would be roughly 3.7 and 5 percent.
8. *Los Angeles Times*, January 29, 1998, p. A11.
9. It is difficult to distinguish between the direct effects of events as they occur and the indirect effect of events as reported in the media. But a research project of Larry Bartels of Princeton University shows how this can be done. With a measure of the "real economy" from the Commerce Department and a measure of the "media economy" from content analysis of media coverage, he hopes to find out which has more influence on presidential approval. Among the auxiliary variables whose impact on presidential approval he will assess is the white-collar unemployment rate in Manhattan. The results will be interesting however they come out.
10. The references were to Ted Kennedy, widely considered at that time to be a future president, and to John Tunney, a photogenic, media-savvy Senator from California.
11. These figures were calculated as follows: Starting with the 1900 election, the percentage of the vote won by the Democrat was subtracted from the percentage won in the previous election, and the average absolute value was taken. For example, William Jennings Bryan won 45.5 percent of the vote in 1900 and 46.7 percent in 1896, for an absolute difference of 1.2 points. The average of these interelection swings in the Democratic vote from 1900 to 1964 is 6.67 percent; for the period 1968 to 1996, it is 7.53 percent. The corresponding figures for Republican candidates are 7.72 percent and 8.18 percent. The averages of the Democratic and Republican figures are those reported in the text.

13. For 1948 to 1992, these data are from Stanley and Niemi (1995, p. 96). For 1996, data are from Gallup polls published on Hotline on January 10, August 30, and October 4. Calculations were made as in the previous note.
14. Data are from same source as in Table 12.2.
15. *Newsweek*, November 4, 1968, p. 28.

REFERENCES

Baum, Mathew, and Sam Kernell (1999). "Popular Support for Franklin Roosevelt in War and Peace: Economic Class and Heterogeneous Evaluations." Unpublished manuscript, UC San Diego.

Brody, Richard (1991). *Assessing the President: The Media, Elite Opinion, and Public Support.* Stanford: Stanford University Press.

Fiorina, Morris (1981). *Retrospective Voting in American National Elections.* New Haven: Yale University Press.

Halberstam, David (1979). *The Powers that Be.* New York: Dell.

Key, Jr., V. O. (1966). *The Responsible Electorate: Rationality in Presidential Voting, 1936–60.* New York: Vintage.

Jacobson, Gary (1997). *The Politics of Congressional Elections.* New York: Longman.

MacKuen, Michael B., Robert S. Erikson, and James A. Stimson (1992). "Peasants or bankers? The American electorate and the U.S. economy." *American Political Science Review*, 86:597–611.

Morris, Dick (1999). *Behind the Oval Office.* Renaissance: Los Angeles.

Mueller, John (1973). *War, Presidents, and Public Opinion.* New York: Wiley.

Rosenstone, Steven (1983). *Forecasting Presidential Elections.* New Haven: Yale University Press.

Silbey, Joel (1994). "The Rise and Fall of American Political Parties, 1790–1993." In L. Sandy Maisel (Ed.), *The Parties Respond.* Boulder, CO: Westview.

Stanley, Harold, and Richard Niemi (1995). *Vital Statistics on American Politics.* Washington, D.C.: CQ Press.

Wattenberg, Martin (1991). *The Rise of Candidate Centered Elections.* Cambridge: Harvard.

Zaller, John (1992). *Nature and Origins of Mass Opinion.* New York: Cambridge.

   (1998). "Monica Lewinsky's Contribution to Political Knowledge." *PS*, 31(2), June.

CHAPTER 13

The Big Spin: Strategic Communication and the Transformation of Pluralist Democracy

W. Lance Bennett and Jarol B. Manheim

Among the several competing notions of how democracy functions, pluralism – the idea that the views of citizens are effectively and equitably represented through competing organized interests – has long held special appeal. The pluralist model is often offered as the democratic ideal in cases such as the United States, where interest formations do not display the broad structural coherence of the "corporatism" common to many European nations. Our analysis applies primarily to the United States, but we draw upon important efforts to bridge the theoretical gap between pluralist and corporatist systems, including Putnam's comparative analyses of civic group life in the United States (1995) and Italy (1993), and, most importantly, Dahl's (1989) general theory of polyarchy.

Dahl defines a general continuum of polyarchy (rule by many), ranging between voter selection of officials in free and fair elections at the lower limit, and an upper limit defined as the democratic ideal of equal governance by all. This ideal is approximated by equal control of the policy agenda and equal opportunity for inclusion in policy decision processes (1989, p. 222). Like many democratic theorists before him, Dahl regards the quality and communication of political information as central to the evolution of democracy. What is relevant for our purposes is that Dahl identifies an informational dilemma common to most advanced polyarchic systems – the capture of many policy processes and decisions by policy elites whose information gives them an exclusive power (i.e., power that often excludes general publics) in complex decisions. Dahl argues that if polyarchy is to evolve beyond a state of capture by policy elites, the key lies in maximizing the free flow of information in the policy process. He recommends creating independent communication channels for transmitting reliable knowledge to citizens, and for facilitating broadly inclusive deliberation on related policy decisions (1989, p. 338).

Our ongoing research on the uses of information and communication by various organized interests in the United States indicates movement in just the opposite direction of that advocated by Dahl. In particular, policy organizations all across the political spectrum have learned to use communication technologies to target the smallest audiences likely to be helpful to their political aims, and to deliver information that is designed not to promote informed, deliberative engagement on the part of those selected citizens. Rather, information is typically publicized to mobilize and demobilize segments of the public to serve narrow strategic objectives, often masking the identity or intent of the communicator in the process.

We can begin to make this point clear by defining two key terms of analysis. *Information transparency* refers to the clear identification of groups sponsoring a political initiative, a clear statement of their purposes for sponsoring it, and disclosure of the known risks and benefits that may flow from the initiative. *Information inclusiveness* refers to the degree to which political information is distributed broadly to publics who might be interested in participating in (deliberating about and deciding on) an issue if they understood its implications more clearly.

In place of transparency and inclusiveness, we observe growing political communication practices that subordinate the identities and motives of the participants, along with the full disclosure of their objectives, with the overriding end of achieving pragmatic political victories. As explained by Jamieson in Chap. 15, both electoral and issue advocacy campaigns often involve deception in the messages and the ways the sources of those messages are identified in communications with target audiences. Indeed, the very transformation of publics into exclusive target audiences is a blow to the democratic ideal of publics as inclusive deliberative bodies, as explained by Gandy in Chap. 7. It is also clear, as Underwood notes in Chap. 5, that these developments in communication practices are associated with a commercially driven media system in which news and citizen information values are easily displaced by the business values of the industrial conglomerates that own much of the national information system. All of these changes in the political communication process recommend rethinking both the research agenda and the theoretical frameworks of our field.

WHAT HAS CHANGED FROM THE OLD
PLURALISM TO THE NEW?

An assumption at the core of pluralist democratic theory is that the competition of organized interests produces enlightened citizen participation. The validity of this assumption is challenged by at least three conditions that distinguish today's society from that of an earlier era: the decline of group memberships, the rise of technologies for assembling audiences from targeted individuals, and the routine engagement of government processes as much for image purposes as for securing policy remedies.

First, interest formations of an earlier pluralist era may have reflected larger, more stable, party and labor formations and higher levels of civic group involvement by individuals. Group origins of interests not only provide people with a socially grounded experiential basis for judging the political information they receive, but personal membership in groups offers individuals a useful information heuristic or short cut in the form of interpretive cues transmitted by group leaders.[1] Thus, it is probably no accident that what we call strategic communication campaigns have evolved over the same period in which the structural coherence of pluralist society has also fragmented (Putnam 1995; Bennett 1998).

Second, communication in earlier eras of pluralist democracy was comparatively uncorrupted by recent technologies for "creating publics" by assessing citizen attitudes and shaping messages designed to mobilize those attitudes into expressions of public opinion. The centrality of these communication technologies may be magnified by the protection of their uses through expanded definitions of free speech, as explained in the Chaps. 15 and 16 by Jamieson and Baker, respectively.

Third, a simple view from the old pluralism is that groups take information to government in order to enlighten and persuade courts, legislatures, and executives of rational solutions to public problems. It is well known that government has long been the primary staging area for so-called hard news about politics (Bennett 1996). However, in the new political environment, groups may engage government primarily to reach target audiences (which may be no larger than other government officials and policy elites) with news that shapes images, damages opponents, disguises motives, and authenticates political claims. This is an extension of Edelman's (1964) vision with a technological sophistication that few students of contemporary democracy have either anticipated or addressed adequately.

In this emerging neopluralist order, the idea of stable groups embodying enduring and relatively transparent interests must at least make room for an alternative reality in which interests arise outside of stable group contexts and communication processes construct publics in strategic ways. This strategic communication – *the scientific engineering and targeting of messages that subordinate the ideals of deliberation and transparency to the achievement of narrow political goals* – calls in question the definitions of groups, information, and interests in the old pluralist models.

Before turning to the workings of strategic communication campaigns, we address several questions that can be raised about the argument thus far. Perhaps the most obvious question is: *Hasn't deception always been a central element of politics?* For example, Timothy Cook reminded us (personal communication) that a campaign no less important than the one advocating the adoption of the U.S. Constitution was waged by a broad ideological coalition of actors representing themselves as a pseudonymous fellow named Publius. We also acknowledge that the history of politics and public opinion in this century can be written in terms of the uses of often deceptive public relations techniques to "engineer consent" among the governed (Ewen 1996).

Our response is that deception, whether anecdotal or historical, must be evaluated in a theoretical context such as our general framework of transparency and inclusiveness of communication within societies undergoing declines in group-based politics. Examined from this perspective, it is clear that *The Federalist* can be defended as an effort to disguise potentially divisive group differences in order to draw diverse readers into common deliberation about complex choices. By contrast, the historical origins of public relations and the engineering of consent are commonly traced to the antipluralist, elitist perspectives of Edward L. Bernays, Ivy Lee, and Walter Lippmann, among others (Ewen 1996). Yet, we now detect a move beyond public relations as a largely intuitive and sporadically employed publicity tool, to the systemic adoption of more scientific methods for shaping images and promoting or undermining causes by political groups large and small, public and private, left and right (Grefe and Linsky 1995). If we detect a movement toward a more systematic corruption of public information quality, should we excuse it on grounds that it is a mere compounding of past problems with democracy?

A second obvious question is: *Does the shift to an increasingly mediated political process mean that individuals are continually deceived by the interest organizations that bombard them?* No. Our point is not that individuals are inevitably political dupes in modern information games. A more serious problem may be that most people, most of the time, are not even addressed in modern information games. And many of those who are targeted encounter information that is alternately confusing, cynicism-inducing, or hard to validate independently of the media experience that delivered it. True, as Zaller argues in Chap. 12, publics display remarkable independence of mind on some judgments such as voting choice and presidential approval, even when – as during the Clinton-Lewinsky impeachment scandal – dominant media framing might suggest a stampede of supporters away from the president. We also accept the idea that people may deploy various heuristics to sort through the barrage of daily news and political information (Sniderman et al. 1991). All of these points conceded, however, none of these rational public theories strays far beyond Dahl's (1989) standards for the lowest levels of polyarchy. Instead, these theories leave information environments largely unexamined, while characterizing citizens as inherently lazy. We simply propose to add to our understanding of democratic communication by exploring more broadly how meaning systems may selectively engage, exclude, and motivate people.

A final obvious question is this: *Does this mean that there are no instances of high-quality public deliberation in contemporary politics?* The answer is that different qualities of policy debate may occur on different issues, and that something like public deliberation with good information undoubtedly occurs on some highly publicized and politically contested issues (Page 1996). For example, Chap. 3, by William Gamson, convinces us that a relatively high quality public deliberation has gone on in America for more than two decades on the issue of abortion. We note, however, that abortion is an issue that has a social group base that is both strong and diverse (e.g., churches and women's groups). These groups tend to be relatively transparent in identifying themselves, disclosing their goals, and rebutting opponents' information with great volumes of fact and moral argument. The dramatic human choices involved with the issue also invite widespread personal engagement and stimulate huge volumes of information through both news and entertainment media. As Delli Carpini and Williams argue in Chap. 8, such issues are prime *infotainment* fare and may well break down the gatekeeping capacity (and therefore the effectiveness of attempts to manage the content) of the news. We readily concede that such issues are not easily captured by strategic communication techniques, and we also note that they are not the typical policy fare.

NEOPLURALISM AND THE EVOLUTION OF STRATEGIC COMMUNICATION CAMPAIGNS

What is needed is a democratic theory for the new communication era – one that recognizes and takes into account the greater sophistication of human knowledge and the willingness to apply it for political purposes. For ours is an era when a half-century of social scientific research has generated substantial understanding of the cognitive processing of individual stimuli and of how those stimuli flow through whole economic and political systems. Put another way, ours is an era when those with the requisite resources to manipulate the democratic system for their advantage have more capability to accomplish that than ever before – and there are many such people in play. For example, one estimate suggests that reporters are outnumbered by communications professionals by a margin of 130,000 journalists to 150,000 communication practitioners, and that the gap is growing (Dowie 1995).

We believe that pervasive uses of strategic communication are now altering the political behaviors of other important "pluralist" institutions such as labor unions, cause groups, and business interests. As an empirical exercise, this new democratic theory must explain and predict a broad range of newly observed political behaviors. As a normative exercise, it must provide guidance for judging these evolving practices and recommending policies to regulate them.

We believe the starting point for developing this neopluralist theory is through an examination of the growth and dimensions of strategic political communication campaigns. The communication strategies that characterize such campaigns are direct descendants of the techniques developed over the last four decades by political marketers as they have sought to advance particular candidates, policies, or ideologies. Among them are appeals to emotion rather than to reason, the reliance on graphic verbal and visual imagery, thematic simplification, and a frequent resort to intense and unyielding negativity. Because these techniques have migrated beyond the electoral arena, with its media spotlight, formal and informal accountability, and other self-regulatory mechanisms, however, their use is far less subject to any type of constraint. In strategic communication campaigns, as opposed to their electoral cousins, there are no inherent limits on time or resources, no meaningful reporting requirements, no systematic media or public scrutiny, no prohibition on channeling messages through seemingly independent surrogates, no boundary between communication efforts and other forms of advocacy, and no expectation of ethical behavior. In other words, there are no rules. In this arena, strategy is king, and whatever it is that "works" is done (Manheim 1998, p. 1).

These campaigns have in many cases replaced traditional grass roots actions and social pressure with astroturf (i.e., artificial) groups and electronic publics. Strategic campaigns transcend conventional political modes such as public relations and lobbying by fully integrating image (e.g., ads, PR events, news story placement, editorials) and power (e.g., judicial, regulatory, legislative, protest, boycott) tactics to advance partisan causes and damage vulnerable opponents. Campaign technologies have been advanced by both the left and the right, and by nonprofit organizations and big business. For example, the rise of the Republican right marks an important chapter in the strategic campaign book (Ferguson and Rogers 1986), as does the resurgence of labor activism centered around communication campaigns (Perry 1987).

LABOR CAMPAIGNS: AN ILLUSTRATIVE CASE

Recognizing the development of important communication techniques by the labor movement is a useful corrective to common assumptions in the communication literature that communication power is the nearly exclusive purview of government and big business, or that the evolving communication practices of the left are somehow more pure than those of the right. Labor variants of strategic communication campaigns, often called *corporate campaigns*, were developed by labor unions as they faced serious erosions of membership, public support, and power. Over the past half-century, through good times and bad, workers have increasingly opted out of the labor movement. Today, only 9.8 percent of the private sector work force is unionized, a decline of nearly 40 percent since 1983 (Manheim 1998). By the mid-1970s, the more forward-looking labor leaders had recognized the emerging crisis that faced their movement to be a long-term structural phenomenon. More importantly, they had identified a potential solution – a move away from their reliance on the National Labor Relations Board, the collective bargaining process, the strike, and the other trappings of traditional labor-management relations, and toward the then-emerging social technology of strategic communication. These leaders saw that, by attacking the reputations of companies, either directly or through surrogates, they could create real pressure of a degree and type that management was ill equipped to resist. Then, in exchange for union recognition, contract improvements or other concessions, they could make the pressure go away. Better still, they could often accomplish this without resorting to the traditional – and for a union very costly – last step in labor-management disputes, the strike.[2]

The trend in the years since has been toward more, and increasingly sophisticated, campaigns, reflecting a transformation of the labor movement as well. In many ways, the key outcome of the 1995 AFL-CIO election was the replacement of an old guard with a leadership experienced in and committed to this new style of labor activity. In the words of AFL-CIO President John Sweeney, "The challenge is to find ways for working people to support each other in their struggles and to plan sophisticated strategies to use media coverage, political clout, community organizing, international support, and even pressure from investors and major companies to persuade employers to come to terms." (Sweeney 1996, p. 142). At this point, perhaps 100 companies have been the targets of corporate campaigns by organized labor. Among the most significant have been attacks upon Bridgestone/Firestone, Caterpillar, Eastern Air Lines, Food Lion, International Paper, Hormel, JP Stevens, Ravenswood Aluminum, and the United Parcel Service (UPS).

The corporate campaign can be characterized as wide-ranging and often long-running economic, political, and psychological warfare waged by a union or other entity against a corporation. The objectives of campaigns generally involve disrupting the target company's relationships with such vital constituencies as its customers, employees, shareholders, bankers, vendors, regulators, and the general public. As described in a recent court case, corporate-campaign tactics "may include, but are not limited to, litigation, political appeals, requests that regulatory agencies investigate and pursue employer violations of state or federal law, and negative publicity campaigns aimed at reducing the employer's goodwill with employees, investors, or the general public" (*Food Lion* 1997). By undermining the corporation's good name – or by the mere credible threat of doing so – those who wage such campaigns seek to pressure its management into complying with their wishes on a range of issues varying from labor contracts, to environmental or human rights practices, to altered competitive postures.

Communication strategy is the central one of many components of a typical corporate campaign. Some others include the filing of class action and other lawsuits, initiation of regulatory complaints through various government agencies, encouragement of congressional hearings by labor- or cause-friendly panels designed to embarrass the target company, other types of legislative initiatives, attacks on the quality or safety of the target company's products or practices, shareholder actions (unions often have sizable holdings in the stock of targeted companies through their pension plans), and secondary boycotts of companies or individuals associated with the target company. Such conventional tactics are increasingly developed around a communication strategy that has the potential to reshape the fundamental perceptions of the company among its key audiences and, in the process, to generate the pressure on management that can lead to success. In this sense, for example, the UPS strike in 1997 was less a direct power tactic than an integral component of the Teamsters' comprehensive communication strategy.[3]

GENERAL CHARACTERISTICS OF COMMUNICATION IN STRATEGIC CAMPAIGNS

Whether we are talking about corporate campaigns waged by labor or about the many variants of strategic campaigns waged by parties, cause groups, and business, common communication strategies are relatively straightforward and remarkably consistent. The basic elements of strategy include:

- Identify the vulnerabilities of the target. This is done through surveys and focus groups, through legal and economic analyses of public documents, and through what the labor movement initially referred to as "power analysis" – assessing the structural and constituency relationships upon which any particular opponent depends.
- Identify the target audiences. Once a target's vulnerabilities have been identified, the next step is to determine which audiences represent potential pressure points on those vulnerabilities, and to determine, again through research, how susceptible those audiences are to influence or manipulation.
- Develop and test messages and themes. Just as in a political campaign, messages are developed and woven into themes designed to

place the campaign sponsor on the high moral ground and the target on the defensive.

- Legitimize themes and messages through third parties. In many cases, partisan sponsors can communicate more effectively with publics (who often hold negative opinions about those sponsors) if they create or enlist surrogate groups to take actions and make announcements.[4]

CAMPAIGNS AND THE TRANSFORMATION OF INTEREST GROUP POLITICS

As a direct result of the effectiveness of these communication strategies, we have seen in recent years a proliferation of strategic communication campaigns. For example, the persistent personal attacks on Bill Clinton, including the uses of lawsuits to publicize image-damaging claims, appeared to have the coherence of a strategic campaign. Corporations commonly invent consumer groups to create appearances of public support for various regulatory policy changes from deregulation of telecommunications markets to lowering fuel or environmental standards in the auto industry. And in recent years strategic campaigns have proliferated among groups that typically describe themselves as members of the "progressive community." This would include such groups as the National Organization for Women (NOW) and the Rainforest Action Network. The "Merchants of Shame" campaigns by NOW – on its own against the brokerage firm Salomon Smith Barney, and together with the Rainbow Coalition and the Rainforest Action Network against the Japanese conglomerate Mitsubishi – are cases in point.

Perhaps the most interesting and complex campaigns involve combat among business interests both in the consumer marketplace and in the promotion of interests within government institutions. In this variant, a target company's business competitors, often working through surrogates to mask or reframe their initiative, attack an industry-dominant company in an attempt to weaken it and distract its management, allowing them to claim portions of its market share.

Increasingly common in business campaigns is a kind of political piling-on in which unlikely campaign partners spanning business competition, labor, and cause groups see different political advantages in joining a campaign against a vulnerable and newsworthy target.[5] The involvement of unlikely and opportunistic partners, the creation of surrogate groups, the increasing resort to Internet organizing, and the attacks from so many sides mean that information transparency (who is doing what, why, and with what methods) often eludes journalists, publics, and sometimes even the targets themselves. One of the clearest examples of such a campaign to date is the one waged initially by corporate competitors and consumer surrogates, and later joined by labor, against the corporate megalith of the 1990s, Microsoft.

THE NEW INTEREST POLITICS AND THE CAMPAIGN AGAINST MICROSOFT

The elements of the Microsoft campaign closely resemble the practices outlined above.

- *Use of litigation.* Microsoft has been the subject of considerable litigation related to its market dominance. The antitrust action brought against the company by the Department of Justice (DOJ) and the attorneys general of twenty states is only the most obvious of these actions. Our research indicates that business competitors were instrumental in engaging both executive and legislative institutions and framing the subject matter of regulatory actions, hearings, and litigation. Not to be overlooked are the series of more specific trade-practices lawsuits brought by Sun Microsystems and other Microsoft competitors, many after the government's filing (Helft 1998; Glasscock 1998). There was also mention in the trade press of a potential shareholders' lawsuit, though none has been filed at this writing (Berst 1998). In the midst of the DOJ trial, the Consumers Federation of America announced its intention to file a $10 billion class action suit based on Microsoft's pricing practices. This pattern of cluster litigation is typical of a corporate campaign.
- *Litigation public relations.* Also typical of such campaigns are efforts to characterize the opposing sides in the dispute in such a way that one or the other may be aided or impeded. In this regard, it is interesting to note the spate of media articles about the attorneys for Microsoft and its nemesis, Netscape, around the time the antitrust case became public. Netscape lawyer Gary Reback and Justice Department outside counsel David Boies were frequently praised, while Microsoft's William Neukom was attacked (e.g., Daly 1997; Hamm 1998). The objective – which in our judgment was

achieved – was to put Microsoft's legal team on the public relations defensive.

- *Reliance on surrogates.* Though Microsoft's competitors are, as we shall demonstrate, behind the scenes of nearly every attack on the company, the campaign itself has been waged largely by surrogates. Among them are: Ralph Nader, the Electronic Privacy Information Center (EPIC), Net Action, and the Project to Promote Competition and Innovation in the Digital Age (ProComp). For his part, Nader challenged Microsoft on privacy issues as early as 1995, when he addressed a meeting sponsored by EPIC and raised the antitrust issue in 1997 (EPIC Alert 1995). Also in 1997, Nader sponsored a conference on "Assessing Microsoft," which brought together a large number of Microsoft's critics (Clausing 1997). EPIC is a project of the Fund for Constitutional Government, one of whose other "projects" played a central role in labor's corporate campaign against the Food Lion supermarket chain.[6] A third player, Net Action, which spearheaded a "consumers" campaign against Microsoft, is tied to EPIC through interlocks with the Board of Directors of yet another group, Computer Professionals for Social Responsibility.[7] The remaining major player, ProComp, took the lead in hiring a Washington lobbying team to support the campaign, a team that includes both Bob Dole and Robert Bork (Chandrasekaran 1998). Behind this coalition of consumer and other groups, however, are some interesting names. EPIC is cochaired by Microsoft competitor Sun Microsystems, and, at the time of the DOJ action, listed the primary adversary in the case, Netscape, as a major benefactor.[8] Serving on Net Action's board is an attorney who represents (or has represented) Netscape, Oracle Computing, and Sun Microsystems, as well as the Consumer Federation of America. In addition, Net Action lists Hewlett-Packard Laboratories as a major contributor.[9] And the members of ProComp include Netscape, Sun, and Oracle, as well as other companies that have thus far chosen to remain anonymous (Chandrasekaran 1998).

- *Issuance of a "white paper."* It is typical in a corporate campaign for attacking parties to issue formal research reports and policy statements designed to define the issues in the campaign in the most favorable light. Several of these reports have been issued in the Microsoft campaign by groups such as Net Action and Corporate Watch, another frequent campaign participant. Report titles tend to have clever names that play on words or themes closely associated with the target company. Illustrative titles in this case include: "*From MS Word to MS World: How Microsoft Is Building A Global Monopoly*" and "*Microsoft: One World Operating System.*"

• *Publishing a "Monitor."* Essential Information, Ralph Nader's core organization, has for several years published *Multinational Monitor*, a magazine that reports on and evaluates the activities of large, but not always multinational, corporations. Companies that are targets of labor-based corporate campaigns are often the subjects of highly critical articles in this publication, which are then cited by the relevant union as further evidence of corporate malfeasance. In effect, the publication helps to legitimize the corporate campaign's themes. In the present instance, *Multinational Monitor* published a report in 1995 attacking Microsoft, and a parallel effort was underway on the Internet, where Net Action published a newsletter titled *Microsoft Monitor.*[10]

• *Reliance on legislative and regulatory action.* Communication strategies often include the use of legislative and regulatory processes to increase the pressure on the target company, and, in the process, to make headlines creating the impression that the company is troubled or embattled. Access to government agencies and officials was used effectively by different actors in the campaign against Microsoft. In Congress, Senator Orrin Hatch of Utah served as the leading critic of Microsoft (Alvarez 1998; Rivlin 1998). Perhaps not coincidentally, Hatch received campaign contributions from individuals or PACs associated with several of the Microsoft competitors. As for the regulatory agencies involved, the Justice Department's antitrust lawsuit was stimulated by complaints and supported by legal briefs from a consortium of Microsoft's Silicon Valley rivals. The subsequent filing of a similar claim against Microsoft ally Intel Corporation by the Federal Trade Commission expanded the offensive. The Intel litigation was settled within weeks of that company's testifying against Microsoft in the DOJ case.

• *High-ground thematics.* In a corporate campaign, and in strategic communication campaigns more generally, the attacker always seeks to position itself on the moral high ground. This is typically accomplished by defining the campaign itself as an effort to redress some grievance with which the public can identify. In the Microsoft campaign, Net Action defined itself as a consumer protection group – a status conveyed by Ralph Nader's participation in the campaign – and the campaign itself as a "Consumer Choice Campaign." By some measures in some polls, public opinion has actually favored Microsoft, with as many as 75 percent of respondents opposing government intervention and a four-to-one margin in favor of integrating a browser with the Windows operating system. The same polls, however, show 80-percent public support for enforcing antitrust laws (*Fortune* 1998; Taft 1998). By filing on these latter grounds, then, the company's antagonists played to their strength. However, abstract polls about antitrust or product development may not tap underlying image damage done to a company over the long course of a campaign, as indicated in the following list.

- *Personalization.* Finally, a common element in many corporate campaigns is personalization – focusing the attack on the CEO or some other prominent individual rather than on an abstract entity like a corporation. The ACTWU attack on the Farah family set this pattern at the outset, and the multiunion strike that drove Eastern Air Lines out of business and its CEO, Frank Lorenzo, out of the airline industry forever refined it to near perfection. Now, in effect, Microsoft's Bill Gates is being defined as the Frank Lorenzo of high tech. Once seen as a hero and role model, Gates is increasingly portrayed as a robber baron, compared, for instance, to John D. Rockefeller (Klein 1998). One Internet site actually featured a real-time counter of Gates' personal wealth,[11] and cartoonists increasingly portray him as an all-consuming monster (e.g., Gateszilla) or as the toll collector on the information highway. *Brill's Content* magazine went so far as to publish Gates' mug shot from a 1970s arrest on its September 1998 cover. When so many stereotypes and formulas enter the media information stream, news narratives begin to take on common frames, and "the story" begins to write itself. Even journalism reviews may begin to cue their journalist-readers about how to play the story, as in the screaming cover of *Columbia Journalism Review* that appeared at the same time the justice department filed its antitrust case: WILL GATES CRUSH NEWSPAPERS? The article was filled with both sourced and unattributed references to Gates and Microsoft that included "software behemoth," "media baron," "the most powerful economic force in the United States," "lust to own the world," "evil company," "naked ambition," and "the Seattle slasher" (Hickey 1997).

The results? While the protracted legal cases churned through the courts, the headlines increasingly told the story of an arrogant, embattled, aggressive company whose CEO had pretensions of ruling the world. Even as Microsoft began to win its early legal battles, it showed signs of losing the public relations war. Various poll results from early in the campaign suggested erosion in public support, particularly among important segments of its customer base. For example, a poll of online users sponsored by *Fortune* magazine showed that 43.5% agreed that Microsoft engaged in unfair marketing, while a large neutral block of nearly 30% waited in the wings to form their opinions. Fully 62.7% agreed that Microsoft had too much power in the computer software market. And 51% agreed with the Justice Department in the conflict, contrasted with only 25.5% siding with Microsoft.[12] Another survey by Techtel, a market research company that tracks brand reactions to technology companies, reported a 10% decline in favorable opinion about Microsoft (to a still strong 70%) among business users during 1997, the year in which the campaign emerged on all fronts. Positive opinion among all consumers fell 5% (to 67%). Negative opinion among general consumers doubled (to 8%), and Microsoft's "negatives" among business users increased to 19.4% from 11.5% during 1997 (Markoff 1998). In response, Microsoft released results of a poll conducted by Hart and Teeter showing that the company still topped the list of most admired companies in America.[13] The battle for public opinion was clearly engaged, and it is this strategic communication battle that can become more important politically and economically than the specific effects of particular legal or regulatory actions.

CONCLUSION

It is true that many of the elemental techniques of strategic political communication were developed years ago in public relations efforts to promote corporations and their products, and then in the political arena to sell candidates to voters in elections. However, the techniques of market and voter research, message development, advertising, and free-media management have now been transported to new arenas where they are of increasing importance, but where their use and its consequences have to date been little studied and are little understood. That lack of understanding, however, by no means renders them inconsequential. To the contrary, these forms of political communication are likely to play an increasingly important role in political life in the future.

The following characteristics of the new interest group politics constitute potential threats to the ideal of enlightened public policy deliberation by masking the identities, motives, and goals of the very groups who "go public" with their causes.

- First, the group structure of the new pluralism is often a symbolic construction. Many of the consumer, citizen, and public interest groups, alliances, and coalitions prominently featured in communication campaigns are virtual organizations that exist primarily (often exclusively) on letterheads, on the Internet, or as offices within other, well-known organizations whose partisanship is well established. In the pluralistic ideal, by contrast, it is established and politically identifiable groups who cue both publics and public officials in thinking about issues and government policies.
- Second, when established partisan groups enter the strategic communication picture it is often as a downstream victim, or as a party privileged by a legal or regulatory action (which they themselves initiated). This blurring of causal roles in political action chains further confuses the issues and the partisan positions that are useful for judging the merits of political conflicts.
- Third, the outward-looking emphasis of campaigns and the coordinated scripting of acts by primary and surrogate groups help to hide the motives and interest conflicts among partners in broad coalitions. This often enables players to appear on the side of a (good) coalition against an (evil) opponent, even though they may engage in similar business or political practices as the targeted opponent.
- Fourth, since news and publicity from multiple campaign sources reinforce similar themes, news stories often report the simplest and most dramatic narratives, and miss the underlying complexities of campaigns. Unraveling the group networks and interests in a typical campaign would require both increased commitments by news organizations to enterprise reporting, and a simultaneous willingness to turn down the dramatic story ideas and public events orchestrated by campaign strategists and placed with news organizations. Trends in the news business are moving in the opposite directions.

Because of these informational characteristics, strategic communication campaigns tend to loop back on themselves. For example, negative news about campaign targets that is reported by prestige news organizations is typically used to convince officials that those opponents are, indeed, guilty as charged, and need to be (further) investigated or regulated. Such investigations, in turn, may prompt journalists to tell even more dramatic stories based on information placed by partisan sources who may recede into the background of news accounts as surrogates assume the role of primary sources. As a result, the core economic and political interests at stake in many campaigns may never enter public debate. As these information cycles play out in the press and through political institutions, the targets of campaigns may end up modifying their behaviors, not in response to principle or public interest, but in response to the brute power of the campaign waged against them. This, we submit, is an inversion of the ideal relations among groups, governments, information, and publics in democratic society.

As media campaigns grow in technical sophistication, the basic assumptions of pluralist democracy become harder to sustain. For example, interested parties may hide behind surrogates who mask and otherwise misrepresent the positions of their sponsors. Community-based groups are increasingly displaced by centralized organizations that sustain memberships through direct mail, and other communication strategies that render members less involved in group interest formation processes. Publics who form opinions about issues passing through the political arena are increasingly assembled as targeted audiences whose understanding of problems is based on market research about their own private fears and feelings rather than more thematic social analysis. Finally, strategic coalitions of groups formed to defeat political opponents or economic competitors may associate groups with principles that they do not seriously support. All of these tendencies challenge the basic assumptions of information transparency, stability of interests, and political coherence of interest organizations on which the quality of democratic communication among specific interests, general publics, and policy makers depends. It is a challenge of some consequence.

NOTES

1. The decline of civic group memberships also implies the weakening of the two-step flow of communication (Katz and Lazarsfeld 1956), as individuals become increasingly separated from civic groups and their related information cueing systems.
2. The conventional history of this phenomenon identifies the 1976 campaign against textile giant J. P. Stevens by the Amalgamated Clothing and Textile Workers Unions

(ACTWU) as the first corporate campaign. Indeed, it was during that effort that the term "corporate campaign" was first developed by Ray Rogers, an ACTWU staff member who went on to form Corporate Campaigns, Inc., the first consulting company devoted to assisting unions in applying this new technology (Jarley and Meranto 1990; Perry 1988, p. 105). But the roots of the J. P. Stevens campaign actually trace directly to an attack by the same union on Farah Manufacturing, a nonunion, Texas-based clothing manufacturer a few years earlier (Perry 1987).

3. From a corporate campaign perspective, UPS was an interesting target. The company had a long history of friendly relations with the Teamsters, and many, if not most, of its top managers had begun their careers at the company as Teamsters themselves. Moreover, UPS had a very positive corporate image among the public, strong financials, a reputation for efficiency and customer service, and good relations with its customers generally. And it was privately held, eliminating shareholder and other potential pressure points. But UPS had a particular vulnerability that the union was uniquely positioned to exploit. UPS workers – unlike those at many other companies – had names and faces rather than mere numbers. They were not just known to their customers one-on-one, but they effectively *defined* the company for those customers. If those workers should become, or appear to be, disillusioned, the image of the company would be undermined. That outcome would best be assured through a strike. So the strike, rather than an act of last resort, became a central component of the union's communication planning. The union's core message was perhaps best summarized by John Wayne Garrett, the southern regional coordinator for the UPS strike, who told the *Atlanta Journal Constitution*, "The public knows what is happening to UPS workers is also happening on their jobs." When the media came to the union for comments on the strike, more often than not the union was represented, not by leaders in suits, but by members – many of them women – dressed in jeans. Campaign organizers worked carefully to time their updates, statements, and news conferences to correspond with the natural rhythms of the news cycle. The result? A CNN survey found that 55 percent of the public supported the union; 27 percent, UPS management. This represents a huge gain over general or "standing" opinion about unions in contemporary America (see Nagourney 1997).

4. In the case of unions, for example, attempts to play into popular distrust of big business were often offset by an equivalent distrust of organized labor, as evidenced in part by the aforementioned decline in union membership. Because of their own weak image, unions have found it useful over the years to channel their messages through surrogates and coalitions – some created by the unions expressly to mask their interest in a particular campaign, and some involving existing and often well-known organizations that happened to share interests with labor, including environmentalists, civil and human rights groups, religious societies, and consumer advocates, among others. The use of surrogates, both real and invented, is now standard procedure in interest politics (Perry 1987, pp. 31–38).

5. Origins of these mixed motive interest campaigns can be seen in the AFL-CIO's long-running campaign against Nike, which involved a network of human rights advocates and other surrogates to attack the company's reputation. Nike's principal competitor, Reebok, played an active role in supporting that network. Perhaps in exchange, Reebok, with many labor and human rights practices that initially

appeared similar to Nike's, was not targeted with anything approaching equal vigor. Reebok subsequently capitalized in image terms by issuing its own global human rights award.

6. EPIC Web site. www.epic.org.
7. Net Action Web site. www.netaction.org.
8. EPIC Web site. www.epic.org.
9. Net Action Web site. www.netaction.org.
10. Available on the Net Action Web site.
11. www.webho.com/WealthClock.
12. Reported in http://www.pathfinder.com/fortune/1998/980202/onlinepoll2.html.
13. Hart-Teeter study #5030 released by Microsoft on November 25, 1997.

REFERENCES

Alvarez, Lizette (1998). "Gates in Spotlight on Capitol Hill." *New York Times*, electronic edition, March 4, http://www.nytimes.com. Archives.

Bennett, W. Lance (1996). *News: The Politics of Illusion, 3rd ed.* New York: Longman.

———— (1998). "The UnCivic Culture: Communication, Identity, and the Rise of Lifestyle Politics." *PS: Political Science & Politics*, 31:December:741–761.

Berst, Jesse (1998). "Microsoft's Next Legal Nightmare Could Be Even Worse Than the DOJ Lawsuit." *ZDNet*. May 19, 1998, www.zdnet.com. Search anchordesk.

Chandrasekaran, Rajiv (1998). "Opponents of Microsoft Open Drive for Wider Antitrust Case." *Washington Post*, April 21, p. C2.

Clausing, Jeri (1997). "Nader Conference Levels Sights on Microsoft." *New York Times*, electronic edition, November 14, http://www.nytimes.com. Archives.

Dahl, Robert A. (1989). *Democracy and Its Critics.* New Haven: Yale University Press.

Daly, James (1997). "The Robin Hood of the Rich." *Wired Magazine*. 5: August 1997, www.wired.com/wired/archive/5.08/.

Dowie, Mark (1995). "Torches of Liberty." Introduction to John C. Stauber and Sheldon Rampton, *Toxic Sludge Is Good for You.* Monroe, ME: Common Courage Press, pp. 1–4.

Edelman, Murray (1964). *The Symbolic Uses of Politics.* Urbana: University of Illinois Press.

Ewen, Stuart (1996). *PR! A Social History of Spin.* New York: Basic Books.

EPIC Alert (1995). "Nader Speaks to Privacy Advocates." Vol 2.01, January 18, www.epic.org/alert/EPIC-Alert-2.01.txt.

Ferguson, Thomas, and Joel Rogers (1986). *Right Turn: The Decline of the Democrats and the Future of American Politics.* New York: Farrar, Straus and Giroux.

Fortune (1998). "Nationwide Poll Results." Electronic edition, February 2, www.fortune.com.

Food Lion, Inc., v. United Food and Commercial Workers International Union, 103 F.3d 1007, 1014 n.9 (D.C. Cir 1997).

Glasscock, Stuart (1998). "Microsoft Blasts Sun Suit." *CMPNet*. May 12, www.cmpnet.com.

Grefe, Edward A., and Martin Linsky (1995). *The New Corporate Activism: Harnessing the Power of Grassroots Tactics for Your Organization.* New York: McGraw-Hill.

Hamm, Steve (1998). "Is Microsoft's lawyer too tough for the job?" *Business Week.* January 26, www.businessweek.com.search.

Helft, Miguel (1998). "Sun Fires at Windows 98." *San Jose Mercury News*, electronic edition, May 12, www.sjmercory.com.

Hickey, Neil (1997). "Will Gates Crush Newspapers?" *Columbia Journalism Review*, November/December:28–36.

Jarley, Paul, and Cheryl Maranto (1990). "Union Corporate Campaigns: An Assessment." *Industrial and Labor Relations Review*, 43:305–322.

Katz, Elihu, and Paul Lazarsfeld (1956). *Personal Influence.* Glencoe, IL: The Free Press.

Klein, Jeffrey (1998). "Billing Us Softly." *Mother Jones*, electronic edition, January/February, www.mojones.com.

Manheim, Jarol B. (1998). *Corporate Campaign Communications: Union Attack Strategies.* Washington, DC: Labor Policy Association.

Markoff, John (1998). "Harm Found to Image of Microsoft." *New York Times*, electronic edition, Business/Financial Desk. April 6, www.nytimes.com.

Nagourney, Adam (1997). "In Strike Battle, Teamsters Use Political Tack." New York Times, electronic edition, August 16, www.nytimes.com.

Page, Benjamin I. (1996). *Who Deliberates? Mass Media in Modern Democracy.* Chicago: University of Chicago Press.

Perry, Charles R. (1988). "Corporate Campaigns: The New Power Game." In Marlin M. Volz (Ed.), *Fourth Annual Labor and Employment Law Institute.* Littleton, Colorado: Fred B. Rothman & Co.

(1987). *Union Corporate Campaigns.* Philadelphia, PA: Industrial Research Unit, The Wharton School, University of Pennsylvania.

Putnam, Robert D. (1993). *Making Democracy Work.* Princeton: Princeton University Press.

(1995). "Tuning In, Tuning Out: The Strange Disappearance of Social Capital in America." *PS: Political Science & Politics*, 28:December:664–683.

Rivlin, Gary (1998). "Orrin Hatch, Microsoft Critic." *Upside.com.* April 28, www.upside.com.

Sniderman, Paul M., Richard A. Brody, and Philip E. Tetlock (1991). *Reasoning and Choice: Explorations in Political Psychology.* New York: Cambridge University Press.

Sweeney, John (1996). *America Needs a Raise.* Boston: Houghton Mifflin.

Taft, Darryl K. (1998). "Microsoft Poll: Americans Oppose Blocking Windows 98." *CMPNet.* May 6, www.cmpnet.com.

CHAPTER 14

The Impact of the New Media

W. Russell Neuman

Everybody has a hypothesis about the impact of the new media. According to recent reports the new media have variously initiated or reinforced trends that have

- Weakened political party systems
- Offered a new platform for hate speech
- Stimulated a new capacity for grassroots democracy
- Permitted the third world to leapfrog painful stages of industrialization into an information economy
- Robbed children of their childhood and everybody of their sense of place
- Sped up the process of government responses to international crises precluding appropriate deliberation
- Isolated family members from each other
- Permanently stabilized the business cycle
- Exacerbated gaps between information haves and have-nots
- Limited the capacity of authoritarian regimes to control the flow of information within and outside of their realm

Readers will recognize many of these as preowned hypotheses, most not particularly low mileage at that. Much of the evidence of such effects is derived from the selective accumulation of anecdotes.[1] Systematic empirical research struggles for methodologies capable of distinguishing the causal impact of new technologies from other historical trends and cycles. Further, the most radical new technologies such as the Internet are still at early stages of diffusion, challenging the analyst to distinguish the characteristics of early adopters and of early implementations from the underlying character of the technology.

I would argue that the academic community should acknowledge and encourage the journalistic battle of anecdotes. Although the question of whether the Internet will turn us into a nation of porno addicts or political know-nothings might seem less than optimally framed for designing research, it reflects the characteristic style of popular journalism and general public concern. Scholars might encourage such popular speculation but should, in my view, aspire to something more substantial. I believe that empirically sound and theoretically grounded research on the impact of new technologies will require us to reconnect these popular hypotheses with our theoretical roots in the social sciences. (Abramson et al. 1988; Bimber 1998c; Castells 1996, 1997, 1998; Habermas 1989).

My background as a sociologist may be evident in the pages ahead. The discipline of sociology has its roots in the turn of the century struggle to understand the impact of the industrial revolution and urbanization on social structure, social cohesion, and politics. Seminal theory and new methodologies for studying social behavior still in active use grew out of that struggle. My hope is that communications research will find equivalent success and a convergent and accumulative research paradigm as we struggle a century later with the transition from an industrial to an information society. I am unapologetically trying to hold out the early stages of sociological theorizing as a model for a more theoretically and historically grounded theory of communications effects organized around the notion of an information society/communications revolution.

Early sociological theorists developed the key analytic concepts of class, status, and power and demonstrated historical and quantitative methods for studying their interaction. They developed models for studying charismatic leadership and the routinization of large bureaucratic structures characteristic of the industrial-age public and private sectors. They pioneered research on the interaction of surviving cultural values and the new political fault lines of industrial capitalism. If we can find inspiration in the inventiveness and breadth of this work in a sister field 100 years ago, we might more effectively sketch out promising directions for theory and methods in the study of political communications at the next century mark. If the goal is theoretical accumulation and refinement, we need the overarching concepts to link and systematically compare what would otherwise be a miscellaneous and incomparable collection of hypotheses and findings. My vote for a theoretical starting point would be a modest area of sociological inquiry that flourished most notably in the 1940s and 50s known as mass society theory. (Neuman 1991a, 1991b, 1996).

THE IDEA OF MASS SOCIETY

A mass society is characterized by homogeneity of the mass population and the weakness of interpersonal and group life. Riesman's (1950) phrase, the lonely crowd, captures the essence of the concept. Various essays in the literature emphasize different factors but the loss of a sense of community and political belonging remains a central theme. The theory posits that since the turn of the century the rapid urbanization and industrialization of Europe and the United States has resulted in:

1. The decline of family life – the nuclear family replaces the extended family; family members spend less time together; children attend large, centralized, anomic school systems; working mothers may be absent; television watching replaces family conversation.
2. The alienating workplace – mobility from job to job and isolating work conditions in large organizations make both the workplace and work associates less important to the individual.
3. The decline of local community – dispersed suburban areas are separated from central, integrating cultural institutions of the city give residents little sense of community.
4. The weakening of religious ties – although the majority of people may identify themselves as religiously affiliated, such affiliation is nominal and participation is irregular or nonexistent.
5. The weakening of ethnic ties – over time ethnic communities blur into a massified urban landscape.
6. The decline of participation in voluntary associations – the lack of group life further weakens the individual's sense of identity and connectedness (Fromm 1941; Riesman 1950; Kornhauser 1959; Bell 1962; Giner 1976; Beniger 1987).

The historical argument asserts that just as these social forces reach a stage of crisis, the evolving mass media technologies including radio and television become available to provide a new nationally centered identity for the isolated and rootless individual who seeks a sense of belonging. Hannah Arendt, exploring the origins of totalitarianism, characterizes the process as follows:

The masses grew out of fragments of a highly atomized society whose competitive structure and concomitant loneliness of the individual had been held in check only through membership in a class. The chief characteristic of the mass man is not brutality and backwardness, but his isolation and lack of normal social relationships. Coming from the class-ridden society of the nation-state, whose cracks had been cemented with nationalist sentiment, it is only natural that these masses, in the first helplessness of their new experience, have tended toward an especially violent nationalism, to which mass leaders have yielded against their own instincts and purposes for purely demagogic reasons (Arendt 1951, pp. 310–311).

Kornhauser (1959) follows this line of argument, tracing the Nazi's mobilization of alienated and restive youth groups in Germany in the 1920s. These young Germans had abandoned their traditional religious ties and community ties and substituted a sense of direction and belonging derived from Hitler's charismatic leadership. An intensive propaganda campaign in 1924 helped to coordinate a number of diverse groups into the Greater German Youth Movement. The character of these propaganda appeals focused on remote and abstract political symbols rather than the more specific and concrete political issues of day-to-day political life. These media symbols represented a pseudoauthority in that they were concocted, manipulative, and designed to sway masses; were shallow in content; impinged directly on individuals through the media rather than being filtered through the community or educational system; and encouraged a compulsive, irrational form of loyalty and attachment (Kornhauser 1968).

The rapid breakdown of traditional norms of behavior may suddenly provide more freedom than the individual is psychologically prepared to handle (Fromm 1941; Riesman 1950). These anomic individuals may find comfort in the pseudo-authority and pseudocommunity of the mass media. But these cultural dynamics lead to political instability because such individuals are easily mobilized by authoritarian and demagogic appeals. This cluster of concerns stimulated a large corpus of social science research on persuasion, attitude change, mass psychology, and political communications (Hovland et al. 1953; McGuire 1969). Michael Robinson developed a theory of how the growing dependence of the mass population on television for political news fosters the growth of political malaise, and he demonstrated the connection in a series of empirical studies (1976). Others found evidence that isolated individuals were more easily persuaded and prone to extreme political views (Kornhauser 1959). The historical fact of Hitler's rise to power in Weimar Germany and a special concern about the fragility of democratic institutions serves as the intellectual backdrop. A haunting question is under what conditions might it happen again (Hamilton 1972)?

Although critics such as Daniel Bell have characterized the concept of mass society as a rather slippery and odd mixture of moral philosophy and systematic social analysis, he describes it, nonetheless, as one of the most influential social theories of the mid-twentieth century (Bell 1962, p. 21). Indeed, it traces its legacy directly to the founding studies of the field of sociology on the maintenance of social integration in times of change conducted at the turn of the century by such luminaries as Weber, Durkheim, Tönnies, and Comte.

CONNECTING THE NEW MEDIA PARADIGM TO MASS SOCIETY THEORY

Few have explicitly tied these ideas to the hoopla over the new media, but it may have occurred to some readers that indeed there is a familiar ring to the theme of social cohesion. The Web, some would argue, will fragment and polarize society, rob us of our political commons (the currently shared space of newspaper and broadcast journalism), and isolate us from each other. Pseudo/virtual community replaces real community. If each of us reads our electronically filtered "Daily Me" we reinforce our own beliefs and opinions and know less about our neighbors' beliefs and concerns.

Bob Putnam has developed a small industry in analyzing the decline of social capital, and currently he seems to place most of the blame for America's apparent cynical withdrawal from politics on the growth of television in our lives. Wait until he discovers the Internet. In my view the social capital argument is very closely allied with the mass society notion, and what started as a catchy soundbite on bowling will evolve into a serious and broad inquiry into the interaction between a society's media infrastructure and its political infrastructure. (Jackman and Miller 1998; Norris 1996; Putnam 1995; Bennett 1998).

Others who have drawn attention to the fragmentation issue include Oscar Gandy, Jr., and Joseph Turow, who have independently explored the (hopefully) unintended consequences of commercially targeted advertising on public identity and the health of the public sphere (Gandy, Jr. Chapter 7; Turow 1997).

If we start with the popular conceptions of political fragmentation, polarization, and cynicism, can we move toward a more tightly framed hypothesis and perhaps even an empirical test? I would like to focus on four interrelated concepts that strike me as especially promising tools for the integration of research and analysis in this field. They deal broadly with the character of the public sphere, the distribution of political information, beliefs, preferences, and behavior.

- The first concept is *social cohesion.* The rules of law, order, authority, and public acceptance of social norms are traditionally conservative concepts. But increasingly, analysts have come to accept social cohesion not as an ideological or xenophobic ideal, but a legitimate and practical concern for managing the democratic process in large industrial and developing societies (Gamson 1968).
- *Fragmentation* represents a counterpoint to social cohesion and refers to the horizontal distribution of beliefs and preferences within a society, that is, the polarization or differentiation among different regions or ethnic or ideological communities. Measurement in this case would focus on dispersion rather than central tendency.
- Likewise, *stratification* refers to the "vertical" differences between elites and masses in political information and other political resources, a phenomenon perhaps best captured by a measure of inequality such as a Gini coefficient or descriptive statistics that would illustrate differences in opinions and beliefs (if any) among different strata.
- Finally, *polarization* refers not just to the distribution of opinions and beliefs but to the psychological intensity and willingness to act out on the basis of perceived social and attitudinal differences.

In this chapter I will focus primarily on the central concepts of fragmentation and stratification as they offer the most immediate promise for empirical analysis. Fragmentation captures a variety of normative and analytic concerns about the character of the public sphere. For a given political unit or region, the analyst attempts to measure the ratio of shared to unshared beliefs and values. Any static parameter is not necessarily informative, but trends could be very revealing, as could comparative analysis. It is an assessment of ideological and political tension across the class, ethnic, religious, or geographic faultlines of a given community. Research methods can focus on informal speech, formal public statements, news and entertainment content, public opinion, and the linkages among them. Analysis can focus on the extent to which cleavages are crosscutting and diffused or polarizing. The relevant subgroups vary from one area of the world to another. In the United States, for example, the highly differentiated reactions of white and black Americans to the O. J. Simpson trial verdict demonstrated a dramatic rift of understanding and belief between two important social groups despite the fact that both groups had been relying largely on the same media coverage.

The concept of stratification is similar to fragmentation as it is also a distributional concept. But stratification emphasizes a vertical dimension of resources, information, and political activity that will be evident within each issue public or affinity group. Thus, typically fragmentation refers to differences between significant social groupings and stratification, to differences within them. We might find that two groups were equivalently differentiated from each other or from some common cultural value (fragmentation), but that the beliefs within one group were internally homogeneous (including leaders and followers) while beliefs within the other were not (stratification).

These overarching theoretical concepts span more concrete hypotheses about political attitudes and behavior, and they allow for the possible grouping and integration of diverse speculations like those listed in the first paragraph of this chapter. Like equivalent concepts in the disciplines of law and economics, they have normative relevance without the complex value-laden language of common parlance. These are also collective-level concepts (akin to Durkheim's conception of social facts), not individual-level phenomena like political opinions or political behavior.

Many of the classic empirical studies of public opinion and political behavior focused on the paradox of low levels of political awareness and on the need for a balance between mass political engagement and political stability (one thinks of the work of Key, Lipset, Lazarsfeld, Berelson, Converse, and Verba, among others.) These concerns are still important and often evident in the evolving literature on new media, but the intellectual linkages are not always clear.

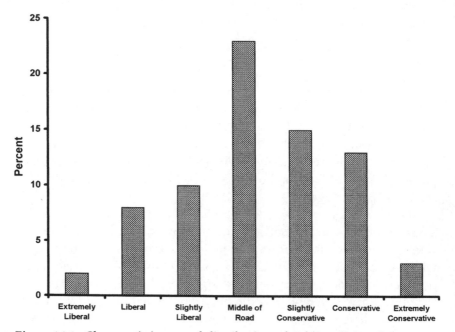

Lib-Con Self ID (US - NES - 1992)

Figure 14.1. Characteristic normal distribution of public opinion. *Source*: *National Election Study,* 1992.

PUBLIC OPINION IN THE AGE OF THE INTERNET

How might we connect the legitimate public excitement and concern about the Internet with a reenergized and theoretically regrounded approach to public opinion research? Return to our roots, I say. Let's start with V. O. Key's fundamental and now neglected *Public Opinion and American Democracy.*

Key starts with chapters that typify different types of opinion distributions. Consensus of opinion is characterized by the characteristic normal curve (Figure 14.1). The weight of opinion may be reflected in the hump of the curve centering on a position to the left or the right of a given seven-point scale. But the tails, that is, the extreme or minority positions, are occupied by fewer and fewer citizens the further one moves from the center, that is, the community norm.

A much rarer but theoretically important distribution is the bimodal distribution, with large numbers of citizens at the extremes with rela-

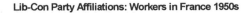

Lib-Con Party Affiliations: Workers in France 1950s

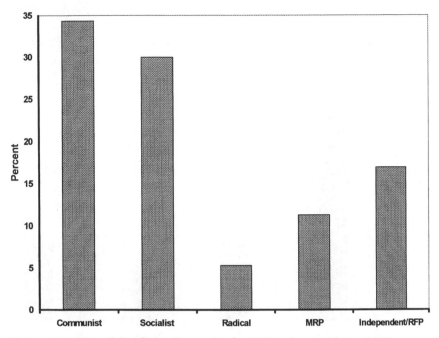

Figure 14.2. Bimodal politics, France in the 1950s. *Source:* Lipset, 1960.

tively few in the moderate middle (Figure 14.2). This would represent the fragmentation and polarization of opinion. These are simple univariate statistical properties of opinion distributions easily captured by a cross-tabular array or an indicator of dispersion such as a standard deviation or kurtosis coefficient.

Assessing opinion stratification, however, requires a bivariate analysis, assessing the difference in opinion distributions among social, economic, or demographic groups of theoretical relevance. Thus, if we find that poor versus wealthy, or black versus white citizens, are attracted to opposite ends of a policy debate, we confront a bimodal distribution of special significance (Figure 14.3).

While these concepts and the illustrative data might appear to be relatively straightforward, making a causal connection to the changing media environment provides a methodological challenge requiring a sophisticated response.

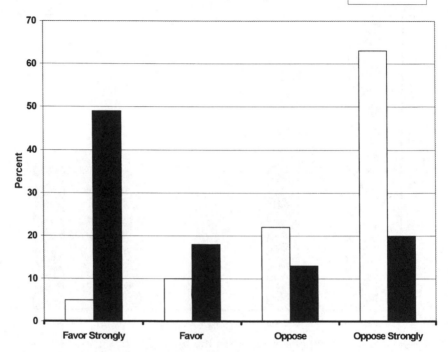

Figure 14.3. Polarized views of racially based hiring preferences (stratification). *Source:* Kinder and Sanders, 1996 (NES 1986).

METHODOLOGICAL ISSUES

The Internet is a moving target. Seven issues demonstrate the diffusion of communications technology and the impact on public opinion and political behavior.

1. *The Diffusion of Technology.* Is evidence of a particular Internet behavior a result of the nature of early adopters or is it fundamental to the character of the technology? Will the Web look like network television as soon as the average Web user looks like the average television viewer? Paths of diffusion generate unique path dependencies in technical architectures and social definitions of technology. Will these qualities evaporate as diffusion reaches mass levels? We must draw on the rich data and experience in studying the diffusion of print and electronic media. This may

prove useful in assessing the digital divide – the correlation of social inequities with new media adoption (Rogers 1995).

2. *The Hawthorne Effect.* We know people behave in predictably different ways when they know they are being watched and assessed. When a researcher with a clipboard and a lab coat is looking over your shoulder, you might find yourself studying candidate policy positions with unusual attentiveness. It is not a new problem; it is just an especially important one here, not just because of social desirability biases, but because those biases are systematically correlated with other variables of interest such as social class.

3. *Heisenberg Effects.* If we find out something about the Web and publish our findings, it may and, perhaps, it should influence behavior and strategy. But it makes the accumulation of evidence and attribution of causation a delicate task.

4. *Assessing Complex Phenomena.* This is a case of the blind men and the elephant again. Field research and case studies can demonstrate interesting examples of use and misuse. But it is hard to estimate the distributions of these behaviors and their relative effects. We need to bridge the gaps between studies, encourage the accumulation of comparable findings, and, if possible, come to a scientific consensus.

5. *Assessing Communication Channel Effects.* Bill McGuire (1985) has reviewed the accumulated literature on how the medium interacts with the message. Clear-cut conclusions are surprisingly elusive. One might characterize the typical finding as taking the form that certain content under certain conditions is marginally more effectively communicated through a particular medium. We might expect that 'Internet-Effects' will have similar character. We would be wise to review and build carefully on the best work in this research tradition.

6. *Stalking the Big Effect.* McGuire (1986) is also famous for his contributions to the big effects – minimal effects debate. Will the Internet have big effects? Some have argued that this is an unfruitful and distracting bit of scholarly dramaturgy that should be avoided. Given a stylized utopian–dystopian continuum, perhaps it cannot be avoided. But serious science can adopt a strategic response to the fact that spin doctors await the chance to have at our findings. It is good that they are even interested.

7. *Technical Obfuscation.* The Internet is a complicated bit of technology, a network of networks, an incredible patchwork of systems. Some engineers persist in believing that their protocols

are simply optimized engineering and that they need not be assessed for their potential social, economic, and political consequences. Leave the engineering to us, they argue. We dare not. Serious analysis of the impact of the Net requires serious study of the technical architecture of the net.

A METHODOLOGICAL STRATEGY

One key in untangling the effect of the Internet from the impact of other changing behaviors, values, public events, and economic conditions is the careful analysis of time series data. Edward Tufte (1974) noted that a lot of things change over time, and it is possible to demonstrate a near perfect correlation between nonsensical variables. He illustrated his point with data on the number of radios in use in Great Britain and the corresponding number of individuals committed to mental institutions. I believe the over–time correlation from the 1920s through the 1940s was $R = 0.97$.

But ultimately to resolve causal linkages the analysis will depend on our ability to triangulate data from very different research traditions. Most research on this issue thus far has depended uniquely on time series or cross-sectional data. We show the time series growth of television viewing or Internet use and correspondingly increased political cynicism or declining participation. (See Bennett 1998 for a review.) Or we examine the cross-sectional differences of poor and wealthy citizens online and conclude that there is a "digital divide" of political consequence (Cooper and Kimmelman 1999; NTIA 1999).

The appropriate methodological strategy requires that we combine the two traditions and examine diffusion over time among significant social strata. Furthermore, we need to incorporate and calibrate with sound experimental research. For example, one frequently noted explanation of the relatively slow adoption of Web technology among African Americans is the statement among black spokespersons to the effect that "there is nothing there for us, black culture is not well represented on the Net." The digital character of the Web makes it a prime candidate for machine-based content analysis. What are the growth trends of black-oriented content? How are such trends related to adoption rates among black citizens of different ages? If diffusion rates among African Americans remain low, can experimental and depth interview research reveal to what extent technophobia, economic costs, and other attitudinal factors might be relevant?

SELECTIVE ATTENTION AS A
KEY INTERVENING MECHANISM

One central causal mechanism of the suspected "Internet effect" is a polarization resulting from increased selective attention to different (and potentially ideologically extreme) news sources. Will political conservatives move from just supplementing their newspaper and television news consumption with a little *National Review* and Rush Limbaugh to an outright abandonment of traditional news media? Will the anti-UN crowd succeed in completely filtering out any international news from their laptops? Will amateur and ideological journalism flourish at the expense of the mainstream media?

Some years ago, Sears and Freedman (1971) provided some surprising experimental evidence that self-interested selective attention may not be as prevalent as originally presumed. Individuals often want to take a look at the evidence on the other side and, furthermore, want to have some familiarity with what is popular and what others are watching. Research thus far on Web behavior reveals diverse personal interests but a surprising balance among specialized and 'mainstream' sites among new and experienced users (Neuman et al. 1996).

WHAT IF THE WEB RAISED LEVELS OF POLITICAL
KNOWLEDGE: AN EARLY EMPIRICAL TEST

Web users do not use news sources on the Web to replace regular media exposure but rather to supplement it. Measures vary, but news may represent about 5 percent of typical non-work-related Web use, and not all of it political news (Kiesler et al. 1997; Neuman, O'Donnell and Schneider 1996; Pew Center 1996, 1998, 1999).

But what if the Web meets its promise and lowers the transaction costs of keeping the citizenry informed about those issues in politics it cares about? If the public were better informed, would politics be demonstrably different? Would the concerns of mobilization, polarization, and fragmentation of mass society and social capital theory prove to be manifest?

My strategy here is to try to tie the question of potential impacts of the new media to an interesting new set of research projects in the field of political behavior and communications, focusing on the impact of increased information on political opinion and behavior. Delli Carpini and Keeter's (1996) recent book anchors this field of inquiry with a comprehensive overview of the literature and a theoretically grounded compilation and analysis of the key findings. Drawing on (and in the spirit of) their work, a fresh set of inquiries has tried to estimate what public opinion would look like if the public were somehow better informed or if public opinion were assessed as part of a deliberative process (Alvarez 1997; Bartels 1996; Fishkin 1991; Fishkin and Luskin 1998; Price and Neijens 1998a, b; Zaller 1991).

The idea is straightforward. Rather than tackle the difficult question of community and identity implied by the mass society frame, let us address a question of which the accumulated political opinion and behavior data archives permit a direct empirical test. The Internet and the Web give the user a lot more control over the flow of information. Rather than a passive recipient of the EyeWitness News of the hour, cybercitizens may at their leisure find out as much as they might desire about the topics that engage them. There are adversarial sites of various stripes; mainstream political organizations; lobbying interests; and searchable electronic repositories of news, legislative debate, and independent policy analysis (Browning 1996; Hill and Hughes 1998). If the Web, as predicted, decreases the transaction costs of being a better-informed citizen (Downs 1957), do the accumulated findings of the literature of political behavior lead us to expect a significant change in mass political behavior? That represents a big "if," of course, but if proven true, my reading of the literature and my fresh analysis of the 1996 National Election Study lead me to the following conclusion. There will be effects on opinion fragmentation and stratification. They will be modest in size. They will be complex in character. It turns out not to be a simple matter of an identifiable "knowledge effect." It depends on the issue at hand. The plot thickens.

AN EMPIRICAL ANALYSIS OF THE KNOWLEDGE EFFECT

My initial question focuses on what kinds of opinion distributions are characteristic of the better versus less well informed citizens. I thought such a basic question would be amply addressed in the literature but was surprised to find it only partially addressed. Delli Carpini and Keeter (1996), for example, have a full chapter entitled "The Consequences of Political Knowledge and Ignorance." They follow the Converse tradition, demonstrating the impact of knowledge on the stability and coherence of attitude structure and developing an interesting argument about the impact of knowledge on self interest. But there is sur-

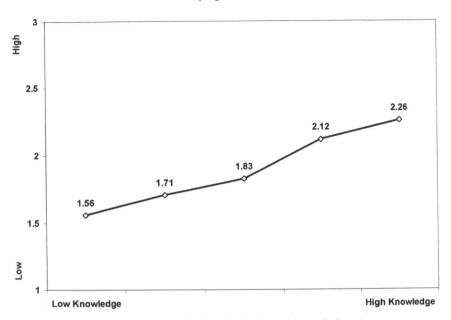

Figure 14.4. Campaign interest by level of political knowledge. *Source: National Election Study,* 1996.

prisingly little descriptive information in their chapter about whether being more informed leads to fragmentation or stratification. Bartels (1996) and Althaus (1998) imply that the differences are significant, but they use complex equations that mysteriously adjust for knowledge effects, so it is frustratingly difficult to get an intuitive sense of how the equations are derived from real behavior. So I turned to the empirical motherlode – in this case, the 1996 National Election Survey – and arrayed the opinion distributions on most of the traditional political issue items by five levels of political knowledge (a cumulative index of respondent knowledge of political figures and events.) I first reviewed the means on a measure of campaign interest by the knowledge index to make sure the oft-cited correlation between knowledge and interest was in evidence, and indeed it was. Figure 14.4 demonstrates that the mean difference between low and high knowledge respondents is almost a full point on a three-point scale.

But an examination of the relationship of knowledge with actual opinion positions on central political controversies of the election pro-

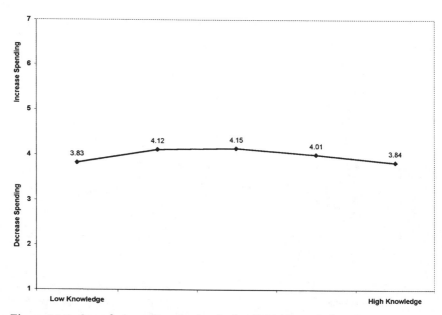

Figure 14.5. Sample issue item by level of political knowledge. *Source:*
National Election Study, 1996.

duces a much more complex picture. It may be a case of the half-empty
versus the half-full glass, but my impression is one of surprise at how
so few of the issues continue to be associated with a consistent
difference of mean opinion position. Figure 14.5 and Table 14.1 review
the group means for the different knowledge levels for a sampling of
the classic NES issue items. There are two general tendencies evident.
When there is a difference, the more knowledgeable seem to be more
conservative in the traditional sense of relying more on private enterprise than government for the provision of services. And when there is
a difference, the more knowledgeable are more enlightened about
the modern norms of gender equality. But the general rule is relatively
small differences or no difference at all. This is especially notable on
self-interest items. The more knowledgeable, of course, are generally
better off, are more likely to have attended college, and expect their
kids to attend college. On strictly self-interest grounds, we might
expect more pronounced differences here. But they are not in
evidence.

Table 14.1. *Various issue items by level of political knowledge*

Knowledge index	Gov't guarantee job	Gov't help blacks	Foodstamp spending	Welfare spending	Help homeless	Border security	Jobs vs. environment	Gender equality
1	4.02	4.87	2.41	2.29	1.68	1.65	3.64	2.57
2	4.50	5.01	2.46	2.29	1.61	1.60	3.47	2.31
3	4.60	5.02	2.38	2.26	1.89	1.51	3.54	2.33
4	4.81	4.83	2.41	2.25	2.02	1.65	3.40	2.01
5	4.89	4.70	2.33	2.26	1.95	1.74	3.38	1.94

Source: National Election Study, 1996.

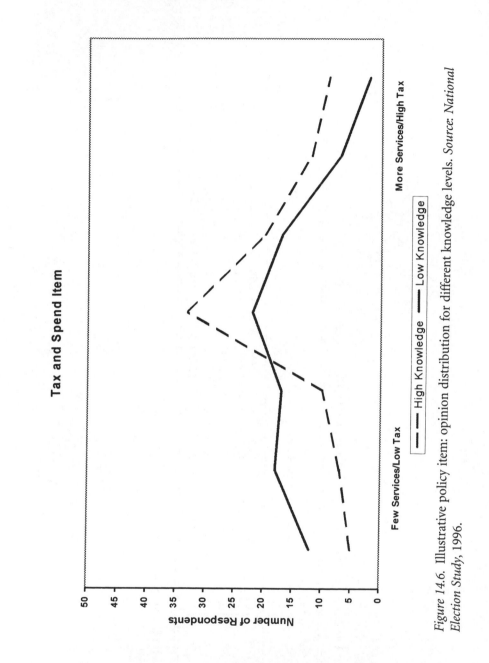

Figure 14.6. Illustrative policy item: opinion distribution for different knowledge levels. *Source: National Election Study*, 1996.

I reran the analysis to examine the dispersion of opinion as measured by standard deviations across the policy items and found they were almost identical across all knowledge levels. The less well informed did tend a bit to cluster around the scale midpoints, as illustrated in Figure 14.6. But such patterns were not strong and consistent. Further work will control for additional intervening variables, such as income, profession, and race, to look more closely to see if the already small knowledge effects are further reduced by appropriate controls.

A CONCLUDING NOTE

These preliminary analyses put us in the company of Davis and Owen (1998) and Bimber (1998a, b, c), who found that the reduced transaction costs of getting political information of interest may be associated with increased participation and attentiveness but are not likely to be associated with large-scale differences in the level of polarization or stratification of political opinion and belief.

The political activists in the Web community have just completed a successful promotion of civic awareness and Web use under the rubric of Web, White, and Blue. There is an entrepreneurial young man traveling the country in a bus filled with Internet terminals and wireless connections, encouraging the unconnected to experiment with the new tools to connect citizens with government. He calls it the *E the People Bus*. (He is traveling the country also to raise money to support his enterprise.) Their impact may well be positive, but in the larger order of things, relatively small.

There may be significant social realignments and social movements that will bring new issues to the fore and reorganize traditional political allegiances. The new groups may use the new media to get their message out. It is likely the journalists and concerned members of the establishment will hyperventilate a bit about electronic politics. But the issues will turn out to matter more than the media of communication.

NOTE

1. The academic literature is still an odd brew of systematic and anecdotal analysis. See, for example, Browning (1996), Davis and Owen (1998), Graber (1997), Grossman (1995), Hill and Hughes (1998), Jones (1995), Kamarck and Nye (1999), Kiesler (1997), Strate et al. (1996), and Sussman (1997). See Neuman et al. (1999) for a review.

References

Abramson, Jeffrey B., F. Christopher Arterton, and Gary R. Orren (1988). *The Electronic Commonwealth: The Impact of New Media Technologies on Democratic Politics.* New York: Basic Books.

Althaus, Scott L. (1998). "Information Effects in Collective Preferences." *American Political Science Review,* 92(3):545–558.

Alvarez, R. Michael (1997). *Information and Elections.* Ann Arbor: University of Michigan Press.

Arendt, Hannah (1951). *The Origins of Totalitarianism.* New York: Harcourt Brace.

Bartels, Larry M. (1996). "Uninformed Voters: Information Effects in Presidential Elections." *American Journal of Political Science,* 40:194–230.

Bell, Daniel (1960). *The End of Ideology: On the Exhaustion of Political Ideas in the Fifties.* Glencoe, IL: The Free Press.

Beniger, James R. (1987). "Personalization of Mass Media and the Growth of Pseudo-Community." *Communication Research,* 14(3):352–371.

Bennett, W. Lance (1998). "The UnCivic Culture: Communication, Identity, and the Rise of Lifestyle Politics." *PS: Political Science and Politics,* 31(December): 741–761.

Bimber, Bruce (1998a). "The Internet and Citizen Communication with Government: Does the Medium Matter?" American Political Science Association Annual Meetings. Boston, MA.

(1998b). "The Internet and Political Transformation: Populism, Community and Accelerated Pluralism." *Polity,* 31(1):133–160.

(1998c). "Toward an Empirical Map of Political Participation on the Internet." American Political Science Association Annual Meetings. Boston, MA.

Browning, Graeme (1996). *Electronic Democracy.* Wilton, CT: Pemberton Press.

Castells, Manuel (1996). *The Rise of the Network Society.* Cambridge, MA: Blackwell Publishers.

(1997). *The Information Age: Economy, Society and Culture.* Malden, MA: Blackwell Publishers.

(1998). *End of Millennium.* Malden, MA: Blackwell Publishers.

Comte, Auguste ([1851] 1875). *System of Positive Polity.* London: Longmans, Greene & Co.

Converse, Philip (1962). "Information Flow and the Stability of Partisan Attitudes." *Public Opinion Quarterly,* 26(4 Winter):578–599.

(1964). "The Nature of Belief Systems in Mass Publics." In David Apter (Ed.), *Ideology and Discontent.* New York: Free Press, pp. 206–261.

Cooper, Mark, and Gene Kimmelman (1999). "The Digital Divide Confronts the Telecommunications Act of 1996." Consumer Federation of America.

Davis, Richard, and Diana Owen (1998). *New Media and American Politics.* New York: Oxford University Press.

Delli Carpini, Michael X., and Scott Keeter (1996). *What Americans Know About Politics and Why It Matters.* New Haven: Yale University Press.

Downs, Anthony (1957). *An Economic Theory of Democracy.* New York: Harper & Row.

Durkheim, Emile (1951). *Suicide.* New York: Free Press.

Durkheim, E. (1964). *The Rules of Sociological Method.* New York: Free Press.

Fishkin, James (1991). *Democracy and Deliberation*. New Haven: Yale University Press.

Fishkin, James S., and Robert C. Luskin (1998). "Bringing Deliberation to the Democratic Dialog: The NIC and Beyond." University of Texas at Austin.

Fromm, Erich (1941). *Escape from Freedom*. New York: Farrar & Rinehart.

Gamson, William (1968). *Power and Discontent*. Homewood: Dorsey Press.

Giner, Salvador (1976). *Mass Society*. San Diego: Academic Press.

Graber, Doris A. (1997). "Building Cyber-Age Bridges Between Citizens and Public Agencies." Paper presented at the American Political Science Association annual meeting, Washington, DC.

Grossman, Lawrence (1995). *The Electronic Republic*. London: Penguin.

Habermas, Jürgen ([1962] 1989). *The Structural Transformation of the Public Sphere*. Cambridge: MIT Press.

Hamilton, Richard F. (1972). *Class and Politics in the United States*. New York: John Wiley & Sons.

Hill, Kevin A., and John E. Hughes (1998). *Cyberpolitics: Citizen Activism in the Age of the Internet*. Lanham MD: Rowman & Littlefield.

Hovland, Carl, Irving Janis, and Harold H. Kelley (1953). *Communication and Persuasion*. New Haven: Yale University Press.

Jackman, Robert W., and Ross A. Miller (1998). "Social Capital and Politics." In Polsby, Nelson W. (Ed.), *Annual Review of Political Science*. Palo Alto: Annual Reviews, pp. 47–74.

Jones, Steven G. (Ed.) (1995). *Cybersociety: Computer Mediated Communication and Community*. Thousand Oaks: Sage.

Kamarck, Elaine Ciulia, and Nye, Jr., Joseph S. (Eds.) (1999). *Democracy.Com? Governance in a Networked World*. Cambridge: Harvard University Press.

Key, Jr., V. O. (1961). *Public Opinion and American Democracy*. New York: Alfred A. Knopf.

Kiesler, Sara, Robert Kraut, Tridas Mukhopadhyay, and William Scherlis (1997). "Homenet: A Field Trial of Residential Internet Use." Project Summary, Carnegie Mellon University. *http://homenet.andrew.cum/progress.hnsum.html*.

Kornhauser, William (1959). *The Politics of Mass Society*. New York: Free Press.

(1968). "Mass Society," in Sills, David (Ed.), *The Encyclopedia of the Social Sciences*. Vol. 10. New York: Free Press/Macmillan, pp. 58–64.

McGuire, William J. (1969). "The Nature of Attitudes and Attitude Change." In Lindzey, Gardner, and Elliot Aronson (Eds.), *The Handbook of Social Psychology, 2nd ed.* Reading, MA: Addison Wesley, pp. 136–314.

(1985). "Attitudes and Attitude Change." In Lindzey, Gardner, and Elliot Aronson (Eds.), *The Handbook of Social Psychology*. New York: Random House, pp. 233–346.

(1986). "The Myth of Massive Media Impact: Savagings and Salvagings." In Comstock, George, ed., *Public Communication and Behavior*. Orlando: Academic Press, pp. 173–257.

National Telecommunications and Information Administration (1999). *Falling Through the Net: Defining the Digital Divide*. Washington, DC: National Telecommunications and Information Administration.

Neuman, W. Russell (1991a). *The Future of the Mass Audience*. New York: Cambridge University Press.

(1991b). "What Ever Happened to Mass Society Theory?" American Association for Public Opinion Research Annual Conference. Phoenix.

(1996). "Political Communications Infrastructure." *Annals*, 546(June):9–21.

Shawn R. O'Donnell, and Steven M. Schneider (1996). "The Web's Next Wave: A Field Study of Internet Diffusion and Use Patterns." MIT Media Lab.

Eric A. Zimmer, Jenny Stromer-Galley, Christopher Hunter, and Elvin Montero (1999). "Caught in the Web: A Research & Policy White Paper on the Evolving Character of the Internet." Annenberg Public Policy Center, April 9.

Norris, Pippa (1996). "Does Television Erode Social Capital?" *PS: Political Science and Politics*, 29(3):474–480.

Pew Center for the People and the Press (1996). "TV News Viewership Declines." Washington, DC, Pew Research Center for the People and the Press.

(1998). "Internet News Takes Off." http://www.people-press.org/med98rpt.htm.

(1999). "The Internet News Audience Goes Ordinary." Washington, DC, Pew Research Center for the People and the Press, January.

Price, Vincent, and Peter Neijens (1998a). "Deliberative Polls: Toward Improved Measures of 'Informed' Public Opinion." *International Journal of Public Opinion Research*, 10(2):145–176.

(1998b). "Opinion Quality in Public Opinion Research." *International Journal of Public Opinion Research*, 9(4):336–360.

Putnam, Robert D. (1995). "Bowling Alone: America's Declining Social Capital." *Journal of Democracy*, 6:65–78.

Riesman, David (1950). *The Lonely Crowd.* Garden City: Doubleday.

Robinson, Michael J. (1976). "Public Affairs Television and the Growth of Political Malaise: The Case of 'The Selling of the Pentagon.'" *The American Political Science Review*, 70:409–432.

Rogers, Everett M. (1995). *Diffusion of Innovations, 4th Edition.* New York: Free Press.

Sears, David O., and J. L. Freedman (1971). "Selective Exposure to Information: A Critical Review." In Schramm, Wilbur, and Donald F. Roberts (Ed.), *The Process and Effects of Mass Communication.* Urbana: University of Illinois Press, pp. 209–234.

Strate, Lance, Ronald Jacobson, and Stephanie B. Gibson (Eds.) (1996). *Communication and Cyberspace: Social Interaction in an Electronic Environment.* Cresskill, NJ: Hampton Press.

Sussman, Gerald (1997). *Communication, Technology, and Politics in the Information Age.* Newbury Park, CA: Sage.

Tönnies, Ferdinand ([1887] 1957). *Community and Society.* New York: Harper and Row.

Tufte, Edward R. (1974). *Data Analysis for Politics and Policy.* Englewood Cliffs, NJ: Prentice-Hall.

Turow, Joseph (1997). *Breaking Up America: Advertisers and the New Media World.* Chicago: University of Chicago Press.

Weber, Max ([1924] 1978). *Economy and Society.* Berkeley: University of California Press.

Zaller, John (1991). *The Nature and Origins of Mass Opinion.* New York: Cambridge University Press.

PART 4

Mediated Campaigns

•

CHAPTER 15

Issue Advocacy in a Changing
Discourse Environment

Kathleen Hall Jamieson

Representative government requires that voters be able to learn about the candidates who seek to represent them. As Madison noted in his 1798 report to the General Assembly of Virginia on the Sedition Act,

> The right of electing the members of the government constitutes more particularly the essence of a free and responsible government. The value and efficacy of this right depends on the knowledge of the comparative merits and demerits of the candidates for public trust, and on the equal freedom, consequently, of examining and discussing these merits of the candidates respectively.[1]

Indeed, in their discussions of what would become the First Amendment the founders even considered giving citizens the power to bind the votes of their representatives (see debate on August 15, 1789). That proposal was not adopted, in part because the founders believed that "Representation is the principle of our Government; the people ought to have confidence in the honor and integrity of those they send forward to transact their business" (Gales and Seaton 1834, p. 762). Such confidence is presumably the by-product of knowledge about the individuals who would serve.

Discussions of the nature and importance of representation occur throughout the *Federalist Papers* (see, for example, numbers 10, 56, 57, 63). Because ours is a representative system of government, the law recognizes that the public has the need to hear the messages of candidates. As a result, the candidate's message is given a privileged space in broadcast law. Specifically, the speech of the candidate is given special treatment not afforded other noncandidate speech (note that the comparable access and lowest unit rate provisions of the FCC apply to candidate speech) and unlike other forms of speech (including issue advocacy and commercial speech) is protected from censorship by stations.

By contrast and without altering any of these FCC provisions, *Buckley v. Valeo* presupposed that all speech is valuable and has a right to be heard. As a result, it refused to give privileged status to the speech of candidates over the speech of issue advocates. That presupposition makes sense in a prebroadcast age when speech was delivered in open-air spaces from the stump or soapbox. But the world has changed dramatically since the day in 1789 when Mr. Sedgwick argued against inclusion of freedom of assembly in the Bill of Rights. In moving to strike "assemble and," he said that such an amendment "would tend to make them appear trifling in the eyes of their constituents." "[S]hall we secure the freedom of speech," he asked, "and think it necessary at the same time, to allow the right of assembling? If people freely converse together, they must assemble for that purpose; it is a self-evident, unalienable right which people possess" (Gales and Seaton 1834, p. 760). In Sedgwick's time, each advocate could claim his own podium without denying others a space from which to speak or the ability to attract an audience.

That presupposition doesn't translate well to television or radio, however, because neither has unlimited air time available to reach the intended audience. When the amount of desirable time (i.e., that time that reaches the intended audience) available for purchase is finite – as it is on television and radio – it is no longer either practical or possible to assume that all voices carry comparable rights, hence the FCC regulations privileging candidate speech.

Whereas in the prebroadcast age candidates and advocates moved about the country delivering the same message to different audiences, in the broadcast age candidates and advocates more often deliver the same message repeatedly to the same audience. The candidate or advocacy group that purchases the largest number of gross ratings points can magnify the power of a given message through repetition. When a group outspends one or both candidates, it is more likely that the audience will remember its message than the message of the candidate.

Because viewers' interpretations of messages is in part a function of the context in which they appear, *Buckley* has spawned two very different types of issue ads. Exploring their character, uses, and impact is the purpose of this chapter. The first, which I call "legislative issue advocacy," addresses pending legislation in a context in which an election is not on the immediate horizon. The second, which I label "candidate issue advocacy," addresses an issue but in the context of a forthcoming election vote. The distinction between the two types is important because communication theorists hold as a basic premise the notion that meaning does not exist in messages but rather in the intersection of a message and an audience.

From the time of Aristotle, scholars of communication have known that audiences draw on their cultural and biographical experiences as well as their knowledge of the conventions through which a society communicates in order to interpret messages. "[O]f the three elements in speechmaking – speaker, subject, and person address – ," wrote Aristotle (1358a–b) in the *Rhetoric*, "it is the last one, the hearer, that determines the speech's end and object."

Audiences routinely invest messages with unarticulated premises in order to draw conclusions. When doing so, the assumptions or premises they bring to the message create what Aristotle called *enthymemes*. The process was so critical that Aristotle called the enthymeme the soul of persuasion. Contemporary theorists capture the same notion in the commonplace expression "meaning is in people." Argument theorists convey it with the notion that "we normally do not make explicit mention of all premises implicit in an argument, especially if they are obvious or noncontroversial" (Kelley 1988, p. 211). "There may be unexpressed premises but also unexpressed conclusions." Unexpressed premises "throw, as it were, an invisible bridge between the explicit premises and the standpoint that is being defended" (van Eemeren and Grootendorst 1992, pp. 60, 141).

Linguists make the same assumption when they note that

1. All utterances are subject to semantic collaboration to establish their effective meaning. 2. In communication, only effective meaning matters: literal translations of utterances could be imposed linguistically but have no intrinsic communicative status. 3. Our ability to use or to understand a wide variety of figurative, indirect, and colloquial forms of language (metaphor, humorous, polite requests, etc.) depends on the process of semantic collaboration (Roberts and Bavelas 1996, p. 143).

The same notion undergirds Grice's (1989) maxims of conversational implicature. These maxims suggest, for example, that when a speaker juxtaposes two seemingly unrelated ideas, the fact of the juxtaposition encourages audiences to assume that they are somehow related.

This fundamental human phenomenon means that an ad that asks you to call a candidate to articulate your approval or disapproval of a position can be interpreted in one context as an invitation to cast a vote while being read in another simply as a request to call and express an opinion on legislation. While legislative issue ads are likely to be regarded as requests to make a call – the cigar is just a cigar – the candidate issue ad is more likely to be regarded as an invitation to factor the information in the ad into one's voting decision. In other words, an issue ad does not have to contain such words as "vote for" or "vote against" for an audience to assume that that is the behavior sought by the ad.

The reasons are straightforward. Among the factors that contextualize messages are the other cues in the environment. When lawn signs, bumper stickers, news accounts, and candidate ads signal that an election is in process, for example, viewers are likely to assume that messages relevant to a voting decision – such as negative information about one candidate or positive information about another – are asking them to use the information in making a voting decision. Enthymematically, such messages solicit a vote when an audience member links the explicit content of the message (the praise or blame) to the context (an election) and recognizes the similarities between the structure of the so-called candidate issue ad and the ads produced for candidates themselves.

BACKGROUND

In the wake of the disclosures known as Watergate, in 1974 the U.S. Congress amended the Federal Election Campaign Act (FECA) of 1971 to limit contributions to a candidate running for a federal office and to limit expenditures made to support such a candidate. Under the amendments, individuals were limited to contributions of $1,000 per candidate in a primary or a general election; political action committees (PACs) were limited to $5,000. Limits were also placed on expenditures by campaigns, by candidates from their personal wealth, and by independent groups that did not coordinate their expenditures with the campaign.

As part of the package, those who agreed to spending limits in a presidential campaign and who qualified by raising a set amount of money in a set number of states from a set number of individuals would receive federal financing for a period in which they garnered a set level of votes in the primaries and for the entire general election period if they were nominated by one of the two major parties. The Federal Election Commission (FEC) was established to administer the law.

The constitutionality of FECA was challenged on the grounds that it violated the First and Fifth Amendments. Among the plaintiffs were Senator James Buckley (R. NY) and former Democratic presidential candidate and Minnesota Senator Eugene McCarthy. The plaintiffs argued that restricting political use of money constituted "a restriction on communication violative of the First Amendment, since virtually all meaningful political communications in the modem setting involve the expenditure of money." The Supreme Court upheld the limits on PAC and individual contributions to a candidate but said of limits on expenditures: "A restriction on the amount of money a person or group can spend on political communication during a campaign necessarily reduces the quantity of expression by restricting the number of issues discussed, the depth of their exploration, and the size of the audience reached. This is because virtually every means of communicating ideas in today's mass society requires the expenditure of money."

At the heart of the *Buckley* ruling is the claim that "the concept that government may restrict the speech of some elements of our society in order to enhance the relative voice of others is wholly foreign to the First Amendment, which was designed to secure 'the widest possible dissemination of information from diverse and antagonistic sources,' and 'to assure unfettered interchange of ideas for the bringing about of political and social changes desired by the people.'"

In *Buckley*, the Court stated, "For the distinction between discussion of issues and candidates and advocacy of election or defeat of candidates may often dissolve in practical application. Candidates, especially incumbents, are intimately tied to public issues involving legislative proposals and governmental actions. Not only do candidates campaign on the basis of their positions on various public issues, but campaigns themselves generate issues of public interest." The Court sidestepped the resulting problem by limiting regulations by the government to "explicit words of advocacy of election or defeat of a candidate."

In the process, it held that reporting of independent political expenditures under Section 434 (e) of FECA be limited to those funds used for communication "that expressly advocate the election or defeat of a clearly identified candidate"[2]. In a footnote (108), the Court said that "[t]his construction would restrict the application of [that section] to communications containing express words of advocacy of election or defeat, such as 'vote for,' 'vote against,' 'defeat,' 'reject.'"

The Court has literally looked for words "exhorting the public to vote" when determining whether an ad did or did not constitute "express advocacy." In FEC v. Christian Action Network a televised ad that aired during the 1992 general election was determined not to constitute issue advocacy on those grounds. "It is beyond dispute," wrote the Court, "that the advertisements were openly hostile to the proposals believed to have been endorsed by the two candidates. Nevertheless, the advertisements were devoid of any language that directly exhorted the public to vote. Without a frank admonition to take electoral action, even admittedly negative advertisements such as these, do not constitute 'express advocacy' as that term is defined in *Buckley* and its progeny." [3]

LEGISLATIVE ISSUE ADVOCACY

The first large scale use of legislative issue advocacy ads occurred during the health care reform debate of 1993–4. From September 1993 through August 1994, the public was subject to the largest, most sustained advertising campaign to shape a public policy decision up to that point in the history of the Republic. Between September 8, 1993, when the first "Harry and Louise" ad began airing and the end of the July 4th congressional recess, a total of forty-nine groups had pledged in excess of $50,000,000 to produce and air more than sixty different broadcast ads and print and distribute more than 100 pieces of print including ads, direct mail, and brochures. By early September, the dollar amount spent on producing and gaining an audience for ads exceeded that expended on ads by any one of the presidential contenders in the general election of 1992.

ADS AS A SURROGATE FOR LOBBYING

Ostensibly an effort to influence the public, the ad campaigns of the health care reform debate were more clearly an effort to persuade print and broadcast reporters that the sponsors were players worthy of coverage and to persuade legislators, particularly those whose votes could be swung on key committees, that risk exceeded advantage in opposing their interests.

The issue-advocacy ads in the health care reform debate forecast two features that continue to characterize this genre: disproportionate use of fear appeal and attack, and use of pseudonymous groups as the source of the message. It is these features that make ads problematic as a surrogate for lobbying. If legislators do not accede to an issue group's agenda, that group can tacitly threaten the legislators with an ad campaign that will attack them and their issue agenda; alternatively, legislators who go along with the group can be rewarded with ads that thank them for their fine legislative records. Because issue advocacy ads are not subject to disclosure requirements, the press and public have no way of knowing who is funding the campaign or how much is being spent. At the same time, funders can camouflage their actual agenda behind an innocuous group label, making it difficult for the public to assess the group's motives and credibility and complicating the rhetorical task for legislators who wish to unmask the group that is opposing them or favoring their opponent.

LEGISLATIVE ISSUE ADS CAN RAISE THE VISIBILITY OF PENDING LEGISLATION AND SYNOPSIZE THE ARGUMENTS OF ALTERNATIVE SIDES

If there is a type of issue advocacy that should gladden the hearts of the majority that decided *Buckley*, it is the multisided legislative issue advocacy that occurs when voices not in the national media agenda are added to the national debate on a topic that is pending before Congress. The debate over flag burning is illustrative. At issue is a proposal to amend the U.S. Constitution, authorizing the Congress to prohibit the physical destruction of the flag of the United States. Proponents of the legislation sought Congressional action in the wake of the 5–4 1989 Supreme Court decision in *Texas v. Johnson*,[4] which held that "If there is a bedrock principle underlying the First Amendment, it is that the Government may not prohibit the expression of an idea simply because society finds the idea itself offensive or disagreeable." The Court also noted that "nothing in our precedents suggests that a State may foster its own view of the flag by prohibiting expressive conduct relating to it."

Public opinion is a function of how the question is framed. In their issue ads, proponents framed the issue as one of desecration of a national symbol; opponents, as support for freedom of expression. Polls indicated that a majority favors a ban on flag burning, but support is weaker for the vehicle that would accomplish that end: an amendment to the U.S. Constitution. A majority thinks that "it should be legal or illegal to burn the American flag": 79 percent said it should be illegal; 17 percent thought it should be legal; 4 percent had no opinion (Roper Poll 1998). However, when asked if "the U.S. Constitution should be amended to make it illegal to burn the American flag as a form of political dissent," the results were equally divided: 49 percent thought it should be amended, and 49 percent thought it should not (Roper Poll 1998).

The House passed such an amendment on June 12, 1997, by a 310–114 vote. On June 24, 1998, the proposal was placed on the Senate Legislative Calendar under General Orders. On September 1, 1998, Senator Hatch of the Judiciary Committee filed a written report (no. 105–298). Senate Majority Leader Trent Lott had promised a vote before the elections in November. Once again in 1999, the House approved the amendment, but it died in the Senate.

In an effort to influence the votes of undecided members of the Senate, two groups have aired issue advocacy television ads and one aired radio ads. The Citizens Flag Alliance and American Renewal favor the bill; the People for the American Way opposes it.

In 1994, the Citizens Flag Alliance was founded by the American Legion. It is a coalition of 123 organizations, mostly national groups that favor a constitutional amendment to protect the flag. The group is based in Indianapolis and reports almost 200,000 members. American Renewal is a conservative group headed by activist Gary Bauer.

The brainchild of television producer Norman Lear, People for the American Way (PFAW) was "founded in 1980 by a group of civic and religious leaders concerned with the rising tide of intolerance sweeping our nation." The group, which both opposes censorship of books and a constitutional amendment to ban physical desecration of the flag, claims a membership of 300,000.

One ad for the Citizens Flag Alliance featured the actor who played a character in the prime time hit *Dukes of Hazard*, who said: "I'm John Schneider. Remember learning the difference between right and wrong? I do. Respect for others is right. Violent acts are wrong. Respect for our flag is right. Desecrating the American flag is wrong. You can right a wrong. Call your senators and urge them to vote yes on the Flag Protection Amendment. Find out where your senators stand and what you can do to help. Call 1-800-530-9444. Call now. It is the right thing to do."

Schneider speaks directly to camera throughout the ad. On screen,

Schneider is identified as "Bo Duke on the Dukes of Hazzard." "Mr. Schneider's endorsement is not compensated," notes print on the screen under his image. The appeal to "call your senators" is reinforced in print, as is the phone number. The ad is tagged, "Paid for by the Citizens Flag Alliance, Inc."

An ad for the People for the American Way also used personal testimony but from a Vietnam war veteran who had been held as a prisoner of war (Figure 15.1).

Adding to the advocacy was American Renewal, a conservative group headed by Gary Bauer that aired radio ads urging people to call their senators expressing support for the bill.

DROWNING OUT COMPETING VOICES DURING LEGISLATIVE DEBATES

One reason that the ads over flag burning are useful is that the opposing points of view were backed by comparable funding. Both sides were heard. The playing field was level. The clash of ideas could inform viewers' judgments. That is not the case when one side has a large ad budget and the other side has a miniscule one. A test case for this principle occurred when the protobacco industry forces outspent the antiindustry side more than twenty to one on broadcast and cable ads about a proposed settlement with the tobacco industry.

Senate Bill 1415, authored by Republican Senator John McCain of Arizona and supported by President Bill Clinton, was voted out of the Senate Commerce Committee in April 1998 by a nineteen to one vote. The bill would have settled the lawsuits brought by the attorneys general against the major U.S. tobacco companies with provisions that: elicited $516 billion from the industry over 25 years; increased the price of a pack of cigarettes at the manufacturing level by $1.10 over a five year period; increased the regulatory authority of the Food and Drug Administration over the manufacturing, sale, and marketing of tobacco products; imposed up to $3.5 billion in annual financial penalties on the tobacco companies if youth smoking failed to drop at least a specified amount; provided $10 billion over a five-year period to help those, such as tobacco growers, whose livelihood was negatively affected by the agreement; and placed a $6.5 billion annual cap on the amounts cigarette companies could be assessed in damages. The funds raised by the bill would have funded medical research as well as a large-scale campaign to reduce youth smoking. The McCain bill would also

Audio:	Visual: Mr. Warner speaking to camera.
I'm Jim Warner. I served in Vietnam and was a prisoner of war for five and a half years. Our battle for freedom was hard fought every day of our captivity.	Text: "James H. Warner, Former POW" Text: "Paid For By People for the American Way"
Once during an interrogation, an officer showed me pictures of American kids burning an American flag.	Visual: File footage of "Hanoi Hilton" Text: "Hanoi Hilton–POW Camp" Visual: File footage of anti-war protest
"This proves your country's wrong," he said.	Visual: Warner
"No," I said. "Those pictures prove that we're right and our country is strong.	Visual: File footage of protests and demonstrations
"We're not afraid of freedom, even when we disagree."	Visual: Warner
The officer flew into a rage. But behind the anger I could see fear in his eyes. It was a victory for me and for freedom.	Visual: Still photo, American POWS released
Now, some folks want to amend our constitution's bill of rights to ban flag burning. That's wrong. I don't want to see my flag burned. I offered my life for it and I'd do it again. But I also fought for the rights and freedoms that it represents, and I'm still fighting to protect it. And you can join me.	Visual: Warner Visual: Statue of Liberty Visual: Children raising flag Visual: Warner
Call your Senators at (202) 224-3121. Tell them to vote against the flag amendment.	Visual: Waving flag Text: "Tell Your Senators to Vote No Call: (202) 224-3121"
Don't let them burn our freedom.	Visual: Warner Final Slide: "People for the American Way (logo)–1 (800) 326-PFAW-www.pfaw.org"

Figure 15.1. Television ad for the People for the American Way. *Source*: Author's transcription of television ad.

have banned billboards advertising tobacco within 1,000 feet of schools and banned human, animal, or cartoon characters in ads for cigarettes. The Commerce Committee bill included financial aid to any tobacco farm owners who experienced a drop in demand as a result of the bill. A related bill was introduced in the House.

After supporting an earlier version of the bill with an issue ad, the five largest tobacco companies in the United States – Philip Morris Inc., R.J. Reynolds Tobacco Company, Brown and Williamson Tobacco Corporation, Lorillard Tobacco Company, and The United States Tobacco Company – lost the protection from liability that they had brokered in the original settlement and initiated a cross-country broadcast campaign against the legislation.

The estimated $40 million issue advocacy campaign by the five largest tobacco companies in spring and summer 1998 was more than two and a half times more expensive than the widely discussed "Harry and Louise" ads sponsored by the Health Insurance Association of America (HIAA) in 1993–4. While the "Harry and Louise" ads were aired for almost a year intermittently in New York, Washington, DC, and in the districts of swing members of committees with legislative jurisdiction over the health care reform legislation, the tobacco industry ads were run at higher intensity in more places for three months. Where the "Harry and Louise" ads ran almost exclusively on cable, the tobacco industry ads were run on both local broadcast and cable. Where the makers of the "Harry and Louise" ads invited media coverage by placing them in the DC and New York City markets, the tobacco industry ads minimized media attention by not concentrating buys in those markets.

The campaign that aired exclusively in the Washington, DC, market was sponsored by a group the public considers more credible than the tobacco industry: The U.S. Chamber of Commerce. Although a much smaller, more narrowly targeted campaign, the U.S. Chamber of Commerce's ads drew more media attention than did the larger-scale campaign by the tobacco industry.

The campaign by the tobacco companies was unprecedented for a number of reasons, including the fact that there was not a week between early April and early August in which industry ads were not being aired; this was the first time in which a large-scale, long-running, nationwide broadcast ad campaign on a piece of pending legislation had run with negligible broadcast response from those on the other side; the only television ad aired by proponents of a "tough bill" against "Big Tobacco" was aired by the American Cancer Society for a single week in May in five states and nationally on CNN. The tobacco industry's ads aired widely (in between 30 and 50 markets); the ads aired on both cable and local spot broadcast; the focused message of the campaign had been consistently reinforced; and the campaign had continued after the demise of the McCain bill. This was the first large-scale issue advocacy campaign with the potential to set the issue agenda for a November election with a nationwide campaign on the air in spring and summer.

The scope of the campaign and the imbalance in the amount of advertising information available meant that a large audience was repeatedly exposed to misleading and uncorrected claims. The most deceptive claims appeared not in the ads sponsored directly by the tobacco industry but by an industry-sponsored group, The National Smokers Alliance. These ads were run not on television but on radio. The argument that the ads were deceptive was made in an Annenberg Public Policy Center report issued in August 1998 and is available on the Annenberg Web site, as is a survey by APPC, which found that those in markets with high exposure to the industry ads were significantly more likely to believe their claims than were those in markets with little industry ad play (APPC 1998).

CANDIDATE ISSUE ADVOCACY

The second type of issue advocacy occurs in the context of an election campaign. In the 1996 election season, more was spent on issue ads than on the ads of three major presidential campaigns combined. A comprehensive review of issue advocacy, conducted by Deborah Beck and Douglas Rivlin for the Annenberg Public Policy Center, found that between $135,000,000 and $150,000,000 was spent airing issue advocacy ads.

Candidate issue advocacy can serve a variety of functions, including agenda setting, mobilizing subgroups, spending in support of presidential candidates outside the caps set by FECA, at key moments altering the balance of messages in favor of the side with the largest amount of issue advocacy money, and occasionally creating a campaign in which the candidates' voices are not the dominant ones on the air waves. Here I will illustrate each use.

AGENDA SETTING

The ads aired by the AFL-CIO in spring 1996 set the agenda in key congressional races by magnifying the salience of the Democratic message that unlike Gingrich–Dole and their congressional supporters, Clinton and his allies would protect Medicare, increase the minimum wage, and preserve pension protection. The early issue advocacy by the

Democratic National Committee (DNC) for Clinton, which ran from summer 1995 through the primaries, performed the same agenda-setting function in key electoral states.

Mobilizing Subgroups

The ads aired by Republican groups such as the National Right to Life Committee were designed to mobilize subgroups of Republicans with messages too controversial for use in the ads of the party nominee. So where Dole soft-pedaled his prolife position out of concern that featuring it would alienate moderate Republican women, issue ads reminded "true believers" that so-called partial birth abortion was an issue that should be at the center of their voting agenda. Part of what is interesting about this process is that the Republican National Committee (RNC) provided some of these groups with funding for their ad campaigns.

Subverting Spending Limits

Both the Democratic and Republican National Committees used issue ads to make the case for their prospective nominees. Because it is unlimited, this form of spending in effect eliminates the spending caps to which presidential candidates agree in return for accepting federal financing of their primary and general election campaigns. So, for example, when Dole became the presumptive nominee of his party but headed a cash-poor campaign that had spent to the limits specified by FECA, the RNC stepped in with issue ads to make his case until his campaign received federal funding at its convention.

Except for the disclaimer, most of the ads aired in 1996 by the Democratic and Republican National Committees were indistinguishable from candidate ads. The candidates recognized the similarity between the party ads and ads directly supporting their candidacy. Speaking on a satellite transmission to ABC affiliates meeting in Orlando in June 1966, the presumptive Republican nominee Bob Dole said, "We can, through the Republican National Committee, through what we call the Victory '96 program, run television ads and other advertising. It's called generic. It's not Bob Dole for president. In fact, there's an ad running now, hopefully in Orlando, a 60-second spot about the Bob Dole story: Who is Bob Dole? What's he all about? It never says that I'm running for president, though I hope that it's fairly obvious, since I'm the only one in the picture!" (Kurtz 1997).

Increasing the likelihood that the Democratic ads – both by the

Democratic National Committee and the state Democratic parties – would reinforce key Clinton themes was the fact that the ads for all three groups were produced by the same ad team. Reporters for the *New York Times* explained the process this way, "The money the committee [the Democratic National Committee] transferred to state parties also came with specific instructions on how to spend it, state party officials say. Within days of receiving the transfers, the state parties sent checks to the consulting team hired by the Clinton–Gore campaign and the national party. The $32 million transferred went to 12 key battleground states." This sort of procedure made it possible for both the Dole–Kemp and Clinton–Gore campaigns to effectively circumvent the $62 million spending limit each had accepted as a condition of receiving federal funding. A Clinton team member told the *Times*, "The whole issue of the ads was the language and on ways to get around the law . . . If you changed a few words, then you could produce them as DNC ads and not as Clinton–Gore ads. It was the nuttiest thing."

Nor did the issue ads necessarily increase the number of voices heard by the electorate. In October 1997, Democrats on the Senate Governmental Affairs Committee obtained documents showing that the Republican National Committee had directed more than one million dollars to other groups in 1996, including the National Right to Life Committee and the American Defense Institute. In the words of reporters for the *New York Times*, "For both parties, the friendly nonprofit groups have become the political equivalent of Swiss bank accounts: places where donors can make contributions that are hidden from public view but still help Democratic and Republican candidates and causes" (Abramson and Wayne 1997).

ALTERING THE MESSAGE BALANCE

The group with money for issue advocacy can set an agenda by airing ads early in the precampaign season but also can follow the polls to determine when issue-advocacy spending would be most useful to its preferred candidate in the election itself. In 1996, RNC head Haley Barber held a large portion of his resources until the final week of the election and then poured them into radio ads in the districts that had experienced the AFL-CIO blitz. In that final week and weekend, the message balance in those districts swung decisively toward the Republicans. The RNC followed the same strategy in the special election to fill the seat vacated by Republican Susan Molinari in the Staten Island district in New York. The race was a dead heat as the final week approached. In that week, the RNC dropped what some estimated to be one million dollars in televised issue advocacy and direct mail. It is impossible to know whether that expenditure should be credited with the Republican win – after all, the seat had been held by a Republican. What is clear is that in the final week, the Republican message received substantially more air play than the Democratic one.

Drowning out the Voices of the Candidates During Election Periods

In some instances, candidate issue-advocacy advertising also has altered the rhetorical structures of campaigns by depriving the candidate for office of the privileged position necessary if the electorate is to determine whether the candidate is worthy of elected office.

Because they explicitly advocated the election or defeat of a candidate, the outside group ads in the California 22nd Congressional District race to fill the seat vacated by the death of Democrat Walter Capps were PAC, not issue-advocacy, ads and as such were subject to public disclosure. However, some have argued that this campaign portends a future in which the ads of competing groups will so dominate a campaign that the voices and agendas of the candidates will be drowned out. I would argue that it is plausible to suppose that that was what happened in at least ten Congressional races in 1996.

The American Federation of Labor and Congress of Industrial Organizations (AFL-CIO) is a labor organization consisting of 78 unions with 13.1 million members. In 1996, the AFL-CIO spent $25 million to air broadcast ads primarily in forty-four Congressional districts. In at least fourteen of those districts, an analysis of the station logs in the districts reveals that the AFL-CIO outspent one of the congressional contenders. In ten of the fourteen, the AFL-CIO outspent both congressional candidates combined. The AFL-CIO is just one of the issue advocacy groups airing material in these districts. Where the Democrats in these districts focused ads on the same topics as the AFL-CIO (i.e., against corporate tax breaks, for pension protection, support of public education, the minimum wage, and Medicare), the issue advocacy drowned out the voice of the Republicans and any independents in the race. Where the Democrats focused on other issues, the AFL-CIO's message drowned out both.

If a plausible case can be made that issue advocacy is drowning out the voices of candidates, then the Supreme Court might reconsider its ruling in *Buckley*. There is precedent for restricting speech that drowns out competing voices. In *Kovacs v. Cooper*,[5] the Supreme Court held that a Trenton, NJ, ordinance forbidding "the use or operation on the public streets of a 'sound truck' or of any instrument which emits 'loud and raucous noises; and is attached to a vehicle on the public streets'" did not infringe on the right of free speech. In a concurring opinion, Mr. Justice Jackson wrote that "No violation of the Due Process Clause of the Fourteenth Amendment by reason of infringement of free speech arises unless such regulation or prohibition undertakes to censor the contents of the broadcasting. Freedom of speech for Kovacs does not, in my view, include freedom to use sound amplifiers to drown out the natural speech of others."

PROBLEMS CREATED BY THE RISE OF SOME
FORMS OF ISSUE ADVOCACY

THE RISE OF PSEUDONYMOUS AND UNACCOUNTABLE GROUPS

The legislative issue ads of 1993–4 and some of the candidate issue ads of 1996 carried forms of self-identification that concealed more than they revealed. Deliberation thrives both on full disclosure and on accurate information about the nature of the problem and the proposed solutions. Knowing who is bringing us the message is important in assessing its substance.

The enthymematic nature of communication means, as well, that audiences may draw inaccurate inferences about the source of a message from its content. Since Aristotle, Western theorists have known that the credibility of a message is determined in part by the credibility of the source, hence the concern in classical rhetorical theory with building what the ancients called the ethos of the speaker and what contemporary communication scholars call source credibility.

Persuasion theorists have found that messages attributed to a source with high ethos are generally more persuasive than those attributed to a source with low ethos (Anderson and Clevenger 1963). The finding is summarized by saying,

> We know an individual's acceptance of information and ideas is based in part on "who said it." This variable, the source's role in communication effectiveness, has been given many names: ethos, prestige, charisma, image, or, more frequently, source credibility. Whichever label is used, research consistently has indicated

that the more of "it" the communicator is perceived to have, the more likely the receiver is to accept the transmitted information. (Berlo et al. 1969)

The advertising groups whose identities were unclear in the health care reform debate included: Empower America, the Health Care Reform Project, Citizens for a Sound Economy, Alliance for Managed Competition, Families USA, and Christian Coalition. What, one might ask, distinguished the American Conference for Health Care Workers from America's Health Care Workers Coalition? Or the Campaign for Health Security from the Corporate Health Care Coalition? Who speaks through The Independent Institute or the National Center for Policy Analysis?

In the 1996 campaign the pseudonymous groups included: Citizens for Tax Reform, Child Protection Fund, Citizens for Reform, Citizens for the Republic Education Fund, Citizens for a Sound Economy, The Coalition, Coalition for Change, Coalition for our Children's Future, Arthur S. DeMoss Foundation, Human Rights Campaign, Tobacco Accountability Project, United Seniors Association, United States Catholic Coalition, and Women for Tax Reform. At worst, such labels trick citizens into misidentifying the source of the message; at best, these labels fail to tell the citizen whose self-interest is served by the message.

THE ABSENCE OF DISCLOSURE IN ISSUE ADVOCACY UNDERCUTS CITIZEN ASSESSMENT

Knowing who is paying for an ad helps viewers determine whether the sponsor is a credible source; part of what makes this possible is knowing the self-interest of the sponsor. Audiences take the possible self-interest or bias into account in evaluating messages. In one study, for example, the "vested interest" of an "expert mechanic whose hobby is the repair and modification of sports cars" was manipulated by describing him to some subjects as a friend of the seller of a car, to some as the friend of the buyer of a car, and to some as an independent person with no relation to buyer or seller. When the "expert" told subjects that the car was worth $500, those who saw him as a friend of the seller interpreted the message to mean that the car was worth $470; those told that he was a friend of the buyer put the value at $530; those who were told that he was independent thought the car was worth $500 (Berlo et al.

1969). In short, knowing who is speaking to us in any form of communication including mass media advertising is consequential to audiences.

Deliberation thrives on disclosure. Knowing who is bringing us the message is important in assessing its substance. If, for example, a Catholic viewer believes that the 1996 ad by The United States Catholic Coalition is actually sponsored by the Catholic Church rather than by a priest and his backers in Montana, that viewer will credit the ad with a level of credibility it would be denied if the viewer knew the actual funder behind the cassock. Disclosure requirements are now on the books in several states. And in one instance a panel of the Sixth Circuit Court of Appeals has upheld them on the grounds that the state's interest in revealing the source of campaign expenditures and the desirability of preventing perceived and actual corruption should prevail.[6]

While legislative issue advocacy backed by comparable funds on the opposing sides of the issue can raise the visibility of important issues and synthesize the positions of the advocates, legislative issue advocacy becomes worrisome when one side substantially outspends the other, a problem magnified when the claims in the issue ads are deceptive. Under that circumstance we should worry with the founders that people will be "misled by the artful misrepresentations of interested men" which may prompt the public to "call for measures which they themselves will afterwards be the most ready to lament and condemn" (*Federalist* 63).

Whether for good or ill, candidate issue advocacy can be used to set the agenda for a campaign and mobilize subgroups. But, when issue ads subvert spending limits and when supporters of one side substantially outspend the other on them, they too become problematic, problems compounded when an outside group drowns out the competing voices of the candidates or dramatically tilts the balance of messages in the closing days of a campaign. If as *Buckley* held, money equals speech, then perhaps our concern here should be that of Hamilton, who wrote in *Federalist* 57 that the electors of federal representatives should be "Not the rich, more than the poor."

NOTES

1. New York Times Co v. Sullivan, 376 U.S. 254, 275 n 15 (1964) quoting Elliot's Debates on the Federal Constitution (1876), 575.
2. 424 U.S. at 80.

3. 894 F. Supp. 946 [1995].
4. 491 US, 105 L Ed 2d 342, 109 S Ct. (1989).
5. 336 U.S. 77; 69 S. Ct. 448; 1949 U.S. LEXIS 3034; 93 L. Ed. 513.
6. Kentucky Right to Life Inc v. Terry. 108 F3d 637 (6th Cir.), cert. denied.

References

Abramson, Jill, and Leslie Wayne (1997). "Nonprofit Groups Were Quiet Partners to Both Parties in 1996." *New York Times*, October 24:A28.

Anderson, K., and T. Clevenger, Jr. (1963). "A Summary of Experimental Research in Ethos," *Speech Monographs*, 30:59–78.

APPC (1998). "Tax and Spend vs Little Kids: Advocacy and Accuracy in the Tobacco Settlement Ads of 1998." Annenberg Public Policy Center of the University of Pennsylvania, Aug. 6, 1998. Web site, *http://www.asc.upenn.edu*.

Berlo, David, James Lemert, and Robert Mertz (1969). "Dimensions for Evaluating the Acceptability of Message Sources," *Public Opinion Quarterly*, 33:563–576.

"Gales and Seaton's History of Debates in Congress." (1834). *Annals of Congress*.

Grice, Paul (1989). *Studies in the Way of Words*. Cambridge, MA: Harvard University Press.

Kelley, David (1988). *The Art of Reasoning*. New York: Norton.

Kurtz, Howard (1997). "Democrats Ask ABC to Release 1996 Dole Tape." *Washington Post*, October 23:A18.

Roberts, Gillian L., and Janet Beavin Bavelas (1996). "The Communicative Dictionary: A Collaborative Theory of Meaning." in John Stewart (Ed.), *Beyond the Symbol Model*. Albany, NY: State University of New York Press.

Roper Poll (1998). Poll conducted for NBC and the *Washington Post* for the Freedom Forum, January 8.

Van Eemeren, Frans H., and Rob Grootendorst (1992). *Argumentation, Communication, and Fallacies*. Hillsdale. NJ: Lawrence Erlbaum.

CHAPTER 16

Implications of Rival Visions of
Electoral Campaigns

C. Edwin Baker

Both our electoral process and our media coverage of elections are a disgrace. High-minded media critics call for more substance in campaign coverage – and then, given the symbiotic relation between campaigns and campaign coverage, campaigns too will have more substance. The media should fully report candidates' views on the issues, especially on issues that the public considers important. Arguably, media should place more emphasis on the areas of commonality between the candidates, and certainly spend less time and space on negative portrayals of political actors and on the "strategic frame," which serve largely to breed cynicism (Cappella and Jamieson 1997; Fallows 1996; Rosen 1996).

My reading of these media commentators suggests that their analyses usually reflect two background assumptions about politics: (1) campaigns for political office are the central embodiment of democratic politics, and (2) the proper aim of politics is a common or public good about which the public is or should become broadly united. Given these assumptions, the health of democracy can be measured largely by the substance and intelligence of campaign discourse and its media coverage. Cynicism, negativity, and even conflict are presumptively dysfunctional and are likely to lead to reduced citizen participation. From this picture, media commentators' various prescriptions follow.

If, however, the conception of politics embodied in these two assumptions were rejected, prescriptions would need revision; current critiques of media performance might need refocusing. Given my quarrels with these assumptions, this chapter offers two media-related theses.

In addition to discussions at the Annenberg conferences, on an earlier draft, I have benefitted from comments of Robert M. Entman, B. J. Bullert, Carlin Meyer, and Michael Madow.

342

First, despite the desirability and some possibility of improved campaign coverage, the actual and *appropriate* nature of elections places real limits on change in coverage. Second, the focus on these proposed changes runs a real risk of diverting attention or energy from a more pressing democratic need for structural changes in the media. In the alternative vision of politics that I offer, the press ought to play a supportive role in electoral horse races while also, over time, serving the needs of the broader polity that extend way beyond elections. These contributions depend as much on changes in the structure of the media industry as on improved journalism, possibly inspired by scholarly critiques and proposals but often undermined by market pressures.

The vision of the role of elections in a democracy affects evaluations of acceptable legal regulation as well as of desirable media practices. In a major 1976 decision, the Supreme Court held that legal limits on campaign expenditures violate the First Amendment guarantee of freedom of speech (*Buckley v. Valeo* 1976). In a recent discussion, I agreed that the Court is quite persuasive if its implicit conception of political campaigns is accepted (Baker 1998a). I argued, however, that the Court's conception is inconsistent with the implicit vision of elections in the Court's numerous other First Amendment decisions and, more importantly, is normatively unpersuasive. Therefore, *Buckley* should be abandoned. I will restate this argument about *Buckley* in the first section.

In the second section, I suggest that media critics, often without much reflection, have adopted a conception of political campaigns much like the objectionable conception implicit in *Buckley*. This observation leads to speculations about how the alternative vision of elections could affect critiques of and prescriptions for press performance.

TWO VIEWS OF ELECTORAL CAMPAIGNS AND THEIR IMPLICATIONS FOR THE REGULATION OF CAMPAIGN SPEECH

Consider two visions of electoral campaigns. First, the dominant concept implicit in popular culture, among defenders of *Buckley* and among many media reformers, views electoral campaigns as the heart of democratic politics, the primary locus for popular formulation and expression of public opinion. The democratic participatory ideal rightly requires that the "public" express itself and be involved. People's meaningful political input, if any, occurs in the campaign and the voting that follows. Although some people engage in some politically oriented activity and discussion at other times, the campaign season invigorates these activities, extends public discussion to the public as a whole, and makes its political activity legally consequential. The campaign calls a busy public to order; during this period (if ever), citizens deliberate about public issues and then choose their leaders. For their deliberation and choice, the mass media should provide the public with information and with discussion of those issues that are or that the public believes are important – and should identify candidates' positions on these issues. (Some commentators also want campaign discourse to help the public find "common ground" and recognize the "public interest" – although this ambition seems somewhat surprising for an electoral system structured to reject the views of nearly half the voting public on the only matter formally decided, that is, who is to hold office.)

An alternative conceptualization also sees elections and electoral campaigns playing an absolutely vital democratic role but one that is much more precise and institutionally limited. This second view conceives of "politics" as discussion of issues, formulation of alternatives, and advocacy of and conflict over values and choices that a person wants reflected in both collective practices and state policy. This politics, however, is not the special province of elections. It occurs continuously within society's unregulated public spheres and, arguably, within the more private realms of life. In contrast, elections have a narrower function, a more formal role. Elections pick particular job holders. Campaigns are essentially part of the job application process where the candidates appeal to the organization's hiring committee – the electorate.

Possibly democracy's most crucial institutional design problem is to systematically connect government "will formation" – i.e., state policy and law, which typically reflect decisions of office holders – to meaningful popular participation that creates "public opinions." Democratic politics is mostly and most importantly the *discursive activity* of creating (formulating, discussing, advocating, and amplifying) these sometimes competing public opinions even if politics also includes more *instrumental activities* directed at getting opinion embodied in law and policy. Thus, this vision distinguishes democratic opinion formation from will formation and treats politics fundamentally as the formation of public opinion and secondarily as connecting that opinion to will formation. Politics in the sense of opinion formation occurs in broad public spheres where the only compulsion, the dominant aim of the actors, is to arrive at the best view. In contrast, the crucial but limited democratic function of elections is to serve as one structural filter that fairly and properly helps public opinion to influence governmental will formation (Habermas 1996).

Even for the portion of politics directed at connecting democratic opinion to democratic will, elections are only one of several institutional foci. Legislative lobbying, legislative committee hearings, agency hearings, rule making, and similar activities at the state and local level allow for popular input. Among these institutionalized connectors, often elections must dilute the focus on substantive issues, partly because they are also crucially concerned with evaluating candidates' personal competence, in its various contested meanings, and partly because of the overwhelming pressures for participation to be strategically focused. Nevertheless, this dilution is less troublesome and broader realms of opinion formation are comparatively more important precisely because, as experience constantly teaches, elected office holders are very susceptible to influence by various manifestations of public opinion.

This second conception of elections assumes that politics takes place primarily in the unregulated public spheres of civil society rather than in elections themselves. The primary mission of elections, with a foot in both civil society and the state, is to advance the proper functioning of the democratic state – that is, to make it more democratically responsive. Like legislative bodies, judicial proceedings, and legislative and agency hearings, elections are instrumentally designed institutions. In order to further effective and proper performance of its particular tasks, each institution creates, structures, and limits specific opportunities for expression. In regard to the regulation of speech opportunities, these institutionally created structures differ from the "wild," "anarchic" practices of the "more or less spontaneously" developed pluralistic public sphere (Habermas 1996, p. 307), in which the broader processes of public opinion formation – of politics – regularly occur.

Because the first vision roughly equates politics and elections, it must view any government action aimed at limiting or regulating campaign speech as seriously problematic. The Court is right that "in a free society . . . it is . . . the people – individually as citizens . . . and collectively as associations and political committees – who must retain control over the quantity and range of debate on public issues. . . ." (*Buckley v. Valeo* 1976, p. 57). If political campaigns are the heart of politics and the central forum for debate, the Court was right to add "and candidates" among those whose hands must control the extent of the debate and to add "in a political campaign" after "public issues" to identify the place of this debate. Restrictions on political discussion and advocacy ignore Justice Louis Brandeis's warning that "the greatest menace to freedom is an inert people." (*Whitney v. California*, p. 375, Brandeis concurring). Given this first view of elections, the Court properly held that all limitations on campaign-oriented expenditures violate the First Amendment.[1]

If, however, the second view of the relation between elections and politics is more empirically and normatively persuasive, then popular "control over the quantity and range of debate on public issues" (Buckley v. Valeo 1976, p. 57) lies in active citizens' capacity to participate (at least, to the extent their varying material and personal resources make possible) in the broader, largely unregulated public spheres. Of course, people do not have direct control over the quantity and range of speech within the various institutionalized realms of government, the places where democratic opinion is transformed into democratic will. These institutions of government, including agency hearings, legislative proceedings, and the courts, have many features in common: Each is a legally created framework, each relies heavily on speech in its processes, and certain speech within each has official legal force – that is, using John Austin's terms, in each, certain speech constitutes "speech acts" (Austin 1962). Most relevantly here, each of these institutions regulates speech. As specific functions of these institutions vary, the permissible regulations also vary. A regulation is widely accepted as proper if it aids the particular institution properly to perform its democratic and governing function.

Elections and electorally oriented speech fit this model. Elections are legally created frameworks, rely heavily on speech, and conclude with expression that has legal force, namely, votes that place one candidate and not another in office. Other speech within a campaign occurs not merely because of a general public interest in an issue. Instead, electorally oriented speech occurs because the legal order first created the election process. Electoral speech instrumentally aims at affecting the binding outcome of this formal process.

In this institutional perspective, the democratic function of elections is to be a fair and open, popularly inclusive process of picking office holders (or deciding ballot questions). Regulations that further these qualities should be permitted, while those that undermine elections' fairness or openness should be struck down. Such a standard permits constitutional objection to particular regulations of campaign speech – but is a far cry from the command announced in *Buckley* that the government keep its hands off.

The most contestable issue within the second view concerns the boundaries of the electoral process. Where is the line between the institutionalized electoral process and the broader public sphere of civil society, how is the line's placement justified, and who draws it? Legal rules determine whether a ballot lists a candidate's name or ballot measure and how or whether to count votes – for example, whether to count write-in votes. The ballot itself and the expressive marks people make on it could be treated as the only legally institutionalized, and hence only regulatable, part of the electoral process. At the opposite extreme, the media's reporting of and commentary about the election might be considered a formal part of the electoral process. Courts in this country once claimed authority to use their contempt power to limit newspapers' commentary about ongoing judicial proceedings. After an initial misstep authored by Oliver Wendell Holmes (*Patterson v. Colorado* 1907), the Supreme Court rejected this claim. The Court now sees newspaper commentary on judicial proceedings as part of the broader public realm and not subject to regulation (*Bridges v. California* 1941). The same should be true of newspaper reporting and commentary in the election context (*Mills v. Alabama* 1966) or, alternatively, the conclusion could be that the regulation here must only meet the standard of not restricting the independent political expression of the press (*Arkansas Ed. Television Comm. v Forbes* 1998; Cook 1998).

The crucial question here is whether electorally oriented campaign speech is an institutionally bound part of the election or, instead, part of a broader, unregulated public sphere. Obviously, the answer is an interpretive and normative, not merely an empirical, matter. At least three criteria are as relevant to the answer: whether treating electorally oriented campaign speech as an institutionally bound part of the election (i) better explains salient features of the electoral campaign, (ii) better supports normatively desirable practices, or (iii) is authoritatively accepted. Without being comprehensive, I offer a few observations.

First, viewing electorally oriented speech as part of the institutionalized realm of elections helps explain fundamental differences between electorally oriented speech and much other political discourse. Most political discourse aims at inquiry, view expression, or value-oriented persuasion. In contrast, electorally oriented speech is overwhelmingly strategic. Its goal is to motivate a particular short-term act, a favorable vote. The first job of any politician, it is often said, is to get elected. Political speech becomes strategic precisely when it becomes oriented toward obtaining an institutionally effective result.

Second, this categorization allows regulation of electorally oriented speech that can significantly improve the democratic quality of elections. It permits structuring the electoral process to promote its fairness and openness. To the extent legal rules limit the devotion of resources to the campaign, this categorization may produce an additional benefit. Predictably, money of those with committed political views will not simply disappear from the public stage. Rather, some money squeezed out of electoral campaigns will migrate to the broader political sphere where the dominant concern can only be the persuasiveness or appeal of views about substantive issues, not the personal qualities of individual candidates or the need to induce a short-term act, a favorable vote. Participatory democratic theory should count such an invigoration of nonelectorally oriented politics as a major plus. Moreover, recognition that elections are only one part – and, as far as substantive value discourse is concerned, not the central part – of politics could encourage those hoping to revive political life not to place all their chips in a single weak basket. Efforts to involve those who realistically or cynically do not and will not value electoral opportunities to choose between centrist candidates could then be placed higher on the civic agenda. This second view of elections emphasizes that citizens' political involvement occurs in many realms of the public sphere, not just during elections. For these reasons, seeing electorally oriented speech as like speech in a legislative committee hearing in that both are part of an institutional realm designed for specific democratic purposes permits real improvements in the quality and vibrancy of democratic politics.

Third, putting aside *Buckley v. Valeo* and its direct progeny, which are the decisions being evaluated here and which I am arguing were wrongly decided, the Supreme Court's electoral-speech decisions are best understood as (unconsciously) adopting this second view – namely, that electoral speech should not simply be equated with political speech. For example, despite the claim that *political* speech receives the highest degree of First Amendment protection and the principle that *content discrimination* (i.e., regulation of speech based on its content) is presumptively impermissible,[2] the Court has upheld extensive regulation of *electoral* speech (Baker 1998a: pp. 4–9). Laws limit the electorally oriented speech of corporations, unions, charitable associations, government employees (think of Hatch Act limits on civil service employees or the prohibition on using the congressional franking privilege for electoral purposes), public broadcasters (cannot endorse candidates), and commercial broadcasters (must make time available at lowest rates and must provide all candidates equal time on equal terms for "uses"). Electorally oriented speech is restricted close to polling places or on military bases. Of course, some regulations of electorally oriented speech have been struck down, but usually only when they ought to be according to the principle that laws restricting the openness (or fairness) of elections are impermissible. The extensiveness of regulation and the Court's general willingness to uphold it suggest that the Court implicitly sees electoral speech not as part of the anarchical, unregulated discourse about public issues but rather as part of a structured institutionalized realm designed for specific democratic purposes. The principle of *Buckley* would be right in the first context but simply does not apply in the second. *Buckley* should be rejected because the second provides the better description of the actual context.

IMPLICATIONS FOR EVALUATING MEDIA PERFORMANCE

Even if the choice between the first and second vision of electoral campaigns determines the permissibility of legal regulation of electoral speech, it may have no bearing on how to evaluate media performance. Nevertheless, here I explore the possibility that it provides some explanatory or evaluative insight into the media's electoral and political roles.

If elections and electoral campaigns are the major embodiment of popular democratic discourse, campaigns and the press both bear huge democratic responsibilities. Any civically virtuous citizen should pay close attention. The press plays the crucial mediating role. These responsibilities are less and different within the second conception, which treats elections as an instrument to choose office holders and as one sluice through which public opinion connects to governmental will formation. However, given either conception of elections, a commentator's specific vision of proper media performance during the campaign season will be partially determined by her theory of democracy (Baker 1998b). One valence on which theories of democracy differ usefully illustrates the point. Some democratic theories emphasize finding or reaching consensus or common ground; the major additional aspect of politics is problem solving on the foundation of that common ground. A second set of democratic theories see politics as much more

Democratic Theory View of elections	Republican (consensus; common ground)	Liberal Pluralist (conflict; competing goods)
Center of politics	Type 1 democracy (D1)	
Limited tasks: choosing office holder; sluice for public opinion		Type 2 democracy (D2)

Figure 16.1. Models of democracy and elections.

a matter of struggle among conflicting or at least competing interests or, sometimes, competing conceptions of the common good. This quick description of what recent scholarship describes as "republican" or "liberal pluralist" conceptions of democracy washes out many subtleties and additional ways in which democratic theories vary.[3] Still, this division among democratic theories can be combined with the two visions of elections to create a 2 × 2 matrix.

All four squares could be discussed. Still, there may be an affinity toward combinations identified as D1 and D2. Given the tendency of winner-take-all elections to push candidates and, even more so, campaigns toward the center, elections may seem more suitable as the primary democratic institution for those who believe in common ground. In contrast, those who view politics as embodying struggles around competing pluralist conceptions of the good are likely to find the electoral focus inadequate and a broader conception of politics essential. In any event, for illustrative purposes, I discuss the media's role from the perspective of these two models.

A democratic commitment requires that the key activities of democratic politics, whatever they are, be inclusive – but that conclusion only begins the inquiry. D1 treats the electoral process as the central participatory democratic institution. The majority vote hopefully finds and embodies in legally effective results the community's best sense of its common good. Conflict and negativity are largely dysfunctional except that people's real differences on issues must be adequately explored so that a community can reach informed decisions. Although individually informed participation is civically valued, partisan mobilization has little affirmative significance and risks unnecessary conflict. Meaningful participation requires knowledge and substantive discourse. If substantive, issue-oriented discourse is to occur, it will occur during elections and the media should take the lead in providing this discourse. Consensus as well as rational problem solving require objective, impartial information; both processes should be open to all constructive suggestions. These informational needs are roughly the same for all people. A media critic can usefully ask whether the media effectively communicates the needed information and whether it avoids frames that generate cynicism, which in turn dampen electoral participation. For example, emphasis on a strategic or horse-race frame does not aid and may discourage participation (Cappella and Jamieson 1997). If elections are the heart of politics and if democratic politics is centered on a common good, then these are the qualities needed in media performance.

In contrast, D2 treats elections as a vitally important, but limited, institutional and instrumental corner of participatory politics. Electoral campaigns' instrumental goal is to win the election. This instrumental goal makes campaigns unlikely loci of serious politics, at least if "serious" means passionate challenges to accepted conventions and thoughtful attempts to explore, defend, promote, and choose state, civic, and personal practices and conceptions of the good. Electoral strategies adopted to put together a winning majority often disfavor mobilization around controversial issues. The need to win often creates an incentive to downplay divisive agendas, appeal to broadly popular themes, or focus on personal leadership qualities – and identify the opposing candidate with the opposite. For issue partisans, this situation would be disillusioning unless they understand elections as only one small part of politics. Many issue partisans who support a particular candidate have a potentially realistic belief that the candidate will favor their controversial goals when in office. These supporters, therefore, may temporarily avoid issue mobilization out of fears of backlash that could undermine electoral success – even though they would never put issue mobilization aside within the broader public sphere of politics.

Given the second vision of elections, the media critic should place still serious but less grandiose demands on the media's electoral coverage. This coverage need not bear the weight of being the center of a democratic discourse; rather it only needs to serve fairly the various actual and potential participants in the electoral process. The often unnoted point is that different members of a politically attuned public will naturally and often appropriately relate very differently to an election's limited and instrumental role. This insight could be difficult for a commentator who sees elections as the heart of politics and politics as about the collective's common concerns. Then everyone's need would seem the same – to have information and discussion aimed at consensus or, at least, aimed at the necessary choices concerning the good. The insight should not be surprising, however, given the conflict frame of politics. It is especially not surprising once the commentator recognizes the limited and more instrumental task assigned to elections. Given people's different relations to elections implicit in D2, media commentators cannot offer critiques based on a single conception of the public's needs for media content. Instead, they must either argue that a particular group's needs should take precedence or recognize that different frames or different types of coverage would serve and be desired by different portions of the public. I will provisionally take the second route.

Here I put aside people whose disinterest in both elections and politics reflects an atomistic concern for solely private interests. Different categories of politically concerned citizens sensibly relate very differently to electoral campaigns. These different groups provide different lenses, none of which has obvious priority, through which to evaluate media performance. First, especially in general elections (maybe less so in primaries), many, possibly most, people who are strongly interested in politics know which candidate they will support before media coverage of the campaign begins. Many "loyalists" hardly consider voting for the "other" party. These loyalists can be intensely interested in substantive, issue-oriented politics; they may even be open to information and discussion that would change their mind on various matters. Still, their discursive and often their substantive political interests are likely best served by politics that occurs independently of and usually at a different time than electoral campaigns. Candidates often strategically avoid the substantive discourse that could truly change people's opinions about issues. Instead, they at best try to capitalize on prior opinion. Therefore, for these loyalists, issue coverage of the campaign often has little personal relevance. In contrast, reporting on the horse-race and (maybe) strategic aspects is not only interesting but also most relevant for their behavior, increasing or decreasing the likelihood of their making either monetary or participatory contributions. Even though these loyalists might piously voice criticism of the media's "over-emphasis" on strategy and horse-race coverage, their criticism probably reflects less their own reading or viewing interests than their desire that the media properly inform and motivate crucial swing voters.[4]

Second are people who do not lack civic virtue, that is, an interest in the public good, but do lack interest in the typical electoral contest between Republican and Democratic candidates. Many "radicals," who are often among society's most politically active, concerned, and informed citizens, find only marginal differences between most mainstream candidates. They wish for more dramatic alternatives. "Activists" constitute the third group. Many activists who are passionately concerned with one or a few specific issues consider organization, discussion, and politics around those issues as central. These activists may believe that more important than the identity of particular office holders is the public view on these issues. They rightly expect that office holders, of whichever party, usefully respond to a strongly developed public opinion but, without this public opinion, will sell out to monied interests. They doubt that the campaign season is conducive to the serious politics they seek. They are especially doubtful that the campaign will include dialogue that could change, modify, or deepen their own views. Many of these radicals and activists regularly vote. If they do, their behavior probably resembles that of the "loyalists" just described, essentially having ruled out one of the dominant parties. When uncertain about their choice, their vacillation is often about whether to vote for a third-party candidate, believing that to do so is more expressive but in another sense wastes their vote. For these skeptical but active citizens, horse-race coverage can be rationally relevant. It can influence their choice between a major-party candidate and a third-party one. However, substantive coverage of the two major candidates will usually be of little consequence. (This is a slight overstatement; coverage could highlight the extent of differences between major candidates, which could also affect their decision whether to vote for a third party.) These radicals' and activists' most common critique of existing campaign coverage is its comparative disregard of the substantive views of third-party challengers. Their real wish, however, is for more and better critical and substantive issue coverage and mobilizing content independent of and between campaigns.

At least three other categories of citizens should be mentioned – the "undecided," the "uninterested," and the "disaffected." Thus, a fourth group is the many, politically crucial, swing voters who initially are undecided because the candidate of either dominant party might best represent their middle-of-the-road views, or their substantive views are too undefined, or their primary concern is with the basically moderate candidates' personal leadership – or some combination of these three factors. Fifth, the "uninterested" includes many people who vote on occasion, usually in particularly "important" elections, but who lack any strong political interest. Sixth are the "disaffected" – those who have potential civic interests and would be interested if only the options (real or perceived) were different. This disaffection is understandable. Our winner-take-all electoral system strongly favors centrist candidates. Walter Burnham observed the demographic characteristics of the voters who in Europe support social democratic or other leftist parties are the same as those who are least likely to vote in the United States – making them the "party of nonvoters" (Burnham 1982, p. 188). Many people find electoral politics to be largely irrelevant for the political issues in which they would be keenly interested.

For the press to serve the democratic needs of these last three groups is complicated. Some "undecided" need more detail about candidates' positions; others need information, including the type given in "negative" ads, about the candidates' personal qualities. As for the "uninterested," mobilization and a stress on an election's importance may increase their participation. They (and some of the undecided) may also need, even though they may be relatively indifferent to, information, discussion, and debate about issues themselves rather than information about the candidate's position. It is curious, however, to argue that media practice should be molded to the needs of this group. Should the media "reward" those who largely lack political interest by emphasizing coverage that serves their weak political interests or mobilizes their participation? Putting aside the "should" question, it is doubtful that a profit-motivated media would do so. In response to those who are uninterested (as well as to the many of those who already know how they will vote), a profit-oriented media might largely ignore the campaign, leaving coverage, as in a recent California gubernatorial primary, to those most intensively interested in mobilizing the uninterested, namely, the candidates, who supply and pay for coverage in the form of advertising (Purdum 1998).

Similarly, it is not clear what mainstream media can honestly and appropriately do to encourage involvement by the (rationally) "disaffected." Many of the disaffected are merely a depoliticized version of the radicals and activists already discussed. These groups have real political needs – but the needs are less for better media electoral coverage than for a different electoral system, such as a system of proportional representation or for more politics outside elections. Of course, the existing electoral system does not exclude them from meaningful political participation, only from particularly meaningful electoral participation. Arguably, the media could best serve their political interests and needs less by engaging in substantive campaign coverage and attempting to find common ground than by reporting that justifies their cynicism about the existing mainstream electoral alternatives. Or the media could serve their interests by stimulating a more vibrant and inclusive political order beyond the electoral sphere. This alternative should include partisan discussions that mobilize around issues in ways that generate response from those in office or that develop sufficient popular support that at least one major political party adopts positions to attract their support. Thus, their media interests may be best served by society devoting greater resources to nonmainstream partisan media and by mainstream media devoting more attention to dissidents and to dissident concerns. In contrast, merely more substantive but less negative coverage of major party candidates is unlikely either to interest or to serve the interests of this large category of citizens.

These six categories are not comprehensive. They overlap and have no sharp boundaries. The categorization has no objective priority over other possible categorizations. Still, it is worth considering what follows for the media from the view that elections are only one institutionalized, strategically oriented corner of participatory politics, that politics involves real conflicts and not just finding common ground, and from the related observation that people are very differentially situated in relation to elections.

THE MORALS OF THE STORY

First, possibly the most important observation is that, given the expanded notion of participatory politics, any critique of the media's role in enhancing democratic politics should not overly focus on its performance in the electoral process. An electoral focus ignores important realms of actual and potential political participation. More importantly, it takes sides in favor of those people adequately served by our centrist, winner-take-all elections. Such a focus is inherently exclusionary, not inclusive. It ignores people whose political needs and interests do not focus on elections, especially not on assessing the views of the two leading parties' candidates.

Second, turning more specifically to elections, the varying relations people have to elections means that different civically oriented people have different needs or interests in respect to electoral coverage differ. These people include those who (1) have virtually no real, personal need for coverage (e.g., for the loyalist, voting is routine), (2) enjoy strategic information and need horse-race information, (3) need information about the candidates' personal qualities because they reasonably consider these qualities substantively most important, (4) need information about the candidates' issue commitments in order to match them with their own commitments, (5) need information or discussion about the issues, or (6) need convincing that favoring one side or the other matters – i.e., need political motivation.

Third, many critiques identify media horse-race or strategic framing of elections as a central problem and try to explain its prevalence. Sometimes, they conclude that it grows out of misdirected journalistic norms – for example, perverse conceptions of professionalism, attempts to maintain objectivity and avoid manipulation by candidates, or the professional unavailability of obvious alternatives such as partisan framing. Sometimes, the explanation connects the problem to the media's commercialism and profit orientation. In contrast, the above observations about different groups' different interests or needs for electoral coverage suggest strategic and horse-race frames may be responsive to real informational needs and interests of a substantial portion of the audience, especially of the more civically responsible members of the electorate who realistically do not expect to find real issues developed in campaigns and who generally know for which of the two main candidates, if either, they will vote. At least in this respect, assuming that fulfilling audience needs is its proper role, the media may not be as bad as sometimes suggested.

Fourth is a point not yet discussed, and that I will mention only briefly here. If elections are the center of public participatory involvement in formulating and furthering notions of the public good – and even more so if public good means "common" ground – anything that turned people away from the electoral process would be presumptively objectionable. Cynicism about candidates and public officials, which particular frames of media coverage may stimulate, probably fits this category. There remains, however, a nagging suspicion that the objection to cynicism should depend on whether the cynicism is justified. Given a perspective that sees politics as more about conflict and sees people factually and appropriately (given their own values) having different orientations toward elections, whether cynicism about and disengagement from the existing electoral process is normatively rational is not a question about which the answer can be presupposed nor one about which different groups can be expected to agree.

For some social scientists, this creates a difficultly. Although any definition of cynicism will be value loaded, an investigator can stipulate a definition and give reasons for that stipulation. To investigate whether the cynicism is justified, however, seems to force the investigation out of the realm of social science and into the realm of politics or ethical theory. But this question of justification may be crucial for evaluating media performance. It would hardly seem appropriate to criticize the press for stimulating justified cynicism. Failure to stimulate cynicism about electoral politics might amount to being a partisan apologist for an indefensible order.

Fifth, even people who share normatively freighted objections to media practices that create potential cynicism and especially to media practices that have politically (or electorally) quietistic results may disagree about the appropriate directions of change. More specifically, although different conclusions could reflect different factual hypotheses or even merely different partisan interests, they could also reflect differing conceptions of democracy. In line with the republican, election-centered conception (D1), the need might be for the media to draw people's attention to their common problems and help them find common ground and common solutions. Media coverage should be substantive and avoid the strategic and horse-race frames that stimulate cynicism. A different conception (D2) recognizes both the conflictual nature of politics and the different relation people have toward the electoral process. It might more broadly respond to cynicism and the problem of disengagement with the claim that the media should help people pursue their vision of more just results, recognizing that people disagree about what this means. Given these disagreements, and because people must find involvement in these pursuits meaningful, this response to the problem of cynicism and disengagement is likely to require competing, partisan media.

Differences between the two responses can be explored in terms of their relevance to different portions of the potential electorate. For "loyalists," neither alternative makes much personal difference – even existing horse-race coverage creates little personal conflict although the loyalist may criticize its presumed (and possibly actual) effect on others. For radicals or activists, existing horse-race and strategic coverage may be more personally helpful than the first alternative, that is, "objective" substantive coverage of candidates' positions on issues. However, partisan media (of their stripe) may better combine serving their informational needs with maintenance of their motivation. A partisan framework that does not normally presuppose answers but that does involve a shared framework concerning what matters may best further their own self-reflective development and their exploration and debate of issues. A well-designed partisan media directly responds to the need of the uninterested and disaffected for motivation. In contrast, the greyness of "objective" journalism may further reduce the accessibility of the issues involved in electoral politics and make differences between candidates seem less meaningful, thereby exacerbating their disaffection. Substantive objective coverage's motivational deficit offers an explanation for the temporal correlation of the decline of electoral participation and the decline of the partisan press (McGerr 1986, pp. 116–122, 135; Baker 1994, pp. 41–43).

Thus, either for energizing broad political involvement or for the narrower goal of promoting better electoral participation, the greatest need may be the need for a strong partisan media. Of course, the United States is media rich, and partisan media certainly exist. Media critics, however, never fall quiet because media entities that fulfill their prescriptions, whether of substance, depth, balance, or whatever, exist somewhere in the country. When the most relied-upon daily (or weekly) media fail, according to their prescriptions, they have a complaint. Although further analysis is needed to support this conclusion, my claim is that partisan media are comparatively underdeveloped and, under current conditions, the market will not support them adequately. If I am right, the changes in the media that could make the biggest democratic contribution require government interventions that would encourage or support more partisan media (Entman 1989, pp. 136–39).

Finally, I remain pollyannish. I accept that many reform proposals directed at how existing media treat the electoral process are valuable. Even if elections are not the center of democratic politics, they are vital as one of the democratic mechanisms for translating politically developed public opinion into legally effective will. In fact, precisely the limited, institutional role of elections suggests that it may be appropriate for the media to treat them differently than other aspects of public life. Maybe fairness in the design of electoral debates, for example, could be demanded even if media generally are free to be partisan (*Arkansas Educational Television Comm. v. Forbes* 1998) To the extent that, for many people, elections are a call to act civically, elections create an opportunity for public involvement that society should not squander. Even if the dominant orientation for major party candidates and their campaigns, which are directed at winning, is strategic, that does not imply that other elements of society should not take the election period as an opportunity for more substantive political discourse. Evidence of this conclusion can be seen in third parties' attempts to raise their own issues. The media, too, whether newly invigorated partisan enterprises or the current dominant firms, could treat election time as an opportunity and accept responsibility not just for reporting on candidates but for introducing substantive political discourse. Most recent reform proposals, ranging from those requiring government action to those proposing voluntary undertakings by existing media, reflect this sense of opportunity. For example, to the extent that most candidates' broadcast ads operate as a diversion from any useful public opinion formation, maybe the United States should follow other democratic countries in barring candidate advertising from the air waves or restricting their permissible formats. To the extent electoral debates add to public understanding, maybe broadcasters should be required to make free time available for candidates willing to debate. To the extent that a major value of elections, in addition to choosing office holders, is to raise public awareness of and interest in issues, maybe opportunity to participate in debates should be extended to any legally qualified candidate who raises issues that resonate with any substantial portion of the public. Such suggestions follow if elections provide a central institutionalized forum for people to be exposed to people and civic views different from themselves and their own.

In combination, the morals of the story call for a pluralism of responses to a democratic distemper and for a pluralism of media. James Curran suggests that the media should be conceptualized as having different sectors that serve different functions (Curran 1996). My claim has been that some democratic perspectives (e.g., D1) fail to recognize adequately the democratic contribution of partisan media, which Curran describes as part of the "civic media sector"; the claim has been that this sector or these partisan media are of vital importance but presently underdeveloped and, therefore, that they need greater structural or economic support. My observations, however, are also consistent with seeing an important role for what Curran calls the "core sector," and that here too reform is needed if this sector is to adequately perform its democratic role.

Notes

1. The conclusion described in this paragraph is the standard civil libertarian view, to which I largely subscribe except for its view of elections. Although inconsistent with the case law and subject to other objections (Baker 1989, pp. 37–46), a popular reformist argument emphasizes that democracy's fundamental egalitarian basis justifies campaign finance regulation either because it overrides the commitment to free speech as a bar on government regulation or because it leads to an emphasis on interpreting free speech in practice, including the distribution of speech opportunities (Wright 1976; Wright 1982; Dworkin 1996).

2. Note that these two common doctrinal principles, although they both provide grounds to object to regulation of political speech, are themselves in tension – that is, giving greater protection to political speech would seem to violate the principle that content discrimination is impermissible. Possibly the two are best combined to say that although regulatory distinctions between content are presumptively bad, content regulations that restrict *political* speech are constitutionally the most unacceptable. However, the reality described in the text is that the content category "electoral speech" is regulated to an extraordinary extent.

3. Elsewhere, I argue that a third approach, which I label "complex democracy" and which takes from both republican and liberal pluralist theories, is both normatively and descriptively superior to them (Baker 1998b; Habermas 1998). For purposes of this chapter, however, the recommendations of complex democracy largely correspond to liberal pluralist or Type 2 democracy.

4. To say that this desire is piously voiced does not mean it is not real, only that it concerns preferences for what others should receive – like a belief that others should watch less violent films and TV programming. Markets are unlikely to respond to these preferences (for what others receive) since the person with the preference is not the person making a purchase. To the extent that the market fails to take into account the preference, the media fails to provide people with "what they want" in any economically meaningful sense of the words. In economic terms, externalities cause the market to be "inefficient" (Baker 1997).

References

Austin, J. L. (1962). *How to Do Things with Words*. New York: Oxford University Press.

Baker, C. Edwin (1989). *Human Liberty and Freedom of Speech*. New York: Oxford University Press.

(1994). *Advertising and a Democratic Press*. Princeton: Princeton University Press.

(1997). "Giving the Audience What It Wants." *Ohio State Law Journal*, 58:311–417.

(1998a). "Campaign Expenditures and Free Speech." *Harvard Civil Rights Civil Liberties Law Review*, 33:1–55.

(1998b). "The Media that Citizens Need." *University of Pennsylvania Law Review*, 147:317–408.

Burnham, Walter Dean (1982). *The Current Crisis in American Politics*. New York: Oxford University Press.

Cappella, Joseph N., and Kathleen Hall Jamieson (1997). *Spiral of Cynicism*. New York: Oxford University Press.

Cook, Timothy E. (1998). *Governing with the News*. Chicago: University of Chicago Press.

Curran, James (1996). "Mass Media and Democracy Revisited." In James Curran and Michael Gurevitch (Ed.), *Mass Media and Society, 2nd ed.* New York: Arnold, pp. 81–119.

Dworkin, Ronald (1996). "The Curse of American Politics." *New York Review of Books,* October 17:19.

Entman, Robert M. (1989). *Democracy Without Citizens*. New York: Oxford University Press.

Fallows, James (1996). *Breaking the News*. New York: Pantheon Books.

Habermas, Jürgen (1996). *Between Facts and Norms*. Cambridge, MA: MIT Press.

(1998). "Three Normative Models of Democracy." In *The Inclusion of the Other*. Cambridge, MA: MIT Press.

McGerr, Michael E. (1986). *The Decline of Popular Politics*. New York: Oxford University Press.

Purdum, Todd S. (1998). "Race for California Governor Is Not Necessarily the News." *New York Times,* May 6:A1.

Rosen, Jay (1996). *Getting the Connections Right*. New York: Twentieth Century Fund.

Wright, J. Skelly (1976). "Politics and the Constitution: Is Money Speech?" *Yale Law Journal,* 85:1001.

(1982). "Money and the Pollution of Politics: Is the First Amendment an Obstacle to Political Equality?" *Columbia Law Review,* 82:609.

CASES

Bridges v. California. 1941. 314 U.S. 252.

Buckley v. Valeo. 1976. 424 U.S. 1.

Arkansas Educational Television Comm. v. Forbes. 1998. 523 U.S. 666.

Mills v. Alabama. 1966. 384 U.S. 214.

Patterson v. Colorado. 1977. 205 U.S. 454.

Whitney v. California. 1927. 274 U.S. 357.

CHAPTER 17

Mediated Electoral Democracy: Campaigns, Incentives, and Reform

Bruce I. Buchanan

INTRODUCTION

The quality of democracy is decisively influenced by the performance of the actors engaged in the process that most centrally defines a political system as democratic: campaigns and elections. To capture the essential dynamic of this core democratic political process, it is necessary to model the communications among candidates, media, and voters, with other players (e.g., parties, interest groups) relegated to lesser roles.

Electoral Triangle Model

The "electoral triangle" depicted in Figure 17.1 is such a model. The practices spawned by these interactions in an American presidential election, for example, represent the most important evidence of the normative adequacy of American representative democracy. Such practices also determine whether the process fosters community or alienation; policy consensus or confusion.

The positioning of the actors in Figure 17.1 is rooted in various classical democratic ideals. Thus, "sovereign" citizens are atop the triangle with candidates cast as "supplicants" and media as "servants." This reflects doctrines of popular sovereignty and protective democracy. The specified behaviors are both consistent with democratic ideals and implied by prominent criticism of contemporary campaign practice. For example, many critics, especially voters, remain unhappy with the candidates' tendency to evade issues and attack opponents (cf. Ansolabehere and Iyengar 1995; Buchanan 1991), practices that have been around in one form or another since the American founding. The implicit wish made explicit in the model is that candidates emphasize

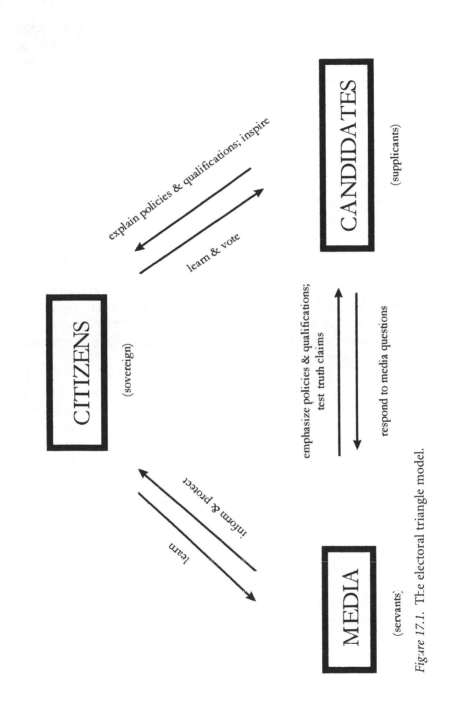

Figure 17.1. The electoral triangle model.

their own plans and qualifications and strike tones more likely to inspire than alienate. The democratic ideal requires a candidate debate that does not repel or confuse but rather interests and informs sovereign citizens.

Other critics, particularly the media scholars who document it, continue to signal disapproval of the news media's consistent preoccupation with the competitive game and horse race aspects of the campaign (e.g., Patterson 1993) many decades after its initial documentation, even as they point out more recent transgressions, such as the overemphasis on conflict at the expense of policy substance (cf. Capella and Jamieson 1997; Lichter and Noyes 1995), and the growing tendency to substitute the faces and voices of journalists for those of candidates in campaign coverage (CMPA 1998a). Implied here, as Figure 17.1 depicts, is that media should let candidates speak for themselves, and more closely mirror reality, except when emphasizing those things, such as candidate policy proposals, qualifications, and distortions, that serve either to inform or protect citizens. Again, the democratic wish is to ensure that citizens have access to accurate and useful information in a form that does not alienate them, as well as to protect from disinformation.

Still other critics, concerned about the general state of American democracy, continue to worry most about a problem that first became apparent in America during the Federalist era, and that has been most heavily documented and regularly lamented since the advent of regular survey research in the 1940s. The problem is a poorly informed and unevenly engaged citizenry (e.g., Brady 1998; Luskin 1990; Campbell et al. 1960) that tends to distrust government and politics (Bennett 1998) and that has no collective sense of responsibility for sustaining the quality of democratic practice (Buchanan 1996). The democratic inference codified by the model is that voters can only obtain the protection of their interests, which is the *raison d'etre* of representative democracy, through vigilant surveillance and participation.[1] Citizens have the power to compel the candidate and media practices identified in the model. American market and electoral systems make both candidates and news organizations almost completely reliant on mass endorsement in varying forms and degrees to achieve their goals. This means that voters-consumers are in a position to make demands that neither candidates nor media can safely ignore. But to use it effectively, they must be well informed and willing to scrutinize candidate and media performance closely so that they may selectively grant and withold the decisive rewards that express their power: vote and audience share.

INSTRUMENTAL CONSEQUENCES

The behavioral exchanges identified in Figure 17.1 are not just normative in value; they also represent the actions most likely to generate such instrumental consequences as community feeling and policy consensus. Logic tells us, for example, that candidates who choose to propose and explain solutions to important problems, and who elect campaign themes and styles that attract and interest voters rather than repel them, will boost the chances for both. Similarly, broadcast and print news organizations that cover campaigns in ways that draw attention to the larger meanings of the choices voters face, accurately portray the content and tone of candidate presentations, repeat key information, and otherwise facilitate mass learning and decision making about national problems and proposed solutions help facilitate policy consensus. And media reduce the likelihood of public estrangement to the extent that they discourage candidate disinformation strategies by exposing them and avoid coverage practices (e.g., overemphasis of candidate conflict) that aggravate mass displeasure with contemporary political practice.

POLITICAL REALITY

Taken together, the specifications in Figure 17.1, like the criticisms that imply them, reflect an idealistic vision of campaign politics that, as the examples suggest, has long endured. But as any casual observer of American politics well knows, the actors rarely behave as either the model or the critics specify. The ideals are more often ignored than implemented, which makes their resiliance both noteworthy and curious.[2]

Why don't the actors meet the critics' expectations? Because the expectations, though widely held, are rarely enforced. Such nonenforcement is due to the interplay of unevenly intense, differentially focused, and otherwise asymmetrical candidate, media, and citizen incentives. Absent unusual situational influence that energizes and mobilizes voters, this incentive mix usually works to dissipate the most powerful available corrective force: citizen agency. That leaves it to the other players, especially candidates, to set the tone.

ACTOR INCENTIVES

DEREGULATED CANDIDATES

The United States features the least regulated political environment among the advanced industrial democracies. The First Amendment prohibits any significant restraint on what candidates may say or do, or what the news media must cover. This rules out decisive measures used elsewhere to discipline candidates, such as banning political advertising, or significantly controlling its contents, or requiring participation in debates or discussion of issues as the price of access to the airwaves.[3]

Candidates enter this deregulated environment with much more at stake and a crisper incentive – electoral victory – than do journalists or voters. Modern candidates are self-selected and highly motivated (Ehrenhalt 1991). In the all-consuming effort to win, candidate organizations strive to control all aspects of the campaign.

Any candidate brain trust faces a complex set of requirements. They must plan, design, initiate, staff, finance, and implement a campaign that can solve several problems at once. They must craft the strategy and message to fit a particular set of political and historical circumstances, and adjust it "on the fly" in response to feedback. They must outmaneuver an equally determined opposition. They must contend with a zealous and complex media contingent that often acts to thwart their efforts and harm their interests. And they must extract a sufficient number of votes from a mass public that is exceptionally diverse, expensive to reach, and hard to motivate.

These realities create certain mind-sets and outlooks. Opponents, media, and voters are all fair game, different kinds of targets in an all-or-nothing war. High-stakes competition promotes both inventiveness and excesses. Modern lore and tradition – shaped by the most aggressive winning efforts, for example, the Kennedy campaign of 1960, the Nixon campaign of 1968, the Bush campaign of 1988, and the Clinton campaign of 1996 – celebrate innovation, guile, and audacity, constrained only by the elastic tolerance of voters. For the most part, the rule is "whatever it takes." At their first post-1996 election encounter, defeated candidate Bob Dole complained bitterly to President Clinton about the latter's "dishonest TV ads that suggested that the Kansan wanted to gut Medicare. To which our insouciant President smiled and replied, 'You gotta do what you gotta do' " ("Moral Authority" 1998).

These incentives and circumstances interact with certain traits of the electorate and the media to produce several recurring candidate strategies that invariably work to thwart the model's ideals. Voter ignorance and aggressive media "prying," for example, combine to invite and offer rationalizations for the use of manipulation and deception. Relentless investigative journalism of the sort pioneered by Bob Woodward and Carl Bernstein of the *Washington Post* during the Watergate episode helped evoke the more comprehensive news management, "spin control," and selective disclosure practices characteristic of the Reagan, Bush, and Clinton campaigns and administrations.[4] And issue evasion, which amounts to deception by omission, is something candidates routinely employ to protect themselves (Aldrich 1980; Page 1978; Downs 1957). Candidates feel they have ample justification to avoid proposing unpopular measures like tax increases or spending cuts even when they make policy sense. They point to examples like Walter Mondale in 1984 and Bruce Babbitt in 1988, both believed to have incurred the wrath of voters as presidential candidates by daring to propose tax increases. Most candidates now believe they must avoid too-specific discussion of just the sort of difficult, no-win issues that campaign-generated policy signals could be most helpful in resolving. Laying out a realistic blueprint for addressing tough problems is perceived as political suicide. Thus, the 1988 party nominees colluded in avoiding serious discussion of the deficit. And the 1996 candidates did the same with Social Security reform. Though journalists typically point out such evasions during campaigns, only rarely are voters moved to put pressure on the candidates to respond. The 1992 election, when economic anxiety spawned an issues discussion, was an exception. Particularly when the candidates collude, there is little or no political price to be paid for evading such no-win policy controversies.

The difficulty of motivating an often indifferent and inattentive public invites candidate appeals to narrow self-interest and to emotions like fear, prejudice, and anger. Emotional appeals, such as television advertising that covertly triggers racial resentment (e.g., the use of black rapist Willie Horton in Republican ads in 1988), attacks against the demerits of opponents (e.g., candidate Bush assailing the liberalism of opponent Dukakis in 1988), or efforts to exploit fear of loss of valued government programs among target voter groups (e.g., the Clinton "Mediscare" ads of 1995 and 1996) are standard candidate practices because of their real or presumed value in the fight for votes. But they contribute to a campaign atmosphere that many voters dislike.

Some political advertising may be genuinely useful to voters as sources of substantive political information. It is argued, for example, that ads can attack the opponent and be contentious, argumentative, and confrontational – i.e., can display characteristics that many would brand negative – while still being accurate and informative and without necessarily being unfair or otherwise illegitimate. In this view, only distortions, exaggerations, and outright lies are never legitimate (Bartels et al. 1998). The point here, however, is not whether particular uses of such tactics can meet the tests set by experts. It is whether candidate presentations and tactics have characteristics that significant numbers of voters experience as alienating.

In fact, voters regularly tell pollsters that they dislike attack advertising and politics, and some claim that it discourages them from voting (Brack 1994). Asked in 1996 to identify changes that would do the most to make things better in future elections, 57 percent of a national sample identified "more honesty and information from candidates," and 35 percent, "less negative campaigning," the two most frequently mentioned changes (Buchanan 1997). Apparently, aggressive campaign rhetoric, even when it conveys factual information potentially useful to voters, reinforces the well-documented public distaste for candidates, politics, parties, and government. In sum, candidate incentives encourage issue evasion and attack politics.

MEDIA AMBITION

Media incentives, though more complex than those of candidates, also evoke campaign coverage practices that contravene the model. Such practices exaggerate the features of political practice that many voters find most repellant. And they discourage policy consensus by minimizing and trivializing the coverage devoted to policy.

The relevant incentives for journalists begin with the ambition to demonstrate their political and professional significance. Political importance is asserted with coverage that goes beyond simply reporting what happens to interpreting the campaign for the mass audience and criticizing the candidates. Ambition for peer respect, on the other hand, is reflected in efforts to uncover "breaking news" and develop important stories, activities that win attention and professional stature. Related to that is the pressure to adhere to news values like novelty and immediacy. And of special concern to those responsible for profits is the incentive of sustaining or increasing audience share or readership, which is thought to require minimal policy coverage and a focus on the most dramatic features of the fight for office.

Political significance incentives have recently bred coverage practices that distort the picture that citizens reliant on mass media for campaign information are able to form of the candidates and the campaign, and that are likely to reinforce mass public dissatisfaction with politics. One such practice is the increasing tendency to substitute the faces and voices of journalists for those of candidates (CMPA 1998a, p. 64; Patterson 1993, pp. 75, 77), thus appropriating from candidates the power to frame the campaign for the audience. Another pattern with roots in the political significance incentive is the increase in interpretive relative to purely descriptive campaign coverage (Patterson 1993, p. 81). The most important impact of both these developments is the *increasingly critical coverage of the candidates.*

During the 1996 presidential campaign, the major commercial television networks all but eliminated the most novel and celebrated form of candidate surveillance, "ad watches" aimed at unmasking misleading or false political advertising, that debuted to wide acclaim in 1992. Instead, the networks emphasized candidate attacks. Coding shows that in 1996 the candidates offered three positive or self-promoting remarks for each criticism of a rival (74 percent positive), but the critical remarks made up a majority (52 percent) of the candidate quotes that appeared in news stories:

> Journalists painted a campaign portrait that was more negative than the reality; then they denounced the candidates' harsh tone. News coverage consisted mainly of criticism – of the presidential candidates, the parties, interest groups, campaign ads, and the electoral system itself. (CMPA 1998b, pp. 5, 7)

The net effect was to exaggerate the extent of the candidates' actual reliance on attack modes and to make the campaign seem more negative than it actually was. Other studies reach similar conclusions (e.g., Cappella and Jamieson 1997, pp. 230–1; Patterson 1993). All of these studies show that media coverage patterns exaggerate the features of political practice that voters find most repellant.[5] The probable result is to reinforce adverse judgments about the political process (Iyengar 1991; Iyengar and Kinder 1987).

The next group of incentives shape coverage practices in ways that obscure the policy implications of candidate choices. The collective

Table 17.1. *Media coverage categories 1988, 1992, and 1996, in percentages*

Coverage categories	1988[a]	1992[b]	1996[c]
Campaign horse race	36	30	48
Candidate conflicts	21	17	35
Candidate qualifications	19	7	1
Policy issues	10	31	37
The electorate	10	7	12
The media	4	7	4

[a] Conducted for the Markle Project by Luce Press Clipping Service (see Buchanan, 1991: 38–74). Based on all campaign news stories and editorials from 13 major newspapers and NBC, ABC, CBS, CNN, and PBS between September 8 and November 8, 1988. Some stories fit multiple categories.
[b] Conducted for the Markle Project by the Center for Media and Public Affairs. Based on all campaign news stories and editorials from *The New York Times, Washington Post, Wall Street Journal*, ABC, NBC, CBS, CNN, and PBS between September 7 and November 3, 1992. Some stories fit multiple categories.
[c] Conducted for the Markle Project by the Center for Media and Public Affairs. Based on all campaign news stories and editorials from ABC, CBS, and NBC between September 2 and November 4, 1996. Some stories fit multiple categories.

effort of major news organizations to capture public attention, market share, and profit are on display in the coverage patterns reported in Table 17.1.[6] Shown is the distribution of campaign coverage during the fall presidential campaigns of 1988, 1992, and 1996. Situational variation produces fluctuations in the cross-year patterns. But in general, we see that the preponderance of year-to-year coverage is devoted not to issues and qualifications but to competition and conflict. Political and professional incentives are also reflected in Table 17.1. They help to explain the prominence of such coverage topics as the horse-race and candidate conflicts. But it is the aim of holding the attention of the mass audience that most discourages extensive or detailed substantive coverage of policies or qualifications. This is particularly true of television coverage, to which most Americans still turn for campaign and other news. There the focus is on the novel, the colorful, the dramatic, and the conflictual. Media adviser Roger Ailes aptly summed the electronic media's focus as highlighting "pictures, polls, attacks, and mistakes" (McCarthy 1988, p. 70).

Not included in Table 17.1 is another routine coding discovery: that such issue substance coverage as there is tends to be quite superficial (CMPA 1998a, pp. 36–41). 1996 coding shows that most references to candidate issue positions are short and insubstantial, with little attention to the proposal's relation to the relevant national policy context, the proposal's potential policy implications, or implications for voters' interests. For example, only 10 percent of 1996 post-Labor Day "issue mentions" were embedded in extensive and detailed policy stories that put issues in a larger context and also spelled out nonpolitical implications. The consequences for the election outcome of candidates' records and proposals received the most attention, appearing in 43 percent of all issue discussions. This pattern held in 1992 as well as 1996, both years in which Table 17.1 shows that issue coverage was relatively high. It probably also held in 1988, which Table 17.1 shows to have featured much less media attention to policy, though comparable data are not available.

THE CITIZEN BALANCE-SHEET

Citizens' incentives to inform themselves and to cast votes are, on average, quite weak, as evidenced by the relatively modest percentages willing to do either in most elections. The American public has historically displayed "minimal levels of political attention and information" (Sniderman 1993, p. 219). And voter turnout in presidential elections has declined from 63 percent of the voting-age population in 1960 to 49 percent in 1996.

In fact, the disincentives to learn and vote are likely to outweigh the incentives for most potential voters in most electoral circumstances, as implied by the lists in Table 17.2.

INCENTIVES. Because it brings tens of millions of voters to the polls during every national election regardless of varying situational incentives, the most consistently powerful and therefore the most important incentive is a socialized attitude: *civic duty*. Civic duty involves the learned disposition to view such activities as acquiring political information and voting as responsibilities and also as sources of psychological satisfaction, or psychic reward (Fiorina and Peterson 1998, p. 175), either as a result of "doing the right thing," by supporting the political community, or simply by evading feelings of guilt.

But civic duty is too narrowly conceived by voters to make them the engine of the high campaign quality envisioned in Figure 17.1. For most, it begins and ends with voting. A November 1996 Markle Presidential Election Watch survey shows that while 70 percent of the

Table 17.2. *Voting and learning citizen incentives and disincentives*

Incentives	Disincentives
Civic duty	Divided government
Competitive election	Multiple elections
Policy anxiety	Workday voting
Political interest	No impact
Clear policy differences	High information cost
Policy impact	Registration cost
Party ID/loyalty	Alienation
	Indifference

electorate identifies voting as an important duty, only about 25 percent identifies "staying informed" as an obligation (Buchanan 1997). Thus, neither political learning nor policing the campaign has achieved "duty" status in the public mind.

When, as in 1992, majorities do become better informed than usual, or signal rare but effective demands to the other actors, it is in response to one or another of the unpredictable situational incentives in Table 17.2, particularly policy anxiety. Economic anxiety, for example, appears to have motivated significant increases in learning, voting, and citizen demand for candidate attention to economic issues in 1992.

As for the impact of other situational incentives, it has long been known that turnout is higher when "issues of vital concern are presented" (Boeckel 1928, p. 517; Key 1966, p. 578), when elections are competitive, and when candidates offer clearly contrasting policy stances (Grofman 1993).[7] And individual incentives such as specific political objectives and interests, or the desire to contribute to the success of a particular candidate or policy, will motivate learning and voting among different aggregations of people at different times.

Party label remains an important information cue for most citizens, and party identifiers who vote tend to be loyal supporters of their standard-bearers (Luttbeg and Gant 1995, p. 45). But party identification is not a uniform incentive to participate for all voters. Strong partisans of either party and all self-described Republicans continue to vote at very high levels (and are often inspired rather than deterred by aggressively partisan campaign styles described here as widely demotivating). But weak partisans, independents, and Democrats, who together comprise some two-thirds of the voting age population,[8] are low turnout groups (Luttbeg and Gant 1995, p. 110). And as noted earlier, political independents are disproportionately discouraged from voting by aggressive political tactics (Ansolabehere and Iyengar 1995; Luskin and Bratcher 1995).

DISINCENTIVES. Taken together, the disincentives to learn and vote are more powerful than the incentives. The reason is that while the incentives often require particular circumstances to evoke them (e.g., policy anxiety, competitive elections), the disincentives more often tend to be structural or recurring. For example, twenty-one of the thirty-nine presidential elections between 1840 and 1992 occurred during periods of divided government. And as Franklin and Hirczy de Mino (1998) demonstrate, divided government (i.e., a president of one party, a Congress of the other) and noncompetitive elections separately and significantly reduced voter turnout in American presidential elections between 1840 and 1992.

These researchers argue that turnout declines because divided government and the separation of powers system work to blur the accountability of government to voters and make the link between the vote and public policy ambiguous. Apparently, the policy link motivates voters by clarifying the stakes.[9] Policy ambiguity, a chronic candidate campaign ploy, is thus an important disincentive to prospective voters, as is the belief, widely held in 1996, that the election outcome is a foregone conclusion.

Other equally demotivating circumstances are also imbedded fixtures of American political life. For example, U.S. voters face a daunting number of state, local, and federal voting opportunities. Even more discouraging is the fact that elections occur on workdays, which can impose financial as well as logistical barriers to participation. As if these were not enough, the U.S. registration barrier is estimated to reduce turnout by around 8 percent (Franklin and Hirczy de Mino 1998).

Finally, rational choice scholars argue that the single most powerful incentive – self-interest – is largely inoperative during elections because individual votes rarely affect outcomes (Downs 1957). For candidates, elections are high-cost, high-reward events. But excepting those citizens for whom participation is psychically rewarding, the potential benefits of participation are likely to seem trivial. That destroys the incentive of many prospective participants to sustain the modest but nontrivial costs associated with learning and voting.

This long list of civic demotivators makes it clear that political alienation is far from the only reason for nonparticipation. But when high levels of alienation are considered along with the structural disincentives, the growth of political indifference among the young, and the universal awareness that one's vote counts for little, alienation may achieve something like last-straw status. Why invest time, attention, and energy in an activity whose content does not interest you, whose outcome does not affect you, and whose result you cannot influence, especially if the process seems repugnant?

REFORM. The foregoing portrayal of candidate, media, and citizen incentives shows why the typical campaign does not feature the preferred behavior modeled in Figure 17.1. It also shows why it is unrealistic to expect such behavior. Still, dissatisfaction with the tendency of elites to dominate an avowedly democratic electoral process intended to privilege the rights and powers of citizens has persisted throughout American history.

Virtually all electoral reforms proposed since the founding have sought either to increase popular control of leader selection processes in the name of democracy, or to elevate citizens' rights and interests above those of economic and political elites. The results have been disappointing, however, because the reforms – from the many expansions of the franchise to direct and binding primary elections to "public interest" broadcasting requirements, to campaign finance reform, to motor-voter registration, to free television time – have but rarely and then only marginally altered the incentives just reviewed.

The enduring realities of power and incentives warrant blunt conclusions. First, so long as the First Amendment is interpreted to rule out coercive regulation of candidate and media practice, the only force powerful enough to compel candidates and media to behave as democratic theorists and other critics want is market demand. But second, market demand can only be created by mass publics, which rarely enforce democracy outside of anxious moments like economic crises. The question for reformers, then, is how to "standardize" such demand.

The only incentive in play among those who make up the relevant political and media markets that could be used to generate consistent demand for the candidate and media behaviors in Figure 17.1 is a socialized incentive: civic duty.[10] It is the impressive power that this socialized incentive has shown to consistently deliver millions of voters to the polls despite the absence of self-interest, despite the many structural disincentives, and whether any particular election happens to be close or otherwise interesting or compelling, that gives it the potential to address the democratic theory–electoral practice gap at issue here.

At present, many fewer actually vote (witness the less than 50 percent turnout for the 1996 presidential election) than profess the responsibility to vote (e.g., the finding that fully 70 percent regard voting as a citizen duty). This 20 percent discrepancy represents a target of opportunty for reforms aimed at increasing voter turnout to levels that better approximate democratic ideals. Recent field-experimental research on voter mobilization suggests that a publicly and/or charitably financed effort to reach these "guilty nonvoters" with nonpartisan appeals to do their duty can be expected to generate as much as a 5-percent turnout increase among registered voters (Gerber and Green 1999, p. 20).

The balance of the reform agenda implied by my analysis, however, is necessarily a much longer-term effort involving the "old chestnut" of political socialization. The reason is that most citizens do not presently regard themselves as responsible for "supervising" the campaign behavior of candidates and media, which they would have to do to function as enforcers of the model. As reported earlier, only about 25 percent even perceive a civic duty to pay attention and stay informed during a presidential election campaign. And the same open-ended survey question about citizen duties uncovered no sense of responsibility for policing the electoral process (Buchanan 1997).

This is why getting voters to accept an expanded role for monitoring elections and for coordinating their own political and media reactions to enforce democratic standards – a tall order under the best of circumstances – can happen no more quickly than the time needed to prepare a new generation of citizens. The preliminaries must include a revised "citizen job description" that calls for strategic learning and voting, and plans for incorporating the new civic curriculum into primary and secondary schools and colleges. Space prohibits detailing either here.

Is this a cumbersome approach to reform? Yes. Is it slow and uncertain? Definitely. Yet where laws cannot be used to constrain candidate and media behavior, citizen demand is all that remains. We cannot expect to cultivate it effectively without significant trial and error. But cultivate it we must, because citizens without portfolios leave us vulnerable to the undisciplined incentives and other centrifugal forces that embitter political practice, fragment the community, and dilute democracy.

Notes

1. Classical political theory is the source of the idea that *the purpose of elections is to enable citizens to protect their interests*, which stems from the power to choose among rival candidates and to vote out incumbents. This view can be traced to ideas of "protective" republicanism and democracy as elaborated by theorists as diverse as Niccolò Machiavelli, James Mill, Jeremy Bentham, and James Madison (Held 1996, pp. 44, 88), who identify regular elections, secret ballots, and competition for votes as practical ways to promote and protect the people's collective interests against the abuse history shows to result from unaccountable leaders.

   But these exclusively procedural protections are not enough by themselves. Elections best protect the interests of those citizens with access to the information (e.g., nonpartisan problem-definition, issue-analysis, and candidate-qualifications data) and the protection (e.g., truthtesting and fact-checking of candidate claims) best offered by a free press. And even with that crucial help, elections can best help those citizens willing to invest in helping themselves by engaging in the self-protective practices identified in the model: learning and voting.

   The debate is ongoing as to whether voters can adequately protect their interests without being well-informed. Some contend that voters are able, through such heuristics as party ID (Schattschneider 1960), low information rationality (Popkin 1991), cognitive shortcuts (Downs 1957) and other forms of cue taking, to accurately perceive how candidates relate to their interests (e.g., Popkin 1991) or to absorb enough low information cues through the course of a campaign to approximate the voting behavior of fully informed voters (Fournier 1997), thus sidestepping the costs of ignorance.

   Others, however (e.g., Luskin 1997; Luskin and Globetti 1997; Delli Carpini and Keeter 1996) dispute the claim that more substantive forms of campaign and other civic learning are irrelevant. But despite the academic debate over "heuristic shortcuts" evidence and arguments, the normative ideal of a well-informed electorate remains a fixture of the democratic tradition. Democratic thinkers from Thomas Jefferson to John Dewey to Walter Lippman to Amy Gutmann have pointed to the informed citizenry ideal while acknowledging that it is rarely achieved and proposing ways to compensate for the shortfall. The ideal is also consistently acknowledged by journalists and editors who continue to publish the latest evidence of mass public ignorance of such things as the identities of their representatives. They regard such evidence as newsworthy precisely because of the informed citizenry ideal.

2. Why do such seemingly unrealistic expectations endure despite their imperceptible influence on political practice, and also despite the fact that much of contemporary political science dismisses them as both unrealistic and misguided? First, because of their moral credibility, that is, they represent deeply felt prescriptive ideals that in many minds intuitively clarify the distinction between political right and wrong. Second, because of their practical potential, that is, they can help facilitate socially useful consequences: community feeling and policy consensus.

3. The same amendment, which the Supreme Court in *Buckley v. Valeo* (1976) interpreted to equate political money with free speech, combines with easily evaded

campaign finance laws to make a flood of special interest money available to candidates strapped for enough cash to finance hugely expensive television advertising campaigns.

4. News management, in the sense of casting presidential news in the most favorable light, has existed since the Washington administration. It took on its state-of-the-art comprehensiveness and artfulness in the post-Watergate campaigns and presidencies.

5. The complaint is not that media fail to be cheerleaders, but that they fail to offer viewers and readers a representative sample of reality and distort reality in ways that make things seem worse than they really are to citizens. ". . . there is a very real danger that a relentless focus on inaccuracies in campaign ads [and, I would add, on the most aggressive rhetoric] will simply reinforce the cynical belief of many citizens that campaigns are "all lies" [and filled with nasty rhetoric] and are not to be trusted [or followed] (Bartels et al. 1998, p. 18).

6. Other recent coding studies include (Zaller 1997; Lichter and Noyes 1995; Patterson 1993; Buchanan 1991).

7. Research on European electorates suggests that "electoral salience," i.e., how much is at stake in terms of allocating government power, is the principal determinant of turnout magnitude (Eijk and Franklin 1996; Reif and Schmitt 1980).

8. A Pew Research Center Poll released in November, 1999, put Republicans at 27, Democrats at 34, and independents at 39 percent. Between 1982 and 1985, independents increased from 26 to 31 percent. See "Six Decades of Gallup Polling in Review," *The Public Perspective*, 8: 52, 60 (April/May, 1997).

9. The idea that low U.S. turnout may be explained in part by the tenuous link between voting and policy is not new (cf. Asher 1992, p. 56; Polsby and Wildavsky 1991, p. 331; Schattschneider 1960: 100–1). The structural disincentive presented by the separation of powers shows that in such systems civic investment and attitudes of obligation are all the more important if the benefits of participation are to be extended beyond the low level equilibrium turnout discussed by Franklin and Hirczy de Mino (1998).

10. "Duty exists to the extent that people are willing to honor obligations in the absence of social rewards for doing so . . . Duty is the way by which people cope with the free-rider problem in the absence of coercion" (Wilson 1993, pp. 101, 115).

REFERENCES

Ansolabehere, Stephen, and Shanto Iyengar (1995). *Going Negative: How Political Advertisements Shrink and Polarize the Electorate*. New York: Free Press.

Aldrich, John H. (1980). *Before the Convention: Strategies and Choices in Presidential Nomination Campaigns*. Chicago, IL: University of Chicago Press.

Asher, Herbert B. (1992). *Presidential Elections and American Politics: Voters, Candidates and Campaigns Since 1952*. Pacific Grove, CA: Brooks/Cole.

Bartels, Larry M., et al. (1998). "Campaign Reform: Insights and Evidence." *Report of the Task Force on Campaign Reform*. Princeton University.

Bennett, W. Lance (1998). "The Uncivic Culture: Communication, Identity, and the Rise of Lifestyle Politics." Ithiel de Sola Pool Lecture, delivered at American Political Science Association annual meeting, Boston.

Boekel, Richard (1928). *Voting and Non-Voting in Elections*. Washington, DC: Editorial Research Reports.

Brack, Jr., Reginald K. (1994). "How To Clean Up Gutter Politics." *New York Times*, December 27:A15.

Brady, Henry E. (1998). "A Review of the Markle Presidential Election Studies." Unpublished Manuscript, University of California, Berkeley.

Buchanan, Bruce (1997). "Presidential Campaign Quality: What the Variance Implies." Paper presented at American Political Science Association annual meeting, Washington DC.

(1996). *Renewing Presidential Politics*. Lanham, MD: Rowman and Littlefield.

(1991). *Electing a President: The Markle Commission Research on Campaign '88*. Austin, TX: University of Texas Press.

Campbell, Angus, Philip E. Converse, Warren E. Miller, and Donald E. Stokes (1960). *The American Voter*. New York: John Wiley.

Cappella, Joseph N., and Kathleen Hall Jamieson (1997). *Spiral of Cynicism: The Press and the Public Good*. New York: Oxford.

CMPA (Center for Media and Public Affairs) (1998a). *Campaign '96: The Media and the Candidates*. Final Report to the Markle Foundation.

(1998b). *Executive Summary*. Report to the Markle Foundation.

Delli Carpini, Michael X., and Scott Keeter (1996). *What Americans Know About Politics and Why it Matters*. New Haven, CT: Yale University Press.

Downs, Anthony (1957). *An Economic Theory of Democracy*. New York: Harper and Row.

Eijk, Cees van der, and Mark Franklin (1996). *Choosing Europe? The European Electorate and National Politics in the Face of Union*. Ann Arbor: University of Michigan.

Ehrenhalt, Alan (1991). *The United States of Ambition*. New York: Times Books.

Fiorina, Morris P., and Paul E. Peterson (1998). *The New American Democracy*. Boston: Allyn and Bacon.

Franklin, Mark N., and Wolfgang P. Hirczy de Mino (1998). "Separated Powers, Divided Government, and Turnout in U.S. Presidential Elections." *American Journal of Political Science*, 42:316–326.

Gerber, Alan, and Donald Green (1999). "The Effects of Canvassing, Leafleting, and Direct Mail on Voter Turnout: A Field Experiment." Paper presented at Midwest Political Science Association annual meeting, Chicago, IL.

Grofman, Bernard (1993). "Is Turnout the Paradox that Ate Rational Choice Theory?" In Bernard Grofman (Ed.), *Information, Participation and Choice: An Economic Theory of Democracy in Perspective*. Ann Arbor: University of Michigan Press.

Held, David (1996). *Models of Democracy, 2d ed*. Stanford, CA: Stanford University Press.

Iyengar, Shanto (1991). *Is Anyone Responsible: How Television Frames Political Issues*. Chicago: University of Chicago Press.

and Donald Kinder (1987). *News that Matters: Television and American Opinion*. Chicago: University of Chicago Press.

Key, Jr., V. O. (1966). *The Responsible Electorate: Rationality in Presidential Voting 1936–1960*. Cambridge: Harvard University Press.

Lichter, S. Robert, and Richard E. Noyes (1995). *Good Intentions Make Bad News: Why Americans Hate Campaign Journalism*. Lanham, MD: Rowman and Littlefield.

Luskin, Robert C. (1997). "From Denial to Extenuation (and Finally beyond): Political Sophistication and Citizen Performance." Unpublished manuscript, Department of Government, University of Texas at Austin.

(1990). "Explaining Political Sophistication." *Political Behavior*, 12:331–361.

and Suzanne Globetti (1997). "Candidate versus Policy Considerations in the Voting Decision: The Role of Political Sophistication." Unpublished manuscript, Department of Government, University of Texas at Austin.

and Christopher N. Bratcher (1995). "Negative Campaigning, Partisanship and Turnout." Paper presented American Political Science Association annual meeting, Chicago.

Luttbeg, Norman R., and Michael M. Gant (1995). *American Electoral Behavior, 1952–1992, 2d ed.* Itasca, IL: Peacock.

McCarthy, Larry (1988). "The Selling of the President: An Interview with Roger Ailes." *Gannett Center Journal*, 2:65–72.

"Moral Authority." (1998). *Wall Street Journal*, July 23:A16.

Page, Benjamin I. (1978). *Choices and Echoes in Presidential Elections.* Chicago, IL: University of Chicago Press.

Patterson, Thomas E. (1993). *Out of Order.* New York: Knopf.

Pew Research Center for The People and the Press (November, 1999). *Retropolitics: The Political Typology: Version 3.0.* Washington, D.C.: Pew Research Center for the People and the Press.

Polsby, Nelson W., and Aaron Wildavsky (1991). *Presidential Elections: Contemporary Strategies of American Electoral Politics.* New York: Free Press.

Popkin, Samuel L. (1991). *The Reasoning Voter.* Chicago, IL: University of Chicago Press.

Reif, Karlheinz, and Hermann Schmitt (1980). "Nine Second-order National Elections – A Conceptual Framework for the Analysis of European Election Results." *European Journal of Political Research*, 8:3–44.

Schattschneider, Elmer E. (1960). *The Semisovereign People: A Realist's View of Democracy in America.* New York: Holt, Rinehart and Winston.

"Six Decades of Gallup Polling in Review (April/May, 1997)." *The Public Perspective*, 8:52; 60.

Sniderman, Paul M. (1993). "The New Look in Public Opinion Research." In Ada W. Finifter (Ed.), *Political Science: The State of the Discipline II.* Washington, DC: American Political Science Association.

Wilson, James Q. (1993). *The Moral Sense.* New York: Free Press.

Zaller, John (1997). "The Political Economy of Election News." Paper presented at American Political Science Association annual meeting, Washington, DC.

CHAPTER 18

"Americanization" Reconsidered: U.K.–U.S. Campaign Communication Comparisons Across Time

Jay G. Blumler and Michael Gurevitch

The notions of "globalization" and its junior brother "Americanization" have become one of the mantras of the end of the millennium. They are invoked in discussion of the global economy, global culture, indeed the "globalization of everything" including, of course, the globalization of the media. The terms are used, by now, with an almost taken-for-granted air, although they have occasionally been subjected to scrutiny and criticism (Negrine and Papathanassopoulos 1996; Scammell 1998). Their compelling power, however, has not diminished.

Discussions of the processes of globalization and Americanization can be regarded as direct descendants of comparative analysis, inasmuch as the comparative approach casts a cross-cultural, cross-national net and seeks to identify similarities as well as differences among the dominant features of economic or cultural or, in our case, media systems in different societies. The logic of the comparative approach has featured quite prominently in our work in the past, and it is not surprising, therefore, that it has led us to reconsider the notion of Americanization in the present chapter.

Its point of departure is an analysis of political party and mass media roles in the U.K. and U.S. elections of 1983 and 1984, which we conducted, with colleagues, a decade ago (Semetko et al., 1991). Many differences and *sources* of difference were discovered – albeit allied to a suggestion that they might lessen or disappear in time. This chapter revisits our 1980s portrait of two quite contrasted political communication systems through the lens of what is known about media performance in the U.S. presidential (1996) and U.K. general (1997) elections. Although our understanding of the latter campaigns is largely based on the research and commentaries of other analysts, this chapter also draws on our own experience of six days of newsroom observation at the BBC in April 1997 (Blumler and Gurevitch 1998). Our key questions are: Have the U.K.–U.S. differences of the 1980s endured into the 1990s? Did the U.K. campaign of 1997 show signs of movement toward the American model? Is the analytical framework devised for the 1980s research still serviceable in 1990s conditions?

This step is an extension of our longstanding interest in the strategy of comparative political communication research (Blumler and Gurevitch 1975; Gurevitch and Blumler 1990). Given a build-up of cross-national enquiries in the recent past, efforts to reexamine some of them in the spirit of unravelling "the interpenetration of space and time" (Blumler, McLeod, and Rosengren 1992, p. 8) could be highly rewarding. Particularly in the present period of turbulent social, political, and media change, the validity of one-time cross-national analyses cannot be accepted unless they are regularly updated.

A SUMMARY OF THE 1980S STUDY

The 1980s research was designed to explore the "discretionary power" of the mass media to shape the agendas of U.S. and U.K. election campaigns. By this, we meant the ability of journalists to tell the campaign story in their own words, scenarios, and assessments (rather than politicians'), to highlight the issues on which they believed the election should turn, and to initiate reports based on their news values and interests. Reflecting macro-level differences between the political and media systems of the two societies, we expected higher levels of journalistic intervention in U.S. campaigns and readier access for politicians' messages in British ones. The essence of our approach can be conveyed through four main points.

First, the study was shaped by an analytical framework for conducting and interpreting cross-national political communication enquiry. This consisted of five systemic factors considered likely to favor or inhibit journalistic intervention into campaign coverage:

1. *The position of politics and politicians in society.* For a variety of reasons,[1] political activity and its practitioners were presumed to enjoy higher esteem among British than U.S. members of the public. This should serve as a constraint on journalistic intervention (Semetko et al. 1991, p. 5).
2. *Newspeople's orientations toward politics and politicians.* The key distinction here was between a "pragmatic" attitude, disposing

381

journalists to cover political events according to assessments of their "newsworthiness," and a "sacerdotal" one, impelling news-people to treat such events with the respect due to them as inherently significant and important – deserving consideration, then, beyond that prescribed by the application of news values alone. U.S. media, we hypothesized, would tend to approach campaigns in a more pragmatic spirit and British media, with a more sacerdotal outlook. And sacerdotalism should restrain journalistic intervention (see Semetko et al. 1991, p. 6).

3. *Degree of professionalization of election campaigning.* Although the influence of publicity specialists on the course and conduct of campaigns had increased in both societies, developments in this direction were said to "have gone farther in the United States than in Britain." This should undermine sacerdotalism and encourage reporters to exercise greater discretionary power (Semetko et al. 1991, pp. 6–7).

4. *Variations of media competition.* The application of this dimension to the United States and United Kingdom was more complex than for the other factors. Whereas competition among British tabloid newspapers seemed fierce, many American newspapers were under less competitive pressure because they enjoyed a monopoly or semimonopoly position in their cities or towns. Competition for the television audience, however, was much greater in the United States than in Britain's then oligopolistic system dominated by the BBC and Independent Television (ITV). The underlying hypothesis here was that higher levels of competitive pressure would render the media more audience oriented and less attuned to politicians' needs and sensitivities (Semetko et al. 1991, pp. 7–8).

5. *Public service versus commercial organization of the media.* In commercial systems we expected a stronger inclination by journalists to set political agendas and not merely reflect party and candidate agendas, though with less news hole space into which to squeeze their contributions. This was of course a virtually defining line of distinction between the U.S. and British television systems at the time – with the former dominated by private networks thoroughly dependent on advertising revenue and the latter geared to public service norms through both a publicly owned BBC and a closely regulated ITV (see Semetko et al. 1991, Chapter 4 and p. 178).

To such system-level influences, we added, in light of the research findings, a few micro-level conditions that could affect campaign agendas (Semetko et al. 1991, pp. 178–9), e.g.:

6. *The partisan or ideological leanings of specific media organisations,* affording preferential coverage for favored parties and candidates.
7. *Candidate status,* with incumbent presidents or prime ministers being "in a better position to influence the campaign agenda than a challenger."
8. *News hole size,* where newspapers and bulletins with more space and time at their disposal can cover issues in greater detail and broaden the agenda.

Second, the validity of this scheme was strongly confirmed by the study's empirical findings. Particularly on television, British election coverage was more ample, more substantive, more oriented to party messages, less free with journalistic evaluation, and more respectful. By contrast, American election television was more terse, concentrated, horse-racist, guided by conventional news values, ready to pass judgement, and ready to be disrespectful in passing such judgment. There were more campaign stories about the political parties in Britain than the United States, and more space within them was occupied by politicians' remarks, which were also on average longer. More campaign news stories were party-initiated and fewer were journalist-initiated in Britain than in the United States. To put it another way, U.S. campaign coverage was considerably more "mediated" than its British counterpart in the 1980s (Semetko et al. 1991, Chapters 7 and 8).

Third, however, we noted that the study's analytical framework referred to certain "traditionally significant features of political communication systems which ... may be undergoing gradual change". Certain trends pointing "in an 'American' direction" seemed to be under way in Britain, and if they were to "hold and persist into the future, the differences between the political communication systems in the two countries would gradually weaken, thus increasing the similarities in the [campaign] performance of the media ... in these two societies" (Semetko et al. 1991, p. 10).

Fourth, we pointed out that the agenda-setting process in both Britain and the United States is a deeply political one. That is, once a campaign is announced, an implacably competitive struggle to control the mass media agenda is unleashed, not only between rival parties and candidates, but also pitting party campaign managements against news organization teams (Semetko et al. 1991, p. 176). Such a struggle for agenda control has become, we argued, a sort of canker in the democratic rose, "impoverishing the election dialogue, probably even undermining its legitimacy" – e.g, through shorter soundbites, increased negativity, and a loss of credibility and interest among voters (p. 184). Nevertheless, we concluded on a note of some hope that a gathering revulsion against the worst campaign excesses (much deplored after the 1988 election in the U.S.) "might help to reverse the swing of the pendulum in the 1990s" (p. 186).

Since the 1980s, however, the political and media environments that shape election communications have been changing in significant ways. According to Swanson and Mancini (1996, Chapter 13), a "modern model of campaigning," including "expanding reliance on technical experts and professional advisers," has advanced throughout much of the democratic world. The media have also assumed more autonomous roles, and relations between politicians and journalists appear to have become more adversarial (Blumler and Gurevitch 1995, pp. 214–215). Citizens' loyalties to parties have weakened and scepticism has increased. At the same time the media system has been evolving through the multiplication of channels, introduction of 24-hour news, the absorption of news media into large conglomerate corporations, the internationalization of communication, and the fragmentation of audiences.

Is our perspective from the 1980s still valid in these altered conditions? Two broad questions arise about its applicability to the 1996 U.S. and 1997 U.K. election campaigns:

First, *is the U.K. election communication system increasingly approximating the U.S. one?* To put the question more pejoratively, are British media campaigns descending to U.S. depths – becoming less substantive, more personalized, more negative, dominated more by soundbites on the party side and journalistic interpretation on the media side – embroiled, then, in a "spiral of delegitimation" propelled by political news management, media scepticism, and voter cynicism (Capella and Jamieson 1996)? It is noticeable that when elections are held outside the United States these days, allegations that their staging has been Americanized often surface instantly.[2] Even though the Americanization label has been dismissed by scholars for simplistically implying a one-way process of change (Negrine and Papathanossopoulos 1996), the assumption that convergent trends are irreversibly remodeling competitive political communication along U.S. lines in most other democracies is widely shared (Swanson and Mancini 1996). Does an updated Anglo-American comparison support this view?

Second, *is the framework of system-level influences generated by Semetko et al. (1991) for comparative political communication analysis in the 1980s still relevant in the 1990s?* Are any of the factors that seemed important then no longer so significant? Are any new variables needed? Among its other advantages comparative research is indispensable as an antidote to naive universalism – or the untested assumption that research findings from one society (normally one's own!) are applicable everywhere (Gurevitch and Blumler 1990, p. 308). In the absence of comparative evidence, we cannot be confident that trends prominent in the United States today (and much discussed in other chapters of this volume) – such as the diminishing centrality of traditional political institutions, the increasing fragmentation of audiences for politics, and the transition from citizens to consumers of politics and media – are similarly prevalent in most other developed democracies. Such evidence will be more penetrating and discriminating if its collection is guided by a suitably considered conceptual framework.

AMERICANIZATION? YES . . . BUT!

British political communication has certainly been swept by currents of significant change in the 1990s. The resulting pattern is far more differentiated, however, than the notion of Americanization can express. Even though certain features of the British system resemble U.S. practice more closely than they used to, in other respects significant differences remain. There is also a further complication with which the concept of Americanization simply cannot deal: *U.S. campaign communication has been changing significantly in the same period as well.* Consequently, new areas of cross-national divergence may arise alongside ongoing processes of convergence.

AMERICANIZING TRENDS

That said, the Semetko et al. (1991) expectation that U.K. campaign communication would shift toward the U.S. model is confirmed by three major trends. These apply to the roles of the three main components of any campaign communication system – its partisan competitors, electoral audiences, and political journalists, respectively.

First, *by 1997 the professionalization of the British parties' approaches to the news media and the electorate had caught up with U.S. practice (especially in the case of Labour)*. Many examples of this trend could be mentioned.

The British campaign, once at only two and a half weeks a model of brevity, has lengthened inordinately. In formal terms, the 1997 campaign lasted six weeks, but by other calculations it stretched back to the election of Tony Blair as Labour leader in 1994 and to the reselection of John Major as Conservative leader in 1995. Thus, what Americans call "the permanent campaign" is now firmly installed in the British calendar. Electoral considerations are *ever* present in leading British politicians' minds (not only in a bounded precampaign period).

News management by party publicity staffs has also been given a much higher priority and become a far more proactive, disciplined, comprehensive, calculated, and incessant activity. The central principle is that all forms of politically relevant communications should be organized professionally with media goals in mind; none should be exempt from the publicity specialists' control.

Of course such an emphasis requires the recruitment of individuals with media skills to manage campaigns and help leaders to handle media demands effectively. In Britain some of those advisers have been elevated into very high positions in the Labour Party and then in Government. Three vaunted "spin doctors" – Alastair Campbell, Peter Mandelson, and Charlie Whelan – frequently appeared in the news during Labour's first year of power and were credited with more influence than some Cabinet Ministers.[3]

Publicity professionalization also entails the invasion of policy domains by communication factors and personnel. Illustrative is the Blair administration's acceptance of radical proposals to transform the organization and workings of the U.K. Government Information Service, designed to modernize "the Government's communications with the media to make them more effective and authoritative" (Mountfield 1997). This includes such changes as a more centralized coordination of government communications to the media through the Prime Minister's Chief Press Secretary, cultivation among civil service information officers of the skills and practices of proactive news management, and a greater integration of communication and policy considerations and personnel.

Reliance on attack campaigning has also increased markedly in Britain. After content analyzing the parties' press releases, Goddard, Scammell, and Semetko (1998, p. 171) reported that 69 percent of

Labour's included attacks on the Conservatives, with 33 percent coded as predominantly negative; while for the Conservatives, 81 percent attacked Labour, with 58 percent coded as predominantly negative. This relates to yet another development in 1997 – the creation by both major parties of so-called rebuttal units to react rapidly to each other's claims and accusations with computer-based research, often presented at special rebuttal press conferences during the campaign. In Labour's case this was a direct import from the Clinton campaigns of 1992 and 1996.

The professional model's insistence on symbolizing the party message in the Leader's image and concentrating its expression in his or her voice has advanced further in Britain as well. Both Labour and the Conservatives relied heavily on the appeals of Tony Blair and John Major before and during the 1997 campaign – at times as if distancing themselves from significant elements of the parties they led. In fact, in midcampaign John Major dramatically begged squabbling Tory MPs to support his controversial position on Britain's relations to the European Union, while much of Tony Blair's campaign could be summed up in a phrase he often used (and still does): Trust *me!*[4]

Second, *evidence accumulated in the first half of the 1990s that many British electors were becoming more like Americans in the wariness and cynicism of their attitudes to politicians and political institutions.* Gallup tracking polls, for example, showed a sharp decline of public confidence in "the way democracy works in this country" between August 1992, when a minority of 38 percent declared themselves "not very satisfied" or "not at all satisfied," and August 1994, when a majority of 55 percent did so. Other polls showed that support for the British system of government (that is, thinking it "worked well") had declined appreciably, while the numbers considering that Parliament worked badly had increased over the same period. Nearly two-thirds said in October 1994 they believed that most members of Parliament made a lot of money by using public office improperly. According to Smith (1995, p. 555), these and other indicators "starkly reveal the extent to which public disaffection had risen over the past four years and few, if any, commentators would dispute the fact." Such attitudes seemed to be reflected in Britons' media behavior as well – for example, in declining audiences for television news programs and more serious current affairs and specialist political programs. Competitive pressures allied to assumptions about low reader interest caused big reductions in the amount of space that many newspapers devoted to coverage of parliamentary debates

(Franklin 1997). It was also identified as a key problem, which the BBC had to face when planning its coverage of the 1997 campaign:

> We are all increasingly aware that there is a degree of alienation from the political process and that applies to political coverage on our bulletins.
>
> In the present climate, we can't just present politics in the old way. (News executive cited in Blumler and Gurevitch 1998, pp. 180, 188)

Third, *British journalism intervened more independently and forcibly in 1997 campaign discourse than at any previous postwar election.*

For one thing, the partisanship of Britain's national press was transformed – no longer displaying virulently Conservative allegiances. Six of the ten daily papers backed Labour at the 1997 election, and of those that still supported the Conservatives, the *Express* "was at best lukewarm," while the other two (the *Daily Mail* and *Daily Telegraph*) joined the uncommitted *Times* in backing Tory rebels against John Major's stance on a European single currency (Scammell and Harrop 1997, p. 156). This was not just a transferral of staunch partisanship from the Conservatives to Labour. Support for any party was altogether toned down and more qualified. As Deacon, Golding, and Billig (1997, p. 9) put it, "the 1997 election was marked by a more hollow-centred partisanship, where derision of the Conservatives only hesitantly translated into an endorsement of 'New Labour.'" Informed observers expect such relative detachment to persist in the future.

Television journalism also injected a more independent voice into the 1997 campaign than before, moving toward the more "mediated" style of U.S. election news (Hallin 1992). This development was particularly striking at the BBC, where hesitations about claiming any agenda-setting role for themselves had long prevailed among its news executives and reporters (Gurevitch and Blumler 1993). Much of its daily reporting of 1997 campaign events was produced from a large and highly professionalized base of political correspondents at Westminster who, instead of concentrating on relaying party messages, were encouraged to assume the role of "the voter's guide" to all that was going on. According to a BBC executive, "What a politician says is not what he means" in a world where publicity is fashioned to cultivate electoral perceptions. It followed that "you really need people who are aware of the nuances and of the forces at play behind the scenes to properly interpret what is being said and what the real truth of the matter is" (cited in Blumler and Gurevitch 1998, p. 184). Greater freedom from party agendas was also sought by drawing up a grid of twenty issues, based on survey data about concerns uppermost in British voters' minds, and instructing BBC news programs to ensure that their campaign coverage overall included reports on a goodly number of them. Moreover, specialist correspondents in BBC Social and Economic Affairs Units were encouraged to be more robust in their commentary than they had been in the past. This policy also stemmed from a pejorative view of present-day competitive electioneering – as trading in oversimplifications, discounting inconvenient facts, and neglecting longer-term problems for immediate advantage. Faced with such campaign rhetoric, it was thought that the specialist correspondent should aim to put politicians' claims in a more factually rounded context – "analysis-setting" (as a BBC editor termed it), "interpreting, in robust terms, whatever it is the politicians have said or done" (p. 187).

Such behind-the-scenes developments demonstrably affected the coverage in several ways. On many days stories derived from journalistic criteria dominated the campaign agendas – e.g., the issue of "sleaze," based on revelations about MPs having secretly accepted cash from special interests for putting their case in Parliament, and Conservative Party splits over Britain's relations with Europe. At times top journalists seemed to be appearing in election news more prominently than the campaigning politicians themselves. According to Harrison (1997, p. 145), who carried out a detailed content analysis, the television coverage was "heavily structured or 'framed' by journalists and experts," with the result that only 17 percent of bulletin time was devoted to what politicians had said. In addition, Goddard et al. (1998, p. 156) found that "the proportion of [television] coverage devoted to campaign conduct[5] increased substantially in 1997," having risen from 13 (in 1992) to 26 percent of the subjects of election stories in the BBC's *Nine O'Clock News* and from 24 to 30 percent in ITV's *News at Ten*. But they also report a decline in the proportion of opinion poll stories and coverage of "a broader range of substantive issues in the news agenda than in 1992" (p. 158). Despite some increased reliance on strategic scenarios, then, British election coverage is still far less saturated with the "horse-race" than is its U.S. counterpart.

The reticent reporting style of the past, however, was evidently displaced by a more judgemental one. This was a particularly dramatic departure from the tone of campaign journalism on British television in the 1980s. Semetko et al. (1991, p. 130) found that during the British campaign of 1983 approximately 65 percent of reporters' contextualizing remarks about campaign events in the main evening news were predominantly descriptive (compared with 27 percent in U.S. network news coverage of the 1984 presidential campaign). According to comparable figures compiled by Goddard et al. (1998), the proportion of straight contextualizing accounts of politicians' activities by British television news reporters had fallen to 56 percent in the 1992 campaign and to as low as 30 percent in 1997.[6] A tendency to bad-mouth both the campaign and its coverage (reminiscent of trends documented by Patterson 1993, in U.S. election reporting) was also noticeable in all British media. As Scammell and Harrop (1997, p. 180) sum up, much of the press complained that the 1997 campaign was "too long, tedious, negative and sour."

What Americanization Cannot Explain

But those three trends, however marked and influential, tell only part of the story of political communication development in Britain since the 1980s. At least five characteristics of the present U.K. system fall outside the Americanization thesis:

1. Campain finance: The one abiding systemic difference that marks off British from U.S. election communication as sharply as ever.
2. Media commercialization with implications for political coverage: There has been some U.K. movement in the U.S. direction, but since the U.S. system has also proceeded *further* down the same path, there is still a considerable distance between them.
3. Volume of coverage: In amount of attention paid to the 1990s campaigns reviewed here, the gulf between U.S. and British coverage was even greater than in the 1980s.
4. New-found populism.
5. Mainstream journalism: Innovations operative in both countries' recent elections are so different in style and consequence as to constitute two new grounds (items 4 and 5 here) of Anglo-American difference not envisaged in the 1980s.

CAMPAIGN FINANCE. One U.K.–U.S. contrast of critical importance that obtained in the 1980s holds true today. *Whereas political com-*

mercials are leading and formative vehicles of the U.S. campaign, paid political advertising is not permitted on British television and radio – neither during nor outside election periods. Instead, free access is rationed by a formula that takes account of the competing parties' past levels of support, in the form of mainly 5-minute party broadcasts up to a maximum of five for any single party during the campaign. The British system thus includes both a principled basis for the allocation of such access and a tight limit on its overall amount.

Even though the style and production qualities of British party broadcasts have increasingly resembled commercial advertising in recent years, four important advantages flow from the ban on political commercials. First, it helps to check rising levels of campaign costs. This is not to imply that money does not talk at all in British campaigns, expenditures on which have increased substantially at each successive postwar election. In media terms, spending tends to be poured into newspaper advertising and billboards (though less on the former in 1997 than in 1992). Nevertheless, the fact that air time cannot be bought sets something of a brake against the wildly escalating campaign costs witnessed in the United States in recent decades. Second, a regime of rationed access is more fair to smaller parties, few of which can afford to mount significant advertising campaigns. Third, Britain is spared the full flood of emotive imagery, negativity, and distortion of the opposition, to which a campaign dominated by short political ads is prone. Finally, the British system ensures that the heart of competitive campaign communication is not lodged within the party broadcasts but in the broadcasters' news and discussion vehicles. In the United States, by contrast, candidates' ads have even come to dominate the news through stories focusing on their dramatic or controversial features and their likely strategic effects (Jamieson 1993).

MEDIA COMMERCIALIZATION. A second basis of distinction arises from the vulnerability of political communication to the increasing salience throughout the developed world of economic and market/commercial factors in the structure and operations of the mass media at a time of increased competition for audiences. *Here the resulting pressures appear to have developed more severely from the 1980s to the 1990s in the United States than in Britain, despite the fact that the bulk of the former's media system was privately owned and advertising-supported from the outset.*

In U.S. television, then, whereas the terrestrial networks enjoyed total viewing shares of 80 percent or more in the early 1980s, today they struggle to win half the audience. News departments in television and the press have suffered diminished autonomy, insistence that they earn their keep financially, and the demolition of firewalls shielding them from advertising departments. In consequence, they are increasingly required "to cover politics only in the ways and to the extent that it is good business to do so" (Swanson 1997, p. 1269). It is not just the amount of attention to politics that is affected. Also favored are "a style of coverage that is driven by entertainment values and a desire not to be left behind by the tabloids in attracting the mass audience" (p. 1269); breakdown of the divide between the public and private lives of political leaders; more emphasis on "scandal" (Lull and Hinerman 1997); and downward pressure on conventional journalistic standards (speculation portrayed as news, unconfirmed information as fact, rumors as evidence, as well as printing of under-sourced stories – cf. Ricchiardi 1998).

Although Britain's mass-circulation newspapers have lavishly, even proudly, displayed all the features just described of tabloid journalism for many years, its television services have not been significantly invaded or transformed by them. Three of its five terrestrial channels (BBC-1, BBC-2, and Channel 4) are constitutionally bound to public service, and advertising-supported ITV is under a closely monitored and regulated obligation to provide large amounts of high-quality news and current affairs. Despite some increase in multichannel competition and active efforts to adapt traditional public service values to modern audiences' tastes and interests, fewer than a third of British households subscribe to cable or satellite television, and the main terrestrial channels' total viewing share remains high at over 85 percent. This is not to deny that many programming changes have been introduced in recent years. *Oprah Winfrey*-type talk shows now litter the daytime schedules (but mainly steer clear of politics). Slice-of-life documentaries have displaced the more analytical brand. Magazine programs are more brisk, arts programs have been pushed out of prime time, and soap operas have become sexier. But traditional journalistic standards still prevail in Britain's television news, including concerns to do substantive justice to the main social and political issues of the day.

VOLUME OF COVERAGE. Non-Americanization also applies to the sheer amount of campaign coverage provided by the two networks' television news services. In the 1980s, BBC and ITV coverage of British elections was far more extensive than U.S. network reporting of presidential races.[7] But although in the mid-1990s British coverage was still of flood proportions, in the United States it had reduced to a trickle!

It is true that British media performance in this respect was somewhat more differentiated than in the past. Four of the five national tabloid papers (excepting the *Mirror*) showed markedly less interest in the 1997 than the 1992 campaign – with a two-fifths drop in front-page lead stories about the election and fewer editorials about it. In the more serious broadsheet press, front-page coverage in 1997 differed little from 1992, though (except for the *Financial Times*) frequency of editorial commentary was down in most of these papers as well (Scammell and Harrop 1997, p. 165). In the mainstream television news bulletins, however, campaign coverage was as massively swamping as ever. To make room for this, 20 minutes were added to the usual length of the BBC *Nine O'Clock News* (from 30 to 50 minutes), two-thirds of the total time of which was taken up by campaign stories (Harrison 1997, p. 134). Although, as in 1992, ITV's *News at Ten* was not extended beyond its usual 30-minute length, 57 percent of its time was devoted to the election (p. 134). These figures differ little from the heavy profiles of coverage of the 1992 election and those of the 1980s in British television news.

By contrast, most available figures suggest that the U.S. networks almost closed up civic shop altogether during the 1996 campaign. Tyndall (1996, p. 4) calculated that network coverage of the primary elections "was down 43 percent compared with 1992 and down a whopping 51 percent compared with 1988." Appreciably less time was also devoted to the Democratic and Republican nominating conventions. And according to Media Monitor (1997), coverage of the Clinton–Dole general election race fell about 40 percent from the already low levels of 1992. In this respect, then, it was not British television but the U.S. networks that were Americanizing in the mid-1990s!

Whether heavy coverage of Britain's 1997 election was the last gasp of a glorious tradition is unclear. More question marks were raised about its appropriateness in 1997 than previously, sharpened by (1) an unprecedented 27 percent campaign-period drop in the audience for the BBC's *Nine O'Clock News* and (2) initiation immediately after the 1997 election of a BBC News and Current Affairs Programme Strategy Review, centering on extensive survey and focus group research into viewers' attitudes. Findings from the latter appear mixed, including evidence both of audience dislike of over-the-top coverage of big events and expectations that the BBC should offer a more serious and authoritative news service than its competitors (BBC News 1998). The implications for its coverage of the next British election could depend on how the balance is struck between these different demands.

NEW-FOUND POPULISM. A fourth area of contrast emerges from another trend noticeable in the campaign and political programming of many national broadcasting systems. Arising from a combination of background factors – the advance of consumerist individualism, plummeting regard for authority figures of all kinds including politicians, and intensified competition for audiences – currents of antielitist populism and attempts to inject popular voices into the coverage have surfaced in the 1990s campaigns of both the United States and Britain. The aims, forms, styles, and relationships to mainstream journalism of these efforts, however, appear to be quite different in the two systems.

"Talk-show democracy" emerged in the United States as something of a political force in the 1992 presidential election with widely publicized candidate appearances in shows with high-profile hosts (e.g., Larry King, Phil Donahue, Oprah Winfrey, and Arsenio Hall) that otherwise often relied on sensational subject matter to attract viewers. Most of the presenters were not professional journalists, and the popular element, introduced through phone-ins and studio participation, was often encouraged to be raw, emotional, combative, and unbuttoned. Such qualities were even more evident in certain radio talk shows with opinionated (mostly right-wing) hosts like Rush Limbaugh. Because politics is not the *raison d'etre* of many of these shows, we observed a few years ago that this genre is "not a *dependable* source of civic communication." When politics was hot, its vehicles would "readily move into the civic arena." But they would "just as readily depart the scene as soon as some more sensational focus beckon[ed]" in the worlds of crime, sports, or entertainment (Blumler and Gurevitch 1995, p. 219). Of course, that warning was borne out by the much less active and prominent role that these shows played in the 1996 campaign (Swanson 1997, p. 1265).

In Britain, the 1997 General Election campaign also precipitated a host of attempts to promote dialogue between voters and politicians in the schedules of all the television and radio services. This thrust embraced a wide range of formats, subject matter, and casts of participants. It included conventional phone-ins, studio panels confronting party representatives, and larger studio audiences putting questions to politicians through a moderator. Sometimes a several-sided exchange was organized, including not only voters, politicians, and experts, but also officials and professionals involved in dealing with the problems at issue.

All this added up to a systemic departure from the classic paternalism of British political programming. Unlike the United States, however, where the main vehicles of talk-show democracy had sprung up outside and even in opposition to the mainstream journalistic establishment (and were accordingly labeled "new news" at times), in Britain the new forms arose within and were adapted to the norms and procedures of public service television. Most of the hosts were also experienced political interviewers. Their aims were therefore different – more principled (to bring the citizen back into the picture and to refresh a political discussion that had become stale and predictable) than pragmatic (to build large audiences and advertising earnings in syndication, as in the United States). Most noticeably as a source of transatlantic contrast, even these "populist" programs were absorbed into the framework of rationalistic civic discourse long characteristic of other forms of political discussion on British television. The producers' objective was to generate more light than heat and to recruit people who could take part in relatively serious and policy-relevant discussions with politicians and other informed guests. As a BBC producer told us, the aim was not to produce "a free-for-all or anything like that." And as another explained:

> The BBC's Producer Guidelines are antitabloid. We wouldn't seek out such emotionalism though we wouldn't stamp it out if it surfaced. But we want to have as much of the discussion as possible focused on the platforms on which these people are standing.[8]

MAINSTREAM JOURNALISM IN THE SADDLE OR ON THE SLIDE? The U.S. system also seems to be moving away from the British one in a related respect. According to Swanson (1997, p. 1274), due to the popularity of alternative media, the shrinking audience for network news, and the advance (admittedly still limited) of the Internet, "the proportion of time and space for information and opinions concerning a presidential campaign that are broadcast and printed, which is controlled by traditional journalists, is steadily declining." As of 1997 at least, no such tendency was evident in the United Kingdom. Public attitudes to BBC and ITV news were still broadly positive, and there was no evidence that those viewers who were watching somewhat less television news than in the past were turning to any *other* source of political information. And according to Ward and Gibson (1998, p. 93), the reach and impact of the Internet on voter choice in the 1997 election "was minimal." In the United Kingdom, then, mainstream journalism still ruled the campaign coverage roost.

Thus, British campaign communication appeared remarkably hybridized in 1997. Despite its impregnation with certain U.S.-style approaches, it had not been completely remodeled along U.S. lines. As in the United States, Britain's party and media communicators faced a less engaged electorate. The struggle between them for agenda control had intensified, party news-making efforts were professionalized to the *n*th degree, and negative campaigning featured more centrally among them. A greater part of the campaign message was also in the hands of more detached and sometimes sceptical journalists, who no longer hesitated to criticize the parties' campaign contributions on both a daily basis and as a less than savory process overall. Had the seeds of a "spiral of delegitimation" (Capella and Jamieson 1996) been planted thereby in British electoral soil? It is not entirely fanciful to link these trends with the fact that the 1997 turnout of 71.3 percent was the lowest since 1935, despite the presence of elements that should have boosted it, such as the extraordinary popularity of Labour leader Tony Blair and the strong determination of many voters to kick out the Tory government.

Nevertheless, the British campaign was still vastly different from how the presidential contest had been presented a year earlier in the United States. Political advertising played only a limited part and did not litter the screens. Campaign coverage was far heavier, especially on television, where it featured in a wealth of diverse formats – party broadcasts, extended news, specialist analysis, numerous interviews, phone-ins, and discussion programs with a wider range of participants than ever before including ordinary voters. It was also predominantly substantive and issue-based, suffused neither with horse-race scenarios nor entertainment values. Even many of the populist elements that were introduced into campaign programming for the first time were accommodated to traditional norms of serious discussion. On the whole, then, Britain's approach to its 1997 campaign was still largely sheltered from those building commercial and competitive pressures that were so much more rampant in the U.S. system.

REVISITING THE FRAMEWORK FOR
COMPARATIVE ANALYSIS

How does our 1980s framework look in light of the above comparisons of U.S. and U.K. campaign communications in the 1990s? In our view, it remains valid but should probably be expanded by inclusion of a few extra variables. Work will be needed, however, on their definition and possible implications.

The abiding comparative utility of the five key dimensions of our original scheme can be demonstrated by reverting to the theme of Americanization. The evidence presented in the preceding section suggests that although the British political communication system has moved *closer* to the American model along three of them:

The position of politics in society,
Journalists' sacerdotal vs. pragmatic orientations to politics, and
The degree of professionalization of campaigning,

the American system has moved *away* from the British pattern along two of them:

Variations of media competition and
Public service versus the commercial organization of the media.

To put it differently, whereas these five dimensions worked well to structure *spatial* comparative analysis in the 1980s research, they have now proved their worth in a *temporal* comparative analysis of many of the complex changes that have reshaped mediated politics in two different societies between the mid-1980s and mid-1990s.

The temporal analysis also highlights points of further interest about two of these systemic dimensions.

First, the suggestion put forward by Semetko et al. (1991) that an increased professionalization of campaigning might encourage journalists to intervene more actively with their own constructions and assessments is strongly supported by the British evidence. Less reluctance to be involved in agenda setting, a more prominent role for senior political correspondents, and more robust commentary from other specialist journalists – all were justified by BBC personnel as essential for guiding viewers through a trickier rhetorical world in which what is said is not necessarily what you get.

Second, the stance of British journalists on the dimension of "newspeople's orientations to politics and politicians" had become more complex by 1997. Sacerdotalism was conspicuously absent from their approach to political institutions, parties, and the political establishment generally. Perhaps in these more sceptical and cynical times, journalists everywhere are more or less alike in this respect – predominantly "pragmatic" with only an occasional sacerdotal twinge! At this level, such pragmatism may be more a transnational constant than a variable nowadays. Nevertheless, the commitment of Britain's public service broadcasters to the task of informing the electorate seemed as strong as ever during the 1997 campaign. They approached the election – even when they predominantly perceived it as being waged by competing teams of sophisticated and artful spinmeisters – as if it deserved more attention than news values alone would justify, i.e., sacerdotally.

But the 1990s analysis has also brought to the fore a few tendencies not anticipated by the 1980s framework. Most important among them was the upsurge in the appearance of ordinary people in the campaign programming of both societies – as reminders of problems on the ground, witnesses to the impact of proposed policies, challengers of politicians' platitudes, voices of concerned down-to-earth opinion, and carriers of dialogue. Can a systemic variable be conceived that would explain cross-national differences (as well as trends over time) in the amount and form of such material? It is intriguing to realize in this connection how much past theorizing about political communication systems has concentrated on political and media institutions and their relative closeness (as in exchange theory) or distance (as in adversarial perspectives) to the neglect of relations between those communication sources and the electoral audiences they address.

If another variable of systemic scope needs to be factored in here, it may belong in the realm of political culture. Thus, political cultures could be said to vary (and to change over time) in *the degree to which they embrace or resist populism – or the principle of vox populi, vox dei*. That principle might be defined as stressing the inherent value of popular experience and belief and the inherent desirability of consulting mass opinion and satisfying mass demand. It should be expected, then, that media operating in more populist cultures would take more pains to include expressions of the popular voice in their political contents and would tend to present that voice on its own terms – less mitigated or contextualized by elite perspectives. Contrariwise, media operating in less populist cultures would tend to marginalize that voice and be more paternalistic in subject matter, format, and style.

Also worth considering when revising comparative political communication theory is Swanson's (1997) idea that the proportion of messages reaching the U.S. electorate from nonjournalistic sources (e.g, talk shows and the Internet) is increasing. If a systemic variable to take account of this should be fashioned, it might be defined as: *the degree of control of political communication by the mainstream journalistic establishment.* At present, this seems to single out the United States from all other democracies, where such bypassing of conventional journalism is still in its infancy. But that might change, and one could hypothesize a multiplication and fragmentation of political agendas, and a broadening of the range of ideas and groups that gain access to the media, in societies where mainstream journalism is less dominant.

Finally, it may be asked whether we have been guilty in some of our comparative scholarship of a naive universalism of Anglo-American proportions! We often write as if the chain of weakening party systems, increased electoral volatility, and increased dependence of politicians and voters on the mass media, which has emerged so prominently in the United States and Britain, was equally developed throughout the democratic world. Yet that may not be so. For example, political scientists have found differing rates of electoral volatility across a range of up to nineteen surveyed European polities (Anderson 1998). The level of such volatility probably depends in turn on the articulation of party systems to large blocs of people with shared experiences, social situations, identities, and attitudes. This suggests that to get at the ultimate sources of media centrality in (or subordination to) politics, cross-national analyses should aim to probe deeper relationships between social structures and political systems. And a system variable to capture this might be defined in terms of: the strength of the linkage of party systems to longstanding sociostructural (e.g., class), sociocultural (e.g., ethnic or religious), or other demographic (e.g., urban vs rural) cleavages. Weaker linkages of this kind might then be hypothesized to favor increased electoral volatility, increased media intervention in politics, and greater adaptation to such intervention, including pressures on politicians to professionalize their campaign communication and news management activities. And such professionalization might be particularly developed in Anglo-American countries because the dissolution of traditional societywide cleavages with ties to the major parties started earlier in them.

CONCLUSION

From the results of this analysis at least two reasons have emerged for avoiding glib uses of the notion of Americanization to explain swirling developments in campaign communication in other societies.

First, it conveys a false impression of an unchanging U.S. system, to which the rest of the democratic world is inexorably adapting. This simplistically ignores certain dimensions along which U.S. political communication may itself be evolving, opening up new or bigger differences from prevailing practices elsewhere. Hence, our temporal comparison of the British and U.S. systems from the 1980s into the 1990s has highlighted both converging *and* diverging trends.

Second, although "Americanization" can manifest itself in different forms, the concept offers an incomplete if not superficial impression of the underlying *sources* of change in political communication arrangements. It can imply direct *imitation* of American styles and practices; it can be based on a selective *importation and adoption* of such practices; or it can involve *adaptation* of American practices to an existing set of practices, assimilating new modes of operation into older ones. But what all this omits is the role of *indigenous conditions* both in sustaining unique features of national systems and in precipitating changes in such systems. For volume and substantiveness of election coverage, for example, and the role of advertising in campaigning, the U.S. and British systems were still poles apart in the mid-1990s. Even those developments that brought the British system closer to the U.S. model than in the past, such as party publicity professionalization, are best understood as responses to the weakening allegiance of *British* voters to the major parties, thereby accelerating electoral volatility and increasing the importance of campaign planning and news management.

This is not to deny that British party strategists have openly sought campaign lessons from the United States. But even this should be regarded as part of a two-way flow of Anglo-American influence. Thus, before and during recent national elections in both countries, campaign experts of the British Labour Party and the Clinton team observed each other in action and shared their tactical expertise with each other. It probably seemed to both sides to make good sense politically as well as being a mutual learning experience. And when they borrowed specific techniques and practices, it is doubtful whether they regarded these as instances of "Americanization" or "Britishization." Such labeling is rather the prerogative of media pundits and academics!

But the processes discussed here are probably still in their infancy. Their future direction may depend on the emergence in other societies of the social, political, economic, and cultural preconditions that have constituted the ground on which the American way of political campaigning has developed to its present form. Thus, we should keep our conceptual and empirical eyes open and watch closely for future trends. For this reason, comparative work, as we argued some time ago (Gurevitch and Blumler 1990), will remain a promising and extending frontier for political communication scholars in the foreseeable future.

NOTES

1. The following possible influences were mentioned: the greater openness of the American political system, the higher visibility of links between U.S. politicians and money, and the more pragmatic, nonideological character of American politics.
2. According to Brants (1998, p. 316), it tended to be deployed during the 1994 parliamentary election in the Netherlands as a *portmanteau* tag for any tendency the critics concerned deplored:
   [The] commentators . . . did not explain what the label exactly meant, but it was obviously no good and a violent contrast with the serious attitude with which they thought politics should be approached.
3. In late 1998, however, Mandelson and Whelan resigned their positions, due in part to intense and hostile media scrutiny of their alleged indiscretions.
4. See Blumler and Kavanagh (1999) for further discussion of the professionalization of the British parties' approaches to campaigning and news management.
5. This included stories about parties' campaign organization, strategy and tactics, advertising, and general campaign trail activity.
6. Based on recalculation of figures presented in Goddard et al. (1997, Table 11.5, p. 169).
7. According to Semetko et al. (1991, pp. 117–119), mainstream British television news carried an average of nine election stories per day in the 1983 campaign, compared with fewer than 3.5 stories per day in network news coverage of the 1984 election. This translated into 19 minutes per day on BBC news and 16 minutes per day in ITN news compared with 3, 4, and 5 minutes per day in the news of the three U.S. networks.
8. The above two paragraphs draw on Blumler and Gurevitch (1998, pp. 187–191).

REFERENCES

Anderson, C. J. (1998). "Parties, Party Systems, and Satisfaction with Democratic Performance in the New Europe." *Political Studies*, 46:572–588.

BBC News (1998). *BBC News: The Future – Public Service News in the Digital Age.* London: British Broadcasting Corporation.

Blumler, J. G., and M. Gurevitch (1975). "Towards a Comparative Framework for Political Communication Research." In S. Chaffee (Ed.), *Political Communication: Issues and Strategies for Research.* Beverly Hills and London: Sage, pp. 165–193.

——— (1995). *The Crisis of Public Communication.* London: Routledge.

——— (1998). "Change in the Air: Campaign Journalism at the BBC, 1997." In I. Crewe, B. Gosschalk, and J. Bartle (Eds.), *Political Communications: Why Labour Won the General Election of 1997.* London: Frank Cass, pp. 176–194.

Blumler, J. G., and D. Kavanagh (1999). "The Third Age of Political Communication: Influences and Features." *Political Communication,* 16:209–230.

Blumler, J. G., J. M. McLeod, and K. E. Rosengren (1992). "An Introduction to Comparative Communication Research." In J. G. Blumler, J. M. McLeod, and K. E. Rosengren (Eds.), *Comparatively Speaking: Communication and Culture Across Space and Time.* Newbury Park, London and New Delhi: Sage, pp. 3–18.

Brants, K. (1998). "Who's Afraid of Infotainment?" *European Journal of Communication,* 13:315–335.

Capella, J. N., and K. H. Jamieson (1996). "News Frames, Political Cynicism, and Media Cynicism." *The Annals of the American Academy of Political and Social Science,* 546:71–84.

Deacon, D., P. Golding, and M. Billig (1997). "Losing Face or Loss of Faith? The Defection of the Conservative Press in the 1997 British General Election." *The Bulletin of the European Institute for the Media,* 14:8–9.

Franklin, B. (1997). *Newszak and News Media.* London: Arnold.

Goddard, P., M. Scammell, and H. A. Semetko (1998). "Too Much of a Good Thing? Television in the 1997 Election Campaign." In I. Crewe, B. Gosschalk, and J. Bartle (Eds.), *Political Communications: Why Labour Won the General Election of 1997.* London: Frank Cass, pp. 149–175.

Gurevitch, M., and J. G. Blumler (1990). "Comparative Research: The Extending Frontier." In D. L. Swanson and D. Nimmo (Eds.), *New Directions in Political Communication: A Resource Book.* Newbury Park, London and New Delhi: Sage, pp. 305–325.

——— (1993). "Longitudinal Analysis of an Election Communication System: Newsroom Observation at the BBC 1996–1992." *Osterreichische Zeitschrift fur Politikwissenschaft,* 22:427–444.

Hallin, D. C. (1992). "The Passing of the 'High Modernism' of American Journalism." *Journal of Communication,* 42(3):14–25.

Harrison, M. (1997). "Politics on the air." In D. Butler and D. Kavanagh (Eds.), *The British General Election of 1997.* Houndmills, England: Macmillan, pp. 133–155.

Jamieson, K. H. (1993). *Dirty Politics: Deception, Distraction and Democracy.* New York and Oxford: Oxford University Press.

Lull, J., and S. Hinerman (Eds.) (1997). *Media Scandals: Morality and Desire in the Popular Cultural Marketplace.* Cambridge, England: Polity Press.

Media Monitor (1997). "1996 Year in Review: TV's Leading News Topics, Reporters, and Political Jokes." *Media Monitor,* Volume XI, Number 1 (March/April): 1.

Mountfield, R. (1997). *Report of the Working Group on the Government Information Service.* London: Office of Public Service.

Negrine, R., and S. Papathanassopoulos (1996). "The 'Americanization' of Political Communication." *Press/Politics*, 1(2):62.

Patterson, T. E. (1993). *Out of Order.* New York: Alfred A. Knopf.

Ricchiardi, S. (1998). "Standards Are First Casualty." *American Journalism Review*, 20(2):30–35.

Scammell, M. (1998). "The Wisdom of the War Room: U.S. Campaigning and Americanization." *Media, Culture and Society*, 20:251–275.

and M. Harrop (1997). "The Press." In D. Butler and D. Kavanagh (Eds.), *The British General Election of 1997.* Houndmills, England: Macmillan, pp. 156–185.

Semetko, H. A., J. G. Blumler, M. Gurevitch, and D. H. Weaver (1991). *The Formation of Campaign Agendas: A Comparative Analysis of Party and Media Roles in Recent American and British Elections.* Hillsdale, N. J.: Erlbaum.

Smith, T. (1995). "Political Sleaze in Britain: Causes, Concerns and Cures." *Parliamentary Affairs*, 48:551–561.

Swanson, D. L. (1997). "The Political-Media Complex at 50: Putting the 1996 Presidential Campaign in Context." *American Behavioral Scientist*, 40:1264–1282.

and P. Mancini (1996). *Politics, Media and Modern Democracy: An International Study of Innovations in Electoral Campaigning and Their Consequences.* Westport, CT: Praeger.

Tyndall, A. (1996). "Why Network Campaign Coverage Is Down in '96." *The Media & Campaign Briefing* No. 3. New York: Media Studies Center, pp. 4–7.

Ward, S., and R. Gibson (1998). "The First Internet Election? UK Political Parties and Campaigning in Cyberspace." In I. Crewe, B. Gosschalk and J. Bartle (Eds.), *Political Communications: Why Labour Won the General Election of 1997.* London: Frank Cass, pp. 93–112.

PART 5

Citizens: Present and Future

Citizen Discourse and Political Participation: A Survey

Roderick P. Hart

There has been a chorus of concern recently about citizen politics in the United States. Etizioni (1993) and Bellah (1992) have sounded these themes, and Putnam (1995) has sharpened the point when arguing that watching television has absorbed energies that voters might otherwise have devoted to political matters. Other scholars argue that economic and historical upheavals (Nye et al. 1997), inadequate amounts of political information (Delli Carpini and Keeter 1996), onerous voter registration laws (Piven and Cloward 1988), and even the emergence of a "culture of cynicism" (Stivers 1994) have sapped people's political commitments.

Scholars in the present volume are also concerned with such matters. In Chap. 8, for example, Michael Delli Carpini and Bruce Williams worry that entertainment television may diminish the public's willingness to think about the world in genuinely political ways. In Chap. 15, Kathleen Jamieson examines how clandestine forms of issue advocacy are now capable of changing people's attitudes without their knowing it. In Chap. 7, Oscar Gandy details the dangers associated with excessive segmentation of the electorate, a condition that depletes what all Americans know in common and, hence, what they feel in common. Finally, In Chap. 17, Bruce Buchanan observes that many Americans now think of voting as their sole public duty, as if citizenship were a sporadic rather than a continuing obligation for them.

Most of these scholars are concerned with citizens' *failures* to be politically active. A more hopeful approach is to ask why some Americans choose the opposite course – to pay attention to politics and to argue and debate the issues of the day. That is my approach here. I report on a series of inquiries into the habits of an unusually concerned set of voters – those who write letters to the editors of their local papers.

My assumption is that by knowing these people we can better understand the reservoir of political concern that sustains them. The citizens described here are neither intellectuals nor activists. They live in small cities in the United States and have ordinary jobs, ordinary lives. But in their spare time they write letters about politics. I wanted to know why.

WHO PARTICIPATES?

Political involvement can include many things – voting, becoming informed about political choices, expressing opinions, working for a campaign, and maintaining system-sustaining attitudes. The most ambitious study yet undertaken of political involvement (Verba et al. 1995) touches on all these factors. Unwilling to restrict themselves to traditional definitions of involvement – turnout alone – Verba and his colleagues inquired into monetary donations, time volunteered, civic groups joined, etc. of their subjects. From this broadened perspective, they found a surprising amount of "civic voluntarism" in the United States. At the same time, they found that political participation increases with education (see also Conway et al. 1996; Nie et al. 1996), that African Americans are much less involved politically (but not civically) than their Anglo counterparts, and that socioeconomic advantage generally predicts political involvement. Other scholars have found that political optimism has dropped off considerably in recent years (Kazee and Shi 1996), while still others find that it also erodes across the lifespan (Luks 1996).

Some scholars have found that political involvement is both a product and a by-product. Having a high sense of political efficacy normally predicts involvement (Brehm and Rahn 1997), as does talking about public affairs in everyday social interaction (Kim et al. 1997). The reverse is also true: Political participation heightens voters' political efficacy (Finkel 1985) as does the calendrical nature of political campaigns (Rahn et al. 1997).

The impact of the mass media on political involvement is complicated. While some find that watching television decreases participation (Brehm and Rahn 1997), a recent study finds that it is the *type* of television watched that most affects civic engagement (Shah 1997). Perhaps the most stable finding in the area is that newspaper reading is strongly associated with political involvement. Studies using N.E.S. data found this to be true (Hetherington 1996), as have studies using *The Civic Culture* data (Bennett et al. 1996), *Times-Mirror* Center Data (Rhine et al. 1996), and a Wisconsin-based dataset (McLeod et al. 1997). With newspaper reading so strongly linked to participation, would not letter writers become a logical focus for an inquiry into the basics of political involvement? That is the logic pursued here.

WHO WRITES LETTERS?

Verba, Scholzman, and Brady (1997) ask a compelling question: If civic engagement is so "costly" from a rational actor perspective, why do people who do *not* profit directly become engaged anyway? Why don't they opt for a free ride, especially those who are best able (intellectually) to calculate the odds of being benefited? Verba et al. do not answer the questions they ask, but they do speculate that affect, not demographics, may best explain certain forms of civic engagement. Dillard and Backhaus (1997, p. 18) agree, arguing that emotion is "a mediating force between civic deliberation and political involvement." For some Americans, political involvement simply feels right. But why?

The former question, at least, is answerable: My studies show that people who write letters share deep commitments to the political enterprise. For many, however, such persons seem ersatz citizens – lonely, disaffected, apart-from-the-people. Buell (1975, p. 440) argues that letter writers have been ignored because they are considered "emotionally unstable, numerically insignificant, methodologically troublesome, and . . . theoretically uninteresting." Davis and Rarick (1964) report that writers are often considered persons of unwieldy temper and dramatically unrepresentative of their communities (a charge echoed by Grey and Brown 1970). Although Foster and Friedrich (1937) observed sixty years ago that letter writers have "thermometric value" for researchers, few have used them to take the nation's temperature.

That is unfortunate for two reasons. First, letter writers may reflect the public mood better than has been acknowledged to date. Studies by Roberts et al. (1969), Buell (1975), and Hill (1981), among others, show that letters can indeed provide an accurate gauge of popular sentiment. Second, letters to the editor represent the only (1) lay, (2) reflective, and (3) not-unrepresentative database about American politics still (4) extant. Even in an age of electronic surveillance, that is, most political conversations vanish as soon as they are held. The few shards of lay commentary that do survive on videotape or audio tape (as represented, say, in street-corner interviews on the nightly news) are often profoundly unrepresentative of the American mindset, chosen as they are to fit a particular reporter's story line. While poll results have great historical value, the questions and answers contained in them are usually restricted in scope. Moreover, because polling is always something of an intrusion into respondents' lives, they sometimes create citizens' agendas rather than tap agendas already organically present.

Letters to the editor are nothing if not organic. In preparing to write a political history of lay politics between 1945 and the present, I have collected some 7,000 letters from across the United States. Faithfully preserved in local libraries, these documents help explain not just what the American people believe but also how they have *reasoned* about civic life during the last fifty years. To better understand such persons, five separate studies were conducted: (1) two mailed surveys in 1993 and 1997 contrasted political letter writers to nonwriters in ten small American cities; (2) a separate survey in 1994 inquired into the media attitudes of citizens in these same communities; and (3) telephone interviews with the editors of the letters columns in these same ten cities were conducted in 1993 and again in 1997.[1]

The ten cities were chosen with care. Averaging about 88,000 residents apiece, each was (with one exception) what Verba and Nie (1972) would call "independent cities," cities removed from the major population centers in their home states. Otherwise, the cities were distinguished by little. They are ordinary cities that, in composite, roughly match the nation's ethnic and demographic profiles. As Table 19.1 shows, these cities also track national norms on several social and demographic variables and conform to the voting patterns for the 1992 and 1996 presidential elections.[2] Each of these cities has longstanding morning newspapers, most of which combined with their former, evening rivals many years ago, and all have active letters columns.

Differences from the national norm do exist, however. The cities tend to be older than the national norm (more long-term residents, fewer college graduates, shorter commuting times, more hospital admissions) and a bit poorer (lower median home value and effective buying income, slightly higher unemployment), and hence probably represent "urban" but not "urbane" values. Home-grown symphonies and ballet troupes were uncommon in these cities; if a given city contained a college or university, it tended to be a "branch" of a major university located elsewhere; no professional sports teams or major foundations or significant tourist attractions were located nearby. The cities reflected the more placid aspects of the American landscape.

Most important, the people in these cities subscribed heavily to their

Table 19.1. *Comparison of U.S. data to 10-city sample*

Relevant trait	U.S. mean	Sample mean
Population change (1950–1990)	+61.3	+25.7
1992 turnout (voters/capita)	40.70	42.70
% 65 years and older	11.90	13.80
% English-speaking only	79.80	82.50
% White	80.30	78.60
% Black	12.10	13.60
% Hispanic	9.20	8.90
% Asian	2.90	1.80
% native to state	61.80	61.30
% 10-year residents	55.10	61.30
% householders renting	28.80	41.80
# crimes/100,000 persons	5,242.00	6,954.00
Mean household income ($)	30,056.00	26,661.00
Median home value ($)	78,500.00	70,030.00
Retail sales/capita ($)	6,007.92	8,517.99
% 1990 unemployment	7.00	8.50
% college graduates	13.80	11.60
% newspaper subscribers	24.40	57.30
ADI television rank	106.10	105.30
% cable subscribers	51.10	60.50

Sources: 1990 Census of Population and Housing; County and City Data Book: 1988; 1993 Commercial Atlas and Marketing Guide; Moody's Municipal and Governmental Manual; 1950 Census of Population: Volume One; Television and Radio City Book: 1990–91; Television PVT Trends: Audience Estimates; Statistical Abstracts of the United States: 1992; Editor and Publisher Yearbook.

local newspapers and were thereby constantly exposed to the political opinions of their neighbors, or so we can infer from previous research. (1) One researcher estimates that as many as 10% of the American people will eventually set pen to paper (Pasternak and Kapoor 1980); another scholar estimates that two million such letters are written annually in the United States (Stotsky 1987). (2) There was a steady increase in letter writing between 1970 and 1990 (Kapoor and Botan 1992), with my ten-city sample also showing a 100 percent increase between 1950 and 1990. (3) Virtually all daily newspapers run letters columns (Hynds and Martin 1979), and most editors report increasing pressure to expand the sizes of letters columns (Hynds 1991; Kapoor and Botan 1989); notably, editors appear to use little ideological bias when selecting letters for publication (Renfro 1979). (4) Editors report that letters are probably the best-read feature of the editorial page (Hynds 1976). (5) Front-page content and the content of letters to the editor match rather well, suggesting that each has a tendency to become a response to the other's stimulus (Pritchard and Berkowitz 1991).

Letter writing is a special sort of political involvement. It represents more commitment to politics than most citizens express and yet it is also quiescent (no door-to-door canvassing, no late-night meetings). As such, it represents a kind of middle ground of political involvement, a space requiring political energy but a space that is neither tangible nor injunctive. Letter writers seem to stand somewhere between the ordinary voter and the impassioned political actor.

SURVEY METHODS

Data were gathered from these cities on multiple occasions. In July 1993 and again in 1997, the editors of the letters columns were contacted by phone and asked a series of brief questions. In addition, four samples of local residents were drawn (two in 1993 and two in 1997), half of whom had written a letter to the editor about politics during the previous eighteen months and half of whom had not. This latter half was drawn randomly from local phone books, with gender being the only variable stratified (to ensure an equal number of women listed individually and listed married).

Identical surveys were sent to 130 writers in 1993 and 175 additional writers in 1997; 570 nonwriters were sampled in 1993 and 350 in 1997. Each potential respondent received an individually addressed envelope; no incentive for completing the questionnaire was offered other than a summary of survey results at study's end. When unreachable residents were subtracted from these totals, and after a single reminder postcard was issued, 183 writers and 418 nonwriters responded to the survey across the two administrations of the questionnaire, representing usable response rates of 60% and 45.4%, respectively, figures that are comfortable for a no-incentive, mailed survey (see Fox et al. 1988 for a meta-analysis of response rates).

The surveys were short (forty questions in all) and simple (three- and five-choice Likert responses). In addition to the usual demographic questions, the respondents were asked to estimate their attentiveness to Campaign 92/96, to evaluate media performance during the campaigns, and to report their political efficacy (both internal and external) and political trust (question wording for these two items was adapted from Newhagen 1993).

In spring 1994 a third survey of similar length was issued to 500 persons from these same ten communities using procedures similar to those just described.[3] This survey was framed as an inquiry into respondents' overall media habits and preferences, although its specific purpose was to discover their attitudes toward letter writers. Respondents' programming preferences were ascertained for television and radio as were their newspaper-reading habits. Their attitudes toward letter writers were collected via seven independent questions (e.g., "writers prefer sounding-off to being constructive," "the writers' views are fairly similar to people I know"), but were preceded by a series of probes about media personalities and programming in order to mask the exact purpose of the study. Nine demographic questions rounded out the survey.[4]

All five surveys were designed to better understand a unique kind of political activity. My reasoning was that people who send letters to small-city newspapers are less jaundiced than those writing to the national weeklies and yet still concerned with politics. They live in vibrant, if unsophisticated, places and experience the normal exigencies of modern life. But unlike their fellow citizens, the writers *reflect* on the problems facing their communities. It was this sort of political energy the surveys were designed to tap.

The data to be reported here are largely descriptive. Tests of statistical difference were run when appropriate (largely *t*-tests, ANOVAs, and chi-squares) and some factor-analytic work will be reported, but no elaborate regression modeling is attempted, given the convenience samples used and the paucity of theory in the area.

SURVEY OF EDITORS

Because interviewing an editorial staff by phone is a hurried and impressionistic task, two surveys conducted over four years were completed. The results were consistent across time and geography. The twenty interviews were brief and focused on utilitarian matters: the editors' tenure on the job, submission and acceptance rates, most common topics addressed in the letters, reasons for rejection, extensiveness of editing, change in submission rates over the last ten years, and the effect of political elections on submission rates. Table 19.2 reports some of the findings.

Table 19.2. *Survey of editors*

Question	1993	1997	Yearly avg.	Overall %
Editorial tenure (in years)	5.5	6.2	5.85	—
Letters received per annum (estimate)	2,034	1,958	1,996	—
% letters accepted (estimate)	85.0	93.0	89.2	—
Letters increase during last 10 years?	80% yes	60% yes	—	70% yes
Letters increase during election years?	80% yes	100% yes	—	90% yes
Letters represent local viewpoints?				
Yes	20%	30%	—	25%
Unsure	30%	10%	—	20%
No	50%	60%	—	55%
Most popular topics (# mentions)				
Local politics	8	9	8.5	25.8
National politics	11	4	7.5	22.7
Religion and morality	4	4	4.0	12.1
Abortion	4	3	3.5	10.6
Environment	4	0	2.0	6.0
Social services/education	3	5	4.0	12.1
Crime/gun control	4	1	2.5	7.6
Reasons for rejecting letters				
Too long	2	4	3	13.6
Form letter	1	5	3	13.6
Not local	1	3	2	9.1
Anonymous	6	2	4	18.2
Obscene/libelous	8	8	8	36.4
Concerns too idiosyncratic	2	2	2	9.1

n = 20.
Source: Author's original research.

While gate-keeping pressures and heavy editing are common in larger newspapers, that was not true in my sample. The editors published about 90% of the letters received, thereby ensuring that the political opinions swirling about in their communities were regularly heard. The editors also reported that submission rates were on an upward spiral and that they were under constant pressure to print more letters. They received an average of forty submissions a week, so each day's letters columns contained between five and eight letters. As expected, elections elicited more letters, although, since elections are constantly held in most cities, the uptick is substantial only during presidential elections. Not surprisingly, the most popular topics were those on the national agenda: taxes, abortion, gun control, education, medical care, etc. Some regional variations were noted (environmental issues in the Northwest, riverboat gambling in the Midwest), but there was considerable topical unity among the ten newspapers.

There were, however, differences in the ratio of submitted letters to local population. The most vigorous cities included a state capital in the Northeast and a rapidly growing city in the sunbelt. The tamest communities included a mill town in New England, a river city in the Midwest experiencing economic distress, and a college town in the inner-mountain West where town-and-gown live in harmony. The four remaining cities moderated the extremes.[5]

Editing the letters column was a long-time duty for four of the editors, with the rest having served from two months to five years. Most of the editors saw their job as keeping an eye out for libel (and correct spelling), but generally let the letters retain their natural color. Because the letters were so colorful, few of the editors thought their correspondents representative of their localities. As one editor observed, letter writers are "highly motivated people with a strong political viewpoint and so the 'silent majority' is not normally represented" in the columns. Another editor claimed that the writers are "the same people who call radio talk shows" (a falsity, as it turns out). This element of distortion could be found in one northeastern city where the editor reported receiving more prolife letters than one would expect for a prochoice city, and in a California farm community that produced precious few Latino letters.

Other editors had different experiences. Some said that the letters columns were "a community service" that naturally "drew from both sides," while others claimed that "there's really no way to determine representativeness," the letters being so diverse and the editors themselves not being practicing sociologists. "We receive very few complaints," argued one editor, implying that the writers were not regarded as aliens by their fellow citizens.

One myth about letter writers can be dispelled – that they are *chronics*, persons who churn out letters by the dozens. There was little repeat publication in the papers sampled here. Between March and December 1992, for example, a total of 1,100 (political) letters was published in the ten newspapers sampled and they were authored by 991 different individuals. Seventy-three persons wrote two letters during that time and fourteen wrote three or more, attesting either to the natural forbearance of the citizenry or to the wisdom of the editors. The latter explanation seems unlikely since, as stated above, the newspapers published what they received.

If the writers are not chronics, might they not be *cranks*, persons from the lunatic fringe who meddle ceaselessly in community affairs? The editors did not speak in one voice on this matter, so perhaps the writers themselves can help answer the question. Before asking them to do so, however, let us examine how they were regarded by their fellow citizens.

SURVEY OF READERS

Given the modest sample size of the reader survey ($n = 164$), one must be careful not to overstate the findings. In general, though, the readers were just as equivocal about the writers as were the editors. Does such equivocality suggest that the writers are more "representative" of their communities than some observers suspect? It might indeed.

Citizens from all ten cities appeared equally often in the sample. They averaged 47.8 years of age, were mostly married (78.7%), and were fairly well educated (40 percent had gone to college). They were overwhelmingly white (93.1%), had lived in the locality for an average of thirty years, and had a family income of $45,000 per year. An equal number of men and women composed the sample and their political affiliations matched the 1992 national vote totals (43.9% Democratic, 30.6% Republican, 19.1% Independent, 6.4% Other). Just under 20% of the sample was retired, with the remainder split between blue-collar and white-collar workers.

Clearly, there are underrepresentations here (particularly with regard to race) and overrepresentations as well (80% of the respondents watched the local news and 67%, the national news each day, higher than the national norm), but the sample seems a fair one when compared to census data for *voters* in the ten communities. Significantly, 75% of the respondents subscribed to the local newspaper, and half of them read it from front to back.

To make sense of the data, four collateral measures were developed from the attitudinal questions asked:

1. *Writer Appreciation* – the sum of the positively phrased questions (the writers are "better educated than most people," they "want to help the community," their views "are fairly similar to my own" and "fairly similar to people I know"), minus the

negatively phrased questions ("they prefer sounding-off to being constructive" and "they seem pretty egotistical to me"), plus a constant.

2. *Political Awareness* – a ten-part measure of respondents' attentiveness to local and national news (television, radio, and print), their interest in political call-in shows, and their reading of editorial columns, multiplied by the thoroughness with which they read the local newspaper (5 = high, 1 = low).

3. *Television Receptivity* – a broad measure of ten TV-viewing habits, including viewership of network morning programs, sports, drama, situation comedies, documentaries, etc., all of which was multiplied by the number of hours of television watched each day.[6]

4. *Media Disapproval* – a summation of the respondents' negative attitudes toward the mass media (e.g., "the people who call in to talk radio seem pretty unstable to me," "today's TV programs undermine the morals of the American people," etc.), minus their positive attitudes ("the publishers of my local newspaper are concerned about the community," "TV newscasters seem genuinely concerned about the American people," etc.), plus a constant.

Many of the findings conform to common sense and previous research: the older a respondent is, the higher their political awareness ($r = 0.411$), but the lower their education ($r = -0.303$) and salary ($r = -0.216$). For the most part, men did not differ from women on the composite variables, although men were slightly more disapproving of the mass media ($t = 1.945$, $p < 0.05$). Democrats reported watching a bit more television than Republicans or independents (F [3, 151] = 2.739; $p < 0.045$); longevity in a community (irrespective of absolute age) tended to heighten political awareness ($r = 0.276$); but income was unrelated to political awareness (perhaps because age was a mitigating factor). In addition, both Republicans and independents expressed slightly more media disapproval than Democrats (F [3, 157] = 2.770, $p < 0.044$), perhaps because they watched television less often. In addition, married individuals were less enamored of the mass media than were singles ($t = 6.481$, $p < 0.012$), retired individuals were more politically aware (F [2, 153] = 5.832, $p < 0.004$) than those still working, and blue collar workers watched more television than white-collar workers or the retired (F [2, 153] = 4.179, $p < 0.017$). Clearly, none of these effects is large, but they do conform to what is known about the sociology of the

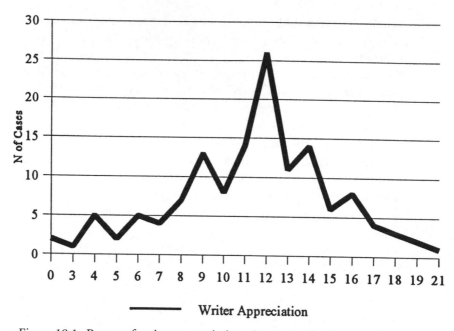

Figure 19.1. Range of writer appreciation. *Source:* Author's research.

mass media, and they set the stage for the disparate attitudes toward letter writers found in the study.

Figure 19.1 shows that writer appreciation is normally distributed in the population sampled. This is an important finding and it flies in the face of the stereotypes: The respondents did *not*, in fact, harbor monolithic attitudes toward letter writers. No doubt, some of them felt that political letter writers were beyond the pale but most did not or, more precisely, most felt a great many things about the writers. Table 19.3 shows what they felt.

On the positive side, writers were thought to have a helpful attitude toward the community and to be more like the norm than different from it. But the writers were not considered better educated than most nor were they thought to be especially constructive. On the remaining items there was less consensus: The respondents could not agree on how biased the writers were or whether they were motivated by ego or something else. Interestingly, the respondents felt that the writers resembled their friends and neighbors but not themselves (a displacement effect?).

Generally, then, there were no general feelings about the writers.[7] The parsimonious explanation for writer appreciation is that there is no

Table 19.3. *Respondents' attitudes toward writers*

Attitudinal options	Balance of appreciation (unweighted)*	Balance of appreciation (weighted)**
They help the community	+23.7	+200
They are similar to my friends	+11.6	+144
They are not egotistical	+9.0	−58
They are not biased	−6.1	+58
They are usually constructive	−13.8	−175
They are similar to me	−25.5	−7
They are better educated than most	−34.9	−31

* % agreement minus % disagreement ("unsure" responses ignored).
** Responses multiplied by Likert intensity before subtraction ("unsure" ignored).
$n = 164$.
Source: Author's original research.

parsimonious explanation. Respondents tended to see in the writers what they wished to see or what they had been habituated to see. In other words, contrary to accepted folklore, no empirically demonstrable, psychologically consistent, or sociologically understandable stereotype of the political letter writer seems to have yet organized the popular mind. This is not to say that individual citizens do not have strong opinions of writers. But it is to say that people in general cannot agree on what they feel.

Perhaps that is why surveys continually show that letters columns are among the best-read features of any newspaper (see Singletary 1976; Sussman 1959). Perhaps we sense that writers are somehow "special," but we do not know how. Perhaps it is our sense of political intrigue, not the writers' alleged biases, that attract us to them. Perhaps it is their willingness to take positions we are not brave enough to take that inclines us toward them. Perhaps we read what they say not because we know them but because we do not know them.

Without question, some people read these letters to reinforce their prejudices. But in my sample these effects tended to cancel each other out, suggesting that it may be the writers' *political energy*, not their political biases, that fascinates us. To be sure, fascination alone cannot sustain a democracy. Commitments are required. But letter writers may be offering the former while the latter awaits development. People who cannot be intrigued by the political sphere, after all, can hardly hope to enter it. Letter writers might be serving as guides to that sphere.

SURVEY OF WRITERS

The survey of writers was conducted in 1993 and again in 1997 in deference to a piece of folk wisdom: that Republicans write letters more often when Democrats are in office and that Democrats pick up the slack when their party is out of power. If true, these conditions would create a partisan sampling bias that could be minimized by polling during both the Bush and Clinton presidencies. As it turns out, this particular folktale is true: 45% of the 1992 writers voted Democratic (vs. 35% Republican and 13% independent), while 59% of the 1996 writers voted Republican (vs. 31% Democratic and 7% independent). Thus, letter writing is in part a contrarian's enterprise, so double-sampling turned out to be a good decision.

On most other variables, the 1993 and 1997 respondents were consistent: They were white (95.5%), educated (over half had attended college), home-owning (86%), faithful voters (94.5%). They were also civically conscious: 30% had made financial contributions to one of the presidential campaigns, most had watched a presidential debate (88.7%) or one of the party conventions (84.2%), and a small percentage (14.8%) had worked on a political campaign in the recent past. These respondents were a bit older than those in the readers' survey (54.6 years vs. 47.8 years), but they reported the same sorts of household incomes (about $45,000 per annum), watched about the same amount of television (3 hours per day), subscribed to the local paper with equivalent frequency (73.5%), and were spread fairly evenly over the ten cities sampled.

Differences from the readers' sample should be noted, however. Although care was taken to sample both men and women equally, 68.5% of the returnees in the writer/nonwriter survey were men (vs. 50% in the reader survey), no doubt reflecting a male bias in letter writing.[8] Also, while the number of white collar workers was similar in the two samples (about 45%), the writer survey contained more retirees – 31.5% vs. 19% – since retirees write a great many letters. Otherwise, the two samples were similar on most sociodemographic variables.

The main dependent variables used in the writer survey included external efficacy, internal efficacy, and political trust.[9] In addition, two master variables were constructed: (1) *political involvement*, a measure of the respondents' attentiveness to the 1992 and 1996 presidential campaigns, including writing a letter to the editor, talking to friends about the campaign, watching political ads, making monetary contributions, working as a volunteer, and watching the evening news, the debates, the conventions, and the political talk shows; (2) *media satisfaction*, a measure of the respondents' attitudes toward the media's ability to inform the public, avoid excessive personalization, treat the candidates equivalently, provide helpful forums for political debate, and give a local perspective on the campaign.[10]

Two of the more intriguing findings of this study are artifactual. One deals with the response rates of the writers and nonwriters (60% vs. 45.5%), an unobtrusive indicator of differential political commitments. A second datum also relates to involvement. As the surveys began to be returned, it was clear that many respondents needed to comment on the questions asked, to expand on their responses, inquire into the researcher's motivations, or (erroneously) correct the survey's spelling. Thus, it seemed prudent to fashion those comments into a measure of *volunteered commentary*. To do so, two recording units were used: (1) the distinct phrase (a long sentence could have more than one) and (2) the emendation, including verbal substitutions and editing marks. A count of 1 was recorded for each such unit found.

Seventy percent of the returned surveys contained no volunteered commentary. The remainder did, even though no open-ended questions had been asked and no correspondence solicited. In other words, volunteered commentary essentially became a measure of political irrepressibility, and so it should not be surprising that writers scored higher than nonwriters on this scale, a fact that can be seen in Table 19.4.

The differences *not* reported in Table 19.4 are every bit as important as the differences that are reported. The writers are, in fact, older than the norm but they are not wealthier. They have no more education than non-writers and their media habits are not substantially different (in terms of total amount of television watched, amount of television news watched, or total newspaper subscriptions). Writers are no more likely to be home owners than renters, to be Republicans or Democrats, or to like political talk shows (although they do watch them more religiously); and, *as a group*, they are no less trusting or externally efficacious than nonwriters.

The most impressive facts in Table 19.4 relate to political involvement. Writers put their money where their mouths (and pens) are,

Table 19.4. *Differences between writers and nonwriters*

Variable	Writers (N = 183)	Nonwriters (N = 418)	Statistical difference*	Signif. (p)
Age (yrs.)	60.4	52.2	$t = 6.04$	0.001
Retired	40.9%	27.5%	$x^2 = 4.14$	0.042
Internal efficacy	8.86	7.77	$t = 5.526$	0.001
Media satisfaction	13.74	15.14	$t = 3.701$	0.001
Voted in presidential campaign	100.0%	92.1%	$x^2 = 15.26$	0.001
Watched political conventions	94.5%	80.0%	$x^2 = 19.39$	0.001
Watched political ads	81.8%	60.4%	$x^2 = 26.29$	0.001
Watched political debates	93.4%	86.6%	$x^2 = 5.57$	0.001
Talked about politics with friend	98.4%	87.9%	$x^2 = 17.15$	0.001
Watched TV talk shows	60.1%	48.8%	$x^2 = 8.87$	0.001
Listened to radio talk shows	54.4%	38.8%	$x^2 = 14.31$	0.001
Gave money in campaign (%)	55.7%	20.7%	$x^2 = 67.06$	0.001
Volunteered in campaign (%)	32.2%	7.2%	$x^2 = 55.44$	0.001
Volunteered survey commentary	1.33	0.64	$t = 3.78$	0.001

* Non-parametric test used = Kruskal-Wallis Test for K Independent Samples.
Source: Author's original research.

being almost three times more likely to make campaign contributions and five times more likely to work on a political campaign than the nonwriters. Not surprisingly, they also vote at a higher rate than the comparison group and pay avid attention to the various goings-on of a campaign, perhaps because their seniority permits them more time to do such things. On the other hand, as Figure 19.2 indicates, political involvement is not easily predicted by any simple factor like age or longevity in the community. In contrast, political involvement is significantly correlated with age, income, external efficacy, and internal efficacy *for the nonwriters*, suggesting that the rational actor model holds rather well for them.

Figure 19.2 shows that most of the standard political and demographic variables are conventionally arranged for the letter-writers – age and income are inversely related to television watching; internal efficacy increases with income, education, and political trust (but decreases, logically enough, with age); and external efficacy is associated with a tight cluster of variables expressing confidence in the political system. But none of these variables leads to political *action*. With the exception of media satisfaction, political involvement is a lonely variable.

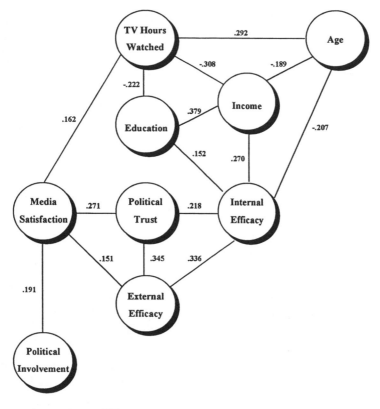

(Writers only, n = 183)

Figure 19.2. Significant correlations among political variables. *Source:* Author's research.

Why? Two explanations seem possible: (1) Letter writers may come in two varieties, thereby suppressing some statistical relationships with their double-mindedness (a possibility to be pursued later in this chapter); (2) it could also mean that political involvement is almost a philosophical requirement for them, since neither psychological nor sociological variables (at least not the psychological and sociological variables tested here) predicted their involvement. Perhaps the letter writers believe, with Rousseau, that civic concern is a fundamental aspect of social identity or, with Locke, that political rights can only be ensured by constant vigilance or, with Mill, that vigorous public debate alone ensures democracy. Or perhaps they are simply arrogant: They were, for example, more likely than nonwriters to agree with the state-

Table 19.5. *Factor structure for main variables*

Variable	Factor One (Urbane Confidence)	Factor Two (Mature Institutionalism)	Factor Three (Mature Skepticism)	Factor Four (Resigned Detachment)
Respondent age	−0.504	0.407	0.416	0.342
Volunteered commentary	−0.123	0.229	0.120	−0.741
Respondent education	0.606	0.102	0.270	0.368
External efficacy	0.451	0.615	−0.152	0.104
Family income	0.587	−0.106	0.359	0.105
Internal efficacy	0.509	0.403	0.312	−0.266
Political involvement	−0.034	0.516	0.460	−0.227
Media satisfaction	−0.030	0.329	−0.635	−0.028
Years in current city	−0.587	0.347	0.175	0.349
Political trust	0.321	0.549	−0.516	0.138
TV hours per day	−0.580	0.350	−0.071	−0.064

Source: Author's original research.

ment, "I feel I could do as good a job in public office as most other people" (66.1% vs. 48.3%) and to disagree with the sentiment "I don't feel sure of myself when talking to others about politics and government" (89.1% vs. 68.2%). Letter writers, in short, may be a political scholar's worst nightmare: They have no need for lectures on civic engagement; they have internalized the public virtues.

A principal components factor analysis was performed to get a more complete look at the writers' underlying cognitive structures (see Table 19.5). When all six hundred respondents were entered into the analysis, four factors with an eigenvalue of 1 or higher emerged. They were labeled thusly:

1. **Urbane confidence** – consisting of younger, better educated, high income, and efficacious newcomers who were also politically trusting but who had low media consumption
2. **Mature institutionalism** – older, efficacious, and trusting respondents who had high political involvement as well as high media consumption and satisfaction
3. **Mature skepticism** – older, involved, internally efficacious

respondents, but persons who had low political trust, low media satisfaction, and low external efficacy

4. **Resigned Detachment** – fairly well-educated, long–term residents who were not politically involved or inclined to volunteer political commentary and who had low levels of internal efficacy

A comparison of factor scores showed that writers were significantly more likely to be higher on mature institutionalism than nonwriters ($t = 7.869$, $p < 0.000$) and higher on mature skepticism ($t = 9.947$, $p < 0.000$) as well. That is, political letter writers come in two varieties – those who embrace politics out of a sense of duty (the institutionalists) and those who do so to keep their political enemies close to them (the skeptics). The "good government" people – the institutionalists – represent the *yin* of the editorial page, championing their causes and bestirring their fellow citizens to action, while the skeptics constitute the *yang*, warning that historic truths are in danger, that conspiracies abound. These forces create the local newspaper's dialectic, with the institutionalists arguing for political involvement along Tocquevillean lines and the skeptics urging the same thing out of Machiavellian fear.

Institutionalist writers were a bit more likely to be female than male ($t = 2.237$, $p < 0.026$) and Democratic or independent rather than Republican ($F[3, 179] = 9.963$, $p < 0.000$). Republican writers had much higher mature skepticism than writers with other political affiliations ($F[3, 179] = 15.605$, $p < 0.000$), and they were also more likely to be male than female ($t = 2.206$, $p < 0.044$). The gender differences may not withstand long-term scrutiny, but the partisan differences are intriguing and seem hardier. The fact that the skeptics have questions about institutionalized politics and institutionalized media suggest a unique perspective on civic engagement, especially since they are highly involved politically *despite their misgivings*. Given the inadequacies they see, what keeps these writers from becoming pure cynics?[11] Similarly, what keeps the institutionalists hopeful when so many others in their same age cohort have long since abandoned politics for private matters? These are mysteries that need solving.

Overall, there was a bit more involvement among the writers in 1993 than in 1997, no doubt reflecting the laxity found in the nation during the 1996 campaign. Writers and nonwriters alike watched fewer debates and less political news and reported lower media satisfaction than they did in 1993, but the letter writers' basic profiles did not change – they still felt more internally efficacious and still scored significantly higher on eight of the nine involvement variables than did the nonwriters. These high levels of involvement are even more impressive when one remembers that the 1993 and 1997 samples differed considerably on partisan identification. Whether Democrats or Republicans, however, political letter writers were systemically allegiant.

The overwhelming sense one gets from the data, then, is that letter writers care about their communities. This was true despite their personal wealth or where they lived (the writer/nonwriter differences could be found in all ten cities). Somehow, the writers were able to act like citizens and they did not do so on paper alone. They also voted, petitioned, and affirmed the political covenant, precisely the things Jefferson and his brethren had expected of all Americans.

Why did they do so? A survey of fewer than two hundred writers provides no firm answers, although it seems clear that no overwhelming structural difference distinguished them from the nonwriters (perhaps because the respondent pool was itself somewhat circumscribed). But none of the usual suspects – money, privilege, party, education, geography, era, occupation, socioeconomic status – predictably distinguished the writers from the nonwriters, so perhaps less quantifiable entities like "habit of mind" or "civic commitment" need to be considered. Clearly, we need to know more about the political energy that sustains such persons.

CONCLUSION

Are the letter writers studied here a collection of exotics or are they the canaries in the nation's cave, persons who point toward tomorrow's politics? In the language of Edwin Baker in Chapter 16, are the writers "issue specialists" who will be somehow insulated from the alienation now threatening to engulf a good portion of the citizenry? In Doris Graber's terms (see Chapter 20), will the "junk news" the letter writers consume reduce the information available to them and hence make them less efficacious? In Russell Neuman's language (Chapter 14), will the "cybercitizens" of tomorrow know more but care less about their communities than the writers sampled here? Finally, in William Gamson's terms (Chapter 3), will the writers retain their sense of agency in the future or will they succumb to a host of new cynicisms as the world moves apace?

Past research on political letter writing has been useful but not definitive. The studies reported here are imperfect, but they do push us in new directions. They find that the editors are not sure what motivates their correspondents and that the average reader is also murky – they have sundry opinions about letter writers but they do not have these opinions sorted out. Our studies also show that a good many of the stereotypes about political letter writers need to be questioned, that the writers are far more variegated than folklore would suggest. If they are characterized by anything, they are characterized by their commitments to the political enterprise.

And now the uncertainties: The available survey instruments and sample sizes clearly limit what one can say about political letter writers. Too, because stereotypes about such persons die hard, no amount of data will keep some people from feeling superior to the writers. Questions about the writers' representativeness will also trouble some scholars. Given their faith in the law of central tendency, many social scientists will always despise outliers, particularly those who write to small city newspapers. "Why concern oneself with the knotty problems of textuality," they will ask, "especially if writers' attitudes only predict writers' attitudes?"

My answer is five-fold: (1) Because they are composed in a *reflective mood*, letters offer a "deeper read" of the American polity than does the opinion survey (which largely probes spontaneous thought). (2) Because letters are *extant, archived,* and *diverse,* researchers can ask questions of the letters today that had not occurred to them yesterday. (3) Because they are *generically similar,* letters offer phenomenological consistency over time and that can prove methodologically beneficial, not to mention theoretically rich, when trying to fathom a nation's political history. (4) Because letter writers often *diverge from* elite political thought, they stand traditional political understandings on their heads, thereby forcing us to ask questions heretofore deferred or dismissed. (5) Because writers (often unwittingly) reflect *communal concerns,* they provide sociological as well as psychological data to the sensitive reader-scholar.

There is a reason why Robert Lane's *Political Ideology* (1962) became an instant classic. In it, he talked to only fifteen men in only one American town, but he asked them careful questions and listened carefully to the questions they asked themselves, questions that were new and fresh and deep (and still are). Given letter writers' political energy, they deserve similar treatment. We do not need better data than the data they offer us. We just need to become smarter about the data they willingly provide. Achieving that sort of intelligence seems a worthy intellectual goal.

Notes

1. Actually, a sixth, more impressionistic data collection was attempted when the author visited each of the cities for a week apiece in spring 1993 to archive letters, gauge the political and social complexion of the ten cities, and meet sporadically with local residents and city officials. The author remains indebted to several dozen such residents, civil servants, and newspaper personnel for their helpfulness and hospitality. He also wishes to thank Mary Triece for her help in some of the data collection.

2. The national-sample vote percentages for the last two presidential elections were as follows: **1992**: Bush (37.5%/37.9%), Clinton (43.1%/41.6%), Perot (18.8%/17.8%), other (0.6%/2.6%); **1996**: Clinton (49.0%/52.3%), Dole (41.0%/38.3%), Perot (8.0%/8.7%), other (2.0%/0.7%).

3. On this occasion mailing labels were used (rather than personally addressed envelopes), a decision that probably decreased the response rate a bit, as did the non-salience of politics at that time. When returned mailings and unreachable addresses were subtracted from the initial total, 164 responses were received for a usable response rate of 36.5%.

4. Copies of all survey instruments can be obtained from the author.

5. The ten cities included the following: Fall River, MA; Trenton, NJ; Roanoke, VA; Lake Charles, LA; Wichita Falls, TX; St. Joseph, MO; Duluth, MN; Provo, UT; Billings, MT; and Salinas, CA. For greater demographic balance, two additional cities were later added to the sample (Utica, NY, and Springfield, OH) but these cities were not included in the surveys reported here.

6. The survey question utilized here was "What sorts of TV shows do you watch on a regular basis? Place an X next to as many as you'd like." Affirmative responses were as follows: Local news (79.9%), national news (66.3%), weekly newsmagazines (59.0%), educational documentaries (51.2%), sports programming (49.4%), network or cable movies (48.2%), weekly comedy shows (37.3%), weekly dramatic shows (30.1%), early morning shows (27.1%), late-night programs (24.1%), political interview shows (18.7%), and daytime dramas (18.1%). Two other demographics are also relevant: 86.7% of the respondents owned a VCR and 68.1% of them subscribed to cable television.

7. Subgroups of respondents had somewhat greater clarity. Older Americans tended to be more tolerant of the writers, particularly in terms of their alleged community helpfulness, lack of political bias, and ego needs, than the younger respondents. But the best predictor of writer appreciation – if there was one – tended *not* to be the traditional variables; neither political party, education, region, job type, nor income usefully discriminated between those who respected the writers and those who did not. Only the attitudinal variable of media disapproval marginally distinguished (using a median split) those with high appreciation from those with low appreciation ($t = 1.838$, $p < 0.073$). That is, people who did not like the mass media also did not like the writers. Even those who themselves wrote letters to the editor

(n = 30) were just as ambivalent about their fellow writers as the general population.

8. Other writers have also noticed this. Forsyth (1950), for example, described the stereotype of the letter writer forty years ago and that stereotype has endured ever since: They are older, Caucasian, fairly well educated, male, conservative, and white collar. Thirty years later, Singletary and Cowling (1979) reproduced these results. Volgy (1977) reports similar demographics but noted that such traits did not push the writers into either authoritarianism or alienation. In our sample, the writers were considerably more likely to be male than female (73.2% vs. 26.7%), but they were not significantly older or better educated than the nonwriters; they were not especially ideologically biased *as a group*; and they were socioeconomically diverse as well. All of these findings suggest how important it is to get a broad sampling of letter writers when investigating them.

9. The survey questions included the following: (1) External efficacy: "The people of the U.S. have the final say about how the country is run, no matter who is in office" and "If public officials don't care what people think, there is no way to make them listen." (2) Internal efficacy: "I often don't feel sure of myself when talking to others about politics and government," "I feel I could do as good a job in public office as most other people," and "People like me really don't have a say about what government does." (3) Political trust: "When government leaders make public statements to the American people, they often mislead them" and "The people we elect to public office usually keep the promises they make during the election."

10. Exact wording for these items was as follows: "In general, the news media increased my political knowledge during the campaign," "The major TV networks (ABC, CBS, CNN, NBC) did a good job of covering the campaign," "My local newspaper did a good job of covering the campaign," "Having the major political candidates appear on talk shows like *Good Morning America* was helpful," "Having ordinary citizens (rather than reporters) question the candidates on TV was a good idea," "Reporters talked too much about the candidates' personal lives during the campaign," "In general, the mass media treated the Democratic candidates better than the Republican candidates."

11. For more on the skeptical–cynical distinction see Pinkleton et al. (1996).

REFERENCES

Bellah, R., R. Madsen, and W. M. Sullivan (1992). *The Good Society*. New York: Vintage.

Bennett, S., R. Flickinger, and S. Rhine (1996). "Political Talk – Over Here, Over There and Over Time: A Comparative Analysis of Who Talks about Politics in Britain and the United States, 1959–1994." Paper presented at the International Society of Political Psychology annual meeting, Vancouver, British Columbia.

Brehm, J., and S. Rahn (1997). "Individual-Level Evidence for the Causes and Consequences of Social Capital." *American Journal of Political Science*, 41:999–1023.

Buell, E. (1975). "Eccentrics or Gladiators? People Who Write about Politics in Letters-to-the-editor." *Social Science Quarterly*, 56:440–449.

Conway, M., A. Damico, and S. Damico (1996). "Bowling Alone or Civic Participants? Patterns of Community and Political Participation." Paper presented at the American Political Science Association annual meeting, Chicago, Illinois.

Davis, H., and G. Rarick (1964). "Functions of Editorials and Letters to the Editor." *Journalism Quarterly*, 41:108–109.

Delli Carpini, M., and S. Keeter (1996). *What Americans Know about Politics and Why It Matters*. New Haven: Yale University Press.

Dillard, J., and S. Backhaus (1997). "An Exploration into Civic Deliberation, Emotional Response, and Political Involvement." Paper presented at the International Communication Association annual meeting, Montreal, Quebec.

Etzioni, A. (1993). *The Spirit of Community: Rights, Responsibilities, and the Communitarian Agenda*. New York: Crown Publishers.

Finkel, S. (1985). "Reciprocal Effects of Participation and Political Efficacy: A Panel Analysis." *American Journal of Political Science*, 29:891–913.

Forsyth, S. (1950). "An Exploratory Study of Letters to the Editor and Their Contributors." *Public Opinion Quarterly*, 14:43–44.

Foster, H. S., and C. J. Friedrich (1937). "Letters to the Editor as a Means of Measuring the Effectiveness of Propaganda." *American Political Science Review*, 31:71–79.

Fox, R., M. Crask, and J. Kim (1988). "Mail Survey Response Rate: A Meta-analysis of Selected Techniques for Inducing Response." *Public Opinion Quarterly*, 52:467–491.

Grey, D., and T. Brown (1970). "Letters to the Editor: Hazy Reflections of Public Opinion." *Journalism Quarterly*, 47:450–456, 471.

Hetherington, M. (1996). "Television News' Contribution to Political Cynicism and Its System Level Consequences." Paper presented Midwest Political Science Association annual meeting, Chicago, Illinois.

Hill, D. (1981). "Letter Opinion on ERA: A Test of the Newspaper Bias Hypothesis." *Public Opinion Quarterly*, 45:384–392.

Hynds, E. (1991). "Editorial Page Editors Discuss Use of Letters." *Newspaper Research Journal*. Fall:124–136.

(1976). "Editorial Pages Are Taking Stands, Providing Forums." *Journalism Quarterly*, 53:532–535.

and C. Martin (1979). "How Non-daily Editors Describe Status and Function of Editorial Pages." *Journalism Quarterly*, 56:318–323.

Kapoor, S., and C. Botan (1989). "Editors' Perceptions of the Letters to the Editor Column." Paper presented at the International Communication Association annual meeting, San Francisco, California.

(1992). "Studies Compare How Editors Use Letters." *The Masthead*. Spring: 5–7.

Kazee, T., and C. Shi (1996). "Alienation and American Politics: 1984–1992." Paper presented Midwest Political Science Association annual meeting, Chicago, Illinois.

Kim, J., R. Wyatt, and E. Katz (1997). "News, Talk, Opinion, Action: Media, Interpersonal Communication, and Political Participation in the Public Sphere." Paper presented at the International Communication Association annual meeting, Montreal, Quebec.

Lane, R. (1962). *Political Ideology: Why the American Common Man Believes as He Does*. New York: Free Press.

Luks, S. (1996). "Political Trust Over Time and the Life Cycle, 1965–1982." Paper presented Midwest Political Science Association annual meeting, Chicago, Illinois.

McLeod, J., D. Scheufele, and P. Moy (1997). "Community, Communication, and Participation: The Role of the Mass Media and Interpersonal Discussion in Local

Political Participation." Paper presented at the International Communication Association annual meeting, Montreal, Quebec.

Newhagen, J. (1993). "Media Use and Political Efficacy: The Suburbanization of Race and Class." Paper presented at the International Communication Association annual meeting, Washington, DC.

Nie, N., J. Junn, and K. Stehlik-Barry (1996). *Education and Democratic Citizenship in America.* Chicago: University of Chicago Press.

Nye, J., P. D. Zelikow, and D. C. King (Eds.) (1997). *Why People Don't Trust Government.* Cambridge: Harvard University Press.

Pasternak, S., and S. Kapoor (1980). The Letters Boom. *The Masthead,* Fall:23–25.

Pinkleton, B., E. Austin, and K. Johnson (1996). "Relationships of Political Disaffection, Voter Sophistication, and Information Seeking to External Efficacy and Political Behavior." Paper presented at the International Communication Association annual meeting, Montreal, Quebec.

Piven, F. F., and R. A. Cloward (1988). *Why Americans Don't Vote.* New York: Pantheon.

Pritchard, D., and D. Berkowitz (1991). "How Readers' Letters May Influence Editors and News Emphasis: A Content Analysis of 10 Newspapers, 1948–1978." *Journalism Quarterly,* 68:388–395.

Putnam, R. (1995). "Bowling Alone." *Journal of Democracy,* 6:65–79.

Rahn, W., J. Brehm, and N. Carlson (1997). "National Elections as Institutions for Generating Social Capital." Paper presented at the American Political Science Association annual meeting, Washington, DC.

Renfro, P. (1979). "Bias in the Selection of Letters to the Editor." *Journalism Quarterly,* 79:822–826.

Rhine, S., S. Bennett, and R. Flickinger (1996). "Patterns of Media Exposure in the U.S. and Their Impact on Knowledge of Foreign Affairs." Paper presented at the Midwest Political Science Association annual meeting, Chicago, Illinois.

Roberts, D., L. Sikorski, and W. Paisley (1969). "Letters in Mass Magazines as 'Outcroppings' of Public Concern." *Journalism Quarterly,* 46:743–752.

Shah, D. (1997). "Civic Participation, Interpersonal Trust, and Television Use: A Motivational Approach to Social Capital." Paper presented at the International Communication Association annual meeting, Montreal, Quebec.

Singletary, M., and M. Cowling (1979). "Letters to the Editor of the Non-daily Press." *Journalism Quarterly,* 56:165–168.

Singletary, M. (1976). "How the Public Perceives Letters to the Editor." *Journalism Quarterly,* 53:535–537.

Stivers, R. (1994). *The Culture of Cynicism: American Morality in Decline.* Oxford, UK: Blackwell.

Stotsky, S. (1987). "Writing in a Political Context: The Value of Letters to Legislators." *Written Communication,* 4:394–410.

Sussman, L. (1959). "Mass Political Letter Writing in America: The Growth of an Institution." *Public Opinion Quarterly,* 23:203–212.

Verba, S., and N. Nie (1972). *Participation in America: Political Democracy and Social Equality.* New York: Harper.

Verba, S., K. Scholzman, and H. Brady (1995). *Voice and Equality: Civic Voluntarism in American Politics.* Cambridge: Harvard University Press.

(1997). "Solving the Puzzle of Rational Participation: Lessons from the Citizen

Participation Study." Paper presented at the American Political Science Association annual meeting, Washington, DC.

Volgy, T., M. Krigbaum, M. K. Langan, and V. Moshier (1977). "Some of My Best Friends Are Letter Writers: Eccentrics and Gladiators Revisited." *Social Science Quarterly*, 58:321–327.

CHAPTER 20

Adapting Political News to the Needs of Twenty-First Century Americans

Doris A. Graber

It is axiomatic in a democracy that citizens must be interested in politics and must be well informed. When it seems like interest in politics is declining and knowledge levels are plunging, red warning flags go up. They have been up for quite a while in the final decades of the twentieth century. Observers are particularly concerned because the decline in interest and factual knowledge about politics has been steepest among the youngest age group – sometimes referred to as "Generation X." The direction that political life in the United States will take early in the twenty-first century hinges on the attitudes and behaviors of this generation. Political scientist Michael Delli Carpini (1989, pp. 11–12) is right when he says that "there is no more fundamental transfer of power, and therefore no more fundamental *potential* for change, than that which occurs between generations. This is so because, unlike any other type of change, it is *inevitable*, it is *all-inclusive* . . . entire populations are replaced every century . . . In the light of personnel replacement of this magnitude, the transfer of power that occurs in elections, or through assassinations, or even in revolutions, pales."

This is why it is important to examine the mind-set of the nation's young adults to assess how safe the heritage of democracy is likely to be in their care. It is equally essential to undertake this examination with an open mind. Major changes in the social, economic, political, and cultural environment in the twentieth century may have produced major changes in the conceptions of the nature of citizenship in a democracy, especially when accompanied by major changes in political news dissemination and consumption patterns. These changes are not ipso facto bad because they do not conform to the patterns of the past (Buckingham 1997; Ichilov 1990).

In this chapter, I will first describe the changes in political interest and news consumption patterns that were apparent at the turn of the century and the major reasons for these changes. Then follows a quick look at current predictions of where these changes may be leading American politics. The chapter concludes with an overview of adaptations in the substance and format of political news that seem essential to meet the needs of Americans in the twenty-first century.

Generation X, as used in this chapter, refers to the 45 million young Americans, aged 18–29 in 1997. "GenXers" were then living in a period of rapid changes where nothing was certain, neither family stability, nor jobs, nor the composition of their communities. Their immediate worlds – the here-and-now, the close-by – therefore were most important. Many of them grew up in single-parent families where ritual family activities, including watching the news were rare and most activities were dictated by their own choices. They also had lived through a major communications revolution, loved MTV, and knew television as an omnipresent baby sitter (Owen 1997).

Their parents, dubbed the "boomers," 78 million strong, were 30–49 years old. They had vivid memories of America's Vietnam, Watergate, and Civil Rights turmoil, as well as basking in the benefits of good economic times. Their grandparents, aged 50 and older, were the 68 million "matures" whose collective lives encompassed the Depression era of the 1930s, World War II, the Cold War, and other tragedies and triumphs of the middle of the twentieth century. Overall in 1997, genXers made up 23.4 percent of the (adult) public, boomers accounted for 40.7 percent, and matures for 35.8 percent.

Comparisons of generational groups at the turn of the twentieth century with earlier groups showed that "Today's young adults are not simply different from older generations, they are different from what older generations were when they were their age. Make no mistake, this particular cohort of young adults, which we label Generation X, is unlike any that came before it" (Zukin 1997, p. 3; also see Abelman 1996; Delli Carpini and Keeter 1996). Of course, there have always been differences in thinking between generations because of unique experiences during their formative years, especially when major political or personal crises or technological changes mark a particular historical period. Because communal experiences are modified by each person's unique situation and personality, sweeping generalizations about any generation are bound to be incorrect for many of its members. But, broadly speaking, most scholars of generational changes in the United States believe that genXers deviate more from past norms than usual, leaving uncommonly broad gaps in beliefs and behaviors between them and their elders, especially their grandparents. Table 20.1 tells the story in terms of interest in politics.

The gap in interest in following public affairs was one percentage point in 1966 between interested youths and their parents and grand-parents. By 1996, the gap had grown to 12 percentage points between youths and their parents and 26 percentage points between youths and their grandparents. Looking at ten-year intervals, the gap surfaces in 1976 when the baby boomer generation, raised on television, diverged by 12 percentage points from their parents whereas parents and grand-parents were still close. Ten years later, in 1986, as genXers came on the scene and boomers moved into their middle years, the youth/parent gap had risen slightly but a 9 percentage point gap had opened between parents and grandparents. That gap widened during the next ten-year span, underlining the fact that the boomers and their children are dis-tinct from each other in their political interests and attitudes as well as distinct from the preboom generation. The attitudinal consensus seen in 1966 no longer prevails.

GENX MEDIA USE STYLES

Public opinion poll analyses by political scientist Cliff Zukin and others reveal five characteristics that make genXers' newsgathering approaches distinctive, particularly compared to their grandparents.

1. GenXers as a group are far more visually oriented than their grandparents and superbly adept at extracting the central meaning conveyed by pictures. They have learned to think con-ceptually rather than in linear fashion (Tapscott 1998). They prefer nontextual information – visuals and graphs – because it resembles actually experiencing situations. It is "virtual" reality.
2. GenXers like diversity in their information supply. As Table 20.2 shows, three out of four relish having hundreds of different news sources at their fingertips; they are not awed by using technology.

    They also are perpetual surfers who move quickly from program to program to find stories that catch their fancy. They often watch several programs simultaneously (Ritchie 1995). In the realm of political information, half want instant access to almost any type of news at any time. While these tastes deviate

Table 20.1 *Age-related differences in following government and public affairs "most" plus "some of the time," 1966–1996*

	1966		1976		1986		1996	
	Age/birth year range	Most + some of the time	Age/birth year range	Most + some of the time	Age/birth year range	Most + some of the time	Age/birth year range	Most + some of the time
18–24	1937–1948	64%	1947–1958	62%	1957–1968	47%	1967–1978	48%
Generation gap		+1		+12		+14		+12
30–40	1917–1936	65	1927–1946	74	1937–1956	61	1947–1966	60
Generation gap		–		-2		+9		+14
50 and over	before 1917	65	before 1927	72	before 1937	70	before 1947	74
Youth vs. over 50 gap		+1		+10		+23		+26

"Only now and then" and "hardly at all" are omitted. Shaded areas = Pre-boomers or mixed pre-boomer/boomer ages.

Source: Adapted from NES Survey data, Virginia Sapiro, Steven J. Rosenstone, Warren E. Miller, and the National Election Studies. American National Election Studies, 1948–1997 (CD-ROM). ICPSR ed. Ann Arbor, MI: Inter-university Consortium for Political and Social Research (producer and distributor), 1998.

Table 20.2 *Interest in technological innovations by generation: percent who are "definitely interested"*

Type of innovation	GenXers	Boomers	Matures
Skip TV stories at will, as in newspapers	74%	69%	49%
Click button for more information on story	66	61	38
Select news mix (politics/sports/weather)	54	53	32
Design program from story menu	50	49	27
Instant access to news any time	50	45	30
Choose from 100+ channels	43	33	14

Source: Adapted from Radio and Television News Directors Foundation, 1996, p. 67.

only moderately from those of their parents, the gap between matures and genXers is substantial.

3. Nourished on videogames, and increasingly adept at surfing the Web, genXers like to participate in shaping their information menu. Half of them, according to Table 20.2, enjoy assembling their own television programs. They like to do this by combining many different media elements as they switch from one media offering to the next. Depth interviews indicate that they pursue intellectual challenges, rather than fluff, and that they learn from their media experiences (Turkle 1997). They look for suspense and high drama and dislike hype and weasel words. They are cynical about news from established social institutions.

4. GenXers prize interactivity. This is the "talking back to your television" concept first mentioned in the 1960s. It is a slap at the notion of the passive audience. GenXers want a chance to respond to questions and to air their own views.

5. GenXers are niche viewers. They skip stories that they do not like and get more information about preferred stories as long as they are readily available at the punch of a button or click of a mouse. In fact, three-quarters of GenXers – compared to only half of other viewers – always watch current news with a remote control in hand. They dislike being forced or cajoled into partaking of a broad information menu just because someone else determines that it is "good" for their civic health.

Knowing and accommodating these five characteristics has become essential for planning the construction and dissemination of political and other news in the twenty-first century. The major shifts in attention to political news recorded during the waning decades of the twentieth century make it amply clear that dramatic changes were needed to satisfy new audience generation.

THE "NEW" MEDIA AND GENX

The communications revolution of the waning decades of the twentieth century has made it technically feasible to satisfy the information proclivities of genXers. It has produced "new" media, such as cable television, satellite transmission, and the Internet, and new programming formats, like interactive television shows and hot-links embedded in news. Six characteristics of the new media are particularly important. They are (1) the predominance of visual formats, (2) the proliferation of media venues, (3) the ending of time-clock tyranny, (4) the weakening of gate-keeper control, (5) the growth of interactivity, and (6) the emergence of niche programming.

AUDIO-VISUAL PREDOMINANCE. The new media rely heavily on audio-visual messages that are the preferred form of news transmission for average Americans. When a national random sample of adult Americans was asked in 1996, "Where do you get most of your news about what is important to you – from television, radio, newspapers, magazines, computer on-line sources, or somewhere else?" 59 percent of GenXers named television. For boomers, the figure was 56 percent and for matures it was 53 percent. Not much difference there! However, true to their heightened visual orientation, GenXers were far less inclined than their elders to use print media. The gap between preferring television as the primary source of news and preferring newspapers was 40 percentage points for GenXers, compared to 33 points for boomers and 23 points for the matures (Radio and Television News Directors Foundation 1996).

There are many reasons why audio-visuals are so stunningly popular now and likely to remain so in the future; most of them relate to human information-processing capacities. They are summed up under the headings of ease of learning, ease of processing, ease of recall, and high appeal. Together, these four characteristics make it imperative to rely primarily on audio-visual transmissions, rather than print media, for satisfying the information needs of twenty-first century Americans (Graber 2000).

Learning from visuals is easy because it is an innate skill that infants master soon after birth. By contrast, learning to read print symbols usually requires schooling. Many people, including many Americans, never master reading printed news, let alone comprehending the complex vocabulary and abstract concepts in which it is couched in the American press. Audiences like processing audio-visuals because they can quickly extract much richer details, and often richer meanings, from them than from purely verbal messages. This happens because human brains can process multiple visual stimuli simultaneously while verbal stimuli can only be processed serially. A picture can tell viewers in an instant what a war-devastated home in the Balkans looks like, conveying the full flavor and meaning of the situation. It would take many words to sketch the scene and be almost impossible to include the many poignant details, such as facial expressions and body language of the occupants, the textures and shapes of the structure, and the nature of the surrounding countryside.

Brain research substantiates that audio-visuals can be recalled more easily and accurately than purely verbal messages because they can be reviewed in the mind's eye. Viewers make fewer errors when reporting what they have seen than what they have heard (error rates for visual observations are 15 percent, for verbal statements they are 32 percent [Graber 1993]). When asked to report memorable events during their lifetime, memories based on television news tend to center around the pictures, such as shocking images about hunger in a third-world country or the faces of prominent people in the news (Barnhurst and Wartella 1998).

Finally, most people find audio-visual messages especially appealing and interesting because their many dimensions come closest to real-life experiences. Audio-visuals provide essential contextual settings that clarify the story and are often missing from purely verbal accounts. They add prized depth to stories by capturing moods, emotions, sounds, movements and spatial relationships to a far greater extent and with more fidelity than printed or spoken messages.

MEDIA PROLIFERATION. Another major aspect of the communications revolution is media proliferation. There has been a geometric increase in over-the-air and cable television channels beginning in the waning decades of the twentieth century. Satellites started to transmit a vast number of radio and television programs to backyard satellite dishes. The Internet system carries a flood tide of politically relevant messages from politicians, pundits, and ordinary American citizens. Increasingly, these messages include visuals of various types, including television clips. It has become easy and relatively cheap for media organizations to collect, edit, and distribute customized information packages widely to diverse audiences. By century's end, access to computers and the Internet was spreading at a pace equaling the diffusion of television in earlier decades. It was growing most vigorously in households with children. By 1997, 82 percent of U. S. children had already used computers (Tapscott 1998; Pew 1998).

Beyond the proliferation of information channels, which offered genXers more diversity than anyone could have imagined a few decades earlier, the new media are increasingly empowering media users to choose freely among a broadened spectrum of incoming messages. In cyberspace, a single private citizen with access to a computer and modem can potentially gather information from thousands of media and nonmedia sources throughout the world, as well as making her or his views available to millions of people. However, as is true of all technological riches, the extent to which the public will use the "new" media to collect and disperse information depends on many idiosyncratic factors, as well as on availability of free time and on competing attractions.

ENDING TIME-CLOCK TYRANNY. In line with genXers' penchant for controlling their news, the tyranny of the time clock has virtually disappeared. Video recorders, audio and video tapes, 24-hour news channels, and a vast array of Internet news sources now make news available around the clock and allow users to obtain political information wherever, whenever, and as often as they wish, rather than at times dictated by media delivery schedules. Much of the available information can be repeated on demand, recorded, or printed. Eighty-five percent of America's households had at least one video recorder at the end of the century.

WEAKENING GATE-KEEPER CONTROL. Another major change is the dilution of the control of professional journalists over the framing and interpretation of the news. Individuals no longer depend on established media organizations to assemble information packages for them or to broadcast messages they want to transmit to large audiences. People who download political information into their home computers from the multiplicity of news sources can edit it to their taste by adding, combining, or deleting visual, verbal, and printed data. These resources are likely to be used extensively when the technology becomes user friendlier. Already, fancy personal Web sites are sprouting like mushrooms after a warm summer rain.

Many events are now broadcast live, often in their entirety. At century's end, CNN or C-Span viewers, for example, could watch many events in full, while they were happening. Polls taken in 1996 record that 56 percent of GenXers watched CNN "sometimes" or "regularly"; the corresponding figure for C-Span was 25 percent (Bennett 1998). Although the initial choice of news is still reserved for journalists who decide which events deserve to be broadcast, news consumers who are inclined to do so can make their own interpretations and draw their own conclusions from full-length replays of major events.

INTERACTIVITY. For those who like to ask newsmakers and journalists questions, or broadcast their personal views, as genXers do, numerous interactive broadcasts offer excellent opportunities over and above the opportunities provided by e-mail, personal Web sites, or participation in chat rooms and similar venues. Most talk-show hosts allow their guests to broadcast their arguments in their own words and from their own perspectives. Talk shows are a public forum where participants who are lucky enough to get on the air can address their remarks to large audiences of their fellow citizens. Interactive television and radio programs provide an unprecedented opportunity for direct interaction between ordinary viewers and listeners and political leaders, as well as media gurus. By the end of the century, average Americans had the option to use e-mail to interact with most major leaders in public life as well as most major government agencies.

NEWS SPECIALIZATION. The mushrooming of news sources makes narrow-casting possible so that a vast array of specialized programs has become available, as genXers prefer. Through media proliferation and channel control, twenty-first century Americans have a worldwide news menu within their reach. They can even obtain personalized responses to their political questions from a plethora of Web sites and e-mail addresses.

HOW GENXERS RATE POLITICAL NEWS

If the news media have become so well suited to the needs of genXers, why has attention to much of the political news diminished? Could the answer be found in changed patterns of information gathering and declining interest in public policy, politics, and civic participation?

Table 20.3, reporting 1996 data, makes clear that genXers put a comparatively low priority on consuming standard offerings of political news.

DORIS A. GRABER

Table 20.3 *News consumption attitudes and behaviors by age groups*

Attitudes and behaviors	GenX 18–29	Boomers 30–49	Matures 50+
Very important to keep up with news	40%	55%	65%
Follow the news every day	36	52	67
Too busy	55	42	22
Follow politics and government most of the time	19	29	51
Follow politics and government hardly at all	21	18	8

Source: Adapted from Radio and Television News Directors Foundation, 1996, pp. 15, 18.

Only 40 percent of GenXers think that it is very important to keep up with current news, compared to 55 percent of their boomer parents and 65 percent of their grandparents. When asked about following news about politics and government – which means Beltway type scuttle and minutiae – a scant 19 percent of the genXers claimed to follow it "most of the time" compared to 29 percent of their parents and 51 percent of their grandparents. GenXers have been saturated with negative news during most of their adolescent and adult years, leaving them with a disdain for politicians, especially at the national level, which has been the chief target of much of the negative news. Currently, only 33 percent of genXers say they enjoy keeping up with news a lot, compared to 38 percent of the boomers and 63 percent of the matures. Obviously, as young Americans admit unabashedly, there is a disjunction between what they want and what they receive from the news media.

The drop-off in attention to political news is greatest for newspapers. When genXers were asked about newspaper use "yesterday," only one-quarter of this age-cohort had read a paper, compared to almost three-quarters of the matures. Thirty years earlier, comparable figures for young adults were 67 percent (Barnhurst and Wartella 1998). Nearly one-fourth of the genXers in 1998 had not consumed any news at all on the previous day – five times the rate of abstinence of the matures (Pew 1998). The decline of newspaper reading puts younger Americans at a disadvantage for scoring well on current tests of political knowledge, which are mostly based on newspaper data. Scores also suffer because younger generations, continuing a protracted trend, are less inclined to memorize details when reference tools are so readily available.

Table 20.4 *"Regularly" and "sometimes" used news sources, April 1996*

News Source	Generation X 18–29	Boomers 30–49	Matures 50+
Local news in viewing area	84%	86%	91%
News magazines	67	72	81
Nightly network news	61	69	80
Cable News Network CNN	56	59	61
Tabloid TV	55	51	48
Print news magazines	54	51	46
M(usic)TV	37	15	15
Daytime 'tell-all' TV	36	23	19
Talk radio show	33	39	32
National Public Radio (NPR)[a]	30	46	26
Print business magazines	22	24	18
Religious radio shows	19	23	31
Tabloid newspapers	16	16	17
Limbaugh's radio show	16	18	19
Court TV	14	18	15

[a] When asked if they "listened to radio news yesterday" 99% in each group said "yes."
Source: Adapted from Pew Research Center 1996 report, pp. 29–45.

Dislike of newspapers cannot be blamed primarily on dislike of reading. It is the content that repels. Book reading among genXers equals that of older generations. By comparison, genXers spend only 10 minutes per day reading newspapers while matures spend 33 minutes. Magazine reading figures are higher for genXers than newspaper reading, averaging 20 minutes per day, much of it unrelated to public life. GenXers also read when they spend time on the Internet, which, in the late 1990s, still involved mostly written information. In 1998, 30 percent of genXers reported going on-line at least once weekly. Again, gathering serious political information was not usually their main purpose. In a list of topics to which Web surfers paid attention, various types of news ranked in the bottom third (Pew 1998, Section 1). "Netters" spent much of their time chatting with like-minded people over the electronic backyard fence of cyberspace or browsing through electronic bulletin boards, or sending and receiving e-mail messages. Some of these interchanges involved substantive information, of course, but available evidence suggests that most did not.

The information in Table 20.4 presents a somewhat more optimistic

Table 20.5 *News interests by generation: percent of viewers who are "very interested" in the topic*

News topic	Generation X 18–29	Boomers 30–49	50+
Local community, home town	59%	71%	67%
State, place of residence	53	63	57
U.S., country as a whole	47	55	64
Weather	45	51	59
Health or fitness	34	33	37
Sports	29	22	23
Other countries, the world	23	18	29
Consumer products	23	24	25
Entertainment, movies, TV, celebs	23	12	9
Computers/technology	18	20	11
Religion	17	19	29
Politics and government	11	23	36
Business, stock market	6	14	17

Adapted from Radio and Television News Directors Foundation, 1996, p. 49.

view about genXers' exposure to various aspects of their political world. It is based on a Pew Research Center 1996 survey in which respondents were asked how often they used a variety of news sources. Table 20.4 combines the figures for regularly and sometimes and omits the figures for hardly ever, never, and don't know. Of course, we do not know precisely what sometimes and other vague quantifiers mean to individual respondents, making it difficult to square audience ratings figures with figures emerging from self-reports.

The array of fifteen information sources listed in Table 20.4 includes many that feature serious public affairs news regularly, such as news magazines, regular audio-visual newscasts, and the offerings of National Public Radio. Exposure to this information was bound to lead to some conscious and subconscious learning. Compared to their elders, a smaller contingent of genXers tapped into newscasts of various kinds but a slightly larger contingent paid attention to print news magazines. GenXers spent considerably more time than older generations watching MTV and daytime "tell-all TV," which are programs that accord with their preferences for fast-paced, music, and drama-oriented fare.

Table 20.5 shows the types of programs in which genXers claimed to be very interested because they care about the type of information presented there. Local community, home town events ranked at the top for all generational groups followed by events in one's state of residence, with news about the entire country ranking third.

Considering that 64 percent of the public, including 48 percent of genXers, expressed interest in government and public affairs in the 1996 polls shown in Table 20.1 and that 88 percent overall agreed in the same poll that local government affects their lives substantially, it seems fair to assume that many pay attention to the public policy aspects of news about these governmental levels.

There is a sharp drop in interested viewers when news focuses on events abroad rather than events at home. Only 23 percent of genXers expressed keen interest in international news in 1996, a period of calm in U.S. foreign relations. Interest in day-to-day reports about the minutiae of politics and government in the nation ranked near the bottom, with a mere 11 percent of the genXers saying they were very interested. That compares to 23 percent of the boomers and 36 percent of the matures.

Overall, the numbers in Table 20.5 are encouraging for observers who worried that large numbers of genXers might be totally alienated from politics. The data suggest that genXers were retaining substantial interests in the world that surrounded them, particularly at the levels where citizen contacts with government are closest and most frequent and where opportunities for participation and influence are greatest. More than half of the group still claimed to be very interested in news about their local communities and their state and nearly half extended that interest to the entire country.

Why, then, does their news consumption behavior fail to reflect this interest? Their crowded lives are a partial explanation. More so than boomers and matures at a comparable stage of life, genXers are burdened with heavy home and work activities including two jobs in many cases and little help from grandparents still in the workforce. In households with young children, time-consuming home chores and childcare tasks are added to the burden. Nonetheless, despite such pressures, genXers spent as much time as older people watching entertainment television. This suggests that there are windows of time into which attention to news programs could be fitted.

More important reasons for GenXer's inattention to political news are the disjunctions between their preferred news topics and the topics stressed by the mass media, the deplorable nature of politics as painted by cynical journalists, and the abominable quality of the content and presentation of much of the televised news which seems neither salient nor attractive to many genXers. In a nutshell, genXers' approach to politics and political information gathering is not well served by much of the news currently reaching them through the media. That goes for story substance and framing and for the manner of presentation.

Many U.S. journalists confirm that current news offerings fall short. In a countrywide 1999 survey, 49 percent of those working for national news venues and 55 percent of those working at the local level admitted to doing only a fair to poor job in terms of striking a balance between reporting news they deemed important and satisfying their audiences' interests. Journalists saw this failure as a major reason for losing audiences. Still, fewer than a third (31%) of national journalists and fewer than half (46%) of local journalists believed that audience interests should be a major factor in choosing and framing stories (Pew 1999). No wonder that young people avoid the news because it bears little relation to their major concerns, as qualitative research clearly shows (Barnhurst and Wartella 1991; Putnam 1995; Buckingham 1997). Rather than blaming decreasing attention to news on self-absorbed, irresponsible young viewers, as has been fashionable, some of the blame – perhaps even most – should be put on a failure to keep the news supply attuned to the needs and tastes of new generations of viewers living in a new technological and political environment.

Can politically rich news, tailored to audience concerns and presented engagingly, attract audiences that are large enough to be economically viable? A 1997 study by the Project for Excellence in Journalism indicates that it can. The Project, which is affiliated with the Columbia University Graduate School of Journalism and other television experts, sponsored an analysis of news offerings by sixty-one stations in twenty U.S. cities. Stations were rated in terms of excellence in content and format, viewed from a civic perspective. Stations that practiced top-notch journalism tended to do well in audience ratings. In fact, more than two-thirds had rising ratings (Rosenstiel et al. 1999). However, that was also true for stations that earned the worst ratings because they focused on tabloid news, including scandal, crime, celebrity news, and bizarre events. Stations that fell in a middle range showed no audience increases. Obviously, there is a demand for sex- and crime-dominated news as well as for news that features politics and public policy. A society as rich in news venues as the United States can supply both types.

POLITICAL DANGERS OF THE STATUS QUO

What political dangers loom if political news is not tailored to the needs of politically interested and concerned young publics so that audiences for political news continue to decline? Many observers fear for the survival of a vigorous democracy in which an interested and informed public participates in political life. When major segments of the public opt out of politics, the relative influence of politically active elites grows while the relative influence of silent, inactive citizens shrinks. The openness of the Internet, which allows hitherto submerged voices to reach larger audiences, may create an open hunting season for demagogues who can use the new technology to mislead unwary audiences. Scholars, like Wendy Rahn and Thomas Rudolph in Chap. 21, also warn that the fragmented interests of young Americans may produce a population of tunnel vision citizens who care only about their special concerns but are oblivious to the broader needs of the nation and the world. The proliferation of narrow interest groups will then make it more difficult for governments to mesh the plethora of special interests. It may foreshadow excessive Balkanization of politics.

Yet, the trends in news-seeking behavior of young Americans also support a far more optimistic interpretation of the current situation. Democracy is not necessarily endangered when young citizens limit their news seeking to a narrower range of issues close to home and use "old" media less. Rather, one can interpret their behavior as a rational adaptation to the realities of the complexities of our age. To stay informed, young people are replacing old media partially with a multiplicity of new media. They are targeting their political curiosity and activity at important aspects of the political process. Political happenings in their immediate environment loom larger for them than far-off events that they do not experience directly and over which their control is minimal.

Many younger citizens no longer regard attention to news as primarily an effort to acquire factual data about the political world in a disembodied way, as was the case for their elders. Rather, they use political information as a tool "to construct and define their relationship with the public sphere" (Buckingham 1997, p. 353). They want to ascertain what the political world means to their own life and role in their community. The outcome may be a more pluralistic, decentralized type of democracy, with more activity at the grassroots level where the citizens' power is greatest and their participation in politics is most likely to bear fruit.

447

Paths to Better News for the Twenty-First Century

How, then, can the supply of political news be altered so that it becomes more meaningful and attractive for twenty-first century audiences? Information processing research suggests numerous ways. Most importantly, the many characteristics that have made political offerings on television so unappealing to audiences of all ages can be corrected. New technologies make it much easier and less expensive to diversify news stories for various types of audiences, cast stories in cinematic-quality visual language, stress local angles in news, and provide salient contexts and interpretations for stories so that political understanding is enhanced.

In political news at the dawn of the twenty-first century, both internal and external contextual data are often inadequate so that the stories are confusing and their impact on the totality of politics and on the audience is unclear. Societal forces that shaped the reported events are left unexplained. Comparisons with related events or appraisals of the story's significance for various groups are missing. While most news stories report clearly who and what is involved and where and when it happened, coverage of the *why* and *how* questions – which interest news audiences of all ages most – is poor by comparison (Graber 1993). These flaws can be overcome as good journalists have amply demonstrated on many past occasions. They know how to weave essential contexts into complex stories and how to link specific stories to larger themes that resonate with various audiences. But they need sufficient resources in time and money for research, production, and presentation to do their job well.

Adherence to journalistic norms of impartiality often makes stories needlessly confusing to audiences by covering an overly broad spectrum of possibilities. Aside from political sophisticates, audiences find it much easier to process a limited number of clearly explained likely outcomes of various policies than trying to make sense out of large numbers of cryptically stated contingencies. Similarly, average audiences can judge more easily what is most and least important when journalists prioritize the consequences. This does not mean that journalists should make evaluations for audiences contrary to norms of objectivity; rather, it means supplying audiences with usable evaluation criteria.

We know that genXers and others flock to the movies, video stores, and selected television programs when audio-visual productions tell interesting, engaging stories tied to human interest themes. This explains why investigative news magazine formats on television, which use these techniques, have become increasingly popular with all age groups – 68 percent of genXers claim to watch them sometimes or regularly. The corresponding figures for boomers and matures are 76 and 81 percent (Pew 1996). Most people (80 percent) claim to gain political knowledge from such programming. Because the stories are dramatic, they increase the viewers' involvement with significant public policy issues. Such programs may even stimulate people with limited political interests to care and become politically active. In good news magazine segments, the visuals are part of the story rather than essentially meaningless decorations for verbal texts. These attractive qualities of cinematic productions have been largely lacking from newscasts. The new digital spectrum can change that by making it easy to produce movie-quality high-definition pictures and sounds which can greatly enhance the attractiveness of broadcasts.

Although Internet technology corresponds most closely to the news selection preferences of genXers, access to off-line and on-line computerized information has remained unduly limited because it usually requires reading skills that some genXers lack. To become more user friendly across the education and sophistication spectrum, access to computerized information must become as simple as selecting a television program. Likewise, computerized news stories must rely far more heavily on high-quality audio-visuals to convey their messages. The needed technological refinements are imminent.

News framing constitutes another problem. There is a disjunction between the way journalists have framed political issues in the past and the way audiences now ask political questions. Presidential debates provide good illustrations. When ordinary citizens frame the questions about future policies in a style that is compatible with their manner of thinking, most audience members report that they can identify much more readily with the questions than when journalists frame their typical questions about campaign strategies and candidate shortcomings. When such "town-hall" formats have been used during public meetings or call-in television, young and old audiences alike have responded enthusiastically.

Besides deciding what manner of framing is most appropriate for the large population of genXers who are turned off by old-style news formats, news producers need to figure out which news topics are most salient for them. Important lifestyle issues, like the safety of the physical environment, the availability of affordable good health care, and the quality of public education all were topics of widespread, keen interest to young audiences at the turn of the century. To accommodate the special needs of these audiences, Cliff Zukin (1997, p. 43) suggested that "news could concentrate more on *transitional* problems, such as jobs or the housing market . . . News could also focus on *solutions*, rather than just on problems, as gen X could use a hand making its way through the world." In terms of framing, Zukin believes that, besides preferring highly visual, fast-paced stories, genXers like greater ethnic diversity among people shown on screen, including reporters and the people involved in the stories.

Zukin also stresses the importance of providing genXers with more specialized programs catering to specific interests, especially at the local level. Narrow-casting should be "in" and mass programming should be on the way out. Programs should cater to audiences of various degrees of sophistication and with various levels of interest in a particular topic. Reporting of political rumors, speculations, transient happenings, and international events should be kept to a minimum. Currently, the technical capacity to carry a vast array of diverse programs to suit the eclectic tastes of young viewers has been wasted by a plague of pack journalism; the offerings on most major news outlets have been like peas from the same pod.

To counteract the danger that a high degree of specialization will lead to undesirable Balkanization of politics, narrowly targeted news could be balanced by brief interludes of more broadly gauged news that place the specialized information into its broader background. Much of the decline in interest in national and international political news has been blamed on the loss of a sense of civic responsibility and failure to realize how greatly the lives of average Americans are affected by events in the nation and abroad. To the extent that young Americans lack civic ardor and are unaware of their dependence on larger social units, remedies rest squarely within the purview of the American educational system. It must put more emphasis on teaching students to discern how directly many seemingly irrelevant and distant political issues affect their personal lives and the welfare of their communities. More often than not, the connections between micropolitics at the local level and the macropolitics of the nation and even the world community are slighted in American schools and by news media accounts (Buckingham 1997).

Nonetheless, it is clear that the twenty-first century, of necessity, will be an age of specialization. The Renaissance citizen of old, who could be reasonably knowledgeable on all major fronts, has become impossible. It is totally unrealistic to expect modern citizens to be able to master all of the political news that interfaces with the concerns that are closest to their interests and attention. Just as Congress breaks its work into ever more specialized committees, so will citizens increasingly confine themselves to paying attention to and making contributions in specialized areas.

The low quality of much political news is often attributed to the stifling influence of profit considerations. Because of market place pressures, junk food news presumably is here to stay, despite its social costs. That is not necessarily the case because many news consumers are turning away more and more from current offerings. If private or public sector programming initiatives demonstrate that there is a sizeable market for truly informative and engaging news, the lure of virtue rewarded with profits could prove irresistible. The alternative of losing sizeable audience sectors, including young audiences, and failing to meet their political information needs is untenable, not only from a civic perspective but from a commercial perspective as well.

REFERENCES

Abelman, Robert (1996). "Can We Generalize from Generation X? Not!" *Journal of Broadcasting and Electronic Media*, 40:441–446.

Barnhurst, Kevin G., and Ellen Wartella (1998). "Young Citizens, American TV Newscasts and the Collective Memory." *Critical Studies in Mass Communication*, 15:279–305.

—— (1991). "Newspapers and Citizenship: Young Adults' Subjective Experience of Newspapers." *Critical Studies in Mass Communication*, 8:195–209.

Bennett, Stephen Earl (1998). "Young Americans' Indifference to Media Coverage of Public Affairs." *PS: Political Science and Politics*, 31(3):535–541.

Buckingham, David (1997). "News Media, Political Socialization and Popular Citizenship: Towards a New Agenda." *Critical Studies in Mass Communication*, 14:344–366.

Delli Carpini, Michael (1989). "Age and History: Generations and Sociopolitical Change." In Roberta S. Sigel (Ed.), *Political Learning in Adulthood*. Chicago: The University of Chicago Press, pp. 11–55.

—— and Scott Keeter (1996). *What Americans Know about Politics and Why It Matters*. New Haven: Yale University Press.

Graber, Doris A. (1993). *Processing the News: How People Tame the Information Tide*. Lanham, MD: University Press of America.

—— (2000). *Virtual Political Reality: Learning About Politics in the Audio-Visual Age*. Chicago: University of Chicago Press.

Ichilov, Orit (1990). "Dimensions and Role Patterns of Citizenship in a Democracy." In

Orit Ichilov (Ed.), *Political Socialization, Citizenship Education and Democracy.* New York: Teachers College, pp. 11–24.

Owen, Rob (1997). *GenX TV: The Brady Bunch to Melrose Park.* Syracuse, NY: Syracuse University Press.

Pew Research Center for the People and The Press (1996). "TV News Viewership Declines: Fall-Off Greater for Young Adults and Computer Users." May 13, 1996 report. (http://www.people-press.org/mediarpt.htm)

(1998). "Media Consumption Survey." Section 3, June. (http://www.people-press.org/medsec3.htm.)

(1999). "Striking the Balance: Audience Interests, Business Pressures and Journalists' Values." Section 4. http://www.people-press.org/press99sec4.htm.

Putnam, Robert D. (1995). "Tuning In, Tuning Out: The Strange Disappearance of Social Capital in America," *PS: Political Science and Politics* 28(4):664–683.

Radio and Television News Directors Foundation (1996). *News in the Next Century Project. 1996. Profile of the American News Consumer.* Washington, DC: Radio and Television News Directors Foundation.

Ritchie, Karen (1995). *Marketing to Generation X.* New York: Lexington Books.

Rosenstiel, Tom, Carl Gottlieb, and Lee Ann Brady (1999). "Local TV: What Works, What Flops, and Why." (http://www.journalism.org.)

Tapscott, Don (1998). *Growing Up Digital: The Rise of the Net Generation.* New York: McGraw Hill.

Turkle, Sherry (1997). *Life on the Screen: Identity in the Age of the Internet.* New York: Simon & Schuster.

Zukin, Cliff (1997). *Generation X and the News.* Washington, DC: Radio and Television News Directors Foundation.

CHAPTER 21

National Identities and the Future of Democracy

Wendy M. Rahn and Thomas J. Rudolph

Even though the essays in this volume focus on the future of democracy, we begin our chapter from a rather old-fashioned perspective, namely that democratic nation-states require some modicum of citizen loyalty and affection in order to induce compliance without costly and inefficient enforcement mechanisms. This is as true for policies, such as military service (Levi 1997), that may involve enormous self-sacrifice as it is for more mundane acts of obedience, such as paying one's taxes (Scholz and Lubell 1998; see also Tyler 1990).

Our chapter also begins with the assumption that the future of democracy, as it is embodied in the form of the modern nation-state, can be glimpsed by studying its youngest members. It is their attitudes and orientations that will come to dominate institutions and infuse politics as older generations quietly or not so quietly leave the population. Drawing on a wide range of national survey data collected in the mid-1990s, we examine the attachments of younger citizens to their national political communities, focusing primarily on the United States and the countries of the European Union. We find that without exception younger citizens are less likely to be committed to a national identity. In some polities, particularly in the United States, these weaker attachments are accompanied by less positive feelings about the "way democracy works." We then try to assess empirically a variety of potential explanations for these patterns.

An earlier version of this chapter was presented at the Communication in the Future of Democracy Workshop, Annenberg Public Policy Center, Washington, DC, May 8, 1998. The authors thank our sons, Aaron and Timothy, for letting us finish this chapter.

453

THE NATION-STATE BESIEGED

According to a huge body of theory, the nation-state is under assault from both external and internal pressures. There are a number of changes occurring in the global political economy that serve to undermine the centrality of the nation-state as the primary unit of political organization. Often collected under the mantra of globalization, these forces are said to impinge on the political economies of even the strongest of states. The number of journalists and academics that have advanced these claims is growing steadily. Susan Strange (1999), for example, chose as the subtitle for her recent book, *Mad Money*, "when markets outgrow governments," signifying her belief that the power of international financial markets has outstripped the capacity of states to control their economies. Arthur Schlesinger, Jr. (1997) worries in *Foreign Affairs* that in the computer age, the creative destruction of capitalism may claim the nation-state as its latest victim:

> The computer turns the untrammeled market into a global juggernaut crashing across frontiers, enfeebling national powers of taxation and regulation, undercutting national management of interest rates and exchange rates, dragging down labor standards, degrading the environment, denying nations the shaping of their own economic destiny, accountable to no one, creating a world economy without a world polity. Cyberspace is beyond national control . . . Where is democracy now? (Schlesinger 1997, p. 8)

The new internationalism has also created a certain breed of citizen, the symbolic analyst or the global cosmopolitan, a person whose professional interests and networks transcend national boundaries (Reich 1991). These people are "seceding," to use Reich's term, from the rest of the nation. In the case of the United States, these globalists,

> send their kids to private schools, insure themselves against medical emergencies by enrolling in company-supported plans, and hire private security guards to protect themselves against the mounting violence against them . . . Many of them have ceased to think of themselves as Americans in any important sense, implicated in America's destiny for better or worse. Their ties to an international culture of work and leisure – of business, entertainment, information, and information retrieval – make them deeply

indifferent to the prospect of American national decline (Lasch 1995, p. 45)

International law, particularly in the area of human rights, challenges the very notion that citizens have a special status compared to non-citizens. The rights and privileges that once were reserved for citizens are now granted to resident aliens in the name of universal personhood. The value of territorially based citizenship, therefore, has declined, according to Jacobson (1997). These and other developments, including the rise of global communications and the creation of supranational organizations such as the European Union, are said to have *desacralized* national boundaries, making them mundane demarcations rather than borders that inspire devotion and connection (Jacobson 1997). Indeed, "time zones have become more important than borders" (Wriston 1997).

Complementing the changes wrought by globalization, the end of the Cold War, according to some, has ushered in an era of state *deformation*. War and other external threats made possible the expansion of most of the world's nation-states and helped maintain internal cohesion.[1] The end of the Cold War, therefore, may make previously secure states weak and vulnerable to internal dissension (Desch 1996). Samuel Huntington (1997) makes the point by quoting the central character from John Updike's novels, Rabbit Angstrom, "Without the cold war, what's the point of being an American?" Huntington predicts that the end of the Cold War will weaken the bond of identity between the American people and the government, leading to increased opposition to its role in American life.[2]

Many scholars of national identity point to the essential role played by cultural institutions, particularly communications systems, in developing national consciousness (Anderson 1983; Gellner 1983; Deutsch 1966). Anderson's (1983) notion of imagined communities, for example, ties the development of national identity to the spread of what he calls print capitalism, of which the newspaper was a primary product. The reading of the newspaper, Anderson argued, involves millions of people in a daily mass ceremony, creating a community even in the midst of anonymity. Network television news, particularly before the advent of cable brought about the decline of the mass audience for national news (Baum and Kernell 1999), may have performed a similar integrative function.

But communication systems may remake allegiances. Smaller

numbers of citizens in the United States, particularly younger Americans, are engaged in the rituals that forged national consciousness in an earlier age (see Table 21.1 and Chap. 20, by Graber). In Europe the trends are similar (see Table 21.2). Instead, people are increasingly likely to be plugged in to these forms of communication that represent the global communications revolution, satellite TV, and the Internet. The communications aspect of globalization has helped to promote the obliteration of place as a meaningful distinction. The global village, with its attendant pleasures of cheap consumer products, exotic foodstuffs, and international tourism has no boundaries and can be purchased on-line with a few quick key strokes. And too, nation-states find themselves increasingly under the glare of a global media, circumscribing their monopoly on the legitimate use of force within their own borders, and thus calling into question the very notion of state sovereignty.

As many an analyst has remarked, increased global interdependence seems to be accompanied by increasing fragmentation and parochialism. Colorful metaphors are often used to capture this paradox, such as Friedman's *Lexus and the Olive Tree* (Friedman 1999). Globalization seems to have unleashed reactionary forces by those who are left behind, sentiments exacerbated by international migration of displaced peoples, many of whom wish to retain their old loyalties rather than assimilate to the culture and values of their host countries. Multicultural ideologies and separatist movements within some established democracies are visible signs of the internal stress facing these states as they attempt to grapple with a new and complex diversity.

These divisions become easier to maintain given the fragmentation of modern marketing and communication systems. Both Elihu Katz (1996) and Joseph Turow (1997) argue that trends in television programming and mass marketing contribute to the fragmentation of national cultures whereas in earlier generations, media and marketing contributed to national cohesion. Turow refers to this transformation as a change from "society-making" to "segment-making media." Bennett (1998) argues further that these technological changes not only weaken national commitments, but collective identities of all kinds, creating what he calls "identity disorders." Oscar Gandy (this volume) sees the same fragmentation at work in the Internet.

Lamented or celebrated, the much-ballyhooed effects of globalization have received surprisingly little empirical investigation at the level of citizens' loyalties, attitudes, and commitments. Is it the case, for example, that heavy users of the Internet or heavy viewers of CNN are less likely to feel themselves to be national? And can developments like the Internet, the upgrading of education, occupational pursuits that involve international connections and travel, etc., account for why young people in many of the world's established democracies are less attracted to national identities than their elders? We will turn to an examination of these sorts of questions.

SOME PRELIMINARY EVIDENCE

An empirical test of some of these more prominent claims reviewed above is hampered by the lack of suitable individual-level measures. While several public opinion surveys now ask about e-mail and Internet access, for example, measures of national attachment are often not included on the same survey. Our analysis will not do justice to the complexity of many of the arguments we reviewed above, but nevertheless we believe that some attempt, however limited and imperfect, to assess the often far-reaching pronouncements about the impact of globalization on the citizens of democratic nation-states is overdue.

In the analysis of political change, the attitudes of young people are of particular importance. In *generational* models of social change, historical changes, such as the Great Depression, wars, and social movements, have differential effects on people of different ages because of their position in the life cycle. While everyone in a society shares the same history, the salient events of a particular time period are more likely to leave a lingering impression on young adults because of their greater susceptibility to attitude change, the so-called impressionable years hypothesis (see, e.g., Abramson and Inglehart 1995; Krosnick and Alwin 1989; Mayer 1992; Rochon 1998; Visser and Krosnick 1998). According to a generational model, then, the national attachments of younger cohorts should be most weakened by the forces of globalization. Older cohorts, socialized in eras in which the nation-state was unchallenged as a form of political organization, may also be affected by those currents, but to a considerably smaller degree.

AGE AND NATIONAL IDENTITY IN THE UNITED STATES

If a generational model of social change is the correct one to employ in the study of globalization, then the political attitudes of today's young people offer the greatest promise in forecasting the politics of tomorrow. We begin our analysis by focusing on the United States. Table 21.1 reports the aggregate means from a series of questions adminis-

Table 21.1. *Age and national identity in the United States*

	New Deal, WW II (pre-1930)	Cold War (1930–45)	Early boom (1946–54)	Late boom (1955–64)	Post boom (1965+)
Media use and other					
Internet access	0.03	0.18	0.32	0.33	0.45
Watch national TV					
News	0.75	0.61	0.49	0.39	0.33
Read newspaper	0.69	0.55	0.50	0.40	0.32
Cable access	0.64	0.70	0.70	0.70	0.70
Own stocks	0.47	0.55	0.61	0.55	0.32
Political Engagement					
General political					
interest	0.66	0.64	0.63	0.51	0.49
Strength of partisanship	0.70	0.65	0.63	0.63	0.56
Reported turnout	0.85	0.81	0.82	0.75	0.60
National Identity					
Satisfaction with U.S.					
democracy	0.74	0.71	0.69	0.68	0.62
Proud of way U.S.					
democracy works	0.81	0.76	0.71	0.67	0.62
Personal importance of					
American identity	0.91	0.87	0.76	0.81	0.76

Note: All variables are scaled on a 0 to 1 range.
Sources: 1996 and 1998 American National Election Studies, 1996 General Social Survey.

tered in recent surveys of the American electorate. To provide a generational perspective, we have grouped respondents according to the generational cohorts proposed by Bennett and Bennett (1990). The columns are arrayed so that respondents become progressively younger as one reads from left to right.[3]

Consider first Americans' patterns of media consumption. As can be seen, the number of Americans who read a daily newspaper declines monotonically across the five age cohorts. Americans born before 1930 are more than twice as likely to read a newspaper as those in the so-called postboom generation. A similar generational pattern exists for watching national television news, as younger generations are far less likely to watch national news than their more senior countrymen.

Each generation, it seems, is less likely than the preceding one to participate in the community building "ceremonies" envisioned by Anderson (1983). The generational story is quite different, however, when we consider participation in more global communication systems such as the Internet. Here the pattern of media consumption is exactly reversed. Internet use among the postboom generation exceeds that of the New Deal and World War II generations by a factor of 15. It is more than twice that of the Cold War generation as well. Clearly, younger generations are not isolated from the media. Rather, they have simply chosen to engage in less conventional and, some would argue, less nation-centric communication systems (see also Graber, Chap. 20).

Generational differences in the United States are by no means limited to patterns of media consumption. Indeed, as shown in the middle section of Table 21.1, levels of political engagement in America are strongly related to age. The decline of parties thesis has been advanced on numerous occasions (Crotty 1984; Kirkpatrick 1978; Wattenberg 1996). Similarly, scholars have documented a rise in split-ticket voting over the last several decades (Beck et al. 1992; Burden and Kimball 1998). Both of these trends are consistent with our observation that strength of partisanship is weaker in each successive generation. Not only are younger cohorts less strongly attached to one of the national parties, but they are less interested in politics generally. Moreover, by their own admission, they are less likely to participate in the most democratic and nation-building ritual of all, voting.

Thus far we have identified two generational trends in America. First, younger generations are less likely to engage in traditional and nationally integrative communication systems. Second, they are less likely to be directly engaged in national politics. Collectively, these two trends have potentially profound implications for the formation and maintenance of a national identity in the United States. If these two trends do in fact influence national identity, we would expect to see a generational pattern in Americans' attitudes toward their country and its political system. Though descriptive, our results are supportive of such a causal story. We find strong generational patterns in three different attitudes toward the United States. As shown at the bottom of Table 21.1, younger generations are less satisfied with U.S. democracy, less proud of the way it works, and, importantly, attribute less personal significance to their American identity. Coupled with Huntington's (1997) concerns about the end of Cold War, these strong age-related patterns, which we are

Table 21.2. *Age and national identity in Europe*

Variable	70+	60–69	50–59	40–49	30–39	Under 30	r
Media Use and other							
Read newspaper	0.71	0.72	0.77	0.77	0.72	0.63	0.09[b]
Watch TV news	0.94	0.95	0.93	0.92	0.89	0.83	0.21[b]
Internet access	0.02	0.04	0.11	0.15	0.18	0.24	−0.22[b]
Satellite TV access	0.12	0.15	0.21	0.22	0.23	0.23	−0.08[b]
Optimism about future[a]	−0.14	−0.10	−0.04	−0.02	−0.01	0.13	−0.09[b]
Political Identities							
Satisfied with democracy in nation	0.49	0.48	0.48	0.51	0.51	0.52	−0.05[b]
Satisfied with democracy in EU	0.43	0.44	0.42	0.45	0.46	0.49	−0.08[b]
National identity	0.86	0.83	0.79	0.77	0.78	0.76	0.11[b]
Support for EU	0.59	0.64	0.66	0.67	0.69	0.74	−0.12[b]
Political Engagement							
Discuss politics	0.37	0.42	0.47	0.46	0.43	0.36	0.05[b]
Reported turnout, 1994	0.73	0.77	0.76	0.76	0.71	0.51	0.16[b]
Projected turnout, 1999	0.79	0.85	0.88	0.87	0.87	0.81	0.02[b]

Note: Cell entries are aggregate mean scores by age categories. Unless otherwise indicated, all variables are scaled on a 0 to 1 range. The seventh column reports the simple bivariate correlations between age and the corresponding row variable.

[a] This variable is a factor score created from ten questions about whether different aspects of life are likely to be better or worse in the 21st century. Higher values reflect greater optimism.

[b] $p < 0.05$, two-tailed.

Source: Eurobarometer 49, Spring 1998.

interpreting in generational terms, mean that in the absence of nation-strengthening events, such as war, to affect the consciousness of subsequent cohorts, we can expect a gradual withering away of the psychological centrality of the nation-state as older cohorts are replaced.

Age and National Identity in Europe

Having considered generational patterns of media consumption, political engagement, and national identity in the United States, we continue our analysis by using data from a recent Eurobarometer survey to focus on trends in Europe. Table 21.2 provides a generational perspective on various political attitudes and orientations in the European theater. Patterns of media consumption in Europe have a similar generational flavor to those in the United States. The likelihood of reading a newspaper or watching national television news declines, though not monotonically, among the younger cohorts. In contrast, younger cohorts are far more likely to have access to "boundary-blind" communication systems such as satellite television or the Internet.

Administered in the spring of 1998, this Eurobarometer survey affords us a unique opportunity to compare Europeans' national identity with their support for a supranational democratic institution such as the European Union. Europe represents an interesting case because its supranational democratic institutions may compete with national institutions for the interest and involvement of Europeans. Respondents were asked how satisfied they were with democracy as practiced by their own country as well as by the European Union. In contrast to the American case, younger cohorts in Europe do not appear to be especially dissatisfied with democracy as practiced at either level. In fact, they are slightly more likely to be satisfied with democracy at both levels. However, when we actually measure individuals' national identity vis-à-vis their European identity and consider their evaluations of the relationship between their country and the European Union, a different story emerges.

To measure national versus European identity, respondents were asked how they would see themselves in the near future. Specifically, they were asked to locate themselves along a four-point continuum, with one end representing a purely national identity and the other representing a purely European identity. As Table 21.2 makes clear, national identity among Europeans is inversely related to age. Not only are younger cohorts more likely to see themselves as Europeans, they are more likely to support their country's membership in the European Union than are their elders.[4] This measure of support is an additive scale constructed from two similar questions. Respondents were asked if they thought their country's EU membership was a good thing, and whether their country had benefited from its EU membership. As illustrated in Table 21.2, support for EU membership becomes progressively stronger from left to right.

The Eurobarometer survey also enables us to examine Europeans' actual engagement in supranational politics by age cohorts. The bottom two rows of Table 21.2 present the mean self-reported turnout levels for the 1994 EU elections and a projection of the mean self-reported turnout levels for the 1999 EU elections. Perhaps not surprisingly, these data reveal an interesting paradox. The youngest cohort of Europeans are the most likely to emphasize their European identity and are the most likely to value their nation's membership in the European Union. However, they are among the least likely to actually participate in EU elections.[5] Clearly, abstract endorsement of the EU does not always translate into concrete action. Dahlgren's (Chap. 2) discussion of public spheres may shed some light on this paradoxical relationship. Dahlgren suggests that in order to participate discursively in supranational political bodies such as the European Union, most citizens of the European Union must go via "national public spheres" (see also Eijk and Franklin 1996). Yet as we have seen, these are precisely the public spheres in which younger cohorts are less likely to be engaged.

MULTIVARIATE ANALYSIS

The preceding tables have provided a generational perspective on various attitudes and orientations in both the United States and Europe. Though suggestive, these descriptive results do not, of course, establish precise causal relationships among such factors as media consumption, political engagement, age, and national identity. To subject some of our causal speculations to greater empirical scrutiny, we construct a multivariate model using the Eurobarometer data. Specifically, we specify a system of structural equations to examine the potentially reciprocal causal relationship between national identity and support for the European Union. At issue is whether national identity affects individuals' support for the European Union and whether support for this supranational body might undermine individuals' allegiance to their own nation. We are equally interested in observing the effects of media consumption, political engagement, and age on these two dependent variables. The results from our model are presented below in Table 21.3.

Consider first the determinants of support for the European Union. Support is higher among those who are satisfied with democracy as practiced by the European Union. Support is also higher among conservatives, the well-educated, and those who are optimistic about the future. Whether respondents read a newspaper or watch television news has no significant impact. The coefficient on national identity is large, but because its standard error is also large, it fails to reach statistical significance.[6] Note, however, that its sign is positive. There is no indication, in other words, that strong national identities interfere with

Table 21.3. *Determinants of national identity and support for the European union*

Variables	Support for EU	National Identity
Support for EU	–	−0.33^a (0.04)
National identity	0.45 (0.54)	–
Read newspaper	0.03 (0.02)	0.01 (0.01)
Watch TV news	0.04 (0.03)	−0.01 (0.02)
Internet access	0.06^a (0.03)	−0.04^a (0.01)
Discuss politics	0.09^a (0.04)	−0.06^a (0.01)
Optimism about future	0.11^a (0.02)	−0.01 (0.01)
Satisfied with EU democracy	0.49^a (0.06)	–
Satisfied with nat. democracy	–	0.06^a (0.02)
Ideology (conservatism)	0.07^a (0.02)	0.04^a (0.02)
Education	0.05^a (0.01)	−0.01^a (0.004)
Age	−0.04 (0.05)	0.04 (0.03)
Constant	−0.03 (0.46)	0.94^a (0.04)
Adj. R^2	0.18	0.11
N	4742	4742

Note: This system of structural equations was estimated using three-stage least squares. Separate dummy variables were also included to account for country-specific effects (results not shown).
Standard errors appear in parentheses.
^{a} $p < 0.05$, two-tailed.
Source: Eurobarometer Survey, Spring 1998.

support for the European Union. Those who discuss politics regularly with their friends or family are more likely to support the European Union. Support for the European Union is also greater among those with Internet access, as use of a boundary-blind communication system increases support for this supranational body. While the effect of Internet access is rather small, comparable to that of education or ideology, it emerges as significant even controlling for age, education, and optimism, control variables that represent substantial hurdles for finding any direct effects. Importantly, the previous relationship between age and EU support has now disappeared, suggesting that its effects are being mediated by one or more of the variables identified in our model.

The second column of Table 21.3 reports the coefficients from the identity equation. As can be seen, the effects of reading a newspaper, watching television news, and optimism about the future do not withstand multivariate competition. National identity is higher among those who are satisfied with their nation's democracy and among conservatives.[7] Education is inversely related to national identity, as the well-educated are more likely to embrace a European identity. Discussing politics reduces commitment to one's national identity, as does access to the Internet. Apparently, then, it is an elite slice of European society, as measured by their greater education, access to new technologies, and political engagement, that is both abandoning the nation-state at the same time it embraces a new form of political organization. As before, the bivariate relationship between age and national identity becomes insignificant when potentially mediating factors such as media consumption, education, and political engagement are taken into account. More importantly, we find that support for the European Union, a supranational democratic institution, appears to undermine national identity, to a large and highly significant degree.

DISCUSSION

Perhaps the most interesting result of our multivariate exercise for the themes of this volume is that access to the Internet seems to accompany a weaker sense of national commitment *and* a stronger endorsement for a new form of political organization as it is embodied in the European Union. We cannot be sure whether it is Internet usage itself or the as-yet-unmeasured qualities of people who use the Internet driving these results. Even if this result is partly derivative of some other set of variables, we view our finding as an important preliminary test of whether the communications aspect of globalization is indeed weakening national commitments as many of its prophets have proclaimed. It is also clear from our results that when an alternative to the nation-state exists and its consequences are deemed to be beneficial, the nation-state can begin to lose its psychological hold on people. This supports a view of identity that is not only constructive in nature, but also importantly instrumental. Whether the instrumental basis of European identity will fade as the European Union ages remains to be seen. Until such identity becomes habitual, it would seem that allegiance to the European Union is vulnerable to how citizens view its performance.

In the case of the United States, there is no viable competitor for citizens' allegiance, at least not yet. Thus, even though younger Americans increasingly see little psychological relevance of their membership in the American polity, they, in effect, have nowhere else to turn. Perhaps that explains, in part, their disenchantment with American democracy, whereas in Europe, there exists something else toward which young people can gravitate. As of yet, however, this new entity has not spurred greater traditional democratic participation on the part of younger Europeans. Increasing cosmopolitanism may not necessarily bring with it increasing democracy.

CONCLUSION

Many things have changed since the end of WWII. As the latest of these developments, globalization in both its internal and external manifestations catches our fancy. We have uncovered strong age-related patterns consistent with a generational interpretation of globalization's impact on national allegiances. An understanding of where the future of democracy lies requires additional theoretical and empirical investigation of these patterns. The nation-state was a modern invention and may be eclipsed by some other form of political organization, perhaps supranational in character, that is capable of creating social order and sustaining allegiance. The weaker national commitments of younger citizens surely make such a transformation more likely. The future of democracy, at least electoral democracy as we know it, in this new world order is by no means assured, however.

NOTES

1. For a valuable look at the role of war bonds in mobilizing support for World War II, see Samuel (1997). What is striking about his account is the way in which major social institutions, including Hollywood and advertising agencies, were engaged in the war effort. Posters that appeared in salient public places were a particularly important aspect of the war bond drive. The themes identified by Samuel in the posters implicated national identity in some way.
2. In another context, we have found strong support for Huntington's hypothesis using time-series data on Americans' level of confidence in national institutions. Controlling for the objective and subjective economy, presidential approval, presidential scandals, and salient foreign policy events, we find that when the public is focused on international issues, they have greater confidence in government. Since the end of the Cold War (i.e., the late 1980s), public concern with foreign policy has decreased substantially, coinciding with sharply reduced levels of confidence, even in an era of robust economic performance (see Chanley, Rudolph, and Rahn 1999).
3. When age-based differences in attitudes appear at one time point, it is impossible to disentangle whether they are due chiefly to life-cycle differences or to cohort differences. We interpret these differences as cohort-based because of their overwhelming consistency and because at least in some cases, such as voter turnout in the United

States (see Miller and Shanks 1996), strong evidence for distinctive generational differences has been accumulated.

4. We must be careful not to push this point too far. Even those in the youngest cohort are closer to the national identity end of the scale than the end representing European identity. However, younger cohorts are further away from a purely national identity than more senior cohorts.

5. When calculating the aggregate means for the voting variables, we excluded those whose failure to vote was due to any age-related ineligibility.

6. The large standard error is probably due to the fact that the identity equation is not very well identified. With a better specified equation, and therefore a better instrument for identity, its coefficient in the EU equation might have attained statistical significance.

7. We note that conservatives are simultaneously more likely to embrace their national identity and support the European Union. We suspect that our measure of ideology is tapping both the cultural and economic dimensions of conservatism. We would expect cultural conservatives to value their national identity, just as we would expect economic conservatives to express their commitment to free trade by supporting the European Union.

REFERENCES

Abramson, Paul R., and Ronald Inglehart (1995). *Value Change in Global Perspective.* Ann Arbor, MI: University of Michigan Press.

Anderson, Benedict (1983). *Imagined Communities.* London: Verso.

Baum, Matthew A., and Samuel Kernell (1999). "Has Cable Ended the Golden Age of Presidential Television?" *American Political Science Review*, 93:99–114.

Beck, Paul Allen, Lawrence Baum, Aage R. Clausen, and Charles E. Smith Jr. (1992). "Patterns and Sources of Ticket Splitting in Subpresidential Voting." *American Political Science Review*, 86:916–928.

Bennett, Linda L. M., and Stephen Earl Bennett (1990). *Living with Leviathan.* Lawrence, KS: University of Kansas Press.

Bennett, Lance W. (1998). "The Uncivic Culture: Communication, Identity and the Rise of Lifestyle Politics." *PS: Political Science and Politics*, 31:741.

Burden, Barry C., and David C. Kimball (1998). "A New Approach to the Study of Ticket Splitting." *American Political Science Review*, 92:533–544.

Chanley, Virginia, Thomas J. Rudolph, and Wendy M. Rahn (1999). "The Origins and Consequences of Public Views about Government: A Time Series Analysis." Unpublished manuscript.

Crotty, William (1984). *American Parties in Decline, 2nd edition.* Boston, MA: Little, Brown and Company.

Desch, Michael (1996). "War and Strong States, Peace and Weak States?" *International Organization*, 50:237–68.

Deutsch, Karl W. (1966). *Nationalism and Social Communications, 2nd edition.* Cambridge, MA: MIT Press.

Eijk, Cees van der, and Mark N. Franklin (1996). *Choosing Europe? The European Electorate and National Politics in the Face of Union.* Ann Arbor, MI: University of Michigan Press.

Friedman, Thomas L. (1999). *Lexus and the Olive Tree: Understanding Globalization.* New York: Farrar, Straus, and Giroux.

Gellner, Ernest. (1983). *Nations and Nationalism.* Ithaca, NY: Cornell University Press.

Huntington, Samuel P. (1997). "The Erosion of American National Interests." *Foreign Affairs,* 76:28–49.

Jacobson, David J. (1997). *Rights Cross Borders: Immigration and the Decline of Citizenship.* Baltimore, MD: Johns Hopkins University Press.

Katz, Elihu (1996). "And Deliver Us from Segmentation." *The Annals of the American Academy of Political and Social Science,* 546:22–33.

Kirkpatrick, Jeane J. (1978). *Dismantling the Parties.* Washington, DC: American Enterprise Institute for Public Policy Research.

Krosnick, Jon. A., and Duane F. Alwin (1989). "Aging and Susceptibility to Attitude Change." *Journal of Personality and Social Psychology,* 57:416–425.

Lasch, Christopher (1995). *The Revolt of the Elites.* New York: W. W. Norton.

Levi, Margaret (1997). *Consent, Dissent, and Patriotism.* New York: Cambridge University Press.

Mayer, William G. (1992). *The Changing American Mind: How and Why American Public Opinion Changed between 1960 and 1988.* Ann Arbor: University of Michigan Press.

Miller, Warren E., and J. Merrill Shanks (1996). *The New American Voter.* Cambridge, MA: Harvard University Press.

Reich, Robert B. (1991). "What Is a Nation?" *Political Science Quarterly,* 106:193–209.

Rochon, Thomas R. (1998). *Culture Moves: Ideas, Activism, and Changing Values.* Princeton: Princeton University Press.

Samuel, Lawrence R. (1997). *Pledging Allegiance: American Identity and the Bond Drive of World War II.* Washington, DC: Smithsonian Institution.

Schlesinger, Jr., Arthur P. (1997). "Has Democracy a Future?" *Foreign Affairs,* 76:2–12.

Scholz, John T., and Mark Lubell (1998). "Trust and Taxpaying: Testing the Heuristic Approach to Collective Action." *American Journal of Political Science,* 42:398–417.

Strange, Susan (1998). *Mad Money: When Markets Outgrow Governments.* Ann Arbor, MI: University of Michigan Press.

Turow, Joseph (1997). *Breaking Up America: Advertisers and the New Media World.* Chicago: University of Chicago Press.

Tyler, Tom (1990). *Why People Obey the Law.* New Haven, CT: Yale University Press.

Visser, Penny S., and Jon A. Krosnick (1998). "The Development of Attitude Strength over the Life Cycle: Surge and Decline." *Journal of Personality and Social Psychology,* 75:1388–1409.

Wattenberg, Martin P. (1996). *The Decline of American Political Parties, 1952–1994.* Cambridge, MA: Harvard University Press.

Wriston, Walter B. (1997). "Bits, Bytes, and Diplomacy." *Foreign Affairs,* 76:172–182.

CHAPTER 22

Communication in the Future of Democracy: A Conclusion

Robert M. Entman and W. Lance Bennett

This book covers considerable ground, raising a variety of empirical and theoretical issues and employing diverse methodological orientations. We have not built a single story here, as different authors read the trends and possibilities in sometimes conflicting ways. What unites the chapters is their fundamental concern with the present and future of democratic political systems in which mass communication and newer communication techniques and technologies play important roles in the exertion of power and distribution of values. In this conclusion we summarize some key themes and issues and lay out directions for future research. First, we suggest a framework for organizing different understandings about the role of communication both as it affects the overall quality of public life and as it shapes citizen engagement in the specific policy decisions in democracies.

A SIMPLE MODEL OF COMMUNICATION IN DEMOCRACIES

From Aristotle's analysis of rhetoric, to Mill's designs for a marketplace of ideas, to Habermas's idealization of the public sphere and Dahl's comparative theory of polyarchy, theorists of democracy have concerned themselves with the delivery, distribution, quality, and uses of information by citizens. We propose here a brief adaptation of Dahl's (1989) account of polyarchy to identify and develop theoretically grounded research into some of the crucial issues emerging from political communication trends apparent at the end of the century.

Dahl argues that democracy in the ideal is defined by the equally empowered rule by all. Even if everyone is unlikely to participate in all decisions, no citizen in a fully evolved democracy is excluded from doing so based on restrictive participation requirements or discouraging burdens for becoming informed and expressing effective preferences. Dahl argues that the ideals of equal control of the policy agenda and inclusive deliberation and decision processes have not been achieved in any society. In fact, most societies loosely classified as democracies display considerable differences in their degrees of citizen empowerment and participation. Rather than corrupt the term *democracy* by using it to refer to vastly different patterns of citizen engagement with government, he proposes a continuum of polyarchy – rule by many – to distinguish different levels of popular sovereignty.

At the lower end of the continuum, the minimum conditions for polyarchy are defined by equality of opportunity to vote and the existence of free and fair elections for government officials. The upper end of the continuum approaches the ideal of democratic governance when citizens are equally included in defining, understanding, and deciding the policy agenda. The distinguishing feature of systems toward the upper end of the polyarchy spectrum is that they offer alternative and transparent policy information to citizens. That is, the information comes from different sources, and those sources and their goals are known. Moreover, this information is delivered in ways that promote inclusive public deliberation and broad control of policy agendas and outcomes (Dahl 1989, p. 222).

In identifying the factors that keep most systems from attaining higher levels of democratic development beyond the basic requirements of electoral competition and freedom of opinion and vote expression, Dahl points to an important obstacle: the control of information by policy elites. This obstacle, he argues, is growing more serious in many advanced systems. His recommendation is for the design of independent communication and information systems tailored to citizens' abilities and needs. Moreover, he proposes that political information systems include deliberative exercises that encourage broadly shared engagement with policies and the decision processes surrounding them. (Dahl 1989, p. 338).

With this continuum, Dahl offers us an interesting way of thinking about how to compare and evaluate political communication processes. For example, we can imagine thinking about the degree to which information is *transparent*, as defined by whether it is identified with its partisan sources, whether those sources clearly announce their political goals (or whether news analysis attributes those goals), and whether such information is clearly connected to different policy alternatives.

We can also imagine political communication processes that are more or less inclusive, as defined by the degree to which information is distributed equally across a public and presented in ways that make it easy for ordinary citizens to assimilate and respond.

There are, we think, several advantages to thinking about political communication in terms of the comparative qualities of, and the deliberative outlets for, citizen information both within and between societies. Above all, we feel that there has been an unfortunate disjunction between different approaches to thinking about what constitutes political communication and its place in democratic process. As noted in the first chapter, for example, we think that there is a tendency among some political communication scholars to dismiss much political content as hype, media spectacle, or noisy propaganda that washes over relatively independent rational information processors. Moreover, there is a tendency to sample opinion on the most commonly surveyed issues, meaning that much research is biased by its unintended focus on those issues most likely to draw publics into the policy sphere.

Indeed, the very focus on opinion as the most obvious core element of the political communication process introduces limits into our thinking about communication and democracy. There is, of course, little point in arguing against opinion as the dependent variable of choice in communication research. The plentiful supply of accessible survey data, along with the behavioral and positivist emphases in much communication research, assures the status of opinion as the leading measure of democratic processes. However, as many of the authors in this volume point out, other patterns of public interaction and engagement are not only measurable but may be of more relevance in thinking about the quality of democratic life. Moreover, the ways in which communication selectively includes and excludes audiences for issues should be incorporated in analyses of survey data as background for interpreting patterns of public engagement or avoidance of policy matters (cf. Eliasoph 1998).

Dahl's information and citizen inclusion criteria for defining various levels of polyarchy offer a framework within which we can think about both the opinion-centered and the process orientation to political communication. For example, it is perfectly consistent with Dahl's continuum to discover that individuals in a given political system may make stable, independent judgments about a few salient aspects of public life and still not achieve higher stages of collective democratic development. This is because higher levels of polyarchy require more broadly informed engagement with a wider range of policy issues. For example, people may demonstrate considerable independent judgment when staking out positions on highly publicized policy issues such as the Lewinsky scandal or abortion. This does not tell us much about citizen engagement with the vast array of less publicized policies that constitute the everyday agendas of government officials – policies that might in fact touch upon many individuals' most pressing concerns (e.g., safety and cost of food supplies, communication law, military procurement). Moreover, even if citizens display some independence and stability of issue judgment over time, assessing the implications for the health of democracy requires determining also whether they are discouraged about politics and government and cynical about their ability to affect policy agendas or decisions. And if they autonomously conclude something based on distorted (or absent) information, and stubbornly cling to that judgment, independence and stability by themselves may not always prove useful indicators of democracy.

Scholars who emphasize the stability and relative media independence of certain opinion characteristics (such as the basis of voting choices or presidential approval) often have little to say about these larger conditions of the communication process. For example, Zaller has argued in this volume and elsewhere that voters continue to base their decisions on much the same durable considerations as they have for half a century. Although important in its own right, this point is not connected theoretically (or empirically) to research on the corruption of voter information, and the dissatisfaction of voters with the electoral process due to alterations in news coverage and campaign message strategies (Patterson 1993; Ansolabehere and Iyengar 1995; Cappella and Jamieson 1997). We merely mean to point out there are important questions that must be framed as complex patterns of citizen response before we reach definitive verdicts on the health of democracy in any political system. We seek a framework that enables us to talk about a combination of factors at the same time. These include not merely voter stability but also shrinking electorates, the varying or perhaps declining quality of policy information over time, the rise of minutely scripted, focus-group-based messages by (often-camouflaged) interest groups and candidates, and the increasing negativity of news frames and advertising, which produces citizen polarization and cynicism.

In short, we sense a disjunction between two ways of studying political communication. In the first, scholars focus on patterns of individual responses to persuasive messages pertaining to particular choices. In the second, they emphasize the characteristics of the communication processes through which messages and political information are constructed and distributed within a political system. We think this disjunction hampers our understanding of the democratic performance of political systems, and the subjective experiences of the citizens within them.

We advocate a more general scheme for describing both information properties within systems and patterns of citizen engagement and disengagement with those properties. For example, for the United States, it is important to put findings of apparent voter independence and stability in the context of a shrinking electorate and alienated citizenry. It is important to weigh cases, like Gamson's analysis of abortion, in which broad and inclusive policy engagement is evident, alongside those such as nuclear or tax policy, in which poor information and less inclusive citizen engagement may have seriously undermined the ideals of popular sovereignty.

The authors in this volume represent a mix of viewpoints about what constitutes mediated political communication, and how such communication contributes to or detracts from various ideals of democratic citizen engagement. Rather than settle on one perspective over another, we conclude this volume with the hope that both individual-centered and process-centered perspectives on political communication will be able to communicate with each other. For example, scholars who find corruption of the democratic information process in strategic marketing that excludes segments of publics from the policy sphere would do well to recognize those areas in which individuals demonstrate impressive autonomy of thought and action – even in the midst of increasingly managed information environments. Similarly, those who currently require individual level measures of information and opinion responses in their models of citizen politics would do well to recognize the importance of ways in which communication processes may undermine ideals of information transparency and inclusiveness on which more satisfying levels of citizen participation may depend. In short, if we establish more sophisticated political communication theories that accommodate a variety of political information properties and citizen performance measures, we may develop better understandings of relative democratic strengths and weaknesses within and between political systems.

COMMUNICATION DILEMMAS IN THE FUTURE
OF DEMOCRACY

The major issues with which the authors in this volume grapple may initially appear as contradictory tendencies that seem inherent in the politics of the information society. For example, new communication technologies may enhance the capacity of individuals to express themselves freely in the public sphere (e.g., the burgeoning Internet traffic in pornography), while also limiting citizen engagement in the policy sphere (e.g., the active rejection of government and politics by those who create such Internet communities). Viewed from the perspective of Dahl's criteria of information transparency and inclusiveness, however, we see that trends that may facilitate individual political expressiveness may work against the growth of inclusive and information-rich policy spheres.

Expansion or Shrinkage of the Public Sphere?

One trend with uncertain implications arises from the triumph of economic efficiency and market values as guideposts to public policy-making in communication. Along with technological innovation, deregulation has produced growing competition and choice among outlets, including the essentially infinite channel capacity of the Internet. We see flourishing sources of information related to politics and public policy, not only on the Internet and specialized cable news channels, but also in "infotainment" and even entertainment programs that comment on public issues and the authoritative allocations of values. As a result of this explosion of channels, people enjoy increasingly inexpensive and powerful means for obtaining information and sharing ideas across group and geographical boundaries. But to what ends is the so-called communication revolution dedicated?

At one level, this future appears to promise expansion of capacity for individual involvement in political communication and networked political activity. However, the simultaneous fragmentation of media audiences and withering of public communication spheres within which to explore issues in common may work against inclusiveness, one key criterion of democratic performance. Dahlgren's contribution describes the complexities of deciding whether a democratic public sphere has in fact been enhanced by the new technologies. Sparks, looking at the possibilities for an even more inclusive public discursive space that crosses national boundaries, suggests that real expansion of public participation is doubtful, even as so-called multinational channels of information multiply. Declining audiences for daily newspapers and evening news broadcasts and the replacement of those common mediated experiences with more individualized and specialized communications may diminish the public sphere, particularly if, like Sparks, we assume such a sphere must set a common agenda for most citizens.

The commercialization of information channels also seems to reduce the resources devoted to traditional hard news coverage by mainstream daily news organizations. In an earlier era, particularly in the United States, government subsidies, greater public service regulation, and lower levels of competition allocated more media resources to public goods. As a result, public affairs information may have better approximated a common agenda of information and issues (although there are many scholars who would disagree). This said, despite the apparent deterioration in quality and audience reach of established daily news outlets, documented here by Underwood and others, the burgeoning availability of information channels may result in a remarkably interconnected citizenry in high-visibility cases such as the Clinton impeachment scandal, when sustained coverage of dramatic events saturates all channels.

Yet with the exception of those dramatic events that produce Wolfsfeld's "waves" of public engagement, ordinary citizens tuned into "society-breaking" media (Turow 1997) may become less knowledgeable and interested in a common public sphere. The decline in common engagement in the myriad routine and less dramatic issues of the day may also undermine citizens' connection to what we have called the policy sphere, where government decisions and resource allocations that affect the entire society are debated.

We are concerned that the shrinkage of the policy sphere may be obscured by increased access to communication channels and personalized information retrieval technologies that enable ever greater numbers of people to steep themselves in personal, narrow-gauged "sphericules" (Gitlin 1998) of interest. Thus, driven by the new communication outlets, the aggregate levels of knowledge and energy devoted to discussion outside the family could increase, even as shared understandings and dialog among a mass public exposed to common news texts deteriorates. As suggested by Slater's essay on trading pornographic files via Internet chat, however, this transition toward a more inclusive yet fractionalized public sphere raises perplexing questions about just what constitutes *political* discourse and behavior.

As we said in the introduction, a central question arises over the political lives of citizens treated as if they were merely consumers waiting to be stimulated and sold like commodities to advertisers and merchants. Will these citizens remain disaffected and cynical, avoiding politics as they retreat into consumer and personal interest sphericules that displace participation in the policy sphere, where collective social issues are made? Even those who remain engaged in the policy sphere may be led by a shrinking civil society and highly personalized voter appeals to make demands on government that are more individualized, and thus less likely to be satisfied, at least by government. This is just one example of how individuals may be engaged, yet still be negatively affected by communication processes that work against our ideal of inclusiveness.

Election campaign news may rest somewhere between the extremes of the wave of attention to sex scandals and the virtual privacy of most legislative committee policy deliberations. Campaigns soak up media resources and public attention at high rates, yet, according to Buchanan's analysis of the United States, all this coverage fails to generate even a moderately well-informed electorate. Although Blumler and Gurevitch show that matters are not as dire in the United Kingdom as in the United States, there is some evidence that the United Kingdom and other countries are converging toward the American model.

Baker might counter this portrayal by pointing to the diverse information needs of different kinds of citizens. Relatively few fall into the idealized model of citizenship implicit in most critiques of election news; a majority may find issue coverage irrelevant to voting, either because all the major, viable candidates are unacceptable to them, or because party loyalty predetermines their votes. In Baker's perspective, it would be incorrect to lambaste the media or citizens for civic dereliction on the grounds they fail to develop expertise on a common agenda of big issues.

Extending a related point, Graber would add that it's hardly fair to blame the message receiver for apathy, when the messenger stubbornly clings to modes of address ill-suited to popular information format preferences, particularly among younger generations. The right kinds of news could bring a lot of currently alienated citizens back into the fold. Hart's research offers a reassuring confluence of evidence on this point as he shows that writers of letters to the editor, the centuries-old vanguard of interactivity in media, are neither crackpots nor cranks. These fairly typical citizens seem quite capable of thinking for themselves and taking part in public discourse. Graber and Gamson both suggest that media can and sometimes do provide resources that enable citizenship. All of these authors point to the need for greater attention to identifying the communication conditions that either promote or discourage broad citizen engagement.

The Institutionalization of Manipulation: Deception, Cynicism or Critical Thinking?

Several authors in this book contend that communication technologies similar to those that cater to individuals as consumers may be manipulating them (or shutting them out) as citizens. The process begins as audiences render themselves susceptible to unwitting influence, not only from the proliferation of direct marketing firms that now collect, store, and sift detailed demographic data, but also from the detailed personal information they automatically provide as they surf the Web or order cable programming. In Gandy's assessment, the usefully informed, independent citizen may be a vanishing breed, targeted by those seeking to guide or control decisions on consuming goods or choosing candidates. We wonder about the quality of information that will be provided by a campaign, such as Steve Forbes's run for the Republican presidential nomination in 1999–2000, that seeks to boost candidate and message recognition through spots crafted by a man who made his mark "repositioning" Mrs. Paul's Fishsticks.

Meanwhile, as Bennett and Manheim's exploration of spin management suggests, citizens and government officials alike may experience less transparent information, as frequent "astroturf" campaigns are crafted to appear as spontaneous outpourings of broad grassroots public sentiment. Deception may become easier as established mechanisms for authenticating the source of information, or the information itself, falter or fail to arise. This holds especially true, of course, for the Internet, where information circulates free of just about any check (with the fitful exceptions of pornography, copyright, and libel laws). Changing information standards also appear to be sweeping through the traditional media. By the end of the 1990s, even traditional media such as *Newsweek* and broadcast news, reeling under competitive pressure, were publishing hot scoops on their Web sites without putting them through the normal vetting process. From Murdoch's transformation of the *London Times* to the tabloidization of mainstream daily news in the

United States, information formats increasingly reflect consumer values that may translate poorly into the policy sphere.

Issue and candidate advertising sponsored by camouflaged interests also adds to the confusing information environment. Not only are claims and appeals based largely on focus group research into audience fears, but the identity of those sponsoring political messages is increasingly obfuscated, further impeding citizens' ability to engage in rational deliberation. Beyond this, as Jamieson points out, the electoral process can be distorted as forces not accountable to the candidates put their own campaign agendas and disputes into play. New forms of interest aggregation, perhaps inimical to the public interest, or at least to democracy, may arise from refined public relations techniques and technologies.

To some extent, the public's own growing cynicism and sophistication could counteract the media savvy of image consultants. Yet even if a cynical public rejects the claims of an interest group, the result may not be empowerment so much as disillusioned withdrawal. In that case, the manipulating groups may still come out ahead as they get to divide up the political spoils with other campaign contributors and intense interests, beyond the constraining reach of public knowledge. Once again, the concerns about democratic participation expressed by Schattschneider (1960) appear to be reinforced rather than assuaged by the uses of mediated political communication.

THE INTERPENETRATION OF IMAGE AND SUBSTANCE

As noted by Delli Carpini and Williams, distinctions between mediated representation of events and their reality seem to be dissolving under this postmodern assault of cynical manipulation met by cynical indifference. Although the problem of differentiating appearance from reality is hardly new, the potential for media images to hold more significance for authoritative allocations of values than do underlying facts docs seem increasingly clear. Perhaps counterintuitively, the contributors here imply that this may hold especially on the elite rather than mass level. Thus, as Entman and Herbst point out, officials may respond to media constructions of public opinion rather than to survey-based evidence on aggregate citizen sentiments, producing a simulacrum of democracy even when making sincere efforts to be responsive. This may account for how the news media in the United States continue to be important for governing (as Cook argues) even as they have lost much of their former public confidence.

As noted earlier, Zaller argues that the mass public remains stubbornly anchored to substance. Resistant to the blandishments of media glitz and hype, for example, when judging presidents, they appear to rely most heavily upon an administration's success in overseeing the economy and maintaining peace. However, the notion that citizens are making a purely substantive judgment when they evaluate presidential performance is challenged by the inevitability of framing. President Reagan was widely perceived as having cut taxes and stimulated economic growth, although for most American families, taxes rose and incomes stagnated. Candidate Bill Clinton successfully assailed President Bush's failure to guide the economy out of recession in 1992 despite data showing the recession had ended in late 1991. The susceptibility of the public to this kind of impression management, and of reality to diverse measures and selective interpretations, makes any dichotomy between substance and image conceptually problematic.

Flattening Media and Political Power Hierarchies as the Concentration of Media Ownership and Cooperation Grows

Traditional media outlets still garner the overwhelming bulk of the news audience and of elite attention. However, one thing that may be changing is the hold that news organizations have on political information, particularly in the case of big stories. Delli Carpini and Williams, and Blumler and Gurevitch, among others, point out that whether in the jokes on the late night talk shows or postings on scandal-mongering Web sites, newer media are distributing power beyond the traditional central elite. Thus an alliance of right-wing interests "outside the Beltway" and external to the traditional party establishments concertedly used revelations and accusations in the new quasi-journalistic media channels to keep Bill Clinton's scandals cooking in the mainstream press. Hillary Clinton invited easy dismissal of this network through her charge that it operated as a conspiracy. Bennett and Manheim would argue that this is simply how many issue campaigns now operate through the use of strategic communication practices, not as conspiracy but as rational political activity.

While the rise of the Internet and niche cable outlets may facilitate stealthy communication campaigns, we are cautioned by Cook, among others, that considerable power continues to reside with traditional media channels. Cook notes that cross-organizational ties and ownership links, such as the Time Warner combination with CNN, or the economy of resources reflected in NBC's global cable holdings, have meant that content across major media remains quite similar. Put differently, diversity of content has not grown apace with profusion of outlets. Cost cutting that accompanies the heightened competition also means reliance upon other media's reports for one's own, meaning networks and newspapers share tapes, photos, and correspondents as much as (and perhaps more than) ever. So long as elites continue to rely upon mass communication outlets in taking the public pulse, the ability to select, amplify, and repeat common frames will continue to give the media institutional power.

CONCLUSION

We bring the book to a close with the conventional plea for more inter-disciplinary and comparative research. In proposing this volume and the conferences that produced it, we argued that alterations in mediated communication technologies and systems are having potentially great, but so far poorly understood implications for politics. In the scant two years it took to complete the book, this hardly startling prophecy has come true. We have seen enough to be certain that, powered by broadband telecommunications networks, the Internet will become a mass medium in which commercial interests will reign uninhibited if not unchallenged; that distributed computing power is here to stay; that an intensifying 24-hour daily news cycle will be driven by mobile telephone Internet access, portable satellite communications, and multi-channel television.

This project sought to begin identifying variables, framing questions, and probing potential effects of these and other transformations. We hope that the new research directions explored in this volume will result in more integrated theories and improved prospects for sharper comparative analysis – in a more systematic and enriched study of political communication for the twenty-first century.

REFERENCES

Ansolabehere, Stephen, and Shanto Iyengar (1995). *Going Negative: How Attack Ads Shrink and Polarize the Electorate.* New York: Free Press.

Cappella, Joseph N., and Kathleen Hall Jamieson (1997). *Spiral of Cynicism: The Press and the Public Good.* New York: Oxford University Press.

Dahl, Robert A. (1989). *Democracy and Its Critics.* New Haven: Yale University Press.

Eliasoph, Nina (1998). *Avoiding Politics: How Americans Produce Apathy in Everyday Life*. New York: Cambridge University Press.

Gitlin, Todd (1998). "Public Spheres or Sphericules?" In Tamar Liebes and James Curran (Eds.), *Media, Ritual and Identity*. New York: Routledge, pp. 168–174.

Patterson, Thomas (1993). *Out of Order*. New York: Knopf.

Schattshneider, E. E. (1960). *The Semi-Sovereign People: A Realist's View of Democracy in America*. New York: Holt, Rinehart and Winston.

Turow, Joseph (1997). *Breaking Up America: Advertisers and the New Media World*. Chicago: University of Chicago Press.

Index

Alperowitz, Gar, 62–3
Althaus, Scott L., 313
Americanization concept, 400–401
Anderson, Benedict, 455
Arendt, Hannah, 121–2, 301–2
Aristotle, 325
Arkansas Ed. Television Comm. v. Forbes
    (1998), 347, 358
audiences
    decline of mass media audiences, 13
    investing messages with assumptions
        or premises, 325–6, 338
    for market-oriented journalism,
        100–102
    for mass media, 11
    segmentation and targeting of,
        147–51

Backhaus, S., 409
Baker, E. Edwin, 56
Barber, Benjamin, 57
Barber, Haley, 336
Bartels, Larry M., 212, 313
Bauer, Gary, 330–1
Bavelas, Janet B., 325
Bell, Daniel, 303
Benford, Robert D., 58
Bennett, Lance, 60, 456
Bennett, Stephen, 190
Bergen, Lori, 104–5
Berlo, David, 338–40
Billig, M., 388
Bimber, Bruce, 317
Blumer, Herbert, 16–17, 207
Blumler, J. G., 388–9

Bogart, Leo, 104
Boggs, Carl, 43
Brady, H., 408, 409
Bridges v. California (1941), 347
Brody, Richard, 260
Buchanan, Bruce, 407
Buckley, James, 327
Buckley v. Valeo (1976), 324–5, 327–8,
    340, 345–8, 348
Buell, E., 409
Burnham, Walter Dean, 270, 354
Bush, George
    economic conditions during
        presidency of, 259

campaigns
    research related to election campaigns,
        381–5
campaigns of strategic communication
    corporate campaigns, 285–7
    evolution, 284–5
    influence of, 288–9
    proliferation of, 288–9
candidates
    in electoral triangle model, 362–5
    FCC regulation of privileged speech
        of, 324
    incentives related to campaign
        strategies, 366–8
    news management and spin control,
        367
Cater, Douglass, 197
citizen letter writing
    as political involvement, 409–12,
        426–8

survey methodology, 412–13
survey of editors, 413–16
survey of letter writers, 420–6
survey of readers, 416–20
citizens
  in electoral triangle model, 362–5
  engagement in polyarchy, 470–1
  incentives and disincentives related to
    political campaigns, 371–4
  of new internationalism, 454–5
  in public sphere, 2–3, 5–9, 36–7
  response to media coverage, 62–72
  role in democracy, 56–7
  territorially-based citizenship, 455
Clinton, Bill, 168–9
  declining popularity during War in
    Kosovo, 260–1
  economic conditions during
    presidency of, 259–60, 269
  judged by performance criteria,
    258–61
  public opinion before, during, and
    after scandal, 263–71
  selection of voter-favored policies,
    261–2
  statement of his record, 269–70
  why public believed, 268–70
Clinton, Hillary, 168–9
Clinton-Lewinsky scandal
  contribution of, 253
  economic conditions during, 258–9
  effect of media coverage, 262–70
  main issue, 253
  new media politics, 168–76
  news coverage, 254–5
  partisanship in response to, 255–8,
    262
  public opinion before, during, and
    after, 177–8, 263–70
  public opinion polls about, 254–5
  saturation reporting, 107
clustering
  cluster analysis, 186
  geodemographic systems, 147–8
Cold War, 455
collective action frames, 58–9
communication
  access to, 2
  channels of, 147–51
  computer mediated communication
    (CMC), 79
  diffusion of technology, 308–9

enthymematic nature of, 325–6, 338
environment of political, 6
global revolution in, 456
model in democracies of, 468–72
in old pluralist democracy, 281
on-line, 50–2
in public sphere (Habermas), 34
revolution of late twentieth century,
  438–41
services and products of mediated,
  9–10.
See also political communication;
  segmentation; targeting
communication, strategic
  characteristics of, 287–8
  designed by political consultants,
    143–5
  growth of campaigns of, 284–7
  in new pluralist democracy, 281–2.
  See also campaigns of strategic
    communication
communication systems
  changes (1980s to present), 10–17
  development of national
    consciousness by, 455–6
  generational differences in attention
    to, 458–9
communicative action (Habermas),
  40–2, 51
community, virtual, 149–50
computers
  computer mediated communication
    (CMC), 79
  network advertising, 14–15
  in U.S. households, 80–3
Constitution, U.S.
  First Amendment's free speech clause,
    327, 329–30, 343, 346, 348, 366,
    374
consumerism
  of on-line libertarianism, 136
  relation to democratic politics, 118
Cook, Timothy E., 184, 196–7, 282
corporate campaigns. See campaigns of
  strategic communication
Curran, James, 359
cyberspace
  censorship, 133–8
  as political domain, 125–30
  politics in, 138
  as test case, 126
  as utopia, 137

Dahl, Robert A., 279–80, 283, 468–9
Dahlgren, Peter, 58, 462, 473
data sources
    Eurobarometer survey, 460–2
    mass opinion, 219
    National Election Surveys, 312–14
    for survey about citizen letter writing,
        412
    telephone interviews, 151
Davis, H., 409
Davis, Richard, 317
Deacon, D., 388
Delli Carpini, Michael, 109, 283, 311–13,
    407, 433
democracy
    activated opinion in, 220
    communication model in, 468–72
    Dahl's argument, 468–9
    future communication dilemmas,
        473–9
    future of, 453
    of Habermas, 40–1
    link to public sphere, 37–40
    mass opinion in, 206
    strong, 57
    trends in Western democracies, 42–5
democratic theory
    of Habermas, 141–3
    role of citizens according to, 56–7
Dennis, Jack, 185
Dillard, J., 409
disclosure
    absence in issue advocacy, 339–40
    state-level requirements, 340
Dole, Bob, 335
Drudge, Matt, 108, 184

Edelman, Murray J., 60, 160, 281–2
elections, 344–5
electoral speech
    First Amendment protection of,
        348
    regulation of, 324, 348–9
electoral system reforms, 374–5
electoral triangle model, 362–4
Eliasoph, Nina, 43, 182–3
Ellul, J., 143
entertainment media, 162–6
enthymemes (Aristotle), 325
Europe, generational perspectives,
    460–2
European Union (EU), 462–5

Fallows, James, 228–9
Faucheux, Ron, 152–3
Faux, Jeff, 62–3
FEC v. Christian Action Network, 328
Federal Communications Commission
    (FCC) regulations, 324
Federal Election Commission Act
    (FECA)
    amendment limiting campaign
        contributions (1971), 326–7
    constitutional question about, 327
Federalist Papers, 323, 340
Ferree, Myra M., 67
Fiske, John, 170, 172
Flacks, Richard, 61
Flowers, Gennifer, 168, 171, 175
focus groups, 151
fragmentation
    of national cultures, 456
    political, 304
framing
    collective action frames, 58–9
    media frames, 229
    of political issues, 449–50
    process of, 203–4, 210–11
    producing mass opinion, 211
    of public opinion, 211
Franken, Al, 160
Frankfurt School, 34–5
Freedman, J. L., 311
Friedman, Thomas, 456

Gamson, William, 5, 67, 283, 472
Gandy, Oscar, Jr., 280, 303–4, 407
Gans, Herbert J., 61, 183
Ganz, M., 143–4, 155–6
General Social Survey (GSS), 189–90
generational differences
    in attitudes toward United States,
        458–60
    in media consumption, 458–9
    in news consumption and interests,
        441–6
    in political engagement, 459
    in political interest, government, and
        public affairs groups, 434–5
Generation X
    defined, 434
    newsgathering approaches, 435, 437–8
    rating of political news, 441–6
    reading skills, 449
    response to "new" media, 438–41

watching television news magazines, 449

globalization
changes influenced by, 455
communications aspect of, 456
contemporary view, 76–7
Goddard, P., 386–7
Golding, P., 388
Grice, Paul, 326
Grootendorst, Rob, 325
Grossman, Leonard, 108
Gurevitch, M., 388–9

Habermas, Jürgen, 3, 33–4, 110–11, 141–3, 208
Halberstam, David, 270
Hamilton, W., 145
Harrison, M., 389
Harris surveys, 190
Hartley, Thomas, 211–12, 216–18
Hatch, Orrin, 330
Hawthorne effect, 309
Heisenberg effects, 309
Herbst, Susan, 194, 208
Herman, Edward, 49
Hertsgaard, Mark, 107
Hibbing, John, 192
Hill, Kevin A., 51
Hughes, John E., 51
Huntington, Samuel, 455

identity, national
of Europeans, 460–2
relation to support for European Union, 462–5
Ilshammar, Lars, 49
information
available on the Internet, 473
control of (Dahl), 469–70
diversity in mediated, xxiv
focus groups as sources of, 151
news media processing of, 229–30
sources related to politics and public policy, 473
stratification and equality, xxiv
transparency and inclusiveness, 280, 469
use in targeting individuals, 151
institutions
news media as collective, 183–6
of public sphere, 35–7
in public sphere (Habermas), 33–4

interest groups
arising outside stable group context, 282
campaign against Microsoft, 289–93
communication campaigns of, 288–9
in Habermas's democratic theory, 142–3
importance to legislative staff, 220–1
public relations activities, 106
segmentation in specialized, 154
strategy under old and new pluralism, 281–2
internationalism, new, 454–5
Internet
advertising on, 14–15
as approximation of global public sphere, 86
generational differences in use of, 459
as global public sphere, 80–9
growth of hosts by domain, 87–9
information sources related to politics, 473
institutional structures, 49–50
literature about, 45–8
public sphere on, 50–2
rapid growth, 150
release of Starr report over, 196
rise of, 13–14
significance for democracy, 44–5
as solution to media problems, 79–80
use in United States, 81
issues
in Clinton-Lewinsky scandal, 253–62
framed in flag-burning debate, 329–40
framing of political, 449–50
issue evasion, 367
management in corporate campaigns, 153, 155
management of, 152–5
issue ads
about flag burning, 329–30
candidate issue advocacy, 325, 334–8
health care reform debate, 328–9, 339
intepretation of, 326
legislative issue advocacy, 324–5
pseudynonymous groups (196), 339
unclear identities of advertising groups, 338–9
used by political parties (1996), 334–6, 339
issue advocacy
absence of disclosure, 339–40

candidate, 325, 334–8, 340
  defined in *Buckley*, 324–5, 327–9
  of DNC for Clinton, 334–5
  legislative, 328–34, 340
  problems with some forms of, 338–40
issue-advocacy ads
  about flag-burning issue, 330–2
  of candidates to alter message, 336–7
  health care reform debate, 329
  of U.S. tobacco companies, 331–4

Jacobson, David J., 455
Jamieson, Kathleen Hall, 280, 407
Jones, Paula, 171, 173–4
journalism
  market-driven, 188
  pack journalism, 188–9
  quality of, 36
  redefinition, 108–10
journalists
  dilution of control of news, 440–1
  framing of political issues, 449–50
  incentives in campaign coverage,
    368–9
  incentives to create political waves,
    248
  visibility of work of, 192–3

Katz, Elihu, 456
Katz, Jon, 109
Kavanaugh, Dennis, 16–17
Keeter, Scott, 311–13
Kelley, David, 325
Key, V. O., 208, 221, 306
Klapper, Joseph, 208
Kluge, A., 89–90
Kornhauser, William, 302
Kovacs v. Cooper, 338

labor movement
  strategic communication campaigns,
    285–7
  transformation of, 286
Larsmo, Ola, 49
Lear, Norman, 330
Levine, Lawrence, 164
Lewinsky, Monica, 168–9, 171
Lewinsky scandal. *See* Clinton-Lewinsky
  scandal
libertarianism, on-line, 136–7
Liebes, T., 244
Lipset, Seymour Martin, 190

lobbying, grassroots
  development of specialists, 153
  focus of, 153–4
  in special interest campaigns, 152–3
Lott, Trent, 330

McCarthy, Eugene, 327
McChesney, Robert, 49
McGuire, Bill, 309
McLuhan, Marshall, 112
McManus, John, 188
Madison, James, 323
majority opinion
  perceived majorities, 221
  as public opinion, 209–10
Mancini, P., 384
Marx, Karl, 122–3
mass communication, xxiii
mass media
  decline of audiences for, 13
  impact on political involvement,
    408–9
  political communication shift in, 9–10
mass opinion, 206–7
  produced by framing, 211
  in surveys related to Clinton
    impeachment, 219–20
mass society
  fragmentation and stratification in,
    304–5
  idea of, 301–3
  new media paradigm linked to,
    303–5
media
  actions circumventing role of, 106–8
  as approximations to public sphere,
    77–8
  channels of communication, 147–51
  as collective institution, 183–6
  convergence in, 15
  distribution of campaign coverage
    (1988, 1992, 1996), 370–1
  in electoral triangle model, 362–5
  as embodiments of global public
    sphere, 78
  global, 76
  incentives in campaign coverage,
    368–71
  increased centralization of, 167
  international and global, 78–9
  public space of, 37–8
  in public sphere, 35–6

traditional, 77–9.
  See also journalists; mass media; news
    media
media, new, 79–80
  audio-visuals, 438–9
  characteristics of, 438
  politics of Clinton-Lewinsky scandal,
    168–76
  proliferation, 439–40
  segmentation in, 15–16
media discourse
  abortion, 67–9, 71–2
  affirmative action, 65–71
  Arab-Israeli conflict, 64–5
  nuclear power, 69–72
  steel industry decline, 62–4
media environment
  changes in United States, 166–7
  in Clinton-Lewinsky scandal, 168–71
  multiaxial, 173, 178 new
  public's interpretation of Clinton sex
    scandal, 177–8
media event concept, 179n9
media frames, 229
media markets
  trends in, 11–12
  trends in newspaper markets, 12–13,
    103–5
Merelman, Richard M., 59–60
Merritt, Davis, Jr., 109
messages, targeted
  delivery systems, 152
  survey research to shape, 151
Microsoft Corporation, 289–93
Mills v. Alabama (1966), 347
mobilization
  related to political waves, 230–1
Mueller, John E., 205
multiaxiality concept, 172–6

narrowcasting. *See* news narrowcasting
nation-state
  as unit of political organization, 454
needs
  intrinsic to politics, 118–19
  outside of politics, 120
  private domain of, 118–23, 133–4
  statements of, 118–19
Negt, O., 89–90
Neustadt, Richard, 197
news
  alteration of political, 448–51

availability in late twentieth century,
    440
  dilution of journalists' control, 440–1
  framing of political issues, 449–50
  Generation X rating of political, 441–6
  homogeneity of, 185–9
  low quality of political, 451
  number of sources of, 441
news media
  coverage of Clinton-Lewinsky scandal,
    254–5
  declining legitimacy, 195
  distinct from entertainment media,
    162–7
  influence on public opinion, 258
  initial content analysis in Lewinsky
    scandal, 263–6
  as intermediary political institution,
    193–7
  linking information to political waves,
    229–30
  as political institution, 183–4
  power of, 195
  role in defining political waves, 227,
    228–9, 237–43
  role in establishing political agenda,
    230
news narrowcasting
  for Generation X, 450
  rise in, xxv, 186–7
Nixon, Richard M., 259–60, 269

opinions
  majority opinions, 209–10
  in political communication process,
    470.
  See also mass opinion; public opinion
Owen, Diana, 317

Page, Benjamin I., 211, 213
party loyalty
  decline in Western democracies, 42
  measuring party allegiance (1952–96),
    271–3
  in reaction to Clinton-Lewinsky
    scandal, 255–8, 262
  of voters, 352
Patterson, T., 228–9, 230
Patterson v. Colorado (1907), 347
Pew Research Center surveys, 185–7,
    190–1, 193, 194–6
pluralism

changes from old to new, 281–4
group structure of new, 294
polarization
  in mass society theory, 304
policy sphere, 3–5, 35
political campaigns, United Kingdom
  1997 campaign, 386
  campaign finance, 390–1
  mainstream journalism, 395–7
  media commercialization, 391–2
  media coverage, 392–3
  populism, 394–5
political communication
  citizen information, 470
  decision in *Buckley*, 327–8
  in democratic process, 470
  disjunction between ways of studying,
    471–2
  mediated, 1, 472
  practices subordinating identity and
    motives, 280
  professionalization of, 16–17
  public sphere mediated, 5–9
  research about media frames, 229
  research about media role in U.S. and
    U.K. election campaigns, 381–5
political communication, United
  Kingdom
  Americanizing trends in, 385–90
  characteristics of present system,
    390–7
political consultants
  segmentation and targeting role of,
    143–5, 152–7
  shift in attention of, 152–5
political environment
  absence of regulation in U.S., 366
  concept of, 226–7
  impact of changes on, 244–7
  political antagonists struggle for
    control of, 228
political information
  stratification in, 304
  used by younger Americans, 447
political knowledge
  analysis of effect of, 312–17
  from television news magazines, 449
Political Marketing Services, 154
political waves
  defined, 226
  effect of, 247–8
  incentives to create, 248

initiators of, 228
linking of information to, 229–30
mobilization related to, 230–1
news media role in defining, 227,
  228–9, 237–43
separate, 227–8
structure provided by news media,
  229
politics
  advertising and consumer culture as
    paradigms for, 124
  citizen involvement in, 408–12
  in cyberspace, 138
  definition, 2
  definition of democratic, 344
  generational interest differences, 459
  of needs, 118–25
  of new interest groups, 294–5
  new interest groups' campaign against
    Microsoft, 289–93
  public domain of, 118–23
  relation to consumerism, 118
  in sense of opinion formation, 344–5
  strategies to achieve goals, 282
  in strong democracy, 57–8
  transformation of interest group,
    288–9
  trends in Western democracies, 42–5
politics, American
  contribution of Clinton-Lewinsky
    scandal to, 253
  party loyalty, 255–8, 262
  political accountability, 253
  political parties dominate, 270
polls
  to characterize individuals, 151
  Reagan administration approval polls,
    209.
  See also public opinion polls
polyarchy theory (Dahl), 279–80, 283,
  468–71
pornotopia, 130–33, 135
president, American
  criteria related to popularity, 258–61
presidential elections
  impact of economic conditions on
    outcomes, 273–5
  outcomes, 273–5
  voter participation, 273
public opinion
  activated public opinion, 207–8,
    220–1

defense spending example of, 210–19
effect of changes in, 212
factors influencing, 203
Habermas's conception, 210
in the Internet age, 306–7
its own conception of issues, 268–9
Key's conception, 306
latent public opinion, 208–9, 221
mass opinion, 206, 219
of Microsoft and Bill Gates, 292–3
perceived majorities, 209–10, 221
representation of, 210–19
shaping of, 106
support for Clinton, 268–71
public opinion polls
about Clinton before, during, and after scandal, 263–70
about Clinton-Lewinsky scandal, 183–5, 254–5
during Clinton sex scandals, 177
General Social Survey (GSS), 189–90
public relations
for issue management, 153
of political consultants, 143–5
public sphere
in common usage, 35
as a communicative space, 37–40
concept of, 76–7
distortions in (Habermas), 142
fragmentation in, 304–5
global, 75–7
of Habermas, 33–4, 39–42, 110–11, 141–2, 208, 468
ideal, 3, 468
idea of, 2–3
information stratification and equality in, xxiv
on the Internet, 50–2
link to democracy, 37–40
mediated communication in, 5–9
national, 462
policy sphere as subset of, 3–5, 35
of present time, 35
segmentation and targeting as threats to, 155–7
spatial dimension of, 37–40
structural dimension of, 35–7
Putnam, Robert, 303

Rarick, G., 409
rationality

of communicative action (Habermas), 40–1
low information rationality, 206
regulation
deregulation, 473
of electoral speech, 324, 348–9
of privileged speech, 324
of U.S. political environment, 366
Reich, Robert B., 454–5
Riesman, David, 301
Roberts, Gillian L., 325
Robinson, Michael, 302–3
Rosen, Jay, 109
Rosenstone, Steven, 276
Ross, Andrew, 136–7
Russett, Bruce, 211–12, 216–18

Sachs, Jeffrey, 75
Scammell, M., 386–7
Schlesinger, Arthur, Jr., 454
Schneider, William, 190
Schoenbach, Klaus, 104–5
Scholzman, K., 408, 409
Schudson, Michael, 165–6
Sclove, Richard, 149
Sears, David O., 311
segmentation
breakdown of news-entertainment, 166–7
as competitive strategy, 145–7
design of strategies, 153–5
development of segments, 151
of news from nonnews, 163–6
role of political consultants, 145
in specialized interest groups, 154
technology of, 147–51
as threat to public sphere, 155–7
Semetko, H. A., 381–7
Shapiro, Robert Y., 211, 213
Shine, Neal, 112–13
Silbey, Joel, 270
Simmel, Georg, 123
Slater, Don, 133
Smith, T., 387
Snow, David A., 58
social cohesion, 304
social space, 37
society
citizen information in, 470
conditions of contemporary, 281
fragmentation within, 304
politics in mediated societies, 9–10.

See also mass society
Soper, K., 118–20
Sparks, Colin, 473–4
Starr, Kenneth, 168, 184
Starr Report
    release over the Internet, 196
Strange, Susan, 454
strategic action (Habermas), 40–1
stratification
    in mass society theory, 304–5
    in political information, 304
surveys
    Harris surveys, 190
    research to develop segments and
        targeted messages, 151
Swanson, D. L., 384

targeting
    as competitive strategy, 145–7
    defined, 146
    design of strategies, 153–5
    role of political consultants, 145
    technology of, 147–51
    as threat to public sphere, 155–7
technological change
    in communication systems, 10–17
    effect of contemporary, 456
Telecommunications Act (1996), 49
television
    effect of trends in programming, 456
    newscasts, 105–6
    news magazines, 449
Texas v. Johnson, 329
Theiss-Morse, Elizabeth, 192
Tripp, Linda, 171

Tufte, Edward, 310
Turow, Joseph, 149, 303–4, 456

United States
    computers in U.S. households, 80–3
    differences in generations' attitudes
        toward, 458–60
    First Amendment rights, 327, 329–30,
        343, 346, 348, 366, 374
    political environment in, 366

van Eemeren, Frans H., 325
Verba, S., 408, 409
voters
    basis for decisions, 471
    demands on political parties, 270
    likes and dislikes, 275–6
    participation in presidential elections,
        273
    partisan loyalty (1952–96), 271–3
    right to learn about candidates,
        323–4

Wattenberg, Martin, 270
Weaver, David H., 186–7
Weber, Max, 123
Whiney v. California, 346
Wilhoit, G. Cleveland, 186–7
Willey, Kathleen, 171
Williams, Bruce A., 109, 283, 407

Young, Iris M., 68

Zaller, John, 208, 471
Zukin, Cliff, 450